CRITICAL ACCLAIM FOR *TULLY*:

"Beautifully written . . . A strong story . . . Hard to put down . . . Highly recommended."
—*Library Journal*

"Simons' literary influences are as much Dostoyevsky as Danielle Steel. The charisma of the writing and pitch-perfect dialogue are apparent from page one."
—*Glamour*

"Startling in its reality . . . Simons crafts this novel in remarkable fashion . . . A complex, diverse, multifaceted story."
—*Denver Post*

"An extraordinary and massive novel . . . Simons piques your curiosity with delicate finesse at every turn . . . Impressive . . . Remarkable . . . Truly exciting . . . One hopes we will see other books by Paullina Simons."
—*Bookpage*

"Keeps poking its way back into your mind long after you've finished it."
—*Chicago Tribune*

"Jane Smiley me
—*Washington P*

Tully

Paullina Simons

ST. MARTIN'S PAPERBACKS

Page V constitutes an extension of the copyright page.

TULLY

Copyright © 1994 by Paullina Simons.

Library of Congress Catalog Card Number: 94-713

ISBN: 0-312-95548-0

Printed in the United States of America

St. Martin's Press hardcover edition/May 1994
St. Martin's Paperbacks edition/April 1995

10   9   8   7   6   5   4   3   2   1

Acknowledgments

I'd like to thank my agent, Joy, for living up to her name. And Bob Wyatt, for his "Greek Chorus"—may it never stop. My thanks to those song artists who did not deny Tully the right to quote from their lyrics, to the ubiquitous hand of the copy editor, and to Anita Miller, for her eleventh-hour help.

Thank you, Kevin, for reading *Tully* three times before anyone else had ever read it, thank you for being there for me and with me. And thank you, Natasha, because you're such a great kid. "Mommy," she said to me in Topeka, "You know, Tully is not real." That's what she thinks.

And finally, thanks to Claudine for writing just the right thing on that "Postcard from Home" long ago.

To Alla and Yuri Handler,
my mother and father

Contents

Straight is the gate
and narrow is the way
That leads unto Life
And few there be that find it

—St. Matthew 7:14

Tully

I

Jennifer Lynn Mandolini

Ah Life,
I would have been a pleasant thing to have
About the house when I was grown
If thou hadst left my little joys alone!
—Edna St. Vincent Millay

Mama's gonna make all of your nightmares come true
Mama's gonna put all of her fears into you
—Roger Waters

1

THREE FRIENDS

September 28, 1978

One warm September afternoon, Tully, Jennifer, and Julie sat around a kitchen table in a house on a street named Sunset Court.

"Tully, go home," said Jennifer Mandolini. "I don't want you at my party looking like this." She pointed to Tully's face.

Tully Makker ignored her, busy stirring the French onion dip she made rarely but well. "One more taste and I'm out of here," she said. But the Mandolini kitchen smelled of apple strudel, while at home the kitchen smelled nothing like apple strudel. Tully was sitting at the table with her feet up on Julie's lap, and Tully was comfortable.

Jennifer reached over and took the dip away from Tully. "One more taste and there'll be nothing left."

Tully watched her put the dip on the kitchen counter and sighed. Jen was right. It really was time to go.

Turning back to Tully, Jennifer added almost apologetically, "We'll have nothing for the guests, right, Jule?"

"Right, Jen," agreed Julie Martinez, sipping her Coke.

Tully reluctantly got up from the table, strolled over to the kitchen counter, and picked up her onion dip. "Jennifer, they're going to be much too busy dancing with you to have dip," she said, running her finger around the rim of the bowl. She began to hum "Hotel California."

Jennifer wrested the bowl away. "Makker, it's five o'clock!" she exclaimed. "You've got a two-mile walk home," she said, getting Glad Wrap and covering the dip, "and a two-mile walk back. And I don't have wheels yet to cart your ass around." She put the dip in the fridge. "Get the hell out of here. Go put your face on." And then to Julie, "Julie, why won't she leave?"

"I don't know," said Julie. "She's never liked it here before."

"Girls, girls," said Tully. "You can leave me alone now. I'm on my way." Tully did not go, however; quite the opposite: she walked back to the table, sat down, and put her feet up on a chair.

Jennifer perched down next to her. "Go," Jennifer said, but

gentler. "I don't want you to be late, that's all."

Tully didn't move. "And it's only *three* miles there and back."

"Get out of here," repeated Jennifer, sighing with exasperation.

Tully reached around Jennifer for the tube of Pringles. It had been a good Saturday afternoon. Quiet. Fun. Warm.

"Listen, Mandolini," Tully said, handing Jennifer a potato chip. "You still haven't told me how many people are going to be here tonight."

"Thirty," replied Jennifer, taking the chip, getting up, and opening the kitchen door. "And I did tell you."

"Thirty," echoed Julie cheerfully. "Half of them football players."

Licking the salt off her lips, Tully eyed Jennifer. "Oh, Jen?" she said. "By the way, how *is* cheerleading?"

"Good, okay, thank you for asking," said Jennifer, standing by the door.

The breeze felt good on Tully's arms. "Ahh," she intoned, glancing meaningfully at Julie but trying to keep a poker face. "Ever get to talk to any of the football players?"

"Not often," said Jennifer, walking over to the sink. "Every once in a while they come around and shout obscenities at us." Tully stared at Jennifer's back.

"So you don't talk to any football players in particular?"

"No, not really," said Jennifer, carefully ripping off a paper towel and wetting it.

Julie cleared her throat and said, "Jen, isn't your locker right next to a guy who looks just like a football player?"

"I don't know," said Jennifer, not turning around. "I guess." And she began to wipe up the counter in earnest, with her back to the kitchen table.

Tully and Julie exchanged a look.

"Yeah, yeah," said Tully, getting up and walking over to Jennifer. "I do recall seeing you talk to some guy who wears those sexy football jerseys with a number on the back. What's his number, Jule?"

"I don't know," said Julie.

"Maybe sixty-nine?" offered Tully, trying to peek at Jennifer's face.

Jennifer didn't answer, just pushed Tully away with her wet hand.

"Jule?" asked Tully. "What does he look like again?"

"Kind of blond?" said Julie.

"Kind of tall?" said Tully.

"Always wears Levi's?" said Julie.

"With stubble?" said Tully.

"Levi's with stubble?" said Jennifer, compulsively wiping the stovetop. Tully and Julie ignored her.

"Really built?" Tully went on.

"And I heard he's really smart, too," added Julie, getting up and laughing silently into her hands.

"Julie!" said Tully. "Smart? I heard he can spell his name but has a little trouble with his address. I guess that's smart for a High Trojan."

Julie shook her head. "Well, if Jen can be valedictorian *and* cheerleader, why can't he be smart *and* a football player?"

Jennifer swirled past Tully to the closet and got Tully's bag.

It was a warm and sunny early evening. Tully thought Jennifer looked warm and sunny, too, wearing a yellow tank top with white cotton shorts. She is so pretty, thought Tully. Does she even know? She's got these nice thin legs and those beautiful arms. Her hair looks so nice permed. I should have mine permed again, except it'll never look like hers, not in this lifetime.

Jen looked Tully flush in the face and said, "Are you two quite finished?"

"Actually, no," said Tully, taking her bag and touching Jennifer's hand with her fingers. "Jule," Tully said. "I didn't go to the Junior Prom, but didn't you tell me that some guy danced a lot with Jennifer? And that Jennifer danced a lot back?"

Julie smiled an unsuppressed smile. "Yeah," she replied. "Come to think of it. But I don't think it was the same guy. I mean, the Junior Prom guy was blond and tall and well built and everything, but he was clean-shaven and wearing a suit."

"Oh, of course, we're being silly, right, Jen?" said Tully. "That was obviously a different guy."

Jennifer folded her arms. "Are you two *quite* finished?"

Julie and Tully looked at each other. "I don't know," said Tully. "Are we, Julie?"

Julie laughed. "Yup, I guess we are now," she said.

"Good," said Jennifer. "Because I have nothing to say to either one of you. Get the hell out."

"We're out of here," Tully said, pulling Jennifer's hair.

"Don't forget my presents, girls," Jennifer said.

When Tully and Julie were at the end of the driveway, Jennifer yelled after them, "Oh, by the way, smartasses!"

They turned around.

"He is number thirty, for your information." And slammed the screen door.

2.

Outside, on the corner of Wayne Street and Sunset Court, Julie turned to Tully. "Why won't she tell us?" she asked.

Tully shrugged. "I suppose she's told us as much as she wants us to know. Have you ever spoken to him?"

No, Julie said, and walked the five blocks from 17th to Huntoon in silence. Tully did not go to the Junior Prom last May, Julie thought. Tully had not seen Jennifer unable to look up into the face of a seventeen-year-old boy who had his arm around Jennifer's back and her hand in his hand. Seeing them together and seeing the look on Jen's face impressed Julie, but since Jennifer never mentioned the Junior Prom, or the boy, and since Julie did not see him all summer, she forgot to make him a big deal to Tully. Not until Julie saw the same look in Jennifer's eyes while talking to a boy near her locker did she connect the dots. *Then* she told Tully. And Tully was a troublemaker. She put the boy in the fan and blew him around Jennifer every chance she got.

"He can't be that important," said Julie, stopping at the corner of Wayne and 10th. "We don't even know his name."

Tully punched Julie lightly in the arm. "But we will. We will. Tonight." As an afterthought, Tully asked, "Is Tom coming with you?"

"But of course," said Julie.

"But of course," mimicked Tully. She rolled her eyes and snorted.

Julie leaned close to Tully. The girls were standing in the middle of the road, in the middle of Topeka, in the middle of America, in the middle of an Indian summer. "I'll tell you a little secret, Tull. He doesn't like you, either."

"What's to like?" said Tully.

* * *

What's to like? thought Julie as she rushed to get ready. What's to like? she thought as she walked down the stairs, unhappy as always with her Mexican face and her slightly rounded Mexican body. Tom wasn't there yet, thank God, to hear her mother. "Oh, *conchita*! Why, you so beautiful! What a beautiful dress, turn around, let me look at you, my, aren't you growing up, your hair looks so lovely, you gonna be such a heartbreaker!"

Tom did hear her mother, though. Angela Martinez continued to gush well after he arrived. "Isn't she beautiful, Tom, isn't she just lovely?" Julie rolled her eyes, a gesture she borrowed directly from Tully. "Mom! Please!"

"Yeah, she is," said Tom. "Now, let's go."

Angela came over and hugged Julie. "All right, Ma, all right," said Julie, hugging her back. "You're messing up my hair."

"Julie! Julie!" Vincent, the youngest of her four brothers, came running from the kitchen, his hands full of raw cookie dough, and grabbed her around the thighs. "Julie!" whined three-year-old Vinnie. "I want to go with you!" She screamed, peeling him off her. "Ma! Get him off my dress!"

"Take me with you!" repeated Vinnie

Julie looked intently at her mother. Angela turned to her youngest boy. "But Vinnie, who's gonna help Mama make cookies? Or did you eat all the dough already?"

Vinnie was torn, but stomach won over brotherly affection, and he bolted back into the kitchen after kissing Julie's dress good-bye.

"Your mother!" said Tom when they were outside.

"Yeah, I know." Julie nodded. "She only likes me 'cause she's got no other daughters." But though she said that, she felt a little defensive. Yeah, that's my mother. Everyone should be so lucky to have a mother like mine. She glanced at Tom. He annoyed her sometimes. Oh, well, she thought. Being in the history club together is fun enough.

3.

After Tully and Julie left, Jennifer sighed and went upstairs into her parents' bedroom. Her mother, just out of the shower, was sitting on the bed, one hand on a towel, one on her cigarette.

Jennifer said, "Ma, did you know that Marlboro just patented a waterproof cigarette?"

"Don't start with me, Jen," said Lynn Mandolini.

"I'm serious. I've seen the commercial. 'Why not enjoy two pleasures at once? Wash your hair and inhale nicotine at the same time. You've always wanted to do it, and now you can. It costs a bit more, but it's worth it.'"

"Are you quite done?" asked Lynn. Jennifer smiled.

No mother and daughter could have looked less alike. It was a running joke in the Mandolini household that Jennifer, Lynn and Tony's only child, must have been born to a Norwegian family who got tired of all those fjords and came to landlocked Topeka, only to get tired of baby Jennifer. "But Mom, Dad," Jennifer would say. "Didn't you tell me you found me in a cornfield where the sun made my hair blond?"

Jennifer was a tall, blond, busty girl, who had always battled with weight. At eighteen, she was still winning; just. But she had the kind of body that with time and kids and plenty of good cooking might get heavy around the middle. Big breasts, small behind, thin legs. She was the only one on the cheerleading squad with a chest larger than 34B. Tully was usually merciless when she described the mammary attributes of the rest of the team when compared with Jennifer, and Jennifer all too frequently had to point out that Tully herself fell into the 34B category. "Yes, but I don't go around parading my tits in a low-cut costume while I dance," Tully would say. At this, Jennifer would raise her eyebrows, widen her eyes, and stare mutely at Tully, who'd say, "All right, all right. But never on a football field, and only very rarely with a pom-pom."

Jennifer's mother was as dark and thin as Jennifer was fair and robust, outwardly anxious as Jennifer was outwardly calm, elegant as Jennifer was casual.

"Everything ready?"

"More or less," replied Jennifer. "Tully ate all the dip."

"Why doesn't that surprise me?" Lynn smiled. Then, "You must be happy Tully was allowed to come tonight."

Tully *and* Jack. Yes. I'm not unhappy. "Sure," Jennifer said. "It's been a long time."

"How's she doing?"

"Okay. Her guidance counselor's giving her a hard time."

"Oh, yeah?" Lynn said absentmindedly "Why?"

Jennifer did not want to talk about Tully at the moment. "Oh, you know," she said, rolling her eyes, a gesture she borrowed directly from Tully. "Guidance counselors." She plodded back downstairs into the living room, where all the furniture had been moved to the walls. Jennifer sat down on the carpet. Her thoughts ran to the calculus quiz she had failed earlier in the week and told no one about; thoughts ran to the calc quiz and passed onto cheerleader practice on Monday. Here the thoughts stopped. Jen, a cheerleader! The valedictorian of her middle school, a former president of the chess and math clubs, a cheerleader! Well, at least she wasn't a very good cheerleader. It seemed every time she threw her pom-poms up, they fell to the ground instead of into her hands. She got up off the floor and lumbered into the kitchen.

Her mother came up close to her and touched Jennifer lightly on the cheek with her floured fingers. "My baby. My eighteen-year-old, grown-up, big, big baby."

"Mom, please," said Jennifer.

Lynn smiled and hugged her. Jennifer smelled Marlboro and mint, and did not pull away.

"Are you enjoying your senior year?" Lynn asked.

"For sure," said Jennifer, remembering her father's exact same question three days after senior year began. At least Mom waited a few weeks, Jennifer thought, patting her mother gently on the back.

Lynn let go of Jennifer and went to look for her bag. "What's the matter, Mom?" Jennifer said. "Too long without a cigarette?"

"Don't be fresh." Lynn lighted up.

Jennifer silently sidled after her mother, watching her make pigs in a blanket and sprinkle a little cinnamon on the apple strudel. Jennifer loved apple strudel. She walked over to the counter and broke a piece off the end.

"Jenny Lynn, you stop that now," said her mother. "Go upstairs and get ready, will you?"

Jennifer went back into the living room instead. She was a little sorry her dad wasn't going to make it to the party. Tony Mandolini, assistant store manager at JC Penney, always worked till ten on Saturday nights, and after work tonight, he said, he would rather disappear to his mother-in-law's than face Sunset Court with thirty howling kids. He promised Jennifer a great present tomorrow when she woke up. Jennifer already knew what it was; she heard her parents talking one evening.

I hope I can gush effectively, she thought. Hope I can satisfy them with my gushing.

She looked outside the living room window onto Sunset Court. Sunset Court. Sun-Set Court. Jennifer had always liked the sound of that. *Sun*set Court. Unlike Tully, who said she hated the name of her own street, Grove Street, and told everyone she lived in "the Grove." Please drive me to the Grove, Tully would say. The Grove.

"Jen, phone!"

She picked up. "How's my birthday girl?" boomed a familiar jolly voice. "Couldn't be better, Dad," she said. Maybe a little better. "Ma, it's Daddy," she called across the house, relieved he didn't want to talk to her again. This was the fourth time he had called today, each time greeting Jennifer with a resounding "How's my birthday girl?"

Jennifer went back to arranging the records. Bee Gees, Eagles, Stones, Dead, Van Halen. The *Grease* soundtrack, the Beatles. A little lone Garfunkel. Pink Floyd. As she worked, her face was soft, her gaze blinkless, her body outwardly relaxed, nearly motionless. But inside her head there was a relentless noise, and to shut it out she started counting her records and then counting sheep. One sheep, two sheep, three sheep . . . two hundred and fifty sheep think of nothing but sheep. Calm, she thought, calm.

4.

Tully walked purposefully but not fast. She knew she had to go home—it was five-fifteen and home was more than a mile away from where she had left Julie. She needed to shower, get ready, and walk back to the party by seven. Yet Tully did not rush. She walked slowly up Jewell.

The three girls lived in a geographical near-straight line from each other, with Jennifer's house on Sunset Court the farthest away from Tully and in the nicest neighborhood. Julie

lived on Wayne and 10th, in a four bedroom two-floor bungalow that housed five kids and two adults. Tully lived closest
to the Kansas River. The low-level rush of the river would've
been soothing to her if only the river hadn't been drowned out
by the endless hum of the Kansas Turnpike and the clanging
of freight trains on the St. Louis Railroad. If not for the Kansas
Pike and the railroad, and the sight of the horrendous structure
that was the City of Topeka's sewage disposal plant, the sound
of the river would have indeed been pleasing to Tully.

On her way home, Tully passed a park so small it had no
name. There the kids from the nearby elementary and nursery
schools played on weekdays. The playground was long on
the ground and short on the play, with only the standard
slide, a swing, and a seesaw to entice the little ones. Not
like the great playground at Washburn University. Now, that
was a playground, thought Tully, sitting down on the swings
and swinging for a while. She was rocking herself gently,
back and forth back and forth, when she heard a woman
with two young babies heading her way. The older boy was
toddling along and griping about something, while the infant
was squawking in a huge pink carriage. The trio passed by her,
the little boy grumbling to his mother to take him to the "baby
sings." Looking at Tully, the woman smiled wanly, walking
after her son. Tully smiled back. She watched them putter
about, watched them aimlessly, without time, without thought,
without feeling—until she remembered Jennifer's party, got up
hastily, and hurried out.

Standing in front of her bedroom mirror, Tully appraised
herself. Her hair needed perming and bleaching again. Skin
was too pale, thanks to the sunless summer, and her cheeks
had on too much rouge—made her look like a clown in the
daylight. But now, in the evening, it was more acceptable.
More acceptable to who? Tully thought. To Mother?

Tully had not been to a party by herself for more than
a year.

Tonight's the night, she thought, straightening her collar and
adjusting the belt on her leather pants. I'm too angly. Not quite
thin, but angly. Arms, legs all over the place. And not enough
breasts to go with them. Wide hips with no meat on them.
She touched her behind. Too flat. To match my chest. She

peered into her face, bringing herself flush against the mirror. Squinted her eyes. Hey, you. You going to a party by yourself? Aren't you a little young to be going anywhere by yourself? Aren't you only seventeen? Hey, you?

Too much makeup, she'll say, thought Tully. Too much eye shadow, too much mascara. Will she even notice? She was sleeping when I came in, maybe she'll stay asleep. . . . In any case, I'm not coming into a house full of people with nothing on this face, that is just not what's going to happen. Say it.

"I am plain," she said. Plain. "Plain Tully, that's what they call me."

But I look all right now. The red blouse's nice (to match my red lips). But tight. Pants are tight, too. She'll never let me out again if she sees me. Seventeen and a half, but just too young to go out, just too young to go. Tully snickered. Now, isn't that just the biggest joke in the Grove. Ah, yes, but I'm so safe here at home. Why, this is the safest place.

Tully found a toothpick. A party! How many people? How many of them guys? How many on a football team? Nice going, Jen. She smiled. Jennifer even promised there might be some guys at the party Tully—remarkably enough—did not know.

Tully started making friends with boys when she was around thirteen, going to a bunch of boozeless kiddie parties. Then boozeless kiddie parties started to bore her silly, and when she was fourteen and fifteen and sixteen but looked nineteen, twenty, twenty-one and had the ID to prove it, she went around with a wilder crowd. Most of the girls she hung out with were not in school anymore. Some were pregnant, all were husbandless. Some were still in school but truant; many were in foster homes. It all seemed kind of fun at the time. Nothing quite like a dozen kids, running around the Midwest, going to College Hill, drinking beer, dancing on the tables, smoking pot, having a good ol' time. She got to know some older boys then, too; some college students. They looked like men and talked deep like men, but when it came to wanting to touch her, they had no self-control, just like boys. Mother did a lot of sleeping back in those days and didn't mind Tully's going out. After working hard for the Topeka refuse plant every day, who would have the energy for anything but sleep? Tully had been telling her mother she was sleeping over at friends' houses since she was thirteen, knowing Hedda Makker would always be too tired to check. That's what it was, thought Tully, as she ran a pick through her frizzy hair. She's always been just plain too tired to ask me where I've been.

The younger boys and the older boys had all watched Tully dance, danced with her, and cheered her when she danced alone. They came up to her, they bought her drinks, they laughed at her jokes. All those boys who kissed her told her she was a good kisser; who fondled her told her she had a good body. Tully scoffed but listened to them all the same. And some had come calling for her in the following few days but did not stay long, disheartened by the stares of her mother and her Aunt Lena, or by the condition of the beaten-down house in the Grove with a broken front window, broken during Halloween of 1973 and boarded up ever since. Or disheartened by the Grove or by the railroad or by the river.

In many ways, Tully minded Topeka more than the Grove itself. Oh, it was just a town, a small, subdued green capital town, with empty streets and lots of cars. But when the town ended, and quickly end it did, after a narrow street, or a road that suddenly became a hill, there was nothing but the prairie stretching out ad infinitum. Fields and grass and an occasional cottonwood, all on their way to nowhere, windblown, ravaged by fires, never broken up by an ocean or even a sea. Just pastureland, millions of miles long, seemingly up to the sky, westward, outward, onward, to absolutely nowhere. Tully never felt more intensely confined than when she thought about the vastness beyond Topeka.

For sure, there were other nearby towns. Kansas City bored her. In Manhattan, there was nothing to do. Emporia and Salina were smaller than Topeka. Lawrence was a university town. Wichita she had been to only once.

The Grove emptied out on the western side into Auburndale Park, right next to the Kansas State Hospital with its Menninger facility for the insane, and on the eastern side into Kansas Pike. Fortunately, the Grove was too far a walk for most of the boys who got interested in Tully. It was just as well. Most of the boys Tully met were not to her mother's taste.

When Tully was sixteen, all the "staying over at friends' houses" had stopped. Hedda Makker, having been too tired for years, suddenly expressed interest in the contents of Tully's desk and found some condoms. Tully swore up and down that they were given to her as a joke, for balloons, that she knew they were bad but didn't know what they were. It was to no avail. The "sleepovers" stopped. That was a shame. Tully had made a lot of money on those dance contests up on College Hill.

Tully went nowhere for six months, except Jennifer's and Julie's, and when she had turned seventeen last year, her Aunt Lena came with her. Loud, laughing, partying teenagers, who drank Buds and told dirty jokes and sang the Dead, and Aunt Lena, sitting in some corner like a fat mute duck, watching, watching, watching her.

Not being able to go out and party, Tully, who for years had tried to shut out her childhood friends, reluctantly returned to the Makker/Mandolini/Martinez circle. They became known around Topeka High as the 3Ms. They were always together again, but it wasn't the same. There were . . . things they did not speak about.

And they never slept outside in Jennifer's backyard anymore, like they used to when they were kids.

Tully kind of missed that. But at sixteen, she missed College Hill more. Missed the dancing.

Tully was not allowed to stay out past six o'clock on school days or weekends. Last February, Tully stayed an extra few hours at Julie's. Upon her return, at six-thirty, she found all the doors and windows locked. No amount of banging and crying made Tully's mother shift from her TV chair before the eleven o'clock news ended. Hedda must have fallen asleep on the couch like always and forgot all about Tully.

In the summer before Tully's senior year, Hedda Makker loosened up. But Tully suspected Mother had simply become too tired again to watch over her.

Tully called the summer of 1978 her "a-storm-a-day summer." It had not been a good summer. She watched a lot of "All in the Family" and "General Hospital." But even sunny summers were a drag in landlocked Topeka. The girls managed to get to Blaisdell Pool in Gage Park once or twice. Tully went to a number of barbecues at Julie's and Jen's and read—a lot, all trash.

The girls celebrated Julie's eighteenth birthday a month ago in August, with Aunt Lena pleasantly in tow.

*   *   *

Tully's bedroom door opened.

"Tully, it's after six, are you ready to go?"

"Yes, just brushing my hair."

Hedda Makker came near and ran her hand over Tully's frizzy locks.

"Mom." Tully pulled away, and so did Hedda, looking her daughter over.

"Your hair looks awful. The roots are growing out."

"Yes, I know, thank you."

"I'm only telling you because I care about you, Tully. No one else would care enough to tell you the truth."

"Oh, I know, Mom."

"I don't have money for your hair, Tully."

"I know," Tully said harshly. Then, "Mrs. Mandolini will need me to clear up all the leaves soon," a little milder.

"So will I."

But will *you* pay me, Mother? thought Tully. Will you pay me to clean up your leaves and dance on your table?

"I'll rake them soon, okay?" Tully said, her mouth stretching into a nominal smile. Hedda stared at her daughter and said, "You should let your natural hair grow out. It looks terrible now."

"Mom, I get the picture."

Hedda squinted at Tully in the dim light. "Tully, you are wearing too much—"

"Makeup," Tully finished. "I know."

"Tully, I know you know, you *tell* me you know, but you don't put any less on. Why?"

"Because I'm ugly, Mom, that's why."

"You aren't ugly. Where'd you get that idea from?"

Tully looked at her mother's drawn, broad face; tired eyes the color of mud; lank hair, roughly the same color; thin, colorless lips.

"Mom, I'm plain."

"But Tully, when you wear so much makeup, do you realize how you look?"

"No, Mom," said Tully in a tired voice. "How do I look?"

"You look slatternly," said Hedda. "You look cheap."

"Do I?" Tully stared at herself in the mirror. Now be very, very quiet, Tully Makker, she thought.

"Yes, you do. And when you look cheap, boys will think you are cheap, they will come on to you and treat you with no respect. And boys your age, they can be very . . ." here Hedda paused, "persistent. You may not be able to fight them off."

Fight them *off*? Tully thought. "Yes, Mom, you know, I think you're right. Maybe I am wearing a little too much makeup." And taking a cotton puff, Tully began to vigorously rub her face.

Hedda stared at her "Are you humoring me, Tully?"

"No, of course not, Mom, I just don't want to upset you."

Hedda said nothing, turning to go. Tully got up out of her chair, then immediately sat back down when she saw Hedda looking at her leathers.

"Tully, what's that you're wearing?"

"Nothing, Mom, nothing. Just some pants I bought."

"Bought? Bought with what?"

With Jennifer's money. "I did some work for Mrs. Mandolini, and she gave me a little money for it."

"And this is what you bought with her money?" Hedda's voice was extremely quiet. She turned on the overhead light in the room to see better.

With *my* money, thought Tully, saying, "Mom, they are just leather, that's all."

"Just leather? Just leather? Do you realize how you look in them? Look!" And she yanked Tully by the upper arm out of the chair and stood her in front of the mirror. "Look! How do you look to boys and to girls? How do you look to Jennifer's parents? Do you know what they'll think of me for letting you wear something like this to their home?"

Jen and her mom helped me pick these out, Tully thought. "Mom—"

Hedda wasn't listening. "I know what they'll see. Here's a girl, a young girl, with bleached permed hair, roots showing. Bright red blush, bright red lipstick, eyes covered with black and blue gop, and those pants. And that shirt." Hedda's voice was stone cold and dead slow. "That slinky red shirt, with the first button right between your tits!"

"Mom! Please!"

"Are you gonna be . . . bending over a lot, Tully?" asked Hedda menacingly. "Are you . . . wearing a bra, Tully?"

Tully threw her hand to the top of her blouse, but too late—

Hedda got there first, pulling Tully's shirt away from her body to reveal two pale, moist-with-sweat breasts.

Hedda's eyes narrowed and Tully's widened.

"Mom, I only have two bras and they were both dirty. I couldn't wear them."

"Shut up, Tully Makker, shut up." Hedda's voice was as slow as before but an octave higher.

"Who else besides you would know that your two bras were dirty, who?" Hedda paused, panted, then sprung again. "Are you wearing any panties, Tully?"

"Yes, of course I am, Momma," Tully replied, remembering just what she was wearing—a black G-string.

"Open your pants."

"Mom, no."

"Tully, you are lying to me? I wanna know how far you stooped, what a dirty trash you become. Now open them."

Tully uttered a small sound. And unbuttoned her trousers; unzipped them just enough to show her mother the top of her black underwear.

Hedda looked at the panties, then at her daughter's face. She let go of Tully's arm, finally, and Tully sank into the chair.

"Get undressed. You aren't going nowhere."

Tully made an inarticulate, throaty cry.

"Mom, please. I'm sorry. I'll change. Please don't do this."

"Tully, you've done this to yourself. You're a tramp. My daughter's a tramp. Where have I gone wrong?"

Tully heard her mother cracking her knuckles. "Didn't I try to raise you properly?" Hedda said. "Didn't I try to put some values into you?"

Tully's eyes were on her mother's hands. "You have, and I am, I mean, I have good values, I *am* moral. Please, Mom."

"What you think your father would say if he was here?"

I do not know, Mother, Tully thought desperately. I really don't know. "Mom, I'm sure he'd accept my apology."

"Oh, you don't know your father, Tully, you don't understand how he thinks."

Hedda's face was purple-red, and her big German body was heaving.

"Truth is," she continued, "what does it matter if you do what I want and wear proper clothes? Truth is, you *want* to go braless, you *want* to show off your tits and have boys pull off those leather pants of yours and see that piss-poor excuse for panties you got on. That's what *you* want, so what does it matter if to make me feel better you do what *I* want?" Hedda's face got a bit redder. The little blue veins in her hands stood out as she clenched and unclenched her fists. Tully saw another question dawn in her mother's eyes. Hedda sat on the corner of the wooden table and brought her face so close to Tully that Tully could smell the sausage and sauerkraut of Hedda's dinner. Well, that's about as close as we get, Mom, thought Tully, intensely wanting to move back.

"Tully." Hedda's voice was quiet again. "Tell me, are you a virgin?"

Tully moved her head away from her mother and looked down at her hands while the little droplets of sweat collecting on her forehead dripped into her eyes.

Hedda persisted. "I mean, all these years I kept you home and sent Lena with you wherever you went and forbade any calls from boys to this house, tell me, Natalie Anne, was I . . . too late?"

Tully finally gazed at her mother in cold disbelief. "Mom, what are you talking about? Have you for—" and then broke off, looked down, and said, "No, Momma, you weren't." Hedda placed her finger, thick as the sausage she had just had for dinner, under Tully's chin and lifted up her daughter's face. And must have seen the fear.

They looked at each other for a few moments, until Tully tried to drop her gaze again.

Hedda's voice was calm, almost reasonable.

"Is that what you wanna do tonight? You want some boy? Any boy in particular, Tully, or are you . . . mmm . . . not particular?"

"Momma, really, honestly, I just wanted to look attractive. But I'll wear something else, I swear."

Tully noticed her mother had stopped clenching her fists and was cracking her knuckles again. Kneading each finger tensely, twisting and turning them until the sound came, the sound of logs popping open in the fireplace. *Crack.*

Nowadays, Hedda did not lose her temper often; Tully would attest to that. Most of the time it was difficult to get Hedda to notice Tully was in the same room. But when Hedda did blow, it was always prefaced by this knuckle cracking.

Last time Hedda lost her temper was the night of the condoms. The time before that was when Tully was thirteen and
got caught kissing some boy outside the front door. When
Tully was younger, Hedda's loss of temper was like Tully's
hunger: sometime, during each day, Tully would feel hunger.
And sometime, during the day, Hedda would lose her temper.
Mother was probably trying to get used to living life on her
own with an uncommunicative and unattractive child ("Come
here, you dumb dog! Come here, you unloving cow, and tell
me about your day!"), and loss of temper was as random as
clouds. Didn't sweep the floor in the corners, left the frying
pan on, broke a table (left too often on her own, Tully once
decided to turn the coffee table into a slide), didn't feed the
cat (it died eventually; nobody fed it), pulled up Aunt Lena's
dress just for fun, didn't take a shower for three days, and so
on and so on.

Sweat trickled from Tully's forehead steadily now, like
syrup. When she was younger Tully had become inured to
Hedda's fury, the way she had finally become inured to persistent lack of sleep. But in the last few years, she hadn't seen
much of Hedda and had forgotten a little. Now, too frightened
to wipe off her sweat, Tully sat immobile in the chair and
watched her mother.

(How did your daughter break her nose, Mrs. Makker? By
walking into a door, was her mother's reply to the hospital
nurse, and two years later, when Tully was nine and had her
nose broken a second time, Hedda didn't take her to the doctor
and the nose healed on its own, though not well. Didn't take
her to the hospital again after that, not even when she chipped
Tully's front tooth with a phone receiver.)

"Mommy, please," whispered Tully. "Please, I am so sorry,
Momma, please. I don't want any boy, I just want to see my
friends, be there for Jen's birthday, I'll wear anything, please,
Mom!"

The fist flew out and caught Tully square across the jaw,
snapping her head backward. The other hand bloodied her
nose. Tully's only reaction was to wipe the blood off with
the sleeve of her red shirt. She did not look up, and she said
nothing. Hedda panted, hovering over Tully.

"Do you know what your trouble is, Tully?" her mother said
through gritted teeth. "You don't learn. That's the trouble with

you. You don't learn at all. All your life, you knew exactly the things that make me *so* angry, but you still defy me. You know what makes me very angry is this sort of thing, this slut way you have about yourself, and still, after all this time, you throw it at me, you parade in front of me like the tramp that you are, flinging yourself in front of me, to say, 'You can beat me, you can punish me, but I'll still do exactly as I please, because I am a slut.' "

Hedda paused for breath. Tully said nothing but wiped her nose again.

"Say it, Tully. It's true."

"I won't say it! It isn't true." The fist came out, knocking both Tully's hands from her face, striking her cheek and mouth, making her nose bleed again.

"Say it, Tully. Say, 'I am a slut.' Say it!" Every letter enunciated.

Tully remained mute.

Another slap, this one with the other hand; her head snapped sideways, her ear and eye hurt; and another, hard on the temple and the ear again; Tully put up her hands to her face to protect herself and only succeeded in having them rammed into her bleeding nose. Then another, another, another—

"All right, Mother, all right," said Tully inaudibly. "I'm a slut."

"I didn't hear you."

"SLUT!" Tully screamed. "I am a slut! SLUT!SLUT!SLUT! SLUT! . . . SLUT!"

Hedda Makker carefully, watchfully, looked at Tully with her lifeless swamp eyes. Her gaze was hard at first, but then it softened; Hedda seemed satisfied.

"Tully, there's no need to scream, but all right." She looked at Tully's swollen face and said, "Go and clean yourself up. And put on something decent."

Hedda reached out to touch her daughter's cheek. But Tully flinched, and Hedda saw it. She drew away and left the room, rubbing her hands together.

Tully stood up and stumbled to the bed. For a few minutes she cried a dry, choking cry, then tried to wipe the blood off her face, shaking in her effort to calm down.

It's okay, it's okay, it's okay, she chanted to herself. *I must get ready. I'm allowed to go.* Now get yourself together, Tully

Makker, and go! Get up, Tully, just one push, you are up off the bed, you are okay, forget it, sit up, pull your knees up to your chin, bury your head and rock back and forth, back and forth and forget, forget, it will all go away, it will all go away, it will it will, rock back and forth, it will; just go on, Makker, go right on. Go on, Tully, don't give up. Don't give up because of her, Natalie Anne Makker. You really want to give up, don't you? What? Do you think all the rest of your life will be an encore of *this* life? Well, if you think that, then give up, Makker. JUST GIVE THE FUCK UP. Or you can just count your sheep, Tully, one sheep two sheep three sheep. I understand: how can a bad pseudo-Catholic girl like you not give up finally? But cut this pathetic self-pity and get up and get dressed and go see your best friend Jennifer on her eighteenth birthday.

Tully stopped rocking eventually and breathed slower. No one to watch over me but me, she thought. Go on. It'll be all right. This is the last year. Next year . . . just think! Hang on, Tully Makker, ignore her and hang on, until next year.

Tully came down the stairs wearing no makeup, a black loose skirt, a beige baggy sweater. All old. All worn a hundred times. She walked quietly past the sofa where her mother and Aunt Lena sat watching TV. Aunt Lena did not look up at Tully. Tully was not surprised. Aunt Lena usually did not look up after hearing the scenes from upstairs.

Tully put on her only coat: brown, gabardine, torn, worn.

Now she had to ask carefully what time to be home.

Aunt Lena looked up. "Tully! You look wonderful!" she said. Tully didn't answer. When taking into account Aunt Lena's impression of the visible universe, Tully always reminded herself that her aunt was registered as legally blind. However, Tully very quickly remembered an episode three weeks ago when she was just about to go over to Jen's for a barbecue and Aunt Lena asked her when she would be back. Tully didn't answer, Hedda threw a cup of coffee at Tully, with the coffee still warm, and Tully ended up going nowhere, no barbecue, no television, no dinner.

"Thank you, Aunt Lena," she replied. "I'm going now, okay, Mom?"

"What time will you be back?" asked Hedda.

Here it is, thought Tully. Again, deliberately trying to stump me, trying to make me pay, trying to make me make myself not go. How many times did I get stuck on this question because I couldn't figure out what time she had in mind? There was no correct response.

Tully held her breath. It's only a stupid party. Stupid party. Fuck you, I say, and I go upstairs and don't go. I'll see Jen tomorrow at St. Mark's. There's never anyone good at these parties anyway. They are all so lame. Fuck you, Mother, I don't want your fucking permission. I don't want to go anymore.

Sweat collected under her armpits and trickled down her sides. But she did. She did want to go. And Hedda was waiting. Tully had to answer. The correct response was not dependent on any particular set time; there was no curfew time in the Makker household, there was only the barometer of Hedda's mood that was certainly not helped by the goings-on in Tully's bedroom a half hour ago.

Asking her mother when might be a good time was a bad idea. Hedda invariably said that if she, Tully, didn't know at the age of (fill in the blank—Tully had heard this line from about seven) when a good time to come home was, then she certainly wasn't responsible enough to go out.

Still, the question lingered in the air and needed to be answered. Hedda would not look at her. Hedda was waiting. Fortunately, Aunt Lena for once meddled to Tully's rescue.

"Will you get a ride, Tully?"

"Yes, Jen's mom will drive me home." That was a lie.

Tully looked at her watch. Six fifty-five. Come on. Come on. Come on.

"Ten-thirty," said Hedda. "Now go."

Tully descended down the porch steps and smelled the rotting leaves. Tomorrow I'll have to clean them up, no doubt. She walked slowly and steadily down from the Grove to Kendall, and then, when she knew she was out of view, she ran.

2

THE PARTY

September 1978

Out of breath, Tully rang the bell with little hope of being heard and then walked right in. Look at this place, she thought, and immediately some guy ran? fell? out of the hallway, spilling beer on her and himself, too. She backed away with distaste; he got up halfway to apologize, saw her, and smiled. "Tully!" he called, ambling up to her and grabbing her waist. *"Be-bop-a-loola, she's my baby . . ."*

"That's nice," she said, trying to get away from his arm.

"I'm not letting you go till you dance with me, Tully. We've all been waiting for you! But I get the first dance, and *'save the last dance for me!'* " he sang.

"I will, I will," she said, prying his arm off her. "Let me go change first."

"Don't go changing/to try to please me . . ." he sang drunkenly, bending closer to her. Tully ducked underneath his arm and saw Lynn Mandolini watching her from the kitchen.

"Hi, Mrs. M.," Tully said when she got loose.

"Hi, Tully," said Lynn. "Who was that?"

Tully rolled her eyes. "Who the hell knows? Never talked to him before in my life. Rick something or other."

"He seemed to know *you* pretty well."

"He seemed to be drunk pretty well," said Tully. "There's liquor at this party?"

"Not anymore," said Lynn. "What are they playing? Listen to this noise."

Music. The Stones? Van Halen? Tully couldn't tell for sure. Ah, yes, The Who. There was a stone in their shoe, apparently, and they couldn't get to it.

"Pretty loud, huh? I rang but no one heard."

"Who'd hear you? And have you lost your key?"

Tully smiled. "Never had a key."

"Well, by God," said Lynn cheerfully, "maybe it's time you got one."

Putting her Marlboro out, she looked Tully up and down.

"Let me take your coat." Lynn stared at Tully a little closer. "You're a bit late," she said.

"Yes, I know." Pause. "I got held up."

"Everything all right, I hope?"

"Oh, yes, fine, fine." Tully became acutely aware of her swollen, bluish face. How well was it hidden behind the cake powder? My nose feels twice its size, Tully thought. I wonder how it looks. "Where's Jen?"

"Upstairs. They're destroying the house," said Lynn, lighting another cigarette and downing her Alabama Slammer. "Simply destroying."

Tully patted Mrs. Mandolini on the arm. "It's a good thing an eighteenth birthday comes only once, ain't it, eh?" she said, leaving the kitchen and heading upstairs. Rick something or other was still out in the hall, now milling around another more willing victim.

Jennifer had the master bedroom. Needing a bigger room for all her junk, she pleaded and pleaded with her parents until they gave in, or so Jennifer had said. Tully and Julie postulated an entirely different scenario. Tully said that Jennifer probably mentioned it once at supper, and Lynn and Tony immediately started clearing out of their master bedroom.

Upstairs, the noise was less deafening. Again, beer cans, plastic glasses, cigarette butts. The Mandolinis really should've waited to install a new carpet, Tully thought. And what a nice clean cream color it used to be, too.

Five or six people stood in the hall, shouting a conversation at each other. They nodded to Tully; she nodded back and pushed her way into Jennifer's bedroom.

"Hi, Tull," said Jennifer. Tully grunted, looking around the room. Jennifer peered into Tully's face and at Tully's clothes. "Hey, you okay?"

"Great," Tully said. "Couldn't be better." She nodded hello to Julie and Tom, who were sitting on the love seat. But Tully wasn't that interested in her friends just then. Instead, her eyes were on someone in the room she didn't know. A young dark boy, nearly a man, very well groomed, who looked up at Tully when she walked in. Unfortunately, there was some bimbo on his lap, marring the otherwise impressive view. Tully would have to ask Jennifer about him when she had a chance. But right now she needed to go and get changed. Trying to look unselfconscious, Tully sauntered over to the drinks bureau.

"Mmm, nice," she said to no one in particular. "I haven't seen so much Coke and lemonade in a long time."

"You know, we are not allowed to drink if we're not eighteen," said Tom from the couch.

"Really?" said Tully, irritated by his self-righteous tone. "Wow, thanks. I didn't know that. That's so helpful." She gave Julie a withering look that made Julie move a foot away from Tom.

"But Tom," said Tully sarcastically, "did you know that though we can't drink, we *can* go to K Mart and buy ourselves a teeny-weeny handgun with super-duper bullets?"

Tom made some kind of a noise. Tully continued in the same helpful tone. "And did you know, Tom, that not only can't we drink even beer, but we can't drink hard liquor until we're twenty-one?"

Tom methodically rubbed his hands together.

"But that's neither here nor there, Tom," Tully went on. "What is here and there, though, is that I distinctly remember seeing you at a twenty-one-and-over club last summer, swilling those twenty-one-and-over cocktails down with an incredible twenty-one-and-over speed—" Tully saw Julie's astounded face.

"Oh," Tully said quickly. "My mistake." She looked at Julie. "Ha! Must have been someone else. So many tall, skinny, freckled guys around. Of course. I'm wrong. Silly me, huh, Jule?"

"Yes," said Julie, glaring at Tully. "Silly you."

Moving away from them, Tully took a beer and peeked at herself in the mirror. *My first party without Aunt Lena in a year and a half and look what I'm wearing.* She sneaked a glance at the good-looking boy with the bimbo. *He must've heard all that entire exchange with Tom-boy. Yeah, but look how I look. Who cares what comes out of my mouth when I look like this?* Tully wanted to speak with Jennifer before disappearing into the bathroom, but Jennifer was all over the place, in, out, in, out. She seemed to be enjoying herself. Tully was mildly surprised. Jennifer was usually a wallflower.

Propped up by a piece of furniture, Tully stood alone for a few minutes. Julie and Tom were kissing. Tully fought an impulse to roll her eyes. Tom held Julie with his right hand

and a beer with his left. Well, I guess he's eighteen, he can do those things, Tully thought. They weren't the only ones kissing. The lap bimbo was making out with the cute guy.

Tully went over and sat by Julie.

"What's the matter?" Julie asked.

"Nothing. I want to dance."

"Let's go."

Tully rubbed her forehead. "Are there a lot of footballers?"

"So many!" Julie said. "You're in luck."

Tully ignored her. "Did Jennifer's *friend* come?"

"I think so. I haven't been watching her every minute."

"Where is he?" asked Tully.

"Downstairs, I think."

"They spend much time together?"

"Dunno," said Julie.

Tully shook her head. "How strange, don't you think, Jule? I mean, don't most girls like guys in the image of their fathers?" Tully looked derisively at Tom.

Tom sat up straight. Julie laughed uncomfortably.

"What kind of guys do you go for, Tully?" he asked. "Do you go for guys who look just like *your* father?"

Julie stopped laughing.

Tully skipped one beat—but only one. "I don't like to limit myself, Tom. I like all guys, but you should know better than most what kind I *don't* like, am I right?" said Tully. "Or am I wrong again?"

Julie was now glaring at Tully *and* at Tom.

Tom looked the other way, mumbling, "Oh, I'm sure you like all guys, I'm sure."

Tully got up and walked out of the room.

"Tom!"

"Julie, calm down."

"What's wrong with you?"

"What did I say?"

Julie leaned close and screamed at him over the Stones, who were screaming they could get no satisfaction. "I'm sorry I ever told you anything about my friends, you shit!"

Tully, at this time, was demonstrating her offended feelings by pinching Jennifer's behind on the way to the bathroom.

* * *

She locked herself in and looked around. Whether she needed to or not, Tully always made sure she visited the Mandolini bathroom at least once. Their entire house was neat and well kept, but the best, cleanest, prettiest, most organized room in the house was undoubtedly the bathroom. Spacious and gleaming, it had spotless white tiles with roses and daisies on them, an ivory white carpet, mirrors on all four walls, chrome taps, soft pink bulbs, blush-pink carnations, fresh-smelling towels and shower curtain. Unlike the Makker household, where everything in their gray bathroom smelled of diseased mildew, the Mandolini bathroom smelled not like seaweed but like the sea. Not that I have any idea what the sea smells like, thought Tully, looking in the mirror.

Her face was puffy. No amount of makeup, no matter how diligently applied, could hide that in the harsh light. She turned off the fluorescent and turned on the soft pink. Ah, that's better, she thought. Now I just look a bit . . . fuzzy. Oh, well. She opened her big bag (Mary Poppins called hers a "carpetbag," but even Mary would've been surprised to find what lurked in Tully's) and took out her makeup case. She put on another layer of cake powder, added another hue of black to her eyes; Tully liked her eyes, her eyes were all right. A shadow of all colors. Yes. Oh, but her dress! She couldn't have looked more frumpy in Aunt Lena's nightgown. She retrieved out of her bag a thin black polyester skirt, with a zipper at the front, a slit in the back, and a length of about ten inches.

She quickly slipped out of her skirt and shirt and tried to stuff them into her bag, but they were much too bulky, sort of like squeezing a brick through a keyhole, and so she ended up dropping them into the hamper.

"Jule, I'm sorry, don't be mad," Tom was saying in the meantime. "I can't help it that she rubs me the wrong way."

"And what the hell did she mean about that twenty-one club anyway?"

"I don't know what she meant," Tom said.

"What club was she talking about?"

"Julie, how should I know? She's got me mixed up with someone else. She knows a lot of men, believe me."

"How the hell do you know?"

Tom giggled awkwardly. "Julie! She's got a *re-pu*-tation."

"How the hell do you know? What does that have to do with anything? And who are you? The Pope?"

"Look," Tom said. "Everyone in school knows."

Julie got up. "Tom, you're gonna have to stop this. You're gonna have to stop talking about Tully that way. As long as me and you are together, you're just gonna have to be nice to her, just gonna have to."

"Why?" he asked.

"Because," Julie said, "I can always get another boyfriend."

"Oh, that's delightful," Tom said. Julie became silent.

"What is it, Tom? What is it? You have something personal against her, or what?"

"Nothing personal," he said grumpily.

"What is it?"

"Don't hound me," he snapped.

"Go to hell," she snapped back, and walked out of the room.

Tully remained in the bathroom, with a long line of footballers lining up outside the door, knocking and muttering obscenities. To complement the black skirt, she put on black high-heeled pumps and a white short-sleeved T-shirt—plain, thin, no bra.

That's me, thought Tully. That's what I am. And when I die, that's what will be on my tombstone. Plain, thin, no bra. The T-shirt was cut off at the navel, showing her young stomach. Some more red lipstick, some more black eyeliner, and she was set.

She strolled out of the bathroom, looked bemusedly at the herd of guys scrambling past her, and then stood against a wall. Lighting a cigarette, she scratched the inside of her bare thigh and smoked. A guy walked by and ogled. Another guy also ogled, until the girl with him pinched him hard; he walked on. A couple was walking up the stairs. The male gave Tully an appraising up-down. The female's glare was less appraising, more abrasive. That girl didn't even notice me before, thought Tully. I wasn't properly dressed before. She smiled.

Tully must have looked good, judging by the reaction of the females; always, but always, she told herself, judge your appearance by the reaction of the females. The more derisive the look, the better Tully was attired. And I haven't even danced yet, Tully thought gleefully.

She stubbed out her cigarette on her shoe and got out a piece of gum. Satisfied with herself, Tully was about to go downstairs in search of Jennifer when Julie stormed out of Jen's bedroom with Tom behind her. Tully sighed.

Julie stopped near Tully and smiled. "Well, Tull," she said, "I'll be damned. I shouldn't be surprised, really."

"Surprised at what?" asked Tully, ignoring Tom's expression at the sight of her. He looked at her as if she were not the same person he had just insulted. Finally, she smiled an obnoxious smile at him and cracked her gum. "Mary Poppins bag to the rescue once again," she said to Julie. "Remind me to take my clothes out of Jen's hamper before I go." She pulled out another Marlboro. "Jule, every day in school you see me metamorphose myself. Why are you looking at me as if I'm from Mars?"

"Tully," said Julie, touching her friend's upper arm, "like I said, I shouldn't be surprised, but you never cease to amaze me." She rubbed some blush off Tully's cheek. "Not too much metamorphosis, eh?" she said.

"Thank you, Julie," said Tully, moving ever so slightly away from Julie's hand. "Earth to Tom, Earth to Tom," she said. He stood dumbfounded and deep red, obviously embarrassed by his own inability to stop staring at Tully's breasts poking through the T-shirt.

Departing for the bathroom, Julie left Tom red-faced, self-conscious, and alone with Tully.

To talk at all seemed impossible—the music was loud and they would have to come close to each other. Tom would have to bend his head down to her mouth, and Tom looked as if the thought of coming closer to Tully were already rendering him insensible. But just to stand there and not talk seemed equally unpleasant, so Tully moved away from the wall and closer to him. He backed away, was stopped short by some guy right behind him. He looked to her as if he would burst. She stood on tiptoe until her mouth was an inch away from his ear and said, "I think you should grow up and not hold it against me anymore."

Tom didn't look at her. "I don't hold anything against you," he said. "So when are *you* going to be eighteen?" In January, she told him, and he said, "That's nice!"

He didn't hear me, thought Tully. He is not even listening. He has not stopped staring at my tits, and this really pisses him off.

Tully stopped trying. A misunderstanding between them—when any conversation was already so undesirable—was too much to take, so when Julie emerged from the bathroom, Tom rushed straight to her, and Tully slipped out of sight and down the stairs.

Watching Tully disappear, Julie poked Tom in the chest. "You've obviously frightened her. I've never seen her go down the stairs so quickly. Why, I think she took them two at a time!" Tom wiped his sweating forehead and apologized to Julie for his earlier behavior.

Tully found Jennifer loading up on apple strudel in the kitchen.

"What a loser," she muttered.

"Ease up, will ya?" snapped Jennifer. "I want to eat it, it's my birthday, so ease up!"

Tully looked at Jennifer as if she were from outer space. She came close, broke off a piece of the strudel, shoved it into her mouth, and said, "Hello, Mars. Not you, you nut. Tom."

"Oh." Jennifer looked relieved. "Him. I thought you were gonna bug me about my weight. Forget him. He doesn't like us. He thinks we are a bad influence on Julie."

"He's an idiot," said Tully. "I think *he* is a bad influence on Julie."

Tully wanted to change the subject and ask Jennifer, who seemed absentminded and listless, about the brown-haired boy, but Mrs. Mandolini came in with a clutter of people wanting more ice, more strudel, more Jennifer.

Jennifer left Tully in the kitchen peacefully stuffing her face and smoking.

"You shouldn't smoke, Tully," said Mrs. Mandolini from behind her. "It's bad for you. And your mother would kill you if she found out."

How right you are, thought Tully, taking a deep drag and moving toward the living room.

Tully stood against the wall in the living room and watched Jennifer offer a beer to a blond guy. In the way Jennifer handed it to him and looked up at him and minutes later danced to "Wild Horses" with him, Tully took a shot in the dark and guessed it was *the* guy. He sort of looked like the guy at the lockers. It was dark and Tully couldn't be sure. He wasn't wearing a football jersey.

Look at her, Tully thought, amused. Jennifer was stumbling over her own feet, looking at them instead of at him. She looked awkward, especially when compared to the boy's tall, fluid grace.

Tully lit another cigarette and sighed. She wanted to dance, too.

Dancing. Tully had learned when she was young how to dance; with a God-given talent and a love for music, both classical and rock, she had learned at twelve how to move, dancing naked in her room late at night in front of the mirror. Tully had spent endless solitary hours in her room, banned from the living room or the dining room, or avoiding sleep—dancing. She had learned to make good use of that mirror, of her naked body in front of that mirror, of music and her naked body, breastless, hipless in front of the mirror; and then, when she began to bud and grow, Tully had already worked out her own private, emotive, erotic act. She started to dance at the spin-the-bottle parties, at first with others and then tentatively by herself in the corner, and soon in the middle of the room. She danced fast and she danced slow, the boys clapped, the girls joined in or just watched; in any case, it became quickly known around Robinson Middle School that Tully Makker was a fine dancer.

But it was at fourteen, when Tully volunteered to dance at a special talent show one Friday night, that the whole faculty was made aware of her "gift" as she danced with her eyes closed to Beethoven's *Emperor*. The principal, labeling Tully's dancing morally reprehensible, called Hedda, who had missed her daughter's performance. Where had a fourteen-year-old learned to dance like that? the principal asked Hedda. Mrs. Makker wrung her big, clammy hands and cried, but Tully was suspended for a week anyway.

The full-length mirror was taken away and Tully was never locked in her room anymore, but it was too late. Tully had grown to love the reaction of her peers and her elders. Feeling that she had a true talent, Tully, in the next three years, proved to the enchanted and drunk patrons of Topeka's nightclubs and bars, to the students and the rugby players and the farmers, just how prodigious and how wasted her talent was. Tully was sure the punishment Hedda meted out when she found the condoms in Tully's room would have been a lot harsher had she been aware of the hundreds of dance contests that Tully had won, of the money her daughter had made, of the boys and men Tully had danced with, and more.

And tonight, Tully stood alone and smoked only briefly, barely managing to finish her cigarette before three guys from school came over to her and asked her to dance, all at once; and she smiled and did. She was so breathless afterwards that she even danced with Julie. Cheek to cheek, Tully danced with her friend, knocking into people and bouncing off. And then she grabbed on to Jennifer, but there were now too many guys around Tully who, having recognized her, would not let her alone, and Tully, still wanting to have a word with Jennifer, managed only a quick whirl with the birthday girl to part of Neil Young's "Hey, Hey, My, My."

Afterwards, Julie got Tully alone for a moment.

"Tully," Julie said, "I'm sorry about Tom."

Tully waved her off. "But Jule, how could you have told him anything at all about me?"

Julie looked embarrassed. "Tull, I'm sorry. He is my boyfriend. I thought I could trust him."

"Oh," panted Tully. "Don't you get it? It's not yours to trust him with."

Julie lowered her head. "I'm sorry, okay?"

"Okay," said Tully, and went back to dance.

After an hour of frenetic dancing, a sweaty and exhausted Tully sat down on the sofa in the living room, soaking up the lights, the music, the smoke, the booze, the guys.

I spy with my little eye something beginning with—ah, but I don't know his name. She spied the brown-haired guy, dancing with his girl, though dancing was a strong word for what *she* was doing. Tully did not pay attention to *his* dancing; she was much more forgiving when it came to the male sex.

Jennifer was talking to her blond footballer in the corner. As Tully studied him, she had to grudgingly admit that with the lights off, strobes blinking, music blaring, cigarette smoke fogging up the room, he did not look bad. In fact, he almost looked kind of . . . okay. He was tall and broad-shouldered. It impressed upon Tully in some visual, nonspecific way that he held his head high, impossibly high, even when he was bending down to hear Jennifer.

The Stones were "Waiting for a Friend," and the brown-haired boy and his girl, deciding to sit this slow one out, snuggled on the couch next to Tully. She watched them out of the corner of her eye. Eventually he got up—to get a drink, apparently. His girl sat still, not turning her head to look at Tully. She sat there with her little skinny doelike legs uncrossed and close together.

The boy came back with the drinks and sat down, not between Tully and his girl, but rather at the very end of the couch. Well, that's all right, thought Tully. Now I can see his face.

After a few moments, he looked away from his date and stared calmly at Tully, then politely smiled and once again faced his girl.

He is even better looking than I first thought, Tully mused, sipping her beer, but older than most guys I know. She appraised his groomed, slick look, his southern European, round, clean-shaven face. When he talked to his girl he tilted his head and smiled, showing perfect white teeth. When he laughed, his eyes lit up. Tully noticed his Levi's were ironed (what kind of a man irons his Levi's!) and even his pink Izod shirt looked freshly pressed. He doesn't look very tall, thought Tully, but in every other way—Tully smiled inwardly—well, let's just say I wouldn't climb over him to get to his date. But it was obvious that the little mouse was not about to let him out of her sight and in fact kept turning around and shooting lethal glances at Tully.

Tully supposed that if she had a hunk like that, she would be throwing lethal glances at everybody, too. Tully was eager to ask Jennifer about him, but Jennifer had not stopped talking to her blond, who by now seemed quite drunk (how come he has a full beer bottle in his hand at all times while the rest of us are still nursing the beer we latched on to at seven?) and was leaning over her, his arm strapped around Jennifer's neck.

Her face, usually devoid of expression, tonight was a happy face. Tully saw it and felt a stab of pleasure and light envy. She looked at the blond's face and immediately felt something else, too—anxiety, small and sharp.

For there was no happiness in the blond boy's face; only beer.

Tully sought Julie out with her eyes and found her talking heatedly to a group of people, including Tom. Probably about whether or not the Americans should have been helping the French in Vietnam in the first place, thought Tully.

Minutes passed. Tully did not move from the couch. The boy got up and offered his girl another drink. She nodded. He was about to walk away, but then moved carefully toward Tully and asked if he could get her anything.

Good voice, she thought. "Oh, yes, please, a Bud, please, if you can find it."

"If that's what you want, I will find it," he said.

He has a good, deep male voice, Tully thought; so what if he's as corny as the rest of them?

Sitting stonily with hands firmly clasped to her knees, the mouse shot Tully another poisoned-arrow glare. Tully smirked and settled back on the couch, uncrossed and crossed her bare legs, one arm on the arm of the sofa, one arm on its back. Tully sat in this pose until the boy came back, handed her a beer, and sat next to her.

"Thanks," said Tully, and smiled. He smiled back politely.

"Yeah," said the girl. "Thanks, Robin."

Robin! That's his name! That doesn't sound too Italian. Tully's thoughts were interrupted by a guy perching himself on her lap, asking her to dance. Tully gave him a hearty push and he fell off, laughing hysterically, and crawled away. Under no circumstances was she about to get up from the couch. Tully could've gotten up and danced—she *had* wanted to at one time—but here, in this smoke-filled, music-filled, people-filled house, she had found what she had come for.

"Tully!" Jennifer yelled in Tully's ear, crouching beside her. "Why are you sitting here all alone? Guys are complaining that you're not dancing!"

"I'm not alone!" yelled back Tully, grinning.

"Why are you sitting here by yourself, then?"

"I'm not sitting here by myself!"

Jennifer looked over to Robin and his mouse. "Tully, uh-uh! Absolutely not! He is taken!"

"Ohhhh. Jennifer! Pooh! I want you to be a good host and introduce me to him."

"Tully, he is taken."

"Be a good host, will ya, Jen?" said Tully into Jennifer's ear. "Just introduce me." And she stared intently into Jennifer's open face. Jennifer sighed.

"Robin," she said, standing up and walking over to him. "I don't think you know Tully. Robin, this is Tully. Gail, you must know Tully from school. Are you in any of the same classes?"

"No," said Gail. "We've never met, but I have certainly *heard* of Tully. Tully Makker, right?"

"Well, that's funny," said Tully. "Because I have never heard of *you*."

"Nice to meet you," said Robin.

"Robin's father," Jennifer continued, "is an old friend of my father's. In fact, my dad started out working for your dad, right?"

"Right," said Robin. "A number of years back."

Tully stretched out her hard, small hand to Robin, who took it into his hard, wide hand. Tully did not offer her hand to Gail, who sat back and said nothing.

"Jennifer! Come and dance with me, Jennifer!" boomed a guy's voice behind them, and Jennifer smiled into a broad, flushed, sloshed face. Pulling him by his arm, Jennifer said happily, dizzily, "Tully, Robin, Gail, this is Jack Pendel."

And Jack Pendel pumped Robin's hand, hard, without looking at him, too busy bending down to peer into Tully's face. In his bloodshot, barely focused eyes, Tully saw a puzzling ray of a sober thought, a clean expression of . . . Tully couldn't tell what, but she stretched out her hand, and Jack took it, held it, and said, "So *you* are Jen's friend Tully," and then, not letting go, Jack bent—nearly *fell*—on top of her and pressed his beery wet lips to her hand. It was a drunken, funny gesture, and Tully had to push him back to help him straighten up. They all laughed. Jennifer and Jack left to dance, while Robin turned to Tully.

"So how do you know Jennifer?" he asked, looking straight at her.

"We've known each other since we were five," said Tully.

"Wow," said Robin. "I don't think I know anyone that long, except my family."

"Well, there you go," said Tully. Then she pointed to Julie fifteen feet away. "I've known her since I was five, too."

"Are the three of you friends?" asked Robin.

"Best friends," said Tully.

Robin leaned over. "Almost like they're your family, huh?" he said.

"Almost," said Tully. Robin smiled. She smiled back.

"Have you lived in Topeka all your life?" Robin asked.

She nodded. "I did go on a trip to Lawrence once or twice," she said. "You live in Topeka?"

"Uh-uh. Manhattan," he said, looking at her face and neck. "You been to Manhattan?"

Tully glanced at her watch. Almost time. "Uh-huh," she said. "Once or twice."

"How far do you live from Jen?" Robin inquired.

"Oh, a few miles."

"Do you have a car?"

"No, I walk it," she replied. "I walk it all the time. It's no big deal." He was nearly caught. Like any good salesman, Tully knew by heart Dale Carnegie's Five Rules of Selling: Attention, Interest, Conviction, Desire, Close. This guy was already attentive, interested, convinced, and desired.

He paused. "You walking home tonight?"

"Yeah, of course. In fact, I kind of gotta go now." She saw his expression and said, "Told my mom I'd be home early. She's sick."

He was thoughtful; she held her breath.

"Want a ride home?"

She breathed out. *Closed.*

"Oh, sure, if it's no trouble, that'd be great, thanks."

"No trouble at all," Robin answered, not looking at Gail. He glanced over at the grandfather clock. Tully looked, too. Ten-ten. Time to go.

"Can you be a little late?"

"It *is* late," Tully said.

Robin looked at her peculiarly. Tully managed a smile. "Gotta cook my mom something to eat."

"But you haven't been here long."

He noticed. "Yes," she said. "But my mother's sick."

Robin did not look at Gail when he said to Tully, "We could go now if you want."

Tully nodded. "If it's no trouble."

Reluctantly turning to Gail, Robin said, "Gail, I'm going to take Tully home. She lives far away and doesn't have a car. I'll be right back."

Gail blinked and said, "I'll come with you."

Robin touched her hair. "I'll be right back. Besides, you know I have a two-seater." He did not look at her when he spoke, and she did not look at him but stood up quickly and walked away. Not so quickly, though, that Tully wasn't able to stare at Gail's chest. Hmm, she thought. Nothing there. *Totally* perplexing.

Robin and Tully got up. "Want a quick dance before we go?" she asked.

He said yes, never taking his eyes off her, while hers were all over the room. "Hotel California" just finished. Tully wasn't sure if Jennifer was hugging her drunken blond or holding him up. Julie was making out with Tom and adjusting the zipper on the side of her dress at the same time. Stones again, and Jagger's hoarse *"You're out of touch, my baby . . ."*

Tully grasped Robin's fingers and skated with him onto the ice. Closing her eyes, Tully saw the music and moved to the music, while Robin moved to her. Tully, eyes closed, swayed her hips and thrust them closer to him, almost grinding against him. With her eyes still closed, she let go of his hands and ran her palms up and down her torso, from her breasts to her thighs, pulsing to the rhythm. When the song ended, she was sweating, panting, grinding up to him. She opened her eyes. Tully saw him looking at her with an expression she knew very well and had seen very often. He was definitely closed. Okay, *now* she was ready to go.

They said their good-byes quickly. Tully ran upstairs and got her clothes out of the hamper. Striding over to Jennifer, Tully noticed Jen had an embarrassed look on her face, having just finished talking to Gail. Jennifer let Tully kiss her on the cheek. "Happy Birthday, Mandolini," Tully whispered. "And thank you."

"Are you coming with us to St. Mark's tomorrow?" asked Jennifer.

Tully shook her head. "Not tomorrow, okay?"

"Tully, you haven't been since school started."

"Not tomorrow, okay? I'm going to have to rake the leaves in the morning."

Jennifer made a skeptical face. "You don't have a rake."

"With my teeth, okay?" said Tully, moving away and waving.

Robin opened the door for her, and they were out. The cool air smelled so fresh after the staleness of the living room. It was quiet and windless, unusual for Kansas. Tully's head throbbed and her ears rang a continual dog whistle, as they always did after hours of loud noise, even if it *was* Jagger noise.

In the car, Tully silently bit her nails.

The walk home was long, but the ride seemed short. If he is going to get to work, he'd better get to work fast, thought Tully.

"Would you like to see me again?" Robin finally said.

"Yeah, sure," Tully replied laconically.

He drove slowly, at one point obeying the stop sign for about a minute.

"Tully," Robin said at the stop sign. "Tully. That's an unusual name."

"Robin. That's an unusual name. Is that Italian?"

"Third generation DeMarco," he answered. "My mother was of mixed blood and my father wanted to Americanize the family. Also," Robin added, "they were bird lovers."

"Were?" said Tully.

"My mother is dead," said Robin, and drove on.

Tully swallowed, and said, "My brother couldn't pronounce my name properly and it stuck."

"So is that your name?" asked Robin. *"Properly?"*

"Yeah, that's me," said Tully. "Properly Makker."

"What's your real name?"

"Natalie," said Tully. "Natalie Anne Makker."

"That's nice," said Robin. "What's your brother's name?"

She paused. "Henry, Hank." She almost did not mind the questions, for this one was particularly cute. Still, she bit her nails furiously. She had no harmless answers. Why do they always have to know so much before they fuck you? she thought. Why?

"There are three brothers in my family," Robin said. "I'm the oldest."

"How old is oldest?"

He looked over at her and smiled. "Oldest is twenty-five. Is that very oldest?"

"Yes," she said. "Ancient."

"How many kids in your family?" Robin asked. "Two?"

He is tough, she thought, shaking her head. She had nearly forgotten how tough they all were. "Only one," she replied. *Only one left.*

"One? I thought you said you had a brother."

"I did," said Tully, "have a brother." Two brothers, even. *Two that I know of.* "He's not around anymore. Make a right at the next corner."

Tully navigated him through the short streets near her house. And then the Grove. Robin pulled up near her house, took one short look at it—broken porch, long grass—and then one long look at her.

"Can I come and see you tomorrow?" he asked.

Nothing would be better, thought Tully. My mother on one side of him, Aunt Lena on the other. And so Tully smiled and gave him her stock answer, the answer she gave to all the boys, the only answer she had. "Sure, great, come. Maybe we could go for a ride in the afternoon." She looked around her. "Am I sitting in a red Corvette?"

"With red leather seats," he replied.

"Cool," said Tully. Right in front of him, she pulled on the big black skirt over her little skirt and a sweater over the T-shirt, then took a tissue and started wiping her makeup off.

Robin watched her. "You live pretty far away from everything, don't you?" he said.

"Oh, but that's not true," she said. "I live very near the railroad."

"The railroad? The St. Louis and Southwestern Railroad?"

"I guess. What does it matter?"

"It's got a lot of history," Robin said.

"Oh, good," said Tully.

"Like you?"

"Me? I'm history-less," Tully said.

"I never would've guessed you live near a railroad. You didn't strike me as the type."

"Oh, but that's not true." Tully smiled. "I am exactly the type. You can always tell."

"Always? How?"

"Because," Tully said, handing him the smeared tissue, "the girl who lives near the railroad always wears the brightest lipstick."

"Hmm," said Robin. "As I recall, when you came in, you weren't wearing any lipstick at all."

The look she cast him quickly prompted him to ask her if he could walk her to the door.

Shaking her head, Tully said, "My mother is very sick." Hedda's room was on one side of the house and Aunt Lena's on the other; the house was dark, the entire street was dark, not too many people were up. Tully leaned over and kissed Robin full on the mouth. His lips were soft and wet; he smelled of alcohol and apple strudel. She liked that and kissed him deeper. Deeper and deeper; his lips were open while his eyes were closed. Tully always watched when she kissed them. What's the point otherwise? Their faces are everything. She groped for him; his lips got more urgent, more and more urgent. She touched his hair, his neck, his shoulders. He groaned softly as he ran his hand under her skirts, over her bare legs, over her thighs, to touch her, one hand under her skirt, one on her breast. She was almost naked underneath her clothes; the Corvette windows got all fogged up. Robin kissed and kissed her. He pulled up her T-shirt and buried his face in her breasts as Tully stroked his hair, nearly shutting her eyes herself at the feel of his brown head. "Tully, what are you doing to me?" he whispered, getting over to the passenger seat, on top of her, grinding himself against her. "What are you doing?"

Tully felt his erection, his need, his want, his breath, oh, this was just what she wanted. It had been such a long time since she had smelled lust and desire, had felt an erection. She moaned aloud, and that only made Robin grind harder against her. She unbuttoned his pants and took him out. He groaned. Really wanting him inside her, Tully moved her G-string over and guided him in. Robin went to touch her with his fingers, but she was already pushing him past them, inside, inside, inside.

Robin was much too excited, and it was over very quickly. As Tully liked it; she always liked it best when they came fast and out of control. It wasn't very comfortable in the car; backseats were better, but the Corvette seemed better altogether. Tully had never been in one. When Robin came, she held him against her and caressed his back. Good, she thought, and smiled. Good. He stayed there, propping himself up but on top of her for some minutes, until she patted him lightly on the arm. "I gotta go," she whispered.

"Oh, Tully," he said. Gently, she pushed him off her, and when he moved back to his own seat, she adjusted her skirts and brushed her hair. Robin buttoned his pants. "So you gotta go. You don't want anything else? Anything else for yourself?"

Tully was amused. How to tell him that in the last ten minutes she got everything for herself she possibly could get from him, and anything else was out of his league, out of his Corvette, and in any case, completely unnecessary.

"Robin, I'm so fine," she told him. "But I really gotta go."

"Can I still see you tomorrow?" Robin said, touching her cheek.

Tully smiled. This one was a real gentleman. Some of them were. "Sure, great. Come," she said, kissing him quickly, and then was out, up the path, up the porch steps, and inside.

3

ROBIN

September 1978

Sunday morning, Jennifer sat by the phone and waited for Jack to call her. Last night he said he would call her, but here it was, noon already. Jennifer didn't even go to St. Mark's for the ten o'clock Mass, waiting for him to call.

The last guests had left by about midnight, and Jennifer spent until two in the morning compulsively cleaning her room before she lay down in her bed. How did he get home? Jen had thought. He left around eleven, mumbling something about getting a ride. But he lived nearby, so he might have just stumbled home.

Jennifer slept poorly, waking up at five-thirty in the morning to sneak into the garage. Then she started cleaning up the house, and at six-thirty her mom and dad got up and helped her. Jennifer went back to her room, vacuumed, dusted, polished, shined. Then she came down to breakfast.

Sunday breakfasts! How she loved the mozzarella and onion omelettes her mom made; the whole family, all three of them, did. But this morning, Jennifer looked down into her omelette and thought about *his* breath, *his* breath on *her* shoulders, on *her* hair, *his* beer breath as *he* leaned over and laughed in *her* ear while she felt *his* sweat-soaked blond hair brush against *her* face.

"Jenny, did you have a good time?" Tony Mandolini asked her.

"Great," she said into her food.

"Did anyone get drunk or embarrass themselves?"

And they danced, oh, they danced together to "Wild Wild Horses."

"Only Mom," replied Jennifer, trying to be jovial, "but everyone knew she can't handle her liquor, so they were real sympathetic."

"Jennifer!" Lynn slapped her daughter's arm.

Jennifer smiled. "No, everything was great, Dad, thanks."

"Hey, your mom did most of the work. Thank *her*." Tony

reached over and patted Lynn's thigh.

Tony and Lynn glanced at each other, and then Lynn said, "We have another surprise for you, Jenny," handing Jennifer a little wrapped box with a white bow.

Jennifer stopped eating, put down her milk, wiped her mouth, looked at her mom and dad, and picked up the little gift. She knew what it was. So when she ripped the wrapping paper, opened the box, and took out a pair of keys, Jennifer summoned all her powers to open her eyes wide and to put on a big surprised smile on her face.

"Dad! Mom! What's this? You know, I already have a pair of keys."

Tony and Lynn were grinning. "Yes, darling, it's what you always wanted," Lynn said.

It's what you always wanted rang in Jennifer's ears as they went outside and her father opened the garage door and showed her a huge white bow, this time wrapped around a brand-new baby-blue Camaro.

To match my eyes, thought Jennifer wearily.

"To match your eyes," said Tony as his daughter stood and stared. She then effused sufficiently. Hugged and kissed them both. But did not take the car for a ride just then and spent the rest of the morning in her bedroom, sitting on her bed in utter silence, not moving at all.

"I told you they were gonna get me a car," Jennifer said when Julie called at nine-thirty.

Julie squealed. "A car! A beautiful car! Your car! You can take us all everywhere in *your* car!"

"Hmm. What are you so happy about? *You* didn't get a car."

"I should've been so lucky," Julie answered.

"Well, maybe if your mom and dad didn't have twenty kids, you might've," commented Jennifer.

"Five," said Julie. "But why were you so sure it was going to be a car?"

Because it's what I always wanted, Jennifer thought, and wearily said so.

"Going to St. Mark's, Jen? My grandmother wants me to take communion today."

"Not today, Jule, okay? I really gotta help clean up."

They talked about Tully a little and hung up; afterwards

Jennifer sat back down on the bed with hands folded on her lap and waited—until Robin called.

"Jennifer, I want to take Tully out," said Robin.

Jennifer sighed. The only phone calls she had received were from Julie and now from Robin to ask permission to see Tully.

"Go right ahead," said Jennifer. "By all means."

Robin was pacing around his bedroom. He could tell Jennifer was not listening to him, and hated finding himself in a ridiculous position of having to confer with a seventeen—no, eighteen-year-old. But he remembered Tully's face and sweet lips as she kissed him. He would have been delighted with her lips alone. The rest of their encounter confounded him. Robin felt vaguely that unwittingly and unknowingly, he was being sucked into some bottomless mire. That last night's encounter with Tully felt like he had been had. With no choice in the matter. Simply sucked in, and *had*. Tully seemed like a mosquito in the summer that sucked just enough blood to feed itself but not to kill him, and when the mosquito was swollen and bloated with the little it took, it buzzed off, to digest Robin's blood and then feed off some other poor slob. Still, Robin felt persisting for Tully was the right thing to do. It *felt* like the right thing to do.

"Jen, can you help me out a little, please?"

"What can I do for you, Robin?"

"I want to take her out."

There was a short pause.

"What would you like me to say?" said Jennifer.

What's she like? Robin wanted to ask. Is there something about her I should know? Do you think I'm her type? Is there something that'll scare me off her? But he already knew the answer to that one. She was scary as hell, devouring him as she did, on a whim, unexpectedly, and then patting him on the back, sort of like, good boy, Robin, good doggie, now sit. But all Robin asked was, "Well, is she going out with someone?"

"No," said Jennifer. "But you are."

Robin ignored her. Gail was strictly short-term.

"She said her mother is sick. Is it a chronic thing?"

Another pause, slightly longer. Robin sighed into the phone. Dentist visits were easier than this.

"Oh, it's pretty chronic, all right," said Jennifer.

Robin was silent.

"Robin," said Jennifer. "Tully is not the easiest person to take out, you know."

"No," he said. "I don't know. I was hoping you'd tell me." Pause. "She told me to come in the afternoon to her house and take her for a drive," he said finally.

"She did?" Jennifer seemed to liven up.

"Yes, uh-huh."

Jennifer chuckled. "She didn't mean it."

Robin's circular pacing around his bedroom speeded up.

"How's your dad?" Jennifer asked him.

"Fine, fine," he said. That was not strictly true, but he really did not want to talk about his dad at the moment. "What's Tully's dad like?"

"He's not," said Jennifer, "around."

"Not at all?" asked Robin.

"Not at all."

"Is he dead?"

"I don't know," said Jennifer.

"How long has he been not around?"

"Ten years," said Jennifer.

"Jennifer, will you do me a favor?"

He heard Jennifer sigh. "Robin, I kinda gotta go. I'm expecting a phone call."

"Jennifer," said Robin. "If he's going to call, trust me, he'll call back—now please, would you?"

"What do you want me to do?"

"Call Tully, find out if she really wants to see me again, and if she does, please find out the best way I can get to her. Can you do that for me?"

Jennifer quickly agreed, and they hung up. Robin sat quietly for a few moments. He was thinking of Tully, of the way she held on to him last night and of her soft needy moans. Then he inadvertently remembered how upset Gail was with him and how he meant to apologize. Robin thought of calling Gail up but decided against it. He did not want to be talking to Gail while he was thinking of Tully.

Tully was the first girl whose smell and taste and expression affected him enough to humiliate his date at a party for a mutual friend. Robin hoped Tully was worth it.

* * *

When Robin was twelve, six months before his confirmation and seven months before his mother's death, he found out that he and his younger brothers were all adopted by Stephen and Pamela DeMarco from some adoption agency that had managed to palm off all three little male siblings to one set of parents. Sort of like a kitten litter. Robin had been three, Bruce a year and a half, and Stevie three months.

Robin had been looking for his birth certificate because he wanted to open his first savings account for the anticipated earnings from his confirmation. His adoption papers shattered him. Robin ran downstairs to his parents, wildly waving the certificate and crying, "Why didn't you ever tell us? Why? Why didn't you ever tell *me*?" The DeMarcos tried in vain to comfort their oldest boy. But for the next six months, young Robin went to school, worked his paper route, came home, ate dinner, did his homework, watched a little TV, and went to sleep. For six months, he hardly spoke to his mother and father. At his confirmation, he coldly kissed Pamela DeMarco and thanked her for going through the trouble of throwing him such a great party, even though he was not her son.

A month later, Robin's mother died unexpectedly of congestive heart failure. Young Robin quickly forgave himself for not forgiving his mother in time. After graduating from high school, he went to work for his dad and proved himself to be a hardworking and smart manager. The family business prospered under Robin. Then money came his way. Money, good clothes, great cars. Robin worked, played soccer, and took in a great many women. He usually had his pick of most girls he met—and he met a great many girls. He was always courteous to them, but often he was not particularly sensitive. He spoke little of himself and regularly broke up with his girlfriends without letting them know about it; one day he would just start going around with a different girl and that seemed to say it all for him—what more was there to say?

Shying away from girls who were in touch with their feelings and wanting to talk all the time, Robin preferred those similar to his adopted mother: flashy, fair-haired, and private. Gail was nothing like his mother.

* * *

The phone rang again as soon as Jennifer put it down. She closed her eyes and let it ring three times before picking it up.

It was Tully. Jennifer sighed.

"No, no, don't worry," said Tully. "I know that you are glad to hear from me deep down."

"Very deep," said Jennifer. "Robin called, asking for you."

"He did? Did you tell him he called the wrong house? I don't live with you."

"But wish you did," said Jennifer, half kidding.

"Well, that's pretty thrilling," continued Tully. "I didn't think I'd see him again. What did he want?"

"He asked if you were going out with anyone."

"And you said . . ."

"I told him that you weren't going out with anyone but that *he* was."

"Nice going, Jen."

"I told him," continued Jennifer, "that your mother might be a problem."

"Well done!" exclaimed Tully. "Nothing a guy likes more than a problem mom."

"Tully, did you tell him he could pick you up at your house?"

"Yeah," said Tully. "I say that to everybody. I didn't mean it. I didn't think he'd show up."

Jennifer said, "Well, he was definitely going to show up. Good thing I talked some sense into him."

Tully was silent.

"Tull, you wanna see him?"

Silence. A grim "A little."

"He's going out with Gail, and Gail was very upset with the both of you," said Jennifer.

"Fuck Gail," Tully said. "Is he in love with her?"

"Tully, she's seventeen and I think she kind of loves him."

"Yeah, so? I'm seventeen, too. Besides," she added, "I'm not responsible that he calls me up."

"That he calls *me* up," Jennifer corrected her, smiling at the phone.

Jen arranged to pick Tully up in her new Camaro and drive her over to The Village Inn, the popular hamburger place on

Topeka Boulevard, where Robin would meet them. Then she called Robin to tell him the plan. Jennifer thought that Robin seemed pleased with that, and this struck her as odd because she always perceived Robin as unemotional. He must like Tully, thought Jennifer.

"Is there anything I should know about her?" Robin asked Jennifer.

Well, there are a lot of things you should know about her, thought Jennifer, but right now, I really want to get off the phone.

"Yeah, she is not much into talking."

"She and you both. What's she into?"

A different kind of communication, Jennifer thought. *Tactile* communication.

"Into? Dancing," Jen replied. "Music. *National Geographic.* Books."

No one knew Tully better than Jennifer, no one knew Tully on such personal terms, but even Jennifer was hard-pressed to define what Tully was into, or what was into Tully. When she was twelve, Jennifer overheard her mother and father discussing adopting Tully; she wished she could have heard that conversation better, but the words were big and vague. Something about Wichita, something about foster care. Then Tully more or less dropped out of Jennifer's and Julie's life. Oh, Tully came over, ate dinner, did some homework, talked, watched TV.

But it was all pretend. Like the games they used to play when they were children. Pretend. Tully was a Stepford Tully during 1975, 1976, 1977. Jennifer knew only a bare skeleton of Tully's life during the years Tully was dancing and getting into dance clubs with her fake ID.

In 1977, things got a little better. Tully showed Jennifer the ID. "Natalie Anne Makker," it read. "Female, 5'6", 105 pounds, gray eyes, blonde hair, b. January 19, 1955." Jennifer had been shocked at how Tully looked in the photo, done up so old. Tully made herself to look six years older, but she might as well have made her lie be sixteen years or sixty, so large had been the chasm separating Tully from Jennifer. And even after 1977. They didn't play softball anymore, Tully and Jen.

"Yeah, Tully is really not much into all that verbal stuff," Jennifer finished.

"Ahhh, a girl after my own heart," said Robin, hanging up.

Afterwards, Jennifer sat back on her bed and did not move for an hour until it was time to go pick up Tully in her new Camaro.

"Nice car, Jen," Tully said, getting in. "Now you can drive us all to school."

"Makker, Julie and I walk to school. And I'm not driving every morning to pick your ass up from the boondocks of town, that's for sure."

"Oh, yes, you are, Mandolini," said Tully. "You got nowhere else to go but to pick me up."

"I got plenty of places," said Jennifer.

"Yeah? Name one. Admit it, you don't really need this car."

"I admit it," said Jennifer. "But Makker, whether I need it or not, you are not getting this car, not even for five minutes. Absolutely not."

"I don't want this silly car," said Tully, smiling and touching Jennifer's hair. "I just want you to teach me how to drive."

At The Village Inn, Robin sat down across from Tully. Or rather, Tully sat down across from Robin. Tully looked entirely different from last night, looking more as she did when she first arrived at Jen's: no makeup. She was wearing old faded jeans and a HAVE FUN! IT'S TOPEKA! sweatshirt. Her eyes were sweet and gray and she had large blue bags under them. Her nose was a little misshapen and her mouth was pale. She had short, kinky hair. She didn't look like a party girl, she didn't look scary, she didn't look much like anything, but as Robin sat and watched her dig into her burger and talk to him, he thought she was the most beautiful girl he had ever met.

"Why did you tell me I could come to your mother's house?" he asked her.

She flashed him a smile. "I didn't think you'd come." Beaming at the waiter, Tully ordered black coffee and lemon meringue pie.

"You really transform yourself for a party, don't you?" Robin said.

"What's the matter? Regret you came today?" Tully asked.

He shook his head quickly. Gray is not an especially warm

color, he thought, never having seen gray eyes before. "No, you look better now, but different."

They sat and talked for an hour.

"What do you do, Robin?" Tully asked him. "With yourself? When you're not accompanying high school seniors to parties?"

"I work for my dad," he told her. "DeMarco & Sons. Fine men's clothing."

"In Manhattan?" Tully seemed surprised. "Is there a market for that sort of thing out there?"

Robin shrugged. "We have no competition. It's not bad."

"Well, that explains why you're so well dressed," said Tully, smiling lightly.

As Tully talked, she gestured with her hands, which reminded Robin of his profoundly gesticulate family, and he found her hand motions very Italian and *very* endearing. They were having a good time. She was funny, nonthreatening, and, well, seemed entirely normal to him. They both smoked. He lit her cigarette for her, and she stared into his face as she inhaled.

But while Tully was holding up her hands—thin, white, and thoroughly pleasing—to imitate a friend of hers during a police raid on a dance club, Robin saw her wrists. On both her wrists, very close to her palms, he saw two horizontal scars, jagged and dark pink, scars about an inch long. He inhaled sharply. She stopped talking and looked at him; Robin could only imagine what his expression looked like to her—fear? pity? more fear? How often had she seen these expressions on the faces of men who encountered her and those wrists of hers? All that mixed with lust and tenderness. How often?

Instantly, her demeanor changed. She wasn't animated anymore, and her eyes were cold.

To sit and say nothing seemed somehow unthinkable, somehow worse than acknowledgment, so Robin steadied himself and acknowledged Tully. Touching her sleeve, he said, "Are you okay?"

"Of course," she said. "I'm great."

Robin looked at her wrists, and so did she. "Oh, these," Tully said. "I cut myself shaving."

"Oh," Robin said, letting go of her sleeve and feeling himself go pale. "I hope you don't . . . shave them very often."

"Not too often, God help me." She attempted a smile.

I love her, Robin thought then and there with a spasm of emotional clarity that pulled at his stomach and tugged at his throat. I love her. How is that possible? How? What has she done?

After leaving The Village Inn, they drove to 45th Street and headed east, in the direction of Lake Shawnee and Lawrence. Tully was much quieter than she had been at the restaurant. Basically, she just sat and stared at the road, commenting that the weather was certainly turning chilly.

"Shawnee County is really beautiful," Robin said. "Look at this place. Hills and valleys and meadows."

"And long grass," said Tully impassively. "It's the prairie, Robin." She looked out the window.

"Yeah, but looking at this, you wouldn't think it was the prairie," said Robin.

"It's the prairie, nonetheless," said Tully.

They parked at Lake Shawnee and had sex again; it was just as brief this time, just as confounding. There was no one around. Tully stroked Robin's hair, and then gently pushed him off her. He sighed and got dressed. "Done with me, are you, Tully?" he said.

"I'm not done with you at all," said Tully, touching his cheek. "But I have to get back."

"What's the matter? Your mother sick?"

"Very sick," said Tully. "If you only knew."

"Tell me."

"Nothing to tell," said Tully.

Robin took a deep breath and told her about his dad's cancer.

"I'm sorry, Robin," said Tully, cracking her knuckles. "My mother is not really sick, nothing like *that*. She is just . . . strict, that's all."

"How strict, Tully?" he wanted to know. "Is there a curfew? Does she insist you do your homework all the time and not go out? Does she make you do housework?"

"If only," said Tully. "No, nothing like that. Robin, it's really hard to explain about my mother. She is not very communicative."

"From what I understand, neither are you," said Robin.

"Right," said Tully. "So, me and my mom, we just don't talk much."

Silently, Robin looked at the lake. "She is still your mother, Tully," he said. "She's the only mother you'll ever have."

Tully glanced at him. "Robin, that's not necessarily a good thing," she said. "Let's go."

It was nearly seven in the evening when they hit 45th Street again. The sun was hiding behind the hills. The trees, the barns, and the oblong grain silos were dusky silhouettes along the road. Robin and Tully had been driving for about ten minutes on 45th when a car coming the opposite way passed them and all of a sudden something hard and black bounced off the other car, and then the Corvette smashed it with its right fender, and the black thing bounced off and fell with a thump to the ground.

"Robin!" exclaimed Tully. Both cars stopped. Two young men in plaid shirts came out of the other car, and all four of them carefully stepped to the middle of the road to see a Doberman, prone on its side, still breathing but unable to move any part of itself.

"Oh, God," said Tully.

"Hey, where did he come from?" said one of the plaid-shirted men excitedly. "I was driving, didn't see nothing, and then all of a sudden this thing just jumps out in front of my car, poor bastard."

"And I hit him," said Robin, shaking his head.

"Nah, he bounced off my car, man, there was nothing you could do. I feel bad, though, he must be a guard dog for one of them barns over there. His owners are gonna be pretty sad when they find him."

"My God," said Tully. "He's not even dead."

And it wasn't. The Doberman was trying in vain to lift its head, but all the while its black eyes were open, staring mutely at Tully and at Robin. They looked at each other, and then at the road. A car was coming. "We gotta move him," said Tully.

"Nah, he'll be better off if a car puts him out. Look at him, he is suffering," said the guy.

"We gotta move him!" said Tully louder, looking at Robin.

All four of them had to move out of the road. The car slowed down but didn't stop as it went barreling past them and over the Doberman, flinging the animal a little closer to the shoulder, but not close enough, because seconds later another car went by, and this one didn't even slow down as it ran over the Doberman. The dog remained in the road, no longer trying to move its head. Amazingly, it was not dead. Its mouth was open as it slowly gulped some air, its black eyes still open, and still watching. The four of them stood motionless. The only sound in the air was the dog's belabored, difficult breathing. Tully wrung her hands and moved toward the three men. "Guys, please! Just move him, move him, don't let him be hit again, please! Robin!"

Robin stepped over to the dog. "I wouldn't do that if I was you," said the plaid-shirted driver. "You don't know how that thing's gonna react, man. It's a Doberman, for God's sake. He may just get crazy right then and there, rip into you or something. I wouldn't do it. Just let him be. He'll die soon enough."

Robin stopped. "He is right, Tully," he said.

"God!" Tully screamed. "The dog is in the middle of the road! Hasn't he been run over by enough cars? Goddamn it," she said, walking over toward the animal, "you'd move it if it was your mother lying in the road, wouldn't you?"

Tully grabbed the Doberman's hind legs, and with great effort dragged it ten feet, all the way into the grass. The three men watched her, and the driver of the other car leaned over to Robin and whispered, "She is crazy, man, crazy. That thing goes for her and she'll be in bad shape. Crazy, I tell you."

Tully wiped her hands on the grass and said to Robin, "Let's go." She did not look back at the dog.

"Well, it sure is pretty eventful being with you, Tully," said Robin, parked in front of Jennifer's house on Sunset Court.

"What do you mean, with *me*? Nothing ever happened to me until I started being with you," said Tully.

"Somehow," said Robin, "I find that pretty hard to believe." And Tully smiled.

"I'd like to see you again," Robin said.

She stared at her feet. "It will be a little difficult," she said at last.

"That's all right."

"I can't get out much."

"Still, though."

"I can't stay out."

"Well, there you go," said Robin.

"Aren't you going out with Gail?" Tully asked him.

"We're not serious."

"*You* are not serious," she corrected him.

Robin smiled. "I'll talk to her. I really want to see you."

"When?" asked Tully.

Robin breathed out. "I work every day," he said, and tried not to show his pleasure. "Uh, except Sundays. How about next Sunday?"

"Sunday is okay," she answered. "Same deal? In the afternoon? 'Cause I usually go to church on Sunday mornings."

"You go to church, Tully?" said Robin with surprise.

"Well, you know," said Tully. "Just to keep Jen company."

"That's fine. Next Sunday, I'll take you to lunch. Somewhere nice. Okay?"

"Okay," she said, leaning over and kissing him on the lips. It was a long time before Robin stopped seeing her serious gray eyes and smelling the coffee and meringue on her breath.

Jennifer and Julie were waiting for Tully in Jennifer's kitchen.

"Well," said Julie. "Do tell all!"

"Not much to tell," replied Tully, sitting down and taking a sip from Jennifer's Coke. Jennifer got up and got herself another one.

"Where did he take you?" asked Julie.

"For a drive. Jennifer, you should've told me his father has lung cancer."

Jennifer stared at Tully. "I didn't think it was my place," she replied. "Did you want me to tell him stuff about you?"

Tully rolled her eyes. "Can you *tell* me if he is nice, Jen?"

"Of course he is, very nice, but what do *you* think?"

"He is very good-looking," Julie put in. "And drives such a good-looking car! What does he do?"

Tully said, "He manages his father's ritzy-glitzy men's fine clothing store," adding, "And he *is* good-looking. He knows it, too."

"This bothers you?" Julie smiled. "But what does a handsome, well-off, grown-up guy like him want from you?" She poked Tully in the ribs.

Tully was unperturbed. "The same thing," she said, "that an ugly, poor, young guy wants from me."

The girls drank their Cokes.

"Are you going to see him again?" asked Julie.

"Next Sunday, if Jen's willing." Tully patted Jennifer on the head and turned back to Julie. "Are you going to see Tom again?"

"Tully!"

"Yes, yes, of course. You *looove* him!" Smiling, Tully turned to Jennifer, who sat there, spaced out. "Jennifer? Has he called?"

Jennifer looked at Tully and Julie as if she couldn't be sure which one spoke to her.

"Jennifer, has he called?" repeated Tully.

Jennifer got up. "I don't know what you're talking about."

"He hasn't called!" Tully and Julie chimed in unison.

"You both are so silly and immature," said Jennifer.

"I agree," said Tully. "But Julie, have you ever seen a guy who wears tighter Levi's?"

"Never," said Julie. "But I hear it's a sign of maturity—"

"To lust after someone with tight Levi's? Absolutely," finished Tully.

"Girls," said Jennifer, "I really think it's time for you to be driven home."

She ran into Jack on Monday.

He walked over to her locker and said, "Hi, Jen, great party, thanks for inviting us, hope we didn't all trash the place, hope you can make it to the Homecoming game in a couple of weeks." Hope this hope that thanks for this thanks for that, blah, blah, blah.

And Jennifer smiled and nodded politely and said of course and yes and I'll see you at practice and I hope you play well at Homecoming, and then he left and she closed her locker, took her books, and went to her American history class, where she had to take a surprise quiz and failed.

Back home, she walked past her mother, went upstairs, closed the door behind her, and lay face down on her bed until her father came home and it was dinnertime.

Jen kept to herself at dinner, slightly amused at the recurring topic of dinner discussion nowadays: Harvard. Harvard and the

SATs. Harvard, the SATs and med school. Harvard, the SATs, med school, and isn't she amazing, Lynn? Isn't she just amazing? And she, their amazing daughter, sat and concentrated very hard on driving each of her fork tines through four green peas. Sometimes she only managed to get two or three instead of the full four and this made her want to fling the entire plate across the room. But she set her jaw and kept on, while Lynn and Tony continued. So what if the mean SAT score was 1050, while Jen got a combined 1575 on her mock SATs last year, out of a possible 1600? Mock SATs! Even Jack got 1100 on them. And Tully got 1400, except no one knew it because no one cared. Nobody cared what Tully got on her mock SATs, and that was really okay with Tully, Jen thought. At least she didn't have to hear *this* during dinner seven days a week for months. Jennifer thought of telling her parents that she had no intention of going to Harvard; Jennifer and Tully had their plans. But she just couldn't be bothered. She excused herself, went back to her room, and spent the rest of the evening calling his number and hanging up before it rang.

Hundreds of times, many hundreds she must have called his number, and hung up many hundreds of times, dialing it with unseeing eyes, in her master bedroom.

2.

Robin finally called Gail. Her voice was like ice, and he was not surprised. His adoptive mother was as warm as the noon summer sun, but Gail was nothing like his mother. Robin apologized to Gail, saying he had never misled her; they were never in any way serious. Gail asked him if he actually thought she would stand, *could* stand him seeing both of them at the same time. Robin was surprised at this: he had no intention of seeing Gail at all. But to her he said, "No, of course. I understand. I could never stand being two-timed, either. I hope we can still be friends."

The following Sunday, Robin took Tully to Red Lobster with Jennifer's help. They ate well. Tully wanted to know if he had said anything to Gail, who had been slithering past her in school like an old cobra.

"I swear, I never saw her before in my life," Tully said.

"And this week, I see her every day and she walks past me and hisses venom in my direction. You haven't talked to her, have you?"

"I have," Robin replied, "but what's there to say?"

"Watch out," said Tully. "Or she'll start telling you things about me."

Robin smiled. "What kind of things?"

"Oh, all sorts of things of a very sordid nature."

"All damnable lies?" he wanted to know.

"Of course not," said Tully. "But of a very sordid nature."

Robin suggested that she tell him about these things herself, but Tully declined politely, saying only that she used to dance well, and for a while everyone knew it.

"Used to? Have you stopped?" he asked.

Tully nodded. "I haven't stopped, I've just . . . cut down."

"How is your mother?" Robin wanted to know.

"Splendid," said Tully.

"Have you always gotten on so well with your mother?"

"Yes," said Tully with mock cheeriness. "We have a very special relationship."

In the parking lot of Red Lobster, Robin kissed her and Tully put her hand on the back of his head, and he touched her hair and felt that old, familiar stirring. They drove out to Lake Shawnee and quickly and efficiently had sex again. The lake was gray and beautiful; the trees had shed many of their leaves; it was windy; but Robin didn't notice the lake much, so busy was he making love to Tully. Afterwards, Robin wanted to touch her, to do something for her; Tully refused. "Not necessary," she said evenly.

"But I want to," persisted Robin.

"I don't," replied Tully.

"You're really something," he said as they were driving away from the lake. "I just can't figure you out."

"What's to figure out?" asked Tully. "I'm an open book."

"Yeah, and I'm your knight in shining armor," said Robin.

3.

"You wanna go for a drive?" Jennifer asked Tully one Sunday on the way back to the Grove.

"Yeah, sure," replied Tully, looking at her friend. It had

been three weeks since Jennifer got her car and this was Tully's first invitation for a drive. The girls usually sat in Jen's kitchen and looked over college catalogs. Twice Jennifer let Tully get behind the wheel. In the driveway.

"Where do you want to go?" asked Jennifer.

"California." Tully smiled. "But I'll settle for Texas Street."

Jennifer smiled back. "It's been a while since we've been there," she said.

"Speak for yourself," said Tully, getting comfortable in the seat. "I go there all the time."

"Oh, yeah?" said Jennifer. "It's four miles away from you. How do you get there?"

"I walk," said Tully, and then, seeing Jennifer's expression, added, "It's worth it, to see it."

The girls drove to Texas Street, a short narrow road between the Topeka Country Club and Big Shunga Park. The southwestern end of Texas Street curved downward to a dead end, but if they walked through the trees, they came out to the Shunga Park fields. That's how Jennifer and Tully found Texas Street the very first time, five years ago. They were still playing softball then, and they left a game early— their team was losing 2–17—and wandered into the woods, coming out onto Texas Street.

The oaks stood ancient and tall on opposite sides of the street and their branches intertwined in the middle, casting Texas Street in perpetual shadow through which glimmers of sunshine struggled.

Tully and Jennifer parked near the dead end of the street, opposite "their" house. They sat on the Camaro's warm hood for a long time, not speaking.

"Still looks magnificent, doesn't it?" said Tully finally.

"Yeah," said Jennifer. "Sure does."

"What are you looking wistful about?" said Tully. "You who live in a master bedroom on Sunset Court."

"Look at that porch," said Jennifer. "Have you even seen a porch that size?"

"Yeah," said Tully. "On Tara."

"I think Tara's was smaller," said Jennifer, jumping off the hood. "Come on, Scarlett, let's go."

Tully didn't move. "I wonder what the houses are like in Palo Alto."

"Who cares?" said Jen. "We're going to live under the shadow of the El Palo Alto, under its leaves and thousand-year-old branches. We won't need a house."

"Still, though," mused Tully. "I wouldn't mind living in *this* house."

"Who would?" said Jennifer, looking at its four wide white columns. "It needs paint," she said. "Imagine having a house like that and not painting it every year. Let's go."

On the way back, Tully looked over at Jennifer and said, "Jen, you okay?"

"Great," said Jennifer.

"How's cheerleading going?"

"Uh, you know."

"I don't know. How are things?"

"You know," said Jennifer.

Tully looked away.

4.

"So when am I going to meet your mother?" Robin asked one afternoon when he called Tully.

"Never," she said jovially, but after they hung up, she sat in her room and did not feel so jovial. So she called Julie. Julie would cheer her up. But Mrs. Martinez said Julie was doing something or other with her history club. Who cares what she is doing? Tully thought as she hung up. She's never around anymore to talk to.

Tully called Jennifer, who wasn't home, either.

Nobody's home but me, Tully thought petulantly.

She turned on the radio and danced in her room with the windows open. Hers was the only room besides the bathroom on the tiny second floor. It almost felt like the attic. *"I will fly away,"* she sang, *"I will fly away/ fly away/ so far/ I will fly away."* She stopped dancing, went to her closet, and took out a *National Geographic* map from one of her milk crates. Spreading the map open on her bed, Tully knelt down in front of it. With careful fingers, she touched the towns, villages, hamlets, cities, oceans, and deserts of the state of California. Palo Alto, here we come, Palo Alto, San Jose. Nowhere else but Palo Alto nowhere else but Palo Alto nowhere else but—

Tully remembered the time. She ran downstairs to the kitchen before her mother came home. Sometimes Tully made hamburgers nicely, putting bread crumbs and egg and fried onions in them. There was no time for that tonight. It was five forty-five. She slapped the patties together roughly, unevenly, and threw them in the frying pan. Then she peeled the potatoes and put them on to boil.

Hedda walked through the door a little after six, hung up her coat, and walked past Aunt Lena and Tully on the couch. Aunt Lena was watching TV, and Tully was reading a magazine. They both looked up and said hello when Hedda came in, but Hedda rarely looked at them, rarely said hello back. Tonight was no different. She grunted past them to the kitchen. They ate in near silence a half hour later. Aunt Lena kept jabbering on about something or other; Tully did not pay any attention. After dinner, Tully cleared her throat and, not looking at her mother, asked if she could go to the Homecoming dance. Hedda, also not looking up, sullenly nodded. "Thank you," said Tully, and went to make some tea before clearing up.

Hedda took her tea into the living room, sat on the couch, and watched Walter Cronkite, then "Let's Make a Deal," and then an old movie. Tully washed the dishes and went upstairs to her room, where she danced quietly so they wouldn't hear her down below.

At eleven o'clock, Tully came downstairs to wake her mother and tell her to go to bed. Aunt Lena had long gone to her rooms. What does my aunt do all day? thought Tully. Every day she's by herself, sitting there, watching TV, knitting; knitting what? She always has the knitting needles in her hands, but I never see any knitting. I'm convinced she's had the same ball of yarn in her plastic bag since Uncle Charlie died four years ago. Poor Aunt Lena. I'm afraid Mother and I aren't such good company. But then, neither is Aunt Lena. If she really is knitting, she's knitting with one needle, for sure.

Upstairs, Tully washed her face and brushed her teeth. After staring at herself in the mirror for a few seconds, she got a pair of tweezers from the medicine cabinet and plucked her eyebrows. In her room she took off her jeans, baggy sweater, socks, bra. She used to not wear a bra under her baggy sweaters, but her mother had recently taken to giving her surprise quizzes, and Tully made sure she was always prepared. Putting on an old summer tank top, Tully climbed into bed. She left the light on, lay on her back, and looked around her room.

The walls were painted light brown and stood bare of all the trappings of obsessive teenagehood—no pictures of the Dead or the Doors, no Beatles, no Stones, no Eagles, no Pink Floyd. Not even her favorite Pink Floyd. No Robert Redford, John Travolta, Andy Gibb. No Mikhail Baryshnikov, Isadora Duncan, Twyla Tharp. No postcards, no photographs obvious to the eye. No bookshelves, no books. No records. Near the window there was an old wooden table that served as a desk, a makeup stand, and a bed for Tully. In front of the table there was one chair. There was an old dresser by the corner near the closet. On the nightstand near the bed, there was a lamp and a phone. Tully did not have a TV, but she had a small AM/FM radio.

And that is all Tully saw as she lay in her bed and fought sleep. But she knew that in the closet, four milk crates belonged to her: one was filled with *National Geographic*s, a subscription gift from Jennifer, and the others with all the books she had read, "presents" from Jennifer or Julie. And in the top drawer of her table, beneath some general debris, there was a photograph of little Tully, about six years old, blond and skinny, flanked by a chubby Jennifer and a dark-haired Julie. In the photo, Tully held a toddler in her arms.

Tully fought sleep for about an hour or two. She turned and tossed. She sat up, rolled her head, rocked back and forth. She laughed, stuck out her tongue, mumbled. Getting out of bed to open the window, she stuck her head out—it was cold, nearly freezing—Tully thought of screaming at the top of her lungs. But the Kansas Pike, the trains, the river, were already screaming. No one would hear Tully. Leaving the window open, she got back into bed and pulled up the covers. Finally she was restlessly asleep, sleeping just as she was awake, tossing and turning, rolling her head back and forth, rocking on her back. Tully kicked back the covers and lifted her arms up above her head, then put them back down again, sweating profusely.

As Tully dreams, she finds herself lying on her bed, trying to keep awake; she sleeps and dreams of trying to keep awake, closing her eyes, her head snapping with presleep, but she is sitting up, and finally lying down, finally sleeping in her dreams, and as she sleeps she hears the door open and footsteps creaking on her wooden floor. The footsteps are slow and careful; Tully tries to open her eyes, but she can't, she shakes her head from side to side, side to side, but it's no good; the footsteps are close to her, they are next to her, she feels someone bending over her—to kiss her?—and then—the pillow, the pillow over her face, as she flails her arms up and twists, but the body is on top of her, holding her down, and she is twisting, twisting, she tries to scream, but she cannot open her mouth, there is no breath, she is choking, wheezing soundlessly; Tully tries to draw her knees up, but there is a body on top of her, holding her down, the pillow, oh no oh no oh no—and then she comes to, sitting up sharply, gasping for breath, drenched with sweat.

She panted and wheezed, her eyes closed; she panted, her hands around her drawn-up knees; she tried to get her breath back. Then she went to the bathroom and threw up. She took a shower, dried herself, put on a sweat suit, and sat behind her desk in front of the open window. She sat there in the cold until her head was too heavy to hold up, and she put it down on her wooden desk. When she heard the first birds, Tully fell asleep.

5.

Robin wanted to come and pick Tully up on Homecoming day. He also wanted to meet her mother. But Tully thought it was a bad idea and said so.

"Tully, but I'm tired of playing these games. Involving Jennifer, lying, sneaking about. There's got to be a better way."

"Sure there's a better way," said Tully. "You can go out with another girl."

"She can't be *that* much of an ogre," said Robin. "Doesn't she want you to have a good time?"

"I haven't thought about it," said Tully vaguely. "Probably not." She only hits me in the face, because she knows it's the only place I care about, Tully thought. Good time? I don't think so.

"Don't you think she'd like me?" Robin asked her.

Tully sighed. "I'm sure she'd like you, Robin," she said. "You're very likable."

"How are you getting to Home Bowl? Are you walking?"

"Sure, why not?"

Tully heard Robin's breathing through the receiver. "Let me get you a bike," he said at last.

She laughed. "Robin, I don't need a bike. Thanks, anyway," said Tully.

Tully walked over to Julie's on an October Saturday afternoon and Julie's dad drove them to Home Bowl at Washburn University. The Topeka High Trojans played all their home games but one at Home Bowl. The girls cheered on the Homecoming football heroes and tried to get Jennifer's attention, but she seemed so busy throwing her pom-poms that she did not notice them.

Robin arrived shortly before the game. Tully introduced him to Julie and Tom and then climbed down the bleachers to say hi to Jennifer, who was sitting on the ground during a short break. Jennifer stared at Tully and didn't say a word.

She's silent a lot these days, thought Tully. Not just quiet, for Tully spent many quiet years in Jennifer's company, but *silent*. Like a voice stopped talking inside Jennifer's head and she was just sitting around waiting for her body to go silent as well. Like a TV with the sound permanently off. Maybe that thing is coming back into Jen again. But so late?

"I gotta go, Tull," said Jennifer at last, getting up from the grass.

"Go on, go on," said Tully. "Go and cheerlead us into victory."

Tully climbed back up, and she and Julie tried to figure out which uniform-clad butt was Jack's.

"Didn't Jen say he was number thirty?" said Tully.

"Is he a linebacker?" asked Julie.

"He's a throwbacker," Tully replied.

"He is the captain of the football team," interjected Tom.

"Yes, *he* is, isn't he?" said Tully icily.

Despite the relentless rain that started in the first quarter and did not let up, the High Trojans won 12–10, and afterward the two couples went to the Sizzler. Robin had to relay drive, since he was the only one with a car—a two-seater. Jennifer stayed with the cheerleaders. Before Tully and Julie left, they hollered on three, "Well done, Jen!" but she didn't look up.

*   *   *

Twirling her pom-poms, Jennifer stood there with rain falling on her face, unable to see in front of her. She thought of being eight and running home with Tully after they got caught in a terrific Kansas summer storm. In the end, they got a little frightened and, drenched, climbed under someone's porch and huddled together. And Tully, getting out her sodden hand-kerchief and wringing it, was laughing and tenderly wiping Jennifer's face—her forehead, her cheeks, her mouth, her eyes. Jennifer could smell Tully's breath—warm fruit gum—and see Tully's own wet face. That is what Jennifer thought of, when she looked and looked but couldn't see Jack in front of her.

The Homecoming dance was in the Topeka High School caf-eteria. Their Senior Banquet later that year, catered and all, would also be in the Topeka High School cafeteria. Not that it was a bad cafeteria—it had a fireplace and everything. It was just amazing to Tully how she never left the school unless she went up to College Hill. I wonder if the Senior Prom is going to be in the cafeteria, too. The Junior Prom was.

Tully killed most of the four hours until Mr. Martinez came to get them at eleven by dancing. Mostly with Robin, but Robin didn't seem to want to be there, not even to dance with Tully. When she rubbed up against him, though, she felt hardness against her leg and thought, Well, maybe he does want to be here after all.

Julie was arguing with Tom, and Jennifer was standing in the corner. Tully went over to Jennifer.

"What's the matter with you?" Tully said, guiding Jennifer onto the dance floor. "You seem so out of it."

Jennifer grunted something incomprehensible in reply, some-thing about bad wet weather and Tully's not being there.

"What are you talking about? I was there."

Jennifer mumbled something.

"What?"

"I said, I couldn't see him . . . the rain."

Tully stopped dancing. "We were talking about me a second ago. Who are you talking about? Jack?"

Jennifer looked at Tully with sweet sad eyes. "Jack," she said, and before Tully could ask, was dragged away by her cheerleader buddies.

In a little while, Tully left with Robin, but the name "Jack" continued to ring in her ears. Jack, Jen said. Or, Jack? Tully wasn't sure if Jennifer meant it as an answer or a question.

Jennifer stood in the corner, sipped her Coke, and watched Tully leave with Robin. Julie was busy with Tom, and Jack was just plain busy. Often, Jennifer couldn't even find him. He would dance with this girl and that, or stand and laugh with his friends. His *other* friends. His team won and he reaped the accolades. He was the captain. Too busy to come near her. Two girls came around collecting ballots for Homecoming Queen. Jennifer had forgotten to fill hers out, so now she scribbled Tully's name and put the paper in the basket. "I think Shakie's gonna win," said the shorter girl.

"Shakie?" asked Jennifer.

"Shakie, Jen! She is only on your cheerleader squad," said the girl. "Last year's Homecoming Queen."

Oh. Shakie. Yeah. I guess. But can Shakie dance? And then Jen saw Shakie dancing with Jack, and all she could think of was that at least it was a fast song and they weren't touching each other. Not like we were touching during "Wild Horses," she thought. Where is that Tully? Tully, Tully, Tully. Please come back.

Jennifer stood there for a little while longer and then decided to go home. She walked slowly around the dance floor. Then she heard *his* voice. "Oh, Jennifer, ohhhhh, Jennifer! Where do you think you're going?"

Holding her breath, she turned around and faced Jack. "Where are you going, Jennifer? I thought we were going to dance." Her mouth began to widen to a smile, and just then two of his teammates and some girls ran up, giggling, talking, and grabbed his arms and pulled him away. Jack just made a face, a what-are-they-doing-to-me face, but not an I'm-sorry-we-didn't-get-to-dance face. Jennifer watched him being dragged away and then went home.

At eleven, Mr. Martinez came to drive Julie and Tully home. Julie was sullen; she was thinking of breaking up with Tom again. She wanted to tell Tom she did not want to see him anymore. All they ever did was argue about politics. They took their history club and their current events club with them everywhere. But what's the point of breaking up? she thought. It's not like I have anyone else I like. At least this way I have someone to go out with. Julie was sad. She really wanted to like somebody. She wondered if Tully liked Robin. She could never tell with Tully. Julie looked over at her friend. Tully was sitting with her head thrown back against the seat and her eyes closed. She is always kind of the same on the outside, thought Julie. What's not to like about Robin?

There had been several boys who were interested in Tully, several who even spoke to Julie about her, but Tully was always so indifferent. Julie would have liked to like a guy like Robin. If a guy as handsome as Robin with a Corvette really liked Julie, she'd never leave his side. Tully, however, was the type who wouldn't care if her guy drove a beat-up Mustang and wore jeans and T-shirts all day. Tully always was the kind of girl, Julie thought, who did not jump up and down for a guy. Any guy. Kind of like Julie herself. Would Tully like to jump up and down? Julie wondered. Would I? Would Tully ever tell us if she fell in love? Julie didn't think so. Jennifer likes Jack, Julie thought, she likes Jack hard, it's obvious as the eyes on her face, and look where it's getting her. Jen's regressing again to her old ways, for sure. She hasn't been this bad for some time.

Julie had been seeing Tom since the Junior Prom, but their sexual relationship had never developed. They made out often, and once or twice Tom felt her breasts, but he was awkward, and she wasn't into it at all; it didn't do anything for Julie when Tom touched her, so they stopped and discussed politics instead. Watching Tully sit there with her eyes closed, Julie wondered if she and Robin had just had sex. If they did, Julie knew it would be far from the first time for Tully. Tully apparently had some pretty interesting years. Tully told her best friends about some of the boys she met in those bars. Julie had felt that some of the boys were disrespectful to Tully, but now, as she said good-bye to her friend, came home, and sat down with her parents to watch "Saturday Night Live," Julie wished someone would be disrespectful to her.

6.

The following week Gail called Robin up to scream at him for ignoring her at the Homecoming dance, and in a heated discussion told Robin some nasty things about Tully that he did not want to hear and did not believe. But something rotten got inside him, so he got indignant and hung up, and on the ride from Manhattan to Topeka to pick Tully up from school, he could not stop thinking about it.

Tully climbed into his car, kissed him on the lips, and smiled. He did not smile back, but revved the engine and drove.

"Robin, what's the matter?" Tully said after a while.

"Nothing," he said, and continued to say it was nothing. He told her he'd had a bad day at work, this and that and the other thing. Tully had to be home before Hedda, around six. Robin and Tully went to "their" deserted lot again. It wasn't actually deserted, it was the after-work parking lot of the Frito-Lay factory. It was far from her house, as far as they could go without actually leaving Topeka, but somehow that Frito-Lay sign was familiar to them already.

They parked in the farthest corner of the parking lot and had sex. It wasn't so cold that afternoon, even though it was nearly November. Robin did not leave the car on, and Tully moaned a little again and he came fast again. He lay on top of her and thought of asking her if she liked it, if she came, if she ever came, if maybe next time she wanted to go to a motel or something, but he asked her none of these things, saying instead, "Tully, are you a virgin?" Knowing full well that she could not be.

Tully laughed. "Robin, that's a very funny thing to be asking me after we just had sex. Yes, Robin, of course I'm a virgin. What else could I be after having sex with you?" She laughed some more, but he didn't laugh. He got off her, pulled up his pants, and climbed over the stick shift to the driver's seat.

"You know what I mean," he said. "Were you a virgin before me?"

She moved the chair from horizontal to vertical, found her underwear, put them on, pulled down her skirt, buttoned her blouse. Then sat and looked at her hands and said nothing.

"Tully, are you going to answer me?"

"No, Robin, I'm not."

"Why? I'm just curious. I simply would like to know."

"It's none of your business."

"What does that mean?"

"That means take me to Jen's, Robin, right now."

He started the car, began to drive. This just was not going the way he wanted it to. Tully was not playing ball. But he was angry with her now and needed her to be angry back.

"Tully, I heard that you had a reputation in school. I heard," he said, feeling braver, "that you were labeled the girl most likely *to*."

"Oh, you heard that, did you?" she sneered. "You must have heard that from one of my friends."

"Well?"

"Well, what? Well fucking what?"

"Do you?"

"Robin!" she shouted. "It's none of your goddamned business!"

He persisted. "I think it *is* my business. You are my girl now, and I don't want people to be talking behind your back about you."

She laughed an awful laugh. "I'm *your* girl? Since when am I *your* girl?"

He was baffled. "I thought it was understood."

"Nothing is understood, Robin. I am not your girl and you are not my boy. We meet once in a while and you take me to lunch and then fuck me in your car! Let's not make a mountain out of that, shall we?" Her voice was loud and cold.

"And tell me something," Tully said. "If you thought for a moment that I was a virgin, is this what I got from you, is this the very best you had to give a virgin, taking my virginity from me in your Corvette, without even keeping the engine on? Is this your very best, you asshole?"

"Okay, Tully, okay," he said. "I got my answer."

"Yeah, you got your fucking answer, all right," she said. He drove her to Sunset Court, and she got out of the car, slammed the door, walked into Jennifer's house, and did not look back.

Robin went home feeling like shit. It did not go as well as he had hoped at all. Maybe it was difficult for a thing like that to go well. Maybe she was right. Maybe it was none of his business. But what should he do? She wasn't his girl? It *had* only been about four weeks, but he liked her; that much was obvious. How she felt was less obvious—Tully always had the mental equivalent of one arm's length, maybe two, separating herself from him. But he didn't want to stop seeing her. Stop seeing her and do what? Go back to Gail?

Robin worked and moped for a couple of days. Being at home depressed him and now there was not even a Tully on Sunday to look forward to. Robin's dad was home from the hospital. There was nothing more a hospital could do. Stephen DeMarco, Sr., had been sick with lung cancer for about six months now and the whole family was waiting for him to die, Robin included, because he could not stand the sight of his father in pain, or worse, on morphine—delirious, debilitated, and dying. The entire house smelled of chloroform and death. To make himself feel better, Robin took Gail out to dinner, apologized to her, brought her back to his house, and had sex with her, all the while thinking of Tully groaning beneath him, her arms wrapped tightly around his neck.

Two weeks passed, and Robin couldn't stand it anymore. One day he left work early and drove over to Topeka High. He sat in front of the main entrance for two hours without turning the radio on.

Jennifer and Julie walked out of the school together, schoolbooks against their chests, and when Robin saw Jennifer and Julie looking at him, he thought: they know. They know, and they think I'm an asshole. Robin asked them where he could find Tully. He was surprised by their answer. Washburn University Day Care?

Driving over to Washburn University, he parked on the southwestern corner of the campus and watched Tully through a wire fence play with a group of children. The sign on the fence read KEEP OUT. PRIVATE PROPERTY. WASHBURN UNIVERSITY NURSERY AND DAY CARE. Robin noticed all the kids clung to her, and Tully, bending down or kneeling in front of them, listened to each of them speak. Then the children chased her around the playground at manic speed and she ran from them a little slower so that they could catch her. Robin saw that Tully was laughing, and the kids were laughing, too.

Robin waited until five o'clock and then beeped the horn. Tully saw him, and slowly came through the gate to the car. She did not get in.

"Please get in, I want to talk to you," Robin said.

She got in.

"I gotta get home. My mother's home by six o'clock." Robin drove to the Potwin Elementary School, a block away from the Grove, and parked there.

"So what's this about the day-care center?"

She shrugged. "Just something I do on Thursday afternoons."

"Every Thursday afternoon?"

"Sure."

"For how long?"

Tully rubbed her hands together. "This is my third year."

"For God's sake, why?"

Tully shrugged again. "All the teachers—they're all older. The kids need someone young to play with."

Robin touched her hair tenderly. "It's obvious they like you."

"Yeah, you don't know what we play. I'm the Wicked Witch of the West, and they're supposed to kill me when they catch me."

Robin smiled. "You like children, Tully."

"Yes, for two hours a week, I like other people's children," she said, moving away from his hand on her hair.

Robin cleared his throat. "Listen, I'm sorry about the other day. I didn't mean to upset you. Please go out with me again, and if you don't want to tell me anything, I won't ask you. You can set the rules, Tull, just don't break up with me."

Tully was glad he had come. She missed him, but she also thought it was a good time to be honest with him about some things. "Robin, I'll be glad to go out with you," Tully said. "I like you, you're a nice guy, but you just have to understand a couple of things about me. One—I don't much like to talk about my business. And two—" Tully struggled to find the right words. "And two, this—we—can at best be a temporary thing." She felt a little tight inside seeing his reaction, his blank stare, a hurt, mute face. What does he expect? she thought. What the hell did he think was going to happen?

"Robin, what?"

"Why temporary, Tully?" he asked.

"Robin, because I have plans. I got plans." *That just don't include you.*

"Plans?" he said wearily.

"Yes. I'm a senior, you know. I'm going to be eighteen years old. I'm going to do something with my life."

"Like what? Dance?"

Tully shook her head. "No dancing. All that practice, all that competition, those grueling hours, that's not a life, not a life for me, anyway. From one jail to another," she said. "No, I like to dance, been dancing since I was young. You could say"—she half smiled—"that dance was my first passion—"

"That's nothing to be proud of, Tully," Robin said.

"Who is proud?" she said defenselessly. "I'm not proud of it, that's just the way it is."

"So pursue it."

"No," she said. "I don't want to be trapped by dancing." She rubbed her hands together. "Classical dance is out of the question and every other kind involves taking your clothes off." *And I just don't want to take my clothes off.* She never had been able to spend the hundred-dollar bill she won the time she took off her shirt during a dance contest in Tortilla Jack's on College Hill.

"You don't seem like you much want to be trapped by anything," said Robin.

"You're right," she said. "So?"

Robin wanted to know what else was there.

"College."

"Good, college is good," he said. "So?"

She sighed. "Jennifer and I are applying to Stanford. My grades aren't great, I'll never get in, of course . . ." she trailed off.

Robin interrupted her. "Stanford. That's an Ivy League–type school. Where is that?"

"California, actually," said Tully.

"California?" exclaimed Robin. "I see. So what do you plan to do at this Stanford?"

"If you'd let me finish, I said I'll never get in. But UC Santa Cruz is nearby, so I applied there too. Get a degree, get a job, dance on the weekends, see the ocean," said Tully.

"A degree in what?"

"Whatever. Who cares? A *degree*."

"What about Jennifer?"

"Jen is going to be a doctor. A pediatrician. Or a child psychiatrist."

"And Jennifer wants to do this, too, does she? Go to California?"

"Of course she does," said Tully. "She suggested it."

"Oh, well, then I guess that's that," said Robin, looking away into the side window. "I guess that's that."

Tully sat quietly.

"So I see," said Robin. "So what do you want to go out with me for? Do you just want me to tide you over till next year?"

"Next year?" said Tully. "I was thinking more like till next week."

"Yes," said Robin. "Oh, yes, I'm sure," he said sarcastically, hitting the wheel. "I'm sure. So, Tully, tell me, what do you want to be, in California, when you grow up?"

"Dream-free," replied Tully.

4

WINTER

November 1978

"What do you mean, you want to go to California with Tully?" said Lynn. Tony stopped eating his steak.

"I mean," said Jennifer, "just what I said. We want to go to California. We *are* going to California."

"What are you talking about?" said Tony. "You are going to Harvard. I thought it was all agreed."

Jennifer shook her head. "We've applied to Stanford. That's where we're going."

Lynn and Tony exchanged a long look. Lynn said, "Jenny Lynn, honey, whose idea is that? Is it Tully's?"

Tony raised his voice. "Of course it's Tully's! Tully, Tully, Tully! I'm tired of hearing that girl's name!" He turned to his wife. "I kept telling you she was a bad seed!" And then to Jennifer, "What do you want to do, Jennifer? What do *you* want?"

"I want to go to California," Jennifer said stubbornly.

"Goddamn it!" shouted Tony, throwing his fork down on the plate. It made a loud noise that rang in everybody's ears. "I will not let that girl make a loser out of you, Jennifer! I will not let that girl make another *her* out of you."

Lynn asked Tony to lower his voice. Jennifer put her utensils down and laid her hands on her lap. "Dad. Going to Stanford is not a loser thing to do. It just isn't."

Lynn and Tony talked for a while, heatedly and passionately at first, then slowly, pretending to be reasonable. Jennifer withdrew completely and watched as her parents argued with one another about just who was responsible for letting *this* happen to *their* Jennifer.

"You're the one who is always here talking to her!" yelled Tony.

"Yes, and you're the one who is never here talking to her!" Lynn yelled back.

Tony said, "I told you and told you about that girl. And you wanted to bring her into this house. I told you: she is no good,

Lynn. She came from no good and she will come to no good, and in between she will do no good for anybody. That's Tully."

"That's not true, Dad," said Jennifer. "Tully *will* come to good. She will. You watch. Tully wants to help kids. Be a psychologist, maybe."

"Help kids? Tully is not *helped* herself!" Tony screamed. "A psychologist? Jennifer, to be a psychologist, one needs to like to talk! And your friend Tully is nearly a deaf-mute!"

"Dad! What are you talking about?" Jennifer said. "To be a *bad* psychologist, one needs to like to talk. To be a *good* one, one needs to like to *listen*. And Tully is not a deaf-mute, Dad. Just because *you* don't hear her, she is not a deaf-mute. *She's* not the one."

Standing up, Jen cut her father off before he began again. "Dad, Dad! Besides! This is not about Tully, goddamn it!" she screamed, backhanding her glass of Coke across the room. It smashed against the dining room wall and shattered loudly, echoing through the quiet house. Her parents sat there and did not react. Lynn finally said sadly, "Jenny, we thought you always wanted to go to Harvard."

"No, Mom," said Jennifer. "No. *You* always wanted me to go to Harvard."

"Well, honey, there is nothing wrong with that. There is nothing wrong with Harvard."

"Yes. And there is nothing wrong with Stanford, either."

How to tell them, how to explain just how *much* she wanted to go to California! How to explain to them that her poor Tully just wanted to be close to her. Alone upstairs, Jennifer laughed softly. They'd never believe it if I told them. They'd never believe that California is not Tully's idea at all. How little it actually has to do with Tully. Jennifer strongly suspected that, left to her own devices and despite all her protestations, despite all the maps and all the dreams and all the talk of palm trees, left to *herself,* Tully would not go to California. Oh, Tull would certainly disagree with that, certainly. But Jennifer just had a feeling about it. Without Jennifer, Tully would never go. But how to tell her parents that? And how to tell them that despite a number of colleges nationwide wanting him to play football for them, Jennifer alone knew that Jack Pendel, nineteen years old this November, captain of the High Trojans

for the second straight year, would be going nowhere else but
Palo Alto.

2.

> " . . . *Take me now*
> *Baby, here as I am*
> *Pull me close*
> *Try to understand*
> *Desire and hunger's the fire I breathe*
> *Love is a banquet on which we feed . . .*"

Robin was singing very loudly in the shower. It was Saturday night, and he was going to see Tully. Somehow—
miraculously!—she made Saturday night happen. He booked
the best room at the Holiday Inn three days ago when she told
him she could make it.

Robin got out of the shower and toweled himself off in front
of a huge floor-to-ceiling mirror. The mirror was all fogged up,
but Robin ran a towel over it and then stepped back to look at
himself. "Hmm, I look pretty good," he said aloud, and got
dressed.

His great mood was marred only by the anxiety of leaving
his family store's money to be counted on the busiest day
of the week by a nineteen-year-old assistant. *I really need to
relax, man,* thought Robin, pulling on his best tan slacks and
a Polo sweater. *Look at my brothers.*

Stephen DeMarco, Sr., too ill to get out of bed, left his store
to be managed by his three sons, but Robin's brothers were not
at all interested in the family business. Bruce and Stevie were
too busy dating and playing ball. Dating and playing ball was
all Bruce and Steve wanted to do.

Stevie was a sophomore at Kansas State University in
Manhattan, majoring in rugby, beer, and girls, while Bruce
had been playing the guitar since his high school graduation
five years ago. He was "trying to find himself." At present, he
had apparently found himself in dairy products. Bruce became
convinced that he could "self-actualize" only through farming,
and, with that in mind, he bought, with his dad's help, a
hundred-acre farm twenty miles north of Manhattan. Replete
with horses, chickens, and corn. So instead of wearing Pierre

Cardin suits and Polo shirts like Robin, Bruce wore overalls and got up with the cows. He played his guitar to the horses, and they seemed to like that; so did the girls.

That left only Robin to work the store. Before Tully, Robin worked the entire seven days the store was open. When he told Tully that he was off Sundays, he wasn't telling the truth. The truth was that Robin hadn't taken off a Sunday in seven years, but seeing that Tully could drag a dying Doberman single-handedly off the road, Robin figured he could also show some backbone and take off one day. He realized, though, that no one knew the merchandise as he did, no one could sell it as he did, no one could offer the customer exactly the right thing or know the customer's style and size and price just by the way the customer dressed and talked, quite as Robin did.

And then, of course, there was the small question of cash. Not much was cash—mostly it was VISA and personal checks. But on a good Sunday, there could also be five hundred to a thousand dollars in small bills. Okay, okay, no big deal, he was insured against theft, and in any case what was a grand to a company whose annual gross sales were nearly $2 million? But theft! And there were plenty of ways to steal from him. There were some expensive Ralph Lauren and Pierre Cardin shirts in his store. Some pricey ties and belts, some $200 Bally shoes. Robin's floor guys could just walk off with three or four $75 shirts, and that wouldn't make Robin happy at all. So he methodically made note of the merchandise on display, and the following day matched what was missing to the receipts in the register. It was neurotic, he knew, but he just hated the thought of being taken.

Robin put on Paco Rabanne and blow-dried his hair. After a few months of taking off Sundays, Robin locked the supply room, locked away the inventory sheets, and began to take off Wednesdays, too. A couple of times he brought Tully to Manhattan on Saturdays to watch him play soccer in the afternoons. Playing soccer on Saturday afternoons felt to Robin like cutting school—wrong and slightly delicious. Usually he went back to the store after a few hours, but not tonight.

" . . . Because the night
Belongs to lovers . . ."

he sang, locking the house and starting up his car.

> " *. . . Because the night*
> *Belongs to us . . .*"

Even though Robin was fretting about work, he was thinking of Tully most of all.

He was stroking her hair after they had just finished making love.

"Tully," Robin whispered. "Tully."

"What, Robin, what?"

"You do this with many guys?"

She laughed. "Well, never in a Holiday Inn." She looked around the room. "Nice. Great bed. I've never been on a bed like this before. This big."

"I'm serious."

"Yeah, I'm sure you are." She smiled and sighed. "Not so many."

"Do you remember your first?"

She stiffened, and her body became lifeless. "Who doesn't?" she said evenly. "Don't you?"

"Sure." He smiled. "It was with an older woman. Meg. She came into Dad's store, you know, to buy something for her husband."

"But was looking for something for herself, too?" offered Tully.

"I guess," Robin said. "A little for herself."

"How much older?" Tully wanted to know.

"I was sixteen, she was twenty-five."

"Kind of like you and me, reversed," said Tully.

"Kind of," said Robin. Except that for Meg he had felt nothing but gratitude. "Was your first older, too?"

"Yeah," said Tully. "He was older."

"How old were you?"

"I," said Tully, "was younger."

3.

"Is this all you got?" said Tully to Julie in early December. The girls were getting ready for their Senior Banquet. As always,

Tully was borrowing a dress from Julie, who was about two sizes larger with bigger breasts. Tonight's dress was a flower print. "Got anything black?"

"No, Tully, I don't have anything black. Don't be so picky."

"All right, all right," said Tully. "I'm a beggar, after all."

"You're not a beggar, Tully. I just don't have anything, all right?"

"All right," Tully said, putting on the dress. "God, look at me," she said in front of the mirror. "I look like a bouquet. Hope nobody comes up and smells me or pins me to their chest like a corsage."

Julie rolled her eyes, and Tully laughed.

"Tully, how did you get your mom to let you stay out so late on a school night?"

"Oh, you know. Jen this, Jen that. Of course I'm not going with a boy, Mom, to even think! This is not the prom, you know! This is a dinner for us seniors! So we can get to know each other better."

"And she bought it, huh?"

"Yeah, well, she's a little suspicious. She wants Jen to come in and say hi to her. At midnight! But that's my mother. Suspicious for the right reasons but at the wrong time."

"How is Robin?" asked Julie.

"Fine," said Tully. "How is Tom?"

"Fine." Julie cleared her throat. "Umm, speaking of Tom, will you ever tell me what you meant by your cute remarks back on Jen's birthday?"

"God, Jule, you got a long memory. Why haven't you said anything before?"

"I've been busy," Julie said. "I just thought of it."

"Don't think so much about it," said Tully.

"Well?"

"Well, what? Julie, I got him mixed up with another guy."

"I don't believe you," said Julie.

"So what the hell are you asking me for?"

"Please tell me, Tully. I won't be upset. It really doesn't matter."

"Well, if it really doesn't matter," Tully mimicked Julie's voice, "then what the hell are you asking me for?"

"He was there, wasn't he? In some club? And he made a pass at you, before he even knew who you were, and you must have turned him down, didn't you? And this really riled him, really really did, because, you see, he was under the impression that you didn't turn anybody down. That's what happened, didn't it?"

Tully bent her head for a few minutes, and when she looked up, she said, quieter, "Well, Julie. Since you think you know everything, what the hell are you asking *me* for?"

"Do I? Do I know everything?"

"Yes," said Tully, taking her friend by the shoulders and spinning her toward the door. "You know everything."

"Is that really what happened?" Julie asked Tully when they were on their way to Topeka High in Jen's Camaro.

"Yes, uh-huh," said Tully. "Don't think about it so much. Does it bother you?"

"No, uh-uh. What Tom did before he met me is his own business. It amuses me, though." She turned around in the front seat to face Tully in the back and saw Tully's slightly embarrassed face.

"What?" said Julie. "What kind of an expression is that—" And then her eyes opened up and her mouth, too. "Ahhhh," she said. "Wait. I don't know everything, do I? I thought of everything, except the *when*, didn't I? Well, Tully, you did say it was over a year ago."

"I was using the term 'year' loosely," said Tully. Jennifer stifled a laugh.

"So *exactly* when was it, then?" said Julie. "Try to be specific."

"August," said Tully.

"What? *This* August? The one that just passed?"

"Yes, uh-huh," said Tully, and her face became blank and inscrutable.

Julie faced the front again, mouth slightly ajar. "What do ya know," she said. "Well, I'll be damned."

"Forget it, Julie," said Jennifer.

"Yeah, Jule, it's no big deal," echoed Tully.

"Yeah," said Julie. "No big deal."

When the three of them were walking toward Topeka High, Julie leaned over and asked Tully, "Listen, tell me, did you refuse him because you were my friend or because you just didn't like him?"

Tully put her arm around Julie. "I refused," she said, "because I am your friend. But if I wasn't your friend, I would have also refused, because I don't like him."

Makker, Mandolini, and Martinez—or the 3Ms—sat at the same table in the decorated cafeteria. The food was nondescript, to go with the nondescript music. But after dinner, everyone was able to walk around to the other tables. Tully saw Jennifer pass by Jack's table. He waved to her, and she waved back but didn't stop. Tully was amused but became less amused when afterwards Jennifer was mute for a half hour until Tully dragged her out to what was passing for a dance floor and the girls danced together, their flushed faces inches away from one another.

Gail was there, looking almost nice in a blue dress and new hair, Tully thought grudgingly. Tully stopped by Gail's table to talk to a guy in her math class, and Gail did not even look Tully's way. Strolling over to Gail, Tully lowered her head and said quietly, "I'd ask you to dance, but I can't take your rejection."

"Get away from me, you tramp," said Gail.

Tully recoiled as if her mother had slapped her. But her face was a Tullyface, and she coldly smiled when she said, "Gail, you're a sore loser."

"Get away from me," Gail repeated, shaking.

"Ooops, what I meant was," said Tully, "Gail, you're just a plain loser."

Tully and Jennifer danced together some more. There wasn't much of a dance floor and there wasn't much dance music, either. Wait till the prom, the girls said to each other, and then Jack, in a suit and unshaven, walked over and took Jennifer's upper arm and asked if he could cut in. When he said it, however, he stared right at Tully, making her go red. Watching them dance, without touching each other, Tully felt even more uncomfortable, feeling another stab of the anxiety that moved her at Jennifer's party. Tully saw in Jennifer's face lost deer and something else, too. Insanity. Sheer, raw, naked insanity. All she needs is a straightjacket for that expression she's got on her face. She never talks about him! thought Tully. She never talks about him, yet where does it all go? Where does all that's behind the crazy look on her face go? Who sees it? Not me. And if not me, who? Julie? No, Julie and I both have no clue. Does *he* see it? I hope so, thought Tully. I fucking hope so.

And then the inexplicable happened. When the song ended, Jack and Jennifer came over to Tully. A new song began, Yvonne Elliman not wanting nobody baby if she couldn't have you, and *Jack asked Tully if she wanted to dance.*

"You're famous, Tully," he said. "Let's dance."

Tully shot Jennifer a quick look. She seemed fine about it, if a bit vacant. And then Tully and Jack danced. Tully toned it down so much that she even heard some guy shout from across the room, "Come on, Tully Makker! Show him your stuff!"

But Tully wasn't going to be showing Jack any of her stuff with Jennifer standing there looking at them. Tully made sure she barely touched him. He was much taller than she was, even with her heels. Tully usually danced with her eyes closed unless she was drunk, but tonight she wasn't drunk and her eyes were open. She casually looked up into his face. Jack smiled at her, and again Tully saw something in his eyes. Something . . . clear.

"Jack-ieeee!" squealed a voice near Tully. She turned around. A girl was standing next to them. Shakie Lamber. Everyone knew Shakie. She was the Homecoming Queen.

"Jack-ieeee!" whined Shakie again. "Pleeeease, can I cut in?"

"Do you want to dance with me or Tully?" asked Jack.

Shakie gave Tully a perfunctory smile. "With you, of course. I'm afraid Tully is just too good for me."

"Well, then, you'll have to ask Tully if you can cut in, won't you?" said Jack.

"Be my guest," said Tully, relieved to get off the floor and not be stared at anymore by Jennifer.

Soon the noise got to be too much for Jennifer. She never liked noise, and Tully joined her in a walk down the school corridors.

"How many lockers on the first floor?" asked Tully, passing by the front doors.

"Counting the ones in the Admin office and the wings? Five hundred and twenty."

"How many handmade bricks did it take to build our school?"

"Nine hundred thousand," answered Jennifer automatically.

"What's Topeka High's minority population?"

"Piss off," said Jennifer, snapping out of it.

Tully smiled. "Want to go upstairs to the library?"

"It's closed," said Jen.

"Let's try," said Tully, leading her friend up the stairs.

It was open. Tully and Jennifer walked in, softly shutting the door behind them. They sat on the bench near the fireplace with their feet up.

"God, this place is creepy in the dark," said Jennifer. "Those stained-glass windows seem so pretty during the day, but at night, boy, are they creepy."

"I wish the fireplace was lit," said Tully, with her back to the stained-glass windows. She wasn't creeped out at all.

"Soooooo," said Jen slowly. "Did you and he talk about anything?"

"What, while we jigged around? No," said Tully.

"Nothing?" Jennifer wanted to know.

"Nothing, Mandolini," said Tully. "If you wanted me to talk to him, you should've sent me there with a mission. I've never spoken two words to him in my entire life. You want me to engage in conversation on the dance floor when your stare is driving me to distraction?"

"I'm sorry," said Jennifer. "I didn't mean to stare. I just thought you might talk, that's all."

"Talk about what?"

"I don't know," said Jennifer. "Something."

"Like? The weather? Politics? Football, God help me? You?"

"You, maybe?" said Jennifer.

"Why the hell would we want to talk about me?"

"Me, then," Jennifer said.

"Now you're making sense," said Tully. "We didn't, though I'm beginning to wish we did, just so you'd stop interrogating me."

"It's okay," Jennifer said. "Let's go home."

Later, in the Camaro, Tully said, "Jen, you know, you lost a bit of weight. I noticed when we were dancing, you're getting this thin waist. Are you dieting?"

"No, I just kinda go on not being very hungry lately," answered Jennifer. "Not thin like yours."

"No, but then I don't have boobs like yours, either."

Jennifer didn't say anything.

"Love your car," said Tully.

"Yeah, it's pretty neat, isn't it?"

Tully sighed. "Okay, that's it. Jennifer, what do I usually ask you? How's cheerleading going? Well, tonight I'm gonna ask you something different. How is Jack?"

Silence. "Great. *You* danced with him."

"Yes, I did. You did, too. You guys looked good dancing together."

"We did?" Jennifer brightened a little. "I always wonder what we look like when we are together. Whether we fit, you know."

"I know," said Tully. "And you do." Tully saw it in Jennifer's eyes again, the mute withdrawal, and changed the subject. "When do you think we'll be hearing from Stanford and UCSC?"

"February," replied Jennifer.

They parked in front of Tully's house.

"Do you really want me to come in with you?" asked Jennifer.

"You must," said Tully. "That is, if you want me to live."

They woke Hedda up, who sat with her head drooped and mouth open in front of the late news. Tully woke her up.

Hedda thanked Jennifer for driving Tully home and asked Tully where she got her pretty dress. Tully actually felt lucky then that she looked like a flower shop.

"Want to sleep over, Jen?" Tully turned to her mother. "Is that okay, Mom?"

"Tully!" Jennifer said. "You want me to sleep over? I haven't asked my own mother."

Tully nodded. "So ask her."

Jennifer looked briefly away but called her mother and made sure it was all right.

"Jennifer, how could anything not be all right with your parents?" Tully said as they were getting ready for bed. "If you told them you were heading for Texas to become a tattooed rodeo girl, they'd pay your way."

"You're wrong, Tully," said Jen. "They're not happy we're going to Palo Alto."

"Are they paying your way?" asked Tully, adding, when she

saw Jennifer's expression, "See?"

They climbed into Tully's bed together. When Jennifer was younger she had many nightmares, many bad things frightened her in the night, and Tully, who used to stay over at Jen's house three, four times a week, would climb into Jennifer's bed to calm her down. Tully did not mention all the bad things that came to *her* in the night. The habits of children die hard, and as they got older, Tully did try to sleep on the floor when she stayed over. When she did, it felt as if she and Jen were fighting, so they continued to sleep alongside each other. When Julie stayed over with them, all three girls slept on the floor. In the last few years, Tully seldom slept over with just Jen.

Tully pulled her blanket over them and spooned Jennifer, the only position in which Jen liked to sleep. Tully occasionally wondered through the years what it would be like to be spooned herself, but never brought it up. It was never *that* important.

Jennifer's hair smelled faintly of Gee, Your Hair Smells Terrific. Tully touched it. Jennifer didn't stir. She seemed tired, or silent. Uncomfortable?

"Jen, your hair smells terrific. Jen?"

"Hmm?"

"Jennifer? Are you uncomfortable?"

"Me? No, why should I be uncomfortable?"

"You go through these things sometimes. You get awkward."

"I'm okay, Tully," Jennifer answered. "I'm glad to be here. I haven't been here in so long. With you for so long." Jen paused. "We missed you, Tully, when you weren't with us."

Tully swallowed and held Jennifer tighter. "I was with you guys, I was constantly over."

"Not constantly," said Jennifer. "Not like before. And never alone with me. Admit it, Tull, you wanted to be away from us."

"No, that's not true," said Tully.

"So why did you do it, then? Why did you stay away?"

"Who knows? I guess I just wanted to be with people who didn't know me at all."

"Yes, but why?"

"Because," said Tully, "I guess I needed some seclusion."

"Seclusion? Like anonymity?"

"Yes, just like that."

Jen was quiet. "Anonymity, like . . . death?"

"Yeah," said Tully slowly. "I guess like death." In the dark, she could almost bear it.

"So would you say that you sort of, like, died during those years?"

"Yes," said Tully. "I guess you could say that."

Jennifer was quiet. "Why did you need that so much, all that anonymity? What happened to you that you needed to . . . die? Did you fall in love with someone? Did someone break your heart?"

Tully shook her head. "Jenny, I didn't fall in love. And no one broke my heart."

"Tell me, Tully," said Jennifer.

After a moment of silence, Tully said softly, "Nothing to tell, Mandolini."

"Makker, you even stopped playing softball. Come on."

"Really," said Tully, smelling Jennifer's hair again. "Believe me."

"Makker, you are so full of shit. You really don't want to talk about it, do you?"

"No, Jen, I really don't."

"Well," said Jennifer, "in any case, I'm glad you came back, Tully. We missed you when you were gone."

And I missed you, too, guys, thought Tully, but remained silent.

"Tell me, Tully," said Jennifer. "Tell me about the first time with your wrists."

Tully moved away slightly. Jennifer reached around and pulled her back. "Go on."

"Not much to tell," said Tully.

"Tell me why you do it."

"Jennifer, what the hell is wrong with you, what are you asking me this shit for?"

"Just tell me, Tully," whispered Jen. "Tell me. Do you do it to die?"

Tully sighed. "No," she said slowly. "I don't think I do it to die. I do it because I want to feel what death feels like. I just want unconsciousness to wash over me, I do it almost like they did it in the ancient times—to heal myself. And then when all the bad is out of me, I come to and go on."

Tully trailed off, thinking of the very first time she sat down inside a bathtub filled with water with a double-edged razor in her hand. She thought her young breastless body was all relaxed, but when she put the razor near her wrists, her fingers were shaking so badly, she had to put them back in the water for a few minutes until she calmed down. Am I going to die? thought Tully. I mean, is that what's going to happen to me? Am I going to die? I'll cut my wrists and lose consciousness and bleed to death like the Romans did, except that nobody will find me until next week, after I will have been stone dead for so long. Am I going to die? I cannot count on anyone to come and save me, that's for fucking sure, so before I put this steel blade to my hand and watch my veins pop open like dough out of a Pillsbury can, I want to be sure that I don't want to die. Tully looked around the bathroom, looked at the towels near her, at the gauze bandage, at the iodine, and thought, *I am ready.* For *whatever.* For *what-fucking-ever.* And she took the blade out of the hot water and sliced an inch-long horizontal gash in her left wrist, thinking *Oh, goodness me, my hands are so steady, oh, my goodness me, look at all that blood.* She put her wrist down and watched the water near her slowly turn pink. She lifted her hand and, fascinated, watched her prepubescent blood pour down her arm. She touched the blood with her fingers, then tasted it. It was salty and slick. And then Tully cut her other wrist. She put both her hands under the water and closed her eyes, but that wasn't as good as watching herself bleed. She opened her eyes and lifted both her hands up high, lying down all the way up to her neck in the blood water, and gazed in disbelief as the bright red blood oozed down her arms. It was when Tully's eyes started to close, it was when she started to hear strange noises and see water and waves and rocks in front of her eyes, it was when she started to smell the salty sea, that Tully thought, *It's time, or I will die. If I don't get up now, I will die.* She felt herself to be in slow motion, moving with all the deliberate speed of a tanker on the horizon—seemingly immobile and soundless—when she lifted her body out of the water and bent over for the towel. Again, rocks were washed over with water in front of her eyes, water broke against the rocks, making gurgling sounds. Gurgling, burbling waves rose up and crashed in front of her, whooshh . . . whoooshhh . . . whoooshhh . . .

whooooshhhh . . . *Let me lie down for a moment*, Tully thought, *just for a moment*. But she didn't. She pulled herself up and grabbed on to the towel instead, pressing it to one wrist, then the other. She kept herself up, kept her arms up, got out of the bath, got another towel, and, wrapping it around the other wrist, pressed her wrists together hard and sat there naked on the cold tile floor, with her arms up and together, eyes closed, trying to will the blood to stop. And it did, eventually. The towels were ruined. Tully didn't even need to dry herself off, so long had she sat on the floor. When she unwrapped her wrists, her gashes were black and swollen, but no longer fluid. That was good. Pouring iodine on the wounds was not so good. Tully whimpered and grit her teeth, and finally bit her lip to blood to keep herself from screaming.

She bandaged her wrists tight, went to her room, and prayed, swearing to God that she would never, *never* do that again.

But time passed, and her wounds healed, ragged, jagged scars though they remained. Tully forgot the closeness to death, remembering only the closeness to the waves and the rocks. And so she cut her wrists again, some time later, and again and again, longing to be washed away by the salty water.

Jennifer's back was to Tully. Nudging her and getting no response, Tully sighed and said, "Jen, what's wrong with you?" feeling tightness around her stomach. "Are you all right?"

"Of course. Why shouldn't I be?"

Tully patted Jennifer's shoulder. "Jennifer, you're not playing ball. Want to talk?"

"Tully, there's really nothing to talk about."

"Don't I know it," said Tully. "There never is. You forget who you're talking to. Still, though," she said, using one of Robin's phrases. "Something you want to tell me?"

"Nothing to tell, Tully," said Jennifer sadly. "Wish there was."

Taking a deep breath, Tully said, "Jennifer, have you slept with him?"

Jennifer didn't answer, and then began to cry. Tully was speechless. Crying! She touched Jennifer's hair and managed only, "Please, please." Crying, my Lord, over what? I cannot believe, just cannot, is she really crying over—

"Oh, Tully," Jennifer sobbed, sitting up against the wall. Tully sat up, too. *Oh, Tully?* What the hell was *Oh, Tully?* Jennifer was smearing tears all over her face with her fist, like she used to when she was young, but God, it had been since about then that Jen last cried in front of Tully. "You just don't understand."

"Then explain it to me," said Tully softly.

"It's nothing like you think."

Tully thought Jen was wrong there. Tully was afraid it was exactly as she thought.

"Jennifer, my God, but are you crying over *him*?" Tully, shaking her head, got up for a box of tissues, sat on the edge of the bed and gently wiped Jennifer's face. It was minutes before Jennifer was collected enough to speak.

"Jennifer," Tully said. "You're fucking crazy. Have you slept with him?"

"No, Tully, I haven't," said Jennifer. "But do you know why I haven't? Do you know why? Because he hasn't asked me. He hasn't asked me!" she cried. "And if he had asked me, I would say, When? Now? And if he asked me to jump before I did it, I would say, How high, Jack Pendel, how high? Here I am, a virgin till I die, as you say, and I would give it to him faster than I could say Jack."

Tully was at a complete loss for words as she wiped Jennifer's face. At a loss, and helpless, too. Helpless in part because she did not understand her. Tully Makker just did not see what the problem was.

"So go after him, Jen, go after him. You want him. Tell him you want him. Let him know you want him. They get it after a while, they do, believe me."

"Oh, Tully, you really don't understand, do you? It's not a matter of going after him, don't you see?" Jennifer began to cry again. "Don't you see that if he wanted me, he would've seen by now what's so plain to me and to everyone else? He would've seen it. But he doesn't see it because he doesn't feel the same way."

Tully disagreed. "Jen, he doesn't get it because he is a football jock."

"No, Tully, he doesn't get it because he doesn't love me. When you don't love somebody you never get how they feel. You don't even look for it."

"Hmm," said Tully. "I know plenty of people who love each other and still don't get how they feel."

Jennifer waved her off. "Who do you know, Makker?"

Tully wavered. "Well, your parents, for one. Julie's, too."

Jennifer was still crying. Tully coughed and switched tactics. "Jenny, okay, so he doesn't get it," she said. "For whatever reason. So you just say fuck you and move on. That's it. Just move right on," said Tully, making a sweeping motion with her hand. "Move right on to Palo Alto," she added. "Where there are so many Jack Pendels, where there will be so many Jack Pendels dying to steal your heart and with it your bikini, you will have to buy twenty just to keep up. Bikinis, I mean."

"Tully, you just don't get it, do you?"

"Honestly, Jen?" Tully said apologetically. "No, I don't. See? *I* don't get it, but *we* love each other." Tully was trying to make a little light of it, but Jennifer hit at Tully impatiently.

"It's not the same, now, is it?" said Jennifer.

"It's not?" said Tully.

"Well, of course it's not!" exclaimed Jennifer. "Makker, that's why I don't want to talk to you sometimes. You're just so obtuse."

Tully saw in Jennifer's face that thing, that crazy crazy thing. She is so far out there that where she is, not even I can reach her.

"Don't you understand, Tully?" Jennifer said. "I love him. I *love* him."

"You *do*?" said Tully distastefully. "So, okay. So, *un-love* him."

"Tully, you don't—you just can't—just stop loving the people you love."

"You can't? Why the hell not?"

"I don't know. *I* can't," said Jennifer brokenly. "He is my first love. My very first. And I will never stop loving him."

Tully sighed and tried to reason with her. "Jen, I know, but everyone says that. Everyone feels that way, that we will never stop loving someone, that we will never love anyone else, that we can never feel more than we do right now, but yet . . . we do, somehow, stop loving. We do get over it. Don't we? We have to. We must. Otherwise, how could we go on?"

"Tully, I know you, of all people, are skeptical. I don't

expect you to understand. I just know the way I feel about him and have felt about him for a long time. I will never love anyone else for the rest of my life."

Tully patted Jennifer's head. "And it may be a very short life indeed, Mandolini, because if you don't stop crying, I'm going to have to kill you."

Jennifer laughed a little and wiped her face with her arm.

"I love when you do that," said Tully, handing her a tissue. "You look soooo attractive."

The girls settled back into bed. Jennifer faced the wall and Tully lay down beside her.

"I'm hot, Tully, I'm very hot. Can you blow on my forehead?" Jen said, turning around. And Tully did, while Jennifer whispered with closed eyes that trickled tears. "Why do I love him, Tully, why? For what good and damned reason do I love him?"

"Because he is beautiful and he moves well?" said Tully.

"You think he is beautiful?" exclaimed Jennifer.

"No," said Tully quickly. "*You* think he is beautiful."

Jennifer closed her eyes again. "I shut my eyes and I see his face," she whispered. "I see his face as it talks and laughs, I see only his face and nothing else. Not even you, Makker, not even you. You know? I don't even see Palo Alto anymore. Just him. My God, Tully, what's happening?"

"You've taken complete leave of your senses," Tully said gently.

Jennifer continued to cry, but softer and slower, and Tully continued to wipe her face and blow on her forehead, but softer and slower. Finally Jennifer fell asleep, but Tully did not.

She lay perched on her elbow, tenderly blowing on Jennifer's face for a long time, remembering the first time she had met her. Julie had introduced them. And Julie had met Tully by finding her wandering on the street not far from Lowman's Hill Elementary School, where Tully attended kindergarten. Tully had gotten lost again—accidentally on purpose—and Angela Martinez brought the five-year-old girl home. Tully played with Julie while Angela called the police. "Oh, it's that Makker kid again," the cops said when they arrived. "She's always getting lost, once a week, about. One day she'll wander out onto the turnpike and that will be the last we'll see of her. She'll just keep going. She's a spunky little kid. We'll drive her home now."

Oh, no, Julie and her mother had objected. Let her play. We'll take her home. They fed Tully dinner: burritos and tacos. Tully had never eaten such delicious food.

Angela was worried that Tully's parents might be going out of their minds looking for her. Tully wanted to tell the nice woman that was not a problem, but Angela found out soon enough when she brought Tully home and Hedda said, "Have you been out again? What did we tell you? Stay in the yard."

From then on, Mrs. Martinez tried to pick Tully up from kindergarten and bring her to the house. Tully remembered that several weeks later during the summer, Lynn Mandolini brought Jennifer over. Jennifer! So plump, so bossy! She came into Julie's house and immediately told the two girls to give her the bike. The three of them played together all summer, and every summer after that. When Jennifer was young, she lost her temper frequently when she did not get her way. Screaming, she would throw toys that weren't hers, throw sand, throw herself on the ground, spit. When Tully was younger, she found Julie a little easier to get along with; Jennifer's tantrums upset her.

Jennifer improved as she got older, and it was only when Tully was older herself that she discovered Jennifer was moderately autistic at the age of two and three, and Jennifer spent years overcoming the remnants of the illness as an adult. Minor vestiges of withdrawal remained: the compulsive neatness and slight detachment from physical closeness were the most obvious. But there were other things, too. Every day, Jennifer counted the number of cracks in the pavement from her house on Sunset Court to the corner of 17th Street and Wayne. She always verbalized the discovery of a new crack and showed it to Tully and Julie. She counted the number of lockers on each floor of Topeka High. She kept careful track of the gross national products of the twenty-five most developed countries, and of the broken streetlights from 17th Street to Gage Park. Also Jennifer got 800 on her math SATs she took last October. Tully pressed her lips to Jennifer's damp forehead.

Before Tully knew Jen was sick, she thought that Jennifer was the luckiest girl on earth. Out of the three of them, she seemed to Tully the one destined to live in perpetual sunshine, having lived a sunshine childhood. After all, Jennifer had the fortune to be born to two people whose sole mission in life was Jennifer's happiness.

While Tully played barefoot and alone in a dirty yard with chickens and stray cats. Dusty and unwashed, Tully spent her summers and afternoons in that yard of the house on the Grove, looking out onto the turnpike and the railroad. Who put suntan lotion on her? Who kissed her boo-boos and washed her face and gave her toys? The early years swam together for Tully. Somewhere in there, there were two brothers and even a father, but then Hedda and Tully were alone, and Aunt Lena and Uncle Charlie came to live with them to help Hedda with the mortgage. When Uncle Charlie died, it became easier to pay the bills with his insurance. Hedda worked as she always had, while Aunt Lena stayed home, having never worked a day in her life. Aunt Lena was gray and heavy, though she had been only forty when she became a widow. She kept mostly to herself in her rooms: she took a bedroom and a dining room after Uncle Charlie died. She said she was entitled to the space since the house now technically belonged to her.

Tully breathed on Jennifer's face. Jenny, so many things you have at God's grace. But I don't care. I don't care, and I mean it. I don't give a shit. I can't believe I'm thinking this, but I swear to you, Jennifer, I would relive my whole life exactly the same if somehow God, by again denying me, could bring you happiness, bring you what you really want, want with all your heart, the only thing you want. Dear Jennifer. It'll be all right.

The next morning, her eyes red and swollen, Jennifer lay in bed and said, "Tull, tell me your story of the turtle and scorpion."

"Jen, get the hell out of here. I am dead tired. The sun is out, isn't it? I'm like a bush baby. Now *I* go to sleep. You slept all night."

"Tell me, Tully, tell me, and please rub my back while you do it."

"God, Mandolini, you're fucking demanding. Oh, all right." Tully sighed, sat on top of Jennifer's rear end, and began to rub Jen's shoulders. "Once upon a time," began Tully, "a scorpion swam all the way to the middle of a big lake. And when he got there, he realized he did not know how to swim and started to drown."

"Not so hard, Tully, not so hard!" exclaimed Jennifer.

Tully sighed and continued. "Help! Help! the scorpion yelled. But no one came to help him. A turtle was swimming by, and the scorpion saw her and said, 'Turtle, please help me. Can't you see I'm drowning?' And the turtle said, 'No, I will not help you. If I come near you, you will bite me, and then I will die.'"

"Tully, now I can't feel it at all. A little harder, please."

Tully stuck her tongue out at the back of Jen's head.

"And stop sticking your tongue out at me," said Jennifer, her eyes closed. "I know you did it. Just go on with the story."

"The scorpion protested," said Tully loudly. "'Turtle, I swear to you, I will not bite you. I'm not stupid, turtle. You could save my life. If I bite you, I will drown, and I do not want to die.' The turtle believed him, swam over, put the scorpion on her back, and started swimming with him back to shore. When the turtle was close to the shore, the scorpion bit her. And as they were both drowning, the turtle turned around and said, 'Why? Why did you do it, scorpion? Now we're both going to die. Why did you do it?' And the scorpion replied, 'Because I am a scorpion. I cannot help myself. It is my nature.'"

Jennifer lay there quietly on her stomach. "I love that story," she said.

And I love *you*, Mandolini, thought Tully.

4.

For Christmas, Robin took Tully to his father's funeral. Mr. DeMarco died on Christmas Eve.

They buried him next to Pamela DeMarco on the twenty-seventh of December. Robin introduced Tully as his girlfriend, and Tully smiled cordially. She observed a lot of grief on a bitterly cold and windy December day. She wondered how it was possible to display so much emotion in public. Robin stood still, dressed in somber black, and his face was a mask. But when he and Tully got back to his house and he smelled the camphor and saw his father's chair, he broke down. Tully patted his back and again wondered. Robin never seemed to talk much or show much feeling about his dad's cancer; yet, here he was, struck.

New Year's Eve was better. Shakie, the Homecoming Queen, threw a party, and everybody went. Even Julie seemed to be having a marginally good time with Tom. But it was Jennifer who held Tully at attention most of the evening, for Jennifer spent most of the evening with Jack. In fact, he never left her side. Tully did not waste time looking at Jennifer's face, knowing already what she would find there. Instead, she watched Jack to see what was in his. It was hard to tell with Jack. For one, he was drunk. And two, his face was the kind of face that would not be read easily. It seemed composed even under the glaze of alcohol. But his hands touched Jen's shoulders and arms, touched her face and her neck. His eyes laughed with her, and so did his mouth. Bending his head down to talk to her, Jack almost seemed tender to Tully. *Tender*—what an absurd word! Yet tenderness was what came to her mind when she saw Jack looking at Jennifer. And familiarity, too. Sort of like he knew her face well. Who can tell? "*So*," she sang softly under her breath,

"*. . . so*
you think you can tell
Heaven from Hell,
blue skies from pain.
Can you tell a green field
from a cold steel rail?
A smile from a veil?
So you think you can tell?"

Jack is a popular football captain, thought Tully. That should tell me everything I need to know about his feelings for Jennifer. But all Tully wanted was what Jennifer wanted, and all Jennifer wanted was Jack.

They said good-bye to 1978 and greeted 1979 with champagne and kisses and "Auld Lang Syne." Robin kissed Tully, and she smiled and squeezed his arm. I don't need to sing a song to figure out what he is feeling, she thought. She lost sight of Jennifer for a moment and then couldn't find her again anywhere. Not her, not Jack.

Jennifer closed her eyes and then opened them again in a hurry. Yes, sir. He is here. Open your eyes, Jen, all you wanna do is look at him and you're closing your eyes? What's the matter with you?

She assumed they were driving to his house. He didn't make it clear. Right before midnight, he whispered to her, "Let's get out of here," and then said little else. Did Jack perhaps think they were going to *Jennifer's* house? He seemed very drunk.

Okay, Jen, hold on to the wheel with both hands, steady on, now, girl, and drive. You'll have plenty of time to look at him. Just drive now. Must be well past midnight, she thought. Did he ask me to drive him home or did I just volunteer? Does he even know where his home is? Look at him, will you just look at him. Jennifer, drive the car, steady on.

At Lakeside Drive, Jack asked her to come in. No one seemed to be home. "No one's home," he confirmed, disappearing into the bathroom. Jennifer sat on the sofa and looked around. She was in the back room—the family room. It had been a long time since the last time she was at his house. Nearly a year, she guessed. She had always liked this room. It had a lot of pretty white-painted wicker furniture and many plants.

Jennifer looked up as Jack handed her a Coke. "Your favorite, right?" he said. She wanted to tell him that no, wrong, *he* was her favorite, but thought that was too trite.

He sat down next to her and touched her hair. "Your hair feels so nice, so soft," he murmured. "You smell so good, I love the way you smell. I've always loved the way you smell."

"Always?" she asked.

"Always," Jack confirmed, moving Jen's hair to expose her neck. She helped him, and he leaned over and kissed it, kissed her neck. Jennifer leaned into him and Jack kissed her throat all over. Jennifer wanted to keep her eyes open so she could look at him, so that she could look at him kissing her throat, but that was just impossible. As soon as his lips touched her neck, her eyes closed.

She wrapped her hand around his neck and with her other hand touched his face like a blind person. At first Jack was kissing her gently, then his kissing got more urgent; his mouth ran up her jaw and he began to kiss her lips, roughly and gently, roughly and gently. Jennifer tried to keep track of what he was doing to her, but it seemed her brain, like her eyes, closed as well. Keeping track was clearly not possible. She stopped keeping track of anything except his mouth and his big rough and gentle hands that ran all around her. Jack knelt down in front of Jennifer and unbuttoned her blouse. Putting his face between her breasts, he kissed her skin between them while his hands fumbled with the back of her bra. "It opens in the front," she said helpfully, and he unfastened her and took her breasts out; looked at them and moaned. "Jen, you are so beautiful, look at you, you're unbelievable." He kissed her breasts under the nipples and over the nipples, sucked her nipples, sucked the skin of her breasts under and over the nipples. Jennifer moaned and moaned, her eyes permanently shut, her hands clutching his blond hair; she was just so lost.

I can't believe I am really here with you. I can't believe you are kissing me. I can't believe *you* are kissing *me*. When Jennifer had dreamed of what it would be like to have Jack kiss her and touch her, when she dreamed of him and his lips every day for the past four years, this is what she dreamed it would be. Being completely lost in his lips.

Jack carried her up to his bedroom, kissing her all the while. He laid her on his bed and began unbuckling his belt. *Unbuckling his belt. I am lying down on his bed.* Jennifer watched him do it, but incoherently; crazed with aching, she just wanted the feel of *him*.

And she got him. Jen managed to wrap her hands around him, seconds before he thrust himself inside her, and her only thought was, My God, it is so big, is this what they are all like, this *big*?

"Oh, you are so wet." He groaned. "You are so ready for me." She could only groan in response; she was here with him, under his smooth wide chest, with his big muscled arms propping him up, with all his blond hair falling into his beautiful drunk face above her. She was here with him, and her readiness just did not matter, for she had fallen so hard for him, she had been perpetually at the ready.

Jack had had a lot to drink, and it took him forever to come. They tried this and that. Jennifer even went down on him, as incredible as that was: she had never even *seen* one before tonight. There was a certain pleasure in that, Jennifer thought, as she rubbed him with her hands. He is my first *everything*. Jack went down on her; she got on top of him; he got behind her; then he got a mirror and brought it to the bed so that they could see themselves. He asked her to touch herself; then he asked her to touch him. Finally they had come full circle and he was on top of her again. It had not hurt at all for him to take her virginity from her, for she was not a virgin in the *strictest* sense. But now, after strenuous intercourse, Jennifer had come back to earth and began to feel some physical discomfort. Discomfort or not, however, all Jen thought of was making him last, and if he whittled her genitalia away by his thrusting, it would be worth it, to feel him above her, to be lost in space, to be lost in *Jackspace*.

He came, finally! collapsing on top of her in a sweaty heap and promptly falling asleep. Jennifer did not care.

Jack was wet and heavy. His hair, all matted up, clung to his head. His breathing was uneven; his legs were between her legs. I think mine are asleep, Jennifer thought. They've been open for so long, I must look like a frog ready for dissection. Jennifer stroked Jack's legs with hers. She ran her fingers on his back and kissed his temple.

How long did she lie there awake? What did she think about? Nothing. Nothing, and everything. She thought about having sex with him again, she thought about him kissing her on the street and impossibly about taking her to the prom. She thought about having used no contraception, about it not even occurring to her to use any. He didn't ask her and certainly didn't wear any himself. She thought about being pregnant, and laughed. And then she thought, "I love him. I am in love with him. I love him. This is what it feels like; this is what it's all about. This is the only way I want to feel when I have someone above me. This is what I want to feel when I look up into someone's face, and if I don't feel this, I feel nothing. Everything else is an illusion. Jennifer continued to lie there stroking his back lightly with her fingertips, thinking of the years they had been friends. Remember softball, Jack? Remember Shunga Park? Before you became a football captain? You remember those days? And then she fell asleep.

Jack was still on top of her when he woke up. He quickly got off her, mumbling an apology, and then went into the bathroom. When he came out, he pulled on a pair of shorts. Sitting on the bed next to her, Jack rubbed his temples.

"Jen, it's six o'clock, are your parents going out of their heads?"

My *parents*? Me, *I* am going out of my head.

"Yeah, I guess." Jennifer smiled at him and Jack smiled wanly back.

"Do you think you should go?"

"If *you* think I should go, I will. Otherwise I can call them."

Jack seemed surprised. "You can call them? The only child and daughter of Italian parents, you can call them at six in the morning and say—say what?"

Jennifer thought for a moment. She did not want to go.

"If you think I should go, I will," she repeated dully.

Jack did not reply, but he did not look at Jennifer, either.

"Okay," she said, getting up out of bed, still completely naked. "I understand totally."

After she got dressed, Jack, clad only in a pair of shorts, walked her to the car. His hand rested on her shoulder. "Listen," he said. It was freezing cold. "I apologize. I really needed and wanted to do this. I'm glad we did. I hope you understand."

She understood. Of course. She stretched her lips into what she hoped was a smile and not a grimace, and Jack bent down and kissed her on the cheek. "I'll call you," he said. "Be careful driving back."

Jennifer drove off, and drove and drove. Instead of going home, she drove to Lawrence, drove around the Kansas University campus, drove to Eudora, drove to De Soto, where she sat in front of a barren cornfield, lost in a timeless vacuum. Then she drove to Tully's house. Came around back and threw rocks at Tully's window until one of the rocks hit the sleeping-at-her-desk Tully on the head.

"Come on, you light sleeper, let me in," said Jennifer from below.

"You almost killed me," said Tully, opening the front door. "Where have you been? Your mother is frantic."

"Okay, I'll call her," said Jen. "After we sleep. Let's sleep." Jennifer undressed to her underwear and climbed into bed.

Tully spooned Jennifer and softly said, "Jennifer, I know that smell. I recognize it. You smell of a guy."

"Tully," whispered Jennifer, "ask me no questions and I'll tell you no lies."

Tully said nothing and lay there for two hours wide awake until Hedda came into the room, saying there was a half-crazed Mrs. Mandolini on the phone. Jennifer talked to her mother for a few minutes and then climbed back into bed and pretended to sleep.

6.

In February, Mr. and Mrs. Mandolini went to a parent-teacher conference and sat grimly with Jennifer's math teacher, Mr. Schmidt, while he told them about the "big problem" with Jennifer and about Jennifer's performance in school.

"There is nothing wrong with our daughter's work, Mr. Schmidt," said Lynn. "She is under a lot of pressure," she continued, not giving him a chance to interrupt. "You know she applied to Stanford, and you've seen her SAT scores; it's just too much for one teenager to take."

Mr. Schmidt was shaking his head. Tony flared up a little. "What? Problem, problem! Why are you trying to make some kind of a big deal out of this? I don't get it. Is it personal?"

Mr. Schmidt took a deep breath before speaking. "Mr. and Mrs. Mandolini. Lynn. Tony. I've known you now for the three years Jennifer's been with us—you know how I feel about her. No, of course it's nothing personal. The only personal thing I feel toward Jennifer is affection. However, her work and her lack of interest in her work gravely concern me."

"Well, it doesn't concern us," said Tony. Getting up, he turned to his wife. "Let's go."

"Tony," said Mr. Schmidt, cracking his knuckles. "Wait. Do you understand, that Jennifer's math grades have slipped from a ninety-nine average last year to an eighty-two in the beginning of this year, and by the second quarter . . ." he paused again, "well, you saw her report card. I gave her a sixty-five, because I like her and am concerned for her. However, you must know that she failed all of the tests I gave last quarter—that's four exams, six quizzes. *Failed every single one of them.* Jennifer could do math while asleep standing on her head in nine feet of water. She used to correct *me,* for God's sake! I've been a teacher for twenty years and have never known anyone to get a perfect score on their math SATs." He paused for breath. "I'm just trying to tell you, her performance is a cause for concern." He looked at them, sitting there with their eyes to the floor. "I'm sure this is not the first time you are hearing this," he said gently. "I've spoken to her other teachers. This is a running problem. She is not doing well."

"Mr. Schmidt." Lynn looked up at him. "It's Senioritis. Senioritis! Have you forgotten about being young? Young, eighteen, a cheerleader!" She swallowed. "You know, we've done nothing all her life but push and encourage her." Lynn looked at her husband, who was nodding vigorously. "But," she went on, "this is her senior year! Let's ease off her a little. Right, Tony? She is going to Stanford next year; let her have a good time before she has to work so hard. Right, Tony?"

"Absolutely!" he said.

Mr. Schmidt sighed. He made one more attempt. "She was valedictorian of her middle school. Now, *how* is she going to be valedictorian of Topeka High, having failed everything?"

Tony got up. "You know, Mr. Schmidt, we are proud of our daughter no matter what she does, and the most important thing to us is that she is happy. If she is happy not being valedictorian because of her own personal reasons, then it's okay with us."

"Is her . . ." Mr. Schmidt began carefully, "is her, hmm, problem, her, hmm, withdrawal . . . is she having withdrawal symptoms? Like she did when she was young? Is it coming back? She is nearly mute in class."

"Jeeezzus!" Tony exclaimed. "You're not a doctor! You're a math teacher."

They did not want to talk to him anymore and left. Mr. Schmidt looked after them and then went next door to Miss Keller, who taught biology, and asked her about Mr. and Mrs. Mandolini.

"They don't want to hear it, Jim. It must be really hard for them. She's always been such an excellent student."

"Well, I'll tell you this. I'll bet we won't be seeing them at the spring parent-teacher conference," said Mr. Schmidt.

Tony and Lynn still had two more teachers to see, English and history, but without saying a word to each other, they just walked out of the school, got into their car, and drove home in utter silence.

"Should we?" asked Lynn, chain-smoking in the middle of the Sunset Court kitchen.

Tony was making himself and Lynn a drink. "No, absolutely not. She'll think we're ganging up on her. Let's leave her alone for a while, okay?"

Two hours later, Lynn said, "She hasn't come down to see us."

"She's probably on the phone or listening to music. Let's leave her alone, okay?"

At midnight, when Lynn and Tony walked past Jennifer's bedroom on the way to bed, their daughter's light was off and there was no music. Lynn couldn't help herself. She knocked and quickly opened the door.

"Mom," said Jennifer's voice from the bed. "What's up?"

"Nothing, babe, nothing," said Lynn. "Sleep tight."

The following night at dinner, Lynn said carefully, "Jennifer, the teachers seem to think you are not doing too well in school."

Jennifer looked up and stared at her mother. "Mom," she said. "Didn't you see my report card a week ago?"

"Yes, honey, of course we did," said Tony. "But the teachers said you were actually doing even worse than what the grades showed. They said you really haven't passed anything at all this quarter."

"That's true, Dad. I haven't."

"Honey, is anything the matter?"

"No, Daddy, why should anything be the matter? I just didn't have a good quarter, that's all." She added, "I'll do much better next report card, you'll see."

Lynn and Tony smiled tensely. "Oh, we're glad to hear that, honey," said Lynn. "We're so glad! We want you to do so well!"

"I know you do, Mom. I'm sorry if I disappointed you."

Lynn reached out her hand to Jennifer. "Jenny, you cannot disappoint Daddy and me," she said seriously. "We're just concerned. We want you to be happy, that's all."

"Mom, it's my senior year. I'm having such a good time," replied Jennifer.

After finishing her dinner, Jennifer went to the upstairs bathroom. Locking the door, she stood there for a moment looking around, and then stepped on the scales, with her sneakers and pocket change. This was the first time Jennifer got on the scales in about three weeks, but she had eaten particularly well the last few days and felt she deserved it. She stood on them and stared at the wall for about a minute (*Please please, please*) before looking down to see the three-digit number on the black line. She let out a small, yelplike scream. But there it was. 102. *One-oh-two. 102!* Pretty soon, it won't even be a three-digit number, she thought frantically.

Jennifer got off the scale and went into her bedroom, where she undressed, got into bed, turned off the light, and let out another scream, another stifled dark groan, and another and another. She had to turn the stereo on to drown out her crying. When her mother opened the door to say good night, Lynn said happily, "Jenny! Music! You're playing music!"

Yeah, thought Jennifer. *Music and the maiden.* She lay there a long time before sleep came. Tully taught her to think of nothing but sheep when sleep or peace wouldn't come, and tonight and every night Jennifer tried to do just that. But tonight Jennifer's sheep were not going to sleep. Over and over and over, her sheep were running through a meadow and going to Stanford and becoming adults and doctors and parents. The rest of their lives seemed *so close* to the sheep.

Late February, Tully, Jennifer, and Julie sat in the Sunset Court kitchen.

"Okay, what are we putting in our yearbooks, guys?" said Julie. "We need to write out a will and a dream."

"We need a will to dream," said Tully.

"Or a dream to will," said Jennifer.

"Makker, Mandolini," said Julie. "Shape up. Let's have it. The yearbook committee is not going to be waiting around for you. The deadline is March second. That's this Friday, for your information."

"Oh, yeah? And who died and made you president?" said Tully.

"Secretary, actually," said Julie.

"Well, inspire us. Let's hear *your* will, Martinez," said Tully, doodling on her sheet of paper. "What are you going to leave Tom? Are you going to leave him your virginity? Or is it too late?"

Julie punched her in the arm. "Stop talking nonsense. Stop drawing nonsense, too. Work, work, work. How are you guys going to go to college if you can't concentrate?"

"My, she is bossy," said Jennifer.

"I learned from the best," answered Julie, smiling and pointing at Jennifer, who didn't smile back.

Tully changed the subject. "Where did you say your loved one was going?" she asked Julie.

"Brown."

Tully smiled. "Yes. And you are going where? Northwestern? How many miles apart is that? A thousand? Knowing how intimate you guys are, I'm sure you'll really miss that physical closeness you two share."

"Tully!" said Julie.

Tully went to get a bag of pretzel sticks. Julie grabbed a handful. Jennifer said she wasn't hungry.

A little later, Tully said, turning to Julie, "Robin asked me again if I'd consider moving in with him."

"He did?" said Julie. "*Again?* That's great!" She saw Tully's face, and Jennifer's face, too. "Isn't it? Isn't it great? Isn't it just what you want? To get out of your mother's house?"

Jennifer and Tully stared at her, then exchanged looks. Tully nodded. "You know what it is, Jen," Tully said. "It's all that great sex she's been having with that Romeo of hers. She's lost her mind."

Jennifer smiled.

"Why do you say that? It's not fair," said Julie, banging the table.

"Martinez," said Tully, banging the table herself in jest. "You haven't listened to a word I've said the last two months. What are you paying attention to? Tom? The crisis in the Middle East, God help you?"

"Tell me already!" said Julie.

"Julie," said Tully, shaking her head. "You know Jen and I are going to California."

"So don't go," said Julie. "So stay. Robin is worth it."

"Worth it, huh?" said Tully.

"Sure," drawled Julie. "You stay, you get married, you have a couple of babies. He'll buy you a house."

"Hell, why stop at a house?" said Tully. "Why doesn't he just buy me a whole life?"

"Ask him, he'll do it for sure."

Tully smiled. "What's wrong with you, Martinez? I don't want to have babies, I don't want to get married. I've been telling you that since I was about ten."

"Well, at ten maybe you didn't want to," said Julie. "Right, Jen?"

"Right, Jule," said Jennifer.

"But you're eighteen now."

"Nothing's changed," said Tully.

"I don't believe you," Julie said. "What do you call Washburn Day Care every Thursday?"

Tully looked at Jennifer with a what-am-I-going-to-do-with-her look. Jennifer shrugged.

"Besides," continued Julie, "what are you going to do with Jen in California? You know she'll leave you first chance she gets. She *wants* to get married. She *wants* to have children. Right, Jen?"

"Right, Jule," said Jennifer, looking at Tully.

"Jennifer wouldn't leave me," Tully said, mock pouty. "Would you, Mandolini?"

"First chance I get," said Jennifer, smiling.

"I don't know. It seems a shame to throw Robin away, Tull," said Julie. "You guys sure do spend a lot of time together."

"A lot?" asked Tully. "What, out of a whole day? A whole week? A year? Out of a life?" Tully laughed. "We sure spend a lot of *purposeful* time together. That red leather in his 'Vette beckons us and seems better than, say, talking."

Jennifer and Julie giggled. Jennifer was drinking a glass of milk and dipping her index finger into the glass, drawing concentric circles on the table.

"But think about all the advantages of moving in with him," Julie persisted. "He's got plenty of money. He'll sire cute offspring."

"And Tull, think about it," interjected Jennifer. "If you ask, I'm sure he'll buy you that house on Texas Street. Dad found out for me who owns it. An old lady." Jennifer raised her eyebrows. "A *very* old lady."

Tully looked from Julie to Jennifer "What is it with you guys? Leave me alone, will you? Jen, what's the matter? What about Stanford?"

Shaking her head, Jennifer patted Tully on the arm and continued decorating the table with milk rings.

"Think about it, Tully," Julie said. "You'll be out of your house."

"Yes," said Tully. "And in somebody else's."

"Oh, yes, but on Texas Street! Just think!" said Jennifer.

"Mandolini!" Tully exclaimed.

Jennifer laughed mildly. "I'm only joking, Tully," she said. "Julie, Tully doesn't think she loves Robin. And how can you reason with a heart? Right, Tully?" Most of the milk from Jennifer's glass was drying on the table.

"Right, Jen," said Tully, looking away.

"Tully, how do you know you don't love him?" asked Julie.

"I don't know," Tully said slowly. "How would I know if I loved him?"

"You'd know," said Julie, glancing at Jennifer. "Right, Jen?"

"Right, Jule," Jennifer replied slowly.

Together, Jennifer, Tully, and Julie accomplished nothing that afternoon. At six in the evening they agreed to give up and surprise each other when the yearbooks came out.

In the car, Jennifer sat in the passenger seat and let Tully drive the Camaro to the Grove.

"You're doing well, Makker," she said. "A few more years, and you may pass your test."

"Get out of here," said Tully. "My test is March seventeenth."

Jennifer shook her head. "I don't know," she said. "Maybe you should pray to St. Patrick."

5

JENNIFER

March 1979

The days spun on. Their pattern was the same, small and uninspired, but each blade of grass brought with it the field of spring, each rainfall washed away the smell of winter. Each breeze carried off the last of winter air. The process was slow, of each tree's and flower's rebirth, of each day's light getting longer by the minute and nightfall's coming yet later and later. Had they all seen what was growing in the spring of all their lives, they would have paid more attention to those petty things that slip by so unnoticed, so unremembered. Time, however, is slow when nothing happens; and those cracks in the foundation seemed so unrelated, so trivial, that each incident was absorbed and forgotten, the way breakfast and sunset are forgotten—as part of the sameness that filled everyone's days, especially theirs, especially the days of the young, when they gulped the air and lived to see the better world, the grown-up world, when they could not wait for the days to end so that they could get on with the rest of their lives.

February snowed into March. And in March, it rained.

The smell of spring came with the winds and the storms. There was a tornado alert every day, and rain every day, and sun every day, too. A typical Kansas March.

Tully was busy with Robin, with keeping him away from her mother, and busy keeping herself away from her mother. She received a small scare in the first week of March when she found a letter addressed to Hedda Makker in the mailbox one afternoon. What surprised Tully about the letter wasn't that it was addressed to Hedda Makker, but that the address was handwritten. Hedda, besides bills, never received anything—certainly nothing handwritten. Upon closer examination, Tully noticed *Hedda* was misspelled. *Heda* Makker, it said. The Grove. Okay, thought Tully, and took it upon herself to commit a federal offense.

She was glad she did when she tore open the envelope. "Mrs. Makker," the note said. "Your daughter is fooling around with my boyfriend. A lot. Every week. She stole him from me and now she's lying to you every Wednesday and Sunday."

The note was unsigned. Tully wasn't so much stunned by the arrival of the note. She half expected some form of sabotage. What surprised her was the depth and accuracy of Gail's knowledge. Not only did she know what days Tully met Robin, but she also knew to a useful extent the difficulties Tully had with her mother.

Tully tore up the letter, deciding to keep very quiet about it to everyone. She figured that Gail must have gotten all that information from the guileless, unsuspecting Julie, who was in the same English class. If Gail now thought her ploy had succeeded in getting Tully in deep shit, then she wouldn't attempt any more war missions.

Julie was busy with the debating society, the history club, the current events club. "Talk is the one four-letter word you and Tom can enjoy together," Tully called it.

Jennifer continued to lose weight.

Monday, March 12, at Sunset Court, when Jennifer left the kitchen for a moment, Tully mentioned the weight loss to Lynn Mandolini. Lynn got a little defensive, saying her daughter never looked better.

"Mrs. Mandolini, yes, twenty pounds ago she never looked better. I'll be surprised if she is a hundred and ten now."

"Oh, Tully!" said Lynn, lighting up and taking a drink. "A hundred and ten! Really!"

"Jen," said Tully when Jennifer returned. "How much do you weigh?"

Jennifer looked as if she'd been hit. "I—I don't know. Why?"

"Jennifer, you used to get on the scale twice a day. How much do you weigh now?"

"Tully, don't badger her!" Lynn said loudly.

"Mom, Mom. It's okay. I weigh about a hundred and fifteen," answered Jennifer.

Lynn looked at Tully with an I-told-you-so look. Tully stared back defiantly.

"Oh, I see," she said. "One hundred fifteen. Would you say that's about a thirty-five-pound loss since September?"

Later, when they were alone, Tully said, "Mandolini, you lie. You lie. How much do you really weigh?"

"Tully, I did not lie—"

"Jennifer, stop! I know your lying face even if your own mother doesn't. Now, how much?"

Jennifer mumbled something.

"What?" said Tully.

"Ninety-six," whispered Jennifer.

Tully was cold for the rest of the evening.

Later that night, in her own home, she slept, after hours of anxious restlessness, after counting 1,750 or 2,750 sheep. She slept at her desk, wind blowing about the curtains and her hair. Her hands were under her face, between her and the wood. Tully slept and dreamed that she was in the desert. She was walking in the desert by herself, she was completely alone, and she was thirsty. It seemed that she had walked for days and had not drunk for days. God! how she wanted to drink. To drink or to die, thought Tully in the desert.

"Julie, there is something very wrong with Jennifer," said Tully, Tuesday morning, March 13, right after homeroom. Julie seemed a little absentminded. "I think she's anorexic."

"Are you crazy?"

"Julie, I know you haven't been paying attention to a lot of things lately, but don't tell me you haven't noticed Jennifer is now thinner than me."

Julie looked thoughtful. "Well, maybe she does seem a little thin, but—"

"Julie!" Tully exclaimed. "She is ninety-six pounds! Ninety-six!"

Julie turned red and said, "Tully, don't scream at me! Yes, that seems very thin. Sick, even. But what do you want me to do about it?"

"Julie!" Tully folded her hands together, pleading. "Don't you care?"

"Tully, of course I care. But I have an English report to write by sixth period, and after school we're going to the Statehouse on a fact-finding mission— Look, she's always been a little plump and she lost weight lately. And you kind of gained weight lately."

Tully shook her head. "Don't you get it? I haven't gained

weight lately. And Jen hasn't just lost weight, she is sick."

"I've got to get to class," said Julie. "We'll talk to her."

"You and your stupid fact-finding mission. Where have you been all these months? Where? I don't know who has more of a problem. Do you know Jen got sixty-fives in all her classes and that's only because the teachers felt sorry for her? Do you know she has not passed one test since January and is still failing everything?"

"How do you know that?" asked Julie, shifting uncomfortably from one foot to the other.

"I know, that's how. I know because I was talking in gym to two girls who are in Jen's math class. They told me Mr. Schmidt is worried about Jennifer. He keeps talking to his students about her."

The bell rang. Julie sped down the hall. "We'll talk to her, we will," she yelled.

Tully stared after Julie dumbly. Wanting to feel better, she had approached Julie, but now she felt worse. Books pressed hard against her chest, Tully went to class with a punched-in-the-stomach worry.

Four days later, on St. Patrick's Day, at eleven in the morning, Tully passed her driving test. Jennifer was with her.

"I guess Saint Paddy listened to my prayers," said Tully, smiling.

"Guess so," said Jennifer.

"Thanks for teaching me how to drive, Jen."

"You're welcome, Tully," said Jennifer.

Tuesday, March 20, after school, Julie gingerly approached Jennifer. She had wanted to do it earlier, or over the weekend, but there was so much to do. The president of the history club asked her to talk about Indonesia's involvement in World War II, and she knew nothing about it. Today she had her current events club meeting, but she hadn't read the paper over the weekend or *Time* or *Newsweek* on Monday, so she decided to spend Tuesday afternoon with Jennifer instead.

"So, Jen, how is everything?" Julie said as the girls ambled down 10th Street to Wayne.

"Fine, thanks," Jennifer replied, kicking stones out from under her feet.

"You and Tully excited about Stanford?"

"Tully's going to UC in Santa Cruz. She's pretty excited."

"What about you? Are you excited?"

"For sure," said Jennifer.

Julie just did not want to ask Jennifer, just did not. She did not want to bring up a subject Jennifer so obviously had no interest in discussing. How long ago did Tully and Julie stop teasing Jen about her crush on Jack? January? When Julie made some silly remark about how Jennifer could not hide her obsession with Jack's butt, and Tully glared at her and Jennifer looked away. Julie never brought the subject up again, but now, two months later, she wondered why she never asked Tully about it. Why she never asked Tully if something happened between Jennifer and Jack.

Julie sensed uneasily that something *had* happened. Something happened to make Jennifer go from a plump, content girl to a darkening shadow. But, truthfully, Julie just did not want to deal with it. *Just did not want to,* and Julie felt ashamed on this windy, sunny March afternoon as the girls walked to Julie's house. Ashamed that Jennifer's heart was too much for Julie to help heal because it would take so much time and so much energy and so much of their day, which, instead of being spent in jokes and TV and their senior year, goddamn it! would be spent in tears.

Julie lowered her head; and when she did, she remembered school days the last few months when she would see Jack stroll by and smile his jock smile and feel Jennifer physically stiffen, remembered her own lowered head at this sight—of smiling Jack and stiff Jennifer—and Julie recognized that then, too, she was lowering her head in shame.

Julie looked at Jennifer's gaunt, pale face. Her lips used to be so red, but now were bluish pink. All the highlights were out of Jennifer's hair and it looked a lot like Tully's hair before she had it bleached and permed for her eighteenth in January. Jennifer's body was well hidden by a long, loose black skirt (Tully's?) and a large sweatshirt. That's all Jennifer wore nowadays. Loose skirts and large shirts. Ninety-six? Was it possible? And what to do about it? Julie cleared her throat.

"Jen, have you lost weight?"

"God!" Jennifer said in a raised, exasperated voice. "What is it with you people? Everybody keeps asking me the same question! Can't you be original and ask me something else?

What about how I'm doing in school—"

"Jennifer, how are you doing in school?" said Julie quietly.

"Great! I actually got a sixty-two on my English lit exam.
Mr. Lederer said I was improving. Anything else?"

"Yes," said Julie. "What the hell is wrong with you?"

Jennifer did not reply.

At Julie's house, they played with Julie's two youngest
brothers, Vinnie and Angelo. Jennifer seemed to cheer up a
little playing with Vinnie, who was her particular favorite
because he would latch on to her and not let go until she left.

She did leave, though, before dinner, saying she wanted to
eat at home. Julie walked her to Wayne and 10th, and they
stopped at the corner.

Julie skipped a beat and said, "Jennifer, tell me what's
bothering you."

"Nothing, Julie," said Jennifer. "I forgot when to stop dieting.
I'm a little low on energy. I'm going to have to start eating
more."

Julie was unconvinced.

"I've been going through a little period of self-doubt,"
admitted Jennifer.

"How long a little period?" asked Julie.

"Oh, about seventeen years," replied Jennifer, and they both
laughed.

"You? Self-doubt?" said Julie. "Jen, what do you have
self-doubt about? You're brilliant, beautiful, strong . . . what
self-doubt?"

Jennifer paused, then said, "Yes, well, it's hard to argue with
all that," not answering Julie's question.

They hugged each other good-bye and as Julie watched her,
a pit developed in her stomach. She loves that asshole, thought
Julie, and was nearly knocked out by sympathy and pity and
envy, yes, envy, goddamn it. *Loves him!* But then pity swam
back into Julie. Loves him with all the bittersweetness of first
love and now she's trying to find a way to cope. Jennifer
should talk to Tully more, thought Julie, heading back to her
house. Tully would teach Jennifer how to cope.

Bright, beautiful, brilliant, billowy, blighted, blind, thought
Jennifer as she meandered home, looking straight ahead with
unseeing eyes. Yes, I'm all these things, I am so many things,

o many of them good, some of them wonderful. I should
know: I've been told nothing else my entire life, so how can
t not be true? Yet it is as I have always suspected. All those
things mean shit, for the world is full of beautiful people, full
of beautiful, brilliant, billowy people. And so what? Ugliness
is now inside me. Beautiful! What does beautiful have to do
with anything? He does not want me. Everyone told me he
was worthless and I was precious, but this worthless guy did
not want precious me.

So if he was so worthless and still did not want me, how in
this world could anyone worthwhile want me?

And he is not worthless. He is serious and strong. He is a
lot like Tully. Maybe that's why I just can't stop. I've tried
to do what Tully tells me to do. I've tried to study and drown
myself in Tully's heart because I know she cares so *much*. I've
tried to eat, to sleep, and to listen to music. I've tried to look
at other guys and think of Stanford. But what's California to
me without him?

I've tried to forget him. But every day I see his face *above
my face. Above me.* I see his smiling face when I was a cheerleader and he was a football captain. When we played softball
together. When he danced with me to "Wild Horses." When he
was my friend. I have but a few memories, but the ones I have
are all in my throat, the ones I have are all in my face when he
walks by and smiles his "Hey, Jen, what's happening?" smile
at me. I cannot even hate him. He has done nothing, this is not
his fault. This is no one's fault. Not even mine. Tully taught me
how to fight, but even she cannot help me heal this sick, tired
feeling inside me. And that's how I feel. Sick. And tired.

Wednesday, March 21, Tully reluctantly went to dinner at
Jennifer's. There was something in the Mandolini household
nowadays that reminded Tully too much of her own.

Silence.

Silence in the kitchen, silence at the table. Jennifer, Lynn,
and Tony Mandolini sat and passed the spaghetti and dug into
the meatballs and chewed on the bread, and around them there
was no TV, no radio, no words, only silence! Just like home,
thought Tully, and swallowed her bread too fast and started to
cough, breaking the sound barrier. When she quieted down,
she thought, I want to go home.

Lynn chain-smoked, unable to wait until she finished he dinner. Tony drank and looked only into his plate.

Tully could see that Jennifer was practicing voodoo sel control. She was counting the squares in the tablecloth an then the number of hairs on her arms.

My God, at least the radio used to be on. Maybe they starte turning the radio off so that they could hear each other.

She's doing it to them. They have no idea what's going on and she won't tell them. They're as lost now as she is. At firs they thought she was doing so badly in school because sh was so happy and having this great time, but they can't eve fool themselves with that one anymore. She is so *obviousl* not happy. Maybe they're afraid that thing is coming bac to stay. I'm sure she's anorexic. I wonder if she throws up Would she tell me if she does? Would she tell even me that Would she speak even to me?

After dinner, the girls washed the dishes and Mr. and Mrs Mandolini went to catch *The Deer Hunter* before the Oscars which were in a few weeks' time.

"So, Jen," said Tully when they were finally alone. "Tel me, Jen, how often do you pass dinner like this?"

"I'm sorry," she answered. "Were we quiet?"

"Quiet?" said Tully. "What the fuck is wrong with al of you?"

Jennifer did not answer her, just kept on drying.

"You gotta snap out of it, Jen," Tully said. "You just gotta.

Jennifer said nothing.

"You are making everyone miserable. We don't know wha to do for you," continued Tully. "And we all would do every thing, anything, to have you back to your usual semi-norma self again."

Jen smiled a little, but again did not speak.

"Jennifer, tell me, are you anorexic?" asked Tully.

"Anorexic? God, no!"

"Are you throwing up in the toilet?"

"Tully, please!"

"Jennifer, you really need to talk to somebody who doesn' know you; you need to do something for yourself." Tully' voice was getting louder. "And if you can't, you have got t tell your parents to open their eyes and take you to a doctor get you healthy again, get you on your feet again."

"On my feet again," repeated Jennifer dully.

"Jenny, you have been taking this lying down, you *lay down* three months ago with him and you are still lying down, you have not gotten up, and you have to."

"I have to," said Jennifer.

Tully turned off the water and turned to her friend. "Yes, *have* to. You have no choice. Gotta do it, Jen. Just think, three months and you're out of school, out of *him*, and then it's summer! We work, we hang out, we go swimming in Lake Shawnee, and then it's August and we're off! Off we go. Hi-ho, hi-ho. Palo Al-*to*. A new life. I'm so excited. A beginning. So cheer up. And keep going. Come on, Jen. You're stronger than all of us."

"No, Tully," said Jennifer. "*You* are stronger than all of us." Jennifer stood there blankly, her hands down at her sides.

The girls watched *Love Story* on the "Million Dollar Movie." They had seen it three times already, and the fourth time found them sitting and watching the flickering screen, absorbed in everything but Jenny Cavilleri's death. Tully sat curled up on the couch entirely dry-eyed, entirely without movement as she looked unflinchingly and frightlessly at Oliver Barrett IV sitting at the Central Park ice skating rink without his Jennifer.

Tully's own heart, however, was as frightened and tight as a narrow path in the dead of night in the dead of winter.

Jennifer did not even see Oliver sitting in Central Park. She was imagining Harvard and meeting someone like Oliver in Harvard. She tried to imagine holding her heart with both hands so it wouldn't jump out of her chest for an Oliver in Harvard and drew a black blank. Instead, she remembered lying out in the middle of the night in her backyard on Sunset Court with Tully when they were kids. When they were about seven, eight, nine, ten. Eleven. Even twelve. Every summer, Tully would come over and make a tent in the backyard, and they would dig and twig, doodle and dawdle, talk and talk, and smell the Kansas night air.

"*Do you think the stars are this bright everywhere in the world, Tully?*"

"*No, I think Kansas is closer to the stars than everywhere else in the world,*" said eight-year-old Tully.

"*How do you know?*"

"*Because,*" said Tully, "*Kansas is in the middle of America. And in the summer America is closest to the sun. Which means it's closest to the rest of the sky, too. And Kansas, being in the middle, is the most closest.*"

"*Are you sure about this?*"

"*Positive,*" answered Tully.

Jennifer was quiet for a while, absorbing, thinking. "*Tull, do you think the stars are still there when we go to sleep?*"

"*Of course,*" said Tully.

"*How do you know?*"

"*Because,*" said Tully slowly. "*I see them all night long.*"

"*You don't see them when you sleep,*" argued Jennifer.

"*I don't sleep,*" said Tully.

"*What do you mean, you don't sleep?*"

Now it was Tully's turn to be quiet.

"*What do you do if you don't sleep?*"

"*I dream,*" said Tully. "*I have . . . bad dreams a lot. So I wake up and look outside a lot.*"

"*Much?*"

"*Every night.*"

Jennifer clicked the TV off, and the girls sat there in darkness, with only the blue light from the street coming in through the bay window.

"Tully," said Jennifer hoarsely. "Tell me about your dream again."

"Which dream?" Tully looked at Jen.

"The rope dream."

"Oh, that old dream. Jennifer I don't wanna tell you about *any* of my dreams. You know them all."

"Humor me," said Jen. "Tell me again."

Tully sighed. "What do you want to know?"

"Do you still have it?"

"Yes, every once in a while."

"How often?"

"I dreamed it a few weeks ago," said Tully.

"Is it still the same?" asked Jen.

"It's a little different," answered Tully.

"What's the same?"

"The rope," said Tully. "The rope is always around my neck.

I fall off the tree and pray that this time my neck would break so I won't have to suffocate."

"Does it?"

"Never. I just can't breathe."

Jennifer was quiet. "What's different?"

"The setting. Last time, I was in the desert. In a musty palm tree. I guess I'm thinking about California."

Jennifer touched Tully with her fingers. "Did you like your palm tree? You've never seen one."

"Its bark was rough like a pineapple's. It was pretty cool."

"Was the rope tight?"

Tully could not see Jennifer's face.

"It's always around my neck," said Tully slowly. "When I fall, it's tight."

"Did you suffocate?" Jennifer was barely audible.

"Yes, and then I woke up."

"Have you ever . . . died in your dreams?"

"No. I don't think you can. I think when you die in your dreams, you die in real life. No, people don't die in their dreams."

"Not even you?"

"Not even me," said Tully.

"What stops you?" asked Jennifer faintly.

"I wanted a drink of water," said Tully. "I was really thirsty. I did not want to die. I wanted to drink. And then I wanted to go swimming."

After a while, Jennifer said, "Well, at least you are getting out of the house."

Tully smiled thinly. "Yeah. I used to do it in front of my mother, in the living room, and Aunt Lena would say, 'Tully, can you move a little? You're blocking the TV,' and my mother wouldn't say anything at all."

Jennifer stared into the dark. "I remember thinking you were sick for dreaming that. I remember thinking that you didn't really want to die, you were just screaming for help."

"Yeah, screaming," said Tully. "Obviously loudly."

"To people who didn't care," said Jennifer.

"Hey, wait a minute. You're talking about my mother here," said Tully. "And we all know how deeply she cares."

"Yes," said Jennifer. "Deeply."

The girls said nothing for a little while and then Tully asked,

"Jennifer, why are you asking me this? We haven't talked about this in years. Why now?"

"We haven't talked about a lot of things in years."

"Like?"

"Like why you stopped coming around here. Around me and Jule."

"I thought I told you."

"Yes, but you didn't tell me *why*. Why, Tully?"

Tully didn't answer. She thought back to the time she was twelve. And thirteen, and fourteen, and fifteen. 1973, 1974, 1975 . . . Bicentennial. July 4, 1976, she went with Jennifer and Julie to watch the fireworks at Lake Shawnee. Tully had called up Jennifer. And Jennifer, as if nothing were wrong, invited her out, and Tully came. It wasn't the first time in two and a half years the three of them got together, but it was the first time in two and a half years Tully did the calling.

Those years, thought Tully. It was as if I disappeared off the face of the earth. I did all the usual things; I went to school, I did my homework, I learned how to dance and made some new friends, and hung out and smoked, and danced in dance clubs and won some money to buy myself clothes. I occasionally slept and occasionally saw Jennifer and Julie. But I don't myself know how I made it through those years. Certainly nothing worth repeating to this crazy person sitting next to me on the sofa.

Jennifer rolled her eyes. "Forget it. Tell me, do you think you love Robin? Honestly."

Tully looked over at Jennifer's shadow in the dark room.

"I don't particularly want to lose him," she said. "Is that love?"

"Tully, have you ever loved any of the boys you've been with?"

Tully did not hesitate. "No," she replied. "I haven't. Not one. Not even remotely."

"Is that why you don't cry at the end of *Love Story*?" asked Jennifer. "Because you can't imagine what it would be like to love someone?"

Tully patted Jennifer's leg. "Who said I don't cry at the end of *Love Story*?"

"Tull, I've never in twelve years seen you cry."

"I don't," said Tully, a brittle rock inside her chest, "cry much."

"Not even in front of me?"

"Obviously not," said Tully, then giving in a little. "I try sometimes to . . . imagine loving somebody like that."

"Like Oliver loves Jenny?" she asked.

"No," said Tully, squeezing Jennifer's leg. "That I understand. Because I love Jenny, too. I know what it's like to love Jenny." Tully smiled. "I want to know what it's like to love *Oliver*."

Tully saw Jennifer press the tips of her fingers hard to her eyes and not let go, and Tully nearly wanted to press her own fingers to her eyes, to *press* out the image of Jennifer suppressing her demons.

They sat there silent and unmoving in the dark. Tick tock, tick tock. Tick. Tock. Tick.

"I want to go home, Jen," said Tully.

"Come upstairs with me," Jennifer said. "Please."

Tully went upstairs. And gasped when she saw Jen's room: usually immaculate, it was now an unbelievable mess.

"My God, Jennifer! Who lives here now? Not you!"

"Well, I've been too busy to clean up."

"Busy. Of course," said Tully.

They sat on the bed next to each other. Jennifer looked at her feet and then pressed her fingertips to her eyes again, hard.

Tully sat on the unmade bed, next to her.

"It'll be all right, Mandolini," Tully said, feeling desperately helpless, nearly angry, when it came to all of Jennifer's unreachable, untamable animals, baring their teeth at Tully's meaningless comforts. Her words sounded dull and void even to herself. "Forget it . . . forget him, Jennifer Lynn Mandolini," whispered Tully. "Please. Forget him."

But inside, Tully thought, Who cares about him? There is a *whole life* to be destroyed by or excited by. A whole fucking life.

Far off, Tully heard Jennifer speak.

"What was that poem you wrote, Tully? Remember?"

"No," Tully said quickly. "I wrote a couple of poems. The summer poem?"

"I don't know the summer poem," Jennifer said. "The disconsolate poem."

Tully cleared her throat.

"I used to sing
I used to be
Disconsolate, alone, yet free
Now that my soul has been encased
Whatever will become of me . . . ?"

Jennifer closed her eyes. "That's nice," she said. "Now tell me the summer poem."

Tully moved slightly away on the bed. "Maybe some other time, okay, Jen?"

"Okay, Tully," said Jennifer.

Tully's heart gripped and ripped as she listened to Jennifer's erratic breathing. A small scared thought ran darkly through her like a roach surprised by light. How's Jen ever going to handle *anything* if she cannot handle something even this minor? Jen had always suspected there would come a time when she would be called upon to deal and wouldn't be able to. No, I told her, don't be absurd. Don't be silly. Everything that happens only makes you stronger. Remember what Tolstoy said? *"All that doesn't kill you makes you stronger."* But yet, here she is, weaker than ever, and I cannot find the right words.

"I want to go home, Jenny," said Tully finally.

Jennifer let Tully drive the Camaro home. They opened all the windows to let the wind in. The March air was cool, but it smelled like spring. As if everything were about to bloom.

"Car handles well," said Tully.

"Tully, you've never driven anything in your life," said Jennifer. "What do you know about handling?"

"That's not true," said Tully. "Robin lets me drive his Corvette."

"Yeah, in the parking lot," said Jennifer. "I'm sure you're a real speed demon in the parking lot."

At the Grove, the girls stood on the porch facing each other. "Jennifer," Tully said. "I'm going to ask you something, and I want you by God to answer me. Jennifer, are you screaming for help?"

Tully could hear Jennifer's belabored breathing.

"What a brave question, Tully," she finally said.

"Give me a brave answer, Jennifer, don't buy time, tell me right now, are you?"

"No, Tully," Jennifer replied. "I'm not."

"Promise?"

"I swear on our friendship."

Tully stood right in front of Jennifer, looking brokenly at Jennifer's thin face. After a moment, Tully's right hand went around Jennifer's head. Tully brought Jen's face close and kissed her hard on the lips, pulled away, and then kissed her again.

"Mandolini, I love you," Tully said, drained and in pain.

"And I you, Tully."

Friday, March 23, in school, Tully, Jennifer, and Julie sat together at lunch—a rare event. Jennifer usually sat with her cheerleader pals even though cheerleading season was long over. Tully thought Jennifer seemed brighter. The heaviness that clung to Tully lifted a little. That Friday night, the girls went to see *The Deer Hunter*.

"I think it will win Best Picture," predicted Jennifer on the way home.

"I think *Coming Home* will win," said Julie.

"Oh, you're joking!" Tully laughed. "They couldn't have been more heavy-handed in that film if they had tied you to a post and beat you over the head repeatedly with a 'War is b-b-b-a-a-a-a-d-d-d' shovel."

"Oh, and here, killing Nick in the last five minutes of the movie, when we were all thinking he was gonna make it, what is that, huh? That's not heavy-handed?"

"I didn't think he was gonna make it," said Jennifer, keeping her eyes on the road. "I thought from the beginning he would die. He wanted to be so strong," she said evenly. "He wanted to be as strong as Michael, but he just wasn't, no matter how he tried, and he tried really hard. In the end, he just lost faith."

"Yeah, but Stephen made it," said Julie. "And he was the weakest of the bunch."

"Stephen never even tried to be strong," said Jennifer. "It wasn't important to him like it was to Nick. To Stephen, Michael was so far out in the stratosphere, to be respected certainly, but never to be understood. But Nick wanted to be as strong as Michael and in the end was shattered by his own weakness."

Julie waved her off from the backseat. "I don't think Michael was so strong. I think he pretended to be strong."

Jennifer shook her head. "No. He was strong through and through. He was invulnerable."

"Nobody is invulnerable, Jen," said Tully thickly. "It's a myth."

"I think you're reading too much into it, Jen," Julie said.

"Yeah, but unlike with *Coming Home,* we're actually able to read *something* into it," said Tully. "I agree with Jennifer. *Deer Hunter* will win."

"When are the Oscars?" asked Julie.

"Monday, April ninth," said Jennifer.

"Well, we'll just have to wait and see, won't we?" said Julie. "And the loser buys lunch."

Julie was dropped off first, and when Jennifer parked in front of Tully's house, she folded her hands across her chest, hung her head, and said, "Maybe you like me too much, Tully."

Tully turned her face away from Jennifer. The fog around Tully was so dense, she could not see well. She blinked, trying to blink back the aching that, like anchors, weighed down her eyes. Shaking her head in short, convulsive strokes, Tully said quietly, "I definitely like you too much, Jennifer, I definitely like you way too much, but . . ." Tully paused, "what does that have to do with *anything*?"

"I wish," said Jennifer, "that maybe you wouldn't like me *quite* so much."

Tully's head did not stop shaking. "Don't be so concerned. Do we seem close to you? We're close with Julie, too."

"Not that close," said Jennifer. "You and me are too close."

"What's wrong with close?" whispered Tully. "Everything will be okay, Jen."

"I just wish you wouldn't be so attached to me, Tully," said Jennifer a little stridently. "I just wish you wouldn't be."

"Okay, Jen," said Tully, "I won't be."

"Promise me you won't be?" said Jennifer.

"I promise, Jennifer," said Tully, her throat so tight she was surprised any words could get through, even little ones. "I won't be."

* * *

Saturday, March 24, Tully, Jennifer, and Julie went to watch Tom pitch his first baseball game of the season. His team won 11–9.

Jennifer was talkative and cheerful. She narrated Tom's game, much to Tully's superficial amusement, and afterwards ate a double scoop of strawberry and chocolate ice cream. Even when she saw Jack with Shakie Lamber on his arm, Jennifer did not flinch. Tully watched her. Jennifer did not say hi or look Jack's way. Only her unblinking eyes gave away the remains of her soul.

Sunday, March 25, Jennifer as usual picked up Tully and drove her to church, and then to The Village Inn. Rather, Jennifer let Tully drive the Camaro to St. Mark's and to The Village Inn.

"I really like my car, Tully," said Jennifer. "Don't you?"

"Great car," said Tully. "Great fucking car."

"I've really come to like it," said Jennifer.

Yes, all the Stanford jocks, Tully wanted to say, will go crazy over you in your Camaro, shiny and baby-blue.

Sunday night, Jennifer sat between her mom and dad and watched the "ABC Sunday Night Movie" with them. Afterwards, she said, "Mom, Dad, I'm sorry, but I'm just not going to make valedictorian this year."

Lynn and Tony exchanged looks. "We know. We understand. It's okay, honey. Honestly," said Lynn.

"I haven't been feeling very happy lately," continued Jennifer. "As I'm sure you've noticed. And my grades have suffered." She breathed in deeply.

"Are you okay, Jen?" Lynn asked. "Do you want to go see . . . someone?"

"Like who?" said Jennifer.

"Like Dr. Collins. Your breathing . . . it sounds . . . not so good."

Jennifer smirked. "Maybe. Yes. We could do that. I *am* having a little trouble catching my breath."

Tony said, "What about maybe talking to him about, you know, to see if, you know—" he broke off.

"If I'm slipping back again, Dad? Don't worry. You guys

love me so much, and I love you back so much, I'm sure I'll be fine. Teenage blues, you know."

"Oh, honey, don't we know!" exclaimed Lynn. "We've all been there. You'll be all right."

"I know I will, Mom," said Jennifer. "And anyway," she added, "the good news is that I haven't lost any of my hair like Dad."

"Good news indeed." Tony smiled.

Jennifer then kissed her mom and dad good night and went upstairs. She brushed her teeth and washed her face. Then she took a long shower, washing her hair four times and deep-conditioning it. She shaved her legs, from her ankles to her thighs, and her underarms, too. After the shower, she put on Oil of Olay all over her body, taking particular care of her face. When she put on an extra long T-shirt and a fresh pair of underwear, she got on the scale. The two-digit number above the black line read 89.

She was having trouble sleeping. So she spent the next two or three hours quietly cleaning up her records and books, picking up her strewn-about papers, putting away her magazines, and throwing out dirty paper plates from months ago when she was still eating. Around two in the morning, Jennifer opened the window, moving the curtains out of the way so that the fresh air could get through, and got into bed. She lay on her back, hands under her head, looked up at the ceiling, and remembered that she hadn't called Tully tonight. Just as well, she thought. Reaching under the bed, she pulled out her notebook journal and flipped it open.

Tully, wrote Jennifer in the dark,

> *It breaks my heart to break your heart, my Tully, my Natalie Anne Makker, my faithful friend. But Tully, I assure you, you would not have wanted me to live my life out with my soul such a screaming raging zoo. You would not have wanted me to live my life out in such pain. You taught me all I know about caging the animals that run rampant inside me, for the monsters have been running rampant inside you for years. But strength is not like a will: you cannot will it to me. And though you tried to teach me, you could never give me any of your strength. Which is really good, because now God*

*is going to call upon you to summon all your strength,
all your ironclad, gritted-teeth, clenched-fisted will to
pull through. And pull through you will have to. Cope
you will. I'm sorry though, Tully. It seems that we all
have done nothing but break your poor heart . . .*

She scribbled a few more lines and then shoved the journal
back under the bed, flinging her head back on the pillow.
Jennifer started counting sheep, and sleep came before the
twenty-seventh sheep jumped over the fence.

Monday morning, March 26, Jennifer was not in homeroom.
After homeroom, Tully pulled Julie aside and said, "Jennifer
was not in homeroom."

"I know. I'm in the same homeroom, remember?"

"Where is she?" said Tully.

"How should I know? Home sick."

"Let's call her," said Tully.

They called from the downstairs cafeteria. Tully let it ring
twenty times before she hung up. "Let's call her mother," she
said tensely.

"Oh, great, Tull!" exclaimed Julie. "Let's call Mrs. Mandolini
and tell her her daughter is not home and not in homeroom."

"Well, where is she, then?" asked Tully.

"Maybe she's taking a shower," replied Julie. "Maybe she
has the music on so loud that she doesn't hear us—"

"Impossible," interrupted Tully. "The stereo is unplugged."

"Why is it unplugged?"

"She says because she doesn't listen to it that much any
more and she doesn't want it using passive electricity."

"Passive electricity?"

"That's what *she* says," answered Tully. "What are we going
to do?"

"What's the matter with you? I don't know what you're
going to do, but I'm going to Health."

"Julie."

"Tully! What kind of a face is that? You are out of your
mind! Listen to me. She is taking a shower. She is listening to
music. She plugged it back in. She went shopping. She went
for a drive. She went to Kansas City. She's a big girl."

Tully stood motionless. "Come with me, Jule," she said.

"Tully, I'm going to Health. I'll talk to you at lunch," said Julie, and ran to class.

Tully continued to stand there. She then slowly went to her locker, stashed her books, and left the school. Outside, she thought of calling Robin and asking him to come and get her. But it was a feeble thought, and Tully dismissed it, wrapping her arms tightly around herself. What am I going to say to him anyway? Robin, please come and drive me to Sunset Court? I just don't want to be alone going to Sunset Court. In fact, I don't want to go to Sunset Court at all. Robin, please come and drive me to a desert, drive me to a palm tree, drive me to drink, but just drive me away from Sunset Court, Robin. Tully sat down on the bench outside the side entrance, sat there motionless for such a long time that the sun moved from the bottom of the trees in the courtyard to near the top of the sky before she got up and crossed 10th Street. She trod to Sunset Court with her shoulders as squared as possible. On the way, Tully studiously counted every car that went by, numbering them at fifty-seven by the time she walked up to Jennifer's house.

Walking past the garage, she held herself tighter with her arms and continued on to the back gate. She sat herself down at the picnic table, arms folded around herself, unyielding, shaking arms, gripping her around the chest, and sat there looking at the grass until she heard the car door slam in the front. Tully ran to the driveway, but it was not Jennifer's Camaro, only Mrs. Mandolini's Chrysler Plymouth.

"Tully, what are you doing here, what's wrong?"

"Oh, nothing, Mrs. Mandolini."

"Tully, you're ashen. What's the matter? Is everything all right at home?"

My home? *My* home is wonderful, here it goes, here it goes, here it falls right now, right here, here we are, I am going to turn around and walk out of this house and I am never going to come back. I just cannot stand here in front of her.

"Want some lunch?" Lynn walked businesslike into the kitchen, swung open the fridge, and pulled out the Tupperware bowl of tuna salad.

"I'm glad you're here. You haven't talked to me in some time. I feel very close to you, Tully. You've been very dear to me, but you know that, of course."

"Of course," mouthed Tully, to whom Lynn Mandolini's

voice sounded as far away as Zaire and just as black.

"And to Mr. Mandolini, too, despite how he acts sometimes. Want something to eat?" Lynn asked Tully with her mouth full.

"Mrs. Mandolini," said Tully, putting her hands to her throat. "Do you know if Jen's car is in the garage?"

"Well, of course it is, we always put it there overnight."

"Could you check, please?" Tully asked, trying to keep the raw edge out of her voice. But Lynn must have seen something in Tully, heard *something* from Tully because she put down her sandwich—though not her Marlboro—and said, "Tully, where is Jennifer?"

"Not in school," said Tully. "I'm thinking maybe she went shopping or something."

"Playing hooky from school? Jennifer?" Lynn shrugged her shoulders and picked up her tuna sandwich. "Well, I suppose anything's possible," she said, her mouth full.

They walked outside to the garage. Lynn turned the key and Tully closed her eyes, wanting not to see. She heard the garage door pull slowly up. When Tully opened her eyes, she saw a brand-new 1978 Camaro, shiny and baby-blue.

Tully did not move and neither did Lynn. Nothing moved except for the ash on Lynn's cigarette, which broke off and fell to the floor.

"Gee," said Lynn. "I wonder where she could be. Where do you think she could be, Tully?"

Tully did not hear her. She was holding on to a low tool shelf, keeping herself steady, and was stunned at the anger that swam over her. Yes. Anger. Fucking, naked anger. Goddamn it, Jennifer, Goddamn it, couldn't you at least go out on the open road, couldn't you do at least that, to spare us all just a little? Just a fucking little?

"Tully, where do you think she could be?" said Lynn, a little more urgently.

Tully looked up at her, met her gaze head-on, and said as calmly as she could, "She is in the house, Mrs. Mandolini." But when she let go of the shelf, her legs gave out under her, and she collapsed to the cement floor.

"Tully! What's the matter with you, are you sick?" said Lynn, helping her up with one hand, the other one still holding on to the Marlboro. "You look so awful, why don't you come in. I'll have Jen drive you home."

Tully struggled up. She thought wretchedly as she walked back into the house that if Jennifer wanted to drive, she would have already driven off somewhere. But the car! The car was in the garage.

"Jennifer!" yelled Lynn Mandolini at the foot of the stairs. "Come and have something to eat. Jenny Lynn!"

There was no answer. Lynn looked at Tully, who was clutching on to the banister. Lynn went up first. Tully trailed behind her. "I hope she is all right," said Lynn. "She hasn't been feeling well these past couple of days. But it's so strange. She seemed perfectly fine this morning. Very chipper and everything. Ate a big breakfast." Upstairs, the door to Jennifer's room was shut and so were all the other doors upstairs, making the hallway a dark tunnel. Tully came to stand near Jennifer's bedroom door.

"Tully! Are you just going to stand there, or are you going to open the door?" She walked past Tully and turned the knob.

Jennifer's room was empty. They both walked in. It was not only empty, it was spotlessly clean. The bed was made, the floor was vacuumed, the window was halfway open. The books and records were in their places.

"Wow, when did she do that?" Lynn wondered. "Last night it was really messy."

Tully sat down on Jennifer's bed. Her hands were wet. "This morning. She did it this morning."

"What, instead of going to school?" Lynn said. "Well, maybe. I thought you said she was in the house."

Tully pressed her fingertips to her eyes so hard that when she stopped she saw red spots. "Mrs. Mandolini. She is not in school and her car is in the garage."

"But she is not in the house, either, Tully," said Lynn, sounding slightly irritated. "Listen, my lunch hour is almost over."

"Mrs. Mandolini," said Tully. "Jennifer is in the house."

"Tully, the house is completely quiet except for you and me. She can't be in the house. Where could she be?"

"Did you try the bathroom?" Tully said faintly, hating Jennifer at that moment.

Lynn Mandolini started to breathe very hard. "There is no noise in the bathroom," she said. "Why would she be in the bathroom?"

Tully carefully got off the bed, slowly walked past Mrs. Mandolini across the hall, and put her hand on the bathroom doorknob.

The door was locked.

Tully stepped away and sank to her knees. "She is in the bathroom," said Tully, putting her hands to her face.

"Don't be absurd," said Lynn. "Here, let me try. It's probably just stuck, it sticks sometimes."

The bathroom door was locked.

"Jenny?" said Lynn.

Tully bit down on her lip until she tasted salt and metal.

"Jenny Lynn," said Mrs. Mandolini, knocking on the door. "Jenny Lynn, honey, open the door, what's the matter? Honey, please open the door, Jenny Lynn. Jenny Lynn? Jennifer! Open the door! Open the door, Jennifer! Open the goddamn door!"

Tully knelt with her eyes closed, her hands to her ears, mumbling incoherently to herself, *"Our Father, which art in heaven, hallowed be Thy name . . ."* all the while listening to Mrs. Mandolini's weeping voice, to her body thudding against the door, to her crying, "Jenny Lynn, Jenny Lynn! Honey, please! Open the door for Mommy! Open the door for your mommy, Jenny Lynn!"

Mrs. Mandolini ran stumbling downstairs, got a screwdriver, ran back up, knelt down in front of the door handle, and started to frantically unscrew the lock, her right hand on the screwdriver, her left wiping her face, and all the while muttering, "Jenny Lynn, Jenny, it will be all right, honey, it will be all right."

Behind her, Tully clasped her hands. *" . . . Thy kingdom come, Thy will be done in earth, as it is in heaven . . ."*

Lynn got one screw out and before the other one was out she shoved the door open with her shoulder as Tully lowered her head and clenched her trembling hands. *" . . . Give us this day our daily bread, and forgive us our trespasses as we forgive those . . ."*

Tully's eyes were shut tight, but she was not deaf, and only the deaf and the dead did not hear Lynn Mandolini scream and scream and scream when she pushed open the bathroom door and found her daughter.

II

Railroad
Days

Be still my soul; be still
—A. E. Housman

6

A HOUSE OF
LITTLE ILLUSION

May 1979

Shortly before Tully's high school graduation, a woman named Tracy Scott approached Tully at the Washburn Day Care Center where Tully continued to work on Thursday afternoons. Tracy Scott was a large-boned woman of about twenty-five whose skirts were short, exposing a good deal more of the fleshy white thigh than Tully cared to see.

Tracy's three-year-old son Damien attended the Washburn nursery. Tully wasn't sure how many credits the parents actually needed to take at Washburn University to enroll their kids in Washburn Day Care. Tully guessed by listening to Tracy that it couldn't have been many.

Tracy Scott wanted to know if Tully would mind looking after her little Damien for the summer, five or six nights a week.

"My new boyfriend's a musician," Tracy Scott told Tully. "And me, I wanna be with him to support him, you know, while he plays. He's real good. He sure is. You'd think so, too, if you saw him. Maybe you can come sometime."

Tully was uncertain. Where did Tracy live?

"Right across from White Lakes Mall. On Kansas. Well, really, it's right behind Kansas. There may be one or two late nights. Dependin' on where we gotta go for a gig. I used to take Damien with me, but I don't think Billy likes that too much, Damien gets cranky. Besides, Dami needs a little . . . what d'ya call it? Peace. He's just a little kid. Maybe staying out so late isn't so good for Damien, don't you agree?"

Tully couldn't have agreed more.

"I can't pay a lot, Tully," said Tracy. "But Damien sure likes you, he talks about you at home. I'll be able to make up what I can't pay you with room and board, how's that? I have a spare room you can use, you're still livin' at home, right? So what do you say? Will you think about it?"

Tully said she would.

* * *

A few days later, Hedda was walking home from work when she was accosted by a thin girl in cutoffs and a tank top. The girl walked behind Hedda for a little while, but finally got the courage to approach her.

"Are you Hedda Makker?" she asked.

Hedda looked the girl over and said, "Who are you?"

"You don't know me," the girl answered. "But I know your daughter."

Hedda immediately sharpened up.

"What's your name?" Hedda asked the girl.

"Gail," the girl answered, trying to keep up with Hedda. "Gail Hoven."

"Gail, is there something you want to tell me?"

"Hmm, yes, hmm, well." Gail seemed extremely nervous. "Did you get my letter?"

"What letter? I'm really tired, Gail," said Hedda. "I'd like to go home now."

That seemed to encourage the girl. "Mrs. Makker," she said. "I think you should know that your daughter has been going out with my boyfriend since September."

"Ahh," said Hedda.

"At Jennifer's eighteenth birthday party she met him and they've been meeting, like, two or three days a week ever since!"

"Three days a week, huh?"

"Yes, ma'am, uh-huh," Gail said. "She's been lying to you. I just thought you might like to know."

"Well, thank you, Gail," replied Hedda. "But I already knew that."

Gail seemed baffled by this. "Oh, oh," she stammered.

"She is a big girl now," said Hedda. "She can do as she pleases. Now let me go home, Gail."

"Yes, of course, Mrs. Makker," said Gail, stopping in the middle of the street.

"Oh, and Gail?"

"Yes, Mrs. Makker?"

"Maybe you should try getting yourself another boyfriend, or doesn't anyone else want you?" said Hedda, walking away without turning around.

At home, Hedda waited for Tully. She did not make dinner.

She did not talk to Lena. The TV was off. Hedda sat and waited. At seven-thirty, she asked Lena to go to her rooms.

Tully did not get home until after eight. She had gone to visit Tracy Scott's home. Tracy lived in a trailer—a trailer, for God's sake! And not just a trailer, but a dirty, run-down trailer, with dirty washing and dirty dishes and dirty Damien all over. But that's not what offended Tully. What offended her was that *Damien* lived in a dirty, run-down trailer, with dirty washing and dirty dishes all over. Tracy apologized for the mess and the smell. "I'm real sorry. I been so busy, I didn't get a chance to clean up." But somehow Tully doubted Tracy Scott ever had a chance to clean up. The trailer's dirt looked *lived-in*. Well, this would certainly be a lateral move, thought Tully as she drove home. Like it mattered, anyway.

When Tully came through the door and saw her mother's face, she said, "Sorry I'm late, Mom, I was over at Julie's."

Hedda got up off the sofa, strode over, and hit Tully full-fist in the face. Tully staggered back from the blow and fell. Hedda, teeth clenched, sweating, completely mute, came close and kicked Tully in the stomach.

She kicked Tully again and again and Tully started to shriek. Her screams carried through the front screen door into the Grove, and a few neighbors came out. They whispered to each other, but no one dared go near the house.

"Ma!" shrieked Tully, still supine, trying to scramble away from her mother's foot. "Stop it, stop it, stop it!" She finally managed to get up and put her hands over her face, while her mother, foaming at the mouth, punched her, hissing, "Slut, slut, slut."

From the time Tully was two, she learned fear, and with fear she learned hate, and with hate she learned silence. But something else, too, came out this evening. As Tully struggled up, hands over her face, trying to protect herself, Tully felt rage rising. It nearly lifted her off the ground with its force, and she grabbed her mother's hand and knocked it against the wall, hissing back, "Stop it! Stop it, you crazy woman, stop it!"

Hedda was much stronger than Tully and seeing her daughter angry only made her crazier and stronger. Hedda flailed at Tully, grabbed her with both hands around the neck and began to shake and strangle her.

For Tully, the sensation of not being able to breathe was an odd one in real life. She had woken up with the sweat and fear of death so often that to not be able to breathe at first felt oddly like a dream, and—as if in a dream—Tully felt her suffocation in slow motion and didn't fight. Quite familiar with the feeling, she did not panic, nor even gulp for air. She finally lifted her knee and hit Hedda with what strength she could muster square in the crotch. Hedda gasped and let go. Seeing Hedda's hands between her legs made Tully braver. Tully gritted her teeth and grabbed Hedda's tangled hair, yanking it up and down and hissing all the while, "You're fucking crazy! Fucking crazy!"

After a few moments, Tully let go of her, and as mother and daughter backed away from each other, they saw they were both covered with blood. They stood there for a long moment, looking at each other dumbly. Hedda stared at her own hands, her own shirt, and then at Tully. Tully stared at her mother and then held up her unstitched wrists, which had opened up. Having been recently cut again—for the first time in three years—they had had no time to heal and were bleeding profusely onto Tully's palms and fingers and down to the floor in the hall. Drops of dark blood formed red quarters on the black and white tiles. Tully pressed her wrists to her chest.

Hedda started screaming. "You slut, you liar!" she shrieked. "You slut! You liar!" And then, out of breath, she lunged again for Tully, who, calmer now and prepared, backed away fast, to see her mother fall on her knees, get up, and lunge for Tully again. And again. Trying to move away, Tully became slower and calmer, as if too much tension and anger weakened all her defenses. But she knew it was not tension and anger that was calming her down, for the light-headed feeling turned into the familiar *Whoooshhh*, and she saw not Hedda in front of her, but the waves and the rocks. Rocks blended in with the visual unreality of her mother, her mother screaming at her for being a *slut* and a *liar* while Tully stood there and bled.

"What are you saying, you crazy woman, what are you accusing me of?" Tully said weakly, holding her wrists to her chest. She knew she had little time. Her legs were buckling under her, and she wanted to hold on to a chair or sofa, yet couldn't while holding on to both her wrists.

"You've been fucking since September!" screamed Hedda. Tully lost all her sensibilities. She charged at her mother, flinging her hands in front of Hedda, her wrists spitting blood into Hedda's face. "Since September? September! You mean since September, '72, don't you, Ma! Since September '72, right, Ma, starting with your brother-in-law—my Uncle Charlie! Right, Ma? Right?"

Hedda, supporting herself by leaning against the back of the couch, looking at Tully and breathing hard, shook her head and hissed, "This will all come to a complete stop, do you hear me? You will not be a slut and a liar under *my* roof!"

Glowering at Tully, Hedda went for her again, but fell on the floor, spent, and from the floor said, "Not while you are living in my house, do you hear me?"

"Great!" said Tully. "Fuck you!" She wanted to shout it, but she had nothing left in her to shout with. Her split wrists shouted "Fuck you!" all over Hedda's face and floor, while Tully turned and stumbled up the stairs and into the bathroom.

Hedda lay there until she got her breath then stood up, wiped her face with her sleeve, and went upstairs. She found Tully on her knees in her room, in front of her bed, wrists sloppily bandaged, stuffing clothes into milk crates.

"What are you doing, Tully?"

"I am getting the hell out of here, Mother," said Tully, not looking at her.

"You are not leaving this house."

"Uh-huh. Right."

"You aren't leaving this house! Tully! Did you hear me?"

"Mother, did you hear *me*?"

"You aren't going anywhere, sit down and calm down. You're hurt. You been cutting yourself again."

"I don't want to talk to you anymore, Mother. Get out of this room and leave me alone."

"Tully, don't you fucking talk to me like that!" Hedda shrieked, and started toward Tully.

Tully got up off her knees and, standing up straight, legs apart, both bandaged hands in front of her, pointed the long barrel of a .45 pistol at Hedda Makker.

Hedda stopped cold and stared at the gun.

"Where did you get that?" she whispered.

"Mother," said Tully. Her voice was weak, but her eyes

were those of a madwoman. "That doesn't matter. What matters is that I am leaving and I am not coming back. You must be familiar with that, Mother, your family leaving you and not coming back?"

Hedda flinched.

Tully laughed. "How could I say that to you, Mother? Because you're fucking nuts! That's how! And you're making me crazy, too." She lowered the gun but continued to stand legs apart in front of her mother.

"Put the gun down," said Hedda.

"Mother, I want you to leave this room. I will be out of your house in just a few minutes."

"I don't want you to go," said Hedda. "I lost my temper."

"Too late," said Tully.

"I don't want you to go," repeated Hedda dully.

"Ma!" Tully screamed. "Get out of this room right now so I can get out of this house! Do you hear me?"

Hedda did not move.

"Because I'll tell you something, and you might be surprised to hear this. If you try to stop me, if you come near me, or if you go crazy on me, I will kill you. I will shoot you dead, do you understand?"

Hedda stared at her daughter.

"I will shoot you like a crazy rabid dog in the middle of the street and spare you the rest of your life!" screamed Tully, panting. "You might think I have *some* bad feelings for you, but Mother, I hate you. Hate you! Now get the fuck out of my room!"

Hedda stretched out her hands and took two steps toward Tully.

Tully lifted the gun, cocked it, and before Hedda could move any further, pointed and fired a foot away from Hedda's face. The explosion was deafening, but the bullet slipped into the wall near the door, making only a small neat hole in the Sheetrock. Tully shuddered.

Hedda stood motionless. Tully recocked the gun and said, "Ma. Get out of my room, because next time I won't miss."

Hedda did not turn around, but backed up toward the door, opened it, and staggered out.

Tully put the gun down, went over to the phone, and yanked the cord out of the wall, not giving Aunt Lena a chance to call the police. Thirty minutes later, Tully got into her not so new car and drove out onto the Kansas Turnpike.

It was night, and Tully drove and drove, heading west, with $800 in her pocket and a gun.

Everything hurt.

She suspected that something in her was broken: either her nose, or her ribs, or both. She didn't know. And then KWAZ put out a tornado alert and Tully stopped the car.

It *was* unbelievably windy, particularly here, she thought, in the middle of Kansas in the middle of the Great Plains. The highway was pitch-black. The prairie must be all around me, thought Tully. There were no stars, and no other cars. There was only Tully, two hundred miles west of home, and a tornado. She pulled over to the shoulder on I-70, ran down the slope, found a ditch, collapsed in it, and promptly lost consciousness.

2.

When she came to, it was morning and raining. Her body ached and her wrists throbbed. She crawled up the embankment, got into her car, turned around at the next exit, and drove 150 miles east, back to Manhattan, to DeMarco & Sons. Her quest for the west had brought Tully as far as WaKeeney on the Central Plain.

In Manhattan, Robin took care of her. Tully spent forty-eight hours at Manhattan Memorial, where the doctors reset her nose for the second time in her life, bandaged up her two cracked ribs, and put a half dozen or so stitches in each of her wrists.

She stayed with Robin for two weeks, until the middle of June. Tully didn't really want to stay with Robin, but she didn't have much choice. He was at work most of the day, anyway. She drove around and shopped and spent some time at the library. Sometimes she went to Topeka to see Julie. Tully did not see Julie very often.

In the evening, Robin and Tully went out to dinner or to bars or movies or nightclubs. Once, Tully entered a dance competition with a handsome Kansas State dance student, and when they won, she said to him that she'd never met an Irish guy who could dance, and he told her he'd never met *anyone* who could dance like her. They won two hundred dollars. He gave her half and bought her a drink. Later that night, she and Robin had a ranting, jealous fight.

The following day, Tully called up the student and drove over to the off-campus house he was sharing with three other dance students. The two had sex in the afternoon. Tully left, concluding that he danced much better than he fucked.

For two weeks Tully didn't know what to do with herself. She often just drove out onto I-70 and turned around somewhere around Salina.

Once Tully drove to Lawrence to visit Mr. and Mrs. Mandolini. Lynn never came back to the house on Sunset Court, but stayed with her mother until Tony could get them a place out of town. They moved to Lawrence and now lived in a one-bedroom apartment off Massachusetts Street. Tony commuted every day, continuing as assistant manager at Penney's. Lynn Mandolini was no longer working. Tully didn't see Mrs. Mandolini. Tony said his wife was not well, and the bedroom door stayed shut. Tully did not stay long.

Before she left, Tony put his arm on her shoulder and asked, "Who is J.P.?" showing her the Will Section in the *Topeka High School 1979 Yearbook*.

When Tully found her voice, she was going to tell him, but the look in his eyes reminded her of the look in George Wilson's eyes in *The Great Gatsby*.

So Tully didn't tell Mr. Mandolini who J.P. was, shrugging her shoulders and shaking her head instead.

They were silent for a moment, and then Mr. Mandolini said, "I'm sorry, Tully. This is hard for us. But if you should ever need for anything . . ."

Tully smiled colorlessly at him.

When she came back to Robin's house, she packed her milk crates and left him a note: "Dear R. I've gone back to Topeka to work for Tracy Scott. T."

Tracy was very pleased to see Tully. She set her up in a tiny little room in the back and offered to pay her a "little extra" if she helped clean up.

A little extra, thought Tully. I don't think she has a little extra to buy her kid a toy, much less pay me. "Not to worry," said Tully.

* * *

It was a scorching summer. Kansas weather was changeable; it had something in it for everyone. But this summer, whether it poured or shined, whether there were thunderstorms or tornadoes, it was always 105 degrees.

Tracy was rarely home during the day, even though during the day she was supposed to be home. Tracy usually caught a quick breakfast and then went out "on errands," staying out longer and longer. Her boyfriend Billy the musician was sapping all her energy. Tracy got dolled up in the morning and said she'd be back by lunch but wouldn't return until six o'clock, when she'd change her clothes while Billy waited in his van. Then she would fly out, kissing Damien good-bye.

Tully frequently took Damien to Blaisdell Pool, where she taught Damien how to swim. After the pool, they would often visit the World Famous Topeka Zoo or ride on the carousel. Every Sunday, Tully went to St. Mark's with Damien. A few times on Sundays, after going to church, Tully, Robin, and Damien would go to Lake Shawnee. Sometimes on Saturdays, Tully would drive to Manhattan with Damien to watch Robin play soccer.

Tully rarely saw Julie.

"Tully, why don't you come around no more?" asked Angela Martinez one afternoon. "My daughter misses you," Angela added as Julie looked down at her barbecued hot dog.

"I'm very busy, Mrs. Martinez," Tully said, patting Damien on the head. "It's not so easy taking care of a little child."

"Don't I know it," said Angela. "I have five of them."

"Mom, I'm not your little child," Julie said sullenly.

"Till the day I die you will be my baby," avowed Angela.

When Tully left with Damien that day, she felt as if she would be really happy not seeing Angela or Julie again till the day *she* died.

In July, Tully became aware of a pattern in Tracy Scott's trailer that displeased her. Tracy would leave with her man Billy about seven in the evening and not get in until late the following morning.

"Tracy," Tully said one day. "I thought our agreement was for five or six nights a week."

"Yeah, and?"

"Well, it's more like seven days a week, twenty-four hours a day. At first you were 'running errands' early in the morning, but now you sleep for six hours and are away the other eighteen."

Tracy Scott was defensive. "I'm paying you, right?" she said rudely. "What do you want, a raise?"

"No, Tracy, I don't want a fucking raise," said Tully. "Your little boy misses you. You are never with him. And no, you are not paying me to work around the clock."

Tracy didn't get it. "He is well taken care of, ain't he? He's got clothes and toys and food. And he loves you—"

"No," Tully interrupted. "He likes me. He loves *you*."

"Look, Tully," said Tracy intensely. "I'm trying to work out my life, you know what I mean? If I work out my life, it'll be good for me *and* it'll be good for Damien. If Billy comes to live with us, it'll be good for everybody. I mean, where is Damien's dad? I don't fucking know. And I don't give a good goddamn. I don't want that bastard back. But I do want Billy. What's the big deal? It ain't like I don't come back every day. What's the big deal, Tully? It ain't like you got anything else to do."

Tully sat outside on the trailer steps and watched Damien dig a hole in the ground with his little shovel.

It ain't like I got anything else to do, thought Tully. Nothing else to do. Nothing at all. Well, she is certainly right. Nothing else to do but look after her kid, her unkempt, ill-behaved kid, who bites his nails and throws things and spits and curses. I'll look up little Damien in the State Correctional Facility for Youths in about a decade. Why not? I'll have nothing else to do. Nothing at all. No money, no job, no home. That woman pays me just enough to entertain and feed her boy. I live in a trailer with a child who's not my own. I keep house in a trailer. My God, what's happened? What has *happened*?

In mid-July, Tully and Damien waited all night for Tracy and her man to come home, but they did not come. Not that day, nor the next. Little Damien was cranky and cried a lot. Tully was plenty cranky herself. All of a sudden, things began to feel totally out of control to her. Here it was July, five weeks in the trailer, five weeks of more and more responsibility with a three-year-old, and now Tracy was not even coming home.

Tully woke up with the boy and spent all day with the boy and went to sleep with the boy and when she woke up the next day, she was still alone and still with the boy.

Finally Tracy Scott and Billy came back. Tracy hugged her son, apologizing profusely. "I'm sorry, honey, I'm sorry, baby, Mama had to go with Billy to Oklahoma, and do you know where Oklahoma is? It's so far away." Tully, who heard this, wondered if Tracy herself knew where Oklahoma was. She doubted it. Tattoo-covered Billy just stood there and smoked.

A week later, Tracy disappeared again, for about four days this time. Little Damien bit his fingernails to blood and started to strike out at Tully. Tully retaliated by snapping at him or ignoring him. They rarely went to the pool or to Manhattan anymore. Tully stopped seeing Julie completely. On Sundays Tully and Damien still went to church.

Mostly Tully just sat in the chair and watched Damien play. They watched the trains go by, not ten yards away, and cars go by on Kansas Avenue. Across the street was the back of Sears Automotive and Carlos O'Kelly's, a Mexican Café.

When Tracy came back, she was less apologetic and more defensive. It seemed to Tully that Tracy Scott was almost *resentful* that she had to come back at all.

"Listen, Tracy," said Tully, not leaving anything to chance. "Next time you go away for more than twenty-four hours, maybe you can take Damien with you."

"Oh, that's really great, that's just great!" exploded Tracy. "And who's gonna take care of him on the road, huh? Who?"

"I don't know," said Tully. "Let's see. Maybe, hmm . . . you?"

"I already told you," Tracy whispered, almost hissed. "I'm in bars, clubs. I *can't* take care of him."

"He is your son, not mine," said Tully. "You pay me ten bucks a day to be a mother for you and I can't do it. I don't want to do it. I want to go back to our old arrangement. You've got to find it inside yourself to do the right thing, Tracy."

"Oh, yeah? And what the hell would that be?" said Tracy belligerently.

Tully was tired. "Listen," she said. "During the day, I don't want to watch him anymore."

"Then you can't live here, if you don't want to watch him anymore," said Tracy.

"That's fine," said Tully. "You've made it very easy for both of us. I don't want to work for you anymore."

Tracy hastily apologized. She said Tully got her all hot and bothered over nothing. "Of course you can live here. And just look after him at nights, that's okay. I'm real sorry."

Tully reluctantly stayed. For about seven days, she went out at nine in the morning and did not come back until six at night when it was time to watch Damien. For seven days, Tracy Scott took care of Damien while Billy slept in the bedroom, or smoked, or went out without her.

After seven days of watching Damien, Tracy Scott went out to watch her Billy be a musician and did not come back the next day. That's it, Tully thought. That's just fucking *it*! As soon as she comes back, I'm out of here so fast. A day went by, then two, then three. Then four, then five, then six.

After eleven days, Tully began to suspect that perhaps Tracy Scott went so far that she couldn't find her way back to her trailer and her son. And every day for those eleven days, as Tully sat there in a stupor, waiting for Tracy to come back, she thought, *I got nothing else to do.* I. Got. Nothing. Else. To. Do. And she looked down at the little boy and thought, There is nothing else I *can* do. Because what am I going to do with *him*?

After thirteen days, she remembered how Hedda took in a boarder about ten years ago, to help pay the bills. A seven-year-old boarder. The State of Kansas paid Hedda a sum of money, including extra for his food and clothes, and the seven-year-old boarder lived with them for about eight months. After eight months, the child's parents claimed back Hedda's boarder, and Hedda, helped out by the arrival of Aunt Lena and Uncle Charlie, refused any more boarders from the state.

The State of Kansas foster home program. Tully remembered it existed, just in time.

She left Damien with Angela Martinez for a few hours one afternoon and drove over to the Docking building, across from the Capitol, going up to the fourth floor, to Social and Rehab Services. The receptionist pointed her in the direction of the door that said FOSTER HOME RECRUITMENT AGENCY and told her to speak to Lillian White.

Tully related Damien's story to Lillian White, who sat behind her big table with her big hands folded and said, "What would you like me to do about it? Bring his mother back?"

"No," said Tully, disturbed by the response. "I would like for you to find him a suitable home."

"Miss, this is Foster Home Recruitment and Licensing. We do not find them suitable homes. We find them homes. If you would like suitable homes, you should speak to a private adoption agency. Besides," added Lillian, "his mother will almost certainly come back. They nearly always do, and always want their kids."

Tully was aghast. "But he has no one to take care of him while he waits for his mother!"

"Ah, but that's not true," said Lillian White. "He has you."

"Me? I'm eighteen. I'm even less suitable than she is, if that's possible. Besides, I am not available," Tully said, helplessly forced by this unfriendly, overweight woman to make *some* kind of a decision on her life. "I start Washburn this month."

Lillian lifted her eyebrows. "You do? What are you studying?"

"Child development," Tully said, suddenly remembering something from her life before March 26.

Lillian stared at Tully intently. "And you're going to Washburn?"

"Yes," said Tully, calmer. "I applied to Stanford, in California, but I didn't get in. So I'm going to Washburn. Eighteen credits. Also I found myself a job," rattled Tully. "Carlos O'Kelly's. It's a Mexican—"

"I know what Carlos O'Kelly's is," Lillian cut her off. "And I know where Stanford is. Well, let's see what we can do for him. Can you keep him with you until we find an available family?"

Tully nodded. "How long do you give the parents to come back before you put the children up to be adopted?"

"Eighteen years," replied Lillian, and when Tully got up to leave, she strongly suspected that Lillian wasn't joking.

Oh, man, she thought when she walked outside. Yuk. And

they have *her* running the Foster Program?

Telling Lillian White about Washburn made it somehow real for Tully. She told that woman it was happening and now had to follow through.

It took Tully less than an hour to go to Morgan Hall—the Washburn Admissions Office—get an application, fill it out, drive to Topeka High, get a copy of her transcript, go to the trailer, find her SAT and ACT scores, and drive back to Washburn. Afterward, she went to Carlos O'Kelly's, lied about her waitressing experience, and got a job. Four days later Tully was accepted for the fall semester—with a late registration fee. It took Tully about two minutes to dig out the cash she had stashed away, and another two minutes to pick out her courses from the catalog—all general education requirements. A little English Comp, a little Religion, a little Communication. "Have you thought about your major?" she was asked by the Registrar's secretary. "Child Development," she said dully. It really didn't matter. She could have said Home Ec.

The State of Kansas quickly found Damien a place: the Baxters on Indian Hills Road. Bill and Rose Baxter were a couple in their fifties, and their two children had married and left. The Baxters said they wanted to make another child happy before the grandchildren came. But there was something about them that bugged Tully. Their house was too small to have housed four human beings, Tully thought. And there were no pictures. No pictures of chubby kids running around the yard or playing in the kiddie pool. Nothing.

"Damien," Tully said to the boy that night. "Until your mommy comes back, you're going to go and live with Aunt Rose and Uncle Bill, okay?"

Damien frowned. "Where is my mommy?"

Tully felt grateful that he was only three.

The next morning she drove Damien to Indian Hills Road, with his clothes and books and trucks, and tried to tell the Baxters what he needed and liked, but she was received with near indifference. How much are they getting paid to take care of Damien? Tully wondered achingly as she hugged him, telling him she was going to come by and visit him real soon. While driving away and waving to him, Tully—in the sideview mirror—saw her own face. It looked as small and pinched as Damien's.

3.

At Carlos O'Kelly's, the manager, a small, pretty Guatemalan woman named Sylvia Vasquez, tried Tully out in the part of the restaurant that did not serve alcohol. The tips were smaller, but it was slower, too; more to Tully's speed, since she had never worked as a waitress.

Sylvia gave Tully a cute outfit—a solid blue shirt and a short, flowery cotton skirt. The first week Tully worked three nights, and with a salary of $1 an hour and tips made about $60. It was Tully's very first $60 that she had made at a real job—a real job that did not involve dancing or running errands for Lynn Mandolini or babysitting. The second week, she made $80; the third, Sylvia gave Tully an extra ten hours and she made $120.

Tully continued to live in the trailer, having moved most of Tracy's stuff to the spare room that once was Damien's.

When Robin saw the trailer for the first time, he could not hide his disappointment.

"Tully, why in heaven's name would you want to live in a dump like this?" he asked her.

"It's not a dump," Tully said defensively. "I cleaned and painted it. It doesn't smell anymore. It's only a hundred dollars a month. And for now, it's all mine. How many trailers can you say that about?"

"Tully, you have my whole house. Five bedrooms, a pool, a maid, and all freshly painted," said Robin. "Why would you choose this instead of that?"

"Because this," said Tully, "is dirty, cheap, near the railroad, and all mine. How many places can you say that about?"

"Who the fuck wants to be near the railroad?" He grimaced. "When will it be time to get away from the railroad?"

"Can I get away from the railroad?" Tully wanted to know. "I'm a railroad girl, after all."

Robin just sighed.

August was nearly at an end when Julie came to visit Tully at Carlos O'Kelly's. Ordering a chimichanga and a Coke, Julie said, "I haven't seen you for a while."

"No," said Tully, looking intently into her order pad. "I've been real busy. Will that be a Diet or a regular Coke?"

"Make it regular," said Julie. "So Tom left for Brown a week ago."

"Oh," said Tully, going to clear off the adjacent table. "How do you feel about that?"

"I don't know. We haven't spoken since he left."

"Now, there's a surprise," said Tully.

"Here's a surprise for you," said Julie. "I don't even miss him."

"What's to miss?" said Tully.

"Tom and I used to talk a lot," said Julie, adding, "More than you and me."

Everybody talks more than you and me, Jule, Tully wanted to say.

"But that's not why I don't miss him," said Julie.

I *know* why you don't miss him, thought Tully, but didn't say anything.

When Julie finished eating and paid up, she waited for Tully to come out of the kitchen. The girls stood awkwardly near the front doorway.

"Tully, I've come to say good-bye," said Julie. "I'm leaving for Northwestern tomorrow."

Tully tried to smile. "Oh, well, that's great, Jule. That's great. Listen, I'm sure you'll have a good time. Be sure to write, you hear?"

Julie looked at her bitterly. "Yeah, sure, Tully. You, too, okay?"

They hugged each other quickly and moved away.

"Where are you living now, Tully?" asked Julie. "Are you back home?"

Tully rolled her eyes. "No way. I'm right across the street," she said. "At the trailer park."

Julie stared at Tully. "Ah," she said. "Well, that's great. Listen, I gotta go. Take care, will you?"

Tully watched her go out the doors and then went back to her tables.

"Tully! Tully Makker, right?"

Tully stared blankly into a blithely cheerful face.

"Remember me? Shakie. Shakie Lamber."

"How could I forget you, Shakie Lamber?" replied Tully. "You were Topeka High's Homecoming Queen."

"Yeah, that's it! And Prom Queen, too, but I didn't see you at the prom."

"I didn't go," said Tully.

"Didn't go to your prom? Wow!" said Shakie. Then, "Did you go on the Senior Trip?"

"Noooo," said Tully, already weary. "How *was* Denver?"

"What a city!" said Shakie.

"I'll bet," said Tully. She liked working at Carlos O'Kelly's, but she sure did run into many of the people she went to high school with. Too many.

"So how's it working for this place, Tully? Not too difficult?"

"No, it's great. Piece of cake," said Tully.

"Good," said Shakie. "Because I think I'm gonna apply for a job here. While I'm going to beauty school," she added.

"On the other hand, Shakie," said Tully, "the hours are horrendous and you have to clean your own tables and the customers don't tip too good, and—"

"You'll help me with this, won't you?" said Shakie. "I've never had a job before." She leaned closer to Tully. "Not even babysitting."

"Great," mumbled Tully under her breath.

Shakie got hired and for the first few weeks Sylvia had her "shadowing" Tully, who couldn't avoid her. Much as she tried.

"Shakie," Tully would say, "you're going to have to stack your dirty plates, you just can't carry them out one by one. The tables remain dirty too long and you're wasting time."

"Well, I just can't do that yet, Tully. I'm new at this. I'll get it right," Shakie would say, and throw her blond mane back. Sylvia finally had to ask Shakie to keep it in a ponytail after one customer left Shakie a $5 bill but commented that he would have preferred a little less hair in his burrito.

Shakie didn't have a car and usually would wait for her mother to come pick her up. One Saturday night in October, Tully offered to drive Shakie home.

The girls walked across Kansas Avenue to Tully's trailer. "You live here?" said Shakie.

"Yeah," said Tully. "What about it?"

"It's real nice," said Shakie. "And it's all yours. Must be great."

"Shakie . . . what kind of a name is that?" Tully asked her when they were on their way.

"Shakira," answered Shakie. "I think Mom was expecting an Indian baby. What kind of a name is Tully?"

"Natalie." Tully gave her stock answer. "My brother couldn't pronounce it properly." How ironic, Tully thought. *I'm* asking her what kind of a name she has. Shakira. She's putting me on.

"Oh, you got a brother?" she asked, but before Tully had a chance to respond, Shakie said, "I have three brothers. All older. I'm the youngest. The baby of the family."

"Swell," said Tully.

"Nice car," Shakie said, touching the seats and the dashboard. "You make enough money at Carlos to afford a car like this?"

Tully waited, breathed, counted to five. Then she spoke. "No, it was a gift."

"What, by your folks? Nice parents. We got too many kids in my family, no one has anything newer than 1975. I don't even have a car yet."

The girls chatted a while longer.

"Thanks a lot, Tull," said Shakie, opening the door, and Tully winced.

"Is it okay if I call you Tull?"

Tully nodded her head slowly. "Rhymes with gull, right?" she said. "Why not? I love birds. My boyfriend's name is Robin."

"Great," said Shakie. "Listen, are you busy tomorrow? If it's a nice day, we're having a barbecue. Come if you can."

Tully thanked her for the offer and said she would make it if she could.

Luckily it rained on Sunday and the decision was spared her.

"So, Shakie," asked Tully one Saturday night when she was driving her home again and the girls stopped at the Green Parrot, "who are you going out with these days?"

"Oh, just here and there," said Shakie absentmindedly, and then leaned over to Tully and said, "Don't tell my mom or anything, but I'm waiting for Jack to come back."

"Oh," said Tully coldly. "Where *is* Jack nowadays?"

"Oh, Jack." Shakie shook her head. "He is somewhere. Nowhere. Anywhere."

"What does that mean?"

"I don't know. Didn't he have a football scholarship to someplace or other?" asked Shakie.

"Why are you asking me?" Tully said. "You went to the prom with him. How should I know?"

"Well, nobody knows for sure. I think he had a scholarship to a college in California. Palo Alto or something. I don't think he went."

"Ahh," breathed Tully, her lips suddenly numb. She tried to bite them. *Palo Alto!* Palo Alto. My God, my God.

"Don't you keep in touch with him?" Tully asked after long minutes passed. Tully was grateful for the dimness of the Green Parrot.

Shakie laughed. "In touch? Nah. He is out there finding himself. People who are finding themselves are always out of touch. So how come you didn't go to the prom?" Shakie asked Tully.

Finding himself? Tully thought.

Shakie repeated her question.

Tully shrugged. "Didn't feel like it."

"Didn't feel like going to your own Senior Prom? Wow!" exclaimed Shakie. "We had a bitchin' time. Bitchin'. Jack and I were King and Queen."

Oh, I'm sure, thought Tully. I'm so sure you were, Shakie Lamber, cheerleader and Homecoming Queen.

Shakie took a sip of her Miller Lite. "I'll tell you something, Tully, because you're a friend. I was pretty crazy about that Jack."

"No kidding," said Tully weakly.

Shakie smiled. "Well, he certainly had some craze-inducing parts to him, yes, I can tell you that right now." She ordered another drink. "But he is gone. I think it was just this high school thing between us. But! I keep hoping, nothing wrong with that, right? Oh, I'm not just sitting on my behind, though, Tully. I'm going to beauty school. The Topeka School of Cosmetology. I want to work at Macy's. In the fine makeup department. Chanel or something like that."

"Oh, yeah?" said Tully. She finished her beer in two gulps. "Listen, it's kind of late. I gotta get to sleep. Let's go."

Tully and Robin were invited to Shakie's for Thanksgiving, 1979. Robin didn't go; he was spending the holiday with his brothers.

Tully went alone and met Shakie's three brothers, her huge six-foot-six lumberjack of a dad, and her five-foot-nothing mom, who got all the male Lambers to help her with dinner by screaming at them at the top of her lungs, while Shakie sat with Tully in the living room.

"I'm the youngest and the only girl," Shakie explained. "I never have to do anything."

"Martha! Dinner!" yelled Shakie's mom.

"Martha? Who's Martha?" asked Tully.

Shakie laughed uncomfortably. "Oh, that's me," she said. "Martha Louise Lamber." And when they got to the dinner table, Shakie whispered fiercely to her mother, "Shakie, Ma, *Shakie!*"

A few days later in Tully's trailer, Robin asked, "So, is Shakie a replacement friend?"

"Replacement for who?" snapped Tully.

Robin looked away. "For Julie," he said. "Maybe for me."

"Certainly not for you, Robin," Tully answered. "But Julie is far away. I can't help it if Shakie likes me. We're not that close, though."

"You're not that close with anyone," said Robin.

"No," said Tully, "I guess I'm not. Still, though, what a brave thing to say to me, Robin DeMarco."

"Do you like Shakie?" Robin asked.

"What's not to like?" said Tully. "And as if I have other options. What would you like, Robin, for me not to be friends with anyone but you?"

Robin sighed and made room for her in the bed, pulling the quilt over both of them. "As if what I wanted really mattered, Tully," he said.

"Jack is back!" said Shakie happily as the girls started their Saturday night shift.

It was nearing Christmas.

"He is, is he?" said Tully. "Why?"

"Oh," said Shakie, brushing her hair in the middle of the restaurant, "his dad died. So he's back! Sounds like a song, doesn't it? 'I've been waiting to happen/till Jack comes back!/ Now, Jack is back/ and I'm ready to happen/ Jack is back/ and it's straight in the sack!'" She sang and danced and flung her blond mane all around the empty tables.

Tully watched her and then laughed. "Shakie, you are so full of shit."

"He really is back, Tully," Shakie said seriously.

"No, that's not it. What about all that bullshit that it was just a high school thing?"

Shakie shrugged and smiled. "You're right. It was bullshit."

"Besides, his father died, how can you be so happy?" said Tully.

"Well, he's gonna need a lot of cheering up, ain't he?" replied Shakie, gleaming. "And I mean a *lot* of cheering up!" She giggled and jumped up in the air.

Tully laughed despite herself.

She saw him a few days later when he came to pick up Shakie. Shakie's station was full, so Sylvia sat him down at one of Tully's empty tables. Tully came up to him, real calm, real cool. "What can I get you?" she asked. He looked the same as ever. Better. Sun-drenched, blond, and hard. But Tully's eyes were all fogged up like wet glasses.

"How *are* you?" he asked Tully.

"Oh, all right, getting along, couldn't be better." She tried not to blink and not look at him, either, while her heart gripped and ripped her.

"What can I get you?" she repeated, her voice cold.

He reached out and touched her fingers, lightly. "I'm sorry, Tully," he said. "I am. So sorry."

He said that at graduation, too. Sought her out—cornered her, almost—and said, "I'm sorry, Tully. I'm so sorry." Now, as then, his serious, intent face made her speechless.

"Ooohhh, Jackie!" squealed Shakie, throwing herself and her hair all over Jack, kissing him and giggling. Jack rubbed Shakie's back. "All right, all right, what's gotten into you?" he said.

Tully left them and finished her tables, married some ketchups, and filled some saltshakers and sugar bowls. She kept her eyes on her unsteady hands.

"Tully, do you need a ride?" he asked her on his way out.

God! I wish he didn't know my name, she thought.

"You must be joking!" said Shakie before Tully could answer. "She's got the most brilliant car. A 1978 blue Camaro. She should be asking you if you need a ride." Jack stared at Tully so hard and so sad that she wanted to smash his face in. Smash his face in or break down right in front of him and his girl.

A week later, Shakie walked over to Tully's trailer after work. She entered, sat down, and burst into tears.

Tully rolled her eyes. Walking over slowly, she sat carefully on the corner of the sofa. She wanted to put her arm around Shakie but just couldn't do it.

"What's the matter, Shake? He leave?"

Shakie nodded, crying. "Going to."

Tully rubbed her hands together. Clenched her fists, unclenched them.

"I thought he'd be staying, I thought maybe he would stay," Shakie was muttering. "But no, he had to go, he said, had to go back. Didn't want to be back here anymore, he said." She continued to cry, and Tully continued to sit there and say nothing. They sat for a long time, until it got too much for Tully, just *too fucking much*, and she said, "Shakie, I'm really sorry, because I like you and wish I could be a better friend to you now that you need someone, but I can't make you feel better about this. Do you understand?"

Shakie wiped her eyes and looked at Tully.

"Shakie," continued Tully, cracking her knuckles, "I will cover your ass for Sylvia, and I will clean your tables, and I will drive you home. I will help you with anything else, but I cannot help you with *this*. I just can't, please understand. I just can't help you."

Shakie stared at her.

"Powerless!" exclaimed Tully. "Yes, powerless, and helpless. And I cannot stand to see you cry over this!" she screamed suddenly and stood up. Tully's face was a mask of pain and Shakie just sat on the bed, astonished. Tully pressed her clenched fists to her eyes and whispered, "I cannot stand to see you cry over *him*."

It was a while before Tully took her hands away from her face. "Please be a friend to me, don't do this in front of me, Shakie, okay? Otherwise I really won't be able to be friends with you anymore. Okay?"

"Okay, Okay," Shakie said quickly, getting up and coming close to Tully. "Okay," she repeated, and went to hug Tully, who backed away.

It was dark but Tully wasn't afraid. After Shakie left, Tully drove up to St. Mark's, parked the car, and walked around back. The gate screeched when she opened it, badly needing oiling. Making her way carefully through the backyard, Tully stopped near a wrought-iron chair, which had been brought out by Father Majette when he had found Tully lying on the ground. "God doesn't distinguish between the dead and the living, my child," he had said. "He loves both equally. You're still living, Natalie Anne. You wouldn't want our Lord to mistake you for the dead, lying as you do among them."

Only barely, thought Tully, moving the chair out of the way and lying down on the December Kansas ground. *Only barely living*, she thought, lying down in her coat and scarf and gloves next to a flat gravestone embedded in the earth. She ran her fingers carefully and gently over the cold stone.

4.

One, two, three, four minutes of screaming. Raw, ugly, horrible screaming. Lynn Mandolini was shaking Jennifer, shaking Jennifer and screaming. Tully pressed her palms hard against her ears, wanting to break her eardrums, wanting just to stop, stop.

She opened her eyes and saw Lynn pressing her lips to Jennifer's face, pressing her mouth to Jennifer in an attempt to, Tully didn't know what, but she shut her eyes quick, pressing the balls of her hands to her eyes to go blind to ward off Lynn Mandolini to stop to stop. But it was too late. The image of Lynn bending over and desperately pressing her lips to what was left of Jennifer burned like a big black tattoo into Tully's head. Tully closed her eyes but continued to see a crazed mother bending over her only daughter.

Still on her knees, Tully moved toward the bathroom. "Mrs.

Mandolini, Mrs. Mandolini," Tully whispered, her head bent. "It's no use."

But Lynn didn't hear Tully, through her bloodcurdling screaming and whimpering, whimpering that made ants crawl on Tully's skin.

"Please, Mrs. Mandolini," Tully repeated inaudibly, briefly looking into the bathroom.

There she is, lying in her mother's arms. Lying in them. She lay in them when she was born and she is lying in them now. Well, it is only right that she should be lying in her mother's arms, and not in mine.

Tully could not see Jennifer's head, covered as it was by Lynn's upper body, but she could see that Lynn's face and hands, Jennifer's white T-shirt, the floor, the shower curtain, the walls, the toilet all were dripping, saturated, soaking in what remained of Jennifer.

The doorbell rang; Tully went downstairs to answer it. She saw the policeman outside.

"Is everything all right?" he said, raising his cap. "A neighbor across the street—" he pointed to an elderly woman, standing still. "She seemed to think," he continued, "there was some trouble."

"There has been . . . some trouble," said Tully blankly, and then Lynn started to scream again. The policeman gently pushed Tully aside and ran up the stairs. Tully continued to stand near the open door. I could just go, go right now, just walk on out, right now, walk down the driveway, down the path, away from Sunset Court, away forever from Sunset Court.

"Miss, miss." The police officer ran back down the stairs. He didn't look the same anymore, thought Tully. "We need to call an ambulance," he said, and Tully noticed he was shivering. She noticed that she herself became calmer and calmer the more tumultuous the reaction around her got. The more she heard Lynn Mandolini's screaming, the more something was swinging shut inside her. The more steady her hands became, the more regular her breath, the less she prayed, and the less she closed her eyes. And now the near-panic of this man for an ambulance made her almost, almost *amused*.

"I think," she said, "it's a little late."

The ambulance came anyway, in about ten minutes. Two ambulances. And another police car. The lights, the blue and white colors, flashed so insistently, they nearly drowned out the image of Jennifer's red blood. The sirens coming up the street nearly drowned out the sound of Lynn's terrible screaming. After the paramedics rang the bell, they stood politely near the door, waiting for Tully to let them in, just like insurance salesmen or plumbers. "Have you thought about insurance?" "We've come to replace your pipes."

Swinging the door open, she pointed them upstairs, where the police officer was prying Lynn off Jennifer. Before he went up there for the second time, he went into the downstairs John and quietly threw up. Tully heard that sound. Compared to the screaming, it was an unchained melody to her. The paramedics had to give Lynn five hundred milligrams of Thorazine before they were able to detach her from Jennifer.

"Miss, what's your name, miss?" said another policeman, touching Tully on the arm. She flinched from his touch.

"Makker," she said, her mouth numb, like it was full of Novocain. Novocain that had been administered only after the dentist had drilled raw into her nerve endings.

"Would you like something to calm yourself?" the police officer inquired, and Tully looked down at her body, completely still, completely immobile.

"If I was any calmer," she said, "I'd be in a coma. No, thank you." One of the paramedics grabbed her wrist and felt her head, uttering, "Shock. Needs to go to the hospital. Needs to be treated. Put her in with the mother."

Tully snatched her wrist back from him. "I am fine," she said. "I'm just fine."

"Shock," the paramedic repeated in the same flat tone he might use for "Left. Right. One, two, three." "Needs to be treated."

Tully did not move from the couch. She turned toward the stairs, and then quickly away, almost losing control of her bladder, seeing two men carrying down a covered stretcher.

Minutes passed. Sound waves stopped breaking through her barriers. The men moved and the blue lights twirled and whirled like party lights for a party girl, for a dancing girl. The crowd of people gathered outside for the party show. A whole crowd at noon. Have they nowhere else to be?

There was movement, and there was vision, but there was no sound, no sound at all. I wonder if he is right, Tully thought. *I wonder if I am in shock. I wonder if this is what she felt like withdrawing from us all at the age of two and three, withdrawing because the sounds we made stopped making connections inside her head. I wonder if this is what she felt like when she was a little girl and was trying to shut out the whole world.*

"Miss Makker," she heard dimly. "Miss Makker. Could you tell us what happened? I know it's hard for you, but you must try. Please, Miss Makker."

I'm not her keeper, she wanted to say. *I am not her keeper. I could not keep her. Could not.*

"I don't know," she said. "Have you called Mr. Mandolini?"

"We need to. Miss Makker, were you here when it happened?"

Yeah, sure, she thought. *Why, I helped her. Me and her mom, together. We helped her and then watched.*

"Was it, perhaps," the police officer was saying, "an accident? That's what we're trying to find out. What to put in the police report. Could it have been, perhaps, an accident?"

Tully slowly shook her head and stood up. She felt a lightheadedness not unlike what she felt when she "healed" herself. She sat back down. *Ah. That was better. Still, though, I'm breathing shallow.* She touched her skin. It was cold and clammy. "Look, I am in shock, right? I cannot help you very well right now. But you know," she said, her voice catching a little, "she was a good Catholic girl. Perhaps if you say it was an accident, she'll be able to be buried by the Church. You know how the Church doesn't approve of those . . . unaccidents. So perhaps maybe you could just do that, what do you think?"

Tully looked him straight in the face and saw his eyes fill with tears. "Miss," he said, "I'm a police officer. I have to do my job. I have to put in what really happened. I'm sorry, Miss."

Tully's eyes went hard. "In that case," she said, "it was an accident. She was playing around, I didn't even know they kept a gun in the house. It was an accident. She had everything going for her. We were going to go to California, you know.

She was gonna be valedictorian of her class." Tully looked down at her hands and began to shake.

"All right, Miss, all right," said the policeman, putting his hand on Tully. "All right."

And they all left soon thereafter. Even the crowd disappeared. Well, why not? The show was over. They all had stood and stared as two stretchers were wheeled into the ambulances. The sirens back on, the police cars forged ahead, paving the way to Stormont-Vail Hospital. The only thing the crowd had the decency not to do after the show was over was clap. Tully stayed behind. She figured if she could walk to the ambulance, she could stay behind. If she could talk, she could stay behind. After all, she would have to do a lot more talking if she went to Stormont-Vail, and then to the police station. If she was okay to walk, she was okay to stay. So she closed the door of her beloved house on Sunset Court and stayed.

Sitting back down on the living room sofa, she listened to the house. It wasn't making much noise. Well, at least I'm not waiting for it to make a noise. Like earlier. At least I know it's not going to be making any more noise.

Tully sat there on the edge of the couch, back straight, hands on her lap, then she got up and turned on the TV. She turned it on full blast and stared at it. Because of the TV, Tully didn't hear a great many things. She didn't hear the doorbell ring, nor the phone ring off the hook. She didn't hear the minutes and the hours strike, nor did she hear the screaming inside her own head. I am not in shock, she kept repeating. I am not in shock. I Am Not In Shock.

Sometime later, when the sun was no longer visible through the living room windows, she thought, Should I go home? I might as well go home. Nothing else to do.

But there was something to do. There was something to do for . . . Mr. Mandolini. Tully wanted, at the very least, to spare him. At the foot of the stairs, Tully's heart nearly gave out. I can't go up there! I can't go up there twice!

But then she thought, I had already said that. Four hours ago. And the worst is over.

No, she thought. The worst is not over.

And so Tully trudged on upstairs. Maybe I shouldn't touch it, she thought. Maybe the police need me to leave it just the way it is. Maybe they need it as exhibit B. But no, they *would've said something. And there isn't going to be a trial. There is no defendant. There is no plaintiff.*

She slowly dragged her weight behind her. Upstairs, the doors were all closed. Except the bathroom door. Light was coming in from the bathroom, and Tully thought, how ordinary it all looks. How normal. Door slightly ajar. The house night-still. As if no one's home.

And then Tully clenched her fists, and with trembling lips and trembling hands looked into the bathroom. The paramedics, or the police, had opened the window. The fresh air barely helped.

Tully fell to her knees and crawled in.

She kneeled in the drying coagulated mess on the floor and wept. She lay down flat, prone in the blood on the floor, and wept, rubbing her hands and face into what remained of Jennifer.

"Oh, Mandolini, Mandolini," she whispered. "I didn't even get to hold you one last time, you pig. I didn't even get to cradle your poor head next to mine. She held you and then they took you away, and look what I have left of you. Look what I have left of you, Mandolini . . ."

Tully was a long time lying on the floor, her face pressed down, her palms down—so motionless that she looked as if life had left her.

But then Tully Makker got up and breathed out heavily. She took all the rugs, all the towels, the toilet seat cover, and the shower curtain and carried them down the stairs, throwing them all into a big black plastic bag. We used to gather the autumn leaves in these bags, thought Tully. Autumn leaves. And again she nearly gave out, and grabbed on to a chair to hold herself up, not pass out, not pass out, not pass out. No. No. NO.

Going back upstairs with a floor mop, Tully got a sponge from under the sink, filled a bucket with cold water, and began to wash the bathroom. She washed the side of the bathtub and changed the water in the bucket. The walls near the toilet; another change. The toilet and the floor; three changes. The far walls, the mirror, the inside of the tub, the floor; four more changes. It took Tully ten clean buckets of water and one hundred and thirty minutes to wash that bathroom of Jennifer. When Tony Mandolini came home, Tully was still *in the bathroom, still finding a brown spot here or there and compulsively scrubbing it.*

She got up off the floor, turned around, and there he was, watching her, standing in the doorway, already an old man.

"What's happened to you, Tully?" he whispered. "You're all covered in blood."

Tony told her the police called him and he went to Stormont-Vail, identified his daughter, sat near Lynn for a while, went to the police station, filled out a report, signed out exhibit A, and came home.

Tully and Mr. Mandolini sat near each other for a little while. Tony had turned down the TV, and now they both heard the phone ring. She looked at him. He shook his head. The ringing stopped after a while, and then Tony pulled the plug.

"Tully, stay here, stay over, if you want, if you can. I have to go to bed now. Stay here. Please."

And she did. She plugged the phone back in to call her mother, telling her nothing except the usual—she was staying over at Jen's. "On a school night?" Hedda had said, but didn't care beyond that.

Tully stayed downstairs, hearing Tony upstairs walking past the bathroom in the hall and shutting its door. She spent the night on the couch with her knees up. She sat there and rocked back and forth back and forth back and forth, until the room started to lighten, and she fell into a state of numbed semiconsciousness.

In the morning, Tully made coffee for Tony.

"Mrs. Mandolini will be staying in the hospital for a while," Tony told Tully. Yes, I thought she might be. Tony himself looked as if he could use a hospital stay.

"Tully, I don't know what to do now," he said to her. "I don't know what to do. What to do next." He looked at his shaking hands.

She reached over and took his hands between hers. Her hands were steady, but her eyes were not.

He is still stunned, but I am already falling off my chair, already can't breathe, already without her.

"Mr. Mandolini, she wanted to be cremated," Tully said; her voice shook like his hands. She should not have trusted it. She cleared her throat.

"No, no, that's impossible," he said. "I'm Catholic. We all

are. We need a service. She needs to be . . ." He trailed off.

"Buried?" Tully finished for him. "I agree. We won't listen to her. But the Catholic Church—they—"

"I already took care of it," he said. "With your help. The police officer says to me, a Miss Makker told him it was an accident. Did I concur? So I concurred. Pleaded for no autopsy. Hasn't she been mangled enough?" He paused to collect himself. "I mean, it could have been an accident, right? She could have just been fooling around, right?"

"Right," Tully nodded, and then shook her head, trying to shut out the vision of the entry wound and the exit wound also. Right. She just sat on the bathroom floor, put a Colt .45, your Colt .45, to her chin and pulled the trigger. She was only fooling around.

"I don't want to wait for Lynn to get out. She is not going to be feeling too well, anyway," he said.

"I hear you," said Tully.

"I don't want a big to-do," said Tony.

Well, this is not a wedding, after all, Tully thought. "I hear you," she repeated.

"Nothing at all, in fact," said Tony. "I just want, kind of want it all over with . . . as quickly as possible."

"I hear you," Tully said again.

They left the house a little later and went to Penwell-Gabel, Topeka's finest. Tony Mandolini had them take care of his mother nearly a decade earlier.

"No service?" Mr. Gabel, grandson of the original Mr. Gabel, asked. "But everybody has a service."

"No service," Mr. Mandolini repeated, while Tully stood by him. "Just a priest at the site."

"Where is she to be interred?" Mr. Gabel asked.

"St. Mark's. Right, Tully? St. Mark's?"

She nodded. It was a good choice. St. Mark's was a beautiful small old church, the church Tully went to with the Mandolinis on Sundays for many years. It had a small, private graveyard, covered with trees and bushes. It was the family church.

"Is there to be a wake?" Mr. Gabel gently inquired.

Tully blinked. A closed coffin was a disgrace. An open one an impossibility.

"No!" said Tony vehemently. "No wake. No autopsy, no

wake, no service. All right? And your best coffin. The very best. That California Redwood coffin. All right?"

Tully blinked again. Thank God for Tony.

"All right, sir," said Mr. Gabel. "When would you like the burial to take place?"

"Today," replied Tony. "If not sooner."

"We'll arrange for the priest," Mr. Gabel assured him. "Father Majette I'm sure will make himself available. Have you thought about a gravestone?"

"I haven't thought about anything," said Tony Mandolini, and Tully looked away.

Penwell-Gabel, true to their word, took care of everything. Mr. Penwell and Mr. Gabel themselves went to get Jennifer from the hospital, the California Redwood coffin in tow. They brought her back to their funeral home on 10th Street, embalmed her, and put her briefly into their "St. Mary's room" while their men went to St. Mark's and dug a hole in a backyard filled with gravestones.

"Are you sure Mrs. Mandolini wouldn't like you to wait?" asked Tully cautiously.

Tony shook his head. "I'm sure. It will be a long time before she is okay," he said.

Tully went home and changed into an old black dress. In her own bathroom, she looked at her face and hair, took a pair of scissors and cut the hair off to within an inch of her head, wrapped a black bandanna around it, put on dark sunglasses, high black pumps, and walked over to St. Mark's on the corner of Canterbury and Pembroke. It was gray and raining that Tuesday, March 27, 1979. Tully's sunglasses served her well when she saw Mr. Mandolini, in his best black suit, and then a little later, Father Majette, and then, still later, the hearse and behind it two cars with their headlights on, coming up Canterbury. Yes, those sunglasses served her very well.

Four pallbearers carried the California Redwood coffin through the small gate, up the narrow path, and to the back, where Father Majette, Mr. Walter Penwell, Mr. Gregory Gabel, Mr. Athony Mandolini, and Miss Natalie Anne Makker stood with bowed heads for fifteen minutes under the March rain while Miss Jennifer Lynn Mandolini lay before them in a Califorinia Redwood.

7

JEREMY

June 1980

Tully's freshman year at Washburn came and went.

It was a year in which Tully lived in Tracy Scott's trailer and waited for Tracy to come back. Tully went to class, went to work, and on the weekends saw Robin. Tully stopped smoking and took up drinking, and then gave up drinking and reading and watching TV and took up sitting in the trailer, alone on Tracy's couch. Tully won forty Tuesday night dance contests at Tortilla Jack's her freshman year.

Tully wrote to Julie once before Christmas and once after. Julie wrote to Tully four times before and six after.

Tully worked with Shakie side by side four times a week and didn't like it. Seeing Shakie so often nagged at Tully. Nagged at her so much, in fact, that Tully quit Carlos O'Kelly's in April and got herself a job at Casa Del Sol a few blocks away.

It was a year in which Tully thought ahead only to Sundays.

2.

In the summer of 1980, Tully did an internship, mainly just filing and matching invoices, for the Social and Rehab Services Department. But Mr. Hillier, the vice-president of SRS, took a kind of paternal, solicitous liking to Tully. He reminded her of Tom Bosley, Mr. Howard Cunningham on *Happy Days*.

Convincing Tully it would be great experience, Mr. Hillier placed her in Lillian White's Foster Home Recruitment Agency, where Tully looked over new foster family applications. She didn't go on location, as it was called when the workers cased the premises of potential foster families and determined whether it was a fit home for a child. As far as Tully could see, nobody went on location, though the prospective fosters went through a rigorous six-hour training session: how to raise a kid in 360 minutes.

The workload for each worker was high: thirty-five kids each, and not just the kids but their entire past dirt, family, drugs, gangs. The workforce was small: seven, including Lillian. Tully was a lackey for the social workers during the summer. Tully heard "Take this application and give it to Lillian" twenty times a day. What Lillian did with the applications was a mystery to Tully.

Tully also had to retrieve "pronto" statistical information on the children for Lillian, children that Lillian was looking to "sell" to a foster family, or so Tully reckoned.

But it was the six-hour training session that offended Tully the most. Six hours. Shopping for a bra sometimes took longer.

"I remember you," said Lillian at the water cooler one day, after Tully had been there a month. "Well, well. I guess you were true to your word. Went to college."

"Guess so," said Tully. "By the way, his mother hasn't come back."

"Whose mother? Oh, that little kid's. Well, he is a terror. He's been through three families already. Nobody seems to like him."

Tully was appalled by her offhand manner and by her insensitivity. The boy has no mother, you asshole! she wanted to shout, but kept quiet. The internship was good experience. But is this what happens to people who work here? They market the kids like a commodity and shuffle them from home to home, complaining about the administrative nuisances the children have become? No, thanks, thought Tully. No. Thank. You.

The same summer, Shakie graduated from beauty school and got a job in Macy's Chanel fine makeup department. Tully thought the most interesting aspect of Shakie's new job was the Chanel training course: a twenty-hour-a-week ordeal for seven weeks.

Julie came back home from Northwestern in the summer. She stopped by Casa Del Sol one Friday night.

"Hey, Jule," said Tully. "You're back. Want a table?"

"No, thanks, Tully," Julie said. "Just came in for a second. I'm on my way to the movies."

"Who with?" Tully wanted to know. "Tom?"

Julie waved her off. "No, I don't see Tom anymore. That pompous asshole."

Tully laughed.

"Well, he is. Just because he goes to Brown. He has this really condescending tone now."

"*Now?*" Tully interjected, still standing near the reception area, a few feet away from Julie.

"He is so annoying. I graduated from Topeka High with honors, too, you know."

"I know," said Tully. Pause. "How long have you been back?"

"Two weeks," said Julie quickly, and Tully looked away.

A week later, Tully stopped by Wayne Street. Angela opened the door. "Tully!" she exclaimed. "Come in, come in, my dear! Julie will be so happy. Julie!"

Julie and Tully sat down on opposite ends of the couch in the living room. "What are you doing tonight?" Tully asked.

"Nothing, just watching TV."

"Oh, 'cause I was wondering," Tully said, "if you wanted to come out with me. Maybe to the Green Parrot."

Julie sat staring at the TV with her hands between her knees. "Yeah, sure, Tull," she said slowly. "That'll be nice."

It was eight o'clock at night when the girls left Julie's house. Julie stopped in the driveway when she saw Tully's car.

"Oh, man," she said, her voice low. "You still driving that thing?"

"They gonna have to carry me from that thing feet first," replied Tully. "Come on. It's okay."

They drove through half of the town without speaking. The radio was on loud.

"This is not the way to the Green Parrot," Julie said at last.

"No, it isn't. I thought I'd pick up Shakie. I think she might like to come with us."

Julie stared coldly at Tully.

"Yeah, sure, Tully," she said. "For sure."

And when Shakie came up to the car, all bursting and smiling, Julie turned to Tully and asked, "Would you like me to sit in the back?"

Tully returned Julie's cold stare and then smiled uncomfortably at Shakie. "Shake, would you mind sitting in the back?"

The three of them sat side by side at the bar at the Green Parrot. Tully lit a cigarette.

"Tully," asked Julie, "didn't you tell me in one of your two letters you stopped smoking?"

"I did," said Tully, playing with her lighter. "I didn't mean forever."

For most of the evening, Tully danced and hung out with a bunch of people at the tables. Julie and Shakie sat at the bar not talking.

When it came time to drive Shakie and Julie home, Tully drove to Wayne Street first and dropped Julie off, even though Shakie was much closer.

After a week, Tully came by again, asking Julie if she wanted to go out. This time Julie refused.

A few weeks later, Julie stopped by Casa Del Sol to ask Tully to go see *Superman II*. Tully lied and said she had already seen it.

They did not see each other again until Julie came by Casa Del Sol one Sunday night to tell Tully she was leaving for Northwestern the next day. Tully asked Julie to wait until the end of Tully's shift at ten. Julie did.

They walked over to Tully's trailer.

"So you're still living here, huh?" Julie said.

"Sure. It's so close to work," said Tully.

Julie didn't want to come in. "Mind if we sit outside, Tully? It's a nice night."

They sat on a fallen-down tree trunk near the embankment at the back of the trailer.

"So how do you like Northwestern, Jule?" asked Tully, lighting a cigarette. She inhaled deeply.

"I don't know," Julie said. "My roommate Laura is nice. The work is hard. I didn't join any clubs last year. Didn't you read my letters?"

"Sure," said Tully. "Over and over. Your letters were the only things I read all year."

"Yes, I have your two committed to memory," Julie said. "It wasn't difficult. Two pages in total and a postcard. Large type."

The girls were sitting next to each other and staring straight ahead. At the Camaro. Finally Tully started digging the ground with her foot. Julie started watching Tully.

"I didn't write much," Tully said, poking at the ground with her sandals, " 'cause there wasn't a lot to say. You know. Same old stuff. Job. School. Trailer. Robin."

"How's your mom?"

"Don't know."

Julie turned to look at Tully. "Have you seen your mother since—"

"I haven't seen her since, no," Tully interrupted.

"Same old stuff, I'll bet. Listen, how do you manage to see *her* so much?"

Tully knew what Julie was talking about. "Not so much. Once a week."

"I don't know how you do it, that's all."

Tully gestured with her hand. "She's harmless, Jule. And she cheers me up."

"Yes, you've really been a Miss Sunshine this summer."

Tully paused. "I don't know what you're talking about. You refused to go out with me."

Julie snorted. "Not with *you*, Tully, dear," she said sarcastically. "With you and everyone else the cat dragged in."

Tully started kicking the ground with her foot. "I thought it might be fun for all of us to—"

"You thought it might be fun," Julie mimicked. "Listen, stop. Okay?"

Tully didn't say anything.

"So, my mom's upset you don't come to visit her anymore," Julie said.

"Tell her I'm sorry. I'm so busy," said Tully.

"Yeah, too busy to come see my mom, too busy to write. Yet nothing's going on."

"Julie, stop, okay?"

"Yeah," said Julie, jumping off the tree trunk. "Listen, I gotta go."

Thank God, thought Tully. "I'll drive you back," she offered.

"No, thanks. My dad's car is at Casa. I'll just walk back. It's all right."

" 'Bye, Jule," said Tully, sitting on the tree, her hands on her lap. "I'll be better at writing. I promise."

"Yeah, sure," said Julie, but came back and patted Tully lightly on the arm. Tully moved her arm away.

Julie coughed. "My mom says she sees you at St. Mark's. You don't still go to that church, do you?" she asked quietly.

"Sure," said Tully as evenly as she could. "Why not?"

Julie moved closer to Tully, who tried to move away, but that would have meant falling back.

"I don't know how you can go to *that* church at all," said Julie, her voice catching.

Tully stared at the Camaro. "Somebody has to bring the flowers," she said at last.

"I don't know how you can do it, that's all," repeated Julie.

"Somebody has to," said Tully.

"Let her parents."

"I don't think her mom's very well," said Tully.

Julie wiped her face. Tully continued to stare at the Camaro. "I don't know how you can *not* do it," she said to Julie.

Julie stepped away. "I really gotta go, Tull," she said. "I'll see you."

"I'll see you," said Tully.

After Julie left, Tully went inside her trailer and sat alone on the couch until she fell asleep.

At the start of her sophomore year, Tully bought herself a new couch and a full-size brass bed. She wanted a queen-size bed, but it wouldn't fit in the tiny trailer bedroom.

Tully's money was steady enough now that she thought of leaving Tracy's trailer. But she couldn't bring herself to do it just yet. What if Tracy came back, Tully thought, and wanted her little boy?

Tully saw Robin every Saturday night, but sometimes during the week she needed to feel anonymity touch her, a soothing, caressing, tepid coldness touch her all over. In her brass bed.

When Tully's internship was over, Mr. Hillier called her into his office and told her, "You've done very well, Tully. Even Lillian said you did good work, and she is real hard to please. My advice is that you get a bachelor's in social work instead of just an associate's in Child Development. More money, greater chance of promotion. And then maybe a master's—"

Tully snorted loudly.

"Think about it," said Mr. Hillier. "In any case, come and

talk to me when you graduate. We may have a job for you. Certainly another internship next year."

"Okay, yeah, I'll think about it," Tully said without enthusiasm.

"What's the matter, Tully?" said Mr. Hillier. "It's a good opportunity."

"Yeah, sure," she said.

"No point for a smart girl like you to just wade through some silly job. If you get a master's, it could mean a career—"

"Yeah, great," said Tully, standing up. "Thanks."

Social work? thought Tully. Social work, where the underpaid go to hustle motherless kids through the system? Just great.

"Social work programs need people with a heart," said Mr. Hillier, as if reading her mind.

"Yes," she said. "Tell that to the foster families," said Tully.

"Oh, they're not too bad," said Mr. Hillier. "They do go through a six-hour course, you know."

"I know," said Tully. "And it shows."

Tully thought about a bachelor's. Mr. Hillier acted as if something might be possible for her, and Tully did not experience that kind of faith very often. Most people who had watched her grow up thought nothing at all was possible for the wayward and undisciplined Makker girl. It was so refreshingly alien to her, *not* to be known by someone, but she didn't really care anymore. Once she had plans, but they all seemed to have vaporized. Now the only thing that mattered was being left alone. Tully remembered her dream to go far away, far away west, and thought, If I go away, I will never be known by anyone. No one will know me at all.

Tully decided to follow Mr. Hillier's advice. Why not? She took Social Welfare 250, Advanced Child Development 302, and Introduction to Social Work 100. Intro to Social Work involved forty hours of volunteer community work. Volunteer! She wanted to ask if taking care of Damien for a thousand hours counted toward the requirement. Instead she did some time in the Shawnee Youth Center Lock-Up, where seventy-five runaways or runners and abandoned teenage addicts waited for a foster family to finish those three hundred and sixty minutes of training and "buy" them from the state. Tully was speechlessly glad when those forty hours were over.

Her two other classes were Business Administration and English Composition. She couldn't stand the homework in English Comp. Professor Macy kept asking them to *write* something. Stream of consciousness, an essay on the summer, a short story about a friend, an autobiography. And then *talk* about it in class! Some of the assignments were even read *aloud* in class. Tully was really turned off. If only it weren't a general education requirement, she thought, looking over one of her assignments. "Write on the four seasons. What they are to you or what you would like them to be."

So Tully huffed and puffed, and huffed and puffed, and then went through her milk crates of stuff that were stashed away in the back of the trailer to see if she could find something appropriate in them. Unfortunately, Tully's milk crates weren't the only milk crates stashed away in the back of the trailer. A year and a half ago, Tony Mandolini came over to tell Tully they had sold the Sunset Court house and were moving to Lawrence, and asked her if she could please come over and clean out his daughter's room. So Tully had gotten some empty milk crates from Dairy Barn and trudged over to Sunset Court. For the last time.

And now in front of her, packed neatly into eight red crates were the books, journals, notes, records, postcards, magazines and posters that once were part of the master bedroom in Sunset Court.

If only I had more room, thought Tully weakly. If only I had an attic. Then I could put them away to collect perpetual dust for years, put them away in the far corner. And me, too.

The Four Seasons, by Tully Makker

It was always a hot summer
In the days we used to play
I could say it doesn't matter
But I'd give me all away
Now an autumn has passed and another one, too,
There will be many springs now,
All without you

Our cold Kansas winters won't see you again
And neither will I
Till my seasons will end
What hurts selfish me is not that you've gone,
But that I am still here,
And I'm all alone.

Spring, winter, and fall run into each other
I hope where you are it is one endless summer.

Tully was walking from Carnegie Hall to the library when Professor Macy tapped her on the shoulder. They walked to the library together.

"So, what kind of a name is Tully?" he asked her.

She laughed. He looked embarrassed by her laughter.

"I'm sorry," she said. "It's just that I am asked practically nothing else for openers. It's a great introductory name, isn't it?"

He relaxed, nodded. She looked him over surreptitiously as he was walking; he was pleasant-looking: not very tall, brown-haired, fair-skinned, a beard. Corduroy pants, blue shirt, blue tie, loafers. Nice hands, nice blue eyes.

"Natalie," she said.

"Ah," he said, "Natalie is pretty."

"Yes, and if someone ever called me that, I'm sure I'd think so," said Tully.

"I can call you that if you want," he offered.

"If you want," Tully said gently.

They walked.

Professor Macy said, "I liked the poem you wrote for your assignment. Most people wrote a short story."

"I'm not much for stories," said Tully.

"Can I read yours in class?"

She shook her head. "I'd really rather you didn't."

"It's a wonderful poem," he said. "I think the other students would enjoy it."

"Enjoy it, huh?" said Tully. "Well, as long as they enjoy it."

"Your poem seems very sad to me," Professor Macy continued. "Do you want to talk about it sometime?"

"I'm not a sad person," said Tully.

"I didn't say you were," said Professor Macy. "Do you want to talk about it?"

"I'm not a talkative person, either," said Tully.

As she stared back defensively at his skeptical gaze, Tully was touched by his honest face a little and smiled. "You can read it in class, if you like."

He smiled back. "I was hoping *you* could read it in class."

She rolled her eyes. "I was hoping you wouldn't ask me that."

But something stirred inside Tully. The following week she read her poem in class, for him, careful not to look at anyone.

A few weeks later, he invited her for coffee at the student union coffee shop. Tully ordered coffee and cheesecake.

"You know, Professor Macy, I don't even know your first name. What does J. stand for?" she asked him, inhaling suddenly. God, I hope it's not *Jack*.

"Jeremy," he answered her. "Jeremy Macy."

Tully let out her breath and immediately smiled. "That's so nice. Pleased to meet you, Jeremy," she said. "Tully Makker."

They spent two hours in the coffee shop.

"So, do you live with your folks, Tully Makker?"

"No," she said. "Got my own place. Do you live with your folks?"

"I'm thirty-five years old!" he replied, laughing. "Besides my family's in New York."

"New York? What are you doing teaching creative writing to us, a bunch of rednecks?"

He smiled. "Yes, but I got to hear your redneck poem."

"Oh, like you're a changed man because of it," said Tully. "I'm serious. What are you doing here?"

He told her he had married a girl from Kansas and they came here to live.

"Ahh," intoned Tully. "You're married?"

He shook his head. "We were divorced three years ago."

"How long were you married?" Tully asked him.

"Three years."

"Any kids?"

No, he told her, and changed the subject. "So what's your degree going to be in?"

"It's was going to be an associate's. But now it's going to

be a bachelor's," she told him, trying to keep the proud edge out of her voice. I'm not hanging around Harrison, doing drugs and going nowhere, she thought. I'm just studying to take care of kids who are. It's quite an achievement. Plus I am still dancing at Tortilla Jack's just like I did when I was fourteen. I'm such a loser.

"Social work," she said as brightly as she could. "Don't ask. Who knows why?"

"What do you want to do with it after you graduate?"

"Frame it?" she said. "Hang it on my wall?"

"No, I'm serious."

"Save a little bit of money," Tully said. "Get out of here."

"And go where?"

"I don't know. California, maybe."

"Why California?"

"Why not?" she said.

"That's a poor excuse to do anything, Tully," Jeremy said. She nodded. Guess it is, Professor Macy, she thought. Guess it is.

"Touché," Tully said. "How about because I've never seen a palm tree?"

"So what?" he said. "I bet you've seen a tornado."

Ain't that the truth, thought Tully, saying, "So what? I've never seen the ocean."

"Yes, but you've seen the prairie."

"The prairie," said Tully scornfully. "Fields with some grass."

"So what's an ocean? Lake Shawnee with salt."

"And sand," said Tully, smiling.

Jeremy said, "The prairies are like seas, and filled with wild animals . . . in such quantities as to surpass the imagination."

Tully looked at him with surprise. "Sounds like you like Kansas."

"I love Kansas," he said. "I never want to live anywhere else. I love the plains, I love the sky. I saw Flint Hills. For the first time in my life. I got into my car, and drove down Sky Line Drive, and then down to El Dorado. God! What majesty, what magnificence. Now that I've seen Flint Hills, I feel I've seen everything. If I die tomorrow, I will have no regrets." Jeremy paused. "Why are you looking at me like that?"

"Because you're crazy, that's why," Tully said. "Does the school know we have a crazy man teaching us English?"

Jeremy laughed. "You think California is better? I've been to California. Believe me, Flint Hills is better."

"I don't believe you," said Tully. "Though I have to say, I've never met anyone from out of town who came here and wanted to stay."

"Have you met many people from out of town?"

"Just you," she said, and smiled.

Jeremy studied her intently. "Let me ask you, Tully," he said carefully. "Are you going out with someone?"

Tully was quiet. "Guess so," she said. "For about two years."

"Is he your high school sweetheart?"

"Well, I met him when I was in high school, and I am his sweetheart. Does that count?"

"Are you guys serious?" Jeremy wanted to know.

"Well, *he* is serious," said Tully, and lowered her head, feeling guilty. Two years ago she humiliated Gail, and now, for no reason at all, she was humiliating Robin. "We *are* sort of serious," she corrected herself apologetically, and changed the subject.

They went for coffee again right before the presidential election.

"So I've never met anyone who'd been married," said Tully. "Except for grown-ups."

"Well, I am a grown-up, Tully," said Jeremy. "I thought you were, too."

"Heck, no," she said. "I'm only nineteen. Still a teenager."

She was kidding around, but he looked seriously at her with his blue eyes.

"You seem very grown up to me, Tully," he said. "You have grown-up eyes."

"Eyes, nothing," she said. "I'm a baby."

Jeremy leaned a little closer to her. "Your eyes are the windows to your soul," he said.

"Can you tell nobody's home in my soul?" she said teasingly, but he didn't laugh.

"Would you like to go out to dinner with me?" he asked.

"Uhh," she hesitated. "Well, sure. Sure, why not? Right?"

"No," he said. "Not why not. Do you *want* to go out to dinner with me?"

"Sure," Tully replied, biting her lip at the *why not* that was ready to follow. "Just dinner, right?"

He leaned back in his seat and smiled. "As opposed to what? Dinner and a trip to Hawaii?"

She was thinking more of dinner and another and another and another. Tully actually wavered for a moment and almost told Jeremy she *was* serious with Robin. But the thought of going out even casually with someone who didn't know her, who would never look at her with that Robin look of sympathy, warmed her. Why not? thought Tully. Why the hell not?

"I'm being silly. Everything is okay," she said.

Ronald Reagan was elected president on Tuesday, and Tully and Jeremy went to Steak and Ale on Friday.

"So tell me why you got divorced," said Tully during dinner.

Jeremy picked at his baked potato. "Because Elsa, my wife, got friendly with her karate teacher." He was quiet for a moment. "She did get her black belt, though," he added, "and that was nice for her."

"Oh, I'm sorry," said Tully. "That must've been tough."

"It was," Jeremy said. "It still is. We had a marriage. It's not like boyfriend, girlfriend, it's a true commitment. I left my job at City University of New York to marry Elsa. I thought it was for life."

Tully chose her words carefully. "I think that that's the sick part about marriage. You always think it's for life."

"That's not sick. That's what it's all about. My parents have been married for forty years."

"Wow," Tully said, and then couldn't think of anything else to add, except, "What are their names?"

"Bill and Ellen," answered Jeremy. "Are your parents still married?"

Tully thought about it. "No, I don't think they are," she said slowly. "They are dead."

"Oh, Tully, I'm so sorry," said Jeremy, looking genuinely sorry.

She touched his hand from across the table. "It's all right. Really."

"When did they die?"

"My father died when I was seven. My mother just last year."

"God. What of?"

Tully made a serious face. "Cancer. Long and painful. She suffered a lot. She is really better off now, dead." How easy this is, thought Tully. I should have done it ten years ago.

"Do you have any brothers or sisters?"

"No," said Tully. "I'm an only child."

Jeremy brought her home and walked her to the door of her trailer. He leaned over and kissed her lightly on the cheek. "Good night, Tully. Thank you for tonight."

She wanted him to kiss her properly. "No. Thank *you*," she said softly. "See you in class on Monday."

They went out to dinner again the following Friday. Tully had a really good time talking to him. They spent the main course discussing the differences between *Breakfast at Tiffany's* the book and *Breakfast at Tiffany's* the movie.

During dessert, Jeremy self-consciously cleared his throat. "Tully, be honest with me. How serious are you with that other guy?"

Tully in turn cleared her throat. "Why do you ask?"

"I ask," he said, "because I want to give you an opportunity to be honest. I'd like to see you again."

"Well, I'd like to see you, too, Jeremy." Tully smiled. "Everything is all right."

"Are you serious with him?"

"It's nothing like that," she said evasively.

"Because that's the only thing I ask of you, Tully. That you be honest with me. That's the only thing that matters. You understand? After Elsa, that's all I ask."

Tully was silent and then said slowly, "I think this is what I meant when I asked if it would be *just* dinner."

They left it at that, and during the week, at their coffee shop in the student union, they talked about books and movies and songs. On Friday before Thanksgiving, Jeremy and Tully went out again.

Jeremy resumed their previous week's conversation as if seven days had not passed.

"Honesty is the only thing I ask of you, Tully. I will be able to forgive everything except dishonesty."

She shook her head and said, "Jeremy, to be perfectly honest, I think it's a little early to be talking about *forgiveness.* I've
known Robin, my boyfriend, for two years, and he doesn't talk
about forgiveness."

"Maybe that's because he is hiding something?" said
Jeremy.

Tully was annoyed by his remark. "What's to hide?" she
said sourly.

Jeremy ate his steak in silence. Drinking his coffee, he said,
"Am I moving too fast?"

"No, you're fine," said Tully. "I just want a simple life. You
know? No complications."

"I know," he said. "You still haven't answered me. Do you
and your boyfriend have an agreement to see other people?"

"Agreement?" That word all of a sudden became unpleasant
to Tully. "No, we don't have an agreement. We don't really
see other people," she said. "We're basically exclusive," she
said, thinking she was not enjoying this conversation one little
bit. "We've never talked about it, actually," she said irritably.
And that felt right to Tully. Not talking about really stupid and
irrelevant things. She and Robin just *were,* that was all.

"Have you gone out with other people besides me?"

Tully smiled, trying to lighten the tone. "Not in the last
month," she said.

"No, I'm serious."

"I'm serious, too. Everything will be all right."

"Does Robin see other people?"

"Frankly," said Tully, getting genuinely annoyed, "I haven't
thought about it. No, okay? No, he doesn't."

"How do you know?"

"Oh, Jeremy!" she exclaimed, throwing down her ice-cream
spoon. "Is there a point to your questions?"

"I'm sorry," Jeremy said quickly. "I guess I just wanted to
know what you want to happen with us."

"Let's just take it one dinner at a time," she said, and
repeated, slower, "One dinner at a time. Okay?"

"Do you love Robin?"

"My," said Tully, "aren't we being a little personal?" Jeremy
waited.

"I like him, yes," she allowed. "He treats me well. He is not cheap, he wants me to move in with him, he wants me. I like him, yes."

After dinner, they sat in his car for a while.

"So am I fighting a lost cause, Tully?"

Tully squinted her eyes to look at him carefully. "Are you fighting, Jeremy? What do you want?"

"To get to know you," he told her. "To take you out."

"I'd like to go out with you. But there's nothing to know."

"Oh, there seems to be a lot you're not telling me. A whole big center, and I'm just being shown the outer edge."

"Trust me when I tell you," Tully said, "there is no center. There is only the outer edge. Inside is a black hole."

"Full of so much," Jeremy said intensely.

"Full of nothing," said Tully. "Big, black, and full of nothing."

He was quiet. She was cold.

"Do you want to talk about it?" he asked her.

"Nothing to talk about," she said. "You want to know what I want? I really want to leave Topeka soon."

She saw his curious expression and went on. "That's all I want. I want to go to California. University of California at Santa Cruz."

Jeremy said, "Tully, shouldn't you visit it first, maybe, before you live there?"

"No. Visiting is dumb. Living there is what matters."

"Do you want to talk about it?"

Tully ran her fingers through her short hair. "Listen, maybe that's what New York teachers do, they sit around and talk about their past and how they feel about their past and how they would change it and what they would change and what different people they would be if they had a different past. But I don't do that, nobody in Topeka does that. I just want to go to California, I don't want to talk about it. I just want to go."

Jeremy leaned over and kissed her cheek. "Okay, Tully," he said. "Okay."

At the trailer, he asked if he could come in, and she said no.

When she was inside, Tully regretted their conversation. Something about him really appealed to her. He was interesting, well-spoken, and Tully had never had anyone from New

York before. Also, he was an older man. But his biggest selling point was Mr. Hillier's selling point, and California's selling point. Jeremy Macy did not know her at all.

Tully and Jeremy went out twice more, saw each other for lunch every day before Thanksgiving, when Jeremy flew back home to New York to spend the holiday with his family. He half-seriously invited her to come with him and she half-jokingly declined.

Tully spent Thanksgiving with Robin and his brothers and their girlfriends. She thought of Jeremy the whole weekend.

On Monday morning in class, all Tully could think of was that she couldn't wait to be alone with him. They went out that evening, and when he drove her home Tully invited him in.

She made him coffee, sat next to him on the couch, and told him she had missed him. Jeremy put his coffee down, cupped her face in his hands, and kissed her.

They made love on the couch, then went to her brass bed and made love again.

Afterwards, they lay together, her head on his chest. Jeremy was stroking her hair.

"Why do you keep your hair so short, Tully?" he whispered.

She stiffened a little, shrugged her shoulders. "Why not?" she replied.

"Is that going to be your stock answer with me? I don't know why not. Because you must have pretty hair when it's long," he said.

"Actually, no. It's thin and mousy." She smiled, touching his beard. "Not as nice as yours."

They lay together for a while. She was thinking of Robin's gifts and photos of her and Robin safely hidden away in a drawer. Jeremy looked around her bedroom. "You keep this room pretty bare, Tully. No pictures on the walls, no pictures on the nightstand. What, do you hide them in your drawer?"

"No. Don't be silly," she said.

He inhaled. "Do you feel guilty?" he asked.

"Guilty?" Tully said. "Uh, like what does that word mean? I never use it myself, is that some kind of an emotion or something, duh?"

He smiled but persisted. "Do you feel guilty about Robin?"

"No, Jeremy," said Tully. "I don't." But I am disloyal, she thought. Robin has been nothing but good to me, and I am disloyal to him. I feel *disloyal*. "I do this once a month just to make sure no guilt creeps in."

"Why?"

"Why what?"

"Why do you do this once a month?"

"Why not?"

"You get something out of it?" Jeremy asked.

"I get someone looking at me like you do, once a month."

"Doesn't Robin look at you the way I do?"

"Yeah, but so what?" She really didn't want to be bringing up Robin. Jeremy already knows too much. California. Instant anonymity.

"So," said Jeremy, "is that what I am to you? Your once-a-month feel-good thing?"

"Jeremy," said Tully, "what's bugging you? The once a month? Or the feel-good thing?"

"Nothing's bugging me," he said, changing the subject. "Do you and Robin talk much?"

"Not much, why?"

"You told me *you* don't talk much. I was wondering if it was different with him."

"It's different with *you*," Tully said. "With him, there was never much need to talk," she explained. "We kinda just sit around together."

"Does Robin know everything about you?"

"No, thank God," said Tully. She rolled over on top of Jeremy and they had sex for the third time.

Tully went to dinner with Robin a few days later. She was quiet.

"What's wrong?" he asked her.

Nothing, she told him. That evening she said she was too tired to have him come back to her place.

"Okay," said Robin. "Now I know something really is wrong. Because I always come back to your place. Now, what is it?"

Tully let him come in, and then let him have sex with her, let him kiss her and run his hands all over her and look at her with tenderness and tell her he loved her.

*   *   *

She called Robin early the following week and told him she had caught a cold and would not be able to see him that Saturday night.

"Are you going to work sick?" he asked her.

"If I don't go to work, I'm out on the street," said Tully.

"No, you're not," Robin said. "You can always move in with me."

"I'm out on the street," she repeated.

In the three weeks before Christmas, Jeremy stayed over at Tully's house three times a week. The weekends were for Robin. Saturday nights she and Robin went out after work, and Sundays Tully went to St. Mark's.

One evening, when Jeremy was over at Tully's, he picked up a letter from Julie she had carelessly tossed on the coffee table.

"You get letters, huh? From friends? I don't get letters from anyone but my parents."

"That's because you have no friends," she said jokingly, but took the letter away from him.

"Do you?" he asked. "Do you have lots of friends?"

Tully pointed to Jeremy. "You," she said. "I have you."

"Not just me, though, huh, Tully?" he said challengingly.

Tully didn't reply, and a little later, when Tully was in the kitchen, Jeremy called out, "So who was the letter from, Tull?"

"Oh, my friend Julie," Tully replied through the partition. "She goes to Northwestern."

"I see that by the stationery. Is she a friend from high school?"

Silence from the kitchen. "No. Childhood."

"Wow," said Jeremy. "I don't know anyone from my childhood anymore. College, barely. You guys must be really close."

Tully came in, wiping her hands on the dish towel. "We're like that," she said, crooking her middle finger over her index finger. "Now come and help me dry."

"Do you write to her often?" Jeremy asked, drying Tully's plates.

Tully bit her lip. "Not as often as I should," she answered. "Come, let's sit down."

"But we just started—"

"Come," she said, suggestively. "Let's sit down."

When it was the middle of the night and Tully couldn't sleep again, she gently took Jeremy's arm off her and came out into the living room, where she picked up Julie's letter and reread it.

December 1, 1980

Dear Tully,

I was in Topeka for Thanksgiving, and guess what, surprise, surprise. I didn't get a phone call from you. I don't know what's going on with you, Tully, I just have no idea. But I'll make it real easy for you, okay? I'm not going to write you anymore. I'm not going to call you either. This is my fourth letter to you this semester. You haven't written back, and I can see that you just don't want to keep in touch with me anymore. Though that makes me sad, Tully, I am not going to make myself a nuisance to you. When you're interested in talking to me again, you can write me. I'll always be happy to hear from you, though obviously it's not vice-versa. I would just like you to know, Tully, that I am very sad for everything that's been happening to you and wish I could help you in some way. I guess we all have to deal in whatever way we can, but I can see that you've chosen to get rid of all your old friends and become a different person, and I'm sorry for that, Tully, because I really liked you before.

Well, that's all for now. Bye.

Love, Julie.

Tully read the letter three times and then put it down, throwing her head back against the couch. Not all my old friends, Jule, Tully thought. Not *all* my old friends. Just you.

Around the middle of December, Shakie came in to Casa, beaming. One look at Shakie's face, and Tully knew. She rolled her eyes.

"Okay, which member of Jack's family is sick now?"

"His uncle," said Shakie happily. "Gravely ill."

"Shake, don't start singing now, please, 'cause you'll be crying in two weeks."

"Oh, Tully! Pooh!" squealed Shakie. "Don't be such a spoilsport!"

Around the same time, Jeremy asked Tully to visit New York with him for the holidays. Tully couldn't believe he was for real at first, but when she did believe him, she thought less of getting a chance to see New York than of getting away from Shakie's impending joy.

But to go meant telling Robin. It meant explaining to Robin, if Robin would even want to hear an explanation, what Tully saw in Jeremy Macy that Robin couldn't give her in triplicate.

Jack Pendel and Shakie came into Casa Del Sol the week before Christmas. Tully served them. Shakie hung on to Jack like a barnacle, while he looked merely amused by her. Man, I've got to get out of here, thought Tully, getting them Mexican meatball soup. I've got to go to New York, I've got to, because if I don't go, she is gonna recognize his look for what it is, and I will have to run from her screaming.

When she brought the soup, Jack turned his eyes up to Tully as she stood at their table, though she made a conscious effort not to look at him.

"How you doing?" he said.

"Great," Tully replied as brightly as she could, taking out the order pad from the apron. "Can I get you anything else?"

"Yeah!" said Shakie. "I'm famished. I'll have the cheese enchiladas, Jack, and you?"

Jack was still looking at Tully. "What are you up to nowadays? Going to school?"

"Sure," Tully said. "Will that be all?"

Jack handed Tully the menus. "I'll have the beef chimichanga. Bring three, they're small."

"Jack! You piggie!" exclaimed Shakie. "Oink, oink. Boy are you going to get fat."

Jack looked back at Tully, who grabbed the menus and walked away.

When he paid, Jack left Tully a $20 tip on a $30 check. "It's Christmas," he said, shrugging his shoulders. Tully winced, remembering the shrugging gesture from high school.

"I really can't accept," she mumbled. "No, really."

"Merry Christmas, Tully," he said. "Drink a cup of good cheer."

Fuck you, Tully feebly thought. Fuck you.

After they left, Tully found his wallet on the dirty table. She ran out into the parking lot, but they had already gone.

"He'll come back," Tully said out loud, standing outside. It's no big deal, she thought, and then her teeth started to chatter. *I could look through his wallet!* She dropped the wallet into her apron and folded her arms. No, Tully Makker, that would be wrong, she thought. Her teeth continued to chatter.

Locking herself in a bathroom stall, Tully sat down on the john, trying to catch her breath for a few moments, and then reached into her apron. Putting the wallet to her nose, she smelled it; it smelled of leather, faintly of coconut and Polo. The image of him sprung up: tall, hard, sand blond, serious. Inside the wallet, she found a couple of credit cards, $60, a prom photo of him and Shakie, a brand-new Trojan. She looked through all the little compartments, finding a dozen business cards and receipts. Tully found many small many-folded pieces of paper with scribbled phone numbers on them.

One of the papers was glossier than the rest. When Tully unfolded it, she read the following: "To J.P., I leave my first softball and my first heart."

The very words Tony Mandolini pointed to in the *Topeka High School 1979 Yearbook* when he asked, "*Who is J.P.?*"

Tully folded the torn paper carefully and slowly. Torn ragged out of the section on Senior Wills, she knew, though she had never opened her own yearbook, never read the section on Senior Wills, or any other section, for that matter. What she was thinking now was what she had thought when Mr. Mandolini showed her the quote: *Why him? Why would she leave her first softball to him? We're the ones who used to play softball at Shunga Park.*

Tully closed the wallet, went to the sink, drenched her face with ice cold water, and left. She promptly gave the wallet to Donna, the head hostess, to keep behind the desk. Jack came back an hour later. She saw him take the wallet, thank Donna, and then his eyes moved across the restaurant and did not stop searching until they found Tully. She looked down quickly, but he stood there until she looked up. When he caught her eyes, he raised his hand.

The following Friday night when Jeremy picked Tully up, Jack and Shakie were at Casa Del Sol again, finishing their fajitas. Tully introduced everyone, and Jack asked if Tully and Jeremy wanted to go for a drink.

"We really can't," muttered Tully.

"We'd love to," said Jeremy.

They went to MaGoo's. Shakie babbled incessantly, relaxing Tully a little and amusing Jeremy. After a couple of drinks, they began to listen to the music. The Bee Gees' "Staying Alive" came on.

"Well, now, there's a blast from the past. A taste of high school," said Shakie. "You like the Bee Gees, Jack?"

"Not much," said Jack. "I like Pink Floyd."

Shakie sang from "Comfortably Numb:" *"There is no pain, you are receding . . ."*

"My favorite song," said Jack.

Mine, too, thought Tully, and quickly quickly looked into her beer glass.

"That one, and 'Wish You Were Here,' " continued Jack.

Tully was very busy looking into her beer glass.

"Oh, that's right," exclaimed Shakie, ruffling his hair. "You think Pink Floyd is the be-all and end-all."

"Sure do." Jack smiled as Tully glanced at him.

"Did you all go to the same high school?" Jeremy asked. They all stared—twenty-year-old kids looking at a thirty-five-year-old man.

"Yeah, we did," Jack replied.

"Cool," said Jeremy. "How was high school?"

"Cool," said Tully, and everyone laughed.

"Were you guys friends in high school?" Jeremy pressed on.

Shakie giggled. "I think *friends* is a strong word for what we were." She smiled suggestively, putting her hand on Jack's thigh. She looked over at Tully. "Jack might've known Tully a little, didn't he, Tull?"

"Sure, Shakie," said Tully, intently studying the coasters.

Jack stared at Tully. Tully stared at her drink. Jeremy stared at Tully and Jack; and so did Shakie.

Jeremy turned to Jack. "So what was Tully like in high school?"

Jack watched Tully scratching the stains on the table with her nails. "I think she was very smart," he said evenly. "Very smart. Smarter than anybody."

"She was?" Jeremy beamed.

"She was?" exclaimed Shakie.

"I was?" said Tully, not displeased.

"You was," confirmed Jack.

"How do you know?" demanded Shakie.

"Did she do well in school?" asked Jeremy.

"Oh, no," replied Jack, ignoring Shakie's question. "She did terrible in school. Never went to class. She learned how to dance and forgot all about school, didn't you, Tully?"

Tully, stupefied at the turn of the conversation, fumbled in her bag for a cigarette, forgetting she quit smoking after the summer.

Jeremy changed the subject. "So, tell me, guys, how was your senior year?"

Tully got up so sharply she knocked her chair over, apologizing to Shakie and Jack for having to leave so soon.

"Jeremy, I can't go to New York with you," she told him later that night. He seemed clearly disappointed and couldn't even look at her for a while. But Tully wasn't thinking about Jeremy at the moment. She was upset about having gone out with Shakie and Jack.

Finally Jeremy asked, "Why, Tully?"

"Because I can't tell Robin," she said.

"Why?"

"Because I don't want to hurt him."

"But Tully, *I* know," he said. "*I* know, and it's hurting me."

"Well, why should I make two people feel bad?" she said sulkily.

"Tully, I thought you didn't love him."

She sighed. "Jeremy, I still don't want to hurt him." She tried to caress him, but he got out of bed, put on his underwear and jeans, and started walking up and down the room.

"Tully, I'm too old for this," he said. "I really am."

She put on a T-shirt and sat up in bed. "Too old for what?"

He raised his voice. "For this!"

She stared at him with wide eyes. He lowered his voice a notch. "For this, for you jerking me around."

"Jeremy, calm down," she said. "And don't raise your voice to me in my house."

"I'm sorry," he said, softer.

"Jeremy, I didn't keep anything hidden from you," said Tully. "You know all about Robin, while he knows nothing about you, so who really is being jerked around, huh?"

Jeremy continued to pace up and down. Finally he stopped in front of the bed.

"Tully, how do you feel about me?"

"Jeremy, I like you very much."

"Do you think you could break up with Robin and go out with just me?"

Tully studied the sheet that covered her and her hands.

"Tully?"

"Jeremy," she said, exasperated. "Help! I've known you for only a couple of months. We've been having sex since Thanksgiving and it's not even Christmas! Give me a break, will you?"

"Yes, I know, I know," said Jeremy. "But I feel we've come a long way—emotionally, I mean. I know I have, and hope you have, too. I like our intimacy. I like our emotional honesty. I don't want to lose that."

She said nothing, but shook her head. "Oh, Jeremy, Jeremy." She looked up at him. "Jeremy, you know nothing about me, nothing." *And I'd like to keep it that way.* "What long way emotionally? You mean our sex is pretty good?"

"I know stuff about you, Natalie Makker," he said tenderly, sitting down next to her and taking both her hands in his. "You're an orphan and you act like one. You haven't found anyone to love yet. You have a good heart. You read Kurt Vonnegut and Stephen King. *Ordinary People* and *The Great Gatsby* are your favorite books, not necessarily in that order. You like Edna St. Vincent Millay, you like white carnations, you love to dance. You believe in God. What else do I need to know?"

"Nothing," said Tully. "*Absolutely* nothing."

Jeremy lowered his head into Tully's hands, saying quietly, "But Tully, how can we know if we can make our relationship work if we don't make some kind of a commitment? Without a commitment, there is no relationship. Please, Tully, let me in."

She closed her eyes and moaned lightly. Commitment. Tully never even thought about commitment. Is that what happened when you grew up? she thought. When we were kids, we didn't need to talk about commitment. We were together, we were friends because we wanted to be together. We wanted to be friends. And when we were kids, when we didn't want to be friends with someone, we just stopped being friends with them, simple as that. And now . . . now we have sex.

But me and Robin have sex, and we don't talk about commitment. Somehow, I like that better.

Jeremy left for New York without Tully, who spent Christmas with Robin at his house. They bought a great big Christmas tree and decorated it lavishly. On Christmas Eve they sat in front of the lit fire and watched *A Christmas Story*. The next morning they made love and then opened their presents. Tully bought Robin socks and cologne and a winter sweater—from DeMarco & Sons, of course. He bought Tully a gold necklace with two rubies flanking her name, "TULLY."

She sighed inside but put the necklace on anyway. One more thing to put away in the drawer. One more thing to hide.

Tully cooked the turkey—"a turkey as big as the tree," said Robin. On Christmas day, they got dressed just in time for Robin's brothers to come over with their girlfriends and eat the turkey with stuffing and mashed potatoes. They played music, opened more presents, talked, watched TV. When everyone left, Tully and Robin made love on the carpet in front of the fire.

Tully stayed with him for seven days between Christmas and New Year's, and every one of those days they ate turkey. She made turkey soup and turkey stew, and turkey sandwiches for Robin to take to work. She made turkey parmigiana, which fooled Robin, who thought he was eating veal. Finally, they threw the last quarter of the turkey out with the Christmas tree after New Year's.

New Year's Eve, Shakie invited them to a party at her house.

"Has Jack left yet?" Tully asked.

Shakie sulked. "Tully, don't be mean. Not yet, okay?"

"Okay, Shake. I'm sorry, but I'm gonna say no to this party, okay?"

"Oh! Why?"

Because I already went to one of your parties two years ago, thought Tully. Two years ago when I sang "Wish You Were Here" to Robin, trying to figure out how *your* Jack felt about *my* best friend.

"Because Robin's brother Bruce invited us over to his farm and we must go."

Tully did not quite lie. They had invited themselves over to Bruce's, where they had champagne and eggnog, and played charades all night. Tully showed everyone her new necklace. Tully sang "Auld Lang Syne" to Robin at midnight while he was kissing her lips.

A few minutes after midnight, Robin leaned over to Tully and said, "Tully, don't you think you should call your mother and wish her a happy New Year?"

Tully's smile evaporated. "My mother is not much into celebrating."

"Still, though, Tully—"

"Still, though, Tully nothing," she snapped. "I mean it, Robin. I'd only wake her."

"Tully, you haven't talked to her since the day you left a year and a half ago. New Year's is a good time to make amends. Don't you think?"

"Robin, I'd only wake her," Tully repeated.

"She is your mother, Tully—"

"That's not my fault," she said.

He ignored her remark. "You don't even know if she is all right."

Tully took a deep breath. "Robin, please." She smiled. "Let's try to have a good time. We can talk about my mother tomorrow. Let's dance."

8

HEDDA MAKKER

August 1941

Hedda Makker, née Rust, was born in 1942 to a wife of a pig farmer just north of Oklahoma City. Hedda's parents, Bill and Martha Rust, were married in 1936, and were still childless when Bill was called up to active duty in August 1941. Martha gave birth to a four-pound fourteen-ounce girl five weeks early—on August 6, 1942. When her husband came back from the Pacific in 1945 to find himself not only a wife but a three-year-old daughter, he discovered that fighting the Japanese had not made him forget the simple math of human gestation.

He beat Martha to within an inch of her life, calling her slut all the while, as Hedda huddled near the sofa and watched, and then Bill Rust kicked them both out of his house.

Martha, with a mauled face, a broken nose, and three bloody gaps in her mouth, hitched a ride with Hedda to the nearest hospital, in Oklahoma City, where she was treated with care, while Hedda stayed in the nurses' chambers. Hedda was a thick, sullen, introverted child; she spoke little and for the most part was left alone.

Martha stayed in the hospital for seventy hours and then left, without a doctor's discharge, without leaving a forwarding address, and without Hedda.

One of the nurses tried to explain to Hedda that Mommy left, but was met with glum apprehension. The nurse finally managed to get out of Hedda that Daddy raised pigs and that his last name was "Wust." After calling thirty-five pig farms around Oklahoma City, the nurse finally found the Rusts. She drove Hedda to her father herself.

Bill Rust, upon setting sights on his wife's bastard child, clenched his fists and barked a thank you to the nurse for her time. She left in a great hurry.

Little Hedda was left in front of the man who had tried to kill her mother. He glared at her. She gazed up at him and then did the only thing three-year-old Hedda could do—she screamed and ran from the house. He ran after her and caught her, she bit him, he then hit her so hard, she lost consciousness.

But Bill Rust brought her back to the house and kept her with him.

He fed her and let her stay in the little bedroom. Bill went out to the fields and the pens during the day, and then got dressed up and went out at night. A few times, he did not come back until the following morning, and found Hedda, frozen with fear, hunched in her room on the floor, behind the door.

Bill had his first marriage annulled and when Hedda was six took in a woman, Sarah, whom Hedda remembers as overweight and bad-smelling. Sarah had a fifteen-year-old daughter, Lena, a dense girl who talked funny. Though Lena kept Hedda company, Hedda was made miserable by Lena's thick-headed, slow-mouthed ways. She tried to stay away from her as much as possible.

After a few years, Sarah discovered that Hedda, at eight, still could not read and write. So Hedda was sent to school.

The seven years she spent in school were seven years of suffering, marked by stuporous incomprehension and twice being left back, by constant fights in the schoolyard and no friends.

At fifteen, Hedda was tall and broad, giving the impression of health and strength. Her eyes were green, her skin was fair, her hair was long and light brown. And at fifteen, Hedda got up in the middle of the night, packed a small bag that contained all of her belongings, took $200 out of Bill Rust's hiding place—in the pantry behind the flour—and left.

Not knowing that Texas was below her and Kansas was above her, she let fate decide the course of her life by walking on the right side of the road. She walked eight miles before a truck driver picked her up. Ten hours later, he set her foot down on Topeka Boulevard, and the first person she talked to when she entered a drugstore to get a soda was Henry Makker.

Henry was twenty-two and just got a promotion to assistant manager at the city refuse plant. He looked over the ragamuffin girl with a bag on her back and thought she would be an easy lay. She had a good strong body, but seemed intensely shy.

He found her a job at the plant, filling plastic bottles with sewage treatment solution—a job Hedda kept for twenty-four years until January 1, 1981. Henry found her a room for $2 a week. She kept that room for a month and then moved in with him.

Hedda's green eyes had found their light and her life had found its course.

Henry Makker was tall and handsome; by her standards he was also well-off and educated. Hedda had sung Baptist hymns in church every Sunday her entire life before he found her, but now Henry was her god. Their first few years were marred by little other than her eagerness to be with him all the time. From his small two-room apartment on Harrison in northern Topeka, he drove them to work. They had lunch together in the factory cafeteria. They drove home together. She learned how to cook so that she could cook for him. She learned how to sew and how to read, and how to make love, so that she could sew and read and make love to him. She sang when she walked and lit up when she was with him.

When they got married in June 1959, Hedda was a beautiful bride. Even the justice of the peace said so. A month before her wedding, she wrote Bill Rust, enclosing a check for $200 and inviting him to the wedding. He never answered her letter, never came, but did cash the check.

Lena came, married now to a seedy-looking man, Charlie, who was an unemployed plumber. Charlie came to the wedding in a blue flannel shirt that fell out of his pants during the reception, exposing a hanging, flabby, enormous beer gut. Lena and Charlie liked Topeka enough that they wanted to live there if Charlie could get steady work. He could, and they did.

Henry and Hedda took their honeymoon in Corpus Christi, Texas, and went back in 1960 and 1961.

The first few years were joyous ones for the Makkers, who bought a home with the money Henry had saved. It seemed so big to Hedda, that blue house on Grove Street. It came cheap and had a great big fenced-in yard, where Hedda kept her chickens so that Henry could have fresh eggs in the morning.

Henry was promoted to manager in 1960 and had to work slightly longer hours. Hedda ran home from work every day so that the dinner she cooked would be ready when her tired and hungry husband came home.

Henry Makker was the only man Hedda had ever loved, the only thing in the world she had ever loved, so in the winter of 1960, when she found out she was pregnant, she thought her life had come to an end.

Understanding very little of what went on between her mother and father, and generally not blessed with particularly acute understanding, Hedda understood this: that when Bill Rust found out Martha had a child, he beat his wife half silly in front of Hedda and then kicked them both out of their home.

Hedda understood that Bill Rust bludgeoned his wife Martha because she had a child.

In Hedda's mind, her mother's one grave error was having Hedda, and her father's one grave regret was his wife's having Hedda. This perception was all the more cemented in Hedda by her mother's disappearance. Mommy left rather than face her Sin every day.

And though Bill Rust kept Hedda when the nurse brought her back to him, in twelve years he had never hugged her, had never kissed her, had never spoken a kind word to her. Between them existed a gruff silence, and Hedda was only too glad to run and was sure Bill was glad to be rid of her, though she had no idea what it must have cost Bill Rust emotionally to raise an unloved child by his wayward wife.

So now Hedda was pregnant. Wanting to make her life better than her mother's, she one day took off sick from work, went to a "doctor" and had a messy, bloody abortion somewhere in Wichita, where there were plenty of hacks with a profitable side business. She returned home, cooked dinner for Henry, and then hemorrhaged in her chair. Henry rushed her to Topeka State Hospital, where the doctor quietly informed him that not only were abortions illegal in the United States of America, but *such* abortions could leave Henry a widower at twenty-five.

Henry said nothing until Hedda got better, but then he sat his wife down and told her that though he loved her very much, if she ever pulled a stunt like that again, he would have no choice but to leave her.

In May 1960, Hedda discovered she was pregnant once more, and she suspected her days with Henry were numbered, despite his undeniable joy. On January 19, 1961, Hedda gave difficult birth to six-pound ten-ounce, eighteen-inch Natalie Anne.

Natalie was a quiet, contented baby, and it was a good thing, too, because Hedda, who left her job to be a mother, put Natalie in the upstairs room and came in only at mealtimes. The rest of the day, Hedda sat in the living room and stared blankly at the wall, while Natalie cooed and tossed in the attic.

Hedda breast-fed for the first three months and then put Natalie on solids, hired her a nanny, and went back to work despite strong objections from Henry. But Henry saw that little Natalie did not object; in fact, the baby was happier than ever in nanny's arms and under nanny's care.

Hedda's real anxiety began when Natalie, a chubby, crawling girl, was around nine months, and Hedda saw the look in her husband's eyes when he came home from work and looked at his daughter. The look was one of adoration, and the look was not meant for Hedda. Henry rushed past his wife to pick up Natalie, and for the first time in her life, Hedda experienced jealousy, and with it hot hate. Until she felt love for Henry, she had felt nothing, but even her love for Henry was not as extreme as the black plague that descended upon her heart at the sight of her husband and her daughter, babbling together.

Hedda got pregnant again when Natalie was a year old, and Henry this time hoped for a boy. Hedda also hoped it would be a boy, so that Henry would stop doting on his only girl. In November 1962, Johnny Makker entered the world, and Natalie sank in the estimation of her dad, who now had eyes for no one but his son.

Though Henry certainly paid less attention to Natalie, it was a small victory for Hedda, for all of Henry's love and affection became wrapped up in his little boy. Hedda grit her teeth and cracked her knuckles, biding her time. She stayed home and nursed Johnny for much longer than she nursed Natalie, because Henry wanted it that way. Natalie was toddling about, playing outside or going for walks with nanny while Hedda was with Johnny. The little boy was eight months when he started to crawl, eight months old when Hedda stopped breast-feeding him, eight months old when Henry received a phone call at the plant from the hysterical nanny, saying that little Johnny was in his bed not breathing.

*   *   *

"Crib death," the death certificate read. The doctor expressed some concern that the boy was quite old. "Usually crib death occurs when infants are very young, when they still have not learned to breathe properly."

"How old?" asked Henry.

"No more than ten weeks," the doctor replied.

They buried Johnny in Topeka's Woodlawn Cemetery and Henry Makker went there every Sunday to talk to his boy.

Natalie was forgotten by her father. Henry did nothing but work and grieve, and Hedda did nothing but work and comfort him.

The Makkers kept the nanny until Natalie was four, and then let her go. Henry asked if leaving such a young child by herself was a good idea, but Hedda dismissed him. "I was left alone since I was three. Natalie is four. She'll be fine. She is a very grown-up girl."

In the summers, Natalie was left in the yard with the chickens. In the winters, she stayed in the house. She watched TV, doodled, talked to her dolls. Sometimes she wandered out and wasn't home when Henry and Hedda came back from work.

When Natalie wasn't home, Hedda kept hoping she would stay lost or get picked up by someone who wanted to keep her.

But the police kept bringing her back, casting their disapproving eyes upon Hedda and Henry. Then Angela Martinez and Lynn Mandolini started keeping Natalie at their homes and bringing her back in the evenings. Hedda liked that, but she did not like their disapproving eyes upon her and her husband. It's none of your business! she wanted to shout. I go to church. I'm a good Christian.

In September 1965, Hedda became pregnant for the fourth time. She was as devastated for the fourth time as her husband was overjoyed. Hedda stopped eating, took up smoking, and drank Southern Comfort every day for three months. But despite her best efforts, Henry Makker, Jr., weighed in at a healthy seven pounds on June 23, 1966, nearly three years to the day since Johnny died.

Henry hired a live-in nurse to look after the boy: literally to live in Hank's room and watch him. Hank lived through his first year and through his second year. When he began to speak, his very first word was "Tuwy," for his big sister, the little person who played with him. When Jennifer heard Hank's nickname, she laughed and called Natalie "Tuwy," too, and then "Tully" as a joke, but the name stuck.

Since the time Hedda was forbidden to abort Tully, she knew it was only a matter of time before Henry Makker would leave her. She did not regret any of what she did to pull back fate, guided as she was only by her feelings for her husband. It took Henry Makker nine years to leave Hedda, but on July 20, 1968, he did.

Hedda was destroyed but not surprised; she was surprised, however, it had taken so long. She attributed the longevity of her marriage to her superhuman efforts to keep her husband.

Hedda continued to work, but taking care of the house and paying the bills became too tough for her. Taking care of Tully was never a problem. Tully could take care of herself.

At work Hedda heard of the Kansas foster family program— the state paid $5 a day for one kid under twelve. That sounded so easy, Hedda thought. So she took in a foster child, Billy Bains. She kept him for eight months, but ignoring him like she could ignore Tully was hard. Social Services kept coming over every couple of months and interviewing her and the boy. And Billy Bains definitely did not look happy. So after a while, they took him away, and Hedda asked Lena and Charlie to come live with her. Their arrival was a mixed blessing at best, but Charlie soon died of massive heart failure, being a godless drunk and all, and his life insurance continued to pay Hedda's mortgage. Having Lena in the house was a waste of time, though: Hedda's common-law stepsister was in many ways a child herself—a difficult child. She was slow-minded and nearly blind; she never helped around the house, just sat around and talked to the neighbors all day.

Throughout the years, Hedda's feelings for Tully had ranged from supreme indifference to uncontrollable anger. Tully was often such an annoying child. So undisciplined. Would leave the house, not come back for a few days, cut school, not eat. She never talked, never, which was fine with Hedda, who had little to say herself, but Tully's abject silence frequently grated on her. Tully was godless, too. All that trouble with her and Charlie back in 1973. Hedda just wiped her hands of it, she just wiped her hands of it all, but when Charlie died some time later, Hedda was secretly glad. She even took her daughter to church with her a few times after that, but Tully was more withdrawn than ever, and Hedda just stopped, just stopped trying to be nice.

Hedda worked such long and hard hours, she had no energy for Tully's truancy, for parent-teacher conferences, for dinner, for Tully. Tully stayed over at Jennifer's a few days a week and over at Julie's a few days. That was okay with Hedda. And on days that it wasn't, she beat Tully with a belt and forbade her to go out of the house for weeks.

Then there was that silliness with Tully's dancing at school, and then with the condoms. Hedda punished her daughter appropriately, but didn't really care about either.

Hedda got up at six every morning, was at the plant in northern Topeka by eight, and worked until five-thirty. When she could she worked overtime. Otherwise, she came home, made a quick dinner, or ate what Tully cooked, and then watched TV. She fell asleep on the couch every night, and Tully, when she had been home, would wake her and tell her to go to bed. Hedda never went out with another man after Henry, never went out with any of the people from work, never went out with Lena, or with Tully. Hedda was thirty-six years old when she found out from a girl named Gail that Tully was screwing some guy, when she flew into a rage, when Tully stood there, bitter as coffee, pointing a gun at her—with the same look Hedda remembered in Bill Rust's eyes when he beat Martha.

After Tully left, Hedda felt more isolated than ever. Hedda thought at first that Tully would soon return, but when days turned into months, and months into a year, she came to believe that Tully really would not be back. Hedda fell asleep on the couch now and woke up on the couch—no one came to get her. Lena knit and cooked and sewed a little and sat on the stoop and watched the street, until one day when Hedda came home from work and Lena told her that she had met a man and they were "gonna" get married. "You met a man? How could you meet a man?" Hedda asked. "You never go anywhere."

"I didn't have to," Lena said. "He came to me. He's our mailman."

So Lena and the mailman got married, and Lena asked Hedda to move out. Move out of her own house. Well, it wasn't Hedda's house anymore, and hadn't been for years.

Hedda moved out, to a small room in northern Topeka. The room was only $20 a week and three blocks away from the refuse plant.

She continued to work and go home, put a TV dinner in the oven, sit in front of the TV, sleep in front of the TV. But on Saturday nights, Hedda would take a bus to Carlos O'Kelly's or, months later, to Casa Del Sol, having called Angela Martinez after many months of waiting for Tully to return. Hedda found out from Angela where Tully worked, and also found out about Jennifer Mandolini. How could Tully have not told her?

At Casa Del Sol, Hedda would wait across Topeka Boulevard for Tully to come out. When Tully walked out after her shift, she looked as dog-tired as Hedda did after all that time on her feet. Sometimes Tully walked home, sometimes she had her car with her. Hedda would watch Tully walk to her car, notice her thin legs, her short hair, her flowery uniform. Hedda would watch Tully walk to Jennifer's blue car. Hedda remembered Jennifer's dad coming to the house one day when Tully was still in high school and giving her the car keys. Tully protested. But he just said, "It was what she wanted," and then Tully took them. Hedda had wondered about the car then, but she hadn't wondered enough to ask Tully about it.

At Casa Del Sol, Hedda watched Tully get in and sit in the car for a few minutes, and then drive away. At Carlos, Tully used to walk to her trailer or drive some girl with blond hair home. At Casa, Tully sometimes walked out with a man, and the man would get into his nice red car and Tully would get into hers. Just recently there was another man that Tully walked out with, and his car was just a plain beat-up Ford.

Sometimes Hedda would follow Tully to her trailer and then watch her from across Kansas Avenue puttering about. When Tully drew the curtains, Hedda would take a bus back to her room.

Hedda worked overtime on Christmas Eve, 1980, sealing boxes full of sewage chemical treatments—bottled twenty to a box for easy residential septic distribution—came home, put a chicken in the oven, and fell asleep. She woke up to the smell of burned fowl. She spent Christmas completely by herself—a first. As usual, there was no tree. New Year's Eve, she was also by herself, and she fell asleep on the couch before midnight. New Year's Day she worked for double-time. On January 1, 1981, eighteen days before Tully's twentieth birthday, Hedda was at work having lunch, bending down to pick up a napkin, when she was nearly thrown out of her chair by a sharp pain just behind her right eye. She swooned, got up, wobbled, lifted her hand to touch her eye, and the pain hit her again, this time knocking her down on the floor. She tried to get up, but it hit her again, and she closed her eyes and saw black and she opened her eyes and saw black, and her last thought was, "Tully."

2.

"Tully! Phone!" Donna yelled at around five-thirty that evening.

Tully came to the front desk. "It's a man," whispered Donna. "He sounds serious."

No one ever called her at work, except Shakie. What more can happen? thought Tully, picking up the receiver.

"Yes?"

"Is this Natalie Makker?"

"Yes."

"Tully, this is Dr. Reuben from Topeka State Hospital."

"Yes."

"Tully, I'm sorry, but I have some bad news about your mother."

Silence.

"Tully, are you there?"

"Yes."

"I'm really sorry."

Silence.

"Tully, your mother had a stroke. She is in intensive care now, here at Topeka State. We don't know if she will make it. If she does, we don't know what shape she'll be in."

Silence.

"Tully? You okay? This must be very hard for you."

"Yes."

"You can come to the second floor of the hospital, tell them who you are, they'll let you in to see your mom, okay?"

"Yes," said Tully, and hung up.

"Tully? Everything all right?" Donna asked.

"Yes," said Tully, and she went back on the floor and finished her shift.

After work, she walked home, took a shower, and went straight to bed.

The next morning, Tully went to the hospital. The nurses took her to the room where her mother lay, and Tully looked at her for a few minutes.

"You can go and sit next to her if you want," the nurse said. "Don't worry. You won't disturb her."

Tully shook her head. She left soon after and drove to St. Mark's.

That evening Jeremy, who had come back from New York, looked at Tully coldly and said, "I called Casa Del Sol. Donna told me you called in sick."

"I'm fine," said Tully.

Jeremy shook his head. "That's not what I mean," he said. "Donna told me you'd gone to visit your mother in the hospital."

"Yeah," said Tully. "She's not very well."

"Tully!" Jeremy shouted. "You told me your mother was dead!"

"Oh, yeah," said Tully slowly. She looked at Jeremy and shrugged her shoulders. "Ooops."

"Ooops? Ooops? What the hell is 'Ooops'? Did you lie to me, Tully?"

"Well, obviously," said Tully. "My mother is still alive."

Jeremy looked very upset. "How could you have lied to me about something like this? About your own mother, for God's sake. Why?"

"Oh, and if I lied to you about something else, that would be okay, would it?" said Tully. "Yeah, right."

"Tully, why in heaven's name would you tell me your mother is dead?"

"We're not that close," said Tully.

"No, I should think not!" he exclaimed. "What else did you lie to me about?"

"I don't know," she replied in a tired voice. "I can't think of anything offhand. But I'll be sure to let you know if I think of something."

"How can I trust you if you lie to me, Tully?"

"Well, if you wouldn't ask so many stupid questions all the time," she snapped, "I wouldn't have to lie to you at all!"

"Why don't you just say you don't want to talk about something?"

"Because it doesn't work!" she yelled. "Because you immediately get that disgusting sympathetic look on your face and say, 'Let's taaaalk about it.' Well, I don't wanna fucking taaaalk about it!"

Jeremy didn't say anything for a while, but finally, in a calmer voice, he asked, "How is she?"

"She's had a stroke," replied Tully, also calmer.

"Oh, Tully," said Jeremy, putting his hand on her back. "I'm so sorry." She moved away from his arm.

"It's okay," she said. "I'm sure she'll be fine."

Jeremy looked at her carefully. "Oh," he said.

"I told you," she said. "We're not that close."

"I know, but she is not well, Tully."

"Yes."

Jeremy was quiet for a moment. "You don't want to talk about it?"

"No."

"Why?"

"Because I don't," said Tully.

"Did you go and visit her?" asked Jeremy.

"Yeah, but she," said Tully, "wasn't very talkative."

"You don't want to tell me about it?"

"Jeremy! There is nothing to tell. I went to see her, she was in the ICU, hooked up to a lot of tubes and wires. She looked a little pale. That's it."

"That's not what I mean."

"I know."

Tully got up from the couch and stormed off to the kitchen. A few minutes later, she came back to the living room and sat on the corner of the couch. "Jeremy, look, I really like you, and we have a good time together, and I certainly want to continue to see you, but there are a lot of things I don't want to talk to you about. A whole bunch. But you keep at it, every day, every time we see each other, questions, questions, questions. We don't even talk about books anymore, or traveling, or California, because of your constant going at me. So I lie, or do this or that, or keep away from you, because I—just—don't—want—to—talk—about—it! I mean, you must respect that, right?"

He sat there dumbfounded. "Tully, I thought we were close."

"We are pretty close. But just because we fuck does not mean I have to hari-kari myself to you."

Jeremy was taken aback. "I just want to help you. Why can't I help you?"

"Help me? Help me how? With what?" She swallowed hard and said, "Jeremy, you know how you can help me? Stop asking me things all the time. Just stop."

"Why can't we talk about the things that are bothering you, hurting you? We talk, and your pain becomes my pain and it won't seem so heavy anymore, and you feel better. That helps, doesn't it?" he said.

"Jeremy, Jeremy." She shook her head. "You want to help? Get me a different life." She lowered her gaze. "Yes, get me a different life. A life I can talk to you about, a life I can talk to Shakie and Robin and Julie about. Otherwise, don't upset me."

They didn't speak for a while. Then Jeremy asked, "Does Robin know?"

"Does Robin know what?" she said sharply, afraid he meant did Robin know about him.

"About stuff, about your mother?"

"Well, he has known me for over two years. He knew my friends. He knows a little. Not much. There is not much to know about my mother. We're not that close. Not everybody is close to their mother, Jeremy!"

Jeremy moved closer to her and stroked her hair. "You're not that close with anybody, are you, Tull?"

"What do you mean?" she said, putting her hand to her throat. "Right now, I'm so close to you I don't even have my own oxygen."

* * *

When she told Robin about Hedda's stroke, he got very upset for Tully, and then very upset *at* Tully.

"Tully! Your mother's in the hospital! She may die! How could you have sat here with me, enjoyed all that food, laughed, told jokes, had this great time, knowing this was hanging over you?"

Tully said, "It was more like waving to me in the distance," and laughed.

Robin hit the table with his fist.

"Robin, calm down. It's okay."

"No! I'm not going to calm down! And it's not okay. This is your mother. Don't you give a shit?"

Tully thought about it as she took a bite of her lemon meringue.

"Robin, I'm really sorry I told you," wiping her mouth. "You're actually annoying me right now, and I think I want to go home. Can you please take me home?"

"Why don't we go to the hospital?"

"Because I don't live in the hospital. I live in my home and that's where I want to go."

"How long has your mom been in the hospital?"

Tully hesitated. "Six days, I think. Get the check, please."

"How many times have you gone to visit her?"

She hesitated again. "She's comatose and wrapped in tubes."

"How many?" Robin repeated.

"A lot of tubes." Tully shook her head. "A half dozen, maybe—"

"TULLY!"

"Once," she said.

"Once!" he gasped.

Tully got up and put on her coat. "Robin! I know it's hard, but try to remember this has nothing to do with you. Just take me home."

Outside it was cold and snowing. Robin stopped in front of the passenger door, blocking her way, and said quietly, "Tully, you know how I feel about this. My mother died suddenly."

"Yes, thank you for trying to make me feel better. However, that was your mother, and I don't know if mine will be so lucky."

Robin inhaled and pulled back his hand to hit her, while Tully just stood there and looked at him. She did not wince, she did not blink, she did not move away. When he lowered his hand, she hissed, "Are you crazy? Have you lost your mind?"

"I'm sorry, I'm sorry, I'm sorry," he said. "I'm so sorry, Tully, I didn't touch you, I'm really sorry."

She turned away from him, and he grabbed her and turned her around, holding her in front of him. She tried to push him away, but his lovely face was so close to hers, and all of a sudden she didn't want to be fighting with him, she just wanted to be close to his face. The last thing she wanted to do was talk about her mother. The second to last thing was to tell Robin about Jeremy.

Finally they got into the car, and Tully sat there, staring straight ahead.

"Tully, look at me. Please. I'm sorry. I've never hit anyone in my life and I don't think I ever could. I just . . . You frustrate me."

She said nothing.

Robin continued. "What's the matter, Tully Makker? You've been so distant lately—"

"Lately?" she said.

He nodded. "I've been able to reach you before," he said. "Before you were reachable. But now we're seeing each other less and less, and I'm a little anxious. I get so upset when I see how cold you are to your mother. Despite everything, she is still your mother."

Still nothing.

He pulled over to the side of the road.

"Tully, please, don't shut me out," said Robin, touching her. "Please."

She sighed. "Okay, Robin. Okay. But it's too cold out here. Take me home. Then we'll talk."

Her trailer was warm and clean. She made them both tea and settled down on the couch next to him. She looked into his earnest face, touched his smooth olive skin, touched his hands cupping the tea, and just couldn't do it. She couldn't do it to him. She didn't want to see him upset, and at the same time she was a little afraid that if Robin found out about Jeremy, he would leave her and not be back. She'd seen him fire people in his store, people who were incompetent or bad for business, she'd seen him call the police on a guy who stole two Christian Dior ties one Saturday. Robin was pliable, she thought, until the moment he was crossed, but after that moment, there wasn't one appeasable bone in his body.

Tully just didn't feel ready to give up Robin. But there he was, sitting on her couch, waiting for her to talk to him, let him in, reach him. And so it was either tell him about Jeremy or tell him about her mother.

She beckoned him into the kitchen. "Robin, let me tell you about little Natalie's first memory," she said with no inflection, getting out two English muffins and putting them into the toaster. "She was two and it was night. Natalie was sleeping soundlessly, and then she woke up. She woke up because she couldn't breathe. She tried to make a noise," said Tully, getting out the butter and grape jelly. "But she couldn't breathe. When she opened her eyes, she couldn't see anything. Something was pressed to her face. She thrashed and kicked and tried to move but couldn't. Her hands tried to grab at the thing pressed to her face. It was a pillow, and she couldn't pull it off. Finally she slowed down, her legs stopped kicking, she was dizzy and drifting away. There was no pain. Then dimly, from afar, Natalie heard her father's voice asking if she was okay. The pillow immediately came off her face. Natalie gasped and started to scream. She saw her mother turn around to her father and yell at him for waking up the baby. Natalie continued to scream, and her father came and picked her up."

Robin's black pupils absorbed his chocolate irises. He and Tully stood there, facing each other, and then Robin said, "The muffins are burning."

Tully pulled the lever up, just in time. She served the muffins and more tea, and they settled back on the couch.

"Tully, I don't believe you."

She shrugged. "Of course. However, it's true, regardless."

Robin put down his cup of tea. "Tully! Mothers don't kill their children."

"She didn't kill Natalie."

"You dreamt it."

Tully smirked. "Robin, you've obviously never been suffocated. It's not the kind of thing you can imagine and dream about at the age of two." She looked away from him for a moment. "Later you can dream about it."

He got up from the couch and paced. She was amused. Why is it that all the men in her life needed to pace when they were around her?

"Is this why you don't sleep very well?"

"I guess."

"Oh. I thought it was because of—"

"No, it's mostly this," she said sharply. "Things relating to this. Just can't sleep, that's all."

Robin continued to pace the living room. "Tully, why would she want to suffocate you?"

"Robin, who the hell knows? Who the hell cares? Because her mother left her, because her father did not love her, because she was afraid my dad loved us too much. Who cares why?"

"I care," Robin said.

"Why?"

When he did not answer her, Tully said, "What difference does it make why? Who cares? You think if you had a reason, you'd understand it better?"

"It would make more sense, yes."

"It would make sense to you that a mother could strangle her fat little baby?" She laughed. "Wonderful!"

Robin was quiet. "You said 'us.' "

"Us?"

"Yes. Us. You said, 'dad loved us too much.' Who is us? You and your brother? I thought you were five when your brother was born."

Tully was quiet, quiet, quiet. They heard the refrigerator hum in the kitchen and the cars outside and the radiators hissing a little.

"I had another brother," she finally said. "He died when he was very young."

"What did he die of?" asked Robin gently.

Tully raised her eyes to him. "Crib death," she replied.

When they got into bed, Robin spooned her close to him and said into her hair, "Tully, that's a terrible story, terrible. I'm having such a hard time believing you."

Tully rubbed her hands. "I know," she said. "And it's okay."

"Poor you. Is this what you dream about when you keep thrashing in the middle of the night?"

"And other things," said Tully, remembering the dream with the head.

A week before her birthday, Tully gritted her teeth, but told Jeremy the same first memory story.

Jeremy cried and hugged her, and all he could say for a while was, "Oh, Tully, oh, Tully, poor Tully, my Tully." Tully lay there generally unaffected. When she did talk about her life, she did it by gritting her teeth and setting her jaw and speaking in an "I'm-rehashing-an-old-news-clip" monotone. But Jeremy's reaction contrasted sharply to Robin's, showing Tully what she needed to know: Robin and Jeremy were not interchangeable. They were as different as the awesomely empty High Plains and the bluestem grasses of Flint Hills— flint more translucent than glass and tougher than steel.

A week later Hedda was better, was over the worst. Dr. Reuben called Tully at home, saying Hedda was asking for her.

"She can talk after a stroke?"

"Not very well," said Dr. Reuben. "But she was calling for 'Tuwy.' "

She came to the hospital, went into her mother's room, sat down, and looked at her for a while. A nurse walked in and Hedda woke up. Hedda sluggishly brought her head around and her eyes saw Tully. She did not move them from Tully's face.

Tully cleared her throat. "How are you, Mother?" she said. "I hear you're going to be getting better."

Hedda shook her head a little and beckoned with her hand for Tully to come closer. Tully got up and leaned over her mother, down to her ear. She smelled chloroform, alcohol, a metal medicinal smell of IV tubes, and something else, too: the pungent odor of Hedda's breath. Tully made a distasteful grimace. She leaned close and heard Hedda say, "They don't think I wiw evah wahk oh move ma ahms."

Moving back, Tully examined her mother's face. "I'm sure you'll be fine, Mom," she said. "You're very strong." She moved away, sat back down. "We should all be as strong as you." She stood up. "You've been through a lot in your life. I'm sure you'll pull through this, too. I gotta go now."

Walked quickly toward the door. "I'll come again soon. Take care, will you?"

Two days before Tully's birthday, Dr. Reuben called, asking her to come in to see him.

"Dr. Reuben," Tully said. She was at work again. "I am very busy. I work in the evenings and have classes during the day. Could we talk on the phone, perhaps?"

"Tully, this is very serious. It's about your mother."

She reluctantly came to see him the next day, January 18. President Reagan is getting ready for inauguration and I'm going to talk to the doctor about my mother.

"Tully," he said, "your mother's condition has improved."

"Oh, good," said Tully.

"Well, not so good." Dr. Reuben was tall, bald, and kind of nervous, thought Tully. He wore glasses, and she noticed that he took them off, wiped them with a tissue, and put them back on about once every few minutes.

Tully hated the hospital smell, hated the white interior, the sterility, the fact that she had to be here at all. She hated that she could not get up and go away that very second. She watched the doctor clean his glasses again and thought, He does not have good news.

"I don't think she is ever going to be able to walk, or move her limbs again," Dr. Reuben said.

Tully was silent. Finally she spoke. "How can you be so sure?" she said. "Physical rehab can do all kinds of things now."

He nodded. "Yes. Yes, it can. But the damage to your mother's brain after the cerebrovascular occlusion was severe. She now has something called peripheral neuropathy, a reaction of her peripheral nervous systems closely resembling that of a muscular sclerotic. She is suffering from hemiplegia on the left side of her body and from paresis on the right. Her aphasia for now is quite pronounced—"

"Dr. Reuben," Tully cut him off, clearing her throat. "Could you please repeat everything you just told me—in English?"

Dr. Reuben took off his glasses again. "Speaking plainly, she is just not going to get well," he said, adding, "certainly not in the next year or so."

"Okay," said Tully.

"The good news is that she can understand nearly everything and we think will regain most of her speech, save for a slight slur."

"That's the good news?" said Tully.

"Of course," replied Dr. Reuben, misunderstanding her. "Judging by the number of blocked blood vessels, she could have been a complete vegetable or worse."

"Or worse," repeated Tully, thinking, Worse than a complete vegetable?

Dr. Reuben took off his glasses again. "Tully, what I'm trying to say is that your mother is going to need daily help. She cannot work anymore and she cannot live by herself."

Tully stared at the doctor for a long while before she answered.

"I'm sorry, but I don't think I understand you."

"Your mother needs someone to take care of her."

"Okay," said Tully. "Okay, I'm sure we can work it out. Aunt Lena, she'll take Mom back."

"And then what?"

"And then what, what? Then we hire Mom a nurse, a physical therapist, whatever she needs. She worked for the city. The city will pay."

"Your mother's insurance does not cover all that."

"What do you mean, it doesn't cover that?" said Tully indignantly. "She worked for Topeka for over twenty years, never missing a day, never being sick, going to work no matter what. She probably got the damn stroke breathing in all those treatment fumes! Are you trying to tell me she doesn't even have disability?"

"No, no, she does, of course. Disability will cover her living expenses for two years," said Dr. Reuben. "She's got very good disability coverage, they tell me. But at most her coverage will pay for a physical therapist once or twice a week, and a nurse maybe once a week. It will not cover the cost of a daily nurse, to cook for her, to wash her, to wash her clothes and bedding, to give her medicine three times a day. Daily care for a sick person, you know?"

"Uh-huh," said Tully. "What's wrong with Aunt Lena?"

Dr. Reuben, who had just put his glasses on his nose, took them off again. "Tully, your aunt has several problems of her own. We've spoken to her, we've gone to see her. It seemed to us, the hospital staff, that she needed some . . . care herself."

Tully almost smiled. "I don't disagree. So what do you suggest, Doctor?"

He put on his glasses, took them off again. "Would you consider moving back home?"

Tully laughed. She got up, still laughing, and walked over to the doctor's desk, leaned over across it, so that her face was close to his, and stopped laughing. "You must be kidding," she said, and there was a blizzard in her voice. "You must be fucking joking."

She straightened out but continued to stand.

"Tully, I know you want to be independent—"

"Independent, my ass!" she interrupted him. "Doctor, I apologize to you, you have no way of knowing. Let me just say, what you're asking, it's completely impossible."

"Why is it impossible?"

"Well, first of all," said Tully, "there is no home. I've driven by the Grove once or twice. My mother doesn't live there anymore. Like Alice. My aunt lives there with some guy."

"Yes, your aunt apparently remarried. We spoke to her. She said she will let Hedda move back if you move back."

"To the Grove?" Tully laughed coldly.

"Tully, you are her daughter," said Dr. Reuben. "You are all she has."

Tully laughed again and shook her head. "Doctor, Doctor. Is this why you got me here? Is this what you had to talk to me about? You can't be serious!"

"Tully, I am very serious. Your mother cannot live alone, you are all she has, it is very simple, there is just no other way."

Tully breathed hard. Then, in a moment of unrestrained frustration, she swiped everything she could off the doctor's desk. Ashtray, photographs, papers, paperweight all fell in a clatter to the floor. There was the sound of broken glass. She lifted her hand in apology and wiped her forehead. I lost my temper, Tully thought. Like *she* used to lose it.

"I'm sorry. We are not very good in my family at handling anger." She picked up her bag off the floor. "I apologize again." She turned to go.

"Tully, please don't go, this is about your mother, after all."

She stopped. He continued. "So then, what do *you* suggest we do with her?"

She turned around. "Doctor, let me ask you, what would you do with her if she had no living relatives? What would you do if she had no one?"

"But she doesn't," said Dr. Reuben, "have no one."

"Believe me," said Tully, "she has no one."

The doctor was quiet. "Well, I suppose we would put her in Menninger, in the ward for the chronically ill."

Tully smiled mirthlessly. "There. You have your answer."

"Tully, maybe you should take a look up there, then you wouldn't say that. All the people there are the saddest people I know. People not taken care of by anyone except underpaid, overworked hospital staff who would all rather be in the maternity ward at Stormont-Vail. It is the place for the living dead. I cannot believe you would want to consign your mother to that. This is Kansas! Not New York, or California. We don't abandon our families here, we take care of them. What you're proposing is a godless thing to do." Dr. Reuben was not putting his glasses on at all, he was just cleaning them, throwing the tissue out, taking a fresh tissue, breathing on them, cleaning them again.

Tully sighed. She came back to the doctor's desk but continued to stand.

"Dr. Reuben, you are a stranger to me, and I don't even speak about my mother to people I'm close to. I certainly don't want to now, with you. However, what you're proposing to me is godless. How can you with any decency consign a twenty-year-old to a life of the living dead? How can you tell me that a twenty-year-old young woman who is working, going to school, trying to make a life for herself, should be subjected to being a daily crutch for an invalid? How can you ask a young woman to clean and wash an invalid, to make an invalid go to the bathroom? To be there day in and day out for? For how long?" Tully paused to catch her breath. "Some stroke victims live paralyzed for twenty years—my mother is not even forty." She raised her voice. "What you are telling me here, what you are asking me, is to end my own life!" She tried not to blink. "And then you stand here and judge me because I refuse! Judge me without knowing anything!" She let out a small, stifled sound.

"I'm sorry, Tully," said Dr. Reuben. "But she *is* your mother. Your mother! She gave birth to you, she took care of you." The doctor put his glasses down and started ripping the tissue he was holding to shreds.

"Yes, my mother!" exclaimed Tully. "I see! So she takes care of me when I'm baby cute and I in return have to take care of her when she is an infirm hag? I get it! Well, that sure is fair. That sure isn't godless!" she said acidly. "She takes care of me when I can sit on her lap and hug her around the neck. When to wash me is a pleasure, when I can play with my ducks and toddle around. And for that I have to drag her fat paralyzed body around the house I hate!" Tully had to stop talking for a moment. She sat down and looked at the floor, and when the doctor started to say something, she waved him off and sat there until she found a voice that did not break. Then Tully got up again, buttoning the coat she never took off.

"You son of a bitch. I cannot believe you made me explain myself to you. I want you never to call me again, do you understand, never, not even if she dies and you want me to pay for the fucking funeral."

Tully opened the door to leave, but before she went, she turned around and said, "My mother treated me like a dog my whole life." Tully's voice was cold. "And that's not even the worst of it. Doctor, I wouldn't take care of her if you offered me true love." Tully spit vehemently on the floor and walked out, slamming the door hard behind her.

9
ROBIN AND JEREMY

January 1981

Tully's first thought when she woke up the next day was: I am twenty years old. Her second thought was: I am still in Topeka.

She got out of bed, brushed her teeth, peed, made herself a cup of coffee, and sat down on the couch. Twenty years old. I have lived for twenty years. For eighteen of them I lived with my mother. Even hardened murderers at Leavenworth sometimes get less than eighteen years. And just like them, I am now on parole. If I don't behave, I will end up back there, back in the Grove.

I've served my time, certainly, Tully thought, but I haven't actually done anything wrong. I'm like Edmond Dantès, the Count of Monte Cristo, serving my time at Chateau d'If, for a crime I did not commit, but unlike him, I don't have the view of Notre Dame à la Garde standing over Marseilles to inspire me. I just have a view of— Tully opened the curtains. Of the Santa Fe tracks and Sears, Roebuck. How majestic. But in any case, she is not my responsibility. She is not my penance. She is nearly not my mother. Tully went outside in her sweat suit. It felt about twenty degrees, and the wind was howling and blowing the snow off the railroad embankment and into Tully's face. She wrapped her arms around herself and looked out onto Kansas Avenue. The road was covered with snow, the plows hadn't been by yet. Tully remembered a nineteenth-century poem. *Why does the wind blow upon me so wild? Is it because I am nobody's child?*

She went back inside and contemplated making herself something to eat, but then decided against it. Tully didn't like to cook, or eat, when she was cooking and eating by herself.

She got dressed and fixed her face up, peering in the mirror. I look as I did when I was twelve, fifteen, eighteen. I look exactly the same. She peered closer. No, that's not true. When I was fifteen, I looked older. All that bleach and mascara then. All those late nights up on College Hill gave me circles under my eyes. All that dancing, all those boys. All that lack of sleep.

Now the bleach and mascara have been replaced by crow's feet, she thought, and the dancing by work—I'm still on my feet—while the boys have been replaced by two grown men. And soon I'll be old. Soon I'll have a degree and will sit under a palm tree. Still with no sleep.

Tully sat down on the floor in front of the old wooden coffee table, back against the couch, and began a letter to Julie.

January 19, 1981

Dear Jule,

Okay, here goes. I'm sorry.

I'm sorry I haven't written to you in so long. Please believe me when I say I really look forward to your letters and read and reread them. Several times each day. I haven't been a good pen-pal, that's for sure, but I don't want you not to write me, Jule.

It's my birthday today, do you care? I haven't received a card from you. Plus, it's already nine in the morning and you haven't called yet. Remember when I used to sleep over the night before my birthday and the night after, just so that I would be around you guys for the entire twenty-four-hour birthday period? Last night, I slept alone, and woke up alone. Most likely, I will spend the whole day alone, and then go to bed alone, too.

I guess that's what happens when you grow up. You sleep alone a lot. Even on your birthday. And you know you're a grown-up when you realize you don't care anymore that you're alone, all the time, making just one cup of tea, and sleeping.

The sleeping part is not an issue.

But you know what? I'm not grown up yet.

And I'll tell you something else too. I almost . . . miss making tea for my mother. I never in my life used to make just one cup of tea. Always two, sometimes three. Even if she didn't drink it half the time. I always made her a cup of tea.

She's had a stroke, you know. How could you know. She's lying there, unable to move, and the good doctor is asking me if I will move back to the Grove and take

*care of my mother. Let me ask you, what can I possibly
do for her?*

*I have a new boyfriend, now. His name is Jeremy, and
he is very nice. He is also thirty five years old, from New
York, and he is not my only boyfriend. I still see Robin
every weekend. I talk to Robin nearly every day.*

*How's your roommate Laura? In your last letter, you
said she was almost your best friend. And that guy,
Richard? You still seeing him?*

*I see Shakie on Thursday nights. We go out dancing,
just us girls.*

*There is snow outside, a lot of snow. All I'm thinking is
that in California, there is no snow, and maybe someday,
on my birthday, I'll actually be able to smell the ocean
instead of having my eyes tear at the cold. I'll look at the
ocean, and feel like it's my "Notre Dame à la Garde."
Never mind.*

*I'm sorry for last summer, inviting Shakie to come
with us, and all. What can I say? Please write. I didn't
even see you for Christmas. That was the first Christmas
I can remember when I didn't see you.*

Please write.
Love,
Tully

Tully put the pen down, and the phone rang. She stared at
it. It rang and rang. It was nine-thirty in the morning, and Tully
moved toward it, but reluctantly, and then it stopped ringing.
She just stared at it, and it rang again. This time she waited
until it stopped and then went to it and took the receiver off
the hook.

Then Tully drove to St. Mark's. *My* Notre Dame à la Garde,
she thought. The chair that was left there for her was covered
with snow. She wiped the snow off and sat down in her coat.
Put her hands between her thighs and blew in and out heavily.

You would have been twenty, too. All three of us, twenty.

Tully sat in the chair for a long time. The wind was howling
in her ears, and she felt her legs starting to freeze. Do your
mom and dad ever come to visit you? Do they put fresh flowers
on you, even now when nothing survives, do they come again
and again to bring you fresh flowers, even in winter, when the

cold wind blows all the flowers away? Or are these only my flowers? No, they can't be, I don't bring you roses. I bring carnations; these flowers are all dead, but they are definitely roses. White roses. Tully peered closer. Who brought these white roses to you? Who sat here with you just recently?

I'm going to go, you know. I've decided, how do you like that? California. Will you forgive me when I go to California and leave you here? Well, why not? You went to California, and left *me* here. You went without me, you said, Fuck you, Tully Makker, make your own way to California. I cannot wait for you. I'm leaving without you. You selfish cow, Mandolini. You selfish, selfish cow. You wanted to go to California because *he* was going to California, and got me involved in your plan, got me believing, got me hoping, got me wanting, and then you just up and left without me. Well, I, too, am going to go. I'm going to go and leave you, and then you'll be sorry. Not to see me every goddamned Sunday. Tully got up, blew in her hands, and crossed herself, whispering, "I hope where you are it is one endless summer. 'Cause it sure is fucking freezing around here."

Tully stayed at St. Mark's till about one. She was supposed to see Shakie for lunch, and Jeremy for lunch, too—somehow—and then Robin for dinner, what a tangled web; in truth, though, she didn't feel like seeing Shakie or Jeremy or Robin. Tully got up off the chair and knelt down in the snow. Taking her gloves off, she brushed the snow off the tombstone with her bare hands until Tully could see *her* name. That's better, she thought. A little better.

And then Tully left, got into the Camaro and drove to Kansas City, where she went shopping for a new, warmer blanket, some goose-down pillows, new tea mugs—she bought a set of four, just in case—and some makeup. She bought herself Lancôme eye creme, for the crow's feet. Shakie will be upset I'm not buying Chanel, but I just won't tell her, thought Tully.

At six-thirty in the evening, Tully went to the movies. A double feature. *Absence of Malice* and *Only When I Laugh*. Tully fell asleep during *Only When I Laugh* and afterwards drove home.

When she got home, she left the phone off the hook, made herself two cups of tea in her new mugs, and fell asleep on the couch with all the lights on. Tully did not have anything to eat, nor did she speak to anyone on her twentieth birthday.

The following day, Tully went to see Shakie at Macy's in White Lakes Mall. Her phone remained off the hook.

"Shakie, let's go to lunch," Tully said.

"Tully Anne Makker!" exclaimed Shakie. It was eleven-thirty and not busy. Shakie raised her voice another notch. "Tully! Where in heaven's name have you been?"

"Oh, you know," Tully said vaguely. "Out and about. Let's go to lunch."

"Lunch. I was supposed to take you out for lunch yesterday. Today doesn't count."

"Great. My treat. Red Lobster. They have fantastic $5.99 specials."

"What, *you*'re buying? Whose birthday is it, anyway?" Shakie said.

"No longer mine, thank God. Let's go."

Shakie had to help a customer, and Tully studied her while she sold a middle-aged woman three bottles of Chanel No. 5. She is beautiful, Tully thought. God, I wish I were that beautiful, *half* that beautiful. Shakie's eyes reminded Tully of Julie's. Nothing behind them but contentment and happiness. Not even *he* could mar those eyes for long. Though Tully had to admit, Julie's had changed. Last summer, the brown eyes looked as sad as a cow's.

Tully and Shakie drove from White Lakes up Topeka Boulevard to Red Lobster. Tully ordered shrimp scampi. Shakie interrupted her, ordering lobster for both of them. "It's your birthday," she said.

"It's not $5.99, either," said Tully.

"It's only money, Tully. It's only paper. Jack taught me that." She smiled proudly. "Good, eh?" she said, opening her bag and pulling out a card and a wrapped present.

Tully smiled. Shakie, who was sitting opposite Tully, leaned across the table and kissed Tully on the cheek and ruffled her hair. "Happy birthday, Tully."

Shakie had bought Tully Chanel No. 5 and a Chanel makeup selection. "Maybe you'll start wearing some again," said Shakie.

In the card, she wrote, "Happy Birthday to my newest best friend, here's to the next twenty years."

"Cool, Shake!" Tully smiled. She reached over and patted Shakie's hand. "I'll wear some next time we go out, okay?"

They ate and talked. Tully even asked about Jack. Shakie waved her off with her hand. "Tully, you don't want to talk about Jack. Something is bothering you." Shakie smiled. "Are you having trouble with your boyfriend*s*?"

"Are you making fun of me, Lamber?" said Tully mildly.

"God strike me dead, no," said Shakie, making a serious face.

"Well, cut it out. Listen to me. I'm not having trouble with them. *They* are having trouble with me. All they want to do is get serious, and all I want to do is get the hell out of here."

"I know, Tully," said Shakie. "So what's stopping you?"

"Nothing," said Tully. Except St. Mark's, she thought.

"Nothing wrong with Topeka," said Shakie.

"Shakie, I want to go to California, you know that."

"Yeah, yeah, yeah. You sound just like Jack," said Shakie.

"God strike me dead, no," said Tully.

"Listen," said Shakie. "I went out with this really nice guy last week and saw him twice this week."

"Really?"

"Yeah," said Shakie. "Frank Bowman. Frank is a good Methodist boy. He's polite to my parents, has a steady job, smiles a lot, talks a lot, wants to see me a lot." She took a sip of her Diet Sprite. "In other words, nothing like Jack."

"Well," said Tully. "Jack is polite. And Methodist. And what are you going to do when Christmas rolls around and another one of Jack's relatives gets ill?"

Shakie shrugged. "There's eleven glorious months to go. We'll see."

They ordered some chocolate ice cream.

Shakie skeptically studied Tully's hair. "Your hair looks . . . great. You look like Mia Farrow at the end of *Rosemary's Baby*."

Tully ran her hands through it. "Lamber, is that supposed to be an insult?"

Shakie laughed. "No. No, it isn't. I wish I had the nerve to cut my hair that short. Or at all, for that matter." Shakie took a big spoonful of ice cream. "So, Tully Makker, what are you going to do when you leave for sunny California? Gonna leave your boyfriends a note?"

"I still have to figure out what to do with my boyfriends," said Tully. "My brain is just not directing me."

"Lower, Tully, lower. It's not your brain that's supposed to direct you in these things."

"Thank you, Shakie," said Tully. "Seriously, though, I feel like I should do *something*. Make some kind of a decision. End it with Jeremy, or tell Robin about Jeremy and let him leave me. Something."

"Stay with Robin," said Shakie. "He loves you."

"So does Jeremy."

"Stay with Jeremy," said Shakie. "He loves you."

"Shake, why don't you ask me who I love?"

"Because you don't love either of them. That's pretty obvious."

"But what if I did love them both?" asked Tully quietly, spooning off the melted part of the chocolate ice cream—her favorite part.

Shakie waved her off. "Love them both. What nonsense. Like that's even possible."

"Why not?" said Tully. "You can love two children. You can love two brothers. You can love two of your friends. Why can't you love two men?"

"I don't know why not," said Shakie, "but you just can't, that's all. Besides, it's a silly point. You don't love them."

Tully didn't say anything.

Shakie said, "Tull, you're still under the impression that you gotta choose something. *Someone*. Just go with the flow. Move with the groove. Have some fun! You don't seem like you're having much fun, Tully. Not at all. Never. Not even when we go out. You don't want to be here in Topeka, do you?"

"Not much," said Tully, slowly eating her ice cream.

"Well, then, up and go. Go to California. Say hi to Jack for me."

Tully shook her head. "I wouldn't go till after the summer. And something's got to be done now. They're both miserable. Robin because he has no idea what's going on, and Jeremy because he does. They're miserable just the same."

"What about you?" asked Shakie, stopping eating. "Are you . . . miserable?"

"Me, miserable? No," Tully let out. "I'm as happy as a pig."

"Okay, happy piggy, so do something," said Shakie. "Go eenie, meenie, minie, mo."

"Stop it," said Tully, reaching over and taking Shakie's half-eaten ice cream. "It's not that simple."

Shakie took her ice cream back but didn't eat it, just licked the spoon. "Why not?" she said. "What else is there besides eenie meenie? There's nothing at stake."

Tully took Shakie's ice cream back. "Shake, you're something else," she said. "You really are." Tully wavered a moment. The same story three times in one week? She wanted to tell Shakie; she looked at Shakie's eager, lovely face. Tully wanted to tell her, to tell someone, as a friend, to make someone a closer friend, to make Shakie a closer friend; and Tully almost did. But she remembered telling that story *outside a tent in the black Kansas night at Sunset Court. Telling that story when she was ten years old. Telling it to her two friends, and how then for an hour, all three of them lay silent, with only the crickets singing their chippery songs to three ten-year-old girls. How hot that night was.*

We were lying there in our T-shirts and underwear, nothing else, and the hot air would fall on me and dry my cold skin And then Julie reached out and said, "Hey, Tull, no wonder you like to stay for dinner so much."

"For dinner?" said Jennifer. "You mean that eternal dinner that begins at twelve-oh-one A.M. and ends at midnight? Tully never leaves. She never goes home."

Tully remembered, and couldn't tell Shakie. Shakie was not her oldest friend.

Shakie watched Tully eat her ice cream. Then, flinging her mane back, Shakie said, "It's okay, Tully. I know you don't like to tell me much."

Tully looked down into Shakie's empty ice-cream bowl. Should I order another one? Damn.

"I know why, too," continued Shakie. "You're, like, thinking, what's the point?"

"Yeah," said Tully, looking away from the ice-cream bowl and at Shakie with surprise. "That's exactly it. That's exactly how I feel. What's the fucking point?"

"Let me ask you, Tull," said Shakie, trying to get the waiter's attention. "Changing the subject and all. Have your feelings changed? For your mom? Now that she's sick?"

"They haven't changed much," said Tully reluctantly.

"Let me ask you," said Shakie. "Would you still go to California even if your mom remains in the hospital? Won't she need someone to take care of her?"

Tully stared at Shakie. "What are you doing, Shake?" Tully said. "Whose side are you on?"

"Yours—of course yours," Shakie assured her. "But still, how do you go about that? Leaving for the coast, with a sick mom behind. Leaving for the coast, with a sick mom, friends, college, a good job maybe, church, dancing, and two men who love you, all behind. How do you do it?"

"Shakie, what are you doing?" exclaimed Tully.

"I don't really want you to go, I guess," admitted Shakie. "*I* wouldn't go."

"No?" said Tully. "Why not?"

"My life's been here and been too good. I'd miss everyone. Wouldn't you? Didn't you miss your high school friends when they went?"

And Tully felt her fingertips go numb before she quickly answered, "Sure, I missed them. And I guess I'll miss you guys, too. But there'll be so many things to do. Go to school, get a job, make new friends. Travel. It'll be all right," Tully said, the feeling in her fingertips still gone.

"Isn't there anything you'd miss?"

"Yeah . . ." Tully drew out. "You know what I'd miss the most? Casa's meatball soup. It's just scrumplicious."

Shakie looked sad. "I wonder how he does it, going away all the time," she said. "You know? Like he's trying to get away. He says it's the snow he hates. But I don't believe him. I mean, there's nothing wrong with Topeka, right?"

"Of course there isn't," said Tully, uncomfortable.

"But he can't stand being here. Can't stand it. Go figure."

Tully touched Shakie's hand. "Ahh, Shake. But now you have Frank Bowman, a polite Methodist boy."

Shakie grabbed Tully's hands and held them tight. "You still miss her, don't you, Tull?" she said. "You still miss *her*."

Tully pulled away. "I guess," she said in a rasping voice. "It's only been six hundred days." *And six hundred nights*, she thought.

"I really liked her," Shakie said carefully. "She was such a nice person. Quiet but so nice. And so smart, too."

"Yeah, she was," agreed Tully. "Real smart."

"Do you know she used to look over the bleachers and tell us how many people there were at any given game? I used to be really impressed by that. How did she do it?"

"She . . ." said Tully with difficulty. "She . . . was like a savant. You know what that is?"

"No, but it was pretty impressive," said Shakie.

"It was just like a way of . . . controlling her environment," said Tully. "Counting stuff helped her not to fear so much."

"Huh," said Shakie. "Well, I'd like to control my environment, too, but in a million years I wouldn't be able to count all the people in the bleachers."

"Well, maybe not being able to is not such a terrible thing, then," said Tully.

"Anyway," said Shakie. "I really liked her. I'm sorry, Tully."

"Thanks, Shakie, thanks," replied Tully. Shakie was trying to be extra nice, extra thoughtful. But Tully was inexpressibly relieved when that conversation was over.

Tully drove Shakie back.

"So what are you gonna do tonight, Tull? Who will have the pleasure of your company?"

"Johnny," replied Tully. "And his guest star Bob Newhart."

At Macy's doors, Shakie hugged Tully around the neck. "Happy birthday, Tull. And don't worry so much about everything. Relax. Keep yourself together, that's most important. Keep yourself together, and you'll know what to do with your boys when the time comes."

"Oh, yeah?" said Tully, not pulling away from Shakie's embrace. "And how do *you* know all this?"

"Tully, because when you love someone, everything is very clear to you. You might doubt if they are right for you, if they might beat you, or cheat on you, or drink, or put the seat down. But you won't doubt your own feelings. Also, you'll never hide yourself from them, like you do now. You'll put yourself out on the table in front of them and say, 'Here I am.' "

"Shakie, I never put myself out on the table for anybody," said Tully.

"Someday you will, Makker," said Shakie. "You'll curse that day, I'm sure. You—the control freak—but someday you will."

Tully shook her head and smiled. "Shake, so who died and left you a philosopher?"

"Jack's father and uncle," answered Shakie.

Before she left, Tully asked, "Shakie, so you put yourself on the table for that gypsy?"

"What do you think?" Shakie replied. "But it's a hardwood table, girl. Hard wood," she added before disappearing into the store.

That night Tully went to St. Mark's and sat in the warm church until it was ten in the evening and time to go home.

2.

Three days following Tully's birthday, Robin drove to Topeka State Hospital. At the hospital information desk, he inquired about seeing Hedda Makker.

"And who are you?" asked the nurse.

"Robin DeMarco," said Robin.

"Are you a relative?"

No, thought Robin. Not yet. "No," he said. "I'm her daughter's boyfriend."

The nurse looked at him askance. "And you wish to see her?"

"Yes." He nodded. "Yes, I really do."

He sat and waited, until a young, pretty nurse came to take him to the second floor to see Hedda. "She is not very well, you know," the nurse said, looking Robin over. "She keeps calling for her daughter." The nurse lowered her voice. "But she never comes to see her mother, you know. It's upsetting all of us. The poor woman's got nobody to come and visit her."

"I'm sorry," said Robin. "I'll talk to her daughter."

The nurse lowered her voice another notch as they walked down a white corridor. "Well, you know what I overheard?" she said confidentially, smiling shyly at Robin. "Dr. Reuben asked Hedda's daughter to move back home and take care of Hedda, and she refused!"

"She did, did she?" said Robin, trying to keep his voice from rising.

The nurse nodded, moving closer to Robin. "They were talking a long while, and then she stormed out. Looking really angry. But we all couldn't believe it, you know? I mean, all mothers and daughters have their differences, right? Me and my mom, we still fight like cats and dogs, bless her, and I'm twenty-two," The nurse gazed at Robin. "My name is Cheryl," she said, sticking out her little hand.

He shook it gently. "Well, Cheryl, I'll have to talk to Tully, I guess," he said. "Don't judge her too harshly, though."

"Sure," said Cheryl. "Well, here we are. Room two-eleven. She was awake ten minutes ago. You might be able to talk to her. And come and see me at my station on the way out," she said. "This is a big hospital. You'll get lost. I'll walk you out."

Robin smiled. If he had a hat he would have tipped it to this eager young nurse. "Thank you, Cheryl. I'm sure I'll be able to find my way out. But you're very nice to offer," he said, opening the door to Hedda's room.

She was lying in her bed, face up, eyes closed. Robin had never before seen Hedda. A number of times he had asked Tully to show him pictures of her family, but Tully said there were no pictures. No pictures of anybody.

The door swung shut behind him, making a slight noise, and Hedda opened her eyes. Robin smiled politely.

"Mrs. Makker, you don't know me, but my name is Robin DeMarco."

She tried to talk, but her voice was hoarse. She cleared her throat. "You're Gail'th boyfriend," she said.

"Gail's! No, Mrs. Makker, not Gail's, Tully's, your daughter's."

"I know who Tully ith," said Hedda Makker.

Robin stepped a little closer. "Here," he said, showing her a bouquet of flowers. "I brought you these."

Hedda stared briefly at the flowers. "I have no vathe," she said.

"Not to worry, the nurses will get you one," Robin said brightly, placing the flowers down on a table near her bed and sitting down.

"What did you thay your name wath?"

"Robin, Robin DeMar—"

"What do you want, Robin?"

Robin started rubbing his fingers. "I just came to see you, Mrs. Makker. I wanted to come and introduce myself to you."

Hedda did not take her eyes off him.

"I'm sorry about what's happened to you. I know you must

be suffering, and I just wanted to come and tell you that everything is going to be all right."

Hedda did not speak, nor did she stop watching him. Robin rubbed his fingers more intently. What a stare! That's a stare that could make me crack my toe knuckles, thought Robin.

"Hmm, I know that you two have not always gotten along," he said. "But Tully just doesn't appreciate your serious condition. My mother," he said, pausing a beat, "God rest her soul, passed away many years ago, quite suddenly. I really sympathize with you. I just wanted to tell you that, Mrs. Makker."

"Tully," Hedda Makker said, closing her eyes, "ith a godleth thlut."

Robin stared hard at Hedda. Moments passed, moments in which Hedda's eyes remained closed and Robin's eyes remained hard on her. But then he slightly nodded to himself, his gaze softened, and he stood up. "Okay . . . well, I'll be going now. It was good to talk to you," he said politely but uncomfortably.

Hedda opened her eyes. "Robin," she whispered. He took a few hesitant steps toward her bed. "Robin," she whispered. "I wanna go home . . ."

Robin was so tense, he nearly laughed out loud. Tully will be so angry I came here, he thought. And I'm beginning to see she has every right. Still, though, I pity this woman, pity her, he thought, nodding gently to himself again. Her face looks like a face that has already lived too long, and has not lived well. I pity her.

"Robin," Hedda repeated, "I wanna go home."

Robin looked over Hedda's body, lying limp on the bed, useless arms hanging down from bed railings. "Mrs. Makker, we'll see what we can do. I don't think Tully will move back to the Grove, if that's what you mean. You need someone else, a professional to take care of you."

She faintly nodded. Robin, overcoming his distaste, patted the blanket covering Hedda. "It'll be all right," he said.

Between the time Robin left Hedda's room and got back downstairs to his car, he had worked out a plan. He only hoped Tully would like it. He looked through the Yellow Pages and found a David's Jewelers on Kansas Avenue, not far from Tully's trailer. Robin thought the proximity was ironically appropriate.

It took him about forty-five minutes to pick out a ring he thought Tully would like—a one-karat blue diamond set in yellow gold—and another twenty minutes to have it inscribed. Good old David could now close for the month of February after selling that ring, mused Robin. Maybe I'm in the wrong business, he thought, driving to Tully's trailer. It would take me three busy days to sell the fifty top-of-the line Dior ties that it takes to buy a rock no bigger than a green pea. But a large green pea, he thought, smiling. A top-of-the-line green pea.

Tully wasn't home. Robin looked at his watch. Three o'clock. He wasn't sure what to do with himself, so he went to the movies. *The Elephant Man.* Actually, he thought he was going to be seeing *The Stunt Man*, an altogether different movie, and it took him about half an hour to figure out that the movie he was watching wasn't what he wanted to see. He mildly enjoyed it anyway; it certainly *was* a great stunt, seeing John Hurt with that pachiderm head. Tully would've liked it. She liked *Eraserhead* a few years back.

When he got out, it was dark and cold. It was still early: only six o'clock on a Friday night. Robin didn't usually see Tully on Friday nights. He hoped she didn't go out straight from school. Did she go out dancing? But no, he knew the girls' night out was on Thursdays and included dancing. Yesterday was Thursday.

Now Robin sat in his car and thought about what he would say to her. "Tully," he said aloud to himself. "Will you marry me? Tully, will you please marry me?"

He didn't know her views on marriage, though he certainly knew them on living together. His Tully preferred a trailer to living with him. She preferred getting varicose veins from being on her feet at Casa Del Sol to living with him. She did not want to live with him, that much she had made clear.

"Tully, will you marry me?" Robin repeated, sitting alone in his Corvette, twenty-seven and a half years old, unmarried, childless, freezing his ass off with fifty ties worth of a rock burning a hole in his pocket. They never discussed marriage. It would probably entail some living together, he thought.

He shuddered a little when he thought of Hedda. Poor Tully. Still, though. Hedda is her mother. Her *biological* mother. Isn't that worth something? Isn't that worth some kind of sacrifice? Surely Tully wouldn't let her mother waste away at Topeka

State, or worse, Menninger, if she knew there were other options besides living in the Grove, next to a muddy underpass that led to the railroad tracks, to the forest, to the river. If she thought she had a choice, aside from the trailer, wouldn't she be happier? Wouldn't she make the right decision? Robin hoped she would. "Please marry me, Tully," he said again.

Soon it was seven o'clock, and he started up the car and drove to 29th Street, made a right onto Kansas Avenue, and then a quick left onto a little road that led to the trailer park. Tully's car was parked in the front. The lights were on in the trailer, the curtains were drawn. Robin got out of the Corvette, closing the door gently, as he always did, to prevent damage to the hinges and the delicate Corvette fiberglass, and walked up to the trailer. He faintly heard noises from inside, talking noises, but it sounded like the TV. Robin knock knock knocked.

Moments later, he heard laughter. Robin's last thought in the instant before the door opened was, Is that a *man's* laughter?

The door swung open, and Robin DeMarco was greeted by a happy laughing face of a man. A man with a beard, Robin noted dumbly.

"Jer, who is it?" asked Tully, sticking her head out from behind the bearded man, her face still carrying remnants of the laughter from a moment ago. "Oh, my God," she said.

Robin gritted his teeth. "Oh, my God, is fucking right," he said.

Tully moved Jeremy out of the way so that she was now standing between him and Robin. Her face was no longer smiling.

"Robin, I am so sorry," she said. "I am so sorry."

He waved her off. She moved to touch him, and he backed away from her as if she had herpes. He stood on the hard ground, a few feet below the trailer entrance, while Tully loomed above him with a look on her face he could best describe as admission. Admission of the worst, and guilt, too. And regret.

He turned and walked quickly to his car, hearing her bare feet coming down the three steps.

"Robin," she said, and he felt her touch his leather jacket. "Please. Please don't go, please, let's talk about this."

He whirled around and faced her. She was half a head

shorter than Robin in her bare feet. She looked cold.

"Talk about what?" he hissed. "What, all three of us? I understand everything."

"Robin, you don't, please—"

"Tully!" he screamed. She put her hands over her ears. "Get the fuck away from me!" Robin screamed again, and then put his hands to his head. "What am I doing?" he said to himself, quieter. "What am I doing?" He quickly got into his car, slamming the door shut and nearly crunching his left foot. Tully came up close to the car with a pleading look on her face and placed her palms on the window. Robin punched the window from the inside, making the glass rattle. Again and again. He smashed the Corvette window with his fist four times before Tully took her palms away.

Robin started the car and put it into gear. Remembering something, he reached into his jacket pocket, rolled down the window, and threw the little wrapped box at her feet. "Happy Birthday, Tully Makker. Happy fucking birthday."

Tully picked up the small box and turned around to look at Jeremy, who was standing at the door. They went inside.

"I'm sorry, Tull," said Jeremy. "He didn't take it well."

"*I* did not take it well," said Tully, still holding the warm box in her hand. She had a terrible urge to smell it. To put it to her nose and smell it, smell *him*, to put it to her lips and touch it. She squeezed her fingers tighter around the box and willed her hands to stay on her lap and not put them up to her face.

Jeremy tried to talk to her, but there was actually nothing at all Tully wanted to talk about with Jeremy at the moment. They were getting ready to go out, but the way Tully felt, she thought she'd be lucky to make it to her brass bed.

Finally, after sitting there, half watching TV, half trying to talk to Tully, Jeremy said maybe it was best he went.

"Yes, I think that'll be best," said Tully. "I'll see you Monday, I guess," she added vaguely.

Tully closed the door behind him, locked it, and went back to sit on the couch. After an hour, she got up, turned off the TV, went back to the couch, and sat there until she fell asleep sitting up. She woke up at dawn. All the lights were still on. Looking down into her hands, Tully saw she was still clutching Robin's gift. She ripped away the wrap and opened the box.

After studying the ring close to the light, she put it on her finger. He's gone mad, thought Tully. I've never worn a ring before. My hand looks nice with it on, doesn't it?

It's heavy, she thought. Feels like it weighs about a pound. What has he done? What have *I* done? She looked at the ring again. I've never even seen one up close. Never one even half this big.

Tully slumped back on the couch. Well, well, she thought again. This will certainly pay for my move to UCSC. And was stabbed with guilt for those words, words she didn't mean. Going into the bedroom, she opened her nightstand drawer, took out the ankle bracelet he had given her, and put it on. Then she took out all the pictures of her and Robin together and placed them on the dresser drawer. There weren't many pictures. A couple of black and white photo booth shots, of Tully sitting on Robin's lap sticking a tongue in his mouth, and of Robin sitting on Tully's lap sticking a tongue in her mouth. Laughing. Two Polaroid shots of them at Bruce's farm on New Year's, and Tully's favorite photo: a three-by-five picture in Robin's pool, of wet Tully and of wet Robin behind her, kissing the back of her wet neck. She swallowed hard, but no use. The lump in her throat remained. A lump roughly the size of the diamond on her finger.

3.

Robin didn't call that week or the next, or the next. Tully reluctantly spent her spare time with Jeremy, all the while waiting for Robin to call her. In the last two years, two days had not gone by without him calling her.

She thought about taking the ring off, but couldn't do it, not even when she was out with Jeremy. The only concession she made was to put Robin's photos back in the drawer, but that gesture was as much for her own peace of mind as for Jeremy Macy's. Jeremy made no comment on the ring, but even if he did, that ring was worth a fight with a schoolteacher.

That ring was worth a fight with Hedda.

Five weeks passed, slowly.

Tully used to spend Saturday nights with Robin. In the wintertime, they slept late on Sundays, and Robin would cook them bacon and eggs or take her out for brunch. And then they would buy some flowers and go over to St. Mark's. In the summer they went to the ten o'clock Mass. In the winter they didn't. Now that she spent Saturday nights with Jeremy and woke up Sundays with Jeremy, going to St. Mark's was no longer an option. To go would mean telling. And Tully would never tell.

She went on Mondays instead, but going on Mondays made Tully feel like she was living at home and lying to her mother. Having to sneak around at twenty, because she did not want Jeremy's prying eyes on her and prying questions, made her feel *caged*. And not a bird that was caged, either; no, something larger than a bird. Something that slept twenty hours a day and roared the other four. *Caged*. At twenty.

To irritate her further, Jeremy wouldn't cook her breakfast, nor would he take her out for brunch. She asked him about it once, and he said going out for breakfast was a silly waste of money when there was so much food in the house. "Uncooked food," Tully pointed out. So Jeremy cooked, but only once. He did not like eggs himself, nor bacon. Breakfast consisted of dried chicken sausage and unbuttered burned toast. Grumbling, she began making and buttering her own toast and having some cereal with it. After that, on Sundays, she said she was not particularly hungry and was happy enough with her Product 19 and a cup of coffee. Jeremy did not drink coffee and occasionally tried to point Tully away from the dangers of caffeine and whole milk. Reminding him that they became acquainted over a cup of coffee, Tully ignored him. She could not ignore the fact, however, that she could not buy flowers and go to St. Mark's.

Fed up, Tully picked a fight with Jeremy one Sunday. She asked him to go so she could study, and he resisted, telling her she was full of shit.

Tully then contemplated taking him with her and ordering him to ask her nothing, but she knew Jeremy well enough by now to know that wasn't possible. She thought about telling him the truth, but the idea of *that* discussion filled her with dread. There was just no way to affect a toneless voice to tell Jeremy about *her*. Not that Tully ever tried, but she had no desire to, either.

Tully would almost rather live with her mother again.

So she picked a fight, and Jeremy left. Waiting what she

thought was a reasonable time, Tully rushed out to the florist to buy some carnations and then went to St. Mark's.

Tully sat in her wire chair at St. Mark's for the first time on a Sunday in five weeks while the Kansas wind blew away all the flowers.

The following Monday night, Tully and Jeremy made up. They were lying in bed together after having some rocking sex, and Jeremy whispered, stroking her leg, "Remember your poem?"

"My poem," Tully said, uncomprehending.

"It was always a hot summer in the days we used to—"

"Okay, okay," she said. "And?"

"Did you write it for Jennifer?"

Astonished, Tully lay very still. One sheep, two sheep, three fucking sheep, she couldn't—

Jennifer! *Jen-ni-fer!* Why, Tully tried never even to *think* those three syllables, much less speak them aloud, and yet, here they were, spoken *at* her by a total stranger. *JEN-NI-FER!*

Tully remembered showing that poem to Mandolini, many many moons before this evening, many many moons before March 26, 1979. After hearing it, she said, "Tully, you're full of it. You didn't write this. You have trouble signing your name to a Christmas card." Tully had argued that she really did write that poem, and Mandolini continued not to believe her. But that was then, when they were just ten . . . and JEN-NI-FER's disbelief was okay with Tully.

A few months ago when Tully had dug up the poem, she dug it up to pay tribute to—among other things—*disbelief*, profound and shocking.

Now Tully lay there, wondering dumbly if she had ever mentioned *her* by name to Jeremy Macy, knowing full well she never had, *never*, because Tully didn't mention *her* to anybody. Already the animals were being let out of their cages, there was a roar inside her, and in front of her eyes was the veil that came down rarely, but come down it did. The last time was when she nearly shot and killed her mother. The veil of red mist.

Yet there he was, lying beside Tully, innocently having asked her something he could have found out one way, and one way only. It was a good thing her back was to him. Tully clenched the quilt between her fingers and bit her lip until she whimpered. She tried to count the number of little black checkers on the dirty wallpaper, and it took her a good few minutes to be able to answer him.

"No," she said finally, clearly and quietly. "I wrote it when I was nine years old for my father."

"Oh. Your father died, right?"

"I don't know," said Tully as quietly as before, lying just as still, her lip still between her teeth. "Is that the same as being dead?"

A few minutes ticked by.

"So, who is Jennifer Lynn Mandolini?"

Tully screamed and shot out of bed. "I knew it! I fucking knew it!" she shrieked, standing naked before him. "You followed me, Jeremy. You fucking followed me!"

"I did," he admitted casually. "First time."

She ran to the bedroom door, opened it, and smashed it with her fists, over and over and over. "Goddamn it! Goddamn it! Goddamn it!" Tully kept repeating. Finally she pointed to the living room. "Get out, please."

Jeremy was still in bed, but now he looked surprised. "Tully, I'm sorry. I didn't realize—I didn't think you'd—I'm sorry, please. I just had this feeling you were hiding something from me."

She was standing at the bedroom door. "Get out, I said."

He stood up and put on his jeans.

"I thought you went to see Robin."

"Uh-huh, sure. What, in church?"

"I didn't know, for God's sake! You bought flowers. I thought you bought the flowers for him, I went a little nuts, okay?"

"Okay," Tully said icily, her lip bleeding. "Now get the fuck out."

"Tully, you're turning me off, you have been turning me off for the past month, now please don't turn me off!"

She said nothing, staring at the floor.

He came toward her, stretching out his arms. Tully furiously swiped her fist across his face. "I said—GO!" she panted.

He backed away, holding on to his cheek. "What is wrong with you?" he yelled. "You're crazy!"

She came after him with her fists, pushing him backward on the bed, grabbing the glass of water on the night table, and throwing it against the wall. Jeremy got up quickly off the bed; his face was red and angry. "Don't touch me! You have no right to touch me!" he yelled.

"GET OUT!" she screamed back.

"Please," Jeremy said, his voice lower. "Please tell me what I've done. I'm sorry. Please."

"You fucking followed me!" Tully shouted. She took several deep breaths, but it came out more like wheezing noises of a dying animal.

"I already said—"

"GET OUT!" she screamed, and Jeremy grabbed the rest of his clothes and quickly left, muttering, "You need help, Tully Makker. You need professional help. You just can't work all your problems out with silence and screaming, you need help—"

"GET OUT! GET OUT! GET OUT!" she screamed, pressing her palms to her ears.

Jeremy left. Afterwards, Tully paced the length of the trailer from bedroom to living room and back again for a long half hour until she was finally calm enough to sit on the couch, hands between her knees, and count sheep and the rust stains on the metal TV stand, and think of trees.

Tully did not see or talk to Jeremy for the rest of the week. She did not go to his class, she did not return his phone calls. The following Sunday she went to St. Mark's. She kept looking around like a cornered raccoon, but could not relax and stayed only a few minutes.

4.

Two days later, Tully went to see Robin. She took Route 24 instead of the turnpike to Manhattan because 24 was more scenic. But it was six-thirty in the evening and pitch black in the Kansas night where the prairie and the cottonwood-covered hills lie underneath the starless sky, with no man-made lights to break up God's darkness.

Tully was worried. She fidgeted with her ring as she drove, thinking, What if Robin really doesn't want to see me again? What if he wants the ring back? Well, I'm not giving it back.

He shouldn't have dropped it at my feet if he didn't want me to have it.

She flicked on her brights and drove slower. She usually liked to drive at least eighty on the highway, constantly getting stopped by the courteous Kansas State Troopers. Tonight she crawled along at about forty, letting other cars honk and pass her on the two-lane road. Tonight Tully was worried. Well, if he doesn't want to see me anymore, I'll sell the ring. I swear I will. I bet I can get a couple of hundred for it. At least two hundred dollars. *"That'll buy my way to San Jose,"* she sang softly.

And then Tully felt guilt again. She had already received and filled out the college transfer application forms from UC at Santa Cruz and sent them off with a $30 nonrefundable registration fee and her college transcript. Her college transcript, with her 3.78 grade-point average. What was the point of driving out to see Robin? Tully slowed down to thirty. What's the point even if he *doesn't* turn me away? I'm leaving anyway. And he's not going to come with me. He loves it here on the goddamn cottonwood prairie. He loves his store, he loves his home, he loves the tall grass and the tornadoes. She slowed down to twenty and then stopped by the side of the road. And what does he mean by giving me a ring like this anyway?

Why am I going to see him? It's been over a month, I should let it go, just let it go. She briefly debated turning back. But Tully wanted to see Robin.

She waited outside DeMarco & Sons. It well after closing time, though the lights inside were still on. Robin's store was one of twenty-seven stores strung together like an outdoor arcade—recently refurbished, the mall offered cobbled sidewalks and protective roofs for the customers' shopping convenience.

Tully got out of her car and walked over to the store. Through the glass, she saw Robin closing down the cash register. One of Robin's assistant managers saw her and waved with his hands. "Sorry, lady, we're closed."

Tully pointed to Robin. The assistant manager mouthed something to him, and Robin looked up. From fifty feet away, Tully could see his dark chocolate eyes. He came over to the door and unlocked it but stood in front of her, blocking her way.

"Hey," he said. "What's up?"

"Not much," Tully said lightly. A long time ago, he used to leave early on Wednesdays to come see me, she thought. Robin looked wonderful. His recently cut hair was razor short in the back and long layered in the front. He had lost some weight. "What's up with you?"

"Not much. Just closing up. What are you doing here?"

"Nothing. Thought I'd drop in."

He studied her coolly. "Well. It's good to see you. Is everything all right?"

"Fine, fine," she said, and then felt awkward. He doesn't want to see me, she thought. Just like I always suspected. He blew up, and now that's it.

"Well, listen," Tully said. "I just wanted to say hi." She stepped back a few feet. "I'll be going now. You take care."

Robin stepped out of the store after her. "Wait," he said. "Do you want to talk?"

"No, actually," she replied, smiling. "I want to eat. I'm famished. Let's go to Mike's. My treat."

"Your treat?" Robin said, raising his eyebrows. "Huh."

They went to Mike's—their favorite Mexican spot in Manhattan.

They ate in relative silence. Tully asked Robin about his brothers, about the store, about rugby.

"So what's up, Tully?" he asked her after she ordered her dessert and he was still finishing his fajitas. "Did you come to return the ring?"

"I will never return this ring," she replied staunchly. "Never."

"Well, that's nice," he said. "You might be able to get a bit of cash for it."

"Robin," Tully said softly. "Don't be mean to me. I'm sorry."

"What are you doing here?" he said.

She shrugged. "You haven't called me."

"Not much to say," Robin answered.

"I thought you might've wanted to talk," she said.

"Again," he replied. "Not much to say."

"I'm sorry," said Tully. "I didn't tell you for ages because I didn't want to upset you."

Robin's eyes widened. "For *ages*?"

Tully corrected herself quickly. "No, well, at first there was nothing to tell." She added, "It seemed like ages. It was only two months, actually."

"How long have you been sleeping with him?"

"Since Thanksgiving."

Robin breathed in sharply. "Gee, and I had thought I had a lot to give thanks for," he said.

She looked down into her fried ice cream and said nothing.

"Who is he, Tully? Who did you take up with?"

She told him.

"Your English Comp teacher?" He smiled humorlessly. "I didn't think any of them liked girls." Tully kept her mouth shut.

"So does he know about your plans to flee this part of the country come your first available opportunity, or are you keeping him in the dark?" Robin had stopped eating and pushed his plate away.

"He knows," said Tully quietly.

"Tully," Robin said, his hands below the table. "Tell me. Why? An English teacher, Tully? Do you do subjects and predicates when you fuck? Does he quote you Milton while he's going down on you? What?"

"Robin, please," said Tully, embarrassed and ashamed. "I'm sorry, okay?"

"Tell me why."

"I don't know why, okay?" she said heatedly. "He's an older man—"

"So am I," interrupted Robin.

"*Much* older," pointed out Tully. "He's from far away, it's just a new thing, it's—"

"A new thing?" exclaimed Robin. "You're telling me that every time a new *thing* comes along, you're going to grab on to it? Oh, that's great, Tully Makker. That's just great."

"I'm sorry, I didn't mean that," said Tully hastily. "Robin, try to understand, I want to leave this place anyway. He's just someone nice to pass the time with until I go."

"Right, Tully," said Robin. "Right. So," he added with mock brightness, "it sounds like he is all you want. What do you call me for, after a month?"

Tully stared at him with feeling. "Because I miss you," she said.

They made love in the car for old time's sake. They couldn't wait. It was cold, but Robin kept the motor running. Then they went back to Robin's house and made love again. Afterwards, they lay in his bed. Tully was in the crook of his arm and was stroking his chest as he was playing with her hair and kissing her lightly on the head. "Tully, Tully," he whispered into her hair. "I missed you, too. I thought I would go out of my head, me and my pride."

And she lay there and nodded her head, listening to him, and to the snow.

"Tully, please, please come back to me, come back to me, you won't regret it. I'll make you so happy . . . I'll make your life so happy . . . I'll buy a big house where we both could live . . ." he said to her, and she chuckled.

"You should see the house I want," she said. "You'd change your tune real quick."

"I know what house you want," Robin said immediately, lifting himself up. "I know the house. I drove by Texas Street once, because you used to talk about a house on Texas Street. I drove by it. I knew it could only be one house, the one at the end of the block with the white picket fence that needs paint. It is a magnificent house, Tully."

"Mmmmm," she conceded.

"Tully, do you like my ring?" He went on before letting her answer. Tully thought Robin's eyes were like live wire. "Because I bought that for you with a purpose, I wanted to do something special for you, listen, you don't have to answer me now, but did you read the inscription on the ring, I have a whole plan, I want to tell you about it, I know you'll like it, I *hope* you'll like it. Listen to me, it's a good plan. And I will sacrifice something, too, I will."

Robin took a deep breath, and so did Tully. "Are you done now?" she said, smiling. "What inscription?"

"You mean to tell me you put my ring on your finger and didn't even read the inscription? Tully!"

"Inscription? Must be a very short one," Tully said, taking the ring off and turning on the light. "I can hardly make it out. What does that say?" She peered on the inside of the band, and then she stopped smiling.

"Robin," she whispered. "Does that say, 'Marry me, Tully'?"

He nodded, a hesitant smile on his lips.

"Robin, are you asking me to marry you?"

He nodded again, muttering, "Marry me, Tully," while the remains of his smile slowly evaporated.

Tully sighed, clutching the ring in her hands. "Oh, Robin," she said, turning to him. "Poor you. You bought this ring and came over to my trailer to ask me to marry you. I am so sorry."

"Tully, I don't want you to see him anymore."

"Of course you don't," said Tully. "And he doesn't want me to see you."

"What do *you* want?" Robin asked.

Tully shook her head sadly. "I don't want to marry you, Robin."

He wasn't smiling at all anymore. "Why?" he said, bowing his head. "Do you want to marry *him*?"

"Even less," she said. "Oh, Robin. Why do you have to bring up marriage . . ."

"Tully, listen to me, we'll get married, and I will buy you that house. I will buy you your house on Texas Street."

She laughed. "While what? While you live in this house in Manhattan?"

"No," he replied. "That will be *my* sacrifice. I love my house, and I love Manhattan, but I will move to Topeka with you. I will live on Texas Street in our house with you."

"You would, would you?" She paused. "How far would you move out of Manhattan for me?"

"Commuting distance." He smiled. "We'll go to California on our honeymoon, how's that?"

She waved him off. "No honeymoon. Robin, you don't understand. I don't want to get married."

"Not at all?" he asked.

"Not at all," she replied.

"Not ever?" he asked, bewildered.

"Not ever," she replied resolutely. "Not ever."

"But children? What about children? You want your kids to be illegitimate?"

"Children?" She laughed. "Robin, no children! I'd rather be married!"

"Oh, Tully," he said, turning away from her. "You're making me sad."

She leaned over and put her head on his back. "Please

don't be sad. How can I possibly marry you? I want to go to California."

"Is that all?"

"That's all."

"You mean if I went with you to California, you'd marry me then?"

She kissed his shoulder. "No," she said. "But going away makes it really impossible."

Robin turned to her. "So what would you do, Tully, if you ever became pregnant? What would you do? Have an abortion?"

Tully turned away, still holding on to his ring in the palm of her hand. "Robin, I'm not going to become pregnant. Have I told you that taking the pill has become a religious rite with me? I kneel down by the side of my bed, pop out one of the pills, put it on a silver tray, look at it lovingly, say a few reverent things to it, cross myself, put it in my mouth, roll it around for emphasis, and swallow it with a full glass of water. I then lie down and wait for it to absorb into my system."

"Ha-ha," said Robin.

"I'm religious about my pill. The pill is my Church," she said.

"I thought St. Mark's was your Church," said Robin.

Tully glanced at him coldly. "Don't talk that way," she said.

He quickly changed the subject. "Okay, the pill. Even the pill sometimes fails," Robin said. "What would you do?" he repeated. "Would you have an abortion?"

Tully tried to count to—

"Robin, I really can't stand that question," she said, squeezing her hands together. "In any case, is that a Catholic boy talking? Or is that the possible father of a child talking? Remember, Robin," she said meanly. "If I get pregnant, the baby might not be yours."

His face got hard. "Thank you, Tully," he said, "for driving that particular point home, as if I missed it." They were silent for a while. Tully felt the drafty cold air coming from the window.

"I'm just asking," said Robin after a while. "Would you have an abortion?"

"Robin, stop it!" Tully snapped. And then said, calmer, "No, I would not."

"But children, Tully," he said beseechingly. "Wouldn't you like to have a wonderful happy baby, to play with, to teach, to love? Wouldn't you like a baby all your own?"

"Holy God, Robin," Tully said, sitting bolt upright. "That is exactly what I do not want." Her fingers were shaking when she lit her cigarette and inhaled. "Listen, what are you talking about? You must know me a little by now. Happy baby? To teach, to love." She let out a dry, sarcastic laugh. "To teach what? To love with what? Look, I have no illusions about myself. I know I have no love in my heart. And babies need so much love. It's like water to them. They become dead inside without being loved. They become fallow. Fallow land cannot grow loving children. It can only grow fallow children, who will in turn pass their barren souls to their children, their stark and empty souls to their children."

Robin shook his head. "Tully, that's absurd."

"Robin, I'm telling you. That's how it is."

"Tully, you're not barren," he exclaimed. "You're not. Look at the way—"

"Look at the way what?" she said rudely.

"Look at the way you loved Jennifer," he quickly said.

Tully stubbed her cigarette out and lay back down, with her back to him, and said quietly, "She was the only one I ever loved. She was the only cactus in my desert. She needed so little. But children have unbelievable needs."

He took her by her shoulder and made her turn to him. "I'm sorry about that. Right. I get it now. You won't marry, won't have any children, but won't have an abortion if you were to become pregnant? Well, Tully Makker, you're not God, you know. Sometimes that *choice* is just not up to us. Anyway, if you feel so strongly about it, why don't you just have your tubes tied?"

She tried to turn away from him, but his hand was still on her shoulder keeping her to him. "That seems kind of extreme," she finally said. "I'm only twenty. Anyway, the pill is ninety-nine point seven percent effective."

They lay in silence again, she trying to put the animals in their cages, imagining what an ocean might sound like, what palm trees might look like.

At last he let go of her, and she turned away. Robin touched her back. "Tull, honey. I'm sorry. I don't want to make you feel bad."

"I'm sorry, too, Robin," she said. "I loved that ring."

"Don't you ever return it to me," he said. "I'd rather you throw it in Lake Shawnee than give it back to me."

They made love again, and afterwards, Tully whispered, "Robin, if I were to stay in Kansas and marry anyone, I would marry you—does that make you feel better?"

"No," he said. "Would you have babies with me?"

"Never, Robin," she whispered. "Never."

After a few long moments, Robin said, "Would you stop seeing *him*?"

"I don't know," she said honestly. "I'll try, okay?"

"Do you love him, Tully?" he asked, and Tully was seized with pain, seized with tenderness for Robin, who had never in two years asked her if she loved *him* and yet mustered enough guts to ask *that*.

"I don't know," Tully said, wanting to be honest, wanting not to hurt him. "Really. I don't know."

Ask me, she thought, ask me, Robin. Have even more guts, if that's possible. Ask me if I love *you*, Robin DeMarco.

But he didn't, and much later, Tully, realizing he wouldn't ask, said, "Robin, would you buy me that house if we just lived together?"

"Never," he whispered back. "Without being able to call you my wife, I might as well live with you in the trailer, ready at any moment to be swept away by a tornado or thrown away when you're done with me."

5.

"Jeremy, I saw Robin," Tully said right away when she and Jeremy saw each other again. He picked her up after work and they sat shivering in the parking lot at Casa Del Sol with the temperature at five above zero.

Jeremy said nothing for five minutes.

"When my wife told me she was leaving me for another man," he said at last, "I said nothing then, too. Now sitting in front of you, I can't find any words. I know so many. Why can't I find just one?"

"I'm sorry, Jeremy."

"You must be saying you're sorry a lot lately, Tully."

She looked out into the parking lot.

"I can't explain," she said.

"Did I ask you to?"

"I missed him a little."

"I understand."

"I'm sorry about the other night," she said, but didn't sound like she meant it.

"No," he said. "*I'm* sorry."

"I lost my temper. Do you know how I felt?" she said. "Like I was on a hospital table, with my legs wide open, and you were sticking a speculum into me and had all your residents right behind you, saying, 'Would you look at that? Would you just look at that?'"

"Let me ask you, Tully," Jeremy said quietly. "If I had followed you anywhere else but there, would you have been half as upset with me? A fraction as upset?"

"I don't know, Jeremy," Tully said coldly. "We'll never know, will we?" And then she added, "Probably not."

He started to speak, then thought better of it and just said, "I'm sorry."

Tully didn't look at him.

Jeremy said, "I was going out of my mind with you. You never ever give me an inch. How can you blame me for taking an inch? I thought you bought flowers for him."

"Okay," she said.

"So what now? You don't want to see me anymore?" he asked.

She cracked her knuckles, then said, "I thought maybe you wouldn't want to see me anymore."

"Is that what you thought?" said Jeremy caustically. "Well, I'm too old to play these games. If you don't want to see me, tell me. Tell me to my face."

She couldn't look at him. "Not for a while, okay? I really need someone not to ask me any questions right now."

"Right now?" said Jeremy. "You mean ever."

Tully didn't speak, so he said, "Okay, I won't ask you any questions."

"No," said Tully. "Not even in your head, Jeremy." She blew out into her hands. "Listen," she said, "it's been a hard few years. Hard, you know. I'm doing my best to keep it all together, but I can't do a good job when you start prying, asking, wanting. You make my job harder. So I want to have time to settle back into my armor while you settle back into not expecting too much from me. Because I really can't give you very much. I may not be clear about a lot of things, but I'm clear on this. I haven't got a lot."

"You've got plenty, Tully Makker."

"I've got nothing," she said slowly. "I'm tired of all of you. Jeremy, you know what your selling point had been with me? That you didn't know anything about me. Anything. That was the best thing about you, Jeremy Macy. Now that you've in one clean swoop taken that away, I don't know what to do with you. I already have someone who pities me, you know."

"I don't pity you, Tully," said Jeremy. And then he added sullenly, "Robin knows about Jennifer."

"Robin used to go to St. Mark's with me sometimes," said Tully, breathing heavily. "He used to wait in church for me."

"Ahh," said Jeremy, and then, "I saw him there. Inside the church."

Tully nodded. "He told me he saw you there. Both of you spying on me."

"What could I have done? Killed him? Beat him to death in front of the altar?"

"You shouldn't have followed me at all."

Jeremy took a deep breath. "Yes. But yet you don't feel he violated you, only I."

"Only you," she replied. "That part of my life he knows about. I can't help that with him. I wanted to help it with you. I wanted you to have that advantage."

"Why does he know about *her*?" demanded Jeremy. "You told him?"

She stared out of the side window. "He knew her." And then, "She introduced us."

Jeremy said, "I thought you met him at a party."

"Yes," said Tully, sinking back into the seat and closing her eyes. "*Her* party."

Jeremy touched her softly. "What happened, Tully? Tell me what happened?"

She replied without opening her eyes, "I don't know what happened." And Tully thought, She just couldn't tell heaven from hell.

10
A POSTCARD FROM HOME

March 1981

It was difficult for Tully not to see Jeremy. She went to
his Advanced English Comp on Mondays, Wednesdays, and
Fridays from ten to eleven in the morning. After their talk, she
didn't stick around after class on Monday, but on Wednesday
they went to have coffee together, and by Friday he stayed
over. When Tully saw Robin on Saturday night, she was so
racked with guilt at seeing his happy face that the following
Monday morning, she informed Jeremy it was really over and
she would not be able to see him anymore. Jeremy, flustered,
said he wanted to meet her later to talk about it.

In the evening, while Tully was waiting for him, she wrote
Julie a letter.

March 23, 1981

Dear Julie,

*Thanks for writing. I can't wait till you come home for
the summer. There'll be some relief from Robin and
Jeremy, and Shakie, too.*

*Last time I wrote, I was being followed to church by
two men. Since then, not a lot has changed. Jeremy is
supposed to come over in an hour or so, so we can talk
about why I don't want to see him anymore.*

I used to like the spring.

*I used to smell the air and look forward to so many
things. The smell of flowers and the warm, strong wind
harbingered the summer. Harbingered? Is that a word?
But nowadays, it's constantly storming. Twenty-four tornadoes this year and it's only the end of March. Remember when we were coming back with Mrs. Mandolini
from a day of shopping in Kansas City, and we saw a
twister? Mrs. Mandolini is screaming and praying and
carrying on, and yelling at the three of us to get out
of the car immediately and run down the slope, while*

we're sitting in the back seat unable to take our eyes off the black thing in the skies. Remember the noise when we got out of the car? It must've been really something because we didn't even hear Mrs. Mandolini anymore, all we saw was her mouth moving as she grabbed on to Jen, dragging her down the embankment, and Jen trying to shout back, "I'm not going if they're not! Absolutely not!" Remember?

I saw Mr. Mandolini at St. Mark's yesterday. It was pouring out. Kansas spring. He had a hat, but a lot of good it did him, between his hands. We put our flowers down; they, of course, got sopping wet. Then we went inside. Lit a couple of candles. He read the rosary. Knelt. I wanted to talk to him, and he was very polite but said he wanted to be by himself. Asked me to come and see him at Penney's.

So I did. After school today. He was busy, so I didn't stay long. Asked him how Mrs. Mandolini was, and he just shook his head, and said, "Not so good, no, not so good. Drinking." No further details, though.

So that's that. He asked me to come and see them soon, but I don't think he meant it, and I don't blame him—I'm surprised they're still in Kansas.

Jack Pendel isn't in Kansas. Oh, speaking of Jack, Shakie is getting on my nerves lately. She's getting serious with Frank Bowman. They see each other nearly every day. He's like her hairbrush: she is never without him. Even on Thursdays—when it's supposed to be the girls' night out. I think he is officially going to ask for her hand in marriage.

Casa Del Sol is good. I'm still in the restaurant part, though. They won't let a twenty-year-old serve drinks. I should tell them about my gun collection. The collection I could have if I wanted to have one.

I told Jeremy on Friday I couldn't see him anymore. I'm already a little sorry. But I can't stand seeing Robin's face. Honestly. And I can't stand him calling when Jeremy is here.

Robin, in the meantime, acts really self-assured. He doesn't take Jeremy very seriously. I don't think Robin believes I would actually leave him for Jeremy. And on the surface of it, he is right. Why should I? How could I?

But you know, Julie, there is something to be said for talking. I'm not a talker, and neither is Robin. I don't know if that's such a great combination. Jeremy on the other hand can't stop talking. Can't stop wanting to talk. And usually, we talk so well. Robin is more like: you don't want to talk about it? fine with me, let's fuck. Whereas, Jeremy is all for talking beforehand and afterhand and duringhand. He doesn't moan sweet nothings during sex like Robin does, but other times we communicate so well, and he is so smart. I really respect him. Though I have to say, Robin's sweet nothings have been turning into sweet somethings just lately.

You know what else? I like sleeping with Robin. He spoons me. Jeremy is always on the other side of the bed.

They both keep asking me what I want. Take me out dancing, I tell them. They laugh and call me funny. And then I think, leave me alone, will you. Forget about what I want. What I want you can't give me. Do what you want. Do anything. Dump me. Call me every name in the book. Stop calling me. Something. Just stop.

But in either case, they are good men, and they don't deserve to have their hearts broken by me. I'm only twenty years old, I don't want to ruin the life of a twenty-seven-year-old, or a thirty-five-year-old. They don't deserve it, and I'm a nobody to do that to them. Imagine, there is so much out there, and they are both wasting their precious time on me, while all I want are some undefined shells under my feet and some pebbles under my toes as I step into the Pacific. So I'm just going eeny meeny minie mo, and choosing Robin. Because in the long run, who cares? Come August, I'm in Santa Cruz. Where I should have been two years ago. I got a response from UCSC. "Admission pending final semester grades." My cum as of today is 3.6. Not too shabby.

Jeremy helps me study. Advanced English Comp with him is a lot of fun. We read Shakespeare and Wordsworth and Whitman to each other. I think they're so depressing.

*I read Edna St. Vincent Millay occasionally to Jeremy,
and she cheers me right up.*

*I'm sorry you broke up with Richard. It doesn't sound
to me like you liked him a hell of a lot or that the sex
was so great. Though I nearly can't believe you actually
had sex.*

I hear Jeremy's car. Gotta go, bye.

Love, Tully

*P.S. By the way, I stopped dancing at Tortilla Jack's.
Reminded me too much of high school.*

P.P.S. I'm real glad counseling helped you, Jule.

Jeremy looked over at Tully from the other side of the
couch. Tully liked the beard on his face, but she liked his
expression less.

"Jeremy, it'll be okay. I promise. Listen, I know this sounds
really dumb, but we can still be friends."

He rolled his eyes. "You're right, Tully. It sounds really
dumb."

She felt exasperated. "Jeremy, I don't know what you want
from me."

"Oh, I don't know. How about honesty? Fidelity? A little
affection?"

Tully moved closer to him on the couch. "Jeremy," she said.
"Please. Let it go."

"I can't let it go!" he exclaimed. "I don't want to let it
go," he said, softer. "Don't you understand? I don't want to
let you go."

"Please," whispered Tully. "Please."

"Tully," he said urgently. "I want us to be together. I want
to make you happy. You seem so unhappy to me, Tully, and
I think I can make you happy. I think I know a way."

Tully thought of Marches, and rains, and sunglasses, and St.
Mark's. "Do you?" she said quietly. "Do you know a way?"

"Yes," he said brightly. "Look." And he pulled something
out of his coat pocket.

"Take off your coat, Jeremy," Tully said tiredly. "What is
that in your hand?"

"A teaching transfer application."

"Transfer application? To where?"

He smiled broadly. "University of California at Santa Cruz."

Oh, my, Tully thought, closing her eyes and leaning back. Oh, my.

"Jeremy . . ." she began.

"No, listen to me. I'll come with you."

Tully shook her head, still leaning back on the couch.

"Listen. I will. We'll go together. We'll just get away from here and start fresh. We'll rent a—"

"Jeremy," Tully interrupted, really tired now. Exhausted. "Please. No. We can't. Jeremy—" Tully stuck out her right hand to him. "Look. Robin asked me to marry him."

Jeremy glanced at her hand. "You've been wearing that thing for two months."

"Yes, and he asked me to marry him. I can't go."

Jeremy stood up. "Well, I certainly can't compete in the net asset department. If you're going to choose him because of his checkbook, I suggest you go and let him buy you into a relationship. Did you say yes?"

No, actually, Tully thought. I said no. Why am I still wearing the stupid thing like I belong to him? Like I'm pretending I said yes.

Tully shook her head. "I'm still thinking about it. But I can't continue this anymore. I can't. It's too much work, and it's not worth it. It's not worth it for you, it's not worth it for him, and it's not worth it for me."

Jeremy sat back down on the couch, close to Tully. "You told him no. You don't want to marry him. You want to go to California. So let's go, Tully. We'll go together. Did you hear me?"

Tully heard him. She just couldn't answer him. "Let me think about it, okay?" she said. "Go now, and let me think." And before he was out the door, she called out to him from the couch, "Jeremy, I thought you said you'd never leave Kansas."

And Jeremy replied, "I'd leave Kansas for you."

On the twenty-sixth of March, Tully skipped her classes and went to St. Mark's. It was about sixty degrees and howling with wind. The skirt of her black dress flapped around wildly and her black sunglasses were blown off her face. Tully had dug the white carnations into the ground, but not deep enough. The flowers were still blown away. In the afternoon she sat in the back pew of the church and listened to Father Majette's monotonous reading of the Scriptures. After an hour, he walked up to her.

"Go, Tully, go," he said gently. "Look at your hands. You've been digging your flowers in. You should know by now that's useless this time of year."

She smiled thinly. "It's all right. Thank you for reading the Lord is My Shepherd for her."

Father Majette put his hand on Tully's head. "For you, Tully. I read it for you."

Tully leaned into his hand. "I'm having trouble," she whispered.

"I know," he said softly. "But Tully, you're not alone. The good Lord is carrying you, and he will see you through. Go on, Tully. Go on with your life."

"I'm trying to," she replied quietly. "I just don't know what that life is."

She continued to sit in the pew long after he left her. She was thinking about Robin.

My life is like a house that has been built too fast and is unstable, she thought. It was built with wood but without foundation, and it trembles when the wind hits it. My house has damp and is cold from the wet hard ground; its windows are broken and hammered shut. It's a house of little illusion. It's a house that's at any moment expecting to fall. Moreover, prepared to fall—having been rickety for twenty years. Nothing should surprise my house anymore. And yet I find that I am still surprised, constantly.

I had never expected nor bargained for one man, much less two. I had never expected nor bargained for two men to want me for themselves so badly that they nearly knock their own houses down in order to rebuild mine.

I had never expected to be bombarded with so many promises, so many pledges, so much intensity. I had never expected to be wanted. And in my house, it surprises and frightens me. I almost want my old house back, with the cold and the damp—one I understand and one I'm comfortable with. I feel, at the moment, everybody's life around me is being built on nothing, nothing substantial, nothing of form.

Is this what human beings go through in their quest for life? How can they stand it? I can't.

I haven't told Robin about Jeremy's quest for my broken-down house. I feel guilt, guilt that sits on my chest like a fat parrot and echoes all my deeds back to me: "What? With Robin again? How convenient! Don't forget to wash your hands after you're done with him! How convenient! Don't forget to look at the calendar. Don't forget what Jeremy looks like! How very convenient! Why don't you tell Robin you and Jeremy are going to California together? Tell him! Tell him! Tell him! Do the right thing. Tell him, and have enough guts to let him hate you. Tell him, Tully! Tully! Tully!" My fat parrot sits on my chest all day and screams all night.

I hope that when it comes time to do the right thing, I will know what it is. I hope I will do it and not look back. Because right now I feel like I belong in a trailer. Like I could be Tracy Scott, *should* be Tracy Scott.

By the middle of April, seeing Robin on the weekends and Jeremy during the week got to be too much for Tully. She gave Robin back his ring.

"Oh, no, please. Tully, why?"

"Robin, I just can't do this anymore."

"Do what? You told me you weren't going to see him anymore."

Guilty and uncomfortable, Tully said, "Robin, I know, but you're working all week, and I see him in class all week and it's just . . ."

"Just what? Just what? Tully, I told you, I'll move out here. Let me buy you that house."

She touched his cheek. "Robin, you've been very good to me. Better than I deserve."

"Then let me make you happy. Let me buy you that house."

Sighing, Tully smiled. "Robin, you just don't give up, do you?"

He stared at her tenderly. "Look what I'd be giving up."

Shaking her head, Tully got up off the couch and walked over to the trailer window. She stood there quietly, staring at Sears Automotive across the road.

"Robin, don't you see, I want to go away. I want to go to California. I mean, I got thwarted a little. *Things* got in my way. But I'm going. I don't want my life to be here."

"Here is home. There is nothing wrong with here. There is nothing wrong with that house on Texas Street."

Tully shook her head again. "Here is not home. Home is the Grove."

Robin stood up, too, and came over to her. "Get out from the Grove, for God's sake. You haven't lived there in years and you never will again. Forget it. It's gone."

"That's what you think," said Tully. "It doesn't go away. Whenever I look out of my window here, I expect to see that sewage plant and that turnpike."

"Yes, but instead, all you see is the railroad. Much better."

Tully was quiet. "Dr. Reuben called again. Or rather, he got one of his more courageous nurses to call me. She told me my mother was about to be put in the Menninger chronic ward and is asking for me all the time. She wanted to know if I had thought about it further."

Robin stood stiffly by her. "And did you? Think about it further?"

Tully glanced at him strangely. "No," she said. "You know I haven't. You just told me I was out of the Grove forever."

"I know, I know," he said quickly. "Just asking."

Tully continued. "Have a nice day, now, I said to the nurse. And that was that. I hope they'll just transfer her and leave me alone."

Robin couldn't look at Tully when he said, "In the chronic ward, Tully. In the *chronic* ward."

"Oh, Robin!" Tully exclaimed. "Give it a rest."

He grabbed her hand and held it. "Tully, what about that house? Let me buy you that house."

She tried to wrest her hand away. He held on tighter. "Robin, I don't want that house. I want to go to California."

Robin let go of her hand roughly, and said, "You're impossible. You're under the mistaken impression that your life is going to change once you get to California. You're forgetting, Tully Makker, you're taking yourself with you. You're not leaving your fucking self in Topeka."

She didn't know what to say to that, but she thought about the trailer and about the Grove and about her mother. And about St. Mark's, too.

"Who said anything about change?" she said slowly. "All I want is the illusion." The illusion of a college degree? The illusion of a good job? The illusion of an ocean?

"The illusion of what?" Robin said impatiently, moving toward the front door. He had the awful struggling face of someone trying hard to stay in control.

Tully saw the face and came after him. "The illusion of a life well lived," she said, standing between him and the door. "Please understand."

"I understand. I don't want the ring back. I only want you back. I told you before. Sell the ring and buy yourself and your poetry teacher a vacation."

Tully was going to tell Robin that Jeremy offered to go to California with her, she was going to tell him how much that meant to her, but seeing his face, she didn't want to tell Robin anything.

"Robin," Tully said in a conciliatory tone. "You don't even know if the house on Texas Street is for sale."

His face softened a bit. "I'll make them an offer they can't refuse," he said without smiling.

She reached for his arm. "Don't go," she said. "Stay here."

April 15, 1981

Hi, Jule,

"Ordinary People" won Best Picture! Can you just believe it? Good old Robert Redford. And we all thought he was just a pretty face. You haven't written. Does a computer science major even have time to go to the movies?

Meanwhile, there is something foul in this state of rainy Topeka. My two gentlemen from Verona are driving me up the wall. And it's only April.

Believe me, Julie, I try. Oh, I do. I go to Jeremy and tell him I don't want to see him anymore. He starts feeling bad. So then I go to Robin and tell him I don't want to see him anymore. He starts feeling bad. I feel bad because they're feeling bad. Robin is offering me the house, Jeremy is offering to go with me to California. But how can I break up with Robin if I'm still wearing his ring, which he refuses to take back from me? And how

*can I break up with Jeremy, who is a tenured professor
and has already applied to UCSC and is waiting to hear
on an interview?*

*I'm so tired of the whole thing. I'm just so tired all the
time. I'm smoking constantly, I'm sleeping worse than
ever, dragging my feet at work, and at school. My exams
coming up and are too important to blow just because I
can't make up my mind. I never knew this, Julie, but I'm
selfish. Selfish and indecisive. I don't like myself very
much these days.*

Please write.

Love, Tully

April 30, 1981

Dear Julie,

*I think if I don't hear from you soon, I won't hear from
you until after the exams. Why haven't I heard from you?
In any case, good old Mr. Howard Cunningham, a.k.a.
Mr. Hillier, is offering me the same internship as last
year. They are really dying for people in Foster Home
Recruitment. I asked him if I could go on "location"
(interview a foster family) once or twice, and he said,
"If there's time." The whole foster thing reminds me of
that game, you know, match the list on the A side to the
list on the B side. The B side is numbered 1 through
20, and doesn't match the order on the A side, so you
have to figure it out, and you only have a few minutes.
The Foster Department is just like that. Except on the A
side, there are about 50 foster families, and on the B side
about 150 kids. No wonder my old boss Lillian White
gives those poor kids to whoever wants them. Better than
keeping them at Youth Lock Up. I worked there. I agree.
There just has to be a better way. More foster families,
families who really want to do something for the kids.
You understand, how many of those 50 families are in
it only for those measly $7 per day? I'd say half, and
that's pretty sick. I guess you don't have any of these
heavy emotional conflicts, working with binary digits
and all.*

*How is Richard? Are you guys still talking? You didn't
tell me exactly why he broke up with you. If you broke
up with him, whatever he'd done must have been pretty
serious, because you went out with that Tom way past
the point of decency.*

*I haven't seen you in nearly a year. It's a good thing
I have Shakie to talk to a little. Though I'm not much for
talking but that's good, because Shakie is not much for
listening, so we get along real well. Plus she is always
with Frank, which makes communication even more difficult. I asked Shakie's advice the other day about this
whole stupid thing. I was telling her for fifteen minutes
straight about California and Jeremy and how educated
he is and how much he cares about my education and
about how we might be able to live near Santa Cruz and
about how Robin wants to marry me and buy me a house.
And you know what Shakie said? She said, "Frank is a
builder, he can build you a house."*

*I almost shook her. She then said, "Gee, I'm sure glad
I don't have your problems."*

"Yeah," I said. "Till Christmas."

She smiled. "Ahh, but my choices are clear."

I gotta go. Please write. Where are you?

Love, Tully.

*P.S. Topeka State Hospital called again. This time I
wasn't so polite.*

May 2, 1981

Dear Tully,

*All right, all right, don't panic. I'm writing. It's going
to be a short letter. Yes, Tully, you want to have your
cake and eat it too. You don't want to make your bed,
you don't want to lie in it, and those two men aren't
stupid. They know, if they just wait you out, one of them
will get you by default. They're in it for the duration, and
they know you won't make your decision. I never knew
you were so indecisive, Tully. I always thought you were
just . . . careful.*

*We'll talk when I see you. I'm coming home. In a
week. I need to wrap up my things here, and then I'm
home for two weeks.*

*You must not read my letters as carefully as you say
you do. I broke up with Richard, not vice versa as you
seem to think. I broke up with him because I didn't care
about him, much in the same way I didn't care about
Tom. But back then it was my Senior Year. I didn't
want to have a senior year without a boyfriend. I didn't
want to go to the prom without a boyfriend. That was
all. Even the fiasco with you and Tom wasn't worth not
having a date for the Senior Prom. And we had a great
time. (The prom was the first time I ever touched one,
you know what I mean?)*

*I'm sorry you didn't go to the prom. Going to K.C.
with Robin must've been fun anyway.*

*I'm still seeing Dr. Kingallis twice a week. She's been
really helpful. What am I going to do without her? But
she says I'm much stronger now and know my own heart
much better, I'll be all right. She has no idea. Hmm.
Maybe she hasn't been so helpful, after all.*

*I'll come to see you at Casa Del Sol when I get home.
Though it sounds like you're pretty busy. You might not
have any time for me.*

> *Love,*
> *Julie.*

*P.S. I don't know Jeremy, so I will reserve judgment, but
I do know Robin, and I feel bad for him. Why did you
have to take up with someone else in the first place?*

True to her word, Julie did come to see Tully in Casa Del Sol,
the week of Tully's exams. "Julie, I can't see you," Tully said
immediately.

"What a surprise."

"I'm only working because I need to eat."

Tully looked Julie over. Julie's hair got longer and curlier.
Also, she had gained weight. Her face was round and her
eyes were round. Her upper arms were round, too, noticed
Tully.

Julie came and sat down in one of Tully's booths and ordered the Casa Del Sol lunch buffet. After having three portions of enchiladas, Julie waved Tully over. Tully eyed the remains on the table. "Full, Jule?"

"I'll have some fried ice cream," said Julie. "Two cherries."

Tully brought it and sat down across from her. "Listen, what are you doing home? It's the middle of the exam week. Don't they have exams at Northwestern?"

"Sure. Didn't you get my letter?"

Tully did get Julie's letter, about ten days ago. But the ten days had been a haze of jealous fights and sleepless nights, of smoking a pack and a half a day and of cramming until the early mornings. Tully vaguely remembered the letter's contents. "Of course I got it. You said you were coming home."

"I'm home."

"Huh," said Tully. And didn't know what else to say. Writing letters was somehow easier. "Your mom and dad happy to see you?"

Julie shrugged. "It's a mixed blessing. Vinnie is happy to see me."

Tully looked around to see if any of her other tables needed help. Unfortunately, they didn't. "So . . . I'm glad you came to see me. Maybe we can go out."

"Maybe," said Julie evasively.

"Is everything all right?" Tully asked.

"Yeah, fine. Listen, I thought of something. You know what would be fun to do?"

Tully shook her head.

"Have a slumber party. Like we used to, remember? In the backyard? I'll get a couple of sleeping bags from my mom, you come over, and we'll sleep outside. We'll roast some marshmallows on the barbecue, how would that be?"

Tully was thinking of the English Comp final tomorrow and the *Taming of the Shrew*, which she still hadn't read. "Well . . ." she drew out. "When would you want to do this?"

"Whenever. Soon. When your exams are over? It'll be our little celebration."

"Okay, I guess," said Tully, standing up and backing away. "Yeah, that'll be good. Sure, let's do it."

* * *

Tully finally went over to Julie's house five days later, when all the exams were over and done with. Angela Martinez made a motherly fuss over Tully and later fed her homemade burritos and enchiladas. But Tully noticed that Angela talked to the kids and talked to Tully and the kids talked to Julie and to Tully, but Angela did not talk to Julie other than to address the perfunctories of the dinner table. Pass the rice, pass the salt, where are the napkins.

When the girls were outside setting up the tent, Tully cleared her throat. "So, Jule, what's the matter with you and your mom?"

Julie didn't look at Tully while she tied the ends of the tent to the posts in the ground. "Oh, you know, this and that."

So there was something. "This and that what?" asked Tully.

Julie looked straight up at her. "I've dropped out of school."

Tully sucked in her breath and didn't say anything for a moment. "You what? Why?"

"I don't know. Why not?"

Tully sat down in a lotus position on the cool grass next to Julie. "And for this you went to counseling? Good work. You call this being helped?"

"Ah, so you did read my letters. Dr. Kingallis says I need to work out my needs before I know what they are."

Tully shook her head. "Julie, that makes no sense at all. How can you work them out if you don't know what they are?"

"I don't know. Look, it's what I'm doing, okay? You and my mother."

"Your mother is right. It's stupid to drop out. No wonder she was upset."

"You have no idea."

"What about your dad?"

"Oh, he is funny. I know he's disappointed deep down, but he just kept saying, 'Angela, stop your whining, she's twenty, she'll figure out what to do, stop your whining.' And my mother is going, 'A commune! She's dropping out of school to live in a commune!' And my father is patting her on the shoulder and saying, 'It could be worse, *mia cara*, it could be worse,' and my mother is shaking her head and saying, 'Not much, not much.' It was a real sight."

Tully laughed and fell back on the ground. Julie lay down next to her. "You want a blanket?"

Tully got up. "No, just the opposite," she said, taking off her shirt and lying back down in her bra and shorts. "I want to feel the wet grass on my back."

Julie put a blanket under herself. "It's better with a blanket," she said.

The night was warm. Julie and Tully lay on their backs, arms behind their heads, and stared at the sky.

"What does your mother mean by commune?" Tully asked cautiously.

"I'm going to . . . Arizona. I met these girls in the college bar. We had a couple of drinks, got to talking, and they told me about this thing they have up in Arizona, called Sunshine Meadow. Every summer they go there and try to make vegetables grow in the desert. If the Jews did it with the Negev, why not them, right? So, anyway, they have this little piece of land. It belongs to somebody—I'm not sure who—and, like, twenty people go and live there, till the soil, get up before dawn, water their gardens, and cook their own food. Very primitive and wholesome. It's something I want to try."

"Sounds great," said Tully without feeling. "Do you know any of those girls?"

"Laura. My roommate. She's coming with me."

"Oh, good. Well, that sounds real cozy."

"What do you mean by that?" Julie asked defensively.

"Nothing. Drop out of school and go to the desert. Very nice."

"It's going to help me grow."

"Julie, you're not a tomato. You're a human being."

"Wait. Let me finish. It's going to help me . . . heal. Dr. Kingallis said it will be a positive experience for me."

"Oh, well, then. Dr. Kingallis should know, shouldn't she?" sneered Tully.

Julie said softly, "Where your treasure is, your heart will be also. Who said that? St. Matthew? St. Mark?"

Who cares? thought Tully. "Summer's almost here," she said. "It's so hot, and we haven't had a good tornado in a couple of days. The air smells real good. Jeremy and I go out to Clinton Lake once in a while, and the air smells delicious there, too. Warm and green."

"Do you see Robin much?" asked Julie.

Irritated, Tully said, "I see him once in a while. He works a lot. And he's taken up rugby, too. He's constantly hurt. Last week he broke his nose."

"Has Jeremy asked you to marry him?" asked Julie.

Really irritated by that question, Tully replied, "No, he hasn't. He knows I don't want him to. He knows Robin has and I said no. He says he wants to have the advantage of being different from Robin."

"Oh, I'm sure he is different from Robin," said Julie.

Tully took a deep breath and turned on her side to face Julie. "What is that supposed to mean?"

"I mean," Julie answered, "that there aren't too many men like Robin in this world. Good men are hard to find."

"Yes, but a good education you can throw away every day."

Julie threw her hands up into the air. "Who cares? Who cares? I want to live."

"Have you thought about where you're going *after* Sunshine Meadow? I'm not unduly worried, but it does sound to me like you're walking one step forward, two steps back."

"Well, I'll just hate to see what happens to you, Tully Makker, when you have your cataclysm."

"I'm not going to have one. I have one every Sunday. Little by little."

"Bullshit," said Julie. "Bullshit, Tully. My God, but where are you in the whole process? Have you even gotten over the anger yet? You can't even get on with the other three steps till you've done that."

"Thank you, Dr. Martinez. Is our hour almost up?"

"Do you ever go there? You ever walk past there? Sunset Court?"

"God, no," said Tully, thinking, God, I don't want to be talking about *her*.

"I went there yesterday," said Julie. "Just walked by on Wayne Street, to see if anyone lived there."

"Ahh," said Tully, looking at the stars.

"There was a car in the driveway, and I saw swings and a slide in the backyard."

"Well, that's great," said Tully. "You're dropping out of school and revisiting Sunset Court. I have a three point six cum and never visit Sunset Court. You call yourself healing?"

Julie turned her body slightly away from Tully. "Yes. I call this healing. *You* can't possibly heal, because you haven't talked about it to anyone."

"Oh," said Tully sarcastically. "You need to talk to heal, do you?"

"You need to do something!" said Julie loudly. "Something."

"I am doing something," Tully said, sitting up. "I'm working, I'm studying hard, I got straight As on all my exams, I'm going to California. I'm in a relationship with someone, for God's sake."

"With two someones, in fact. I'd say that's real progress, for sure."

"Oh, fuck you," said Tully. "Going to raise tomatoes in Arizona with some hippie chick, what do you call that?"

"Healing," answered Julie. "What would you call sleeping around with two men?"

Tully shot up from the ground and kicked the tent post. "Goddamn it, enough already!" she yelled. "Don't you get it? SHE'S DEAD! Dead! She's not dead for a little while, she's not even dead for a long while. She is dead forever! Who the fuck cares what guy or what state or what commune? When she was alive, you were too goddamn busy with your stupid history club to pay any attention to her. What do you think, now that she's dead, you can just drop out of school and heal? That's such bullshit. Go ahead, grow your hair real long and don't shave for days. See if that will bring her back!"

Julie stood up, too. "God, Tully, you're vicious." And she started to cry.

Tully watched her, tried to get her breath back, looked up at the stars and rolled her eyes, and then walked up to Julie and hugged her.

"She is dead," Tully repeated, her voice breaking. "Nothing will bring her back, Jule."

Julie cried harder, her arms tight around Tully. She cried for a long time, sobbed and sobbed, while Tully stood there and stared off into space, patting Julie lightly on the back.

"I miss her, Tully," Julie said, disentangling herself.

"We all miss her," said Tully, sitting back down on the ground in a lotus position and fumbling around the grass for her pack of cigarettes. She smoked one while Julie slowly stopped crying and settled back on the grass. Then Tully lit a second one. Her eyes were dry.

"You never cry, do you, Tully? Not even for her."

"I don't cry much," said Tully, taking a deep deep drag and closing her eyes.

They lay back down on the ground.

"I used to love school," Tully heard Julie saying. "Remember how much?"

"I remember," Tully said tonelessly, not knowing where to put her hands.

"Remember all those clubs I was in—Debate Society, Chess Club after *she* got me to join only to quit herself, International Pen-Pal Society. History Club?" Julie said sheepishly. "Remember all that studying? Not that you would remember the studying part so much. It was so funny. *She* would help me with my math, and we'd all be sitting together at her kitchen table trying to study. You didn't study, you were just along for the ride, for the company, right? You pretended to work, but you'd be munching chips and talking, and soon we'd all be munching chips and talking, and pretty soon it was time for dinner. We finally had to study in pairs, because as a threesome, we never got any work done. Remember?"

"Sure, I remember," said Tully, wanting to get up, light another cigarette, leave, maybe.

"I hope you're not disappointed, Tully, in me. I don't want you to be disappointed in me."

"I'm not disappointed in *you*, Julie Maria Martinez," said Tully, and thought, I am disappointed in *her*. Goddamn her.

"It's taken two years, but I've gradually stopped caring about school," Julie continued. "It was everything to me once, but it's nothing to me now. I couldn't fake it anymore. So I quit. Besides. I'm only twenty, twenty-one soon. There'll be plenty of time to go back to school, don't you think?"

No, Tully thought. You'll never go back once you leave. The statistics are against you, my friend. But she said, "Sure, you'll go back. If you want to."

"It's like . . ." Julie paused and blew her nose. "It was everything to *her*, remember? Everything in her life was for school. She took private lessons and had a tutor, and played the piano and danced ballet, and was surrounded by books,

books, books. She was going to be a doctor. She knew she wanted to be a doctor all the time I knew her, and I knew her before you. When we were five, she wanted to examine me, saying that she was going to be a doctor when she grew up and she wanted to start young."

Tully raised her eyebrows at this, in the darkness, and turned to Julie. Now, this was curious. The curiosity almost got the better of Tully, but Julie was crying again, and now was not the time, Tully knew.

"She was the smartest, the hardest-working one of us," Julie said. "She had a goal and her eyes were set. And yet, yet . . . when it came right down to it, her calling, her intelligence, her drive, her *life* all were just not important. All of it, not important enough! I sit here, and I'm amazed that all those things in her life weren't enough to outweigh *him*."

She stopped talking, and Tully was glad. She stared off into the sky and tried to find the Big Dipper. There's the North Star . . . The difference between her and us, Jule, is that we want to live, thought Tully. There's the Little Bear. . . .

"Tully, do you think she wanted to live, too? You think she did? Stood there, ready to fall, hoping somebody would catch her, and we . . . we just didn't catch her. Do you think that, Tull?"

"No, Julie," said Tully firmly. "She wasn't waiting for us to catch her. She wasn't calling out, she wasn't kidding around. The whole point was that she didn't want anyone to come and get her and bring her back. She wanted to be done with life like no one I've ever known. She wanted peace. She shot herself in the head with a .45. She was waiting for nothing but to fall."

Julie sobbed. Tully found the Big Dipper and then closed her eyes.

Minutes passed. "Have I told you about my latest addition to my dream collection?" said Tully mock brightly.

Julie wiped her face. "No. Tell me."

"I had it for the first time two Christmases ago, after Shakie came to me crying because Jack was leaving. I'm in my university dorm room and my mother comes to visit me. I take her to my room so that she can meet my roommate, who is not there. We're standing in the middle of my room, and all of a sudden my legs start to shake, and I realize I'm sweating. I smell blood. I smell that pungent smell of blood. I'm numb and afraid to move. I look slowly around the room, and I realize the air in the room is not clear, it's hazy and thick, and the haze is pink, pink from blood particles in the air. I turn to my mother in slow motion and ask her, inaudibly, 'Ma, can you smell that?' and she says no. I say, 'Ma, can you see that?' and she says no. And then she leaves the room. I'm left alone and I am too terrified to look, but that smell is coming from somewhere, from somewhere in my room. And then I become certain that there is a body and the body is under my bed. There is a bleeding body and it's under my bed. So I get brave, because I think: this is just a dream, this is ridiculous. I kneel down in front of the bed, pull up the bedspread, look under, and scream. Because Jennifer's severed head is bleeding under my bed."

Julie crossed herself twice. "Oh, my God," she said. "God help you."

"Amen," said Tully.

"Can you share something else horrible with me? Or is that all you got?"

"No, that's it."

"How can you sleep at night? Knowing *that* can come? How can you sleep?"

"Not well," Tully said. She coughed. "Once, I was so utterly disgusted with myself after waking up that I got dressed and drove over to St. Mark's. And slept there."

Julie crossed herself before she asked, "Tully Makker, please don't tell me you fell asleep in the—on the—"

"Hmm," said Tully. "The church was closed."

"Tully!"

"Julie, I fell asleep. Right on the ground. And it was all right. When I woke up, Father Majette was standing over me, praying. I think that upset me more than the dream."

"Tully, I'm sorry," said Julie, "but that's sick. Really. I'll take Sunshine Meadow any day. At least I could talk about Sunshine Meadow to people. I bet you haven't told that story to many."

"Not many," agreed Tully. "But Sunshine Meadow seems to me like walking in place. You know?"

"I know. But going to California is walking in place, too."

"No, it isn't. I sat in Tracy Scott's backyard for the whole summer two years ago, and in front of me as far as my sight could see was Tracy Scott's backyard. Now that was walking in place."

"You snapped out of it, though."

"Sure, I snapped out of it. When I realized I was going to be stuck with a little boy. And I didn't want to be stuck raising anything, not even chickens, much less little boys. Not anywhere, but particularly not in Tracy Scott's backyard."

"So you went to school and that solved everything."

"Everything. School is my ticket out of here. I'm going to UCSC on a scholarship. School is my ticket out of Tracy Scott's backyard."

Julie didn't say anything. And Tully didn't want to ask what Julie was thinking, so she didn't say anything either, just looked up at a sky that was so rich and bright it hurt her eyes. "*Stars,*" she sang, "*they come and go they come fast, they come slow . . . they go like the last light of the sun all in a blaze . . .*"

"Are you lonely, Tully? Have you been lonely ever since she died?"

Tully's hearing dimmed and her sight, too. She couldn't hear Julie well, and couldn't see the stars, either. Tully minded not seeing the Kansas stars more.

"Forgive her, Tully. God, forgive her. She didn't do it to hurt us."

"Oh yes. Oh, yes. She did it to hurt me. She knew I had nobody else. Nothing else. She knew, but she didn't give a shit."

"Tully, don't be so angry. What's the point? Go on with your life."

"What life? And this is you talking?" Tully smirked and quickly turned her face away. "How can I?" she whispered. "I still can't believe it, you know."

"Oh, I know. Abject denial," said Julie. "But it has been two years."

"It might as well have been two days," said Tully. "Two *numb* days."

"So let's talk about her, about *it*. I talk about it to Dr. Kingallis. It makes me feel better."

"I don't want to talk about *it*," said Tully. "Or about her."

"Tully."

"Tully, nothing. I look up at that sky, I look at the prairie hills around Topeka, and I feel such a vast emptiness, I think it's eaten me whole. I feel sick. I want to end it all. I wish she had never become my friend. And you, too, because it was through you that I met her. I wish I never knew her. There's nothing worse than this. Nothing. Not even the mute miserable years with my mother after my father left us."

"But Tully, do you feel lonely now? When you're with me?"

Tully turned on her side and rolled into a ball. "More than ever," she said, squeezing her eyes shut.

And then, Tully and Julie slept. Julie on the blanket, and Tully, half-naked, on the wet ground.

Tully dreamed of Jennifer. They were walking aimlessly through the rocky sands of Mexico, with nowhere to go, and no water with them. Jennifer asked Tully, Where are you taking me? and Tully replied, Where are you going? Following you, Jennifer said. I have no idea where I am, Tully replied. So they struggled but kept on walking. It was hot and they were thirsty. Eventually they began to slow down and thought of stopping, but they were in the middle of the desert.

So on they went and talked a little. Tully saw Jennifer's face. Round and burned by the sun. Her eyes were blue and her lips cracked.

Tully was glad to see Jennifer's face again.

They seemed to have walked for miles or years—the sun never stopped parching their lips and blackening their skin. They walked hardly speaking, but then after a long time, they saw a familiar-looking cactus and realized, terribly, that they had gone nowhere. This upset Jennifer. She stopped, turned around, and saw a man. He was a Mexican man, and a fellow traveler. She walked back, toward him, while he held out a flask of water. Oh, how Tully wanted that water, too! But she would not turn back. Could not turn back.

So Tully went on without Jennifer. She walked for miles, or years. Tully thought she was moving, but she couldn't tell because everything looked the same.

And then, in front of her, Tully saw the same Mexican man. Jennifer was no longer with him, but in his hands he held the flask of water. His hands were outstretched to Tully.

Tully woke up in the blue light of dawn and the first thing she saw to her right was the tent. *The* tent. The same gray tent that they all used to sleep in when they were children, and in the first moments of the morning, in the grogginess of being half asleep, Tully turned to her left and whispered, "Jen . . . ?"

She saw Julie. Tully turned quickly away. She breathed silently, and then lay on her stomach and rubbed her face into the dewy grass.

A few minutes later, she got up off the ground quietly, got dressed, and left.

2.

Julie woke up in her tent, stretched, looked over at Laura sleeping next to her. It was not a bad life, here in the middle of the desert, but getting up at dawn was a killer. It was her turn to go and get water from the well. She got out so as not to wake Laura, went to the outhouse, brushed her teeth, took two big buckets, and walked over to the well. After she got the water, she went to the young tomato seedlings and took the plastic off them that kept them warm in the cold night. As soon as the sun came up, the tomatoes turned into tomato sauce if someone didn't take off the covering.

She then went to the communal tent and made a big pot of coffee—enough to satisfy twenty groggy and cranky coffee drinkers. Finally Julie sat down, and while the coffee percolated, she leafed through a pile of newspapers and magazines and letters that was delivered to the compound twice a week by a mailman from the local post office, forty-five miles away. Julie saw a postcard of an aerial shot of Topeka. Plains, hills, and in the middle of it, Topeka. She would've recognized it anywhere. Smiling, she turned the card over. It was from Tully, dated August 5, 1981, and the inscription—exultation!—said only: *"I chose my teacher!"*

III

The
House
on
Texas
Street

III

The
House
of
Tezis
Street

Straightway I was 'ware,
So weeping, how a mystic Shape did move
Behind me, and drew me backward by the hair;
And a voice said in mastery, while I strove,—
"Guess now who holds thee?"—"Death," I said.
But, there,
The silver answer rang,—"Not Death, but Love."
—Elizabeth Barrett Browning

11

BACK HOME

September 1982

Julie rolled down her window with one hand and steered with the other. "Laura!" she feverishly exclaimed. "Smell! Smell that air! It's Topeka. I'd recognize it anywhere."

Laura shook her head. "Great."

Julie ignored Laura. She had gone away willingly from Topeka and traveled because she wanted to. She had chosen this life over a year ago. It wouldn't be forever, Julie kept telling herself. It was just for now. Because we're young, and it's fun, and why not.

Julie had stayed away for fifteen months because whenever she thought of the lushness of the Kansas cottonwoods bowing their leafy wings to the fertile earth, of the smoothness of the hills covered with the long grass, she felt a pain akin to only one other pain in her life.

Julie hated coming home. Hated it ever since the days of Northwestern. And hated it for hating it. She so wanted to love it again as she once had loved it. Topeka was still undeniably, interminably, pathetically *home*.

She brought a forced smile to her lips. "No, really, I've missed it, I've missed home. My parents are going to murder me for being away so long." *And Tully, too,* Julie thought, her smile fading. Tully, too, will murder me for not writing to her for fifteen months. I don't even know where she is now, Julie thought. The spasm of guilt that lately gutted her whenever she thought of Tully gutted her now.

She got off the Interstate 70 South that circled the city. There was the Ramada. There was the Holiday Inn. She took Laura past Capitol Plaza. Laura absentmindedly looked out of the window. Julie crossed over Topeka Boulevard and continued down 10th Street.

"How do you like it?" Julie asked, trying to sound jovial but still thinking of Tully.

"Hmm," Laura said. "A typical Midwestern town. No one on the streets. No one. Where is everybody, huh?"

Julie slowed down, looking to her right.

"Now, that's an impressive place," exclaimed Laura. "What is it, a Catholic school?"

Julie glanced at the stained-glass windows, the Tudor tower, the landscaped front. "That," she said woefully, "is my Topeka High School."

Laura studied Julie for a moment and then shrugged her shoulders. "Huh. So what's the big deal? Just a high school, right? We have a life now." She scratched her head and watched the road. "I don't even remember the name of *my* high school. I barely remember the year I graduated."

Julie drove slowly and watched the road, too, thinking that *she* remembered the name of her high school. *She* remembered the year she graduated. Thinking that high school had indeed once been a big deal.

Clearing her throat, Julie said, "Well, did you know that you're looking at the most expensive high school built in the United States?"

"Get the hell out of here." Laura waved her off.

"No, really," insisted Julie. "At the time they built it, it cost one point six million—"

"Jule, Jule. I don't mean 'Get the hell out of here, I don't believe you.' I mean 'Get the hell out of here, who cares?' Forget the fucking past already. We have a life."

Julie fell quiet. A life. Huh, Julie thought, borrowing the word directly from Laura. Some life. We have a station wagon and a tent. We drive around the country working as farm hands. We haven't shaved our legs in seven months, we don't know when we're going to get a shower next. Spectacular.

She turned right on Wayne, halfway down the block, and there was her house, freshly painted as always. I know when I'm going to get a shower next, Julie thought. It will be in about thirty minutes, in my beloved bathroom.

"Julie!"

"Mom!"

Angela Martinez embraced her daughter with great physical feeling, and Julie had to catch her breath. "Mom, Mom."

She laughed awkwardly, pushing slightly away. "Mom, this is Laura," Julie said, ushering her friend to the forefront. Angela looked the girl over and smiled. "Nice to meet you, Laura. We've heard a lot about you." She turned to Julie. "I wasn't expecting you home till next week."

Julie glanced at Laura. "I know, but we got freed up in Lincoln sooner than we expected. We have another job, though. Soon. A corn harvest. Near Des Moines. I'm afraid we can't stay as long as I wanted to. September is a busy month for us."

Angela shook her head. "Don't I know that? Your grandfather and my father, God rest his soul, was a migrant worker. Migrated his way from Mexico and worked like a slave in September and all the other months of the year so that his family wouldn't have to live a migrant life. It's nice to know his work wasn't in vain."

"Ma. Ma."

Angela just waved her hands. "You just got here, and already you telling me you can't stay long? You hungry? Dinner won't be ready till six. You know your father. Can I make you a sandwich?" The girls nodded. They followed Angela into the kitchen.

"Seen Tully, Mom?"

"Why don't you ask me about your brothers before you ask me about Tully, Julie Martinez."

"I know where my brothers are, Ma. I don't know where Tully is."

"Yeah," said Angela with a disapproving stare at her daughter and Laura. "I guess it's hard to find a pen and paper in the middle of a field."

"I guess it is, Ma," Julie said, thinking, I deserve it, I know I do, but why does she have to give me a hard time anyway? "Have you seen her?"

"Not seen Tully for a long time, Julie. Ten months? A year?" Angela said. "Last Thanksgiving, I ran into her at Dillon's. You were in her bad books."

Julie bowed her head. "I know. I haven't really been in touch."

"Haven't really been in touch?" Angela mimicked.

After what seemed like a long silence, Julie asked awkwardly, "How was she?"

"You know Tully," said Mrs. Martinez. "Couldn't get a word out of her. She didn't look so good. Wasn't taking good care of her face and hair, you know?"

"Did you ask her about California?" Julie said, biting her fingers. "She was supposed to be going to California."

Angela sighed. "The sum total of our conversation was: 'How you doin'?' I asked her. She mumbled something. Asked after you. I told you were traveling the country with no forwarding address. Told her to come over and read your letters. She never came."

"Where is she living now?" Julie asked.

"Julie, what am I, a mind reader? I don't know. She is *your* friend." She put the turkey clubs on the table. "Here, eat."

Laura ate, but Julie had lost her appetite, further upsetting her mother. She went to take a shower, but even the strong pressure of the hot water didn't feel good on her skin. What was Tully still doing in Topeka at Thanksgiving? Tully wasn't supposed to be in Topeka anymore by Thanksgiving time.

Exactly a year ago, last September, was when Tully's junior year was supposed to start at Santa Cruz. Why was she still in Topeka in November? Where was she? Well, maybe she just came back for the holidays, Julie thought, drying herself off. Yeah, right. What, to visit her mother? To visit Robin with Jeremy by her side? Right, thought Julie. Right.

Julie and Laura drove to Casa Del Sol, where they spoke to the hostess, who wasn't overly friendly, saying only that Tully had quit a long time ago and had not been seen for months and months. After a little prodding, Donna mentioned that Tully's old friend Shakie was still working at the Chanel counter at Macy's. Julie and Laura went to see Shakie at the White Lakes Mall.

Shakie was very busy, and the girls had to wait nearly a half hour before she could talk to them. Shakie looked better than ever, radiant, fresh-faced and well groomed.

Julie leaned closer to Laura. "She was our Homecoming Queen," she whispered.

Laura moved away, not taking her eyes off Shakie. "That's nice," she said.

"Julie!" exclaimed Shakie, finally coming over. "Tully wants to kill you."

"I know, I know," said Julie. "Where is she so I can let her?"

Shakie smiled. "Tully's prodigal friend. You been gone so long." Shakie cast a look at Laura. "Is this your friend Laura?"

Julie got a little flustered, apologizing hastily. "Yes, this is Laura," she said. "Laura, this is Shakie Lamber. Where is Tully, Shake?"

"Where is Tully, where is Tully," Shakie said.

"I guess she's not in California, huh?" Julie said, her face falling.

"I guess not," said Shakie. "But she's got plenty of palm trees in her sunroom. Her California room."

"Where is she?" repeated Julie weakly.

"Fifteen oh one Texas Street," said Shakie, and then the two of them stood silent as the Muzak played. Correction: Julie was speechless.

Leaning back against the counter, she wiped her brow in the air-conditioned department store.

Shakie looked askance at Julie and then at Laura standing nearby looking at herself in the mirror. "Tully's okay, Julie. Go and see her."

Julie turned to go, and then as an afterthought remembered Shakie herself and said, "Shake, how are you?" but couldn't hide her boredom.

"I'm well, very well. Do you know? I'm getting married in two weeks."

"In two weeks? Really? Well, that's great, Shake, that's great." And again as an afterthought added halfheartedly, "Congratulations. To who?"

Shakie's friendly gaze cooled a little. "To my fiancé Frank, of course. To who else?"

"To Frank! Of course! To who else?" Julie exclaimed, embarrassed.

"Tully must have written you about Frank. When you were still writing to each other."

"Oh, yes, she said you were getting real serious with him." Julie turned red.

Shakie stared at Julie coolly. "Two weeks," she repeated. "We're very happy."

"Of course, of course," Julie said uncomfortably. "I haven't written to Tully in a long while."

"No," said Shakie, casting a sideways—nearly derisive, it seemed to Julie—glance at Laura. "You haven't. Go and see her."

In the car, Laura said, "She is beautiful."

"Yes, she is," said Julie. "Very beautiful."

They drove in silence the rest of the way, straight up 29th to Texas Street, a dead-end street backing into the southernmost and sunniest side of Shunga Park. Number 1501. Julie heard even the unemotional Laura whistle when she saw the house with its red roof, its four columns, its sprawling porch. Julie sucked in her breath to keep herself from breathing out. She was trying to forget . . . *Jennifer's and Tully's flushed faces when one day ten years ago they brought Julie to this house they found. This three-tiered house with balconies bracing the second-floor dormers. With bay windows upstairs and downstairs, with fresh paint, with a huge front yard. A house belonging to somebody's dream. "What do you think of it, Jule?" asked Tully, nudging her, and Jennifer in turn nudged Tully, saying, "What can she think of it? What can anyone think of this house other than, it's just the most awesome house?"*

"The house needs paint," Julie heard Laura saying. "But I can't believe she lives in this house. Didn't you tell me she doesn't have a dime?"

"She doesn't," said Julie, breathing out. She slowly got out of the car.

The white picket fence in Julie's memory was torn down and replaced by a wrought-iron one with a creaking wrought-iron gate.

The lawn was sunburned, the grass long and flat to the ground. The weeds near the house looked like sand reedgrass and were as tall as the fence—about four feet, or fifteen months, fifteen months of having no idea what Tully had been up to. There were a few neat flower beds, but near the porch the brambles were ten feet high, reaching up sloppily to the second-floor balconies. Julie and Laura walked up the dusty, sandy path and up the stairs to the porch.

There was a swing on the porch and on the swing was a blanket. Julie knocked tentatively. When there was no immediate answer, she turned to Laura and said, "Let's go, there's no one home."

"Wait a minute," Laura exclaimed. "Knock again. Louder."

Julie backed away, shaking her head. "I should've come alone," she mumbled.

"What's the matter, Jule?" said Laura coldly. "Ashamed of me?"

"I'm not ashamed of you, Laura," Julie said, feeling ashamed. "For Tully I should've just come alone. Let's go." But now she heard footsteps, the large door opened, and in front of her stood Tully.

Julie stepped back.

"Tully?" she said inaudibly. Tully looked only vaguely like the Tully of old, and in her arms she held a naked baby boy. "Julie," Tully said, her voice low and flat, like the grass. Tully did not smile, Tully did not look surprised.

Julie noticed there was not a gram of makeup on Tully's pale plain face. Her hair was shoulder-length and straight, burned-out ash, almost the color of the grass, and before she heard Tully's voice, Julie thought that maybe this wasn't Tully at all. If it was, how come she, Julie, had forgotten how similar to Jennifer's ash hair Tully's hair was without all that bleach? "Come in," said Tully, and Julie knew it must be she. "Come in," Tully said, in a pale, plain voice, but deep, too, coming from somewhere in the throat. It was Tully.

"You must be Laura," said Tully. "Nice to meet you, Laura. This is Boomerang," she said, pointing to the squirming naked body in her arms. "Hold him, please, Jule," Tully said, stretching her arms out. "And for God's sake, whatever you do, don't put him down—he's an unstoppable force." She looked at him. "I'll be right back, I gotta get his clothes from upstairs. We were just having a sun bath."

Tully went away, while Julie stood and awkwardly held him. He was very naked and very squirmy. A passing thought occurred to her that he might pee, and soon enough he did. Julie held him away from her. Laura laughed. The boy was okay for about a minute and then started to cry.

"It's okay, it's okay," said Tully in the same flat tone, coming back with his clothes and a pitcher of iced tea and crackers. She sighed. "Mommy is here." She took him from Julie and they all sat down.

A long silence ensued, during which Tully poured the drinks, cleaned up the floor, and then dressed the boy in a sailor romper. Julie watched Tully and wanted to cry.

"So," Tully spoke at last. "How've you been?"

"All right," picked up Julie eagerly. "How have *you* been?"

"Very well," said Tully. "As you can see."

"How old is your little boy?" asked Laura.

"Little? He is huge. Weighs twenty pounds. That's five times as much as the fattest neighborhood cat."

"How old is he?" repeated Laura.

"Six months. Born March twelfth," said Tully without inflection.

"And his name is Boomerang?" Julie asked.

"Yes," said Tully. "Do you like it? I chose it myself."

"Very nice, yes. Why did you call him Boomerang?"

"I thought it sounded macho, like a football player or something. Nobody to be messed with. Boomer for short. Do you like it?"

Julie ignored the question. "Boomerang what?"

"Boomerang what," repeated Tully, without the question mark at the end. "I guess Boomerang DeMarco."

"Aaahhh," said Julie, glad she was sitting down, glad she could pour herself another ice tea and not have to look at Tully's face. *DeMarco!*

"So you got married," said Julie, not looking at Tully.

"Sure, I got married," said Tully. "Somebody's got to take care of us."

Julie couldn't look at Tully. "Are you still working for Mr. Hillier?"

"I'm a mother now. Boomerang is only six months old."

"Are you going to school?"

"I'm a mother now," Tully repeated, and again Julie could not look up to see her friend's lips move.

"So tell me, what are you doing nowadays?" asked Tully. "Still at Sunshine Meadow?"

Laura laughed; Julie didn't. "No," said Julie. "We gave that place up a long time ago."

"We went traveling," Laura explained.

"You did, did you?" said Tully. "That's nice."

Tully didn't ask, but they told her anyway. Mostly Laura told her. New Orleans, Key West, Mississippi, Georgia, New Mexico, Mexico, California.

"California," repeated Tully, and something in her gray eyes flickered momentarily, like the light of a firefly.

"How do you live?" Tully asked.

"Just the clothes on our backs, a tent, and a car," Laura replied. "Great life. No responsibility."

"No, none," said Tully, and Julie was surprised to feel herself wanting to tell Laura to shut the hell up.

"How many tents?" asked Tully.

"Just one," said Laura. "Great house you got."

"Yeah, thanks," said Tully. "Just one, huh? So you're kind of like sharing a home."

"A home, a life, everything," said Laura.

"That's nice," said Tully, and narrowed her eyes at Julie. Julie knew Tully's look of silent and mortifying reproach. *I should have come alone,* Julie thought for the twentieth time in twenty minutes. *I should have come alone to see my old friend Tully. Then I could have told her everything myself. I could have apologized, I could have explained. Maybe I could've heard her* really *talk to me. What happened?*

Tully rose. "It's naptime," she said.

"Okay," said Julie. "We'll wait till you put him down."

Tully looked at Julie and at Laura; her gaze was cold. "It's naptime for both of us," she said pointedly.

Julie bent her head in pained understanding. When she came over to hug Tully, Tully backed away. Julie kissed Boomerang's head and whispered to Tully, "I'll see you soon."

"Yes, you do that," said Tully loudly. "It was nice to meet you, Laura. Good luck." She walked Julie and Laura to the door and shut it behind them before they were across the porch.

2.

Later that day, Julie knocked on Tully's door around six in the evening, alone. Tully let her in.

"Boomerang sleeping?" Julie asked.

She heard his cry.

"Not anymore," said Tully. Bringing him downstairs, she opened up the top of her old cotton print dress and began to feed him. Julie sat there quietly and watched them both. Tully's hair was the longest she had ever seen it. The straightest. The most colorless. Tully's face, not enhanced by makeup, was pale and dry. Her mouth that never smiled easily bore traces of being permanently shut—those four or five little columnar furrows above the top lip showed Julie that Tully must've kept her mouth tightly shut the last fifteen months.

"Where are all your eyelashes, Tull?" asked Julie jokingly.

"In my drawer," said Tully. "You didn't think those were real, did you?"

Tully was plumper than usual, and her breasts were big, white and full of milk.

"I see you've gained some weight, Tully," said Julie, trying to make polite conversation.

"And I see *you've* gained some weight, Julie. You also got a nice tan. Is that intentional? Or is it just being in the sun year 'round?"

Julie gulped. "I'm sorry, Tully."

"No, don't apologize. I have gained some weight. Sorry for what?"

"For not writing, for not calling. I'm real sorry."

Tully waved her off. "Julie, we're all so busy. We used to have kind of one life, but that was a long time ago. And now we've gone our separate ways." She paused. "Don't worry." After feeding Boomerang, Tully buttoned her dress and kissed him on the nose. "Let's go out back, it's pretty there in the early evening."

Tully was right. It was pretty. The yard was huge and faced southwest. Around the edges of the fence were some red and white impatiens and some sunflowers, too. Julie even saw a neat row of gayfeathers poking their pink heads around the side of the house. The sun shone mercilessly and gloriously on the grass it burned.

"Nice flowers, Tull. Who planted them? You?"

Tully stared at her incredulously. "Me, plant flowers? No, Millie does this. Millie is our housekeeper and cook and gardener."

Julie lightly smiled. "Lady Chatterley also did not plant her own flowers. You're not Lady Chatterley, by any chance?"

"No, and Millie is not my lover," said Tully, attempting a smile, as they sat down on the patio chairs and Tully put Boomerang on the blanket near their feet. "No playpen?" asked Julie. "I thought all new moms had a playpen."

"Not this new mom," said Tully. "My son is not going in a cage."

"Is his name really Boomerang?" Julie asked.

"Really."

They sat for a while, not talking.

Finally Tully spoke. "I married Robin," said Tully.

Julie nodded but did not respond.

Tully looked away, but she didn't really have to do that, because Julie wasn't looking at her anyway. *Couldn't* have looked at her.

"I don't understand," said Julie softly, watching Boomerang. "I got a postcard from you last September saying, 'I chose my teacher!' "

"Yes. I did choose my teacher. But I guess God had other plans for me."

"Tell me," said Julie. "Tell me what happened." But it was so lovely to sit here in this backyard that smelled of cottonwood and sunflowers, that smelled of Kansas, to have the sun set on her face, to see Tully again, that Julie almost, *almost* didn't want to know what happened. Being here was good enough. She caught her reluctance and was shamed by it. I'm ashamed of a lot of things lately, she thought.

"After you left," said Tully, "it was back and forth for a while. Jeremy went to California in June for his interview." Tully paused. "I spent June with Robin," she said with difficulty, not looking at Julie. "When Jeremy came back and said he got the job, I went with Jeremy. When he asked me if I had seen Robin and I told him yes, he got mad, and didn't see me for weeks. So I saw Robin. But then Tracy Scott came back."

"Did she?" said Julie with surprise.

"Hmm. She wanted her place back."

"What about wanting her son back?"

Tully repeated woodenly, "She wanted her place back."

"I see. So what did you do?"

"I gave up my trailer and moved in with Jeremy. We decided to go to Santa Cruz. He was going to start in January. And I was already accepted for the fall term. But it didn't matter too much. I was prepared to skip one semester." Tully swallowed.

Julie was silent. "You moved in with him."

"I had no choice, really. I didn't have my trailer."

"What about Robin?"

"What about him?" said Tully. "I'm with him now."

Julie shook her head. "I still don't understand," she said.

"I got pregnant."

"Oh," said Julie, adding, "I see," but honestly, she saw nothing. Nothing except the sunset and Boomerang trying to eat some grass.

"I had no morning sickness, no discomfort, no nothing," continued Tully. "I was pregnant since June but only realized it in September. A whole month after I moved in with Jeremy."

"Weren't you on the pill?" asked Julie.

"Yes, and I stopped bleeding in between pills. But I paid no attention. I've always been irregular, and thought, Well, this is strange, but then it's always been strange with me."

"I thought the pill was baby-proof," said Julie.

"It is. I had a bit of an infection in June. Had to take a course of penicillin. Supposedly it lowers the pill's effectiveness. Who would've known?" said Tully flatly.

"Oh," said Julie. "Huh. Since June," Julie said. "Since June." *June*. Like June was supposed to mean something. Since last June, fifteen months have passed. Fifteen months during which Julie'd seen a lot of dust on the road. "What happened in June?"

Tully sighed. "I just told you. Jeremy was in Santa Cruz in June."

Julie's eyes widened; suddenly things were becoming clearer. Julie tried to see what Tully was feeling, but Tully was looking down into the grass, and in any case, her gray eyes did not lend themselves to feeling. They were not bay windows to her Texas Street soul.

"Tully," said Julie. "The baby—it wasn't Jeremy's."

"Good, Julie."

"Could it have possibly been Jeremy's?"

"Julie," said Tully wearily. "There is no mistaking the due date, there is no mistaking the time, and Jeremy could count. We could all count."

Julie rubbed her temples. "So, Tully, wait a minute. Who cares about who and when and how and what month? You told me you never wanted to have a child. It is 1982, for God's sake. So you pay a nice doctor three hundred dollars and have the problem well taken care of and you're on your way." And then Julie saw Tully's face.

Hello darkness my old friend. I've come to talk with you again.

Tully did not speak for a long time. Julie felt the breeze and heard the birds celebrating sundown. She heard little Boomerang cooing, rustling, munching on grass. It was hot, and Tully did not speak. In the silence of Tully, Julie again began to feel ashamed at her casual unthinking words. Maybe Jeremy absolutely did not want Tully to have an abortion, and so Tully *had* to tell him the truth. And after the truth she had to leave him. And after she left him, and told Robin, maybe Robin didn't want Tully to get rid of the baby, either, and maybe Tully became resigned to it. Or maybe Tully thought getting rid of a baby was like losing her whole soul instead of gaining her whole world. Maybe Tully just didn't believe in getting rid of babies. Maybe. They had never talked about it when they were in high school. Tully had always studiously avoided the subject in conversation.

Tully stared at her son, unblinking. "Oh, we tried," she said, collecting herself. "*I* tried. Well, first of all I had to tell Jeremy. I couldn't do the math fast enough, and to lie . . ." she trailed off. "Your whole future life then. Not an illusion. Not a delusion. Just a plain lie." Tully breathed hard. "You know, I said it was due in March, and Jeremy said, March? and then counted forward, and then did the math faster than me, and what could I do then? Tell him I was mistaken? Ooops, not really March, just kidding. April, really, yeah, that's right. And then when the baby would be born looking like—" and here Tully pointed to the dark-eyed, dark-haired boy. "What could I say, that there was some Spanish blood in my family?" She shook her head. "Couldn't do it. I had to tell him the truth."

"How did he take it?"

"Well," Tully sighed. "According to what Aunt Lena had once told me, better than my mother's father took it when he found out he wasn't 'it.' But not that much better."

"Did he tell you to go?"

"Among other things, yes." Tully fell silent.

When she resumed, she said, "We couldn't continue as we were. Jeremy was simply unable to continue. Unable. Not for lack of wanting. But he couldn't come near me, couldn't touch me, couldn't say yes to me without getting the look in his eyes that said, you ruined my life. So in the end I had to leave him. In October. I said, 'I'm going,' one Sunday morning and he couldn't even look up from his coffee at first. So I left. Trouble was, I had nowhere to go." Tully laughed hollowly. "Nowhere, Jule. My internship with SRS at Docking had long ended, I had quit Casa in the beginning of the summer. I wasn't working, just living with Jeremy, reading a lot. Watching TV. Shakie was still living with her parents. My mother was finally in Menninger, Aunt Lena hated my guts." Tully breathed in the air. "I had only one place to go. Manhattan."

"Oh," said Julie. "Oh, boy. You went back to Robin. Oh, my. How did he take it? How did you tell him?"

"It was Sunday and he was playing rugby. I got him at halftime. 'What are you doing here?' he said. And I just said, 'I left Jeremy.' He said, 'So? I don't want his leftovers.' And I said, 'I'm pregnant.'"

"Oh, God! Just like that?" Julie exclaimed. "Good Lord, deliver me. What did he say?"

"Nothing," answered Tully. "He went and finished his game of rugby. His team lost, I remember. His nose bled. Then he came back to the sidelines, all muddy and bloody, and said, 'So what are you telling me for?' I said, 'Because it's yours.'"

Tully didn't stop looking at her son. "Then Robin asked me if I was sure. Look at him, Jule. Could there have been any doubt?"

Julie looked at Boomerang DeMarco. "No," she said. "He looks just like him." Thinking, He is a beautiful baby boy.

Tully continued. "We went back to his house and sat for an hour, pretending we were talking about what to do. He asked me what I wanted to do." Tully's jaw was set and her teeth were clenched together, the four furrows on her upper lip standing out like the white columns of the house on Texas Street, but her eyes, her eyes! Julie had to put her head down and look at the little boy. She was wrong about Tully. The soul swam around even in Tully's gray poker eyes. "I told him I didn't want to get married. He said who said anything about being married. I said I didn't want to have children. He said I had told him a few months ago I would never get rid of it. He wanted to know if those were just words. He asked if he should find a good doctor for me. I said, where, in Wichita? He said we didn't have to go all the way to Wichita to find a good doctor and then stared at me for the longest time. I finally said I didn't want to get rid of it. He asked if I wanted to keep it. No, I said. Not that either. He told me those were my only options. I asked him if he would let me get rid of it. He said only because it was not real to him. I asked him if he would let me give it up for adoption, and you know what he said? He said that he assumed I came to him because I was really desperate. That I came back because I had nowhere else to go, just like the time I left my mother. He said that, God help him, he was here. But even he would not watch me in his house for nine months only to have me give away his little girl."

Julie had an intense desire to go and pick up Boomerang. To go and pick him up and feel the top of his head. "He said that, did he?"

"He said that. I asked him why was he so sure it was a girl, and he said because he had always wanted a baby girl."

At that moment, Julie almost, almost loved Robin herself.

"But Jule, I was fourteen weeks pregnant," Tully went on. "Something had to be done. So the following week, he made an appointment for me in Topeka, and we went." She fell silent again. It was the silences that screamed to Julie, not Tully's short and stilted words.

"It's okay, Tully," Julie said comfortingly. "It's okay."

Tully shuddered, got up, and picked up Boomerang. "On the way to Topeka, I asked Robin if he would marry me if I kept the baby. And he sounded really worn down, *worn out,* and said he would."

"So you turned around and got married?"

"Yes," said Tully. "We turned around and got married. Last Thanksgiving."

Last Thanksgiving! Well, that explains the happy encounter at Dillon's with my mother, thought Julie.

"And Jeremy? Did you see him after that?"

Tully shook her head. "No, of course not. I found out he quit teaching that October and went back home to New York." Tully paused, squinting into the sun. "He didn't deserve it."

"Of course he didn't. Robin didn't, either," said Julie.

Tully grunted.

"Tully, it was a lose-lose situation. Two guys and one girl. There is just not enough to go around."

"Guess not," said Tully blankly. "There's barely enough of me for one," she whispered, cradling Boomerang to her cotton print dress.

Julie squeezed Tully's arm, trying to think of something to say. "It's not that great, anyway, California. Really."

"I'll bet," said Tully.

They sat. "How have things been with Robin?" Julie asked cautiously, wanting things to be good with Robin. Hoping Robin would come home early, so she could see him. So that she could see her oldest friend Tully be a wife to Robin DeMarco.

"How *can* they be?" said Tully.

Julie's shoulders sagged. "How is your mother?" she asked to change the subject, and then saw Tully's hard expression and said, "What? What? Did she die? What's happened?"

Tully turned in her chair to look at her house. Pointing to the windows on the left, she said, "Robin's always had big plans for me and my mother. Big plans."

"What does that mean?" Julie cried.

"See," said Tully, "Robin always thought that if we took good care of my mother, she might get better. And if she saw the kindness heaped on her by others, after a lifetime of so little kindness, she would perhaps come around and grow to be a good grandmother."

"What has he done? What are you saying?"

"He took her out of Menninger, is what I'm saying," said Tully harshly. "Back in '81, remember I told you he bought me this diamond ring and came to my trailer to propose marriage to me? He was proposing marriage to me and wanting to buy me this house so that he could bring my mother here. You might even say he was proposing marriage to my mother *through* me."

"Oh, no," said Julie. "He must have known how you'd feel about it. What was he thinking? Didn't you tell him?"

"He knew," said Tully. "I told him."

"Oh, my, oh, my," was all Julie could say. Looking back at the house, Julie saw a glimpse of what Tully saw when she looked at the house on Texas Street.

"How's it been?" she asked. "Has it been better than you thought?"

"No, Julie," said Tully. "It's been no better than I thought. Nothing's been better than I thought."

Julie thought of Robin, of his kind face, of his kind eyes whenever he had looked at Tully when they were in high school. Julie refused to believe that Robin would bring Hedda Makker to Texas Street out of meanness. Maybe out of stupidity.

Tully tapped Julie on the arm. "Tell me," she said, "how's traveling been for you?"

"Oh, good," lied Julie. "Great. I have absolutely no complaints."

"You like it better than going to school?"

"Oh, yeah, much!" Julie lied again. "It's nice. We work outdoors. We feel healthy. You know, the body feeds the mind, as they say. We're real happy."

"Uh-huh," said Tully.

Julie wondered if Tully would ask. Julie would tell her if Tully asked.

They sat for a few minutes longer. Then Tully said Robin was going to be coming home soon and she had to go cook dinner. "You cook?" Julie said. "Now I'm surprised."

"Yes," said Tully, "me and my twelve minutes at the microwave."

"Robin must like you cooking for him."

"Loves it," said Tully, getting up. "Eats it right up."

"What time does he usually come home?"

"It depends," said Tully evasively. "He works late a lot."

Tully and Julie slowly walked around the south side of the house to the front. Tully sat with Boomerang in the swing on the porch. Julie stood in front of her. "I hear Shakie is getting married."

"Frank is a good guy," said Tully.

"Didn't Jack come back last Christmas?" Julie asked.

"Oh, he came back, all right," said Tully. "Shakie was already engaged to Frank."

"Ah," said Julie. "So she ignored Jack?"

"Ignored him? No. She broke up with Frank and spent two weeks with Jack."

"And then Jack left?" guessed Julie.

Tully nodded. "And Shakie went back to Frank. They made definite plans to marry."

"I see," said Julie. "But what happens this Christmas?"

"I suspect more of the same," said Tully.

Julie shook her head in disbelief. "Is Frank the kind of guy who will take that?"

"Who isn't?" said Tully.

Yes, Julie thought, who isn't? The things we do for the ones dear to us. The things we put up with. We sleep in tents and eat raw corn. We don't see our mothers. We don't shower. We miss our friends until we can't breathe. *All* our friends. All our friends who went their separate ways.

Julie cleared her throat. "I haven't been in touch as much as I should've—"

Tully interrupted her. "It's all right. I understand. Really I do."

"Do you still go to St. Mark's?" Julie asked carefully. "My mom says she hasn't seen you there at Sunday Mass."

"Oh, we still go," said Tully. "We go every Sunday. But not to Mass so much. All those people. Boomerang gets a little cranky. And me, too. I come later. I usually leave Boomer with Robin and come for a few minutes. Sometimes I just take the afternoon and go to church and then go shopping or something."

Julie cleared her throat. "Well, I'm glad you go, Tully. I'm really glad."

She bent down to kiss Tully and Boomerang. " 'Bye," Julie whispered. "I promise, I'll try not to be a stranger."

"Don't promise me, Julie," said Tully. "Just come back once in a while."

Julie touched Boomerang's head. "I can't believe you're a mother, Tully," she said tenderly. "I can't believe you have a son."

"You're not the only one who can't believe it," said Tully, playing with Boomerang's legs. "But tell me, Jule. Tell me about Laura."

Julie moved away and looked at Tully, whose eyes were twinkling a little, and Julie's heart lifted. It's not going to be so bad to talk to her about it, after all.

"What'd you want to know?"

"Who is she?"

"Laura," explained Julie, "is my friend."

"Your friend."

"My . . . companion."

"Companion. I see." Tully reached over, pinching Julie's hand, and smiled. "So now I understand why you never knew what to do with Tom." Tully's whole face softened. "You made my day," Tully said, and then her smile slowly dissolved. "Jen would've laughed if she had known," Tully said.

"She had known, Tull," said Julie.

Tully was quiet.

"She had?" Tully said at last. "Did she laugh?"

"Laughed and laughed," answered Julie, her words catching in her throat. I wonder if Tully is seeing what I'm seeing, she thought. I wonder if Tully is seeing Jennifer's laughing face.

Leaning back down, Julie gently pressed her cheek to Tully's. "I miss her all the time, you know," she whispered.

Tully didn't answer.

Julie nodded in understanding. "Take care you, Tully."

"Take care you, Julie," said Tully.

"And if it means anything," Julie said, "I think you did the right thing. You did the right thing, Tully Makker," she repeated. "I think there is always time to go to school, there is always time to do all that. But look at all you have."

"Yeah," whispered Tully, her lips tight. "Look at it all."

"I've always liked Robin," Julie said, rubbing her wet cheek against Tully's dry cheek.

"I know," Tully said. "Maybe *you* should have married him."

"I love you, Tully."

Tully just nodded. Julie wiped her own face and saw

Tully's eyes up close. While walking away, she thought how hard it was to see Tully's gray soul imprinted on her gray eyes.

At the gate, Julie looked back and yelled, "You have a lovely home!"

"Lovely!" echoed Tully, waving. "Have a good harvest!"

12
WICHITA

September 1982

After Julie left, Tully continued to rock on the porch swing. The front of the house faced northeast and she couldn't see the sun, but she could see the street. She and Boomerang sat there and rocked for a long time. He fell asleep, woke up. She fed him, thinking about Julie. What's happened to her? What is she doing?

Her house seems just a little bigger than mine. Her house is a field in Iowa and a desert in Nevada, and a prairie somewhere just west of here, but still she sits and looks out of her tent, out of her car, and thinks that there it is. Out there, somewhere, but not in here. And we both don't even know how to find it.

Oh, that's bullshit. We know, all right. We know full well. Where that frailty that is all our dreams waiting to be blown away by the harsh Kansas winds lies. We know where it lies, and it suffocates us. We used to race from school to Sunset Court to touch it and now I slowly amble to St. Mark's to put flowers on it.

Tully rocking with Boomerang in the swing crooned an old Janis Ian song to him, in a low, hollow voice.

Boomerang cooed. "A lovely home," sang Tully. "It's what I always wanted. And your daddy, Boomerang, he paid for everything."

Tully had told Julie the truth: Robin was coming home soon. However, she was *not* going to cook him dinner. Robin was going to come home and nuke whatever leftovers there were from yesterday that Millie had cooked. Millie cooked every day, but today was Tuesday, and Tuesday was Millie's day off.

So Robin was going to fend for himself, and Tully was not going to care. She was barely on thinking terms with Robin. They barely spoke. Tully was going to continue to sit on the porch until the sun stopped shining off the leaves and making the world auburn. And then she would go inside the house and bathe little Robin and get him ready for bed.

What does Jeremy look like? she thought. I've nearly forgotten. He was the man I almost went fifteen hundred miles away with, the man I lived with, the man I chose, and now I don't even remember what he looks like. No, but I remember our plans well. We had all these *plans*. He was going to be with me and I was going to see California. He had these blue eyes that could barely look at me when I was packing to go away from him forever and there was nothing he could do anymore. He said, "I don't care whose baby it is, I don't. Tully, please. Please don't leave. I didn't mean it. Please don't go."

But Tully knew they could not have lived that life. Not he. Not she.

Dear Jeremy. Did I break your heart? Yes. I might not remember what you look like, but *that* I remember.

She looked down at her sleeping boy. There was a tune softly spinning in her head, but she couldn't place it. Tully hugged him a little closer, rocking and rocking. I have a porch and a swing on the porch, a swing on the porch that swings, and me and my Boomerang sit here every day and we sing and swing, sing and swing. And watch the street. When I was young I sat on my bed and rocked to rid myself of what was all around me, and now I sit in this swing and rock me and my son. Because the truth is, I sit here and though I see my front yard and see the porch and the fence and the windows and the oaks and the cedars, what I really see is Tracy Scott's trailer.

I see her trailer behind me and her son in front of me, and the railroad and Kansas Avenue in front of me, too. And that's about it. I sit *here* but I see *that*.

Now I have my house, and what a house it is, too. It is everything I ever imagined it would be—and more.

The first time Tully saw the inside of the house, she was seven months pregnant and her back hurt. Robin had just closed the deal with the eighty-four-year-old widow who had been living at 1501 Texas Street. Tully didn't want to see the house until it was bought. No, that wasn't it. She didn't want to see the house at all, but when it was bought she had no choice.

Texas Street, number 1501. The living room took up nearly the whole first floor. From the front door to the back door stretched the parquet floor of the living room, with a bay picture window to see the street and the sunrise and a bay picture window to see the backyard and the sunset. When they moved in, Robin positioned the couch just right, so that during the day Tully and Boomerang or little Tully could see out both picture windows.

To the back of the house was a huge kitchen. There was room for an oversized oak table, a two-seat wicker sofa, book-shelves, plants. The kitchen door opened into the yard, so when Tully was actually in the kitchen, she could put Boomerang in the swing in the backyard and watch him from inside. On the north side of the house, there was a dining room with an adjacent den. Once or twice when they had first moved in, they used the dining room to dine in.

On the south side of the house there was a little sunroom, where Tully grew her plants. Her California room. There were only two kinds of plants in the sunroom—cacti, of which there were hundreds, and fledgling palm trees, of which there were a dozen. Robin bought her the palm trees before the summer began.

He couldn't leave work to go on vacation, so he bought her palm trees instead.

There was another two-seat wicker couch in the sunroom, wicker tables, wicker baskets. Little Robin liked the noise wicker made, so during the day Tully sat with him and played with wicker. Little Robin listened and she watched the palm trees.

Upstairs there were five bedrooms. The sprawling master bedroom with its three windows faced northeast and north. Little Robin's bedroom faced southeast and sunrise. And the other three bedrooms were spread over the rest of the second floor. Two of them were untouched, and the third was given to Hedda Makker.

When Robin and Tully got married and he began to nego-tiate the Texas Street house, his only stipulation was that Hedda not remain in Menninger. "As if she belongs to no one."

"But she does belong," Tully said, "to no one."

Robin did not hear her. "That's it, Tully. That's all I ask. I don't ask that you be a good wife, I don't ask that you be a good mother. I ask that you let *me* show a little kindness to Hedda."

Tully said she would not live in any house with her mother again. "Don't you understand? Any house I live in with her is going to turn into the Grove."

Robin was immutable, promising her that contact with Hedda would be limited, but Hedda would have her room in the new and large DeMarco household. Robin would hire her a nursemaid and a physical therapist.

Tully said no. "No," she said. "Don't buy me this house. I don't want to live here. We'll live in Manhattan. I don't care at all."

"Hedda will not stay in Menninger no matter where we live, Tully," Robin said. "And the Texas Street house is so big. You'll hardly have to see each other."

"No," Tully said. "No."

Robin said that he could not *"Bear!"* the way Tully was treating her own mother.

"Haven't you listened to a word I ever said to you, Robin?" Tully asked.

"Very carefully. But this is your mother."

"Yes, but not your mother!" Tully cried.

Robin stood still.

"You think that by ruining every fucking one of my days in this house you would bring your own mother back?" she cried.

He paled but continued to stare implacably at her.

"Robin, she is infirm, she is paralyzed," Tully pleaded. "She can barely move from the neck down. She needs help to go to the bathroom. She needs a dialysis machine. She needs a nurse and a cook and a masseur. The only thing she can move is her mouth. I don't want her in my house! I cannot take care of her, I'm going to be busy enough with a child. With our child," she added for emphasis.

He grimaced. "Don't give me that shit, Tully. You wouldn't take care of her even if you had nothing else to do. And we'll have to see about the *'our'* part, now, won't we?"

Tully was nearly at the end of her rope. She said, "Robin, why are you being so heartless? Don't you understand? I spent sixteen years trying to not be with her anymore. It's the only thing I lived for—why are you doing this to me now?" Her voice was weak. "You got what you wanted, you got me, I married you, what more do you want?"

"I got what I wanted, did I?" Robin said sarcastically. "Did I indeed? I got my girlfriend screwing someone every time she went out dancing, until finally she found herself a poet she wanted to screw on a regular basis, and then she jerked me around and him, too, till the cows came home, halfheartedly chose him by default, and then found out I knocked her up and she wanted a father for her child. Is that what I wanted, huh?"

Tully stood mute before him. It was Thanksgiving Thursday, and they had just gotten married six days ago. They were supposed to be going over to Bruce's for Thanksgiving dinner.

"I see," she said. "I've been bad and so you are bringing my mother into *our* home to punish me? Is that what it is? Is this my penance? What are you, God? Are you fucking God, Robin?"

No, he said, but she understood. She made one more attempt. "Robin," she said weakly. "Please. You know how I feel about her. I beg you, don't do this to me. Don't do this to us. This is no way to start our marriage . . . our . . . life together."

How hard it was to get the words out. The previous Friday she had stood near him in a simple dress, which was neither white nor cream, before the justice of the peace, and she heard those words. "Life together." She saw the judge and his black robes. She saw the sun outside the courtroom and the bare trees waiting for winter. Waiting for Thanksgiving. The judge's voice and Robin's voice were echoes inside her head, bouncing off as distantly within her as Ping-Pong balls in the canyons a thousand miles away. "Tuuulllllieeeeeeee . . . Tuuuuu . . . llllieeeeeeee. . . ."

Life together. She said this to Robin while he stood still as silence. Calm as morning prayer. Calm as a morning paper, in which nothing touched her.

"No way to start our life together," she repeated, and he sneered at her and said, "Don't say it, Tully Makker. Don't say it."

"Robin," Tully tried again. "I know I must've hurt you, and I'm sorry. I'll do my best to make up what I can to you. I'll try to be a good wife, even a good mother, though God knows I haven't had much of an example. I'll do what I can. But don't hurt me back by doing this, Robin. Don't ruin us before we've started. Don't end us so soon. Don't hurt me back."

"Tully," he said. "You're being melodramatic, plus you misunderstand me. I'm not bringing your mother here to hurt you. Really, I'm not. For once, this is not about you. But you can try to do the right thing, you can try to make peace with your mother as a grown woman, as a mother-to-be yourself."

"Robin, you're full of shit!" Tully snarled at him. "You're so kind to point out this has nothing to do with me, you got *that* fucking right, it's got zero to do with me, doesn't it? You're so kind to my mother, but you let yours die without speaking a word to her, you pseudo-noble bastard!"

Robin paled further and clenched his fists, but so it was.

The house was bought and paid for, new crisp one-hundred-dollar bills, all three thousand and five hundred of them. And Tully's mother was bought and paid for, too. And Tully. Everyone was nicely bought and paid for and they all lived together in a little crooked house.

Tully and Robin moved in from Manhattan on February 10, 1982, shortly after Tully turned twenty-one.

Robin brought Hedda Makker to Texas Street himself about a week later. Tully wasn't home for homecoming. She had gone to the movies to see *Tootsie*. And then she stayed at St. Mark's until night fell, going to visit Shakie afterwards. When she came home at two in the morning, Robin was up waiting for her. He stared at her accusingly from his chair, then got up and went to bed.

Tully didn't go upstairs to say hello to Hedda. The following morning, Robin carried Hedda down to breakfast, and Tully snickered: a 170-pound man carrying a 200-pound dead weight. Tully nodded hello to her mother, whom she had seen maybe three times in nearly three years, and then remembered it was Monday and Robin had to leave for work.

"Don't forget to take her back upstairs before you go," Tully said.

"Oh, Tully," said Robin.

"It's okay, Robin," said Hedda slowly. "She has never been good to me."

Robin took Hedda upstairs.

Every night that week, Tully went over to Shakie's. On Saturday, Robin went to Manhattan to visit his brothers and Tully went to Lawrence to visit Mr. and Mrs. Mandolini.

The following week Tully went to the Washburn library during the day, or to the movies. In the evenings, she went to visit Shakie. When she came home late at night, Robin was always in his armchair waiting for her, looking at her coldly.

Hedda's nurse came and went every day. Occasionally she stayed overnight on a cot in one of the unfinished bedrooms. Hedda's physical therapist came and went every day, too.

A few times in the several weeks before Tully gave birth, the physical therapist asked Tully to take her mother outside in the fresh air.

"Well, maybe we can lower her by rope out of the window," responded Tully. And he looked at her with cold reproach. The second time he looked at her that way, she fired him, and Robin had to get a new physical therapist.

In April, Robin finally got a contractor to come in and convert the dining room and the adjacent den into Hedda's rooms. "Now my mother has her quarters in my house, just like Aunt Lena had quarters in her house," said Tully.

Hedda's few attempts to start a conversation with Tully met with stony silence. A few times Tully left the room. Often she left the house.

Three weeks after Hedda came home, Robin finally had to say something. "Tully, this is ridiculous," he said.

"Oh, I agree," replied Tully.

"You're hurting your mother," he said. When she did not reply, he said, "When she talks to you, you give her a yes or no answer and then actively ignore her. When she is brought down to see you, you leave the room. When she is in the garden, you go inside, when she is inside, you leave the house. Can't you see she is reaching out to you?" His voice cracked. "Can't you see that? Doesn't it matter to you that she is your mother, that she wants to make amends?"

When Tully still said nothing, he shouted, "Well? Fucking say something!"

She gave him a level gaze. "Has she made any progress?"

"Yes!" said Robin, sighing. "She can move both her hands now and is starting to bend her knees." Tully was silent.

"Why do you ask?"

She narrowed her eyes and stared at him coldly. "Because, I suggest you figure out a way to keep her away from the baby when it's born," she said. "Now that her hands are moving."

*   *   *

On Friday, March 12, at around nine-twenty in the morning, when Tully was sitting in the library, reading Dostoyevsky's *The Idiot*, her water broke. At first she felt the wetness and thought, My God, did I just pee? So she contracted her pelvic muscles, but the water kept coming. Tully was slightly embarrassed to get up, so she pretended for a while that nothing was happening, hoping that maybe it would just stop.

She went back to reading *The Idiot*.

After a few minutes, she decided that she absolutely had to get up, even if people were going to stare. Fortunately, she was wearing black baggy pants and a knee-length sweater that covered most of her wetness.

In the bathroom, she confirmed that, yes, indeed she was wet. There was less water now—most of it was on her underwear, pants, and the chair she had been sitting on. Hmm, she thought. Am I having a baby? She thought of calling Robin from the library, but figured, What if it's a false alarm? And drove herself to Stormont-Vail in the Camaro.

"I think I'm having a baby," she said to the admissions nurse. "But I'm not sure."

"Are you having contractions?" the nurse asked her.

"I'm not sure," said Tully. She had been having some clasping of the uterus, but nothing more or less than the Braxton Hicks contractions of the last few weeks. Little more troublesome than period cramps.

She was admitted, put into a room in the emergency ward and left alone. There was an ugly round clock on the wall that told her the time. 10:35 A.M. Tully lay on her back, breathed deeply, and clutched the sides of the bed with both hands. Every once in a while her belly would contract and she would hold on to the bed tighter. And then let go. Tighter, and then let go. She closed her eyes. Tighter, and then let go. Opened them. Closed them again. Tighter, let go, tighter, let go. Tighter, tighter, tighter, tighter—

When she opened her eyes again, her hair felt wet and the clock said 10:55 A.M.

The doctor came to examine her. Tully was not letting go the sides of the bed anymore, and forced through her teeth, "I think I'm having a baby."

"Well," said the doctor kindly, "why don't you let me be the judge of that?"

But when he took one proper look at her, he gasped, "Don't move, don't, I'll be right back, right back," rushing out of the room. Tully heard him shouting outside, but inside she was getting a little dimmer. Clutching on a little tighter. Breathing, but not evenly anymore, no, more like panting panting panting like a Labrador.

The doctors and the nurses rushed back in. Tully opened her eyes and deliriously saw 10:59 A.M.

At 11:06 A.M. Tully gave birth to a boy. He was a little purple at first, but turned a nice pink when he started to wail. That was good. The doctors and the nurses just managed to get to Tully in time to catch the boy's head as it popped out around 11:03 A.M. Tully did not reach down to feel his head, she was too busy gripping the sides of the bed. But when he came out, and the nurse took him, Tully felt sad. *She* wanted to take him. She wanted someone to put *her* child on *her* belly. Tully dimly watched the nurse putting something in his eyes, weighing the little guy, and washing some of that red gook off him. The doctor was saying something to Tully, all the while injecting a needle into her thigh. All Tully wanted at that dreamlike moment was to hold her little boy.

And then she got him, ahh, here. All wrapped nicely in a white blanket, just his head sticking out. His head, with lots of hair. Lots of black hair. Yes. We really would have been able to pass you off as a Jeremy baby, wouldn't we, now? She touched his nose. Here. Here, now. And she bent down and pressed her lips to his soft moist head.

The doctor was shaking his head in amazement and relief. "Well, you are one remarkable lady, Tully DeMarco, aren't you? One remarkable lady. Made of tough stuff. Not a peep out of you, not a peep. And yet look at your son, nine and half pounds, and you, poor you, you need to be sewn up right away, you ripped a little, but it won't be so bad. My, you did well. And by yourself, too. I hate to think what would've happened if I stayed with my last patient just a minute longer, and I could've, too, easily. Why did you wait so long to come here? Weren't you in pain?"

Tully shook her head. "I didn't feel any pain," Tully said.

* * *

Afterwards, Tully got seventeen stitches, nine of them internal. She ripped pretty badly, and then apparently the uterus was failing to close, even with the oxytocic injection, and Tully continued to bleed. Robin was asked to donate a pint of blood when he arrived. Tully was AB positive, the universal receiver. Robin was O positive, the universal donor.

"Only a pint?" Robin said, rolling up his sleeve. "Why so little? She usually takes a whole body full."

"Have you seen the baby?" Tully asked him.

"You're holding him, of course I've seen the baby," said Robin.

Tully reluctantly let Robin hold him, and then said after a few seconds, "Here, I think he is hungry. Let me have him."

Robin watched her for a while as she tried to feed the boy, and then sat on the corner of the bed and said, "Why didn't you call me right away?"

"I didn't know I was having it. Him. It happened so quick. One minute, I'm on page three forty-three, and the next I'm getting stitch three forty-three."

"Yeah." Robin cleared his throat. "The doctors say your uterine lining had been damaged before the birth, that's why you were having tightening problems."

"Is that what they said," said Tully, not looking at him.

"Yeah, you know what they asked me? They asked, is this her first pregnancy?"

"They asked *you* that?" Tully said inaudibly.

"Yeah. I told them, yes, as far as I knew. They shook their heads." Robin paused. "Is it?"

"Sure," said Tully, almost to herself.

Robin patted her hand. She moved it ever so slightly away. He moved his away, too.

"What should we name him?" Robin asked. "Do you want to name him Henry? After your dad?"

Tully shook her head. "Robin."

"Yes?"

"No. Robin. That's what we'll name him. Robin DeMarco, Jr."

Robin protested, but not for long.

The next few days in the hospital, Tully continued to bleed, requiring yet another pint of Robin. She stayed in Stormont-Vail for five days instead of the customary three, but it was no big deal. Robin's blood was plenty to tide Tully over.

After Tully came home with the baby, several more futile attempts were made by Robin, by Hedda, and by Millie to get Tully to accept a truce and live halfway amiably under one roof with her mother. But two more months went by and Tully's behavior didn't change, so they all gave up. Robin said he didn't like Tully to be away from home as much as she was, day in and day out, not back until late evening with his son in tow. So the household worked out a schedule. When Tully was anywhere in the house, Hedda stayed in her rooms, and when Tully was in the backyard, Hedda did not go outside. Hedda didn't seem to mind. Tully had Robin buy her mother a TV and Hedda stayed in her room and watched the box all day.

The isolation of Hedda mollified Tully a little bit. She started staying at home more. That's when Robin started to stay at work later and later. Well, why not? reasoned Tully. He paid up. He gave at the office.

Tully rocked as twilight descended on Texas Street. She heard Robin's car, and in a few moments he pulled up to the house. He got out of his Corvette and, like always, waved. Tully feebly waved back. Opening the gate, he walked up the path and up the steps, across the porch. He glanced to his right, where Tully was sitting, and she looked up briefly, caught his eye, and then, unblinking, looked away. Robin straightened his shoulders, went up to his son, kissed him on the head and kissed Tully on the cheek. She smelled Paco Rabanne. He always smelled great. Robin turned away and walked into the house. Tully rocked. She sang softly to Boomerang, who was awake and playing with her hair.

> There was a crooked man
> And he walked a crooked mile
> He found a crooked six-pence
> Beneath a crooked stile
> He bought a crooked cat
> Which caught a crooked mouse

And they all lived together
In a little crooked house.

Boomerang laughed. She smiled. "Like that, huh, well, aren't you cute. How about this, now? Tell me if you like this." She thought for a moment.

Let the little birds sing;
Let the little lambs play;
Spring is here; and so 'tis spring—
But not in the old way!

I recall a place
Where a plum-tree grew;
There you lifted up your face,
And blossoms covered you.

If the little birds sing,
And the little lambs play,
Spring is here; and so 'tis spring—
But not in the old way!

All the dog-wood blossoms are underneath the tree!
Ere spring was going—ah, spring is gone!
And there comes no summer to the like of you and me,—
Blossom time is early, but no fruit sets on.

All the dog-wood blossoms are underneath the tree,
Browned at the edges, turned in a day;
And I would with all my heart they trimmed a mound
   for me,
And weeds were tall on all the paths that led that way!

Boomerang began to wail. Tully laughed. "Boomer, don't take it so much to heart! It's only a silly poem. It's only Edna." He continued to wail soundly. "Shush, shush, Boomer." Lifting him up above her head, Tully bounced him up and down a little, and then stood up and went inside.

She sat down at the dinner table, watching Robin eat. They looked at each other mutely for a few moments. He came over and took Boomerang from her.

"The guys are playing cards tonight," he said.

"Great," she replied.

"Want to leave Boomer with Millie and come?"

She shook her head. "Millie's day off."

"We can call her."

"She's busy enough. Leave her alone."

He threw his plate in the sink. "Her *and* you, huh?" he said, handing Boomerang back and going to change for the evening. She followed him upstairs, carrying Boomer with her. "Why don't you stay home, while *I* go out?" she suggested.

"You go out all the time. You're never home," he said.

"Oh, and you are?"

"I work."

"I take care of our child."

"Yes, yes, I know," he said tiredly. "But why do you always have to take care of him away from Texas Street? Why can't you take care of him here and not in Lawrence or Lake Shawnee or Clinton Lake, or Shakie's?"

"You know why."

"Oh, ease off, Tully," Robin said. "It's getting old. Really."

She stood propped against the bathroom door and watched him shave. He sighed. "Do you want me to stay home?"

"Do you want to stay home?" she said. Actually, Tully did want Robin to stay home tonight. She wanted to talk to him about Julie. Tully remained calm on the outside in front of her old friend, but seeing Julie reminded Tully of she wasn't quite sure what. Some song. And she wanted to talk to Robin about it.

"I promised the guys," he said.

Tully put Boomerang down and followed Robin into the bedroom, watching him with her arms folded as he put on a nice pair of beige slacks, a white cotton shirt, a black Izod sweater. He looked good. In her high school yearbook, he would have been voted Best Dressed, hands down. She tightened her lips. A few moments later, she felt Boomer tugging on her dress, lifting himself up against her, looking up at her, and babbling a smile to her. She smiled back and picked him up.

"Well," Robin said, brushing past her and kissing his son as he went out the door. "See you later. Don't wait up. You know how it gets."

"Oh, yes," she said, kicking the bedroom door closed behind him.

After Robin left, Tully bathed Boomerang. He was having so much fun in the tub that Tully after a while decided to get in herself. But she didn't have nearly as much fun. Afterwards, Tully dried them both off and sat naked in the rocking chair in the nursery and nursed him until he felt asleep.

Boomerang was a good baby, a better baby than she had expected. She had expected very little. The five days she was in the hospital, Tully did nothing else but sit and watch him. Robin arranged it so that Tully had a private room and the baby stayed with her. All he did was sleep, swathed in white cotton blankets. Tully sat in her bed or in the chair near the window, and she would roll little Robin around the room in his cot and watch him. She touched his hair and his lashless eyes and his lips. Twice every day she lifted him out of the cot and woke him, whether he wanted to be awakened or not. When he was awakened, he cried, and then Tully would put him on her chest and rock him. Back and forth, back and forth, she rocked him and thought, I am a mother. My mother is a mother, and so am I. The feel of his head on her chest, now, that was a sensation she had never experienced before. His sleeping downy head, soft, silky, tiny, lying on her chest. My baby, she thought. My baby.

After she brought him home, the sitting and watching him continued. Though he certainly tired her out. Sometimes she sat, but often she fell asleep.

Boomerang loved to be fed. Regularly. Every three hours or so he would wake up and cry. And every three hours or so she would drag herself up from somewhere and feed him. In between he slept. In between she slept and watched him.

Then he started to smile. Indiscriminately at first. He would smile at Tully and at Robin, but also at the green bush outside and at the car. Soon, though, Boomerang started to smile for Tully. When he would see his mother, Boomerang's face would melt into this dizzying happy face, a face he had only for her. He smiled for her like a little boy who knew he was going to be fed, and Tully never disappointed him. In the mornings, she nearly couldn't help but be enchanted, looking forward to going into his room when he was crying because she knew her appearance would light him up, and light her up in return. Tully felt it, felt the pull. Certainly the physiological pull. Every time he cried, her nipples would start to drip milk. And when Tully picked him up, Boomerang would smell the milk, and his little head would start heading south immediately, his mouth opening wide, his eyes already glazed over with pleasure. He would already, before even tasting Tully's milk, stop crying. Just smelling his mother's milk was enough for Boomerang.

When Boomer was five months, he started to reach out to Tully. He would be sitting on the floor stretching his pudgy little fingers to her, saying not just feed me, but hold me. Oh, she picked him up, all right, and she held him and nursed him and bathed him and clothed him. She read to him, and carried him with her in a sling, carried him shopping, and to church. She never left the room without him, and often took him into the bathroom with her. Boomer cried when he was left with Millie, he cried when he was left with Robin, but with Tully he only cried when he wanted to be fed or wanted to be held. Robin and Tully nicknamed their son Boomerang when it became obvious that no matter where he was put, he would end up, somehow, being near his mother.

Tully did what was demanded and required of her, but mostly Tully did it because she wanted to see Boomerang's face dissolve into a smile. She did it because she couldn't *believe* the feelings she had for him.

She could not help thinking, however, that any moment Boomerang's *real* mother was going to ring the doorbell and take little Robin from Tully, and Tully would breathe a sigh of relief and hand him over. Hand him over as she had handed over Damien, because he wasn't hers, because she couldn't take care of him. Tully felt that any minute now, Tracy Scott would come knocking on the door, and Tully would look down at her Boomerang and see Damien Scott. But that day had not come yet. When Tully looked down at Boomerang, all Tully saw was her little boy.

Sometimes Tully wouldn't have minded having Robin's freedom of paternity. Revolving fatherhood, come right in, folks, here I am, I am the dad. Look at me, look how I've provided for my boy and his mother. Why, I've given them everything they want. They will never lack for anything, I've seen to that. I go to work and I sell thirty ties a day because I know that will feed my son. I go to work and I stay there from sunrise till sundown taking care of *my* son. Isn't he lucky?

Tully's reward was that despite all that fatherly nurturing, Boomerang did not want his father. Boomerang had eyes only for Tully. Reminding her with his babbling and his nursing that she was the real McCoy. She was her son's mother.

Tully thought she heard her mother calling her from downstairs and tried to ignore it. But then the calling got more strident. She walked downstairs to her mother's bedroom and stood outside the door. "What?"

"Tully, I finished all my water, can you get me some more?" Hedda said.

Tully grunted, but before she walked away, said grudgingly, "You want some tea, maybe?"

"It's too hot for tea, Tully. Just water."

Tully brought her some, and held her breath not to smell the air when she walked inside her mother's room. She put the pitcher on the night table and poured her mother a drink. Hedda gulped the water down. Tully watched her.

"Thanks, Tully," said Hedda. Tully waved her off as if to say don't mention it, but didn't speak. Tully looked around the room. It was painted hospital white, with only a bed, nightstands, and a TV which was on. Magazines strewn about. Agatha Christie books. Hedda liked to fall asleep to the sound of the nurse's soothing voice, narrating the mysteries of murder and bloodshed.

"Can I open the window, Ma?" said Tully.

"Just a little, Tully. I get cold," said Hedda.

"Ma," said Tully, walking over to the big window and opening it. The warm breeze refreshed the room immediately. "It's September. It's hot."

"Yes," said Hedda. "But soon it will be the middle of the night. I might get cold."

Tully went to walk out. "Call me, I'm up with Boomerang anyway. I'll close it for you."

"Thanks, Tully," said Hedda, and Tully shut the door behind her.

She checked on him; he was sound asleep. Tully sat in the rocker in his room for a while, but sitting in little Robin's room, smelling him, baby powder, blankets, hearing the sound of his breathing, seeing the Mickey lamps and the Minnie curtains, made Tully somehow forget for a moment that there was anywhere else but Boomerang's bedroom. Forget until she heard the song in her head again and recognized the tune. It was another Janis Ian song, written at age fifteen. Tully hummed the tune a little bit, eventually letting out a small gasp of disbelief that fifteen-year-old Janis Ian, homely, lonely, and dogged by pain, could write a song like "Hair of Spun Gold" at *fifteen years old*. I'm lucky I didn't write it at twelve, thought Tully.

She had two hours before Boomer woke up again to be fed. In her darkened bedroom, Tully closed her eyes and started to hum another song and move to the internal music, touching the insides of her thighs with the palms of her hands, running her hands up, tight against her crotch, her lower stomach, her waist, her breasts. Her head was moving from side to side and she was humming, while her legs moved to a rhythm only she heard.

> *Once I ran to you*
> *Now I run from you*
> *This tainted love you're giving*
> *I gave you all a boy could give you*
> *And that's not even all*
> *Tainted love.*

> *. . . Don't touch me please*
> *I cannot stand the way you tease.*

Suddenly she stopped. She thought of Jeremy, who left his beloved Kansas all because of a woman who broke his heart, having followed another woman who broke his heart. "Couldn't you be just a little different, Tully?" she whispered. "Just a little?" She folded her arms around herself and her throat made low, plaintive sounds as she paced up and down her bedroom, up and down, up and down. Up and down. The curtains were not drawn and the streetlights threw light and shadows into the room, onto Tully. Shit, she thought. Shit.

Was it for this I uttered prayers, and sobbed and cursed and kicked the stairs, that now, domestic as a plate, I should retire at half-past eight?

"What's happened to you, Tully?" she whispered. "Where is your husband?" Far away. He is far away. He got me by a fluke of fate, by a fluke of God, he knows it and can't forgive me for it. Who can blame him? She went to the window, cradling up on the sill.

Over and over and over. It's all over. All over because I would not live a lie with one man and could not let another buy me a D&C.

Still rocking, she touched the insides of her hands. Six months ago and two weeks before Boomerang was born, Tully with her eight-month-pregnant belly sat in the bathtub and slit her wrists in her new home on Texas Street. She cut her wrists, and hung on for as long as she could, but hearing the sound she yearned for, hearing the sound of the waves was just too much for her. Too beckoning. Too soothing. She wanted to get up out of the bath, but not that much. Less than ever. What she wanted was to hear the sound of the sea for eternity.

She lowered her hands and couldn't get them back up again, and Tully thought, that's okay. So she let her head fall on the rim of the tub and her hands fall into the water. That's okay now. It will be okay. . . .

Robin got her out, desperately clutching her wrists with his hands. Holding her to him, it was Robin who lifted her wet pregnant body out of the tub and fell down on the bathroom floor with her, shouting something, crying something, pulling down a towel, wrapping it around her wounds, lifting up her hands as she lay prostrate before him, whooshing in and out of consciousness.

And now, when Tully Makker was married to Robin and was not in California with Jeremy, when Tully had a six-month-old son, when she was living again with her mother, she sat on the windowsill, rocking, touching her wrists, and thought back to the very first time she cut them, nine years ago. Fall 1973. Wichita. The unhealed nerve endings in Tully's scars began to throb. *Wichita.*

Nine years ago, Tully, twelve-year-old, skinny-as-a-rail Tully, started throwing up. She started throwing up and stopped eating. Bacon didn't look good to Tully anymore. Neither bacon nor spaghetti sauce.

She'd look in the mirror, every day looking more pale and drawn, but couldn't see in the mirror the answer to why she wasn't eating bacon. Neither bacon nor tuna sandwiches.

Weeks went by and Tully went around as she always went around, silent and still. She continued to throw up, and then after a while she couldn't sleep on her stomach. It hurt. So Tully slept sitting up at her desk, and after five weeks of not eating bacon and not sleeping on her stomach, she stopped throwing up. Tully was glad; glad, too, that no one in the house noticed her morning-time habits. But her stomach still hurt.

The summer spilled over into September, and Tully finally complained to her mother about her stomach pain. Hedda told Tully to stop eating potato chips and gassy foods, to stop drinking orange juice in the morning and to take up some form of exercise. After a few weeks, Hedda offered Tully some of her heartburn tablets after Tully further complained that bubbles were exploding inside her belly. Tully kept looking at herself in the mirror, but the heartburn would not go away.

It was Mrs. Mandolini who finally took Tully to her own family doctor. When they came out of the doctor's office, it was Lynn Mandolini who was holding on to Tully, while Tully walked to the car with her shoulders squarer than ever.

"Tully, what have you done?" whispered Lynn in the car. "What have you done to yourself, girl? What have you been up to?"

Tully wasn't even sure what Lynn meant. Tully wasn't up to anything that she hadn't been up to most of her life. Except . . . yeah—but so what? Who the hell cared? What did that have to do with anything?

It was a crying Lynn Mandolini who brought Tully home to the Grove, and it was a crying Lynn Mandolini who told Hedda.

"Five months pregnant? How can that be?" said Hedda, reddening. And lunged for Tully, who hid behind Lynn. That day was the first day Tully would hear her mother call her "slut." Tully didn't know what it meant.

Lynn tried to interfere but was only shown the door, and left, unthanked. "Pregnant? Pregnant at twelve? Pregnant? How can you be fucking pregnant?" Hedda shrieked. "You never leave my sight!"

"No, I don't, Ma," said Tully, standing straight and narrow as an arrow. "Not yours, not Uncle Charlie's."

Hedda looked at Tully with a stupefied gaze and then slapped her. "You lying wench, what the fuck are you talking about?"

"Not yours," Tully repeated tonelessly, "not Uncle Charlie's."

Confronted with a pregnant twelve-year-old Tully, Uncle Charlie did the only thing he could do. He ranted and raved, threw his hands up in the air, yelled that he would not even honor that with a response, and left for the local bar.

Hedda caught a nasty viral flu a few days later and stayed in bed for ten days. Aunt Lena took care of Hedda, and Uncle Charlie stayed away from everybody.

Lynn and Tony Mandolini finally drove Tully to Wichita when her frail body could no longer hide Uncle Charlie's drunken attentions. It was the fall of 1973, when legal abortions were hard to come by and very expensive. They had to drive all the way to Wichita to get one. There was some explaining to do, how and why it was that Lynn and Tony would let their daughter—for that is what they called Tully—get "so far along" before they took any "action." So far along? Action? What were they talking about?

The only thing that made any sense to Tully was being called Natalie Mandolini for a day. That she liked. It was the only day she and Jen shared the same name.

Lynn and Tony sat with Tully in the waiting room until it was time. "Natalie Mandolini," the nurse called. And Tully got up, liking the sound of that once again.

Tully was the youngest one in the clinic for whom dilation and curettage was no longer an option. Tully was the youngest one in the clinic, period. She was put to sleep, given a saline solution, and induced.

When she came to, she screamed and screamed. Lynn Mandolini was finally summoned by the nurse to come into the post-op room and calm her daughter, who was scaring the other patients. But Tully was beside herself, grabbing at Lynn, the nurse, her bed with unseeing, unblinking eyes, screaming, screaming, screaming. . . .

Finally, she had to be given Thorazine. Tony and Lynn came back for Tully the following day. It rained miserably all the way home.

Back in Topeka, Lynn and Tony took Jennifer, Julie, and Tully out for ice cream and to the movies, but when it was time to bring Tully home, she started to whimper, huddling in the backseat and asking if she could stay over at Jen's for a few nights. Jen clapped her hands yes, and Lynn and Tony readily agreed. Back at Sunset Court Lynn asked Tully to call her mother, but Tully would not. "She'll be worried about you, Tully," said Lynn. Tully shook her head. "She is sick. I don't want to disturb her."

Eventually, though, Tully Makker did go home to Hedda, Aunt Lena, and Uncle Charlie.

"Smile, little Boomerang," whispered Tully, mindlessly rocking in her bay window at 1501 Texas Street. "Smile."

13

INFANCY

September 1982

Two weeks later Shakie got married.

She wasn't the only one. Robin's two brothers were finally getting married, too. Stevie was marrying his long-term girl-friend Karen—and it was about time, frankly, thought Robin, since they already had two little kids. And Bruce was marrying Linda, a broad-shouldered girl he'd known for only a couple of months, but she was a farmer's daughter and therefore very appealing to him. Linda liked his farm, and Bruce couldn't say that about many of the girls he'd dated.

Shakie's wedding reception on September 20 was a sump-tuous affair at the Shawnee Country Club, one of the best places in Topeka. Shakie and Frank got married in a Methodist church, and Robin felt a little rueful that he and Tully could not have had a more traditional wedding. But then, of course, he ought to have been feeling lucky that Tully married him at all. I must have done something right, he wanted to think, but knew it was a lie. He suspected that he himself had nothing whatever to do with Tully's reasons to have a baby, even though having Boomerang meant giving up a life she thought she wanted to live.

This line of thinking was doing nothing for his mood. He tried to focus on Corinthians.

Someday Robin might ask her why, but he was sure Tully wouldn't tell him the truth. Someday Robin might ask Tully if she thought she did the *right* thing by having Boomerang and marrying him. Robin suspected he'd be long bald before he could ask that of his Tully and expect a reasonable reply.

Robin turned his head to look at her and at the baby—pudgy and sweet-toed, sitting on her lap wondering when he'd get fed next. Tully briefly caught his gaze and motioned him to look on ahead.

Shakie looked glorious as a bride in white. Frank in his white tuxedo and maroon cummerbund was the epitome of an elated groom. They both looked exalted as they exchanged their vows. Robin remembered his own wedding—himself standing there looking at the ground, and Tully standing there looking at the ground. She wore beige, though she said it wasn't. He wore a suit. It was a nice suit, a black Armani, one of the very best, but it was not a tux.

Robin leaned over to Tully. "Shakie certainly does look good."

"She always does," Tully said. "Shhhh."

"Jack is a fool," Robin said quietly.

"Shhhh," whispered Tully, louder, looking around. Robin looked around, too. Jack himself was sitting a few pews behind them, impeccable in a black and white tux. Robin shook his head derisively. A tux. What's a man doing wearing a tux to the wedding of a woman he would not marry?

Outside the church, while they were waiting to congratulate the bride and groom, Robin asked Tully how Shakie felt about Jack's presence at her wedding. "*She* invited him. And just look at her," said Tully.

Robin had to admit, Shakie looked unfluttered. She never stopped brimming with joy. She kissed everybody on both cheeks, thanked them for coming, complimented the women's dresses. Robin watched to see if Jack would pay his respects and congratulate the newly married couple. Jack did not disappoint Robin. Coming up to Frank, Jack pumped his hand twice, looked him right in the eye, and said, "Well done, man." And then he stepped toward Shakie. Her demeanor cracked a little then. She blushed; she became flustered. Jack, in his self-assured style, took her hands in his, kissed her on both cheeks, and said, "Well done, Shakie, well done."

Robin shook his head, amazed. Bending over to Tully, he whispered, "You've just *got* to introduce me to that guy." Tully didn't respond, though Robin was sure she heard him. Instead of replying, she turned away slightly, hardening her mouth.

At the reception, Robin got to dance with his wife.

This must be the first time she had danced in . . . he didn't want to think about it. He did not want to think about how long it had been since he had danced with her. Still, though, the thought crept up. Since last summer. Fourteen months ago? He held her a little closer, marveling at her grace and sexiness, marveling at her hair, getting so long now. Her eyes, usually so solitary and toneless, were twinkling. She looked so good when she danced, and she knew it. Robin kissed her right there on the dance floor, as they were waltzing and the lights were on them. He kissed her without breaking their rhythm. She kissed him back, and laughed, deliciously, continuing to dance. When he pulled her to him, he felt her breasts through the thin dress. Tully had gained weight after Boomerang, thank God for that. This was better now.

Tully wouldn't get off the dance floor. "You're upstaging the bride," Robin told Tully as he led her to their table. "How can I be upstaging her?" said Tully. "Look at her."

Shakie must have been in a particularly odd humor when she was making out the seating arrangements for the reception because she put Jack at Robin and Tully's table, next to Tully. The table filled up with people, and finally even Jack sat down. Tully nodded at Jack but did not introduce him to Robin.

Robin waited a few minutes and then gently nudged Tully under the table.

She let out a little breath and said, "Jack, this is Robin, my husband," she said. "Robin, this is Jack." Jack smiled and reached across Tully to pump Robin's hand. Robin noted that Jack's handshake was in character—firm and full of confidence.

"I'm not sure, but I think we've met," said Jack.

"Have we?" Robin asked, taken aback, and then all three of them looked down at their plates.

"This endive salad sure looks good," said Tully.

Have we met? thought Robin. He looked at Tully. She was examining the endive salad very closely. He looked at Jack. He was staring at Tully.

We met, did we? He reminded himself to ask Tully about it. Vaguely, music played in his memory. Music, and something else, too—beer, the smell of beer.

During dinner they chatted amiably. Robin watched Jack. He watched Jack eat and drink. When Jack was offered a cigarette, he shook his head. When he was offered another beer, he nodded. When he was talked to, he listened intently and seriously. When he talked himself, he was animated and descriptive. He spoke well and laughed loudly. He is good, Robin thought. When Jack was asked to dance, he stood up willingly and politely but not enthusiastically. He danced because he could not refuse the embarrassed faces of dolled-up girls who came up to him, and he tried to act the gentleman to the end.

Jack danced with each one, brought each one a drink, and in his polite way charmed all the girls. He maintained a perpetual distance in his own face, however. Robin supposed Jack needed to remain aloof, seeing the perpetual eagerness in theirs.

Even Shakie had to come up to Jack and asked him to dance. And when he got up and smiled at her and took her hand to lead her to the dance floor, Robin saw the same polite, friendly expression Jack gave the other nameless dancers.

Shakie and Jack danced fast to J. Geils' "Freeze-Frame" and then Shakie stepped over to the DJ for a minute, and John Cougar's "Jack and Diane" played. Shakie pulled Jack to her.

Robin was surprised. Shakie, having just been married so beautifully, was now looking up longingly into the polite face of a man who was not her husband.

Robin leaned over to Tully and whispered, "They are playing 'Jack and Diane.' How convenient."

"Not convenient at all," Tully responded. "I know Shakie. She asked the DJ to play it."

Robin shook his head. "I give her and Frank six months."

Tully turned away from the dance floor to look at Robin. "How long do you give *us*?"

Robin in the next two silent moments thought back to the last year, to mute evenings, to eating alone, to sleeping alone while she sat awake at the windowsill, to coming home and seeing no one there. He thought back to staying in the store until nine or ten at night, to playing soccer Saturdays *and* Sundays, to spending his evenings with his brothers. But still. She married *him*.

Robin's heart tightened as he put his arm around Tully's waist and said, "I give us forever, of course, Tull. How long do *you* give us?"

She did not reply.

Robin watched Jack and Shakie, thinking, They look perfect together. Then Robin remembered that Jack looked pretty good with all the girls he danced with. There must be something about Jack that rubs off on his partners and lifts them out of mere pink chiffon into something else. Maybe some natural fiber. Maybe just taffeta.

"So, Jack," said Robin when Jack got back to the table. "You're not living in Topeka these days?"

"No, haven't lived here for some time," said Jack. "My mother's here, so I come back every year at Christmas."

"Only at Christmas?"

"Well, it's not Christmas now and I'm here," Jack said pleasantly. "Mostly at Christmas."

"I see," said Robin. "So what do you do the rest of the year? Where are you living these days?"

"California," said Jack. "These days."

Robin glanced at Tully. Her eyes had been glazed over as if she weren't listening, but summarily her gaze cleared, and she smiled the smile of someone who had not heard the conversation but has the vague feeling she was the main subject.

"So what are you doing with yourself these days, Jack?" asked Robin.

"Not much," Jack replied. "Keeping busy. Traveling a lot. Been everywhere. It's great to travel."

"Not a lot of expenses?" said Robin.

"No, man, plenty. Plenty. But I do okay. Work a little, make some money, move on. Tulsa, Lincoln. Richmond, Charleston, Miami. New Orleans. Work a little, make some money, move on."

"Much like Julie, hey, Tull," Robin said to Tully.

"Uh-huh," said Tully flatly. "Much like Julie, I guess."

Robin turned back to Jack. "Are you working the fields like Tully's friend Julie is? Living out of tents and cars?"

"No, I did that for the first year I was out of school," said Jack. "It's no way to live."

"Oh, so you went to college?" Robin said.

"Yeah, I guess," Jack replied. "One semester, maybe two. Played football, you know. But . . ." he trailed off.

"But what?" Robin pressed.

"But nothing. It's just not the same, playing football for college. High school football, now, that's fun, that's great fun. But college football. They take themselves too seriously."

"So where did you go to college?" asked Robin.

"Berkeley," replied Jack. "California, near San—"

"I know where it is," Robin said, seeing Tully squeeze her palms together on her lap. Well, well. She *is* listening, to every word.

Robin wanted to ask Jack what exactly it was that he did for a living, but Jack cut him off by saying, "Tully, are you still going to school?"

Tully shook her head.

"Oh, that's a shame," Jack said seriously. "Shakie had told me you were doing so well. Why not go back?"

"I have a son now," said Tully, and Robin couldn't read the inflection in her voice.

"A son!" said Jack. "Congratulations." And Robin couldn't read the inflection in Jack's voice, either.

"What have you named your son?" asked Jack.

"Boomerang," said Tully.

"Boomerang!" Jack smiled. "Great. Boomerang Makker?"

"No," Robin interjected pointedly. "Boomerang DeMarco."

"Boomerang DeMarco," Jack slowly repeated. "And you are now Tully DeMarco?"

"Sure," said Tully. "Why not?"

"You've named your son Boomerang?" asked Jack.

"Sure, why not?" said Tully in a leaden voice. She was happier when she was dancing, thought Robin.

"Oh, I do hope Boomerang is his nickname," said Jack, picking up his drink.

"It is," said Tully.

"Let me guess," Jack said. "He once had a regular name, something like Tully, Jr., or Robin, Jr. Robin, Jr., yes, that's it!" Jack seemed proud of himself and, still holding the wineglass in his hand, continued. "But as the boy started to grow up, he started to display a fierce, nearly supernatural attachment to his mother. When she left the room, he would cry. When she came back, he would smile. When she put him down, he would cry. When she picked him up, he would smile. And when he started to crawl, there was no stopping him anymore. When his mother would leave the room, he would crawl after her. When she would put him down, he would climb back up her leg. When she went outside, he crawled outside. When she went upstairs, he would putter and putter up the stairs after her. So he was renamed Boomerang. Boomerang, I'll-always-find-my-mother, DeMarco. Am I right? I'm right, aren't I?" he said, as Robin and Tully sat stunned. "I'm completely right. Well, hooray." Jack raised his glass and said, "Cheers, Tully. Cheers, Robin. Here's to your son."

They raised their wineglasses. "Cheers," Robin said, thinking, Is he always this friendly or has he just had too much to drink? Again, the smell of beer came back to him. Beer and seventies music.

A little while later, Robin asked Jack what he did for a living. "Besides surfing."

"Ah, no. Surfing doesn't earn me a dime," Jack said. "No, I paint houses."

"Painting, is that a lucrative business?" asked Robin.

"Unbelievable," said Jack. "Houses, businesses, storefronts. I do all my own work, very fast, make a real killing."

"Are you now doing most of your painting fifteen hundred miles away?" Robin wanted to know.

"Mostly. I have a little bungalow in Manhattan Beach that I sublet when I travel. I did do some painting here in Topeka last month. Not much, two houses. But there's a lot of work here. What's your house like? Need painting?"

"No, it's fine," said Robin.

"Actually, the paint is chipping, Robin," Tully said.

"It's fine, Tully," Robin repeated.

"So where are you living nowadays?" Jack asked, looking Tully flush in the face.

"Texas Street," she replied. "It's by Shunga—"

"I know where Texas Street is," Jack cut her off mildly. "I'm very familiar with Texas Street. I used to go there with a friend of mine. We would walk up and down the street, marveling at the houses, wondering what it would be like to live there." He broke off. Tully didn't say anything. Neither did Robin. Blondie's "Call Me" blared.

"There was a fine house on Texas Street," Jack resumed. "We thought it was one of the finest."

While in the background the number-one-selling single of 1981 plunged on.

"So which house do you live in?" Jack asked.

"Fifteen oh one Texas Street," said Tully.

"What does it look like?" Jack went on patiently.

"Cream," Tully replied with difficulty. "Red roof. Bay windows. Dormers. Four columns. A big porch."

"A white picket fence?" Jack said, almost gently, Robin thought.

"There used to be a picket fence," Tully replied, holding her wineglass with both hands. "But we took it down. We didn't like it."

Jack sat there and looked at Tully for what seemed to Robin an interminable amount of time. Interminable. Robin couldn't quite put a finger on it. Jack stared at Tully and she stared back at him and they were both mute with a kind of a profound understanding of fuck knew what. Jack downed his wine, stood up, and said, "Tully, would you like to dance?"

She nodded. She never had to be asked twice.

Robin filled his glass to the brim and watched them.

Amazingly, she outclasses him, he thought. Outclasses Jack Pendel on the dance floor. Who'd ever think that when they danced like swans for Tchaikovsky it would be Tully who was making Jack Pendel look good?

She should've been a dancer, thought Robin. She said she never wanted to be one, but I don't believe her. I think she just never wanted to be one in Topeka. Just like she never wanted to be *anything* in Topeka.

Robin had to admit Jack wasn't far behind Tully, not because he was as good a dancer, but because he had the fluidity and self-possession of movement that only comes to few very good-looking people.

Robin tried to read Tully's face, but there was nothing on it but remains of sparkling wine. She had on her dancing face. And then "The Sweetest Thing" by Juice Newton came on. They were already standing together, they could do nothing else but come close to each other and dance. Shakie danced with Frank, and Tully danced with Jack. Robin filled his glass again and, downing the wine, looked at Jack's face.

Jack's face wasn't so *polite* anymore.

It was Jack's face that made Robin leave the table, walk as casually as he could over to Jack and Tully, and ask if he could *possibly* cut in. Jack gave a slight bow to Tully and to Robin and walked to the edge of the dance floor, where an eager female came out of nowhere and extended her hand to him. And his face became polite once more.

On the way home, Robin, as casually as he could, asked if he and Jack had met somewhere before.

"No," replied Tully. "I'm sure you never met."

"Still, though, I keep thinking we have," persisted Robin.

"It must've been someone else," said Tully.

Robin wanted to ask something else. He wondered how to ask it best, but in the end just asked it and damn the torpedoes.

"So what did you guys talk about out there?" he said.

"Not much," said Tully. "Nothing, really. We were too busy dancing."

"Well, you sure danced a lot not to say a word to each other," Robin kept on.

Tully shrugged. "I'm sure we said one or two words to each other, I really don't remember."

"Which two words?" he pressed.

"I might've said to him, 'You lead.'"

But Tully and Jack did talk. Tully was thinking about it while sitting on the windowsill the night after Shakie's wedding, smoking, unable to sleep, watching the street, watching Robin, feeling the night breeze on her face. From her vantage point, if she stared past the tall oaks, she could see the Kansas sky. It wasn't the same as lying on the grass on her back, looking up, but the stars were still there, still quietly incandescent.

Tully was thinking about her and Jack's conversation.

"Julie's left Topeka, too, Tully?" he asked her.

"She did, yes."

"She drop out of school?"

"She did that, too, yes."

"You drop out of school, too?"

She looked up at him. "I have a son, I told you."

"When he is a little older, maybe you can go back to school?"

"Maybe. What difference does it make?"

"All the difference in the world, Tully," Jack replied. "Me, I'm going to be forever painting houses, and Julie, she's going to be forever picking corn, but you, Tully, you were doing so well. Shakie told me. What a shame it would be to lose all that."

"Who cares?" said Tully. "I have a son now."

"You can have both," said Jack.

2.

Two days after Shakie's wedding, Tully sat down with Robin at the dinner table and said, "I want to go back to school."

Robin finished chewing his steak. "Okay," he said slowly. "Great."

"You don't believe me, do you?"

"No, of course I do. This time of the year has always been a time of action for you, hasn't it? Every fall, you start something new. So why not this fall?"

"I want to go back to school," she said stubbornly.

"Okay," he said. "What about Boomerang?"

"I've been thinking about that," said Tully.

"You have, have you? Well, you've had plenty of time to think, certainly."

"Why are you so hostile?" she said. "Why don't you want me to go?"

"You're still breast-feeding Boomer," he said sourly.

Since little Robin was born, big Robin forgot what Tully looked like without the small, neat, powder-fresh appendage constantly fastened to her, either by arms or by sling or by breast. Especially the latter. Tully was a nursing institution, where Boomerang came to quench his thirst for motherlove and his hunger for motherfood, and Tully gave and gave and gave. But when it came to big Robin, she had nothing left. She did not let him touch her, nor did she touch him herself. He brought this up a few times, and then dropped it. His own needs seemed just so irrelevant compared to his son's.

But now, for nothing more than college, nothing more than a couple of lectures, she was willing to throw all that motherlove away, and Robin was offended.

"I'm not going to stop nursing him," Tully replied.

"Oh, good," said Robin. "Where is this college thing coming from, anyway?"

"Robin, I've been thinking about this a long time."

"How long?" Less than a week ago, she was still sitting in the backyard, not moving from dawn to dusk. Less than a week ago, she had been sitting on the front porch as she had sat for the last six months. Rocking with Boomerang in her arms. And before Boomer was born, my God. She had had no plans at all, other than plans to fester in her own self-pity. Tully had sat too long looking at the trees, Robin was sure of that. But less than a week ago, Tully didn't seem to have any plans at all. "Since when, Tully?" he repeated.

"Since I saw Julie and Laura. Since I saw how unhappy Julie is."

"Julie is not unhappy. She is doing exactly what she wants to do."

"She is doing nothing. She is going to look back in a few years and regret that she did nothing."

"I see," said Robin. "Is that how you feel, being a mother? That you're doing nothing?"

"Robin, stop. You know very well I don't. I'm not going to stop being a mother. I'm just going to go to school and get my degree."

"Uh-huh," said Robin skeptically. "So what do you want to do? Go back to Washburn?"

"No, huh-uh. I want to go to Kansas University."

"Kansas State University in Manhattan?" he inquired mockingly. What irony it would be indeed.

"No, Kansas University in Lawrence."

"Lawrence?" Robin slowly nodded. That wasn't funny, wasn't ironic. Okay, that's how she wanted it. For the past twelve months she had been checked out of the life she had asked him to give her and now she wanted to be checked out of the house, too. Okay.

"Okay, Tully. If that's what you want."

She came over to his chair and patted him on the shoulder. "Thank you, Robin," she said without any feeling.

When she was upstairs bathing Boomerang, Robin sat listlessly at the kitchen table. KU. Lawrence. Tully was difficult to live with. He never suspected just how difficult. When he had stayed over in her trailer on the weekends, it didn't feel the same as having her in his house in Manhattan or in this house on Texas Street.

For one, Tully's sleep habits upset and frustrated Robin. She now attributed her lack of sleep to Boomerang, but even before Boomer was born, Robin at various times in the night would have to go looking for Tully and ask her to come to bed. Sometimes he found her downstairs, sometimes in another bedroom. Sometimes in the bathroom. The bathroom scared him most of all.

Pink water. That was the main course his memory served up in grainy diffused color. *Pink water.*

At 1501 Texas Street, Tully got up around seven in the morning. She would also get up at three in the morning and before that at midnight, and generally would sleep in three- or four-hour stints throughout the day. Robin used to call home from work half a dozen times, but gradually he stopped. Whenever he called, he was always interrupting something: a feeding, a washing, a reading. Something he was not a part of. Or worse, sometimes she was not home.

The last months of her pregnancy, Tully had been like a vicious bull, ready at any moment to attack the red cloth that was Robin. When he stayed out of her way, she screamed he was leaving her alone too much; when he was around her, she yelled at him to leave her be. She gave birth to little Robin without him and proceeded to devote what little energy she had to the baby.

The first few months after Boomer was born, Robin rushed home every night to see his family. But after a while, he started working later and later. He didn't want to be eating Millie's cooking. He wanted to be eating Tully's. He didn't want to be coming home to an empty kitchen. At first he would call to tell Tully he'd be working late, but soon he stopped calling. Tully never asked him where he was. She took it on faith he was working, and if she was home when he came home, she always asked him how work was. She seemed to trust him, or not care. Sometimes Robin wished she would ask. It just wasn't normal. If only once she said to him, where were you, or stay. If only once she said to him let's go out, or let's eat in, or watch TV or play a game. Or make love. *If only once.*

So now Robin doggedly got up and washed his plate. Millie was a good cook. Thank God for her.

All Robin wanted to do was stay home and come home, but he just didn't know what to do for Tully. He didn't know how to help her. He didn't know what she wanted. So now she came to him and said, "I want to go to KU." And Robin felt he had no choice but to do what he could. She was only twenty-one. Her life was not over yet. She told him of her wanting and he had no choice but to help her.

*   *   *

A few months later, in December 1982, Robin and Tully went to pick out Tully's very first Christmas tree. She wanted the biggest tree; but Robin put his foot down. They got a twelve-footer in the end—a huge compromise compared to what she wanted to get—and paid extra to have it delivered. Thank God for the high ceilings. They trimmed the tree together, though Tully was not very good at it. She kept putting all the red balls on one side and was useless with snow and lights. Still, though, it was her first Christmas tree. Robin found that unbelievable. Unbe-fucking-lievable, but didn't mention it, remembering that one of the causes of Tully's moodiness was living in their house. Remembering that it was his poor judgment and then his pride that had been responsible for carving a canyon between him and Tully that Robin for twelve months had been trying to mend. How *could* he have known, though? How could he have so underestimated Tully? he thought remorsefully, atop a ladder, attaching a Christmas angel to the tree. How could I have *under*estimated Tully and *over*estimated Hedda?

But here was the twelve-foot tree. And Boomerang, nearly nine months old, was trying to climb up the ladder. Robin felt Tully tickle him behind the knees, and before he reacted to her, he closed his eyes, hoping she would touch him again. She did. He kept his composure, saying only, "Hey, stop that right now. Stop that." And then promptly fell off the ladder, falling right on top of Tully and Boomerang, who laughed so hard he threw up. Tully went upstairs to clean him up, while Robin lay on the floor and looked at their tree. Tully didn't say anything, but Robin thought they had done a great job.

That night, when he woke up and she wasn't there, Robin couldn't find Tully upstairs. But when he came down he found her. She was sleeping in front of the tree, with all its lights twinkling their rainbow colors. He knelt down beside her on the floor and brushed the hair away from her face. "Tully," he whispered. "Tully."

She woke up.

"Tully," he said. "I think I remember. Jack. He was . . . she was . . . birthday, New Year's Eve, football . . . I think he was the one she was . . ."

"Yes," said Tully sleepily. "You're such a detective."

3.

Tully convinced Robin to come to St. Mark's with her for Christmas morning Mass, and he did. He hadn't gone in quite some time. Last Christmas she went alone. Things between them were so bad then. He was bringing Hedda to their house on Texas Street then. Tully didn't go to Mass at all after last Christmas. She didn't want to run into anyone she knew. She didn't want to run into Julie's mother, nor let Julie find out she was pregnant and still in Topeka.

But Tully continued to go to St. Mark's every Sunday, usually after everybody had long gone. Robin was now playing sports in Manhattan on Saturdays and Sundays. He played softball in the spring and summer, rugby and football in the fall and winter. During January and February, when there was too much snow on the fields, he worked in his store from open to close. Sometimes he watched the Chiefs. Sometimes he cooked dinner. But he didn't go to St. Mark's with her anymore.

Today was a fine crisp Christmas morning, however, with snow in their backyard, so Tully asked Robin to come. And he did.

The entire Martinez clan except Julie was in church.

Tully, who wore the blue crepe dress Robin gave her for their first wedding anniversary and held a bouquet of white carnations in her hand, smiled at Angela walking by. Angela stopped, smiled, and leaned over. "It's nice to see you here again."

Was I ever christened? Tully thought as Mass began. Never mind.

She closed her eyes and breathed in the incense. *Wichita*.

What did she tell the nurse that Monday morning in Wichita? Religion? It never occurred to her that she should have one. She had stared dumbly, standing small in her flat twelve-year-old shoes, with a big black Evel Knievel sweatshirt covering her five-and-a-half-month-old baby. It was Lynn Mandolini who broke the silence by shouting. "Religion? Why are you asking her what religion she is? What does that have to do with anything?" The nurse was calm. "In case she requires a priest," the nurse told Lynn. And Tully knew right away. They needed to know what religion she was in case a prayer had to be said over her. In case she needed those, what do you call them? Last rites.

Someone ought to say last rites over me, Tully had thought weakly, but could not speak.

Lynn, not knowing, wrote Tully down as a Catholic.

Well, why not? Tully and her mother hadn't been to church in years at that time. Back when Tully's father was still around, they went to bow their heads once or twice a year. Christmas and Easter. Aunt Lena had told Tully that Bill Rust and his family were Baptists. But that was back in Oklahoma. In Topeka, Hedda waxed Congregational. But Congregational did not soothe Tully. Catholicism and incense and psalms soothed Tully.

In Wichita, Tully had kept her mouth shut about her religion, but boy, did she wish she hadn't. Because after that Monday in 1973, for months in her nightmares, a Catholic priest in full black robes and a Bible in his hands stood under her as she hung from the rope, and said over and over, "But Tully, what religion are you? I can't save you, Tully, if you don't belong to God. How can I save you if you don't belong to God, Tully?"

Tully still woke up in the middle of the night, holding on to the bed, seeing his eyes turned up at her, hearing the priest's kindly voice telling her she was beyond eternal redemption.

She opened her eyes and smiled bloodlessly at Robin, who was staring at her. "Are you all right?"

"Fine, great," Tully answered, looking straight ahead. But she didn't close her eyes again.

Giving the bouquet to Robin and taking Boomerang, she got up for Communion and went to drink the blood and eat the flesh of Christ. Tully had never asked her mother if she was christened, but no matter. Boomerang was christened, she thought, bending her head to receive the bread and wine. And I am christened by umbilical proxy. We're all God's children, she reasoned, crossing herself and kissing Father Majette's hand. We all deserve redemption.

After Mass, she left Boomer with Robin, motioning to him where she was headed, and walked to the back of St. Mark's, where she sat on the rusty old chair and then knelt down in the snow to arrange her white carnations around the tombstone. The flowers blended into the snow; only their black stems and green leaves were visible. She did not stay long. Robin and Boomerang were waiting for her. It was cold. In the summer it was better. In the summer she took Boomerang with her, and he crawled a little bit around the graves while she sat in the chair.

Before Tully left she noticed yet again that hers weren't the only flowers there. Every Christmas someone would carefully lay out white roses in the white snow. Tully sometimes would come earlier than usual and hang around way past frostbite time hoping someone would come. Tully wanted to thank that someone.

Jennifer had loved fresh flowers.

After Mass, Robin and Tully went to visit Shakie and Frank in their new home in one of the developments near Lake Shawnee. Shakie seemed cheerful, until Tully got her alone. In Shakie's eyes Tully saw pain.

"So, Shake, did I tell you I'm starting school next month? KU. I'm gonna try to finish in a year and a half."

Shakie completely ignored Tully. Shakie's face, drawn, tense, tight-lipped, made Tully heave a big sigh. Tully shook her head. "Shakie, what's the matter with you?"

"Tully, you gotta help me. Jack is back home. What am I going to do?"

"What are you going to do?" Tully said loudly, then looked around, lowered her voice, and leaned closer to Shakie. They were standing in the middle of the kitchen. "Nothing, Shakie, that's what you're going to do. You're going to work, you're going to cook, you're going to get pregnant. Then you're going to have a couple of kids. Maybe in the middle of all that, you're going to have a decent marriage. What are you even talking about?"

Shakie shook her head.

"What are you shaking your head for? Are you prepared to throw your marriage away? For what? For some gypsy who comes once a year to screw you and leave? Come on, Shake, wise up. What are you doing?"

It sounded like a good reproof to Tully, but looking at Shakie's anguished face, Tully saw the words meant nothing. In any case, Tully knew that Shakie was not asking Tully for advice on what to do. Shakie was asking Tully to lie for her.

Tully tightened her jaw. "What is wrong with you, girl? So go ahead, it doesn't matter to me, go ahead. Do you want to tell Frank now or after you've packed? God, I just can't believe he is worth risking all you have. Is he *really* worth it?"

Shakie's expression gave Tully her answer. Disgusted, Tully sharply turned around and left Shakie standing alone in the kitchen.

A few days later, Tully came to see Shakie at Macy's. She wanted to stop by JC Penney to see Mr. Mandolini, but just couldn't face him. Didn't want to ask him again about Lynn. Didn't want to hear his words, didn't want to see his face.

Shakie quickly went on her break when she saw Tully. "Thanks for coming. I was afraid you wouldn't come at all for a while."

"Sure I'd come," said Tully. "After he left."

They stood near the jewelry. Tully, while listening to Shakie, was at the same time trying to read the prices on some of the solitaire engagement rings that were locked up under the glass. She was squinting at the diamonds and then back at Shakie.

Shakie was talking but Tully was thinking, My ring is nicer than any of those other ones.

"Tully, will you help me, please?" said Shakie. "Tonight. Will you help me tonight?"

Tully looked silently at her friend.

"What?" said Shakie. "You're not going to help me?"

"No," said Tully quietly. "I'll help you. You're my friend. But Shakie," she said, "can I just ask you one question. Why did you get married? I mean, I know why *I* got married, but why did *you* get married? What was the point?"

"Oh, Tully, you're so naive," said Shakie.

For a moment Tully stopped paying attention to the diamonds. "Shakie, don't fucking tell me I'm naive. You don't think I understand your little game? I understand just a little more than you think I do. For one thing," said Tully, wanting to stop herself from saying it but at the same time wanting to be mean, "I'll bet Jack's not the one asking to see *you*."

"Here is where you're wrong, Tully DeMarco."

"Oh, really? I see." Stop it, Tully, stop it, she told herself. But there was a four-year-old fury still running around her zoo. Tully said, "So this guy, who's decided to leave Topeka and you behind, this guy who *chose* to go away and not to take you with him, this guy has all of a sudden started to pine, and can't spend a week back home without seeing his ex-girlfriend, who is now married to someone else? Shakie, who is being naive?"

Shakie spoke back in low tones. "Goddamn it, Tully, can you get out of your judge's robes for a moment and listen to me? I don't care if it doesn't make sense to you. That's not why you're being naive."

"Why, then?"

"Because," Shakie said in a low voice, "you have no idea what I'm feeling at all. None whatsoever. You think it's all as simple as turning off the light."

Tully coiled up inside. Well, I've heard that somewhere before, haven't I? she thought.

"Who cares if I have no idea?" she declared. "All I want to know is, why did you marry Frank if you don't love Frank?"

"Who says I don't love Frank?" Shakie said defensively. "I love Frank. I'm not going to see Jack anymore. Tonight is the last time. Really. I just want to see him for a few hours, to talk about the old times. Just to see him." Shakie's gaze turned pleading, and she touched Tully's hand. "Please, Tully. Will you help me?"

That evening, Shakie came over for dinner. She came with Frank, and Robin cooked a roast beef with potatoes. After dinner, Tully excused herself and went upstairs to put Boomerang to bed. I don't want to do this, she thought, holding Boomerang in her arms, comforted by his suckling feeding noises. I don't want to do this for her.

When Tully came back down, Shakie had already asked the men if she and Tully could go see *Terms of Endearment*.

"But Tully and I already saw it," said Robin.

"Yes," said Shakie. "And Tully loved it."

"She did?" Robin asked, and looked at Tully, who had just come downstairs and sat down. "You loved it?"

Tully nodded.

"I don't remember you loving it," Robin said.

"Didn't I cry till I couldn't stop?" said Tully.

"No," said Robin. "You didn't, actually."

There was a brief pause, during which Robin and Tully looked away from each other. They saw *Terms* last February, two evenings after the incident in the bathroom. There wasn't a dry eye in the house, except for Tully's.

Tonight, the men settled down to watch TV and the girls went to the movies. Shakie directed Tully to Lakeside Drive.

So that's where he lives, thought Tully, pulling up to a small white house on Lakeside Drive. No wonder I saw him in St. Mark's a few years ago. Lakeside Drive joins Pembroke and Canterbury.

Instead of going to the movies after she dropped Shakie off, Tully walked to St. Mark's. It was too cold to stay outside, so Tully went in and breathed in the warm incense until it was time to get Shakie.

When Tully got back to the car, Shakie was already in it, sitting there teary-eyed rubbing her hands together. Tully didn't ask, and Shakie, for the first ten minutes, didn't offer.

"Where did you go?" asked Shakie.

"St. Mark's."

Shakie glanced sideways at Tully. "You went to church at night? That's what Jack told me you did, when we saw your car outside, but I didn't believe him. Why would you go to church at night?"

"Inside," said Tully. "I sat inside."

Shakie was quiet. "I don't think I should see him again," she said tightly.

"Amen," said Tully.

"You don't approve, do you?" Shakie said, not facing Tully.

Tully patted Shakie's knee. "Shake, I neither approve nor disapprove. I'm not in the approval business. I'm just upset at you for not knowing your heart before September 20, 1982."

"Oh, Tully, Tully," said Shakie. "I knew my heart."

"Well, Shakie, then why did you get married?"

"Because," she replied, rubbing her hands, "with Frank I have this real thing. A thing that works, a thing that can live, that can have a house, that can have children. A thing that's real. And with Jack, I have this impossible thing. I just couldn't base my life on an impossible thing." She looked at her hands. "I didn't think me being married would bother Jack. But apparently it does. Imagine that."

The women said nothing for the rest of the ride to Texas Street. Tully was thinking that if she ever ran into Jack again, she might thank him for having the decency to leave Shakie alone.

"Do you love Frank?" asked Tully, parked in front of her house.

"Of course I do," Shakie replied, shivering. "Like you love Robin."

Tully shook her head, and shivered herself. "No. Not like me. I don't have anyone else. *Anything* else. I don't have Jeremy. I don't have California. I don't have very much at all. All I have is Robin. And my mother."

"And Boomerang."

"Yes," Tully said. "And him." Thinking that he meant more to her than she had ever hoped for. "But nothing else."

"But not for lack of trying, Tully. Besides, you don't need anything else."

"Neither do you."

"No," Shakie said sadly. "I guess neither do I. I guess I don't have anything else anymore, either." And then, a little later, "You think it's just an excuse for him, me being married and all? You think there's someone else?"

"No, I don't think so," said Tully uneasily. "I think he just can't sit still."

Shakie was silent.

"But who can, right?" Tully replied, fidgeting. "Julie can't. He can't."

"You can't," finished Shakie. "But *I* can. And so can your Robin. And so can many people. Most people in Topeka. Those are the happiest ones. The ones who are not itching constantly to be someplace else."

"Oh, yeah," said Tully. "You don't seem so happy to me."

"I want to be someplace else," replied Shakie.

"Who doesn't, Shake?" Tully said quietly. "Who doesn't?"

They sat in the cold car. "Listen," said Tully. "Forget him. I think I've said those two words more often than any other two words in the English language."

"Except 'Fuck you,' " Shakie smiled.

"Yes, except that," Tully smiled back. "Forget him, Shake. Get on with your life. Get pregnant. Move. Something. Just forget him."

"Well, I don't have much choice, do I?" Shakie said. "He doesn't really want to hang around with me, now that I'm an old married lady." And she cried.

"I'm sorry, Tully," she said. "Better in front of you than in front of him, right?"

Tully was remarkably calm. Stroking Shakie's hair, she said softly, "Right. Have a baby. Have two. Forget him."

As they were getting out of the car, Shakie turned to Tully. "You don't like him very much, do you? He's a really good man, a wonderful man. I mean, your best friend thought he was all right. And I do, too. But you have little sympathy for him. You just wish he'd go away and never come back, don't you?"

"I do, actually," said Tully honestly. "You're much happier when he's not around."

Shakie said, "I'm a happy person generally. I think it would take a lot to bring me down." She paused. "Like, as far down as he brought *her*."

"He may've brought her down," said Tully, biting her lip, "but most people get up."

A few days later, Tully and Robin met 1983 at home. Tully was irritable at first, but by the end of the night, she was glad they stayed home and did not go to Bruce's farm as they usually did, because around ten in the evening, December 31, Boomerang took his first steps. Wobbly, uncertain, but delighted at himself nonetheless, Boomer took the four necessary steps from his father's arms into his mother's arms. He squealed with delight, and so did Tully and Robin. They sat around and tried to keep him up until midnight, to celebrate his first New Year's, but Boomerang couldn't hold out and conked out on the couch. Robin prepared shrimp in beer and Tully opened Asti Spumante. They greeted the New Year, sang a little "Auld Lang Syne," and tentatively kissed each other. The shrimp went uneaten and the Asti Spumante undrunk. It was the first Tully and Robin made love since Boomerang was born.

In early January, a few weeks before the spring semester was starting at KU, Tully went to St. Mark's alone. She was earlier than usual and even made it for the last bit of Mass.

"Tully," said Angela, coming up to Tully afterwards. "So how come you don't bring the rest of your family? You got such a nice family."

"Boomerang is sick," Tully said. "Robin is watching him."

"That's good, he's a good man. So you two, you ever go out? Me and my husband, we never went out when the children were small."

"No, we don't go out much, either." Tully smiled.

"That's too bad," Angela said. "You should catch a movie once in a while. Bring Boomerang to me. I take care of him. I look after your boy. My kids will love him."

Angela looked at the flowers in Tully's hands. "More flowers. For her?"

Tully nodded. Angela shook her head. "Too many flowers. Just light a candle. That's what I do. Some guy came with flowers, too—"

"A guy?" Tully interrupted. Angela glanced around the nearly empty courtyard. "He left. Didn't you see him? Sitting in the last pew? How could you miss him? He had the biggest bunch—"

But Tully stopped listening. She waved a quick good-bye and slid through the side gate, down the narrow path.

And there he was.

Tully should have known. Brown leather jacket, black dress pants, head down, arms crossed. Tully came closer. How could she have not known? He turned around and politely nodded to her. They were silent for a few moments; Tully was intensely uncomfortable. Besides the politely nodded hello, Tully didn't know what else to do. What do I say? Thank you? That's what I had wanted to say to the person who was bringing her flowers, but who would have thought that person would be him? Saying thank you to him seems so absurd.

On the surface, Tully felt what she always felt when she was confronted with him. Slightly embarrassed at all the stuff she knew about him. Slightly hostile. Slightly awkward. She could compartmentalize him well enough, but not so well when she was forced to stare into his face.

But somewhere deeper, Tully was . . . grateful that he had not forgotten *her*. *She*'d be pleased to know that. Be pleased to know she was dead but not forgotten. *Johnny Rotten, Johnny Rotten.*

"How are you?" asked Jack.

"Great, fine," Tully replied curtly. "She doesn't like white roses, you know. She likes white carnations."

Jack half smiled. "I beg to differ. At the Junior Prom, she wore a white rose corsage."

"Maybe," Tully said reluctantly. "I didn't go to the Junior Prom."

"No," said Jack, "but you did go to the Senior Banquet, and she wore a white rose corsage then."

"Gee," said Tully coolly. "I don't remember her wearing a corsage then."

"I do," said Jack. "I gave it to her."

"Ahh," said Tully, her breath momentarily taken away.

"Do you want to put those down?" asked Jack, pointing to the carnations.

"Well, that *is* what I came here for," answered Tully, thinking, I'm not being very pleasant, but who cares?

"Is *that* what you come here for?" he asked intently, moving out of her way as she walked past, being careful not to brush against him. As Tully was putting down the carnations, something hot came up into her throat, kicked in, and began to scratch. What did he ask me? She straightened up and looked at him coldly. "Yes, that's why I come here," she said. "Why do *you* come here?"

Jack stared at her, shrugged, and zipped his jacket up higher. "To put down my flowers, of course. Why else?"

"Don't you think it's a little fucking late to bring her flowers?" she snapped, shoving her way past him in the snow. Okay, maybe more than *a little* hostile.

Tully heard Jack's footsteps following her down the path. "Maybe," he said to her back. "But I only bring mine twice a year. Shakie tells me you bring yours every Sunday. Why?"

"Fuck you," said Tully fiercely, crossing herself for cursing in the cemetery.

He ran around and stood in her way. "Why, Tully? Tell me."

"Fuck you," she said, trying to push her way past him without falling in the snow. "Stop talking to me! Leave me alone."

Jack stepped up onto the mound of snow so Tully could walk by. "You hate me, don't you?" he said to her. "You really hate me."

"You're wrong," she said. "I don't hate you. I have no feelings for you at all, you bastard."

He sneered. "Don't give me that shit. You hate me. For both of them."

Shakie. Yes. Tully was so angry at that moment, she stopped *wanting* to thank him for leaving Shakie alone, finally. But she just couldn't stand to look at him any longer. "Fuck you," she said loudly and clearly for the third time, and stormed out of the cemetery.

4.

The days became too short when Tully started school at the end of January. Up through the night—with Boomerang and with herself—Tully left the house at seven-thirty in the morning for her eight-thirty social welfare policy. She was taking twenty-one credits and was on her feet from sunup to sundown. By the time she lay down with Robin sometime around midnight or one, Tully hardly had time for nightmares, but still she couldn't sleep. She started taking ice-cold showers in the middle of the night to rid herself of the sweat and the wakefulness.

Aside from her social welfare courses, she took modern dance again. She couldn't help herself; the practice was grueling, but at least she got to dance a little bit. English Literature, History of the Republican Party, and Readings in Child Development. English Lit was a killer because she had so little time to read, and usually she was blind tired by the time she had time, late at night, after Boomer was asleep. So she read Thomas Hardy aloud to Boomerang. *Tess of the D'Urbervilles* became one of Tully's favorite books and one that Boomer particularly liked to fall asleep to.

On those evenings when Boomer played at her feet and Robin was home on the other end of the couch watching TV, Tully read *Tess* to both of them. Robin ignored *Tess*, but when Tully started E.M. Forster's *A Room with a View*, Robin turned off the TV. Over a period of several weeks, Tully read the whole book to them, as Boomerang played and Robin pretended to look at a newspaper. The night the book was finished, Robin volunteered to bathe Boomerang and put him to bed. When he came downstairs again, Tully was asleep in the kitchen, head down on the table. Robin gently woke her up, and when they were both in bed, he leaned over and whispered, "Tully, what do you think? Do you think of me as a . . . *room with a view*?"

"Robin," said Tully, turning to him and stroking his cheek. "You're a whole fucking house."

Thereafter, television rarely went on in the DeMarco household. Robin came home earlier and earlier, Millie cooked dinner for the whole family. Including Hedda. And after dinner, Tully read.

Shakespeare, Dante, Milton, Dickens, Henry James, occasionally Tennyson. Boomerang for the most part ignored her. Once, Hedda, sitting in the living room with them, asked if she could turn on the TV.

Robin glanced at Tully and said, "Hedda, we don't watch TV now, Tully likes to read aloud to Boomerang. To us." Hedda sat there, moving her head from side to side, her eyes never leaving her daughter's face, listening to *Portrait of a Lady*. After a while, she asked to be taken to her rooms and didn't sit in the living room with them until the spring, until one Saturday night Hedda asked Tully to read Agatha Christie to her. And Tully did.

The reading and dancing paid off. Tully finished her first semester at KU with a perfect 4.0 grade-point average.

She liked the drive to KU, straight through the long-grass Kansas hills, but she missed her son and her breasts ached for him. He was home with Millie, who was great, and that was good. But she wasn't his mother. When the spring came, Robin hired a young nurse to take Boomerang to Lawrence so Tully could spend some time with Boomer between classes. Robin hired the nurse unbidden. Thank God for Robin.

Mr. Hillier welcomed Tully back for an internship the summer of 1983 after her first semester at Kansas University. (Robin told Tully Mr. Hillier had a bad crush on her. "Mr. Cunningham?" said Tully. "Mr. Cunningham has eyes only for Mrs. C.")

A couple of people quit in the department, and Lillian White was stuck and was forced to delegate two full-blown cases to novice Tully. Tully's first assignment was to "conference" with Mr. and Mrs. Buckle, really, to *ask* them to reconsider giving their 13-year-old, booze-addicted son Jerry to foster care. To *beg* them to keep their son. There just weren't enough foster families to go around. They were like the rotten dried-up old food that was so hard to come by in Africa. So Tully was supposed to *plea* bargain. Wouldn't Jerry be much better off getting dry with his own parents' help? And the city would help with clinic costs.

Tully came at eleven o'clock in the morning, to an apartment on top of a garage in the heart of east Topeka. Mr. and Mrs. Buckle were screaming at the top of their lungs at each other through the screen door, but Tully couldn't understand any of the words because Mr. and Mrs. Buckle were slurring them. The conference was over. Tully turned around and returned to Docking. When she was asked by Lillian about the conference, Tully replied that Mr. and Mrs. Buckle felt that Jerry would be better off taken care of by someone else.

Tully's second case put her into the home of Mr. and Mrs. Arnuther, a foster couple whose foster children had complained of abuse. The last two were taken away from Mr. and Mrs. Arnuther, but the couple had since gone to counseling and reapplied for foster family status. Lillian had accepted them with "probation," but that was just a three-syllable word on paper. Tully wanted to know why the Arnuthers weren't just scrapped from the program altogether. "That's fine, Tully," said Lillian. "And kids like Jerry Buckle stay with their parents. The Arnuthers need to be monitored, that's all."

So Tully went to monitor them.

After going to see Mr. and Mrs. Arnuther and their seven-year-old charge, Sharon Muske, Tully wondered if kids like Jerry Buckle wouldn't be better off staying with their parents. Sharon did not say a word to Tully during the hour they were together, not even when the two of them went for a walk around the house. Not a word. Sharon just walked and stared straight ahead. Not even Tully's arm on her shoulder could precipitate a word from Sharon Muske. Tully understood.

Tully thought of talking to Lillian, but she didn't even know how to approach the woman. Lillian smoked nonstop, breathed haltingly, looked dumpy in her size-eighteen clothes.

Approaching fifty, Lillian was unmarried and had no children. All Lillian had was this job and Tully knew it was as futile to talk to Lillian about weeding out inappropriate foster families as it was to talk to her about the tenderness of breast-feeding.

So Tully kept her mouth shut and did what she could.

One Sunday in August, she saw an abundance of white roses at St. Mark's. After touching the flowers with her fingers, Tully reluctantly felt better for a Sunday.

Julie and Laura came back in August, before the September "corn crunch," as Tully called it. Tully was privately happy to see her friend.

At first she came over to Julie's house several times a week, sometimes for lunch from work, often bringing Boomerang. But Laura was always there. Julie wasn't Tully's anymore. They never had a chance to talk alone. A few times on the weekends, Tully invited Julie and, sigh, Laura to come to Lake Shawnee with her and Robin and Boomer. Finally, Tully asked Julie to come to St. Mark's with her. "Just you, okay, Jule?" and heard Julie breathe into the phone. Sunday came and Julie came, alone.

"I really don't want to go in the back, Tully," Julie said.

"Who fucking does?" said Tully. "Let's go anyway."

They stood there for a few moments in front of the small gravestone.

"Look at all these white roses," Julie said with surprise. "I thought white carnations were her favorites. Have I forgotten already?"

"They are," said Tully. "You haven't forgotten."

"Who brings her white roses?"

"Jack," said Tully.

"Jack," Julie echoed hollowly. "I didn't know he came here."

"Well, yes," said Tully. "Apparently. Every time he comes back to Topeka, he remembers."

"Who cares?" Julie said harshly. "Who cares now?"

I suppose . . . thought Tully.

Julie glanced at Tully. "How do you feel that he comes here?"

Tully shrugged. "It could be worse," she said. "I'm glad he remembers her once in a while."

Julie bowed her head and crossed herself. "I hate coming here, Tully. I hate it. Please, let's just go."

Tully continued to stand in front of the grave. "The three of us, together again," she said. "Is this the first time since she died? Have you ever come here?"

Julie pulled Tully by the hand. "I've come here. Not often, I'll give you that. Come on, Tully."

Tully didn't move. "I like that he comes here," she said slowly. "I like that out of all the people to bring flowers to her, *he* comes."

"Goody for him," said Julie, looking at her friend. Tully was gritting her teeth. "Tully, you're not still angry with her?"

Tully kicked the gravestone. Goddamn it. And incredibly, desperately lonely.

On the way back to Wayne Street, Julie said, "Does Shakie know he's in town?"

"I don't think so," Tully replied, remembering she had once wanted to thank him for that. "I think he's ended it with her once and for all. Shake got married and he left her alone."

"How does she feel about that?" Julie wanted to know.

"Oh, thrilled," said Tully, and Julie smiled.

When they pulled up to Julie's house, Julie said, opening the Camaro door, "You still driving this thing? It must be a thousand years old by now."

Tully just nodded, patting the wheel.

That was the only time Tully was alone with Julie. Later that week, Julie and Laura left for Iowa.

The following Sunday, Tully was in St. Mark's, sitting in the very last pew so she could look around the whole church. He was at the front, listening to the Lord's Prayer. Angela was there, too, on her knees.

After Mass, Tully walked out first and fast. She didn't want to spend time talking to Angela. She put her flowers down, sat herself down on her rusted wire chair, and waited. She didn't have to wait long.

"Well, here we are again," he said, coming near her and crouching down. She looked down at his head, and he looked up at her and smiled. She nodded politely and turned forward again. Jack arranged his flowers around Tully's flowers.

"So how's it going?" he asked.

He looked well tanned and well groomed. "Fine, thanks," she said civilly. "What are you doing here in August?"

"My mother lives here all year round. Am I not allowed to come to my hometown in August?" he said, standing up.

She clasped her hands together. "You can do what you like."

"Thank you," he said.

"Personally," Tully continued, "I thought you didn't have a home. My impression was that you lived in a bag."

"I do," he said, "live in a bag. But this month, my bag happens to be in my home. I'm visiting my mother."

"And here, too," stated Tully.

"And here, too," replied Jack.

Tully got up from the chair and stood in front of Jack for a moment, looking not so much at him as at his shirt buttons. "Yeah, well, see ya."

"I'm sorry about the last time," Jack said quickly. "I realize you didn't expect to find me here—"

"No, no," Tully interrupted, moving sideways toward the path and away from him. "I was not myself. I *was* a little surprised, actually."

Jack followed her down the path. "I don't know why," he said. "She was my friend, too."

That made Tully turn around to look at him for a moment. "Somehow," she said, proceeding down to the gate, "I find that very hard to believe."

"Yeah, she told me you were a skeptic."

This startled Tully even further, but this time she didn't look back. "I find *that* even harder to believe," she said.

Jack reached in front of her, opening the iron gate. Tully saw his face, and he was smiling. "What?" he said. "That you're a skeptic?"

Tully cleared her throat. "I didn't know you and *she* talked," said Tully.

"Sure we talked," Jack said. "I know a little bit about you, Tully Makker."

She squinted into his eyes. The sun was behind him and it was hard to see if he was teasing. "You know nothing," she said uncertainly.

Jack just smiled, and Tully had to admit as she unlocked the Camaro and got in that she was a bit curious. To talk about *Jennifer*! Just the thought of being *able* to tightened Tully's gut.

She revved up the Camaro and unrolled the window. Jack leaned in. "How is Shakie?" he asked.

"Good, great," said Tully. "Better for not having heard from you," she added.

Jack smirked. "She never hears from me," he answered, and Tully knew it was true.

"She is pregnant now, you know," Tully told him. She was going to tell him what Shakie was pregnant with, but kept quiet. Tully didn't want to talk about Shakie to Jack.

"Oh, yeah?" He seemed genuinely pleased. "I didn't know that. I'm happy for her. Listen, though." He paused. "Don't tell her I'm here."

"Not to worry," said Tully sarcastically, and put the car into drive. "That's one thing I will not do."

Jack stepped away from the car. "Natalie Anne Makker," he said, "have you gone back to school yet?"

"I have, yes," she said. "Kansas University. I graduate next May."

"Good for you," he said sincerely. "Good for you."

Tully wanted to say something, but the only thing coming to her tongue was *Thank you*.

So she bit her tongue and said instead, "By the way, Jack, it's Tully DeMarco."

" 'Bye, now, Tully DeMarco," he said, smiling lightly.

When Tully came to St. Mark's the following Sunday, he wasn't there, and there were no fresh flowers—only the ones from a week ago. They were dried and wilted, but Tully left them there until they rotted into the ground, and continued to put her fresh ones around his.

5.

When the summer ended, Tully needed to place Boomerang. He was just seventeen months old, too big to be carried constantly, too big to be breast-fed, though she still managed. And Millie, for all her culinary talents, was not a baby-sitter. So

Tully gently asked Angela Martinez if she could look after Boomer for $60 a week.

"Money, I don't want your silly money, Tully. I take care of him for you for free."

"Free is out of the question," Tully said, relieved that Angela would look after her boy.

"Money is out of the question," said Angela. "I did not pick you up off the road when you were five, I did not feed you dinner every night and drive you home every night, and let you sleep over every night, so that you give me money for your son," Angela said indignantly. "One thing more," she said. "I will not call that poor child Boomerang. What's his proper name again?"

"Boomer," said Tully. "And you will not look after him for free. You will let me pay you for being so kind. It will help you, you know it will, I will not take no for an answer."

"No," said Angela stubbornly.

Back and forth, back and forth. Tully went out to the car and got Robin, who was waiting patiently behind the wheel. Finally it was agreed between the three of them that Robin was allowed to pay Angela because Angela did not know Robin since he was five. Just as long as Tully never showed her face in Angela's door with money in her hands. Tully agreed and back home asked Robin to pay Angela generously. For the times she picked me off the street and fed me tostadas, thought Tully.

And so Boomerang stopped being with Millie, stopped going to Lawrence with Tully, and adjusted very well to being on Wayne Street and playing with eight-year-old Vinnie. Too well. When Tully came to pick him up at six o'clock, he barely looked up from his toys and kicked up quite a fuss when it was time to go home. Robin told Tully that he received similar treatment at the feet of his only child on those few occasions that he came to pick up Boomer.

Tully was about to go back to school, but Mr. Hillier asked her if she would mind continuing to monitor her two cases. "What for?" Tully asked.

"The children like you," Mr. Hillier replied. "The foster parents like you."

Tully shook her head.

"Sharon Muske likes you," Mr. Hillier said.

Tully just shook her head. Yeah, she thought. So did Damien.

"She does," he repeated. "She asked after you. Mr. Arnuther called me. Sharon asked for you. Your visits help her. And us. Just the two cases. We'll pay you. I'll see what I can do, maybe we can give you ten dollars an hour. How would that be?"

Tully sighed. She wanted to say that there was no need to pay her $10 an hour, she was already bought and paid for. But instead she quietly agreed—she felt less angry now at the whole world, knowing Jack was bringing Jennifer white roses.

In the fall, Tully carefully brought up to Mr. Hillier the easygoing manner with which the foster families were recruited.

"Are you criticizing Lillian, Tully?"

"No, no," she quickly said. "Well, yes. A little. Lillian is a true professional."

"Lillian knows her job," said Mr. Hillier. "We have too many needy kids. Without more foster families, the program falls on its face. Lillian knows that."

"With some of the people Lillian is getting, the program more than falls on its face," Tully remarked. "It fails."

"So what do you suggest, Tully?" Mr. Hillier asked. "What do *you* suggest?"

"A longer training period for the folks wanting to take on kids. This six-hour deal, I mean, you have to take ten hours of driving lessons and a three-hour course just to take a test you can fail three times, but here, after shorter than a working day, shorter than a ride to St. Louis, shorter than a doubleheader, these families are taking care of children. I mean, if these kids wanted slipshod parenting, they could have just stayed home, right?"

"Longer training periods cost money," Mr. Hillier said. "How much longer are you talking about?"

"Two months," said Tully. "Eight weeks. Five days a week. Four hours a day. Before they even lay their hands on a child. Before they even lay their hands on a government check. Pay them something for their training trouble. Nominal. But make sure they really want to help these kids. I'm telling you, Mr. Hillier, you'd immediately get a lot of folks dropping out when they realize that to pick up their first kid and their first check they'll have to train longer than the time it takes to cook a twenty-pound turkey."

Mr. Hillier smiled and shook his head. "You're real earnest, Tully. But families dropping out is the last thing we want. We don't have enough foster help as it is."

"No, Mr. Hillier, you will have enough. You'll just have to train and advertise to get better people."

"Advertise?" Mr. Hillier asked skeptically.

Tully was cheerful. "Advertise," she said. "Put the ads in all the malls around the Topeka area. Put the ads in local newspapers. Post billboards. Ask them to do something for their country. Recite John Kennedy. Or John Donne. I don't know, but do something."

In October, Tully got to put her mouth where her money was. Mr. Hillier asked Tully to make an appeal for more money to the Appropriations Committee before the beginning of the next fiscal year. Lillian absolutely did not want to talk along with Tully. I think she hopes I will be put off by twenty unfriendly men, Tully thought, but I'm not to be put off by unfriendly anybody.

"I came to Mr. and Mrs. Arnuther over the summer," said Tully in closing after her long presentation, "and I asked them why their foster child Sharon Muske did not speak. 'She is not very talkative,' said Mrs. Arnuther. Well, no, she is not. Who would be? Sharon lives in the middle of Douglas County surrounded by hay and cows. Her parents are dead and her aunt and uncle decided to take a long vacation. Sharon does not go to school; instead Mr. and Mrs. Arnuther are teaching her at home. But at seven years old, she still doesn't know how to read or write. What Sharon does know how to do is milk a cow. She knows how to weed. She knows how to wash the floor. I asked Mr. and Mrs. Arnuther what made them take little Sharon on, and Mr. Arnuther looked me straight in the face, knowing I was from Docking, knowing I represented the State of Kansas, and said defiantly, 'We need the money.' They need seven dollars a day? Seven dollars a day. Ladies and gentlemen, it's not money we need to swing in front of the people of Topeka as the carrot," she said, "but kids. We need to swing these Sharons in front of the people of Topeka and say, the money is terrible. Terrible. It's only seven dollars a day. Just enough to feed a child. The money is terrible, yes, but who cares? Sharon needs your help, Sharon needs your care. These kids are sad kids. These are kids whose parents drink, kids who drink themselves, who steal, who smoke pot, who steal to smoke pot. Kids who don't go to school because no one told them they should. Some of these kids are going to grow up and rape your sister and rob your brother. Some already are.

"And I'm telling you that those families who want to help will not care about the money. Those who only want the money will not come forward. Good riddance to them. But the other ones, you know what those fewer families will do? They will get these kids off the streets. They will get them out of Lock-Up and out of Drug Rehab. They will get them out of your brother's pocket. And the money we will have spent on advertising and proper training will pay for something that has no price. Their future. Ours, too.

"As it is right now, our agency has forgotten what it's here for. And if we ourselves have, how can we remind the folks out there? But we need to remind them. The Foster Home Recruitment Agency is not here to give poor families an extra income, an extra seven bucks a day to wash their floors. We are not here to push a lot of paper, do a little filing, and go home at the end of the day. We are not here to justify our own employment so that the State of Kansas doesn't eliminate the agency from its budget next year.

"We are here first and foremost, and in fact, the only reason any of us should be here, the only reason why I am here, we're here because there are children out there who are not too lucky. There are kids out there who did not have the good luck to be born into . . ."

Tully stumbled. She wanted a good analogy, but the only one that came to mind was Sunset Court.

" . . . Into goose down," she went on. "Sharon Muske was always a quiet child, and so occasionally her aunt and uncle forgot to feed her because Sharon didn't tell them she was hungry. Wouldn't it be nice if Sharon could have had breakfast, lunch, and dinner without having to ask? Don't we owe Sharon a foster family that doesn't look us in the eye and say, 'Seven dollars'?

"No, we say. There are at any given time two hundred kids from three months to sixteen years either in foster care or waiting to be put into foster care. Some of them are in Lock-Up. Some of them are still with their parents. And there are only fifty to seventy-five families taking on kids. So we leave the kids with their parents. We go to the natural parents every two months asking them if they want their kids back. We say to the potential foster families, 'Seven bucks a day, come on, what do you say?' We forget what we're here for. And when we see mute Sharon Muske or drunk Jerry Buckle, we remind ourselves that we have seen a mute Sharon Muske or a drunk Jerry Buckle thirty times before. The first time we cried, and the second, too. The third time we took up smoking. The fourth we took up eating. The fifth time we clenched our fists, the sixth time we gritted our teeth. There are thirty rationalizations we have had to make not to go crazy at what we saw. But by the thirtieth time, we've clenched our hearts. We've *gritted* our hearts.

"And what I'm saying now is, unclench them. Ungrit them. Intensive training. More money. Closer monitoring. Better counseling for the natural parents. Better counseling for the kids. An advertising campaign that shows our new direction. Come! we'll say to the folks of Topeka. Get out of your car and drag that still-living dog off the highway before it dies. Drag it off. Drag it off before it dies, or worse, lives without you, lives with bared teeth and a shallow pant, with black eyes and a black soul, a soul that will be ready at any moment to drive over *you* with its car.

"But in the meantime, Sharon Muske is still mute, and Jerry Buckle is still drunk, and Mr. and Mrs. Arnuther are still getting seven dollars a day."

Two weeks later, the Appropriations Committee voted twelve to eight to increase Foster Home Recruitment's budget for 1984 by $3 million, but refused eighteen to two to allow an additional $2 million to finance the change in the training period from six hours to eight weeks as Tully had wanted.

"Did a great job, Tully," Mr. Hillier told her in private.

"Did a great job, Tully," Lillian White told her in public, but somehow Tully doubted Lillian's sincerity.

"Did a great job, Tully," Robin said to her when she told him of what happened, and Tully knew he meant it.

6.

Tully went to school Mondays, Wednesdays, and Fridays, taking twenty-one credits, and, at the request of Mr. Hillier, worked at Docking on Tuesdays and Thursdays. Tuesday was administrative, Thursday she visited Sharon Muske. Also on Tuesdays and Thursdays, Tully walked over to Angela's for lunch. That she liked and looked forward to. It was like having tostadas when she was five. She looked forward to them. Only the tostadas had been replaced by tuna sandwiches, and Julie wasn't there, but Boomerang was there. Tully figured it probably comforted Angela to see Tully at the kitchen table, just like the old times, so she tried hard never to miss a lunch.

"Angela, I like your yellow curtains," Tully said one afternoon. "You've had them for as long as you've had this house on Wayne Street."

"Wrong, Tully. I change them every two years. I just buy more yellow curtains."

Tully smiled. What an illusion. The sun made those yellow curtains so bright for as long as Tully could remember.

"You miss my daughter, don't you, Tully?"

Tully shook her thoughts off. "Sure."

"I miss her, too. Things just haven't been the same since she went traveling."

They sure haven't been, thought Tully.

She later waited for Angela to say something about Julie's choice of partner, to show Tully some emotion, but Angela spoke only of having her daughter so far away. Shaking her head, she said, "Couldn't stay in Topeka, my Julie. Not like you, Tully, not like you. You're a real survivor. How's your husband nowadays? He's a good man."

"He *is* a good man," said Tully. "And he's fine."

Angela leaned closer. "Personally, I think Jule is still not over Jen. You know?"

Tully knew.

Angela continued. "It's like she pretends real well, but deep down, she just can't face being disappointed or something. You know?"

Tully knew.

"Not like you, Tully. You're a survivor. Not like Lynn Mandolini, huh?"

Tully looked down into her hands. No, not much like Lynn Mandolini.

"That poor woman. That poor woman. I must say I can't blame her. I wish she would pick herself up, but I can't say I blame her. What'd I do if Julie was my only baby? Why, I'd go crazy, I would. Nobody should have just *one* child, nobody. You can't get over them. I don't think God intended for us to get over just *one* child."

"I don't know if God intended for us to get over *any* of our children," said Tully, looking at the yellow curtains.

"No, I suppose not. How can you? At least, if you have others, they keep you busy, they keep you on your feet. You can't sit around and cry all day, there are too many things to be done. But poor Lynn. And Tony, too. But at least he works, tries. But she . . . what's she to do now? Drink herself to death, that's all that's left, what else? You know, I invited her to my house a few years ago, she refused. Like my Julie. Julie comes back here so rarely. And won't go to St. Mark's with me. Everybody goes there, except my Julie. But you, Tully, you hold yourself together. That baby of yours and your husband, they must help you. Am I right? Isn't it hard to mope when you're so busy?"

Not so hard, Tully wanted to say, but Angela was not done. "I always said to Julie that if anyone was going to pull through, it would be you, even though you were closer to her than anybody. You always had that strength."

"Is that what I had?" said Tully.

"Oh, yes, oh, yes," said Angela. "Tough as nails, you." She smiled. "You were always going to make it no matter what. And look at you now."

Yes, look at me now, Tully thought. I hold myself together, by ropes from which my head hangs every night when I go to sleep to dream of peace and palm trees, dream of the sea, of no one to bother me, of someone to take the rope off me, of someone to let me dance on the beach . . . of someone to stop her from suffocating me, but yes, that is how I hold myself together. Because I dream of death.

Tully got up to go. This lunch was getting to be too fucking much.

"How is your friend Shakie? Bring her sometime," Angela said. "Bring her, I feed her, too."

Tully got Shakie to come for lunch at Angela's a few times during that autumn.

"Shakie, you looking so big," Angela said the first time she saw her.

Shakie waddled in. "Thanks. Twins. It's God's punishment to me for always being so thin."

Tully smiled. She remembered neglecting to tell Jack about Shakie's twins.

"So how many months are you now?" Angela asked after the turkey and tuna clubs American style were on the table. Tully missed the tostadas.

"Seven," Shakie answered. "The babies, God help me, are due January fifth."

"Shakie," Tully said. "Poor you. You don't know how hard it was with just one. He didn't want to come out, I wasn't dilating properly, I was in agonizing labor for twenty-nine and a half hours, finally they broke my water and I screamed for two and a half hours straight while he was being born. It was the single worst experience of my life. I really wish you luck with two."

Shakie paled, frowned, stopped eating. Angela mockingly berated Tully for her insensitivity. "Even if it was horrible and awful, how could you make poor Shakie feel so bad? Look at her. She stopped eating. Eat, honey, eat. Don't listen to her. She's always been a troublemaker."

Shakie looked dubious when she asked, "But Tully, you told me when Boomer was born he was out so fast and easy, you read three chapters of Dostoye-something while he was being born, and said that Dostoye-something was harder? Did you or did you not tell me that?"

Tully shrugged, rolling her eyes. "Yeah, yeah, but I only said that so you wouldn't be put off having children. You didn't believe me, did you?"

Shakie grew paler and spent the next few lunches pressing Angela for *her* labor details.

"Well, I just hope I'll be a good mother," Shakie finally said. "I just can't imagine taking time away from my hair."

"You'll be a good mother, Shakie," Angela assured her. "We're all good mothers at heart."

Tully scoffed.

"Well, Tully," said Angela. "At your job, you deal with the extremes. The bad extreme. You deal with mothers who have forgotten God. Most mothers haven't, Tully. You haven't."

"You'll be a good mother, Shakie," Tully said, getting the words out. "We all are good mothers."

7.

Shakie gave birth to a boy and a girl by cesarean section on Christmas Eve, 1983. When Tully came to visit her in Topeka State with Robin and Boomerang, Shakie was less concerned with her two babies than with the fact that she was now going to be scarred for life.

"I had them tie my tubes, you know," Shakie told Tully when they had a chance to be alone.

Tully said nothing, thinking *more is better*.

"What have you named them?"

"The boy is Anthony, and the girl ..." Shakie warmly smiled, holding Tully's hands, "Natalie."

"Natalie!" Tully exclaimed. "Natalie," she repeated, quieter, and hugged Shakie.

"It's nothing. I've always liked that name. Even before I knew you," but Tully continued to hug her, and Shakie finally said, "Look, your name is not even Natalie. No one calls you Natalie. Cut it out, you. You're hurting my stitches."

Then Shakie lowered her voice. "I called *him* a few days ago to wish him a Merry Christmas. He's home again."

Tully's gaze hardened a little. "I figured he might be," she said.

"I wanted to tell him how I'm doing. He wasn't home," Shakie continued. "I was thinking maybe *you* could call him? You know, real casual like. Hi, how you doin', Shakie's had twins, that sort of thing?" When Tully didn't immediately protest, Shakie hurriedly continued, "Maybe you two can come and visit me. Together, like. Not really together," she pointed out. "Totally separately, but just kind of both at the same time. That way no one will get too upset. How about that? Would that be okay? Please."

Tully rolled her eyes. "It sounds like a war mission. Bring him to me, dead or alive. Alive is preferable—"

"But only just," interjected Shakie, catching Tully's hands. "So you'll do it?"

"I'll do it, I'll do it," replied Tully.

Shakie squeezed Tully's fingers. "But call me, like, two or three hours before you come. I have to get ready."

"Yeah," said Tully. "You have to put on a fresh clean hospital gown."

Tully didn't have to call Jack. She saw him at St. Mark's on Sunday, with a bouquet of white roses. They laid their flowers down. After a few minutes Jack asked, "What's Mrs. Mandolini doing these days?"

"Not much, I think," said Tully. She didn't mind to be talking to him. "No one has seen her for years. Tony doesn't talk about her much. He just keeps saying she is not very well. He told me a while ago that she's drinking heavily."

"I'll bet," said Jack. "I'll bet she's numbing herself real good with Southern Comfort. I would. Wouldn't you?"

She looked him flush in the face briefly. Yeah, well. We all have been numbing ourselves real good these last five years. Real good. Taking a real low road. She sighed and shivered.

"It's kind of cold, wouldn't you say?" Jack said to her at the Camaro.

"Kind of freezing, I'd say," Tully replied. "Where's that ocean moderating our Kansas weather?"

"Too far away," answered Jack. "But how about a hot cup of coffee?"

"No, thanks," Tully replied quickly and curtly, fumbling with her car keys. Then she remembered her assignment and sighed. Trying to sound as chipper and casual as possible, Tully said, "Oh, by the way, guess what? Shakie had twins. Boy and a girl."

Jack's eyes widened. "Twins, huh?" He laughed. "Well done, Shakie," he said. "Did she name the boy after me?"

Tully couldn't believe it. "God, you have some nerve! Like she would."

"Tully, Tully," he said. "You're losing your sense of humor. I was only joking. And she would if she could."

"I don't think so," said Tully.

"What did she name the girl?" And when Jack saw her stunned face, he laughed. Uproariously. Laughed a chortling, loud laugh, and Tully couldn't help but smile. Jack bent his head down to look into Tully's eyes, asking, "Shakie named her child Tully?"

Tully nearly told him to forget the whole thing. "I really don't want to discuss this with you. Natalie, of course."

"Of course," he said, smiling. "So, *Natalie*, what do you say we go and see Shakie and her two kids?"

Tully put on an indignant air. She couldn't understand why. She was assigned a war mission, and he was falling *alive* right into her lap. Still, she couldn't help feeling indignant. "Well, do you think it's really appropriate for you to go visit Shakie?" she said.

Jack straightened up and put his hands in his pockets. "I'll just call you Natalie Righteous Makker from now on. It'll be perfectly appropriate. I am going to come bearing gifts. I am going to come with you, and I am going to stay only a little while. It's going to be okay," he said. "Let's go."

"Natalie Righteous *DeMarco*," she corrected him as they drove off in the Camaro, still shiny, still baby-blue.

"Natalie Fucking Righteous DeMarco," said Jack.

And Tully laughed.

Jack was completely bewildered in Macy's at first, walking around racks and racks of playsuits. In the end, though, he didn't need Tully's help at all and nearly bought out the entire infants' department as she stood there and watched him. Look at that, she thought. I didn't even need battle fatigues.

"Get out, please," Shakie said when they opened the door and came in. "I have to get ready for you." Tully turned to go, but Jack didn't move. Instead, he came over and sat down on the bed, staring at Shakie.

"Shake, you look like you've just had a baby—two babies. How often are you going to have that look in a lifetime? Nine, ten times?"

She shook her head. "Never again. Tully was right."

Tully sat down in the armchair, and they stayed for a while. Shakie opened the babies' presents. Jack sat on the bed, occasionally getting up and walking around. Every couple of minutes, though, when Jack would look at Tully or at his watch, Shakie would try to brush her hair. Tully hoped Shakie didn't notice his restlessness. She is so pleased he's here, Tully thought, but he has already done his job. He's done enough. He wants to go. And when she is dead, he'll come twice a year and put flowers on her grave. And twice a year will also be enough. Tully stared at her hands and wished she were someplace else.

The nurse brought the babies in. Shakie asked Jack if he wanted to feed one of them. Jack looked nearly knocked over with that suggestion. Tully stifled a laugh. Jack got up off the bed and said, "But I don't have breasts."

"They are not having breasts," said Shakie. "They are having bottles."

Still, he was not convinced. Especially when he realized he would actually have to hold the little infant as he fed her. Tully rolled her eyes. "Look, Jack," she said. "It's like this." She went over to the bassinet and picked up little Natalie, gently handing her over to Jack. "Hold her close to you, that's right. Are you right-handed? Okay, this is good, put her in the crook of your left arm, that's it. Now hold the bottle like this and plop it into her mouth, and that's all there is to it."

Tully was close enough to him to smell his hair. Beer on Tap. Beer on Tap and Polo. He is quite blond, isn't he? she thought, backing away. Jack looked up at Tully, smiled, and said, "You're an old pro at this. How am I doing?"

"Great!" Shakie cut in, looking from Tully to Jack and back again. "What would Tully know about bottles? I don't think she's weaned Boomerang yet, and he's nearly two."

"Off the bottle?" asked Jack.

"Off the breast," said Tully, and had to look away from Jack's unwavering gaze. Shakie stared at the two of them, and Tully became uncomfortable. She got up. "Listen, I gotta go."

Jack got up, too. "Me, too."

"Congratulations, Shakie," Tully said, kissing her on the cheek.

Jack kissed her on the cheek, too. "Yeah, well done, Shake, well done."

Outside, Tully breathed a sigh of relief.

"What's the matter?" said Jack.

"Oh, nothing," Tully replied. "Can I give you a lift somewhere?"

"Yeah, how about Casa? I'll take you to lunch."

Tully shook her head. "No, thanks. I have to get home."

He said, "Then don't worry. I'll walk around a bit. I'll get home."

They stood three feet apart in the parking lot, and for some reason, Tully remembered dancing with him. Not at Shakie's wedding, but at the Senior Banquet, five years ago. The look of recognition, it was in his eyes again, and it confounded her.

A week later, Tully came to St. Mark's. Jack wasn't there, but Jennifer's entire tombstone was covered by white roses. The flowers looked fresh, despite the heavy rain, or perhaps because of it. Tully sat down.

Mandolini, your Jack, I might've misjudged him. Where are you nowadays? Do you look in on us? Do you sleep when I can't sleep? Do you smile when I can't smile? What's it like, to be free of wanting? I hope it's peaceful where you are, because we here cannot get any fucking rest. Oh, we all manage, we all go on, all except your mother; we work, we get married, we even have children and paint houses and travel all over our great and vast land. But sometime, once or twice during our days, we return to pain. We lay down with it, and when we get up it's still there, looking up from our pillow. I continue not to be free, like there hasn't been enough to tie me, to chain me, to blind me. Mandolini, goddamn you, you are the weight that I carry upstream. And when someone asks, I say—what weight? And they say boy you're a survivor, Tully, boy you endure, boy this, boy that. That's right, Tully says, *picking up a bunch of Jack's wet white roses and putting her face into them*. Tully feels no weight. Tully is light and Tully is free of pain.

14

LAKE VAQUERO

May 1984

After taking twenty-one credits a semester three semesters in a row, Tully graduated summa cum laude, with near recognition from the Pope. Hey, it was just no big deal, just a little reading, look at all the time she had to spare late at night when the Texas Street house slept.

Tully decided to stay on one more year for her master's in Social Work. She said it was because she would have more clout in the department, because she would be able to accomplish more and to be listened to more, but she wanted another year of readings and seminars and dissertations—activities removed from reality—before she embarked on a job that squeezed her throat at nine in the morning and didn't unsqueeze it till five at night.

Tully continued to work part-time at the Foster Home Recruitment Agency, slowly doubling her original caseload to four. Compared with the other people in the department, who carried fifty cases, Tully was free, but Tully thought four was too many. Tully would get in the bath with Boomerang every night to press her face against his wet naked back to forget her four Damien Scotts.

"You would have liked him, Boomer," Tully would whisper in the bath. "He was a nice little boy."

But there were now two little boys like Damien and two little girls that Tully had to keep track of.

Mr. Hillier, noting Tully's reluctance to have a permanent place at FHRA, offered her a position of assistant to the director upon graduation, but that didn't comfort Tully. One, assistant to the director meant assistant to Lillian, and, two, she just didn't want to do it. Work was like watching Damien play all day. Occasionally she would feed him or teach him how to swim. But aside from those cosmetic aids, all Tully did at work as she went from foster family to foster family, from Sharon to Sam to Mary to Jerry, who was still drunk in his nice new foster home, was *watch Damien play all day.*

So Tully would get into the bath with Boomerang and soap him between the toes, with her face pressed into his wet back.

"Come on, Boomerang, do me a favor, put these shoes on," Robin beseeched his two-year-old son. "We're going to be late for Mommy."

"Mommie," said Boomerang, running around Stride Rite. "I want Mommie."

"I'll bet you do," said Robin, running after his boy. "Well, why don't we try on these shoes and go and see her. She's going to be getting her diploma."

"Dip Loma?" said Boomerang. "What's Dip Loma?"

"Come on, Boomer, just put these damn shoes on," said Robin, exasperated. Tully was right. Buying shoes was no picnic. It was harder than managing a retail store. "Come on, let's do it, son, let's not be late for Mommy," said Robin, trying to fit a dress shoe onto a squirming foot. "Your mother has been buying you these things since you learned to walk, no wonder she always looks so exhausted when she comes back from the mall. You need someone to hold you down. Boy, you're strong. Keep your foot still, Boomerang!" Robin exclaimed, panting. "So, do you remember when you got your first pair of shoes? You were nine months. You had just taken your first steps."

Boomerang quieted down, and Robin continued. "Remember? It was New Year's Eve. I remember. You know how come?" Leaning closer to his son's ear, Robin whispered, "Because it was the first day your mom and I made it since you were born."

"Made what?" Boomerang said.

Robin rolled his eyes. "Never mind. Keep still, Boomerang. Keep still."

He managed the sixty-five-mile drive from Manhattan to Lawrence in what was a record time even for Robin—forty-two minutes. "Watch out, Boomer," Robin warned Boomer, strapping him in. "This is Mach Two."

"Who's Mack?" Boomer asked, grabbing a handful of Robin's hair.

They got to the Kansas University Memorial Stadium just in time for the ceremony. But it was crowded. They couldn't see Tully very well.

Afterwards, they found her, in a hat and gown, near the stadium exit. She waved her diploma at them.

"Robin! I thought you were going to buy him new shoes! Boomerang, how come Daddy didn't buy you new shoes?"

"We tried, Tully. Oh, how we tried," said Robin, rolling his eyes.

Tully got separated from them by other graduates, who stood in a circle congratulating Tully and each other.

And then Robin saw Jack.

Jack was standing near Tully, too far away to be talking to her. But near her, talking to other people. Robin picked Boomerang up and walked over. Jack recognized him and smiled. The men shook hands. "What are you doing here, man?" asked Robin. He didn't get to hear Jack's answer because Tully came up to them, her hat off, beaming in full robes. She took Boomerang from Robin, who noted she was not the least bit surprised to see Jack.

"Master Tully," Jack said. "Who would've thought?" He patted her on the shoulder. "Congratulations."

"Not a master yet," Tully corrected.

"Master Tully," repeated Jack, and they smiled.

Then Jack said something like, "Soon we'll be calling you *Doctor* Tully."

Tully didn't say anything, but the remark grated on Robin because he had no fucking idea what Jack was talking about.

They all made way to the student union for the undergraduate reception. Jack got separated from them by some women who seemed to know him well. Robin and Tully both watched him. And then Robin watched Tully as she watched Jack. Her face was impassive.

He decided to ask anyway. "How come he is here, Tull?"

She pointed to Jack's entourage. "Need you know more?"

"How come you weren't surprised to see him? I was shocked as hell," said Robin.

"Who says I wasn't surprised?" asked Tully. "I wasn't one way or the other."

"You weren't surprised," said Robin.

Tully carefully looked away. "Well, if you must know, I don't know. I think he sits in on some classes or something. I really don't know, Robin. He knows a bunch of people, as you can see."

"Have you seen him around campus?"

"Oh, Robin, I don't know. Once or twice. Who cares?"

He cared. But he saw by her expression that she was annoyed and that she didn't seem to care much.

They didn't talk about it anymore. Nor about much else.

In the car on the way back he was alone; Tully drove her Camaro, and Boomerang was with her. The nearly six-year-old Camaro was recently fixed. It needed a starter and a timing chain. Robin had offered to buy Tully a brand-new Camaro, but Tully had looked at him as if he had cursed in church.

Robin was sorry he questioned her; he didn't like questioning Tully. After all, she never questioned him.

Tully wasn't surprised to see Jack because Jack had been coming to the Kansas University campus intermittently for the last six months. He went away briefly during the blizzard days of February and the windy days of March. But even before February, around her birthday, she ran into him downstairs in the game room of the student union. She was playing Galaga, and he was playing Asteroids or Star Wars or something. Tully walked right by him, but he called after her ("Tully Makker!") and then asked her to go for coffee.

She said yes, because she had nothing else to do. "But Dutch."

"No, no, let me buy you a cup of coffee. Please," he insisted.

When they sat down, he said, "Tully, I think this is the first time in three years that I'm seeing you somewhere other than St. Mark's."

That's strange, she thought bleakly, because it's St. Mark's I see all around *you*.

She didn't stay long, but a few days later there he was again. Sitting in a low, comfortable armchair in the union, hands stretched out. Talking to three female students. When he saw her, he smiled a big, happy smile, got up, and walked toward her without looking back.

"Jack, what are you doing sitting there? Holding court?"

"Court? Why, no. Tully, you nearly offend me. I was mingling."

"You were holding court," she repeated. "Were you casing for a queen?"

* * *

Tully decided to stay on at school in the spring before her graduation, but she didn't decide that until she spoke about it with some frequency to Jack. They saw each other every once in a while at KU or at St. Mark's on Sundays. She never went for coffee with Jack on Sundays, she went back to Texas Street after talking to him, but they did sit around the church a little. Sometimes Jack and Tully walked to the little green at the intersection of Pembroke and Canterbury and sat there on one of the benches.

2.

After graduating, Tully took the month of June before she "interned" for the rest of the summer. It was hard to call it something as temporary as interning when Mr. Hillier was offering her the position of assistant director. She called it interning anyway.

Tully spent most of June hanging around with Boomerang. They went to Lake Shawnee, to Blaisdell Pool, to the park. She taught him how to stay afloat in the water with swimmies on. They sat in their own backyard, and Boomer played in his little pool, dragging all his trucks and occasionally his mother in there with him.

Millie continued to cook for the whole family. In the evenings, Hedda occasionally wheeled out of her room to hear Tully read. Once in a while Tully would call her mother. She would knock on the door and say, "Ma, David Copperfield's getting married, Are you coming?"

That June for the first time, Tully watched Boomerang climb on Hedda's lap. Hedda did not react one way or the other, and her arms remained where they had been—on the chair rests. Her eyes were vacant.

Eventually, Boomerang got up, and Hedda said, "Hank . . . where are you going?" Two-year-old Boomerang didn't react. He just came back to her and climbed on her lap again. Tully was unable to go on reading.

Summers were very busy in the store, and Robin continued to come home late. Usually Tully sat with him while he ate, and then they watched TV together. Tully would tell Robin about Boomerang, and they went to bed around midnight. That is to say, Robin went to sleep. Tully then either woke him up to make love or got out of bed and sat by the window. Sometimes the dreams came, sometimes they did not. Tully had no way of knowing when to expect them because all her days were the same. Lazy and still.

Now that Boomerang was two, Robin would take his son to Manhattan. Robin always asked Tully to come with them, but she declined. Once or twice every summer she would come to watch Robin play rugby or soccer. Tully was so happy, though, to see Robin spend the time alone with his boy that she preferred to stay home and go shopping. She did a lot of shopping on Saturdays. It was her day to be alone, to shop, to go visit Shakie and the kids, to ride to Lawrence to walk around Massachusetts Street and look for Mrs. Mandolini. Sundays, Tully went to St. Mark's. And Robin did not come with her. He was either in Manhattan working or playing softball or home watching TV or reading the paper or cooking Sunday dinner. Tully went alone, or with Boomer. Boomerang liked to stay with his dad on the weekends, and it warmed Tully's heart to see them together.

One Sunday in June, Jack got a chance to meet Boomerang for the first time. He shook Boomer's little hand in the St. Mark's courtyard. After shaking Jack's hand, Boomer hid behind his mother's skirt.

"Do you think," said Jack as they all walked around to the graveyard, "that it's such a good idea, introducing *this* to a young child?"

"He doesn't know it's *this*," said Tully. "He knows it's *church*."

"Ahh, what a fine distinction for a boy of two," Jack said. "And when he gets older, then what?"

Tully ignored him, but the following week came without Boomerang.

"I didn't mean don't bring Boomer," said Jack as they laid their flowers down. "Funny, that faced with an alternative, you choose to leave your son at home."

"I don't know what you mean," said Tully defensively. "He was tired and cranky."

"I'll bet he was," said Jack. "Who wouldn't be, knowing they are going to go watch their mother mope?"

"Oh, get lost," said Tully, and started to go.

He followed her to the car. "Tully," he said, "have you ever considered perhaps coming with your son to church but *not* to the graveyard?"

She whirled around. "Would you ever consider perhaps coming on a different day?"

"Of course not," was his cheerful response. "If I came on a different day, why, then, I wouldn't get the pleasure of your company."

"Get lost," she said again, getting into the Camaro.

He smiled. "That's an improvement from 'fuck you.' "

"Only just," said Tully.

He waved to her. "See you next Sunday," he shouted.

Next Sunday, she deliberately avoided coming for Mass. She came much later, around three in the afternoon, and walked around back. There was no Jack and no cut flowers there, but instead a rosebush.

He planted the silly thing so close to the tombstone that it nearly covered it. Tully shook her head, but she had to admit the bush was pretty—thick with white bloom. The earth where he dug smelled good—fresh and grainy.

A week later, Tully made sure she was at Mass with Boomerang. Jack was sitting without flowers in the last pew. Tully brought hers.

"I see you're not heeding my advice," he said to her when they got outside. Before she could answer, Jack squatted down in front of Boomerang, who held fast to his mother's hand. "Boomerang," said Jack. "Wouldn't you like to go and play in the sand?" Boomerang smiled. "I know this great lake not too far away," continued Jack, "with a little sand, lots of water, lots of trees, and no people. Maybe even a few ducks to feed. What do you say we go there?" Boomerang nodded vigorously.

Tully frowned and pulled him away. "This is all very nice," she said, "But we have other plans."

Boomerang started to cry, and tried to pull away from his mother's grip. "Wake!" he whined. "I want wake!"

Tully glared at Jack with a "look what you've done!" expression. Jack stared brightly back. "Let's go," he repeated.

"I told you," Tully said. "We have other plans." He looked skeptical. "I do have a husband, you know," she said quietly. "We are going to go to Lake Shawnee."

"Of course you are," said Jack, the expression in his eyes less bright. "Well, have fun," he offered, patting Boomerang on the head and walking across the street to his car. Tully watched him for a second, then grabbed Boomerang's hand and hurried to the graveyard with her flowers.

The summer flew by.

A few months later, on a Saturday in August, Tully took her usual route to the shopping mall, passing Madison Street, a quiet street off 29th. She drove slowly in case there were any children playing (how would it look if a future assistant to the director of the State of Kansas Foster Home Recruitment Agency knocked over a well-loved three-year-old because she was driving fifty in a thirty-mile-per-hour zone?) and noticed three or four houses all in a row that were immaculately painted. The fifth house looked only half done, and Tully slowed to a near-stop just in time to spot Jack, in white gear, coming out the front door with a Coke in his hand. She beeped the horn. He looked around and waved. Tully thought he would come across the street to talk to her, but he went around the side of the house and disappeared. She parked the car and walked up the driveway. "What are you doing?" she asked him as he was pouring white paint into a pan.

"It might not look like it," said Jack, looking up at her, "but actually, I'm hang gliding."

"You ought to be careful," parried Tully without missing a beat, "hang gliding in this area. The kids might think you are a giant white bat."

"No, Tully Makker. Only you think I'm a giant white bat." Jack smiled at her, and she smiled back.

"So you're painting Topeka houses now?" she asked him.

"You wouldn't believe the amount of work there is to be had in Topeka," he replied. "Why, on this street alone I'm going to do six houses before I leave."

Tully wanted to ask him just when that would be but decided against it, saying instead, "How much do you charge nowadays for painting a house?" shielding her eyes from the sun.

"I'm really glad you ask that, Natalie, because I was passing your house the other day and it looked ready for some serious paint."

Passing my house? "It looks fine to me," she said. "How much?"

"Fifteen hundred for a more or less standard house. Not including paint. But since I know you, in a manner of speaking, I'll give you a good price."

"Oh, no. I would insist on paying the going rate," said Tully.

"Well," he said, standing up and sidling closer to her. "If you insist."

She backed away down the driveway. "I'll call you if I need you," she said.

"I can't wait," he muttered, and then, louder, "Having your usual chipper Sunday tomorrow?"

She stopped walking. "Oh, that reminds me," she said. "What's the big idea with planting that bush? You've hogged that whole area. There's hardly room for my flowers now."

He tipped his painter's cap. "That's the big idea," he said.

"Oh, and who's going to take care of it when you go?" asked Tully. "Rosebushes need a lot of clipping and trimming and watering . . ." She faltered a little, watching him stare at her. She was glad to be going.

"Well, Natalie," he said, tipping his hat. "I guess *you* will take care of it."

She wanted to ask him why he hadn't come to the church for many weeks now, but could think of no way to ask that without inviting some kind of verbal intimacy from him, and worse, implying a degree of intimacy from herself. Like she noticed or something. She hastened her step.

"Bring Boomerang," Jack shouted after Tully. "We'll go to Lake Vaquero."

She pretended not to hear him and drove away. But Sunday she did bring Boomerang, careful not to overdress him. Or herself.

Jack was sitting in the last pew, and for the first time, Tully sat down in church next to him. When Mass was over, they ran into Angela in the courtyard. Tully reluctantly introduced them, only slightly amused by Angela's confused and curious face as Jack shook her hand.

And then in his green 1968 Mustang, Jack drove Boomerang and Tully to Lake Vaquero.

Lake Va-*kwerō*, a deserted lake, surrounded by woods and weeds. Dozens of weeping willows soaking their leaves in the water. There were no paddle boats, no playgrounds, no picnic tables, nothing like Lake Shawnee. Here, there was nothing but sand and ducks. And weeping willows. Boomerang played happily in the sand while Tully, behind him, stood cautiously next to Jack, who finally sat down, and she had no choice but to sit down, too, next to him on the sand.

After a while, they got up and walked around to feed the ducks and geese, roaming freely around the lake. Finally, an exhausted Boomer fell asleep in his stroller before Tully even had a chance to strap him down. Jack pushed him while they walked around the lake paths a couple of times. The trees and flowers still smelled wet like spring. The paths were a little rough for civilized family outings, which was why she supposed no one was here. But maybe, Tully thought, no one even knows about Lake Vaquero.

"So tell me, Jack, how did you find out about this place?" she said.

"It's on the map," he replied.

"Then how come no one is here?" asked Tully.

"But that's not true, Tully," he replied. "*We* are here."

Tully saw sand, she saw weeping willows bending down in their perpetual thirst, and dirt paths, smelled the water and earth, and felt the sun on her face. The wildflowers were ripe with all the colors of the rainbow. The sun did not just shine; it beamed.

When Tully came to Angela's for lunch the next day, Angela immediately said, "So who was that guy with you in church?"

Tully took a deep breath. "He wasn't *with* me," she said. "He comes to church once in a while."

"No, he doesn't," said Angela. "I would've noticed him."

"He doesn't live in town," said Tully, kneading her fingers. "He comes here to visit his mother."

"Good boy. Umm, how do you know him?"

Tully got up from the table. "Angela, what's going on? Is this a game? Because I don't want to play."

"Tully, you're being secretive. I know you since you was five, and I know you're being secretive now."

"Now?" said Tully.

"You got to admit, it's a fair question," said Angela. "So how is it that you know him?"

Tully sighed. She wanted to tell Angela that Jack went to the prom with Shakie, but what if Angela mentioned to Shakie over turkey clubs that Tully talked to Jack?

"We went to high school together," she said reluctantly. "And you have too seen him in church before. Remember? He was the guy with the white roses."

"Ahh! The guy with the white roses!" said Angela. "You mean the same guy you hurried after fast as a boat in a race?"

Tully turned red at having been so misunderstood. "Angela, I wanted to know who was bringing white roses to—" she faltered, "the cemetery. That's all. I kept seeing white roses there for several years and couldn't figure out who brought them."

"Who was he bringing the roses to?" asked Angela

"To *her*. Of course," said Tully, resentful that she had to even point it out.

Tully left to go back to Docking and for the rest of the summer avoided coming over to Angela's for lunch, though Angela continued to watch Boomerang.

At work, Tully's co-workers had stopped looking at her as if she were just another inexperienced intern, and she stopped pushing their paper. She was now out on the town, or the outskirts of town, mostly. Stepping over chicken coops to take the kids away from the parents and give them to Youth Center Lock-Up.

Angela wasn't the only one Tully didn't see for the rest of the summer, the summer Robin turned thirty-one. She didn't see Jack, either. Not in church, not on the streets. She assumed he had left, and in fact was surprised that he had stayed as long as he had. She meant to ask him about it at Vaquero, about him staying so long, but forgot to. What *did* they talk about? She couldn't remember. She only remembered the sun on her face.

3.

Four months later, on Christmas Day, 1984, Tully ran into Jack in church. She came with her entire family, including Robin's brothers, sisters-in-law, and their kids, who were all going to be feasting at Texas Street on turkey à la Millie. Jack, untroubled as ever, shook everybody's hand, including Tully's, and even said hello to Angela, who was standing nearby to get a better look. Tully snorted inwardly. I never knew Angela was such a busybody, she thought.

"Angela, where is Julie?" Tully asked.

Shaking her head, Angela said, "Don't ask. They're in Ohio. Laura's got family there, I think. She doesn't even come home for Christmas anymore."

Tully was embarrassed, but Jack took one of the roses out of the bouquet in his hands and gave it to Angela. "Merry Christmas," he said. And Angela smiled. Tully looked down into her own bouquet.

After a few minutes of polite discussion, Robin looked at Tully's flowers, and then at Jack's flowers, and said quietly, "Why don't you go and put your flowers down. So we can leave."

In the graveyard, Tully asked Jack if he *had* to come today.

"But today is Sunday," he replied. "I always come on Sundays."

"You're real smooth, aren't you?" Tully said, her mouth nearly forming a smile. "Giving that rose to Angela."

Jack bent his head to look into her face. "Hey, Tully," he said softly. "Watch out. Or you might actually smile."

They carefully laid down their flowers. "But you already have a bush," said Tully. "What do you need to bring more flowers for?"

"In the winter," Jack explained patiently, "the bush doesn't grow and the flowers on it are dead. I bring fresh flowers."

She shrugged; was quiet for a while. "Have you seen Shakie?"

"Of course I haven't seen Shakie," he replied offhandedly. "Don't you think these are beautiful white roses?"

"Where do you get them from, anyway?" Tully wanted to know, fidgeting a little. "These are pretty rare in the wintertime, in Topeka."

"Yes, they are," he said. "Aren't they beautiful?"

"Yes, yes," she said, averting her gaze from his. "I gotta go."

"Okay," said Jack. "I'm gonna stay here for a while." He turned away from her. "See you, Tully."

Walking away, she didn't answer, but when she was near the path, Tully turned around to look at him before he became obscured from her view. Jack was sitting down in the chair, his hands between his thighs.

Seeing him sit there, Tully felt . . . *just a little pinprick* . . . a nearly familial connection to Jack. They were here paying respects to a mutual relative. But the bond wasn't warm, it was more like cold leaves underneath her bare feet when she was a little girl. They smelled good but didn't feel so good on her skin.

Tully didn't see Jack the following Sunday, because it was New Year's Day and Tully and Robin stayed in bed nursing hangovers. Early in January she ran into Jack again, and he asked her to go for coffee. Tully refused, but didn't want to go home yet, either, so they stood outside, and later sat on the stone wall surrounding the church courtyard and talked a while. They were freezing, and the wind was bitter. An hour passed before Jack said again, "You sure you don't want to go for coffee?"

"Positive," said Tully, standing up. "I gotta get going."

At the end of January Jack said to Tully, "This is getting way cold for me. I gotta get out of here, gotta get someplace warm."

Someplace *warm*. Someplace to dry his feet and run the sand through his hands. I wonder if when he gets to California he gets away from the rocky abyss above which I hang myself every night.

"I don't blame you," she finally said, looking at their flowers, pleased with the arrangement. They interweaved their roses and carnations into the bare rosebush, to make it look like it was blooming.

She did not see him again after that, and on January 19, 1985, Tully turned twenty-four. When she came to St. Mark's a few days later, Tully knelt down into the snow in front of two dozen of the freshest, crispest, biggest, whitest roses.

Something gave out in Tully then and collapsed inside her as she uttered a little groan and sank deeper into the snow. And then she saw a white card pierced on a bare branch of the rosebush, and inside the card it said, "Tully, these are for you. Happy birthday. Jack."

Tully was gratefully surprised. Thank you, Jack, she thought.

Thank you for not forgetting *her*. Someday maybe I'll say that out loud to you. Thank you. For not forgetting *her*.

And someday maybe I'll tell you why it's so hard for me to look straight at you.

Because when I look at you, when I talk to you, when I watch you, when I see your blond hair and your—blue? eyes, when I listen to you talk and laugh, it's not you I see, Jack Pendel.

I keep thinking that only a blink ago in the eternity that she now lives in, *she* watched you as I watch you, heard you laugh as I hear you, listened to you speak as I listen to you. Seeing you is almost . . . almost like having her pull my hair . . .

God help us. You still roam the earth, while I struggle to beat back the tundra of my own soul, but who gives a shit about us, so long as *she* has found peace.

Tully got up. Thank you for your flowers.

4.

When spring came and the azaleas were in full bloom, Tully, driving through Topeka on the way to visit a foster family, saw a man painting a house and wondered if Jack was going to come home in the summer.

June was almost a quarter over before Tully saw him.

It was Saturday, and she was home by herself—by herself if you didn't count Hedda in her rooms. Robin had taken Boomerang with him to Manhattan for the day. The windows were open. Tully opened them herself; it was a beautiful morning. She was even contemplating taking her mother outside when the bell rang. Tully ambled downstairs and opened the door. It was noon, and though it had been a while since she had gotten up, her hair was still unbrushed, she had on no makeup, and was wearing an old seventies-style short peach terry dress.

She opened the door and sucked in her breath, because Jack stood in front of her, in his painting whites, with a paintbrush in his hand and a big smile on his face.

"God! What the hell—" she began, but he interrupted her.

"I'm sorry, but is the man of the house in?"

"No, but—"

"In that case I guess I'll have to come back," he said.

Tully stood there, little amused. Still, though . . . deep inside her, something small had opened and warm milk was running through it.

"What do you want?" she said.

"Mrs. DeMarco," said Jack, bowing his head to her a little. "As I told you last year, your house—your beautiful home—" he added, "badly needs painting. I've passed your house several times now, and the paint is peeling. The house looks gray and unkempt. Chipped paint does not protect the wood around the windows, which tend to rot when the paint starts to go, and generally speaking lowers the quality of the impression for people passing Texas Street. Why, I remember, as a young boy, coming here with my friend and marveling at this house, thinking it was the most beautiful house around." Without giving her a chance to speak, he went on. "I give free estimates and will be glad to begin work next week. I also do interior painting, but since I have not seen the inside of the house," he pointed out, "I am not in a position to evaluate."

Tully managed a smile and tried to smooth her hair. Clearing her throat, which felt a little froggy all of a sudden, she said, "You were going to spew all that to the man of the house, were you?"

"Yes, of course," said Jack. "I even brought a rate sheet with me, in case Mr. DeMarco was actively interested."

Tully felt mentally and physically disheveled. She had never even thought about having the house painted. She and Robin had never discussed it. They discussed having someone over to landscape the front garden, or to install a swimming pool in the back and a patio, to replace the wrought-iron fence, or possibly to insulate the attic. But they never talked about painting the house. Then she remembered something.

"Jack Pendel, you're full of shit."

His eyes went wide.

"No, you are. Really. I don't know who you came here with when you were a small boy—"

"A young boy," he corrected her.

She went on. "But as I remember, this house was always in need of paint. It always looked a little like this."

"No, Tully, it didn't," said Jack. "Once upon a time, it used to have a white picket fence."

His words struck home. She had just been thinking about the white picket fence she had torn down in a pre-Boomerang fit. "Yeah, but . . ." she trailed off. "The fence needed paint."

"Okay, well, how about if you think about it, and maybe talk it over with Mr. DeMarco," said Jack, handing her a leaflet and starting to back away.

"No, wait," Tully said too quickly, too loudly. He stopped and looked her over. "Just got up, Tully?" he asked lightly.

She snorted. "I have a young child, I don't have the luxury of lying in bed all day."

Jack looked at her hair and said, "I've never actually seen your hair quite so . . . styled." Tully blushed, and he smiled. "Why, Tully, you blush."

She pointed to the leaflet quickly. "I'll talk to him about it, okay? We haven't actually discussed it, you know."

"Of that," said Jack, "I have no doubt." He walked down the porch steps. "Nice porch," he called out. "It must be such joy to sit in that swing, listen to the crickets, and watch the weeds. Not to mention that nice black wrought-iron."

"'Bye, Jack," she said, dragging her words out of her mouth.

"Good-bye, Tully," said Jack, walking to the gate.

"Will you be in church tomorrow?" she called after him. He turned around and said, "What for? My rosebush should be in full bloom soon."

"Some roses are already blooming," Tully replied. "You should see them. They're beautiful."

"Of that I have no doubt," he replied, and waved.

After he left, she remembered wanting to thank him for the roses he had brought and left for her last January. She remembered wanting to ask him if maybe they could go to Lake Vaquero again.

That evening at dinner, Tully spoke to Robin about painting their house. Boomerang was busy eating corn on the cob, and Hedda was, too.

"I see," was Robin's response. He wasn't very talkative. Somebody had kicked him in the mouth while he was goalie. He looked a little swollen.

"Remember Jack Pendel? Well, he's painting houses here for the summer," Tully explained nonchalantly. "And he thinks ours ought to be painted."

"He does, does he?" Robin said slowly, studying her face for a moment. Then, dropping his gaze, he said, "If you think it needs to be painted, then have him paint it. Does he need work?"

"Robin, I have no opinion one way or the other, and no, he does not need work. I will leave this decision up to you." She added, "He said he'll do it for a good price."

"Have him do it," said Robin, not looking at her. Tully got up from the kitchen table and with her back to him said, "It's your money, Robin. Do what you want."

"It's our money," he corrected her. "You're in this house more than I am. He is your friend's old friend from high school. It's okay. Go ahead. With our money, have him paint our house."

They watched a little TV. Tully read aloud. Long after she left school, her habit of reading aloud in the evenings continued. It soothed everybody, though nobody really listened to her anymore except Hedda. So this evening Tully read. What, Robin did not remember. Something about England. He sat there and nodded, his vacant eyes like two empty parking lots at night.

Robin wheeled Hedda to her rooms around eleven in the evening, came back, and sat. Tully went to get ready for bed. "Coming?" she called down to him.

After they made love—twice—she fell into exhausted sleep, while he, for a change, lay there interminably awake, spooning her, waiting to be released.

Finally he got up and sat naked in the bay window where Tully usually sat, moving the curtain to see what Tully usually saw when she sat there naked, unable to sleep. God, this is pretty dreary, thought Robin. Sitting here like this.

He thought back to the first time he saw Tully, the first time he laid eyes on her face, so plain. She held her head high despite her drab attire, but then went and hid her lovely face behind black and red gloop. Tully didn't like her face then, hiding it every chance she could. But Robin loved that face, loved those eyes. He remembered how she sat across from him at The Village Inn and enjoyed her lemon meringue pie. He remembered when she dragged a dying dog off the road while three men watched.

Managing a high-end retail store was a snap compared to being with Tully. At DeMarco & Sons, Robin knew what days were going to be busy, knew when to order more inventory, knew when to close shop and go home. But with Tully, he didn't know much of anything. *Have I been of some help to her?* Robin thought. *Or does she still feel alone when she sits here, as alone as those streetlights—not even a night breeze to keep them company as they burn in the July heat?* Tully had always been alone, but never as alone, he suspected, as she was after the March of her senior year.

Does she still hanker for California? Will she leave me the first chance she gets? Robin closed his eyes, rubbing his temples. *Is that what she's waiting for? For the first chance to leave me, as she sits here?*

And sometime later, Robin thought, *I don't really want her to go. Despite everything that's been. Despite everything that might be. Despite her silence and her dejection, despite that stupid job that saps what life she has out of her.*

Robin got off the windowsill and knelt by her side of the bed, touching Tully's hair. *I like the way her fingers feel on my back. I like to see her holding our boy. I never wanted another life, another wife. I don't want her to go.*

He went back to sit by the window. *Does she feel less alone when she talks to Jack? She must, otherwise why this contact? Maybe he reminds her of high school. What I'd like to know, though, is does Tully see he cares for her? What happened to her lust detector?* It occurred to Robin then with aching clarity that perhaps Tully could not detect anything with her oft-tried-and-tested lust detector because it wasn't lust Jack was feeling for Tully. And Robin intimately, painfully, knew that Tully had no other detectors.

She is blasé about him. If he wants to paint the house, let him. As long as she is blasé, I don't care, Robin thought, drumming a beat on the windowsill. *I don't care. She can have all the rope she wants unless she hangs herself with it.*

Robin sat and sat—but there was no sleep. Only a tune that went around in his head like a carousel without children, a faraway sound on an old and nearly broken Victrola.

Hey!
Did you happen to see

The most beautiful girl
in the world?
And if you did,
Was she crying,
Crying?
Hey!
Did you happen to see
The most beautiful girl
Who walked out on me . . .
Tell her I'm sorry,
Tell her I need
My
Baby
Hey . . . won't you tell! her
. . . that I love her . . .

5.

Tully's first formal full day as assistant to Lillian White went as well as could be expected, considering Lillian White's distaste for Tully. Lillian, in all her fervor to take good care of her foster children and foster families, forgot to allocate Tully some office space. After Tully stood and stared for a while, Lillian put her in what looked like an old storage room, with dust on the floor and cobwebs in the corners.

"Surely you're joking," Tully said to Lillian. "Haven't you forgotten something? Haven't you forgotten an old cardboard box I can sit on?"

"I'm sorry, Tully. All in due course. I know you were promised an office, but we've been very busy around here, as you can well imagine," said Lillian.

"Very good," said Tully. "In the meantime, where am I supposed to sit?"

"Well, hopefully you're not going to be doing much sitting." Lillian smiled. "After all, you've been hired as our on-site special projects director, am I right?" she said sarcastically. "You're going to be on the road a lot, training our new foster families to . . . umm . . . care."

Tully rolled her eyes.

Lillian continued. "Plus maintaining our existing foster family base, making sure they're all adhering to the *caring* standard.

So you see, you're not going to have a lot of time for sitting down."

Tully sighed. "I understand. Thank you. I will do my best. However, I need a table and a chair, and a filing cabinet, maybe, and a phone, too, I guess, so I could monitor that *caring* standard without leaving my office."

"Mrs. DeMarco," said Lillian, "I have been doing this job for twenty years now. This is the way we do things around here—slowly. You came in here off the street, practically, six years ago. We've allowed you to intern here, we've treated you well, I think, even when you decided you were going to be changing things," said Lillian with contempt. "Now, good for you, you got the Apps Committee to increase our budget two years in a row. But that does not give you the right to start making demands on your very first day. First you work. Then you get what you need."

Tully turned around and walked toward the office door. "I see," she said. "So this is how things are going to be around here. Terrific. Well, I'm going home. If you want to get me a desk and a chair and clean up my office, I'll be glad to come back. If not, I wish you every success with the agency and with your personal life. Now, if you'll excuse me, I'm going to take my son to the lake."

Tully left, and Mr. Hillier called her a few hours later, asking her to please come to work tomorrow and not make him look bad. "Never mind Lillian," he told her. "You should know that by now. She knows what she is doing, but she's been at her job too long."

"She sure has," said Tully acidly.

"We are not all as full of fire as you are, Tully," he said. "We can't all be crusaders for better this and better that. You must understand you're going to get some resentment."

Actually, Tully didn't understand. *Crusader* was not the word she would use to describe herself. *Dogged*, maybe. She remained silent.

"You tend to lose your ideals a little," continued Mr. Hillier, "when you work in this place, especially when you work at that place. You want a happy job? Go work for the Gentle Shepherd adoption agency. But I'll tell you right now, they don't need you there. Their job is comparatively easy. We need you down here. But it's tough where you work. What are *you* going to be like in about twenty years?"

Tully didn't hear a word after his first sentence. "Lose your ideals a *little*!" she scoffed. "Mr. Hillier, this is important stuff. Without ideals, what is this, after all?"

He was quiet for a moment and then said, "Work, Tully. This is work."

It got somewhat better after that first day. Tully was one of four assistants to Lillian—another two women and one man. Tully was, however, as the rest of the staff snidely pointed out, the only "special projects director." "As if that gave her some 'special' dispensation to have fewer cases than the rest of us," complained a staff caseworker one afternoon at the watercooler, and Tully overheard, ignoring her.

Tully worked directly with two women, Sara and Joyce, and a man, Alan, who seemed to be decent enough workers. They helped Tully with her "special projects," namely processing new applications, interviewing, and training. But they had their regular work, too, the unending stream of kids and the ending stream of foster families willing to take them on. The better part of the day was spent either talking to the parents, trying to allay an escalating problem, or talking to the kids who were awaiting placement. Who had time to recruit and train potential foster families? Who had the nerve to refuse potential foster families when there was so much need? The dozen or so caseworkers in the department clapped their hands for every new foster family that signed on, and Tully was looked at as a pariah for contesting any new application.

Tully tried to spend at least the mornings working on the special projects. She got in at eight and spent until nine looking over new applications and calling people, and then until about ten-thirty upstairs in the marketing department, helping to lay out a new campaign to target the middle and the upper middle classes for foster work.

The rest of her day, like everyone else's, was eaten up by a bunch of hungry teenage kids looking for something Tully couldn't give them. Though the agency received a dozen or so new foster applications a week there was just no time to go and see them, train them. No time. There was no time even for the kids. Sara and Joyce once, jokingly, said that the criteria for acceptance of new foster families should be, can they fill out the application?

Tully didn't find that funny. "Oh, yes," she said, "Lillian trained you well, guys. Except her criteria is, if you can find your way to City Hall, you should be entitled to at least one troubled kid, maybe two." She wanted to add that Lillian turned away more kids that needed help than families who needed money.

Tully finally ordered new applications to be made up that included more specific questions about why couples chose to make their homes foster ones. She rejected many applicants herself, well before they met Lillian's eye, or Sara's, or Joyce's, or Alan's. *All those people think when they see a potential foster family is, I've got a dozen kids I could send to that family right now. And I know how they feel. Because I got a dozen kids, too. All in a row, as the Eagles say.*

Very soon after Tully started there was trouble. Tully was convinced it wasn't the first time. Lillian's eagerness to take on any Tom, Dick, or Jane to play mom and dad was accompanied by a perverse eagerness to give the children back to their natural parents. One boy named Timothy cried hysterically at the thought of returning home, and the outpatient psychologists at Stormont-Vail recommended that he continue to stay with his present foster family, even be adopted by them. Tully went up to the sixth floor to see what could be done, but Lillian refused to go further with the report and Timothy was returned parcel post to mom and dad. A few weeks later, the boy was hospitalized for second-degree burns. And Lillian raised her eyebrows at the Monday morning meeting. "These things happen," she said, looking directly at Tully, and Tully thought, *I need this. Oh, yes. No, of course. I mean, I could be suntanning with my boy. I could be counting my flowers. I could be at Lake Vaquero. But no. What I need is this.*

"Lillian," Tully said. "We never should have given Tim back." Tully said *we,* but meant *you.* And everybody knew it.

Tully went over to Angela's for lunch less and less. Tully just couldn't turn off work for an hour, and she did not want to talk about work to Angela. Work was not something Tully could talk about easily.

Plus, there was another feeling in there, a strange feeling of discomfort when she saw Angela's questioning gaze about the way Tully spent her Sundays.

During the first couple of weeks of work, Tully had lunch with Sarah and Joyce, but Tully couldn't put her feelings for them away. She couldn't put her resentment away at them all treating her as the enemy. As if she were doing something wrong. Something bad.

Somebody should tell Sara that the sixties are over, thought Tully whenever she looked at the woman's heavy eye makeup and ungroomed hair. Joyce looked better; she was blond and benevolent-looking.

One lunch, Tully discovered Sara and Joyce couldn't put away their feelings for Tully, either.

"So, Tully, tell us," said Joyce. "Are you planning to have more kids?"

"I'm planning only to get through the next day," said Tully. Why is she asking me this odd question? Does she think I don't have enough to do at home?

"Why do you ask, Joyce?" Tully finally said. "Do you think I don't keep busy enough?"

"No, no, it's not that, Tully," said Joyce, looking at her sandwich and then at Sara. "It's just that, well, I guess it's just that it's hard for us all to maintain your level of enthusiasm, Tully," she said, looking down at the table instead of at Tully.

"What enthusiasm?" said Tully. "What does this have to do with enthusiasm? I just do my job."

"Well," interjected Sara, "you just seem so eager to do good, Tully."

"Wait a minute, wait a minute," said Tully, still not catching—*refusing* to catch—the drift of the conversation. "Do good? What are you talking about? Come out and say what you mean."

"We all kind of wish you would stop trying to make a mission out of this, Tully," said Joyce.

"Yeah, Mission Impossible," said Sara, and laughed slightly to lighten the mood.

Tully's face remained dark. "A mission, huh? Okay, that's right. Why don't we all stop trying. We're not in the do-good business, are we? No, of course not, we're in the . . . I've-just-gone-to-college-and-got-my-masters-so-that-I-can-help-people business. I'm gonna help people," Tully said in a sarcastic voice. "Aren't I a nice person. I'm gonna help all those poor children out there, who are just *dying* to get my help. Who are just dying for me to do good. Oh, no, wait! I'm not in the do-good business. I'm in the let's-get-the-dog-off-the-street-to-look-after-this-kid business, and if it's a really nice dog, we'll take the kid away and throw him back on the street, and give another kid to this nice dog on the street. Yeah, why don't we do that? That's what we got our masters for, isn't it? To give those kids to every dog on the street. Right? Am I right?"

Slightly embarrassed, Sara and Joyce briefly glanced at each other.

"Tully, we have to work within the confines of what is possible."

"What are you telling me?" Tully demanded. "That what I want is impossible?"

"Well, kind of," Sara hedged a little. "Sometimes we think you have unrealistic expectations. But you're making it hard for the rest of us."

Tully laughed a mirthless laugh. "Sara, I have no fucking expectations at all. I come here every morning hoping only to get through the day without some kid dying or getting drunk or getting burned up. All I want is to begin to raise the standard just a little, just a fucking notch, and you're right, that is hard, harder than the status quo. Let me ask you, Sara, since you're studying for a doctorate and I'm not, see, all I have is a lowly master's, and I guess I wasn't taught right. Let me ask you, what do you recommend?"

"Tully, you can't single-handedly make it all better, you know," said Joyce.

"No, I sure as shit can't," said Tully. "But I thank you in advance for your support and encouragement."

Sara and Joyce were silent. Tully breathed hard. "Why are you guys even here? I don't understand. I mean, what's the point?"

"We're not here to change things, Tully," said Joyce. "We're just here to help the kids. And you turning away potential foster families because they don't meet some lofty ideal of yours is wrong. That doesn't help the kids at all."

"No, but tossing them from one rotten home straight into another is God's work, is it?" snapped Tully.

"Most parents love their kids, even those who abuse them. Kids are usually better off with the parents. I mean, we want to help," Sara said defensively. "But we know what's possible."

"No, Sara, you have no fucking idea what's possible!" Tully said, getting up out of her chair. "That's right, kids are usually better off with their natural parents. So if I may, what the hell are you doing here? What the hell are we all doing here? I mean, what's the point of having an agency that takes kids away from their loving homes? Sounds kind of cruel to me. Home with mom and dad is where their kids belong, so why are you working for an agency that takes kids away from caring mom? What's the point? If the best deal the kids are ever going to have is at home, then why not just leave them there and go straight to the unemployment line? And I make it hard for you, poor you, how you must hate me," Tully finished.

"We don't hate you," said Joyce. "But this job is not a personal crusade or something."

"No, obviously not. How silly of me to think we were here to help those who couldn't help themselves."

"We are!" Sara exclaimed.

"And some of our foster families are already excellent," added Joyce. "Some love their foster kids. Some want to adopt them."

"Oh, like that means anything at all in your and Lillian's philosophy," retorted Tully. "Who cares how good they are if we all agree the kids belong with their parents? I mean, they could be the Lindberghs or the Rosenbergs, right, it really wouldn't matter one fucking whit." Tully threw her napkin down. "Well, I'm sorry I make it so hard for you guys. Really sorry."

Tully did not have lunch with Sara and Joyce again, and noticed a change in their attitude in the next several weeks. They completely stopped talking to her. Only Alan, tall and awkward, would come over to Tully and help her with her new foster applications. Oh, well, she didn't care if no one talked to her. It was hard enough to come to work every day. Come to work full of fucking enthusiasm.

6.

One late June afternoon around midday, Tully got a phone call.

"Well, Tully Makker, you're actually at your desk. That's a rarity for you." *Jack*. Actually, Tully was standing in the middle of all the desks in an open plan room and smiled when she heard his voice.

"Come with me," he said. "We'll lunch. I know this great place."

"I'm sure you do," Tully said. She was about to say no, but a look into the closed faces of the people she worked with made her say yes in a hurry. She wanted to see an open face.

"Do you want to come up?" she asked.

"I really don't think I should, Tully Makker," he said. She, wanting to correct him, Tully *DeMarco*, didn't.

"So where's your car?" Jack asked her when they met in the parking lot.

"It's not here. It's at home," she said. "I walk to work nowadays. And back."

They got into his Mustang. "Why do you do that?" Jack wanted to know.

"I kind of need to walk off work before I get home," Tully said.

"Yeah, I'll bet you do," Jack said. "Great thing about painting. You never need to walk it off."

They rode quietly in the car while they drove through Topeka. Tully was humming.

"What is that thing you're humming?" he asked her.

" 'My Hometown,' " Tully replied. "By Bruce. *This is my hometown, this is my hometown* . . . I'm really starting to like him."

"You know," said Jack, "somehow I think Bruce Springsteen didn't write 'My Hometown' for Topeka."

"You know," Tully said, half kidding, "somehow I think you don't understand anything. He wrote it for every hometown. What, I have to go to New Jersey to sing that song?"

Jack smiled lightly. "Well, well. I apologize. I didn't realize you felt that strongly about Topeka."

"I don't," she said. "I only feel strongly about Bruce. In any case, I don't want to talk about it anymore."

"Done." Jack smiled and didn't say anything else.

He drove her to a remote little Mexican restaurant behind Washburn. The place was half-deserted, dimly lit, and in the basement. They sat in the corner near a fake window.

"Well, well," Jack said, pulling out a chair for her. "You look so different in your business suit."

"Different from what?"

He sat down. "Different from St. Mark's. From Texas Street. From high school."

"You didn't know me in high school," said Tully, digging into the chips.

The look on his face puzzled her, made her uncomfortable. Tully quickly changed the subject. "Good salsa. Where do you find these places?"

He didn't answer her, but ordered margaritas for both of them despite Tully's protests ("I'm working!"), and when they arrived, lightly clinked his glass to hers and said, "Cheers."

She grunted.

"Do you still smoke, Tully? I saw you looking around the table for an ashtray."

"No, I stopped when I was pregnant with Boomerang," Tully lied. "That was just a high school thing."

"Good," said Jack. "I hate smoking. Can't stand it. Never smoked in high school and still don't. You know, I don't think I've ever even had a girlfriend who smoked."

"And I assume you've had a lot of girlfriends," said Tully.

"I've had my share." Jack smiled. "You didn't talk to your husband about painting the house, did you?"

"As a matter of fact, you don't know everything. I did," responded Tully.

"And?"

"And what?" she said. "And nothing. I'm still thinking about it." Tully noticed how she didn't say "we," feeling her discomfort like wet hands.

"Summer will soon be over and I'll be gone," said Jack.

"I'm surprised to see you here at all."

"No one's more surprised than me," said Jack, adding, "My mother is happy when I'm here. She hasn't been well. Plus, it's hot, and there is plenty of work."

"How is your mother?" asked Tully.

"Fine," replied Jack. "How is *your* mother?"

He doesn't want to talk about his mother, thought Tully. "Ahh." Tully raised her eyebrows. "I didn't know you knew I had a mother."

"Everybody's got a mother, Tully. Even Orphan Annie you. Besides, Shakie's told me some about your mother. Not much, but some."

"So what did Shakie tell you?"

"That she got sick. That your husband moved her into your new home. That you don't particularly get on with her."

"Hmm," intoned Tully. "No, not particularly." I do make her a cup of tea in the evenings, though, she thought. Robin doesn't like tea much, I've found out, but my mother drinks the tea I make her.

Jack took a sip of his drink and said carefully, "Jen told me that. That you didn't get on with your mother."

Ahhhh. Now, this is where the conversation gets interesting.

The waiter came around, speaking mostly Spanish. They managed to order some fajitas and burritos and guacamole despite the language barrier.

"I'm sure she did." Tully picked up where they left off, not sure at all. "So tell me, how did you get to know her?"

Jack smiled. "Gee, you weren't really interested before. You didn't want to go for coffee with me when I offered to tell you."

"Stop. That was such a long time ago."

"Not so long ago," he averred, "for such a change of heart."

"I'm still not particularly interested," she answered, but seeing his raised eyebrows, said, "I don't think you know anything about me. I think you're just bluffing."

Jack leaned over the table a little. "I think you *hope* I'm bluffing, Natalie Makker," he said. "But you know I'm not."

"I really don't know any such thing," she said loftily, but inside she wanted to ask it, she *wanted* to ask her question again.

"What do you want to know, Tully?" said Jack, as if reading her mind.

"When did you get to know her?" she said instantly, thankful for the opportunity. There. The first half of the Family Feud question. The Jeopardy question. The $64,000 six-year question: *When did you get to know her? When, and what did you do to her that she went crazy for you?*

"I met her playing softball at Shunga Park," Jack said. "I was the pitcher for the other team. We got creamed. She hit a line drive off me and ran all the way home."

Shunga Park. This surprised Tully. Stunned her. She fought an impulse to close her eyes. Tully had played softball at Shunga Park, too. She played softball there with *her*.

"I used to play softball, too," Tully said, struggling with the words. "Where was I that I didn't see you?"

"I don't know," Jack said, his eyes half serious, half mischievous. "Dancing at Tortilla Jack's, perhaps?"

That's when Tully couldn't help closing her eyes, mostly at the pain of biting her lip hard enough not to let that gasping sound leave her throat. She clamped her teeth around the imaginary metal bit that allowed her some measure of facial control at his off-the-cuff words.

Almost a whole life went by Tully before she could open her mouth to speak. *Dancing at Tortilla Jack's.* Four words. Four words and with them twenty years.

Jack knew Tully. He knew her! Tully was certain he didn't get the Tortilla Jack's information from Jennifer, because Jennifer had not known where Tully danced. Jack knew Tully separately from high school. He knew her at the time she had been oblivious to the whole world, thinking blissfully that no one had known her at all. There she had been, dancing into nothingness through the town of Topeka, and there he had been, knowing her.

"I don't get it," she finally muttered. "What do you know about Tortilla Jack's?"

"Nothing at all about Tortilla Jack's," Jack said. "Only that you danced there."

"How—how do you know that?"

"Because I saw you there," Jack said.

The words rang in her head like the bells of St. Mary's. *Because I saw you there.* I saw you there.

"How did you know it was me?" Tully said, hoping he was wrong. "A lot of girls dance at Tortilla Jack's."

"Nobody dances like you, Tully Makker," replied Jack.

"I had a lot of makeup on," Tully persisted. "I didn't look like me. How did you know it was me?"

"Oh, I had no idea you were you, don't get me wrong. But there you were, regardless."

Tully thought back. It was at Tortilla Jack's that the unfortunate topless dance took place. Could he have been there then? Tully felt her face get hot. Something else occurred to her. She danced with a lot of guys at that club over the course of two wild years. Danced, and then some. There were so many guys she made out with, and then some. She had forgotten the faceless, countless lips and hands and faces. Would she have remembered the face of the man sitting across from her? She lifted her eyes at him.

Yes. She would have.

And then there was that other thing to think about. Shunga Park.

"How—how old were you when you met her?" Tully asked Jack.

"Fifteen or so, I guess," he replied.

Tully thought for a few minutes. "That's so strange," she said. "I never knew you two had been friends."

"Really?" He seemed genuinely surprised. "She never told you how long we knew each other?"

"Never," said Tully.

Never, not once, during all the times they had talked about him, did Jennifer Mandolini ever say to Tully, he was my friend when you weren't there. When you stopped playing softball with me, I found him. I talked to him about you because you had disappeared, and I missed you.

Tully sat there unblinkingly, lost in Shunga Park. Playing softball in Shunga Park.

So Jennifer knew Jack a long time. Knew him a long time before she let on to Tully and Julie that there was anything *to* know.

And there was Tully, all along thinking Jack was just a football vacuum, sucking in Jennifer by flagging his captainship and his face into Jen's heart. But no, they had been friends! And Tully didn't know.

And here in front of her sat the man who talked to Jennifer when Tully didn't talk to Jennifer. Here in front of her sat the man who was nothing more and nothing less than Jennifer's eight milk crates, stacked neatly in Tully's attic. Except the milk crates were in the attic. But he was right here. Eight milk crates at a Mexican restaurant.

"So what made you start to play football?" Tully asked.

What an inane question. A total non sequitur, but she couldn't think clearly. She was still dumbfounded by Tortilla Jack's.

Jack had been staring at her for some time. "I thought I might be good at it," he answered her. "For the same reason you took up dancing?"

Tully recovered her usual firmness. "Somehow I really doubt it," she said coolly, her senses collected. "I don't want to talk about my dancing anymore, okay?"

"Sure, anything you like," said Jack. "How's work?"

"I don't want to talk about work, okay?"

"Sure," he said. "What would you like to talk about?"

Tully looked around. "I'd like to talk to the waiter about dessert."

After that, Tully tried to make small talk, but small talk with him was ruined for her. In front of her sat a monument to her cluelessness. A monument to all the things Tully didn't know, and apparently there was fucking plenty Tully didn't know.

Things she possibly never would have known, had she not looked around a room full of people at Docking and felt the need to make contact with just one person. Well, here he was. Just one person. And she was sitting across from him and he was tugging at her insides. Hey, Tully, hey, hey, Tully, did you know I saw you dancing there, did you know I played softball with your best friend when you did not play softball with your best friend? Did you know all that, hey, Tully?

How she got through the rest of lunch she didn't know. Jack may have asked her what was the matter. Tully may have asked him about softball some more. How many games did they play? How many Sundays? How many questions?

Jack asked her about Jeremy; had she seen him? No, she answered, licking the fried ice cream off the spoon. I have not heard from him.

All Tully saw was the six-year specter of eighteen-year-old Jennifer before her. Jack sits here, and he is in disguise, for he is taller and blonder and the wrong sex, but make no mistake about it, it is *her* specter just the same.

That's what she *saw*.

What she *felt* was a hurting throat and . . . warm milk.

Tully asked him about California. Jack told her about the beaches and the mountains; about the palm trees, the deserts, the blue cold up north, the amber heat down south. She wanted to know about the oceans.

"One ocean," he said.

"Yes," she said distantly. "One ocean. *The* one."

Jack told her of how big the waves were and how white the sand and how cold the water. He talked about the cliffs and the narrow paths along them, he told her about the white houses looking out into the sea. Tully closed her eyes. She could almost feel the waves beating against her legs. She could almost smell the salty water, but when she opened her eyes, all she saw was eight milk crates.

"Tully," said Jack. "Why don't you ask Robin to take you there? If you want to see it so much, why haven't you gone?"

"Because I don't want to go with Robin," Tully said honestly, instantly regretting it. "It wouldn't be the same, going with him," she explained. "Besides, he works all the time. He would never leave his store."

"That's a shame," said Jack. "Anyway, the sea is the sea," said Jack. "You *were* going to go with Jeremy."

Tully stared at him incredulously, then sighed. "Didn't you and Shakie have anything better to do than talk about me?" she asked.

"Not really." Jack smiled, adding, "Shakie really likes you."

"Yes, yes, I know," said Tully. "But tell me, is there something you don't know about me?"

"Tell me," he said, "is there something *you* don't know about *me*?"

"I didn't know you played softball," she immediately said.

Jack leaned over the table, closer to her. "Not even at Shakie's wedding when I told you about the house on Texas Street?" he said quietly. "Didn't you think I played softball then?"

Tully fought to forget the memory of Shakie's wedding, of Shunga Park, of softball. Jack Pendel had always been just a little too hard on Tully, just a little too hard on Tully's insides.

"Take it easy, Jack," Tully said, putting her hands on her stomach.

He leaned closer. "What's the matter?"

"Well, Jack, you haven't exactly brought me *old* news,

have you? I mean, I never for a second thought you knew I existed until September 28, 1978, when *she* introduced us. I, for one, never had any idea about you."

He leaned closer still. He was almost out of his chair. His voice was low, but Tully could hear him very clearly. "You didn't think I knew you, Tully? Not even when I kissed your hand?"

Her face started to burn. "I thought you were drunk," she said hoarsely.

"Oh, make no mistake about it, I was," said Jack, leaning back, his hands flat on the table. "But that wasn't why I kissed your hand."

Tully felt droplets of sweat run down her temples.

"Do you want to know why?"

She shook her head. Not really.

"Because, Tully. I knew you way before then," he said with an intensity that stupefied her.

"Because your Jennifer never stopped talking about you, never stopped talking about her best friend Tully who did not want to be friends with her anymore." Tully's eyes felt hot as she fought an impulse to exhale.

" . . . because I saw you dancing at Tortilla Jack's," he said, and Tully wanted to cover her face.

After lunch when they got outside, it took a while to adjust to the blazing sun. Tully's pupils were blanched, and the world was washed out until Jack was waved down by a friend of his and went to say a brief hello. As Tully watched him walk away, that's when she noticed his jersey.

Jack was wearing a pair of Levi's and a jersey. The jeans were faded, but the jersey was a brilliant red, glaring bright fire-engine red. She noticed it for the first time as she watched him and thought hotly that she had never seen a red jersey quite so red on a man quite so tall with shoulders quite so broad. Something closed and opened inside her. The milk rushed in, and the milk was hot.

When he came back, Tully hoped her face was not as bright as his shirt. "What's the matter?" asked Jack at once.

"Let's go," she said, without looking at him. "I've been out too long."

Tully tried not to look at him anymore, and in the car that

was easy. She just stared at the road, hoping they would get to Docking soon.

Jack pulled up to the front. Turning to her, he said, "Want to have lunch tomorrow?"

"I—can't," she stammered. "I have an interview at one, I gotta go and check out this family, I really do, I gotta go and check them out."

"I believe you, I believe you," Jack said. "Want to have lunch ever again?"

She squinted her eyes at him. Was he teasing her? Making fun of her? "Sure," she said. "Why not?"

"Why indeed not?" said Jack. "Thursday?"

"Jack!"

"I thought so," he said. Tully held her breath, trying not to make a sound, and opened the car door.

"How about if we go to Lake Vaquero again?" Jack asked. "Would you like to do that?"

Very much, she thought, still holding her breath. "Sure," Tully said. "Why not?"

7.

A week later, in the beginning of July, when Jack and Tully were sitting on the little patch of sand at Lake Vaquero with trees filtering the sun that fell on them and Boomerang, Tully, without looking at Jack, said, "She was the one you used to go to Texas Street with, wasn't she?"

And he did not look at her when he answered, "She was."

A little while later, they sat on a tree trunk immersed in water. Tully took off her sneakers and swung her feet back and forth in the lake.

"Let me ask you," she began cautiously. "You were friends for quite some time?"

"Some time," he said. "We played softball for a few years."

"And then what happened?"

"Nothing happened," said Jack. "In my junior year, I started playing football."

"You stopped playing softball?"

"Yes, gradually. I wanted to be a football player. I had to practice."

"Of course," said Tully. And then, "So, did you and she stop being friends?"

"No, we just didn't see each other as regularly. Not every weekend like before. Not so much after school, either. I started to hang out with people Jennifer didn't hang out with. We kind of . . . you know. Sixteen," Jack said by way of explanation. But all of Tully's questions didn't even begin to get answered. She stopped swinging her feet, got off the tree trunk, and started wading in the water. Pacing in the water.

"Let me ask you," she said. "Did you ever think she had a crush on you?"

"Not for some time," he replied. "You didn't, either, I guess."

"No, like I said, I had no idea you existed, until September of our senior year."

Jack looked at her peculiarly. Or rather, half peculiarly, half—Tully didn't know what. Sadly?

"So we can assume," Jack said, "that she must not have felt very much if she didn't discuss me with Julie or you."

"No, she had always been very secretive. She was the first in our class for three years in a row and I had no idea."

"Well, you were quite busy during the years she was first in our class."

Tully kicked the water with her foot.

Some minutes passed before she asked. "Well, when did you first realize she had a crush on you?"

"Junior year, I guess," Jack said a little reluctantly. "She kept staying after school to watch me practice."

"She told us she was in the chess club," exclaimed Tully.

"Well, there were certainly plenty of pawns on the field behind Topeka High," he said jokingly.

"Yes, but no kings," she said, and Jack's smile evaporated.

"I was sixteen years old, Tully," he said. "And not to put too fine a point on it, but do you know how many girls at various times kept coming to watch us—me—play?"

"She was your friend."

"Yes, she was. All the more reason for me to dismiss her. I thought she was coming *because* she was my friend," said Jack.

"And when she joined the cheerleading squad, did you think she did it because she was your friend then, too?"

"I'm sorry," Jack said. "I didn't think that much about it."

Tully kept wading in the water, watching Boomerang play nearby. "Did you like her?"

"I liked her plenty. I liked her very much."

"Obviously you finally liked her *well enough,* didn't you?"

Shaking his head, Jack said, "I'm going to ignore that. I've always liked her well enough."

"Let me ask you," said Tully, coming to stand in front of him. "If you knew she had a crush on you, if you knew you didn't return most of her feelings, why didn't you just do the decent thing and stay as far away from her as possible?" *Why didn't you stay far away from her on New Year's Eve?* Tully wanted to ask.

"Because I felt a little guilty for neglecting her. We had been friends. And I did stay away from her as much as I could. But she always took it so personally. So I'd try to make it up to her."

"Well, you really made it up to her, didn't you?" said Tully, and grabbed his arm, instantly sorry. "I'm sorry, Jack," she said, and felt terrible, even before she saw his stricken, fallen face. "I'm really sorry," she said, patting his arm, pulling it downward, beseeching him to sit down again.

"It wasn't my fault," he said resolutely, sitting back on the fallen tree trunk.

"I know," Tully said sadly. "I know. But I almost wish it were. For a long time, I wished it was."

"It's not your fault, either."

She looked away into Lake Vaquero, still standing in the water next to his legs. "It's somebody's fault, though, isn't it?" she said, staring back into his face. "It can't have happened for no reason at all, could it?"

Jack looked at her gravely, seriously, woefully. And then he caught her hands in his hands and turned them over. Staring at the insides of her wrists and then into her face, he said, "It could've happened to you anytime, anytime at all, yet you're still here."

Tully pulled sharply away, but Jack was stronger. He did not let go. "Tully, you're lucky, I know you don't think you are, but you are lucky. And you're strong. She wasn't as lucky. She wasn't as strong."

Tully again tried to yank her wrists from his encircling hands. "Listen, Jack," she said, struggling. "Lucky? Strong? What the fuck are you talking about? If I picked up that Colt .45 and put the barrel against my chin and pulled the trigger, I wouldn't be so fucking lucky, either."

Jack brought her wrists close to his face. "No," he whispered. "But you haven't picked up that .45. That's why you're lucky. That's why you're strong." And he bent his face down to her wrists and kissed her scars. First kissed one, then the other.

"Stop it," Tully said, slowly pulling her hands away. "Your stubble is hurting my hands."

"I'll shave," said Jack, letting her hands fall, staring hard at her.

"You should," said Tully, stumbling back. "High school's over."

When Tully and Boomerang came back home in the early evening, Robin was home waiting for them. "Where did you guys go?" he said, picking up Boomer and kissing him on the chest. "I came home and no one was here. I missed you guys."

Boomerang stuck his dirty hands in Robin's hair. "We went to the lake."

Tully stood quietly near them. If he asks me, I will tell him, she thought. I haven't done anything wrong. I will tell him.

Robin, however, must have just assumed it was Lake Shawnee, because he said, "The lake. How pretty. Did you go in the water?"

Yes, Boomerang told him, and then wanted to get down from his arms. "Boomerang!" Robin yelled after him as the boy ran into the backyard. "Tell me about your day!" Boomerang ignored him. Robin turned to Tully, who was standing in the middle of the kitchen with her arms folded around herself. "He is like you," Robin said, smiling as he walked up to her and hugged her. "He doesn't tell me a thing."

Tully hugged him back and felt something stab her in the chest. After Robin went out in the yard after Boomer, Tully went through her bag, took out two unfinished packs of Kent Lights and three lighters, and threw them in the garbage.

* * *

Jack did not paint Tully's house that summer.

But she started rearranging her appointments so that she could have lunch with him every day. Tully kept hoping to see that red jersey again, but he didn't wear it. He wore painter's whites a lot. Shorts. Tank tops. It was another hot steamy summer.

On her morning rounds around the hospitals or the farms, Tully would keep checking the time to see how close she was to lunchtime.

On Saturdays, when Robin was in Manhattan with Boomer and Tully was shopping with Shakie, she would against her will look for him on the streets. On Sundays Jack and Tully went to church bearing flowers. Tully continued to bring her carnations, while Jack brought shears for the rosebush that bloomed all over the tombstone. Tully sat in the wire chair and watched him.

"Tell me, Jack," she said one Sunday. "Where do you get such nice white roses all year round?"

He turned to her and said, "Wouldn't you like to know."

"Yes, I would, actually," she said.

Jack moved to stand closer to her. "Well, Natalie Makker, I'm just not going to tell you. I'm a very simple man, you see. But I've got to have at least one secret from you."

"If you are simple," snorted Tully, "then I'm the Queen of Sheba."

"But, Tully, you are," said Jack, "the Queen of Sheba."

And then, after the white roses, Lake Vaquero! June, July, August. Nine Sundays. Nine Sundays at Lake Vaquero.

"Jack you're clean shaven," Tully noticed one Sunday.

"Yeah," he said. "Never know when I'm going to be rubbing your wrists again."

"Never, I hope," said Tully, flushing.

That Sunday Jack asked her about her dad.

"My father was a nice man," Tully replied. "He used to watch TV with me, I think. Or just watch TV. And I was in the same room with him."

"How old were you when he left?"

Tully looked at him sharply, slightly irritated. "Did Jennifer tell you he left?"

He nodded.

"What? Did she forget to tell you how old I was?"

"You can't be mad at her anymore, Tully."

Mad? I'm furious at her, Tully thought. Still furious.

"I forgot," said Jack patiently.

Tully got up off the sand. "Unbelievable. My entire life. For public consumption."

"Not your entire life," Jack said. "And not for public consumption."

"Yes, public, Jack. You're forgetting. I had no idea you even existed. You were the quintessential public. Jack Q. Public."

"How old, Tully?"

"Seven." Tully sighed. "I was seven."

She felt him lightly touch her arm with his fingers. "Why are you so upset we talked about you?"

"I'm not upset. Who's upset?" said Tully.

"You were pretty floored that day at lunch when I told you she and I had been friends."

Floored? thought Tully. The only thing I was floored by that day was your red jersey, Jack Pendel.

When Tully didn't answer him, Jack said, "I was about eight myself when my dad left."

"Eight?" exclaimed Tully. "What do you mean, dad? Shakie said your dad died just a few years ago."

"My stepfather died just a few years ago," explained Jack.

"Oh," said Tully. And sat back down on the sand again. He sat down next to her. Their arms were almost touching. "Well, at least you *had* a stepfather," she said.

"Yes," Jack replied stonily. "At least."

The question Tully wanted to ask him was at the tip of her tongue. At the very tip, nearly falling out of her lips. *Why did he leave, Jack? How did he leave? Tell me about your father, Jack Pendel.*

But she clamped down on that metal bit between her teeth again. I don't want to in return tell him about my own father.

"You know, Tully," Jack said, as if reading her mind, his voice flatter than before, "you seem to think that nobody else but you feels anything, but that's bullshit."

"What are you talking about?" said Tully. "I don't think that at all."

"You think you're the only one who's got anything to hide."

She got up off the sand again. Jack continued to sit, his knees drawn to his chest.

"Jack, what *are* you talking about? I don't think that at all."

"Then why are you always so secretive? You never share."

Tully looked around, saw Boomerang's pail and shovel, and, picking them up, handed them to Jack, and said, "What are we, five years old? Here, I'll share, let's make mud castles."

When he looked at her scornfully and didn't take them, Tully dropped them on the ground and crouched down. "Share what? What do you want me to share? And do you think you share? You won't even tell me where you get your stupid roses."

"Oh, so now they're stupid," said Jack.

A short silence ensued. The birds weren't silent, though.

"Jack, what's the matter?"

"Why are you so silent, Tully? I mean, I know the worst thing. The worst is out between us. What else is there?"

"Nothing," she said. "Nothing."

"So why do you clam up and bite your lips?"

"Because I want to be plain," said Tully. "I just want to be Tully ordinary. That's all I ever wanted. Just to be the normal kid on the normal block, with the normal life. That's it. I figure, my face is plain and the less I'm heard, the more plain I'll seem."

"Tully, you're anything but plain," said Jack. "But no one has a normal life. No one's the normal kid."

"That's not true," said Tully. "Look at Shakie."

"Yeah, look at Shakie. Now, she is the true Queen of Sheba—her mother, four brothers, and father have made Shakie's bed her entire life, and now I'm sure her husband is, too. Shakie's had her whole life handed to her as a breakfast in bed, but she thinks she's got a raw deal because she is not sleeping out on the beach and not washing for three days."

"She thinks she's got a raw deal because she is not sleeping on the beach or washing for three days *with you*."

"Again, do you think that's normal?"

Tully could not answer that question.

Jack continued. "She now has a husband who has to do the work of two adults and four brothers to keep Shakie comfortable and happy. And by all accounts, he is doing a fine job. But do you think *that's* normal?"

Tully kept quiet. She wanted to say Julie's family was normal, but she couldn't say that. Tully didn't think they felt normal anymore with their only daughter a nomad and in love with a woman. She wanted deep down to say that Jennifer's family was normal; after all, it was the family she had always longed for. But she couldn't say that, either.

"You," she finally said. "You're kind of normal."

"Kind of average, would you say?"

"Yeah." She smiled. "Kind of Jack average."

"Jack average and Jack public. I'm really quite something, aren't I?"

You really are, Tully thought, but said, "Quite average."

"My father left us when I was eight," Jack said. "Nothing seemed average to me after that."

"Left *us*? You're not the only child?"

"Do I seem like the only child to you, Tully?"

"Yes," she said honestly.

"I'm an only child," said Jack. "I meant left me and my mother."

Coming back home, Tully cleared her throat and said to Jack in the Mustang, "You know . . . hmm, there was nothing particularly wrong with your stubble."

Smiling broadly, Jack said, "Oh, really?"

"Yeah," she said, wanting to remember, *willing* herself to want to remember. "I remember when we danced at the Senior Banquet. You had stubble then. It was messy. But it didn't look half-bad."

He shook his head. "Oh, I was a scruff. Was trying to grow a beard, you know. But never had much hair. My dad had a beard."

The following Sunday at Vaquero, Jack said to Tully, "*She* must have told you plenty of things about me."

Tully rolled her eyes. "Oh. Plenty."

"Like what?" he said, lightly and seriously at the same time.

"Uh-uh." Tully shook her head. "You tell me about the white roses and I'll tell you what she said."

"Tully, it's my only secret from you. Can't I have just one secret? It's like the Wizard of Oz showing Dorothy and her friends all his tricks. The tricks just didn't seem so special after he showed them how."

"You are not the Wizard of Oz, Jack Pendel," said Tully.

"Wizard of Oz?" Boomerang said, sitting nearby. "I want Wizard of Oz."

"Well, here he is, Boomer, apparently," said Tully. Boomerang climbed on Jack's neck.

"We off t' see/ de Wizahd," sang Boomerang, *"De wonduh-ful Wizahd of Oz/ becawze/ becawze/ becawze/ becawze/ BECAWZE!/ becawze de wonduh-ful tings he duz!"*

After Boomerang went back to sit in the water, Tully said to Jack, "Well, what exactly are your magic tricks?"

"The roses," replied Jack.

"What else? Can you send Dorothy home? Or give Scarecrow some brains? While you're at it, could you give yourself a heart?"

"No, but I was," said Jack, "thinking of giving you one."

A little later, Jack said carefully, "So what advice did you give her after she told you the things you won't tell me about me?"

"I said you weren't worth all the commotion," Tully stated, immediately and acutely ashamed that she herself could be heard talking aloud about Jennifer's impossible feelings in such a flippant way.

"But she defended you," Tully continued, her voice lower. "She told me you were."

Jack smirked. "That sounds like that old insult," he said. "You said I wasn't fit to live with pigs. But she defended me. She told you I was."

She said you were worth it, thought Tully. That's what she told me. She told me you were worth everything. But I hadn't believed her.

Tully found it harder and harder to face Shakie. Though they continued to see each other, Tully saw Shakie less and less often on her own. Usually she made it a two-family thing when Robin could take off from work or from sports: the boys and girls all together, having a barbecue, a dinner, or going to Lake Shawnee. Tully wanted to talk to someone about Jack, her new friend, and she felt uncomfortable spending her time with a woman she couldn't talk to about Jack.

On Saturdays when Shakie and Tully went shopping, Shakie was usually saddled with her babies, who were at that wonderful stage of being old enough to get into some terrible mischief but not old enough to control their own impulses. (Jack laughed when Tully told him this. "Who is?" he said.) The twins, nearly two years old, were a small irritation to Tully, who wanted to shop, not babysit. Still, Shakie and Tully managed, kids and all. Without much personal conversation.

Tully and Robin went over to Shakie and Frank's a few Sunday evenings after Tully would rush headlong home from Lake Vaquero, having sat on the sand and fed the ducks too long, having lost track of time. Every time she and Jack sat on the sand, she was afraid they would run out of things to say to each other, but the more they sat, the more they talked. The more they sat around each other, the easier the talking became, and the easier the silences became. They had the sand to fill their silences, the sand, and Boomerang, and the rowboat. And the ivy. They had Lake Vaquero to fill what they couldn't say.

Incredibly, Tully told Jack about her childhood. The sun must have been extra hot that Sunday. Jack told her about his. She told Jack about her mother; he told her about his. Tully talked about Shakie, and so did Jack. And when they ran out of words, they would feed the ducks or row a boat. Jack had found an old beat-up boat on its side near the lake and bought some oars for it. So they went rowing. Tully rowed Jack. Jack rowed Tully. One Sunday afternoon in August, as Jack rowed her, he made up a kid's poem for her.

> *There was a girl named Tully Makker*
> *Who pretended she was brave*
> *But all this Tully Makker did*
> *Was sit so bravely at a grave*
> *She pouted*
> *Sulked*
> *She even cried*
> *But never never did she see*
> *Pacific ocean with her eyes.*

And when Tully rowed Jack, she made him up a poem, too.

There was a girl named Tully Makker
Who had a friend named Jack the Wacko
She told this Jack
I am not black
I will not cry
I will not die
I'll see the ocean with my eyes.

"I'll bet you will," said Jack, taking off his shirt.

"Excuse me, what are you doing?" said Tully, averting her eyes. White shorts, tanned chest. Tanned arms.

He yelled, "AHHHHHH!" and plunged into the lake. Boomerang squealed with delight. "Mommy, Mommy, jump in, too!" he cried.

"I'm not taking off my shirt," Tully declared, and jumped in, shorts, T-shirt, and all.

"Come on, Boomerang," said Tully, stretching out her hands. "Come to Mommy." And then three-year-old Boomer jumped in. How they got back on the boat, Tully did not remember. But she remembered the kid poem they tried to make together, wet, rowing back to the shore.

Jack Pendel and Tully Makker
Jumped together in the lake.
Jack Pendel and Tully Makker
Caught Boomer, too, and his small rake.
They said
Watch this
They said
Jump high
They said . . .

They got stuck on the last line. Jack said, *"It's time to say good-bye."* And Tully said, *"Please give me back my tie."* But that wasn't what she was thinking.

8.

Tully and Robin had a barbecue on a Sunday at the end of August. Tully reluctantly agreed to have it. Sunday was the

best day, of course, for a damned barbecue. For everybody
else. Shakie and Frank came with their two kids and one on
the way, Bruce and Karen with their one and Stevie and Linda
with their three. It was a madhouse, but fun anyway. Robin
even wheeled out Hedda, who sat and ate a little food and
then asked to be taken back to her rooms.

"How is it, Tully?" asked Shakie, pointing to Hedda. "Is it
getting better?"

"It's great," she replied laconically.

Later, when dusk settled down on 1501 Texas Street, when
the adults were all sitting there, having eaten and drunk aplen-
ty, not talking about anything in particular, just listening to the
crickets and watching the kids trying to catch fireflies, Frank
said, looking at Robin's house, "Rob, man, you need a coat
of paint bad."

"How can you see in this light?" Robin asked him.

"That's what I mean. If even in this light, you need some
paint . . ." replied Frank.

"Well, speaking of painting," said Robin, looking peculiarly
at Tully who was looking at Frank who was looking at Shakie,
"we actually *were* looking into having the house painted,
weren't we, Tully?"

"We were kind of thinking about it," said Tully vaguely.

"Well, you'll never guess who I saw painting houses around
Topeka," said Frank. "Jack Pendel. Maybe you should ask
him."

"Well, strangely enough," said Robin, glancing at Tully,
"that's who offered to paint our house."

"Offered?" said Shakie, smiling thinly. It was the first time
she had spoken since the conversation started.

"Apparently," said Robin. "I didn't talk to him myself, but
he came over to our house some months ago and talked to
Tully. Didn't he, Tully?" Robin said.

Tully was mortified. "He did," she said, but didn't look at
anybody.

Frank bent his head to Shakie. "You haven't seen him, have
you, Shake?" he asked right there in the dusk, in front of three
other couples, in front of the crickets, in front of the moon.
You haven't seen him, have you, Shake? How could he even
ask her that? thought Tully. Goddamn Robin.

"Uh—no, I haven't seen him," Shakie replied absentmindedly, never taking her eyes off Tully. "I didn't realize he was in town. I didn't realize he was in town for the whole summer."

Tully returned her friend's stare. I have nothing to be ashamed of, she thought. He has not painted our house. He has not been by to see *you*. We have not talked about him. I have nothing to be ashamed of.

"Well, he hasn't painted your house, Tully," said Shakie. "Why not?"

"We haven't gotten around to it," said Tully, wondering about the "we" and deciding to elaborate. "Robin and I've been spending our money on other things," Tully said. "The Camaro needed a lot of work."

They all left soon thereafter, and after they left, Tully faced off Robin. "You had to," she said. "You just had to."

He laughed, but coldly. "I had to nothing. I didn't bring up painting our house."

"Yes, but you brought *him* up. In front of Shakie's face. Why would you tell her he was here?"

"Well, actually, Tully," said Robin, "it interests me why you didn't tell Shakie he was in town. Why would you do a thing like *that*?"

"Because!" she shouted. "Why would I tell her? He is not interested in her, and she is trying to forget him and have a good marriage. You know she's got no self-control, she'd be running down to see him every week. So why would I tell her?"

"Well, why is he coming back to Topeka, knowing it's tormenting her?" asked Robin.

"His mother is here!" she yelled. "Robin, what are you doing? Why are you being this way?"

"Because," he said, and his voice was as cold as his face, "I had been wondering if you had told her he was in town, and now I'm wondering why you haven't."

"Oh, don't be so fucking absurd," Tully said, turning on her heels. "Just get sane, will you? Get a clue. We're friends, okay? Friends."

"Who is friends?" said Robin. "You and Shakie?"

"Yes," she said, walking up the stairs away from him. "Me and Shakie."

* * *

Tully got a phone call from Shakie barely twelve hours later, asking her to come over after work. Tully cringed but came after picking up Boomer at Angela's.

Shakie did not beat around the bush. The front door did not yet close behind Tully when Shakie said, "You've known Jack was in town and you didn't tell me?"

Tully walked over to the couch, sat down, and smiled convivially. "How are you, Shake? You look well."

"Why?"

"Why?" Tully repeated, smiling pleasantly. "Why what? Where is Frank?"

"Working. Why didn't you tell me?"

Tully let out a small thin laugh and rubbed her eyes. "Shakie, why do you think I didn't tell you?"

"I don't know, Tully. That's what worries me."

"Well, don't be worried."

"Then why didn't you tell me?"

"I didn't tell you because you told me you weren't going to see him anymore. I didn't tell you because you're married and are busy with your two kids and being pregnant. I didn't tell you because I didn't want to upset you. Okay?"

Shakie got up. Tully rolled her eyes. Is she going to start pacing now? Shakie started pacing. Tully almost laughed, except she was a little afraid Shakie would cry. Shakie did cry.

"Tully, you have no idea. No idea at all. Jack thinks that now that I'm married I don't want to see him, but he is wrong."

Tully tightened her lips. "Shake, how could he think that? You know he doesn't think that at all. Have you forgotten already? Have you forgotten Christmas, nearly two years ago? You called him, I lied for you, and then you told me he didn't want to be involved with you anymore. You told me you weren't going to see him anymore."

"Oh, Tully, that was then," Shakie was saying, wiping her eyes. "Didn't you know I was full of shit?"

"No, Shakie," said Tully. "I thought you were full of self-control."

"Tully, you're full of shit. You know I've got no self-control. The neighborhood frog knows that."

"That's why," said Tully patiently, "I didn't tell you."

"He's been in town the whole summer! He's leaving soon, isn't he?"

Tully hadn't thought about it. But her face must have fallen a little, because Shakie said, "You've seen him, haven't you?"

Tully thought about telling Shakie the truth—that she had indeed seen him—but Tully did not want to tell Shakie the *whole* truth. After a silence, Tully answered her. "No," she said, "I haven't seen him. Boomerang! Let's go!"

Shakie started to cry again.

"I'm sorry, Shakie," said Tully, taking her son by the hand. "I'm sorry I'm upsetting you. I feel like I've made things worse." Shakie got up to walk Tully out.

"Shakie, listen," said Tully at the door. "Don't upset yourself over nothing. Don't upset your wonderful husband. You and Frank had such a great summer together, you love each other so much, why are you doing this to yourself? If you didn't know Jack was in town, you'd be happy still. And you ask me why I didn't tell you? I just don't understand. Why do you want to hurt Frank? I can maybe understand if you and Jack couldn't live without each other, if you were going to leave Frank and start a new life. But look at all you have." Tully opened her arms and pointed to the room, to the house, and to the kids. She lowered her voice so Boomerang wouldn't hear her. "What? All this, for a fuck?"

But as she left Shakie and, downhearted, got into her car and drove to Texas Street, Tully thought perhaps it wasn't all just for a fuck.

As soon as Tully left, Shakie called Jack and arranged to see him. The next morning she brought the kids over to Angela's, because Shakie had nowhere else to bring them.

"Sure I look after them," said Angela. "What's the matter, Shake? Hot date?" she joked.

"Something like that," Shakie replied wanly, but she shivered in the car on her way to see him. She sat in the Morgan Hall parking lot at Washburn for fifteen minutes before she willed herself to get out. Not sure what she wanted to say to him, Shakie nonetheless knew she wanted to say *something*. She wanted to try something. She looked at herself in the rearview mirror and put on some Chanel lipstick and perfume. She was the Chanel girl. Oh, the hell with it, she thought, her fingers on the keys still in the ignition. I should get out of here right now.

Jack was waiting for her, sitting on one of the benches in front of the Memorial Union. "Hi." He waved. "You're late."

"What else is new?" she said, wanting to put her arms around him like she used to.

"You look good, Shakie," Jack said. "How are the kids?"

"You, too," she replied. "Fine, fine."

Jack looked up at her. "Should I stand up, or will you sit down already?"

Shakie sat down. The pebbles on the ground got into her sandals and she fought the impulse to pick them out of her toes. She didn't want to be touching pebbles. She wanted to touch his blond head.

"So, Jack," she finally, quietly said, clearing her throat and not looking at him. "How come you didn't tell me you were in town?"

Jack smiled a little. "I didn't know I was supposed to."

Yes, but . . . Shakie thought. "But you saw Tully," she said. "Her house needs painting."

"Mine needs painting, too." Shakie smiled. Kind of smiled. She wasn't sure what was on her actual face because she had on her Chanel face, the face she put on at the cosmetics counter for the women who drove her mad if she let them.

"I don't think your husband would be very pleased if I painted your house."

"Hmm, and hers would?"

Jack rubbed his palms together and said after a moment, "Shake, what's up?"

"You didn't want to see me at your mom's house, did you?" she said, more as a statement than a question.

"No," he admitted. "I didn't think it'd be a good idea."

Changing the subject, Shakie said, "I didn't know you came out this way in the summers," thinking, I gotta get focused here, I don't know what I'm saying. I don't know what to ask. Why did I come here at all? At all, except to see his face, to maybe touch his hair.

If he answered her, she did not know it. There *was* something she wanted to ask him.

"You've been seeing her," Shakie said flatly.

"Seeing who?" Jack said, glancing at his watch.

"Her," said Shakie. "Tully."

Jack didn't answer Shakie, but did lift himself up into a straight sitting position. He had been leaning on elbows which were leaning on his knees.

"I'm getting confused, Shakie," he said firmly. "What's up?"

"Is this something you don't want to talk about?" Shakie asked.

"Yes."

"Yes, what?"

"Yes," Jack said, "this is something I don't want to talk about."

Shakie was silent for a few long moments, and so was he.

"Tully doesn't want to talk about it, either."

"So what?" Jack said a little sharply. "She doesn't want to talk about anything."

Shakie was dully curious. "How do *you* know?"

"Know what? Shake, what do you want?"

I want you not to be so mean to me, she wanted to say, but she wasn't going to say it. Not she, no, not Martha Louise Lamber née Bowman, not the Topeka High Homecoming Queen two years in a row, not the Prom Queen. No, not she.

So then Shakie just came out and said it. Just for effect. He hadn't answered her question, but then she really didn't have much to suspect. It was true, Tully never talked about anything. Shakie had no reason to think anything, but she asked her question anyway. After not seeing her for nearly two years, Jack didn't act like he had missed Shakie at all. He didn't look at her longingly even though she tried to look her most summerlike best. He didn't touch her. He didn't sit close to her on the four-foot-long bench. She had nothing to lose. So Shakie said, "Is there something going on between you and Tully?"

Jack sighed. "Nothing is going on between me and her, Shakie. She is a nice person. Come on, now. We all knew each other in high school."

His words jolted her memory, and she nodded. "Yes, of course, how could I forget? There's that bond between you. Her best friend was sweet on you."

Jack eyed her levelly. I'm being mean, Shakie thought. Well, I don't care. She was upset that Jack didn't look at her when he told her there was nothing going on between him and Tully.

"She is happily married, you know," said Shakie.

"Of that," Jack said, "I have no doubt."

"She is," insisted Shakie. "Really. Robin is very good for her and to her. He really loves her."

"Of that I have no doubt," Jack repeated, looking around restlessly. Shakie persisted. Okay, here goes. She moved a little closer to him.

"Jack," she started suggestively, and then stopped suddenly, seeing him move away from her on the bench.

"Sorry, Shakie," he said. "Sorry."

"Jack, why are you moving away from me?"

He stared at her. "Shake, you've always been a fine one for self-inflicted pain. Always asking me to upset you. I'm sorry. I didn't mean to move away, I just don't want there to be a problem, okay?"

"Jack," she whispered, trying to control the twitch in her fingers. "Has me being married and having kids and all really changed your feelings for me so much?"

He didn't answer her.

She continued breathlessly. "I mean, when you came to visit me in the hospital when I just had my kids, you seemed so happy for me. Weren't you sad just a little inside?"

"I was very happy for you," Jack said.

"Well, I wish you wouldn't be so goddamned happy for me all the time!" Shakie exclaimed. "I wish you wouldn't be so happy I'm married to someone else and having babies with someone else!" And then, remembering something about that hospital visit, she asked, "Are you happy for Tully, too, that she is married to someone else and has a baby?"

"Less happy," Jack muttered, and Shakie heard.

The belltower struck noon. They continued to sit there.

"I gotta go, Shake," Jack said at last. "I gotta go paint."

She grabbed his arm. "Jack, wait." And then, seeing the expression in his face, took the arm off and said, "Okay, Jack, okay. If that's the way you want it. I understand. Just tell me something." She coughed. "Why? I know you think I'm a masochist, but I want to know, really. I can't stand not knowing. Why not me?"

Jack rolled his eyes. "Oh, Shake," he said.

"Jack, you have been seeing her. You roll your eyes just like Tully. Everybody who knows her begins to roll their eyes just like her. Don't roll your eyes. Just tell me. There is nothing more you can do to me. Tell me why."

"Why what?" he said gently.

"Why not me? You had me, and I was yours. We were so young and looked so good together, and were so happy. What went wrong?"

Jack patted Shakie's back, and she willed herself to sit still at his touch. "Shakie, please. What can I tell you? I don't know anything. I don't know why. You're right. We *were* young. We did look good. And we were happy. How simple our lives would be if we could choose the people we loved. But we don't choose them. God chooses them, or fate. The stars and the sky choose them, or darkness and light. Not us, okay? If it was *us,* you'd be loving Frank, or I'd be loving you, or Tully'd be loving Robin. I don't know why."

Shakie mumbled, not looking at him. "Jack, are you telling me you never loved me?"

"I liked you very much, and I cared for you. I still do."

Shakie straightened her back and moved away from his arm. "Jack, I'm really all right. Really. But I want to know something. Was there something . . . wrong with me? Was there something you just couldn't—" her voice faltered, "love in me?"

Jack shoved her lightly. "Shake, stop this. Stop. This is going to lead to no good."

Shakie folded her hands on her lap and sat still. "Tell me, Jack, please. I swear I'll be all right. I really need to hear it. Tell me I'm a masochist, tell me I'm crazy, but tell me. What was it?"

"You're a masochist. You're crazy."

"What was it?" she repeated.

He shrugged. "Shakie, you're beautiful. But it could never work between us. I knew it always, and I know that deep down you knew it, too."

"I didn't know it," she said, trying to keep the petulance out of her voice.

"Shakie, I'm not your man. You kept thinking for a long time that I was, but I am not it. Really. Frank is it. He is perfect for you. He adores you and he will take care of you and he will cater to your every need. That's the kind of man who is right for you, not me."

"Why not you?" she said.

"Because I cannot take care of you. I wouldn't *want* to take care of you. I wouldn't want to cater to your whims and be at your every beck and call. That's what you need, but I could not give it to you. And never will," he added.

"You think I'm spoiled," said Shakie.

"Yes, I do," Jack said simply. "That's not such a bad thing, but I barely take care of myself. I roam around, I paint, I live free. I'm still trying to find something, you know? I don't spoil even myself. I couldn't spoil you."

She sat silently.

"I gotta go," he said one more time.

They got up. Shakie was outwardly calm and she was glad for that. "I'm glad we talked, Jack. I understand better now," she said.

In the parking lot, she was about to get in when she turned to him and whispered, "Listen, would you do me a favor, for old times' sake?" coming closer to him. "Would you do me a favor and give me a kiss? For me?"

He sighed but bent his head downward to her. She nearly lost her composure at the feel of his warm lips. For a second she was wearing white chiffon and had a crown on her head.

"'Bye, Shakie," Jack said quietly. "Everything will be all right."

"Of course it will." She managed a bright smile. "It'll all be just fine."

Waiting to make a right onto 17th Street, Shakie looked at herself in the mirror and saw her lips were trembling. I hope he didn't notice, she thought.

A few days later, on a Saturday night, when Robin was staying at Bruce's farm in Manhattan, Tully and Boomerang met Jack to go to the annual Labor Day Crooked Post Fair. Robin did ask Tully to come with him, but Tully knew he didn't mean it. He was going to work until the store closed and then he wanted to go out with Bruce and Stevie. He only asked Tully as lip service, and Tully knew it and refused. Besides, she didn't want to go to Manhattan with Robin.

When she and Jack met, Tully was quieter than usual.

"What's the matter?" asked Jack.

"Nothing," she said shortly.

"What?" he asked again when they got into his Mustang.

"It's nearly 1986," said Tully. "Tell me, when are you going to mature into owning a real car and not a relic?"

Jack looked at her first with disbelief, and then with irritation. "I see," he said at last, raising his voice. "And what you drive is the latest model?"

"Shhhh!" Tully pointed to the backseat, where Boomerang sat babbling, oblivious to Tully and Jack in the front.

Tully was mute, and Jack in return drove in silence down Wanamaker.

"I invited you to the fair because I *had* thought it might be fun," he said at last.

"I'm sure Boomerang will have a great time," said Tully, folding her arms.

The fair was packed. They parked the car on the grass and walked across the field to the entrance. Trembling with excitement, Boomer gasped, "This is gonna be so much fun."

"Is it going to be so much fun, Tully?" asked Jack.

"For Boomerang? It's gonna be a blast."

Jack stepped in front of Tully, and she stopped reluctantly. She tried to get around him, but he moved this way and that until finally he took her by the shoulders and looked down into her serious face. Tully did not wriggle free from his hands that held her and Jack did not let go.

"Will you talk to me, please? What the hell is wrong?"

"Let's go!" shouted Boomerang. "Let's go now!"

Tully shook her head sulkily.

"It's something I've done, isn't it? What is it?"

Tully was pouty silent. "Oh, and I suppose you feel you haven't done a thing?" she finally said.

Jack let go of her shoulders, laughing lightly. "Not a thing," he said. "Not a blessed thing." Tully did not respond. They walked after Boomerang. Jack paid their way in, though Tully made noises about paying for herself and her son. Boomerang immediately ran to the Indiana Jones Obstacle Course. Jack and Tully stood below and watched him walk on a precarious-looking rope.

"Tell me what I've done and I'll apologize," he said. "Tell me what I haven't done and I'll apologize, too."

"I see," said Tully. "But if you didn't do anything wrong, you wouldn't need to say you're sorry, now, would you?" As she smiled a little, with turned-down lips, Jack smiled back.

They all paid twelve tickets to go on the Ferris wheel. It was seven o'clock and not dark, but the lights were already on. Boomerang sat in between Jack and Tully. When they moved up and got suspended in the air a hundred feet above ground, Jack shoved Tully with his shoulder, and she shoved him back, sighing. "I'm sure you didn't do anything wrong," she said.

"I'm sure of that, too," he said. "But tell me what I did do."

When she didn't speak, Jack shoved her lightly with his shoulder again. She shoved him back. "Jack," she began, "why didn't you tell me you saw Shakie?"

They were still sitting way up in the air. Grinning from ear to ear, Jack shook his head and took a deep breath. When he turned to Tully, she was studying the ground below. Bending his head sideways, Jack peered into Tully's face with his laughing eyes. Pressing her lips together, Tully refused to look at him. Jack lifted his arm up and put it around Tully's shoulder, squeezing her to him a little.

Boomerang protested loudly. "Jack! Stoooop! Mommy, he's squishing me!"

"Jack, stop squishing Boomerang," said Tully, and Jack let his arm rest on Tully's shoulder and grinned.

"Tully! Why, Tully Makker. Is it possible that you are . . . could it be? That you are jealous?"

They started moving down again, as Boomer squealed. Tully had her arm around Boomerang, and Jack had his arm around Tully, still peering into her face over Boomer.

"Oh, don't be so ridiculous," she said, still not looking at him and moving slightly away. "I just wish you had told me, that's all."

He did not take his arm off her. "Oh, is that all?" he said teasingly. "Well, I'm sorry. Had I thought you wanted to know, I certainly would have told you."

"I didn't particularly want to know," lied Tully. "Shake just embarrassed me. And this pleased her in some way, I think. Embarrassing me."

Jack touched Tully's bare knee, patting it a little. Goose bumps broke out all over Tully's body. "I'm sorry she embarrassed you," he said. "I only saw her once, recently, and there is nothing to tell."

Tully thought a moment. "So why didn't you tell me anyway, as kind of matter of course, in the same breath you tell me, oh, I painted Mrs. Muir's house, oh, I helped my mother in the garden, oh, I went to Lawrence, oh, I saw Shakie. Like that."

He took his arm off her. "I don't know," he said. "Habit, I guess. I never tell anything to anybody. It's not important, Tully."

They got off the Ferris wheel and walked over to the basketball hoops, where Uncle Oz hit in three in a row and won a bear that he then had to carry. On the way to the kiddy boat ride, Tully said, "Oh, but hiding it from me was going to make me think it was trivial?"

"I didn't hide it. I just didn't tell you. I didn't think you'd be very interested."

After Boomerang and the bear, Jonathan, were going around and around in a little boat, Tully said, "Just out of interest, what did you guys do?"

"What did we do?" Jack repeated incredulously. "We sat at Washburn and we talked. What do you think we did?"

"I think nothing. I didn't even think you saw her," replied Tully pointedly. She had been taken by surprise by Shakie, who couldn't hide her delight that Jack didn't mention meeting her to Tully. And it was Shakie's delight that Tully was still reacting to, among other things.

"So what did you guys talk about?"

"Tully," said Jack slowly, "are you interrogating me? Or is this a fight? If this is a fight, then let's come right out with it and fight about what the real problem is and not beat around the bush. If you're interrogating me, I'm not interested."

She brooded after that, walking silently to a little carousel for Boomer and then to a Bugs Bunny ride.

After they got some cotton candy, Jack said, "What did Shakie tell you we talked about?"

"Jack, are you playing games with me? Because if you are, *I* am not interested."

He sighed. "What do you want to know? We talked a little about you."

"Uncle Oz, Uncle Oz, I want that! I want that!" cried Boomerang, pointing to a huge dalmatian. Jack had to land just one quarter, and only one, on a greasy plate to win the Godzilla-sized Patch. After ten bucks in quarters, they walked on, without Patch.

Tully said, "Shakie told me you talked about you and her."

"That's true, we did," said Jack. "But Tully, let me ask you something. Are we establishing a precedent here? You want the right to know what I talk about with the people I see? I'll be glad to give you that right," he said. "But I'll want some rights back."

She wanted to ask him what rights he wanted, but her throat got scared, so instead she said, "I don't want that right. You don't have to tell me anything." Tully was still mulling over what Jack thought might be the real problem between them.

When they were all sitting in a cabin waiting for Tilt-A-Whirl to start, Jack said, "You want to know what we said about you?"

"Not particularly. I can only guess," Tully answered, playing with Boomerang's hair.

"Do you want me to tell you anyway?"

"Not particularly," she replied, and then said, "Shakie told me that I should be careful not to misinterpret you."

"She said that, did she?" Jack said coolly. "And?"

"And nothing," said Tully. "I told her I could never misinterpret what I didn't interpret in the first place."

"Great," said Jack. And then the ride started spinning them into nausea and they stopped talking.

When they got off, Boomerang was running out of steam. It was fortunate they had brought his stroller. He sat there with his Jonathan and fell asleep despite the loud music, the flashing happy lights, the smell of sausage and peppers and fried dough. Tully and Jack walked around the arcades. Jack won her a big duck at a shooting gallery.

"Does Robin ever ask where you go on Saturdays or Sundays?" Jack asked quietly.

Tully did not want to talk about Robin. "If he was ever home, he might," she said vaguely.

"Doesn't he ask Boomer?"

"Sometimes, and he tells Robin we were at the lake. It's all right. Robin is so busy with work and with football, I don't know if he'd notice we'd gone and left him."

"I'm sure he'd notice," said Jack.

Tully was sure Robin would notice, too. Nearly every week, Robin asked Tully to come watch him play, or to come to Manhattan with him and visit his brothers. And every Sunday, Tully said no.

Clearing her throat, Tully said, "Hmm—but Shakie's saying that, about misinterpreting you, it got me wondering. That perhaps I did misunderstand something in some way."

"In what way?" said Jack.

"Well," said Tully, "I thought we were friends—"

"We are," said Jack.

"Yes, and friends tell each other things. Trivial things. So when I found out you didn't tell me about Shakie—"

"There is nothing to tell," Jack interrupted.

She continued. "—I thought that perhaps you didn't tell me because I had led you to misunderstand my feelings."

"Your feelings?" said Jack, smiling. "Your feelings toward me?"

She got embarrassed. "Perhaps feelings is too strong a—"

He hushed her. "No, no. Don't take it back."

"You misunderstand," she said. "I thought we were friends, but when you didn't tell me, I began to think that perhaps you thought there was more there, that I would be, as you said, jealous."

"Of course," said Jack. "And that's clearly not the case."

"Right," said Tully. "I just wanted you to know that."

"Of course," said Jack. "Thank you. Thank you for being completely honest with me." But his eyes were twinkling as he said it, and she became flustered again.

He doesn't believe me. Well, why should he? We've been rowing a boat the whole summer.

They were standing near the caramel apples and the water balloons when he said, "Don't be concerned about Shakie. It's nothing. She is upset and she might say things to upset you, but you don't listen to her, Tully Makker."

"I understand," she said. But there was one more thing Tully wanted to bring up. "Uhm . . . Jack? Shakie told me you kissed her."

He ran his hand through his hair. "She told you that, huh? Don't pay attention to her, Tully."

"So you didn't kiss her?" she asked, a little too lively, a little too animated.

"No," he said slowly, breathing out. "I did kiss her. Because she asked me to. Because she wanted me to kiss her for old times—"

"Jack!" Tully interrupted. "I didn't ask you why. I just asked you if you did."

"Never mind her, Tully," Jack said soothingly. "It's over between me and Shakie. You know it, she knows it. Never mind her."

Tully remained skeptical. "If you say it is, then it is. It's hard to believe you, though. She is so beautiful."

Jack reached out to move Tully's long hair away from her face, not saying anything for a moment.

"You want to go for one more ride before we go?" he asked softly.

Yes, she said. They went on the Ferris wheel again. Tully held the sleeping thirty-five pounds of child on her lap as they rose into the air, while Jack sat next to her.

There was no sun now, just lights and darkness and the stars and the sky.

"Tully," he said, turning his face to hers.

Jack was so close, Tully could smell his warm breath. Her throat became wet. He was so close, she was afraid to look at him, afraid that if their eyes met at such proximity, sitting there up in the air, music blaring, the lights shining, total anonymity, total intimacy, that he might kiss her.

"You know, painting season is over."

She said nothing for two turns around, as if she had not heard him.

"It's not over in California," she said at last, her voice low.

"No," he agreed. Then, "I still didn't get to paint your house. I hope it's still standing by next summer."

"Yeah, we've been too busy playing with the sand," said Tully, looking at the fair below. A little while later, "So when are you thinking of going?"

"This week," said Jack, and put his arm around her. And she, a little bit, wanted to cry. Just a little bit.

The Ferris wheel came to a stop. Reluctantly, Tully got up. She had so wanted to smell his warm breath again.

When they were walking across the dark field to the Mustang, Tully asked Jack if she had wanted him to tell her everything he and Shakie had talked about, would he?

"If you wanted me to tell you, I would tell you everything," said Jack, staring at her through the darkness. The noise of the fair dimmed behind them.

Tully didn't speak for a while and then said, "Shakie said I misinterpreted your feelings. Tell me, did I?"

"Yes," he replied.

She let out a short laugh. "I did?"

"Yes."

"How could I?" She smiled, taking his upper arm and not letting go for a couple of moments. "I didn't know you had any."

"There you go," Jack said, not looking at Tully. She gradually took her hand away from his arm, and they did not speak the rest of the way to the car, or to St. Mark's, where they parked Tully's car. Jack kissed Boomerang, putting him in the Camaro. Straightening up, he faced her, and she looked away. Coming a little closer to Tully, Jack pressed his palm to her cheek. "Thank you for a nice summer," he said softly, not taking his palm away. With her hand, she patted his that held her face. "No, thank *you*," she said hoarsely. "Thank you for tonight."

Jack got into his Mustang. "So long, Tully," he said, revving up the engine. "See you at Christmas."

9.

Tully came briefly to the cemetery by herself a week later. The following week she brought a pair of shears, knelt down, and trimmed the rosebush where it looked expansively sloppy. Then Tully left and did not come back for a month.

When she came again in October, Tully did not bring carnations. She brought white roses. After that she came every Sunday, always with roses, though the white ones were truly hard to find, forcing her to buy pink or yellow. Instead of putting the flowers on the ground, she weaved them between the rosebush's bare branches. "It'll be okay, Mandolini," Tully whispered. "I've been hard done by you. But it'll be okay."

In October, Hedda had another stroke, though a less severe one, and needed to be hospitalized again. She had been regaining the use of her legs through rigorous physical therapy paid for by Robin, but the second stroke wiped out most of the improvement, and she lost the use of her good arm, too. Hedda was fed intravenously until just before Thanksgiving. Robin and Tully visited her every couple of days and even brought little Robin to see *Grandma*. But not having Hedda in the house did not bring Tully relief. She could still smell her mother. Hedda's smell permeated the entire half of the first floor, and even the housekeeper's bleaching of the rooms did not help, for now half of the house smelled like ammonia, offensive and pervasive.

When Hedda could speak again and Robin asked what he could do for her to make her more comfortable in the hospital, Hedda said, "Take me home." Tully heard this and sighed. She had hoped her mother would see the light of day, see she was better off taken care of daily by professionals.

They took Hedda home in time for Thanksgiving. While Hedda was gone, Robin had had her walls painted and the hardwood floors refinished. It was better. The smell was nearly gone.

"Robin, you know," Tully said one evening before Hedda returned, "you don't have to do this anymore. I think the Catholic God has already reserved a nice little heavenly cloud just for you." Robin assured her he was not doing it for God's sake. "Then for whose?" said Tully.

Robin looked at her unflinchingly, but said only, "Did you say you wanted the spare rooms upstairs done?"

"I was thinking about having them painted. You never know. We might need one of the rooms."

"For what?" asked Robin, sitting himself next to her on the couch and handing her a cup of tea. Now it was Tully's turn to look unflinchingly at him. "We might need it for a nursery," she said.

"More plants? God, Tully, enough already!"

She laughed, but Robin was serious.

"Oh, Robin," she said, a little exasperated. "Baby, baby, we might have another baby."

Staring at her gravely, he said, "Another baby? Are you crazy?"

In early December, Tully wondered if she should call Jack's mother. Deciding against it, Tully now went to church Saturdays and Sundays.

At work, things were slow. Even dysfunctional families wanted their kids with them for Christmas. Tully brought a collection of toys and clothes and books for the kids at the Lock-Up. When she saw they didn't have a Christmas tree, she got Robin to buy the biggest tree they could find, and they both helped the kids from Shawnee Youth Center Lock-Up trim it.

10.

During Christmas morning Mass, Father Majette spoke of Christ bringing Lazarus back from the dead. But Tully, looking around the church for the sight of Jack's head, hardly heard him. Robin wasn't with her, only Boomerang.

Is that Julie sitting next to Angela in the front? Julie came to church? I don't believe it. Where is Laura? Tully continued to look around. The church was packed. Where is Jack?

After Mass, in the courtyard, Tully stood awkwardly with Boomerang. She was afraid that she looked like she was waiting for Jack, and if he saw her that moment, he would've definitely thought so, too. I'm actually waiting for Julie. C'mon, Jule. Come out of the goddamned church.

Finally Angela and Julie were out, and they walked over to Tully and Boomer.

Tully hugged Julie, noticing her friend had lost weight and looked a little sad.

"Julie, where is Laura?" asked Tully.

"Oh, she is . . ." Julie waved in an indeterminate direction. "Visiting her stepmother in Ohio."

"But I thought you usually go with her."

"Shhhh," said Angela loudly. "Bite your tongue. My only daughter is home for Christmas."

Tully and Julie smiled at each other.

"Hello, Tully," a voice behind her said. Tully willed her face to remain flat as she turned around and looked up at Jack. "Well, hi," she said, not bothering to hide the smile in her voice.

"Uncle Oz!" screamed Boomerang, burying himself in Jack's legs. "Uncle Oz!"

Uncle Oz? Julie mouthed to Tully, and then addressing Jack, Julie said, "Jack, how are you? What are you doing here?"

"Hello, Julie," he said, bowing slightly to Angela. "Same thing you're doing here. Visiting home." Then, turning back to Tully, he asked, half smiling, still holding on to Boomerang, "How are you?"

"I'm fine, I'm good."

Angela said, "How is your mom, Tully? I heard she is not well again."

"She is okay," replied Tully, reluctantly turning to Angela. "She is eating solid food now and knows all her vowels."

Angela did not crack a smile.

"She is fine, Angela, really," said Tully, wanting only to turn to Jack.

"Tully," said Julie after they had left him and were alone at Julie's house. "I have a feeling you're keeping something from me. Who is Uncle Oz?"

"Jack, obviously," said Tully, grateful for an opportunity to say his name aloud to someone other than him.

"Jack, obviously," mimicked Julie. "So, Tully, tell me."

"Tell you what?"

"Anything," said Julie. "But do tell all."

Tully thought about it and then said, "Boomerang wants a baby sister."

"Tully!" bellowed Julie. They laughed.

"You never come to Topeka anymore."

"I'm sorry. Laura and I are always so busy. How is your mother?"

"Less of a pain in the ass than your mother. My mother asks no questions."

Julie agreed. "But tell me, Tully," she said quietly. "How is Robin?"

"Fine. Working a lot. Why?"

"Why wasn't he in church with you today?"

"He is cooking. I have to go now and eat his dinner," said Tully. "Why isn't Laura with you?"

"We're meeting up in two weeks. We thought . . ." Julie hesitated. "*Laura* thought," she corrected herself, "it might be a good idea if we had a few days apart. And she is right, for sure. I mean, we're together constantly."

Julie looked so sad that Tully didn't know what to say, except, "Where's her real mom?"

"Dead, I think," said Julie.

"Ah," said Tully. "Well, I'm glad you came by yourself. This way we can talk a bit."

Julie tried to sound cheerful. "Is there anything you want to talk to me about?"

Tully did, actually. She'd wanted to talk to *some*one for sometime. But she had to go home. Robin really was cooking. A great big turkey.

"Nothing in particular, if that's what you mean. I gotta go, Jule. Robin will kill me if I don't come home. It's his first turkey."

"If there is nothing to talk about, then how come you were so happy to see Jack?"

"Was I happy?" said Tully, still happy. "Besides, I didn't say there was *nothing* to talk about. I just said nothing in particular."

Julie squeezed Tully's hand softly. "Tully," she said quietly. "Poor you. You must be so lonely."

Tully took her hand away, still happy. "I'm not lonely. I have my husband and my child and my work, and my mother, God help me, to whom I've read every Agatha Christie novel twice."

"And Jack," Julie pointed out.

Tully shook her head. "I have not read him any Agatha Christie novels."

"Tully!"

"No, really. Not one."

"Tully!"

She leaned into Julie and said, "He's my friend. You know. My friend. It's okay."

Julie just stared at Tully with wide eyes and shook her head. "Oh, my, oh, my. Tully, the rest of us have been trying to get over Jennifer the last seven years. You're just starting. God help you. And God help Robin."

Tully stood up. "I don't know what you're talking about," she said. "Yeah, Mrs. Mandolini has been doing a real good job of getting over Jennifer. And I'm all right, believe me. It will be okay."

"I hope so," said Julie.

She walked Tully to the door. "You've lost weight, Julie," Tully said. "Quite a bit of weight. Long hair, skinny. You're a regular hippie now."

"Hippie, corn picker, gypsy," said Julie sadly. "That's me."

Tully put her arm around Julie. "Yeah, you and Mrs. Mandolini both have been doing a fine job of getting over her. Really good."

"Cut it out," said Julie. "Just be careful."

Tully still didn't take her arm off Julie. "What's the matter, Jule?" she said tenderly. "What's wrong?"

Julie waved her off. "Never you mind. It's all right. I'm just not used to being without her, you know?"

Taking her arm off, Tully said evenly, "It has been *seven* years, Jule."

Julie stared at Tully with incomprehension and then laughed. "Oh, God, you're so sick. I meant *Laura*, Tully. I meant Laura."

A few days later, Tully came to St. Mark's, without Boomerang, and Jack was there waiting for her. How good he looks, thought Tully, her breath catching. How good, in his brown leather jacket, his black scarf, and his Levi's. She came up to him and they smiled at each other. Jack pulled his hand from his back and handed her a bouquet of white roses.

"Where do you get them from?" Tully asked. "No florist I know has them in the winter."

"They're for you," said Jack.

Tully stood still. "Well, thank you, Jack," she said quietly, not looking up. "Perhaps we can put them on her rosebush. After all, what will I do with them?"

"What will she?" asked Jack.

On New Year's Eve, at Bruce and Linda's farm, Tully wondered what Jack was doing for New Year's. And then she remembered him falling over Jennifer, bending over Jennifer on a New Year's Eve seven years ago, and she stopped wondering, while a dull motor idled in her, idled through every capillary, making every capillary dully ache with want. With wanting Jack to bend over her.

Jack took Tully out for her twenty-fifth birthday. On her actual birthday, which was a Tuesday, Robin took her out. On Saturday, Robin took Boomerang to Manhattan to stay at Bruce's. He asked Tully to come with them, but Tully, as was her wont, said no. Robin didn't ask Tully what she would be doing that Saturday night, and Tully didn't offer.

Tully drove to St. Mark's and waited there for Jack. Dressed in black pants and a white dress shirt, Jack picked her up around seven in the evening. He drove them to Kansas City, where they went to a small French restaurant with a funny name.

Tiny. French. Violinist. A few feet for a dance floor. Sweet wine. She drank and he talked. She laughed and he joked. They ate. And somewhere during the meal, sometime between main course and dessert, after the third time they raised their glasses but before their plates were taken away, after she asked him when he was leaving again and before he asked her about work, she looked at him across from her, looked at his face as he was talking, talking the way he always did, animated and alive, and thought, but my God, doesn't he have the most beautiful lips.

This stunned and embarrassed Tully. She looked down into her food and found that she had lost her appetite. Looking up, she saw his eyes, and was thrown against them like the Pacific surf against the cliffs. His eyes were serious and exquisite. There they were, his eyes and lips. His lips were blood-red, but his eyes in this light were of an indeterminate hue—some kind of green, or light blue. She didn't know. She didn't know the color of his eyes. How could that be? All that time she had looked into his face. All that time they had sat on the sand and watched Lake Vaquero—all that time he had rowed her in the brightest, brightest sunlight, all that time he had laughed at her and she at him, she did not notice the color of his eyes. Tully stared at him, dazed.

"Why, Natalie Anne, you haven't listened to a word I've said."

Tully palmed her face. It was warm. She didn't know how to answer him. *Look at his mouth. Where have I been? What have I been looking at? He has been talking to me with that mouth for so many years, and I have never noticed how beautiful it is, how full, how perfect.* Tully was unable to look at Jack anymore. She stared down into her old and dry food, and his index and middle fingers came up under her chin and lifted her face up. He kept his fingers under her chin for a few brief moments. "What?" he said quietly. "What?"

I've lost my speech, thought Tully. *And it's all on my face. Everything I'm feeling is on my face.*

"Nothing," she said thickly.

"Why aren't you paying attention to me?" he asked.

Attention? Why, I'm rapt. Have I not been paying attention? "I am," she said. "Have you?"

"Tully, I do nothing *but* pay attention to you," he replied.

"That's not true," she said bravely. "You travel. You paint. You live in California."

"When I'm with you," said Jack, "I do nothing but pay attention to you."

Tully almost wanted to flirt. She couldn't help herself, she wanted to shake her hair at him, tilt her head, smile coquettishly, wanted to . . . something. All she managed, though, was to put her hands over her eyes and say, "Paying attention? Oh yeah? What color are my eyes?"

Jack was silent for such a while that she had to peek through her fingers. Watching her with an expression Tully could not adequately define, he was shaking his head.

"Tully, Tully, Tully," he said at last. "Natalie Anne. Better I ask you. What color are *my* eyes, Tully Makker?"

"I asked you first," she said. She had long stopped correcting him with her past perfunctory "DeMarco."

"Gray," he replied instantly. "Like Mondays."

Gray like Mondays. Gray. Like. Mondays. She squeezed her eyes shut behind her hands.

"Gray," he repeated, taking her hands away. "Like mine."

She peered at him, grateful for an opportunity to gape without feeling ashamed. "They look green to me," Tully said.

"Gray," he corrected her. "Like yours."

Gray like Mondays. Gray like mine. Jack Pendel. Tully looked at his soft-looking, beautiful lips, and all she wanted at that moment, with the dull motor humming and revving, all she achingly wanted was Jack Pendel to kiss her. I want you to kiss me. Kiss me. I want you to touch my face and to kiss my lips. Gray Mondays. Gray mine. Kiss me. Here, right now, lean over, tilt your head to the right, look at me with your Gray Mondays, gray mines, and kiss my lips with your lips, oh, Jack, please, forget ten years of gray Mondays. Forget I danced topless on a table when I was lost, forget my bestest, deadest friend who loved you, forget the most beautiful girl in Topeka who loved you. Forget I'm married and have a son, forget California beckons you, the palm trees beckon you, because you beckon me, my Mexican friend, come to me, closer, come, and give me that water. Stop talking, touch me with your big wide hands, take my face, and those white roses? Give me. Give me those white roses with your lips, kiss my lips with your lips, look into my gray Mondays with your gray Mondays and kiss me. My longing, you could touch my longing to have you kiss me if you really wanted to, you could reach out and *feel* my need to have you kiss me.

Jack talked and Tully listened. When he asked her something, she answered him, aware that inside her the milk bubbled hot, and all doors were open. The motor was running and the milk was gushing through her veins. It was as if she saw him for the first time. It was as if this was the first evening of their acquaintance. It was as if the violinist had said to her, "Tully DeMarco, meet Jack Pendel." Jack Pendel. Even the name did not sound the same. It was as if many things just stopped dead making sense.

"Do you want to dance, Tully?" he asked her.

"Huh?" She looked at him. He reached out his hand to her. "Let's dance."

She shook her head. "I don't know this song."

He walked over and took her by the arm. She got up.

They went over to the dance floor, a twelve-by-twelve parqueted area. There were four or five other couples on the floor. Other *couples*. The words sounded unreal even when not spoken aloud. We're not a couple. We are Jack and Tully, with the only bond between us receiving our flowers every Sunday. Jack and Tully, we're not a couple. Jack put his hand on Tully's back, on Tully's purple silk dress, below her bra and above her pantyhose. With his other hand, Jack took Tully's hand and held it. His hand was big and strong and warm. She was sure hers was clammy. Her other hand went on his shoulder. It should have gone around his neck, but he was a little too tall and it was not a comfortable reach. She remembered when they danced together at Shakie's wedding. She remembered what they talked about, she remembered having a good time, and smiling, and Robin coming over and breaking in, but one thing she did not remember was feeling. Tonight, they danced close and slow. They did not move much, but they were close. She smelled Polo, and under her hand, his shoulder felt hard. And something else, too. Her right leg was between his two legs, and just being pressed against him, against his tallness, against his body, against *him*, Tully began to feel unsteady on her feet. They did not talk much, she didn't dare look up. Because the way he held her, the way he breathed, he seemed like he was *feeling*, too.

Tully's chin was in Jack's white shirt, and his head was bent down to her. Sometimes she felt his jaw brush against her temple. Experiencing an acutely unfamiliar aching in her lower stomach, Tully did not want the dance to end. But the song played out and they walked back to their table. Jack paid the check, held her coat for her, opened the car door for her, and drove her back to Topeka.

As they parked in front of St. Mark's, Tully heard Jack talking, but she wanted him to stop talking. All Tully wanted at that moment in the cold green Mustang with the snow outside, all she wanted was to feel his lips. Her entire life had no story compared with the fierceness of her longing at that moment. Her hands were shaking; she was afraid to speak.

"Thank you for letting me take you out on your birthday," said Jack.

"No, Jack," replied Tully as best she could. "Thank *you*."

He smiled. "When I first saw you at Tortilla Jack's, I thought you were twenty," he said. "I was a fifteen-year-old kid, illegally drinking beer with my buddies, watching the dance contest, needing to be home and in bed, and I saw you and thought you were wasting your talent. Why isn't she in some dance school on the East Coast? I thought. Why is she wasting her gift on fucking Tortilla Jack's?" Tully smiled politely, not paying a dime of attention to anything but the sound of his voice. Jack continued. "But the second time I saw you—you won again, of course—but I knew then you were a kid. A skinny kid."

She stretched her lips in a thin smile, remembering. "Not like now, huh?"

Jack shook his head. "Not like now."

"Was skinny good?"

"Now is better," he said, and Tully kept the aching in her lower stomach out of her smile.

"But you know what?" he said. "Your eyes gave you away. They were always so sad. Full of—I don't know. Kid pain."

She stirred. "Not kid pain, Jack. Not sad. Just drunk."

Slowly shaking his head, he said, "I don't believe you, Tully Makker."

When Tully didn't say anything, Jack said, "Cheer up, Tully. Let your husband take you dancing."

"He does sometimes," Tully replied, a little deflated. Robin was the last thing she was thinking of that moment.

"Let him take you more."

"I still dance, you know," said Tully.

"I know," Jack said. "But alone doesn't count."

She took a deep breath. There was something she wanted to ask him, and here, in the dark of the car, with only the barest of light from the street, was as good a place as any, to ask him what she wanted to know since two summers ago.

Clearing her throat, she said, "Um, Jack, speaking of Tortilla Jack's, I've been wondering, um, did you . . . ever dance with me?"

He got a look in his eyes that made Tully go red. She was glad it was night, she was glad night did not give adequate light to that expression Jack had in his gray eyes.

"We did dance, Tully," he said, with a thick, tinged-with-memory voice. "I suppose it was always too much to ask to have you remember, you dancing with me."

She knew the other side of that answer. It was always too much to ask her to remember him out of so many other guys. Tully breathed deeply. At the same time, he still struggled with that expression in his eyes. What is it? she thought. What is it that he is remembering that I had never known? What is it that he is incredibly remembering about us when I never remembered him at all?

"I'm sure you're mistaking me for someone else," said Tully.

"Why do you say that?"

She wanted to say something nice, something that would ease those eyes of his a little bit. "I would have remembered you, Jack Pendel," Tully said quietly.

He shook his head. "Oh, Tully, give me a break. You must have been on the Hill for a couple of years before I ever laid eyes on you. You must have been so jaded from all that . . . dancing."

Tully studied her hands. Jack went on. "I must have been less than a face to you on a Saturday night. I wasn't even good enough to stick out one dance with." He smiled. "I wasn't good enough for you, Tully Makker." Before she could cut in, he raised his hand and said, "No, don't protest, there's no point. I know what happened."

"Do you want to tell me about it?" asked Tully.

"Not really," said Jack. "It'll make you uncomfortable. To sit and hear what you don't remember about the time we were sixteen."

She was already uncomfortable. Already red. Already warm. "Tell me, Jack," said Tully in a low voice. "It's all right. I want to know."

Jack took a deep sigh and turned to face her. "It was late one Saturday night," he began. "You had just won another one of your contests."

"You mean I just finished dancing on the table?"

"Yes, uh-huh."

Was I dressed? Tully wanted to ask. He is right, how awful. How uncomfortable.

"You weren't . . . umm . . . wearing much," Jack said.

She stopped looking at him completely.

"Just a little halter or something, and a short, short skirt. High heels."

Tully was marginally relieved.

"And then you came down from the table and there were a bunch of guys wanting to dance with you, me included, but I was far off in the corner, and you seemed so busy. I must have waited twenty or thirty minutes. Six songs." Jack smiled. "I counted. Six songs, and then I saw you were dancing with my friend, not really a friend, just some guy I knew, so I walked over, and you . . ." here Jack paused, "you grabbed my hand and danced with the both of us."

"It sounds like I was drunk," Tully said. *I wish I were drunk now.*

"We all had plenty to drink. We all had beer in our dancing feet. Then my friend left in the middle of the song, and I got to dance with you alone."

Tully wanted to cry. What a terrible time that had been in her life. What terrible wasted drunk years that she had tried to fill and couldn't, tried to erase and couldn't, and yet here was this person, this Jack, this total stranger to her, remembering something from the black hole that had been her life with a tender nostalgia.

"How was it?" she said.

"Short," he replied. "It was 1977. I even remember the song."

"1977? It must have been 'You Make Me Feel Like Dancing.' "

"Actually, it was 'Don't Leave Me This Way,' " Jack said. "The middle of it. You could hardly see, you had so much to drink, but you were smiling, and you said something to me as you came up close. You said something like, 'My, aren't you a shy one.' "

Tully put her hands to her face.

"It's okay, Tully," said Jack. "Just a memory."

. . . A snapshot in the family album, Daddy, what else did you leave for me? DAD! What'd you leave behind for me . . . ? Pink Floyd sang in Tully's head as she put her hands down. "Is that it?" she asked.

"Do you want it to be it?"

"Yes," she said. "But tell me everything. Is there more?"

"Not much more, unfortunately. You were very sexy then,

Tully. Too sexy for a horny seventeen-year-old like me. I just didn't know what to do with you."

"I've kind of matured down after those years," Tully said. "I've kind of *im*matured after those years."

"Guess there was no other way for you to go."

"Did I stop dancing with you then?" Tully wanted to know.

"Soon. Too soon. But not before you . . . came up really close." Jack cleared his throat. "Very close. You kind of . . . danced on me, you know what I mean?"

My God. Did Tully know what he meant. She had liked doing that particular dance, it nearly always got the eyes she wanted to see in the guys she *danced on*. But how unbearable those eyes were to her now. How unbearable and mystifying.

"This is nearly too much," she said.

"Yes," agreed Jack, his voice sounding much like Tully's. "But you did your dance on me, and I, you see . . . Well, I responded. In a manner fitting for a seventeen-year-old. And you felt my response." Jack stared at the wheel when he said it, not at Tully. Her hands were between her knees, and she was staring at the dashboard. She felt sweat.

He continued. "And you said, 'Well, my, my, you aren't so shy, after all,' and you lifted yourself up on your tippy-toes to kiss me."

Tully's entire body stuck to her clothes. Her hands between her knees were wet. She was all wet.

"Did I?" she half said, half groaned. "Did I?"

He smiled sadly and turned to her. "Well, isn't that a sixty-four-thousand-dollar question. Maybe that should be my second secret."

"Jack, please," she said.

"No, Tully," Jack replied. "You didn't kiss me. It was only a moment on your tippy-toes, and before I bent down, and you can be sure I did bend down, the moment was gone and you were gone, too, whisked off by someone else. Or maybe you were just teasing me, maybe you didn't want to kiss me, but you were whisked away nonetheless, and I have never forgotten that."

They sat on that for a couple of minutes. Tully closed her

heavy eyes, wanting more intensely than she had ever wanted anything in her entire life for Jack Pendel to kiss her lips with his lips.

"Well, I guess you'll be going back to surfing," she said at last.

"Yeah, this time of year, the sun beckons me. San Diego. Mexico," he answered.

"There's painting in Mexico?" she asked, not caring, just wanting to keep him there, to keep him talking.

"I don't paint in Mexico. I worship the sun."

"Yeah, but after a while," said Tully, "doesn't it burn your eyes? Topeka sun is so bright. I can imagine the Mexico sun is even brighter."

"Yes," Jack said. "And when it does, I come back to Topeka." He smiled. "Well," he drew out slowly. "It's getting cold."

"Yeah," she said with the reluctance of a dentist's chair. "I better go."

"Are you talking to your mother, Tully?"

"I read to her," she replied. "I make her tea. Is that the same thing?"

"No," said Jack. "Are you angry with her?"

"Only for living so long," said Tully, and then, seeing Jack's expression, quickly said, "I'm not angry at my mother. We just have nothing to talk about."

"Who are you angry with, Tully?"

There were only two people in the world Tully was angry with, and both of them were gone. She shrugged in reply and moved to go.

"Wait," Jack said hoarsely, taking her arm. She turned back, and he brought her to him and hugged her, left hand on the back of her coat, right on the back of her hair. He hugged her quickly and hard. "So long, Tully," he whispered. "Happy Birthday." Tully's face was near his neck and hair. His hair smelled sweet and masculine and blond, and she brought her hand over and stroked the back of his head. " 'Bye, Jack," she whispered back. "Come home soon."

He let go. When she got out and walked over to his side, he rolled down the window and Tully didn't know what to say, so she said, "Maybe next summer you can paint the house." She missed him then, in that instant, missed him terribly already, with his gray eyes and red lips as he sat in front of her in his green Mustang.

"I've wanted to paint your house for the last three years," he said, starting the car. "And it needs painting, Tully."

15

PAINTING THE HOUSE

January 1986

The next four months were tough months for Tully. She worked and took care of her boy, who turned four. She went to St. Mark's and read to her mother and saw Shakie and went out with Alan from work once in a while and made love to her husband, but inside the only feeling that ran with meaning was missing Jack.

Tully missed him as she read aloud to her family, wondering if Jack had ever read Dickens, if he loved Dickens, if he would love having Dickens read to him.

Tully missed him as she walked to work and walked home, as she walked home and picked up her Camaro and drove back across town to Wayne Street to get Boomerang, who didn't like walking.

Tully missed him as she ate spaghetti and wondered whether he liked spaghetti, or whether he would like to have spaghetti cooked for him. Tully was almost going to ask Shakie if she had ever cooked for him but stopped herself just in time.

As she bathed, Tully thought about Jack bathing, becoming acutely turned on with no release. Tully would walk around all day aching until the night.

Sometimes, shamefully, when Robin made love to her, calling her name aloud, "Tully . . . Tully . . ." calling her all sorts of tender things, Tully DeMarco closed her eyes and touched Jack's blond hair, touched Jack's shoulders, touched his chest, reached over and put her hands on his back, reached under . . . never opening her eyes until Robin was done.

Tully took up cooking. Robin came home one night and found Tully in the kitchen, poring over a Julia Child cookbook.

"What are you doing, Tully?" he wanted to know.

"Shhhhh," Tully said. "I'm concentrating." But by eight-thirty, she managed a potato au gratin.

The next day, she attempted meatballs, and the day after that, roast beef.

Desperately in need of someone to talk to about him, Tully

had no one. Julie was God knows where.

And so, not having anyone, Tully had to turn to the only person she could turn to—Robin. And Robin obligingly came home early in the winter and spring to eat Tully's food. Tully couldn't talk to Robin about Jack, but having her husband eat her food, and eventually even praise it, albeit modestly, was enough for her. Her mother was even more enthusiastic. "This is not bad at all," Hedda said one night, after tasting a liquidy beef concoction, her speech unaffected by her last stroke. And that was good enough for Tully, too. She, who thought she never had a need for anything, now had two needs that lived unfilled: a need for Jack and a need to talk about Jack. So she cooked, and imagined she was cooking for him and he was eating her food.

Tully nearly stopped having her dreams. *Nearly.* When she did, the dreams had a sick twist to them. She dreamed: I stand under my tree with a chair under me, or in the bathroom with a chair under me, and Jack comes over, and he holds me with one hand and pulls the chair from under me with the other. I don't like that dream. I wake up and can't get back to sleep. But at least I get to see his face. I get to feel his hand on my leg.

And every once in a while, usually after strenuous love-making with Robin, Tully would dream that she was sitting with Jack on a boat, while Boomerang was on the shore playing with his buckets. Everything seemed normal and as it should be. But at the end of the dream, Tully would look over at the shore, and it wasn't Boomerang sitting there on the sand anymore, but Robin. Then Tully would wake up, awash with sweat and guilt. Robin would be sleeping; peaceful, tired, long day, busy, busy, and Tully would watch him and softly stroke his hair.

Work was numbing, but she did not give up. She fought with the department to increase the training period for foster families. Nobody was really listening.

Over Lillian's objections, Tully was promoted to associate director in April. This was a step in the right direction. Alan, Joyce, and Sara now reported to her. Master Tully, she had thought, remembering Jack at Kansas University. Master Tully.

And once in a while Tully's efforts paid off. Though more often than not, they didn't. Twisted as it seemed to Tully, the kids who got plucked from homes full of abuse and neglect wanted only one thing: to return to their natural parents. The worse the home, the greater their desire to return. Tully's efforts in finding exceptional foster families didn't matter to these kids. What they wanted was mom and dad.

Usually the children were returned to their parents, if the parents wanted them.

One of Tully's best foster families, Diane and Paul Shannon, had offered to adopt a five-year-old girl, Christa, who'd been living with them for the past two years while the parents were finding themselves. When Tully went to talk to Christa's parents for the first time, they just sat there silently for most of the interview. They briefly talked about how much they loved Christa, how she was their only child, how much they had to offer her. Apparently they had little to offer her at the moment.

So Christa went to a home where Mr. and Mrs. Shannon showered the kind of love on Christa that reminded Tully of Mr. and Mrs. Mandolini.

Now, two years later, Christa's parents finally realized what they had been waiting for. What was missing in their lives. They were waiting to have another baby! And when Christa's mom got pregnant again, she wanted little Christa to live with them again.

Tully fought tooth and nail against giving Christa back, fought against Lillian, against Mr. Hillier, against the psychologists, who kept reiterating to Tully that the job of Foster Home Recruitment was not to provide homes for kids whose parents wanted them but to provide "temporary" homes for children whose parents were "temporarily" unable to take care of them. There is a whole fucking lot of "temporary" going on, Tully said to them.

Understanding explicitly, Tully argued that in two months not only Christa but her little baby brother or sister would be back as wards of the court, and Mr. and Mrs. Shannon might be tied up with another foster child.

It was all to no avail. Christa was returned to her parents.

Mr. and Mrs. Shannon, however, did a smart thing. They refused to take on any other foster children, preferring instead to wait for their Christa to return to them. Tully advised them to file adoption papers on Christa with Gentle Shepherd, just in case.

Diane and Paul Shannon did not have to wait long. When Christa's sister was not yet three weeks old, the mother decided that she had been wrong, that perhaps she had been too *hasty*, not just in having Christa back but also in having Christa's sister.

"I haven't found my place in life yet, Mrs. DeMarco," she said to Tully when Tully came to take Christa and the baby away. "Oh, but you have," replied Tully, holding the infant to her with one arm and Christa's hand with the other. "You have."

Tully never imagined that on her job she could have a moment of watching ecstasy on the faces of *anyone*. But Tully did see ecstasy. She saw it on the faces of the childless Diane and Paul Shannon as they crushed Christa with their arms, saw it in their eyes as they brought the baby close to them, faces filled with intense tenderness.

Driving away, Tully thought, I'm in the wrong business. I gotta get a job with the Gentle Shepherd Agency. Their sole aim in life is to spread happiness as far as they can. Whereas *mine* is to diffuse misery as much as I can. Whereas mine is to give out Band-Aids for third-degree burns. Not the same, is it? Not the fucking same.

Tully was lonely, and she missed Jack. At nights at home, Tully stood naked in front of the mirror and ran her hands over her breasts and her stomach. I don't look like I did when I was sixteen. I don't look like I did when I sauntered up in the smoked-out bar with a hundred dollars in my pocket and *rubbed up* against adolescent Jack.

I don't look like I did when he leaned over at Jennifer's party and recognized me, the girl from the Hill. Look at me now, look at my belly and my thighs, they never regained their former shape after I had Boomer. She had to admit her breasts looked sexy, but she couldn't walk around without a bra anymore. My hair looks nice long and straight. What bugged Tully most, though, was that she no longer looked like a skinny sixteen-year-old with bleached hair and black mascara. She looked like she was a mother.

Whenever Tully saw Shakie, she was abrim with bad feelings. She resented Shakie's blue eyes and her red lips and her trim body even after just having another boy but Tully resented Shakie most of all for looking better now than during their senior year.

Occasionally Tully remembered that she and Jack had the same color eyes, that they both liked Pink Floyd, and that they both rowed a boat and both played softball in Shunga Park with one friend. But even all that did not comfort Tully when she looked jealously at Shakie's blond mane.

For four months, Tully tortured herself with her inadequacies, remembering Jack's hair, the color of the sun. Remembering his red jersey. Remembering him as he jumped into Lake Vaquero.

When the first of June came, Tully forgot about work, forgot about Shakie, forgot about everything, while she waited for Jack to come to her.

Robin, who never took vacations from his store or his softball in his life, asked Tully if she wanted to take a vacation this year.

Tully was taken aback. Out of all the years, this was the one year she categorically did not want to take a vacation.

"How about if we go to California? We've never been on a honeymoon, you know," said Robin.

"I know," Tully replied hesitantly. She did know. But this year she didn't care. Last year. The year before that. Then she cared. But then Robin had always been too busy and Tully never mentioned it. This year, she did not care. Tully thanked Robin and said, "Maybe next year, huh?"

"Yeah, sure," he said, going back to reading the newspaper. "Maybe."

She watched him for a moment, and then came over and sat on his lap. "Robin DeMarco, put your paper away for a minute." She was aching.

He put it away. "And do what?" he said, his hands already unbuttoning her jeans.

When Robin came home late on June second and saw Tully seating defeated at the kitchen table, he asked her if she was all right.

"I'm fine," she said, with a pale face.

"I'm sorry I was late. Busy day."

"Of course. It's fine," said Tully, not looking up.

"So," said Robin. "If you're not feeling well, I guess you won't be cooking." Tully glared at him, and he rolled his eyes and ordered pizza.

The following day, Tully took off sick and spent the day in readiness, jumping to the door at every rush of leaves in the front yard.

Millie studied Tully through squinted eyelids, commenting to Hedda over lunch that the mother was perhaps not the only one who needed a nurse around here. June fourth, fifth, and sixth and still no Jack.

June seventh was a Saturday and Robin had gone to play soccer, taking little Robin with him. Tully sat in the kitchen and in the backyard all day, unable to do anything but move from one side of the yard to the other. She did not eat, she did not drink. She thought about sitting in the front porch swing, but she didn't want it to look as if she were too eager, sitting there waiting for him, and though she had been at miserable attention the whole week, it would do Jack no good to know that. Tully might as well have swung in the swing all day, for he did not come.

Robin did not return home till very late. When she saw Robin coming up the path with sleeping Boomerang in his arms, Tully ran to bed and shut her eyes.

On Sunday, June eighth, Tully went to St. Mark's in a white print dress with a bouquet of white roses, feeling unsteady on her feet. Angela was there, but Jack was not.

Tully's only activity during the first eight days of June was to drag the chair that had been at Jennifer's grave for seven years, put it in the front seat of Jennifer's Camaro, and take it home with her. The white roses she threw on the ground near the tombstone.

"Back so soon?" said Robin, coming into the garage where Tully was trying to rub the rust off the chair with steel wool. She eked out a barely audible sound. "Tully, what are you doing?" he asked, coming closer to her.

"It might not look like it," Tully said painfully, "but I'm hang gliding." She looked up just in time to see Robin's cold gaze before he turned on his heels and walked back into the house. He didn't deserve that, she thought, turning her attention back to the rusted chair. But then, he doesn't deserve a lot of things.

What I want to know, she thought, futilely rubbing salt and lemon on the rust spots, what I want to know is: is this what it's going to be like every year? Is this what it's going to be like for me every goddamned year between January and June and between September and December? And what if he doesn't come back this summer? Is this what my life is going to become?

By June ninth, Tully's dreams returned without Jack. They returned without him, and she sat by her window until Monday night and cried into Tuesday morning, and the night after, and the night after that, not wanting to go to sleep, not wanting Jack not to be there in her dreams even if he was trying to kill her in them.

By Wednesday, Tully had calmed down. Having thought only of him for four months, having run madly to the front door every time the bell rang for eleven days, having looked through her mail more thoroughly than a quality control inspector, Tully realized he was not coming. He was not coming, and she was getting ready to live with it. But Friday night, she put her hand on her heart before she went to sleep and silently prayed, *Dear God, when I sleep, please let him be there, please let me see his face and his arms and his hands. Please.*

Tully was still in bed at eleven in the morning on Saturday. She had gotten up briefly around nine to dress Boomerang for his soccer game with his dad and to feed them some oatmeal and scrambled eggs. Tully found out in the last four months father and son both loved oatmeal and scrambled eggs. The oatmeal was always too thick and the eggs were always too runny, but they ate it all up anyway, and asked for more.

After they left, she went back to bed. Tully was not asleep, she was not awake, she was in that tired, dreary state in which reality drifts hazily in and out of consciousness. When she heard the car door slam outside her open window, she did not move because she was dreaming of a car door slamming and it seemed vague and far away.

But when Tully heard the unmistakable screech of her front

gate, which had been squealing for oil for years, she got groggily out of bed and looked out of her bay window onto Texas Street.

It was Jack.

There he was, closing the gate behind him, Jack, in white shorts and a blue tank top, closing her gate behind him. Tully bit her lip so as not to exclaim aloud, but it was too late. She drew in her breath and emitted a guttural sound. Jack heard her and looked up.

"Tully Makker! Are you telling me that on this beautiful Saturday morning you're still in bed?"

"Shhhhhh!" she said.

"Am I talking too loud?" he asked without lowering his voice. "Or are you embarrassed you're still in bed?"

"Jaaack!"

"Jaaack!" he mimicked her, smiling, looking up. "Well, are you going to come downstairs and open the door or should I stand here and recite some poetry?"

There were a number of things Tully wanted to say, because there were a number of extreme things Tully was feeling, but all that came out was, "I don't know, do you know any poetry?"

"Do I know any poetry?! Do I, Jack Pendel, know any poetry? No, of course I don't. Come down this minute."

Tully ran her tongue over her teeth. "Jack, wait, sit down for a minute, please, and give me a second, okay?"

"Okay," he said, walking up to the porch, not taking his eyes off her. "But I demand that you put some clothes on."

Tully stepped away from the window and covered her mouth. But still, her lips quivered, and she jumped on the bed, up and down up and down up and down, jumped off the bed and back on, keeping herself quiet as best she could.

What am I doing? Tully thought. What the hell am I doing? she thought, standing on the bed. I'm so fucking happy.

After she quickly brushed her teeth, washed her face, and combed her hair, she put on a pair of peach shorts and a matching peach top and ran downstairs barefoot, taking the steps two at a time.

Tully opened the door and came out on the porch. Jack stopped whistling and without getting up turned to look at her. He seemed perfectly casual, perfectly at ease, smiling his usual big smile. And all Tully could do was inhale and hold her breath, because Jack Pendel, sitting on her swing, smiling, with his lips and teeth, his gray eyes, his blond hair, was more beautiful in real life than anything she had conjured up in her miserable memory and her miserable dreams.

"Well, Tully," he said softly. "You brushed your hair. You shouldn't have."

"Don't be silly," she replied. "I always brush my hair."

"That's not true. You didn't last year. I came about the same time, about the same Saturday, and you didn't brush your hair then."

"Did you," she said as casually as she could, "come about the same time? I thought it was about two weeks earlier."

Coming closer, Tully sat down on the edge of the swing. Jack was sitting right in the middle and did not move, not even when she sat down. Their bare legs almost touched each other.

"Do you sit here often?" he asked her. "It's incredible to sit here. The summer morning air. Smells great."

"Does, doesn't it?" Tully said, without having the least idea what he was talking about.

"So, what's new?" said Jack. "Let's see. Are you still walking off work?"

"Are you still living in California?" Tully asked.

"No, I've been in Mexico the entire four months. Backpacking."

Four and a half, she wanted to correct him. Four and a half. "How can you afford to live?" she asked.

"I'm broke," he said. "I have just enough to take you to lunch."

"Save your money," she said. "I'll make you lunch."

He leaned into her a little. Just a little, and she tensely backed away. "Make me lunch," he said, "and I'll paint your house."

"Jack," Tully said. "You don't know what you're saying. You haven't tried my food."

"Believe me, after what I've had in Mexico, your food will be gourmet fare to me."

"So how long you been back, then?"

"Since about the middle of the week," Jack replied. And maybe seeing her expression, maybe driven by his own motives, he added, "I like to wait till Saturdays to call on you, knowing how you hate to sleep past noon."

Tully had already forgotten what she had been like in the middle of the week.

She invited Jack inside and showed him the entire house except Hedda's rooms.

"Tully," Jack said thoughtfully, after they were back in the kitchen. "Let me ask you. You carefully avoided showing me half of the downstairs. You showed me your palm trees and this here kitchen and your backyard, but you didn't show me what should be the dining room. How come?"

"My mother is there," Tully replied, lowering her voice.

"Oh, oh," he said, nodding his head. "I thought for a minute you were hiding your insane first wife."

"I'm not Mr. Rochester," Tully said. "And you're not Jane Eyre, no matter how poor you are."

"But you are kind of like Mr. Rochester," said Jack, leaning into her again. She stepped away.

"Like how?"

"Kind of like him," said Jack, "you cannot see very well."

"*Very well?*" she exclaimed. "What does that mean? Jack, he was blind!"

Jack raised his eyebrows, and Tully was about to continue when she heard Hedda calling.

"Will you excuse me, please?"

"Only if we can have lunch on the swing."

"Maybe in the back. The backyard smells good, too," Tully said, moving toward her mother's rooms.

"What?" Tully snapped, nearly barked, opening her mother's bedroom door but not walking in.

"Tully, is there somebody in the house?" asked Hedda. "I thought I heard a man's voice."

"It's okay. I got everything under control."

"Who is it, Tully?"

"It's nobody, Ma, would you like me to turn the TV on for you?" said Tully, walking over and turning on the TV.

"No, I was thinking of having a bite to eat. Help me in my wheelchair?"

Tully stared at her mother disbelievingly, unblinkingly, saying at last, "Ma, you just had breakfast. I brought you your coffee and your cereal myself. You don't eat lunch till two.

You never eat lunch till two. What are you saying?"

"That I'm a little hungry, Tully. Please help me up."

Tully came closer to the bed, clenching her fists. "No, Mother, I will not help you. Why don't you watch some TV, and I will bring you a sandwich if you wish, but I will not help you up right now, okay?" She backed away toward the door. Hedda's eyes became like slits. "Who is there? What are you hiding, Tully? What are you ashamed of?"

"You, Mother," Tully said, opening the door and going out. "I'm ashamed of you."

She needed a couple of minutes to catch control of herself before she went back into the kitchen. But the control was escaping her. It was floating wild and free, while her third eye was showing her the summer ahead, with Jack painting the house while Hedda and Hedda's nurses kept him company. Oh, endless woe, she thought, slowly starting toward the kitchen. Endless fucking woe.

Jack and Tully sat in the backyard for the rest of the afternoon.

At four-thirty, Tully walked him back to his car.

"So when does your husband come home these days?" Jack said.

"In the summers? Late. Sometimes he stays at his brother's house."

"Just in time to see you off to St. Mark's."

"Just about," said Tully.

"Why don't you go with him?" said Jack. "It somehow doesn't seem right that you should be alone on Saturday nights."

"I don't mind," said Tully quickly. "When do you think you can start?"

"Monday," Jack replied. "Thanks for lunch."

"Monday," Tully said feebly. "Great. How long will it take you?"

"I don't know," he said, peering at her. "I'll stop when it's done. Maybe three weeks. Going to church tomorrow?"

Tully nodded.

"Oh, that reminds me," Jack said. "The chair is gone."

"I know," said Tully. "I took it." Then, "I thought you've only been back a few days."

"I have. I went there a few days ago," Jack explained.

Not knowing what to say, Tully said, "I tried to get the rust off. Salt and lemon."

Jack laughed. "Tully, you're so funny. Salt and lemon take off tiny little rust spots. I don't think there is an inch on that chair that's not covered in rust. That chair has received a rust paint job over all these years and the rust is there to stay. What did you do with it?"

"I spray painted it."

"You used paint? Yourself? Well, that's very good."

She nudged him with her elbow. "Stop teasing."

"Okay, I'll stop," he said seriously. "Why did you take the chair?"

"I don't know," answered Tully. "Nobody sits in it anymore."

Jack smiled, reaching out and touching her cheek with his fingers. "Well, now, that's good news, Tully Makker. Good news indeed."

That night, near eleven, Robin was still not home. Tully thought of calling Bruce because she wanted to talk to Robin, but she stopped herself. Tully *never* called to find out if Robin was with his brother. Not in the last several years, anyway. Sometimes he was with Bruce, sometimes with Stevie. All three brothers went out occasionally, to play pool or to catch an action flick. Tully's only concern was Boomerang, though she knew that with Linda, Boomer was in good hands.

But Robin and Boomerang could've left the farm and gotten into an accident, thought Tully, crouching down near her mother's door. Robin is such a maniac when he drives. He and Boomerang, strapped in or not, could right now be turned over three times in a heap in a ditch. Tully sat on the floor, her back against the wall, her knees drawn up. They could both be lying on the side of the road, the car could be overturned, they could have burned to death, they could be dead. All like a bad dream, she thought. And she shuddered and crossed herself quickly in a reflex. God strike me dead for thinking that. But still . . . somewhere deep down . . . echoed, *How simple, how clear*.

Crossing herself again to scrub the top thought layer clean, Tully sat there near her mother's door and tried to figure out what to do about Hedda. When Tully was young, it was simple.

Stay out of her way and pray a lot. Cook, clean, run errands. Wait her out.

Well, she thought she had done just that. But now Tully was twenty-five, still waiting her mother out.

No, Mother has waited me out. Waited me out to once again become the THING that I can't conquer.

When Tully was an adolescent, she had yearned for something, something that sent her out dancing and sitting in bathtubs. Then, when she stopped dancing, Tully yearned to go away. To go away with *Jennifer*. And then yearned to go away by herself. And then, indefinably, indescribably, just . . . yearned.

Now Tully had a longing once again, and her longing had a name and his name was Jack Pendel. And Tully was willing to do whatever was necessary to satisfy the first such longing she ever had.

Robin slipped into her consciousness again. Tully had thought for many years that Robin somehow . . . owed her. Since last January when she ached to be kissed by Jack Pendel, Tully felt Robin owed her more and more. Tully felt that *Robin owed her Jack Pendel*. Jack was going to be Robin's payment for giving Tully a life she did not want.

Earlier in the evening, Tully had called Aunt Lena and asked her if she would mind taking Hedda for a little while, kind of on a sisterly visit, just for the summer. Aunt Lena said that the Grove house was small and her husband would not like someone living in his house. "Besides, Tully, she is your mother."

"Haven't I paid my dues?" Tully said dejectedly. "And besides, it's only for a little while. For the summer." She was not thinking past the summer.

"Tully, your mom took care of you for ten years after your father left you both. It was real hard for her. All the time she wanted to give you up, but she didn't. Don't that count for somethin'?"

Those years Hedda took care of Tully stuck like a pike bone in Tully's throat, right next to the walleye bone of the first seven years when Hedda took care of Tully.

"Eleven," Tully said quietly and hung up. "Eleven years," she repeated, going to sit by Hedda's door, back against the wall.

Give me up. Give. Me. Up. She wanted to but didn't do it. My mother took care of me for eighteen years without giving me up. Without giving me up. Well, isn't that something. Tully swallowed hard, but couldn't get the spit past all the bones in her throat.

Sitting on the floor next to her mother's bedroom in a darkened solitary house, Tully tried to think of other things. But there was only one thing that kept washing up ashore like a dead fish.

Only her and me in the whole silent house.

How easy it would be to kill her.

How easy, right now, with not a soul in the house but me and my mother, to open her door and walk right in. See her sleeping mass, get a pillow from the chair, come near her head, look into her sleeping face, closed eyes, and put a pillow over the head that took care of me for eighteen years. How easy and remorseless. Put the pillow on her face and apply the force. She can't move her body anyway, except for her right hand. Keep the pillow, apply more force. Her head would turn this way and that, but I would keep the pillow down. Her hand would try to flail, but I'd be sitting on it.

More force, her head tries to move but can't. The bowels are released. Intense stench. Can't be any worse than what it smells like every day. Her body jerks, jerks, jerks, convulses, shudders, and then . . . stops. The head stops trying to turn. The hand goes limp. I keep the pillow there for a few more seconds just to be sure. Just in case. Then I take it away to reveal her face again. I close her mouth, which is open trying to gasp the last bit of life's air. But not too much air. Not too much life. I close her eyelids. I get up off the bed. Smooth out the covers. Touch her hand. Still warm. Then I take the pillow, put it back on the chair. Pull up the covers. To take another look at the face that took care of me for eighteen years. Then I swallow. Swallow easy. And leave . . . just like that.

Tully opened her hands and touched her palms together. They were completely dry. Could it really be that easy? Getting up, she opened the door to her mother's room. Hedda was lying on the bed, eyes closed, unmoving. Hardly breathing. The grubby pillow was on the chair where Tully sat when she read to Hedda. Yes, she thought, yes, coming closer. That easy. All my bones wrapped in that blanket on that bed in front of me, what release, what relief, go, just walk on over, pick up the pillow and . . .

"Paint the house," said Robin. He had returned home that night and found Tully asleep on the floor outside Hedda's bedroom. "I really don't care if you paint it or not."

"Not so quick," Tully said groggily, coming up to bed. "We've been thinking about it for several years."

"I haven't been thinking about it at all," said Robin.

"*I've* been thinking about my mother," Tully said, in bed.

"What?" he said wearily. "Do you feel she'll prevent him from painting?"

Tully suddenly felt very tired of him reading her all the time. "Cut it out, Robin. I just can't be trusted around her anymore."

"Anymore?" he inquired.

"I don't trust myself, Robin," Tully whispered. "I want her to die."

"And if she died, Tully, how do you think you'd feel?"

"Relieved," said Tully.

She watched Robin stare at the white curtains rustling at their open window, finish his Marlboro, and say quietly, "And if *we* died, Tully. How would you feel? Would you also feel relieved?"

She was just so *sick* and tired of him reading her all the time. "Oh, don't be so fucking ridiculous!" she snapped.

Monday Tully had to work, but the entire day her mind was at 1501 Texas Street, which Jack was painting! And for the next two weeks, her mind was on little else but 1501 Texas Street.

She would rush over for lunch. She'd rush over to make him lunch, to snatch thirty minutes with him before she had to run back to work.

Sometimes Tully stopped by later in the afternoons and watched him, happily. She watched him go up a ladder, watched his arms scrape and wash, the same arms that pulled a chair from under her in her dreams. Sometimes, at around three or four, Tully would say, "You want to take a walk?"

And if he agreed, they would take a walk. They would walk out of the house to the dead end, climb over the metal railing, and walk through the brush and the wood, through several ditches and over numerous tree trunks, until they came out onto a field, onto Shunga Park. Tully and Jack would walk around the baseball field, up and down on the bleachers, across the baseball diamond, and then back home. Sometimes, but not often, they sat in the bleachers.

Tully would pick Boomerang up by five-thirty or six in the evening, and by the time she returned, Jack would be gone. Robin would get home around eight, and Tully, who had stopped cooking around the first of June, watched Robin eat Millie's dinner. Sometimes she'd eat with him, but mostly she just watched him.

It was not ideal, but Tully did get to see Jack every day. And Tully had seen too few horses' mouths to look into them.

The last week of June, Tully sat in on a counseling meeting with a Mr. and Mrs. Slattery and the contracted-out psychologist, Dr. Connelly. It was not unusual for Tully to sit on these meetings, but it was a little unusual for her to sit in on this one.

She didn't want to be here because she was missing lunch. Also, she couldn't stand Mr. and Mrs. Slattery.

Tully had been introduced to the couple about six months earlier and afterwards made her recommendation to Lillian that the three Slattery children be made permanent wards of the court and put up for adoption. The recommendation was denied. Lillian did not like to make foster children permanent wards of the court, specifying in her own report that Mr. and Mrs. Slattery, with counseling, could easily overcome their problems of "overzealous" discipline and become stable enough for their children. Tully was particularly appalled with this case. Mr. and Mrs. Slattery had a six-year-long history of being intensely . . . *overzealous* parents. Their middle girl was born in the hospital and promptly taken away from Mrs. Slattery, who was caught by the nurse slapping her two-day-old daughter across the face for refusing to drink from a bottle. With the third one, Mrs. Slattery wasn't taking any more chances with the "buttinsky" nurses, as she called them. The second boy was born at home.

The police were summoned a month or so later by the oldest son, Jason. The first three numbers Jason learned were

911. The police dealt with Mr. Slattery's jealousy, his wife's broken nose, his children's beaten backs, by taking the children away, for the seventh time. If Mrs. Slattery wanted to go, they would've taken her away, too.

That was a few years ago. Six months ago, the Slatterys wanted their children back. Tully stated in her report that no counseling sessions, no monitoring sessions, no foster sessions were going to do Mr. and Mrs. Slattery a jot of good. They would never become even modestly safe parents for their children.

Even before Robert Slattery got married and became a father, he had a rap sheet in Salina as long as Salina's white pages. Assault, aggravated assault, battery in the first degree, deviant misconduct, disturbing the peace, DWIs, solicitation of illegal services, et cetera, et cetera. But even criminals are allowed to be married and have children and become good husbands and loving fathers. Mrs. Slattery, née Cooley, a lifelong resident of Salina, provided the small town with one of its very few recreational services. Compared to the rest of the men who came her way, Mr. Robert Slattery was heaven-sent. But too many men knew Miss Cooley in Salina, even after she married, so the newlyweds moved east to Topeka in search of a life and some work. The life was certainly there, but the work was not abundant for a woman who had few skills and a man who had even fewer. Mr. Slattery worked as a contracted bricklayer, a dishwasher, and a farmhand. Finally they settled down in a ramshackle house on an unpaved alleyway between 28th and 29th, off California Street.

Unfortunately, their nocturnal struggles got to be too much for the neighbors. After Jason's birth, the Slatterys moved out to Belhaze, a more isolated community, with houses few and far between. Young Jason's only connection with the outside world late at night was the telephone.

Based on Mr. Slattery's past record, Tully had gently suggested to Lillian that perhaps it was in Mr. Slattery's nature to be an ugly violent pig.

Lillian disagreed, and Tully and she exchanged some hot words. In the end, Tully had to back down, because Lillian wouldn't budge. "People can change if they try, particularly parents," was Lillian's defense. "Bob Slattery has a bad childhood to battle—"

"Who doesn't?" snapped Tully.

"He came from an abusive, broken home," Lillian continued.

"Who doesn't?" repeated Tully.

"Well, then, if you understand, you should be more sympathetic—"

"No, Lillian," said Tully. "Because I understand, I should be *less* sympathetic."

"He deserves a second chance," said Lillian.

"Does he deserve an eighth chance? Haven't the kids been returned to them seven times already?"

"Enough, Tully," said Lillian. "I will recommend a six-month probation for Bob Slattery."

Tully's only response was to ask that she herself not "sit in" on any more counseling sessions between the Slatterys and *anybody*. That was six months ago, and now the six months of probation were up and they were back, trying to get their three kids back. Tully refused to take on the case again. "I'm too busy," she said through gritted teeth. "Let Joyce take it. One of her kids ran away without a trace the other day. She's got some free time."

But Lillian insisted on Tully. No, said Tully. Lillian asked Tully to at least sit in on the counseling session. Tully refused.

"Give it a chance, Tully," cajoled Lillian. "Give them a chance."

In the end, Lillian *insisted* that Tully attend the evaluation session with her. And Tully had to do it.

She sat at the meeting with her arms folded. At times she rolled her eyes. At times she squinted her eyes at the Slatterys. Once in a while she interjected with a question, only to retreat into silence. By the way Lillian talked to the Slatterys, by the way she cajoled them, analyzed them, spoke warmly about their *change* and their love for their children, Tully would have bet the Slatterys were Lillian's relatives.

"Tully? Our meeting has come to an end. Is there anything you'd like to add?" asked Dr. Connelly.

"Add? No," said Tully.

"Do you feel the children are well treated in the foster home?"

"Very much so," said Tully. "So much so that all three of them, as you know, have been asked to be adopted by the foster family. It would be a shame for the state to lose the foster family, but Jason, Kim, and little Bobby would be well taken care of."

"They my children!" cried Mrs. Slattery. "I want 'em back! I never give thems up to good God knows who!"

Tully studied Lillian, the Slatterys, Dr. Connelly, and said as slowly and patiently as she could, trying to keep hate out of her voice, "Dr. Connelly. The children are very happy. They are happier now than they've ever been. Having moved through nine different foster homes in the last six years, they've finally found a decent family they like. I think I can speak for all of us when I say perhaps a longer period of time is needed to establish the children in their foster home. And to give Mr. and Mrs. Slattery a little more time," Tully added.

"A longa time's the last thing I wanna give'm," said Mr. Slattery, a balding, unkempt man in a plain shirt that could not hide his gut. "There's nothin' unstable in the children bein' back with their real mom and dad."

Tully started to crack her knuckles trying to keep in control. She *hated* Mr. Slattery. Tully looked to Lillian for support. Lillian was looking compassionately at him.

"A longer period of time," Tully said steadily. "That's all I recommend. A longer period of time before we can judge your I'm sure considerable improvement, Mr. and Mrs. Slattery. It's best for the children. You will be allowed to visit with them on Sundays. If adoption is out of the question, that's fine. I will recommend that the children remain in the foster home for another six months, during which time—"

"I don't want my children to be in some sleazy, disgusting racist foster home!" Mr. Slattery interrupted Tully. "I want'm home where they belong! I want'm with us!"

Tully gripped the end of her seat. She didn't want to look at Lillian anymore. And the silent, sweating Dr. Connelly was of nominal help himself.

"Mr. Slattery, I am sure you do," said Tully. "I'm sure you love them very much. But these children have been treated less than well. We cannot be too hasty. I know and appreciate how much you must miss them. But we have to think of the children first."

"I'm thinkin' of'm first!" exclaimed Mr. Slattery. "Them children weren't treated badly! They been disciplined!"

Ahh, there it is. Well, thank God. I knew that given enough time to open his fat fucking mouth, he'd slip, and he did. Thank you, God.

Tully raised her eyebrows and looked meaningfully at Lillian, who sat there with her gaze to the floor, and then at Dr. Connelly, who looked very sweaty.

"Dr. Connelly?" said Tully.

The good doctor cleared his throat. "Uhm, Mr. Slattery. Excuse me, but, uhm, I think there is no question that those children have been treated badly. Uhm . . . I think the question before us remains, are they going to be treated badly again?"

"We give youse our word," said Mrs. Slattery tearfully, "they won't be treated bad again."

"Shut up!" Mr. Slattery barked to his wife. She shut up. Though Tully wondered what she had to be scared of. In all ways, she looked much like her husband. *I know what the children have to be scared of, but what does she have to be scared of?*

Lillian glared at Tully with an expression Tully could best describe as withering. "Myself, I am certain," said Lillian, looking defiantly and coldly at Tully, "that there will be no question of future improper behavior by Mr. and Mrs. Slattery. Having sat in on this meeting, I am completely satisfied on this issue. The children need their parents. I shall recommend that the children be returned to them."

Tully quickly turned her disbelieving gaze to the psychologist, who was clearing his throat and wiping his forehead. "Uhm, Lillian, I . . . uhm, perhaps we can discuss it further?"

"Thank you, Dr. Connelly," said Lillian, getting up. "That will be all."

They all got up, but Tully could barely stand. She was behind the desk on Dr. Connelly's side when Mr. Slattery smiled at her and said, "Disciplined, Mrs. DeMarco, that's all. Haven't you ever been disciplined? Don't you discipline your own children?"

Tully breathed in, but it was too late. The *red mist* had escaped and descended all around her like night.

"Yes, I'm sure I do, Mr. Slattery," said Tully, gritting her teeth. "But never with a scalding iron. Never with a curtain rod. Never with a two-by-four. And I never, never put a gun in my son's mouth, cock it, and tell him that either his apology or his insides will come out of his mouth, you FAT FUCK."

Dr. Connelly paled, Lillian smiled, and Mr. Slattery shot screaming across the desk, lunging for Tully, who moved quickly back but could not escape Mr. Slattery's whole blubbery body sliding across the desk, slamming into her. She also could not escape his hands around her throat.

Dr. Connelly, a fifty-eight-year-old gray man, gasped and rushed from Tully and Mr. Slattery, out the door, shouting, "Police! Somebody call the police!"

Lillian backed away and stood there as if mesmerized. Mrs. Slattery just whimpered. "Easy, Bobby, easy, easy," not even getting up from her chair.

Mr. Slattery was strong, and when his 275 pounds rammed into Tully, her head rammed into the wall. He did not let go of her throat, nor did he stop screaming. "You bitch, you sick ugly bitch, I'm gonna kill you! I'm gonna fuckin' smash your brains in!" Ramming her head against the wall again. And again.

Tully, her mouth agape, begging for breath, her eyes dazed, feeling tremendous pain and with pain faintness, somehow drew her knee up, kicking Slattery in the groin.

He cried out and let her go. Tully, choking, coughing, breathless, staggered to the side, but she was still covered by the *red mist*, and while Mr. Slattery held on to his crotch with both hands, she grabbed the office stapler from the desk and smashed it into his bent face.

Mrs. Slattery screamed, seeing her husband reel sideways from the blow and collapse to the floor. The security men arrived then, but the matter was done.

At Stormont-Vail, Tully needed six stitches at the back of her head. She was lying in the emergency room for an hour or two, dazed and bandaged, when Robin rushed in.

"Robin," said Tully. "What are you doing here?" Tully had been thinking of what Jack was doing on Texas Street. She had missed lunch. Damn.

"I got a peculiar phone call from your office. From Alan."

"Oh, yeah," said Tully. "What did Alan have to say for himself?"

"He told me you got hurt on the job. I panicked," said Robin, leaning over Tully and kissing her bandaged forehead. "I said, how bad? He said, she'll be all right. But the other guy, Alan told me," said Robin, kissing Tully's eyes, "the other guy's got it worse."

Tully half smiled and told Robin what happened.

"Oh, Tully," he said when she finished. "He's a crazy fuck. What did you do that for?"

Tully turned her face away. "I lost my temper. I couldn't stand the sight of him anymore."

"Well, now we have to press charges."

Press charges? It hadn't even occurred to Tully. Imagine pressing charges every time someone had hit her. She'd be spending most of her life in court.

"Not we, Robin. Me. And I'm not up to pressing charges."

"When you get better, then."

"I'm not up to pressing charges, ever," she clarified.

"But Tully, why? He'll go to jail."

"He won't go to jail, Robin. He hadn't gone to jail the first fifty times he cracked someone's head against the wall. Maybe for a night or two. To rest up for later. No. Okay?"

"I think you should, Tully."

"Robin? Why don't you get us some food? Okay? And maybe we'll talk about it some other time."

Robin left and came back an hour later with some food and Boomerang. Little Robin lay on top of his mother as she stroked his head and played with his fingers.

"I have to say, the only thing that should satisfy you in this whole mess is what you did to that—" Robin glanced at Boomerang and then spelled it out. "F-u-c-k-e-r. I'm sure it must be killing him right now, not only that he was bested but that he was bested by a woman."

"It's nothing," said Tully. "Have you seen his wife? He must get bested by a woman with some frequency."

"Huh," said Robin. "I thought he bests her and she bests the kids."

"No, not quite. They both best each other, and then they both best the kids."

Robin told Tully that Mr. Slattery had a ruptured testicle and a broken jaw that would require surgery. "Do you know how hard you had to hit him to break his jaw? Have you any idea? Also he's missing three of his back teeth."

"Well, I'm glad it wasn't all in vain," said Tully. "Maybe Mr. Hillier will think twice before returning his kids to him."

"Who'd return a dead chicken to that bastard?" asked Robin incredulously.

"Lillian," said Tully.

Robin stroked Tully's head. "You don't need this shit, Tully," he said quietly. "Why don't you quit?"

Boomerang looked up. "Ooohhh! Daddy said a bad word!"

"Daddy's sorry!" said Robin and Tully in unison.

Robin and Boomerang stayed for a while. Boomerang wanted his mother to come home with them. Robin had to explain that Mommy had a little bit of a swelling of the head—"More than usual," he added jokingly—and had to stay in the hospital for one night to make sure she was okay.

Boomerang then wanted to spend the night in the hospital with his mother. It was an effort to get him to leave quietly.

After they'd gone, Tully tried to erase the feeling of Mr. Slattery's hands around her throat by turning on the TV.

Tully was awakened by the nurse, sticking her head in the door and saying gently, "Mrs. DeMarco, your cousin is here to see you."

"But I don't have a cousin," Tully muttered groggily as Jack pushed his way past the nurse, who never for a moment took her eyes off his chest.

"Cousin!" said Jack, walking in and smiling. "How could you say that? Have you forgotten how we played as children?"

Tully smiled. She felt better. "Why, cousin, how could I forget *how* we played as children?"

"You're only allowed a few minutes, please," the nurse said. "Otherwise I'll get into real trouble, okay, Jack?"

"Okay, Jack?" Tully mimicked when the nurse left. "What is that?"

Jack walked over to Tully's bed and sat in the chair a few feet away. "What's happened with you, Tully?" he asked seriously.

"Well, you wouldn't believe it," she said. "But I was walking up a hill and fell into a ditch and hit the ground and rolled down. But I'm okay now." *I'm okay now, Jack.*

"What's happened with you, Tully?" he repeated.

"This man tried to kill me," she said jocularly. "But I didn't let him."

"No, I wouldn't think you would," said Jack. "But what did you do to make him want to kill you?"

"I called him a fat . . . umm . . . fuck."

Jack laughed. "Oh, that'll do it." He sat by her on the bed.

"Thank you for coming," said Tully.

"Well, I got a little concerned. And then Millie got a phone call from Robin. That's how I found out."

Tully smelled him, sitting on the bed with her. She felt an urge to lift her head from the pillow and kiss his arm. You don't have to explain yourself to me, Jack, she wanted to say. You don't have to explain anything.

"So what's going to happen now?" asked Jack. "Don't tell me you're going to go back to that godforsaken place."

"Somebody has to," Tully said. "And they may not want me. I think Lillian was hoping for something like this. I think she wanted me to make a really huge error."

"Why do you say that?"

"Well, because, for one, she never sits in on counseling sessions. They bore her, you see. Bore her silly. She'd rather knit. Lillian likes theory. She doesn't like practice much. In any case," Tully continued, "you can't get her to sit on the borderline cases, much less on such clear-cut ones like this one."

"But she didn't think so."

"She doesn't think anything. She just does," said Tully. "She hoped I'd lose my temper if the parents got custody of the kids again. They don't deserve custody. They barely deserve to be alive. Lillian knew I could easily lose it. So she *orders* me to go in there, even after I flatly refuse. She's hoping for a confrontation. She's hoping I'd make a fool of myself, make the mother feel bad, do something. Get the father defensive. And then," Tully said, "Lillian recommends that the Slatterys get the kids and I get the boot."

"But I thought you said Mr. Hillier likes you?" asked Jack.

"He does," said Tully. "He's the reason I haven't been fired yet. But they're all skeptical of me. No one is skeptical of Lillian."

"Who is this Lillian?" Jack wanted to know. "It really seems incredible that without a soul she should be heading a foster care department."

Tully lowered her voice. "No one knows anything about her. We know she has never been married and has no kids."

"I've never been married and have no kids," Jack said sharply. "What does that prove?"

Tully raised her eyebrows. "That you have no soul?"

"Stop it," he said. "Be serious."

Tully's eyebrows continued to be raised.

"Stop it." He smiled, pushing her lightly. And all of a sudden, the last thing Tully wanted to talk about was Lillian. She is a miserable ugly woman with no life. Who cares about Lillian? Nobody, Tully suspected, and that may have been the problem.

But Jack was sitting on the bed with Tully, and Tully cared about that.

"You're in the wrong fucking business," said Jack. "Quit this minute and raise your family. You can help your family. And they will not try to crack your skull against the wall."

"You've obviously never met my mother," said Tully.

"She is not your family anymore," said Jack. "Boomerang and Robin are your family. Help *them*."

Tully let her head fall back on the pillow. "I don't know if I can help even them," she said, not looking at him. "They all have so much . . . *need*."

"We all do, Tully," said Jack quietly.

He patted her arm. She wanted him to touch her face, but he just patted her arm and asked if they had to cut her hair to stitch her. She nodded. "Just a chunk. I have a bald spot now. You don't like that word, do you?" she said, smiling lightly.

"What word? Spot?"

"Bald." Tully smiled.

Jack ran his hand through his thick blond crop.

"You're still young," Tully told him. "Just you wait. Why do you think there are no blond middle-aged men?"

"Because they're all gray?" Jack offered.

Tully laughed, wanting to touch his hair.

The nurse returned and asked Jack to go. Getting up, he stared at the nurse until she backed out the door.

"When are you coming home?" he asked.

"Tomorrow. Robin is coming to pick me up in the morning."

Jack was quiet for a moment. "Should I paint tomorrow?" he asked.

"Sure, why not?" said Tully, thinking, He's just painting the house. I have nothing to hide. But the thought of pretending to Robin that Jack didn't know about the sorry incident with Mr. Slattery made Tully feel a little tired. Made her feel not up to pretending.

"Why don't you come on Thursday instead," said Tully. "Thursday is better."

Jack agreed, pressing his hand to her bandaged head. "I hope you feel better soon, Tully," he said.

She smiled. "I feel better already," she replied.

That night she slept badly, and instead watched TV mindlessly, numbingly. She had nearly forgotten about Mr. Slattery. Tully's first thought when she drifted in and her last when she drifted out was of Jack Pendel.

The day after she came home, Tully got a visit from Mr. Hillier. She wasn't feeling so well and wanted to rest, but he seemed bent on explaining away everything: the policies of the Kansas Department of Social and Rehabilitation Services, the policies of the Foster Home Recruitment Agency, Greek philosophy, Lillian. Even himself. Something else, too, about the policies and the principles of providing what by definition is temporary care at best, and how sad he was that Tully had such a large problem with that, though apparently her heart was in the right place, blah, blah, blah.

Tully was in serious intercontinental drift during the hour-long talk. Asia, Africa, the Antarctica. Some oceans, even. The Indian. The *Pacific*. Where were those *National Geographic*s? Upstairs. In my four red milk crates.

"What's the bottom line, Mr. Hillier?" Tully said finally.

"You've always been a bottom-line girl, haven't you, Tully?"

"I've never been a bottom-line girl," Tully replied sharply. "But after a whole hour, I'm still not sure whether you came to apologize for Lillian or to fire me. Or both."

Mr. Hillier shook his head. "Neither," he said. "I can see you're not feeling well. The hospital says you have a slight concussion."

"They say that, do they?" *They had also once told me I was in shock. You're in shock, the intern had told me. Shock. Hospital. Shock.*

Mr. Hillier cleared his throat. "I had spoken to your husband a few days ago. About the possibility of pressing charges. He said you weren't sure yet. Is that right?"

That wasn't exactly right. "Yes, that's right," agreed Tully.

"Well, I wanted to tell you that Lillian continued to staunchly recommend that the Slatterys take the children, but Dr. Connelly and I told her that the man who is going to be up on assault charges doesn't have a good chance of getting his kids back. At best, we will be seen as irresponsible. At worst, we could be sued for criminal negligence. So we asked Lillian to reconsider. To say the least, she wasn't happy and nearly threatened to quit. She thought we were bucking down to you."

"To *me*?" said Tully. "Not to *me*, Mr. Hillier. Not to me."

"In *any* case," he said. "I don't want to force you to press charges. If you don't want to, for some reason, that's all right. Just hanging the threat over the whole mess will be enough to keep those kids away from him. You've done the kids a favor, Tully."

"Some favor," scoffed Tully.

"I'd like to put this all behind us and start on a new foot," said Mr. Hillier. "Please take as much time as you need to get yourself in order. It'll give Lillian time, too, to calm down. You have four weeks vacation coming to you. Plus a few weeks of sick leave. I'm sure we can stretch it out till September. Alan said he'll be glad to take over your cases in the meantime. Relax, Tully. Remember, we're all trying to do our best."

"What, Mr. Slattery, too?"

"For him, I apologize to you."

What about Lillian? Tully thought. Are you once again going to apologize for Lillian? Lillian had been close to threatening to quit. But Mr. Hillier was not close to threatening to fire her. What will it take? What will it take for Lillian to leave a job she hates?

But Tully wasn't concerned about Lillian or Mr. Hillier or Mr. Slattery all that much. The whole summer! she was thinking, the whole glorious, hot, sun-filled, paint-filled summer. Thank you, God, for your mysterious ways.

Tully stayed home while Jack painted. But what she had thought would be fun turned out to be tortuous. Neither the sun nor the summer could fill the ache that Tully walked around with each and every day.

Every conversation with Jack got more difficult the more the summer progressed and the hotter it got.

As Tully convalesced and pondered whether to apply to Gentle Shepherd for a job, she helped Jack paint. Either she mixed paint for him or brought him new paint or brought him lemonade. She covered the furniture with old sheets, and dusted, and cleaned up the wooden debris from the windows.

There were days Tully talked to Millie more than to Jack, who was busy working. Tully wanted Millie to take a vacation. She wanted the whole damn house to take one long vacation.

Millie occasionally offered to make Jack and Tully lunch, but Tully would refuse. Tully made lunch for Jack and Tully. Tully made the patties and Jack stood at the grill. Every day around noon, they had a barbecue. Hamburgers, chicken, corn on the cob. He had a hearty appetite, while she had none. After lunch, they went back to painting. When Tully helped him, she'd occasionally joke that he was going to have to pay her a whopping salary for her efforts. But that was at the beginning of her stay at home. After two weeks together all day, talk became limited to paint mixing and the state of the windows. And even this Tully barely understood; barely, through her red, thick, aching sexual haze.

At nights, Tully stood nude in front of her mirror, running her hands over her body, whispering, *"He wants me, he wants me not, he wants me, he wants me not, he wants me, he wants me, he wants me. He wants me, I want him, he wants me, I want him, he wants me I want him him him I want him."*

And in the mornings, when Jack rang the doorbell, she still took the stairs down two at a time, still barefoot.

She would climb up the ladder in front of him, passing his hands and face on her way up, and having him hold her elbow on the way down. There were days when Tully was dressed to the hilt, in a dress and stockings. There were days when she was barely clad. There were days when she wore a lot of makeup and days when she wore no makeup at all. She braided her hair or left it loose, she curled it or blow-dried it straight, she starved herself or ate nonstop. Tully had no idea what attracted him, she had no idea even if she did attract him, and because his manner toward her was always constant and cheerful, she had no indication from him in which direction to alter herself so that he would ease her aching.

Jack just continued to paint, and Tully continued to have sex with Robin. Now at a feverish pitch, she needed an intense amount of lovemaking that Robin, overworked, overtired, oversported, overused Robin, just could not give her. Sex with Robin did not sate her; Tully wanted Jack.

"Tully, what are you doing?" said Jack to her in early July, when he came into the kitchen and saw her rubbing ice into her face and neck.

"It might not look like it," said Tully, flushed and burning, "but I'm hang gliding."

At night when she could not sleep she sat by the window and stared at the road and thought of his hands. His hands on the surfboard, his hands on the paintbrush, his hands on Jennifer. His hands that touched salt water, that touched hot sand, that touched *Jennifer*! What need, what misery. *I just want to be next to him. I want his lips to kiss my lips, I want to feel the ecstasy of being allowed to see him naked, of being allowed to feel his naked body, of being allowed to sit on top of him and kiss his face. I want the ecstasy of being allowed to touch him.*

"So Tully, Millie says you're having a Fourth of July party," said Jack.

"Yes, uh-huh," said Tully.

They just stood there in the front yard and looked at each other. "Well, that's too bad," Jack said at last. "It would have been nice to finish the whole house so that your guests could oooh and aaahh."

It would have been nice to ask you to come, Jack. It would have been nice to have you make hamburgers like you do for us every day. "They are not guests," said Tully resignedly. "They're family."

And at the barbecue, everybody did oooh and ahhh. Only the north side of the house, Hedda's side, needed to be painted, but nobody noticed because nobody went around to Hedda's side of the house.

Robin and Tully smiled politely, fielding the house compliments. Robin grilled burgers and shrimp. Tully entertained the troops.

"Tully, you are so lucky," said Karen, addressing her sister-in-law and everyone else. "We are all so lucky."

Linda was vociferous in her agreement. Shakie nodded. Tully said nothing.

"Yes," said Shakie. "We have these wonderful, beautiful children, loving, devoted husbands, gorgeous homes, though none, of course, as gorgeous and freshly-painted as Tully's. Why, Tully's got the freshest-painted house in Topeka. Right, Tully?"

"Right, Shakie," said Tully, thinking mean thoughts about her friend. Thinking of saying mean things to her friend.

"Tully, you don't seem very happy," said Linda, touching Tully. "Are you happy, Tully?" asked Linda, tickling Tully's lower arms. "Are you happy?"

"Who wouldn't be happy, married to Robin?" said Karen. The girls laughed, sparing Tully the need for a response. Shakie, not looking at Tully, said, "Robin is a wonderful husband."

"The best," said Linda. "All the DeMarcos are pretty good, of course. But I'll bet Robin doesn't make Tully get up at four in the morning to milk the cows."

"I'll bet he doesn't," said Shakie. "Because Tully is already up. He usually tells you to come to bed around that time, doesn't he, Tully?" said Shakie, smiling congenially. Tully nearly wanted to slap her. "Tully has trouble sleeping," explained Shakie.

"Well, maybe Tully should make better use of that four o'clock in the morning," Karen said with a smile. "When are you going to have another baby? You're behind all of us now. Even I had my third, and I kept saying no after the first."

"I didn't know it was a race," Tully said, not smiling. "But you're right. Even Shakie's had another one, even though she said she had her tubes tied after the twins."

Shakie smiled thinly. "They weren't so much tied as folded once or twice," she said.

"Come on, Tull," said Karen. "You don't want Boomerang to be your only kid."

"Yeah, Tully. It's hard being an only kid," agreed Linda. "I should know, I was one."

Tully squinted into the green grass, her face an impenetrable mask. "Well, that must be tough."

"How many kids in your family, Tully?" asked Karen.

"One," said Tully, thinking of her brother Henry's little GI Joe figures still on the seat where he had sat and ate his cereal.

"Oh," squealed Linda, "I didn't know you were an only child, just like me, well, no wonder we're so much alike and both fell in love with the DeMarcos!"

"Wait a minute, here!" said Karen. "I was one of seven, but I also fell in love with a DeMarco!" She looked over at Shakie. "Too bad there wasn't a fourth brother, Shake, huh? You could have married him," she said.

"Yeah, sure," said Shakie, turning away.

And Tully turned away, too, wanting at that minute only to be at Lake Vaquero.

At Lake Vaquero, Tully began to walk a little closer to Jack, desperate to touch him. When they got into the boat, she held on to his arm. When they went swimming, she tried to bump into his wet body with her wet body. When they crouched down in the sand, Tully crouched down close to Jack.

At home on weekdays, they continued to paint. When they were bending down to pour the paint, she stood so that their bare arms touched. When he was helping her to open a jar of something, Tully did not let go of the jar so that her hands could be close to his hands. When they sat at the kitchen table with Jack's legs open and outstretched under it, she stretched out her own legs and put them in between his. In the doorways, when he walked past her, she did not move out of the way. She smelled him, and it made her feel faint. She didn't know what the control was, what the button was that she could push, the button that would let her touch him.

Never did Tully hate her mother more, hate the house more, hate Millie and Robin and her life more than when she was at 1501 Texas Street with Jack each and every day, yet could not touch him.

* * *

"So Tully, how come Boomer doesn't come with us to Vaquero these days?" asked Jack. They were sitting in the boat. Not rowing. Just sitting. The sun was so hot, it was making Tully dozy. Tully wanted to sleep.

"He's playing softball with his dad," Tully lazily replied.

They were sitting side by side at the foot of the boat, leaning back and into each other. The oars were up and the boat was floating in the lake. Much like Tully was floating in the lake. She closed her eyes.

"How about if we play a game?" said Jack.

"Yeah," said Tully slowly. "I sleep, and you watch me. When I wake up, you win."

"No. I ask you a question and you answer me without thinking."

"Uh, no, I don't like that game. How about if I sleep and you look at me without thinking?"

"Who was your first boyfriend?"

Tully pretended to snore.

"Tully."

"Robin," replied Tully without thinking. "Who was your first girlfriend?"

"This girl Donna," he replied. "We were fourteen. Rather, I was fourteen. She was a year older. I was really smitten."

"You're thinking, Jack. I didn't ask you how old you were." She squinted at him and smiled. He flicked a fly off her arm.

"Was Donna your first kiss?"

"Not my first kiss," said Jack. "But my first. Was Robin your first kiss?"

"Not my first kiss. Not my first."

"You remember your first?"

"I remember my first," said Tully. "I don't much want to talk about it."

"Ahh," he said, nodding, staring at her wrists. "I guess you must've understood Jen pretty well."

Tully pulled slightly away from him. Still leaning back. "I didn't understand Jen at all," she said. "You misunderstand me."

"Oh, I see," he said. "It wasn't really love with your first."

Tully didn't answer him and Jack changed the subject. "Who did you know first, Jen or Julie?"

"Julie. What was the first thing Jennifer told you about me?"

"She said, my friend Tully is a better pitcher than you. My friend Tully could kick your butt."

Tully smiled. "That sounds just like Jen. And you said?"

"My turn, Tully. What was the first thing Jen told you about me?"

"She never told me anything about you at all. She told me I underestimated you."

"Did you?" said Jack. "Did you underestimate me?"

"My turn, Jack," said Tully. "Were you attracted to her?"

"Sure. I was sixteen. I was attracted to everybody," said Jack. Then, "*Did* you . . . underestimate me?"

"I underestimated you a little," she replied, leaning into him on the boat floating through Lake Vaquero. "Were you in love with Shakie?"

"I was in love with being the captain of the High Trojans," Jack said. "I was in love with being Prom King. Did you ever fall in love with any of the boys you danced with?"

She turned her head up to look at him.

"No," Tully replied, thinking, *I'm lying.*

"Never?" asked Jack, not looking at her.

"My turn," said Tully.

"Wait, that was not a question. That was more like an incredulous exclamation. Like 'Never?!' "

"I see. So you don't need a reply to it," said Tully. "Have you had many girlfriends in your travels?"

"Well, I've had many girls. Is that the same thing?"

"Is that a question, Jack? Are you wasting your turn on that question?"

"No," he said quickly. "Did you love Jennifer?"

"What do you think?" said Tully.

"I don't know. Are you wasting your question on that, Tully, or are you going to answer me? Did you love her?"

"Sure," Tully replied evenly. "I was sixteen. I loved everybody." But she thought, *Jennifer had been the only one I ever loved. Until now.*

Tully asked, "Did you . . . love any of the girls you were with during your travels?"

"Well, I told them I loved them. Is that the same thing? That was not a question," he added quickly.

"Too late," said Tully, and before he could speak, added unsteadily, "My turn. Did she ever tell you she loved you?"

"Never," said Jack "Did she ever tell you she loved me?"

"Yes," replied Tully.

"She should have told *me*," said Jack quietly.

It was still blistering hot when they got out of the boat. Wading through the water, Jack pulled the boat up on the sand in the little alcove behind the ivy where they hid it. Tully was already on the sand, sitting looking up at him as he continued to gesture and talk and laugh, standing there, his bare thighs not four inches away from her face. From her eyes, from her lips. Tully just sat there, keeping him silent company, sat there looking at his legs. *Inches* away from her face. She watched him longingly. His thighs were so close. *How easy it would be, how easy it would be, no effort at all, no strain, no courage, to just lean over literally two inches and press her lips to his legs, just lean over and touch his thighs with her lips, feel his blond curly hair against her lips* . . . She closed her eyes and heard him say, "Tully?"

Opening her eyes, she saw he had stopped talking and was staring at her intensely. Answers. Time. Longing. Years. Jennifer.

"Tully," he muttered, pulling her up and standing close to her. "What did you do?"

What did I do? She looked at him, puzzled.

"Did you just kiss my leg, Tully?" said Jack Pendel.

"Oh, God!" she exclaimed, her aching like a bad burn. "I'm sorry."

He took her hands away from her face, and, holding her by her wrists, repeated quietly and hoarsely, "Did you just kiss my leg?"

His head was bent down to her, his lips an inch away from her lips as she breathed into him, "Jack, I'm—"

"Oh, Tully," he whispered fiercely, pulling her down to her knees and going down with her, kneeling with her, pressing her chest to his chest. "Oh, Tully," he breathed into her mouth, and kissed her lips.

Feverishly, hotly, he opened her mouth with his and kissed her lips, and Tully groaned into his mouth, grasping for his head with her hands. She could not touch him fast enough.

Frenzied, she ran her hands over him, touching his face his hair his neck she was pressed against him hard, so hard, her bare legs were rubbing against his bare legs and their lips and tongues moaned and cried, moaned and cried into each other's lips. He pushed her down on the sand, and she fell back, never letting go of his neck never letting go of his lips. He was on top of her, opening her legs, between her legs, grinding against her, still in his shorts, and she lifted her hips and ground against him and he moaned and kissed her harder while his hands, oh she did not notice where his hands were, but the sun was hot on her closed lids. How they got their clothes off she didn't know, but she was still wearing her tank top while he pulled down her shorts, sat up to pull down his own shorts as she lay half-naked in front of him; didn't even take the shorts off all the way, he just pulled them down, then pulled up her tank top and bent his head into her breasts, wet from sweat, wet red nipples, he only said, oh, Tully, and fell on them, she moaned and held his hair she wanted him she wanted him now, she didn't know whether to faint, close her eyes, or never close her eyes again so that she could look at his face, full of everything she had ever wanted. Tully pulled her face up to his, kissing him, groaning Jack, please, please, please Jack. *Please.* He opened her legs wider, and she let go of his neck for a moment to reach down to touch him, moaning at the feel of him. She thrust her hips up, aching, and he was inside her. Tully tried to hold on to something, but there was nothing to hold on to but him. He was slippery and out of control, Jack, Jack, yes, oh yes, just like that, yes, go on, go on, go on . . . panting panting, yes . . . hard . . . yes, Jack . . . blond hair, matted and wet, wet back, wet lips, wet cock, yes . . . harder, harder.

He moved so fast and she came so hard, came and let go of his neck for a moment trying to hold on to something else while he continued to thrust inside her and she continued to come because he would not stop and there was nothing to hold on to, and then he came, too, and eventually stopped moving, and when he stopped moving, she cried.

Cried, holding on to him with both hands, crying into his neck, into his weight on top of her. He was heavy, but she did not feel it, she welcomed it wrapping her legs tighter around him.

He lifted up his face to look at her. "Why, Tully," he said, still panting. Smiling. "Did you kiss my leg?"

Tully closed her eyes and smiled back, feeling his lips on her eyes, hugging him tight, feeling his back. I still haven't gotten a good look at him. But I touched him.

Stroking her head with his fingers, Jack was looking at her and saying something, but she hardly heard him, so loud was the feeling inside her, shouting, running on the rooftops, shouting, Jack, Jack.

"Hmm," she said softly. "Now I know what all the fuss was about."

Was there a fuss? he asked. Oh, yes, she told him, a big fuss, huge, and now she knew why, kissing his wet bristly cheek, "I sat by the lake, and looked at the sky," quoting one of Boomer's children's stories.

Jack got *out* of her, after a while, rolled off her and onto his back, placing one of his hands on her stomach. "I was there," he said happily. "Finally. There I was . . ."

Tully sat up. "Let me have a good look at you," she whispered, hunkering over him. "God. You're so beautiful," she said breathlessly, stunned. All that *body*. All that blond hair. On his chest, and on his stomach, leading down, getting thicker, coming down into a V. Yes, Tully thought, kneeling down between his legs and looking at him. Very beautiful.

It was still hot in the late afternoon, so they crawled naked into the water to wash themselves off, to wash off their sweat. Not talking much, just murmurs, sweetness.

Afterwards she spread out a picnic blanket and they lay down on it and made love again. This time he lasted longer, this time she got on top of him, put him inside her, and made love to him and made him come and then she slid down and went down on him again until he got hard hard, coming into her mouth, panting, whispering things to her she would never remember.

When the afternoon was over, Tully didn't tell Jack how it was, nor did she ask him how it was for him. She didn't need to. She knew what it was.

At the end of a sweltering August, Tully went over to Shakie's for a Saturday afternoon. Plodding after Shakie and the kids, Tully was lost somewhere in Lake Vaquero of the last two months of the last two years, when Shakie asked, "So, is he done? Painting the house?"

"Done?" Tully echoed absentmindedly. "Done? Yes, of course he's done. He was done ages ago."

"Have you gone back to work?"

Tully shook her head. "Soon. I need to speak again in front of the Appropriations Committee. If they don't give me what I want, if they don't give me my foster training period of eight weeks, I'm quitting. Plain quitting."

"Quitting and doing what?" asked Shakie.

Tully hadn't thought about it. Not *concretely*. Oh, things swam around her head.

"I don't know," she replied vaguely. "Transfer to adoption." At least that would be a better illusion. Like I'm actually making *something* happen for those kids.

"Why would you want to transfer?" Shakie asked, sitting down on the grass. "I should think after what had happened they need you more than ever. It's obvious that Lillian will eventually dig her own grave. They'll need someone to replace her."

"Maybe," said Tully. "But after what happened, I need *them* less than ever."

"Think about your little ones," said Shakie. "Those kids need you to care about them."

"No," said Tully. "They need mom and dad to care about them. I'm just a poor third cousin." Tully pressed her hand to her heart. "Everybody is just a poor third cousin. It's really a lost battle. Running in place. In space."

"It's not a lost battle," said Shakie. "You think I give up so easily when a lady comes up to my counter and all she wants to do is try on perfumes? No, I say to myself. She's not leaving here without a hundred dollars' worth of merchandise and free gifts. I don't give up."

"That's good." Tully smiled, thinking, no, Shakie did not give up. She was perfect for the Macy's job. She'd be perfect for Tully's job, too.

"So," said Shakie, looking at Tully oddly. "What have you been doing with your summer? I haven't seen that much of you."

"Oh, you know," said Tully evasively. "This and that. Nothing special."

Shakie waited a moment. "I've seen you," she said. "I've seen you around town. Painting. Painting with *him*."

Tully didn't miss a beat. "So?" she said.

"Painting with *him*."

"So?" repeated Tully.

Shakie said nothing for a while, just looked at the grass. "It's happened, hasn't it." More a statement than a question.

And Tully replied, also looking at the grass, "I don't know what you're talking about." Yet how she wished she could talk about it! She wished Julie were in Topeka.

Shakie nodded slowly. "Yeah. You do. You can't even say his name out loud, because then everyone would know it's happened."

Tully rubbed her hands together in a gesture heavily borrowed from her mother. Tully knew it and hated it, but during times of stress, it was like biting her nails. She could not help herself.

"Shakie, I don't want to talk about it." Yet how she did. How.

"Tell me, is it true, Tully, is it true?"

Tully sighed. She wanted Julie to come home.

Standing up, Tully said, "Shakie, I am not your captive audience. I don't want to talk about it."

Shakie studied her with a disappointed, sad look. After an awkward moment, she said, "We don't have to talk about it. It makes no never mind to me, you understand." And then, seeing Tully's disbelieving face, said, "It doesn't, I have no more feelings for him, no more good feelings anyway, it makes no never mind to me. I have three wonderful children. Macy's is closing down and becoming Dillard's. We're all moving to the West Ridge Mall across town and I'm going to be the manager of the whole Chanel department. I've got a life. I'm over him. High school is over. But let me ask you," Shakie added, almost as an afterthought, but Tully knew better. "What do you hope to accomplish?"

"Accomplish?" said Tully in a vague way as if the word had no meaning for her. "Accomplish?"

"Oh, Tully, don't you think I understand? Do you forget? I understand better than anybody. You forget I wrote the book," she said bitterly.

Now, that struck something specific in Tully. "No," she said, blinking away . . . something. "*You* didn't write this book."

Shakie dismissed her. "Huh. He did not come back for *her*, but he did come back for me."

"He never came back for you," said Tully. "He comes back for *her* every year. He comes to bring her flowers every year."

Shakie said in a measured tone, "A little late, wouldn't you say?"

"Yes," said Tully grimly. *But not for me.*

Shakie must have read Tully's thoughts because she laughed and said, "Tully Makker! Tully DeMarco!" She enunciated, "Tully DeMARCO! This is not some fucking knight in shining armor we're talking about here! This is Jack Pendel. What do you think, he is going to climb through your freshly painted window late at night and take you away on his horse to his hut? Let me remind you that he doesn't even have a hut, he has nothing but himself, nothing," Shakie said sadly. "Himself and a lot of armor." Looking over at Tully, Shakie shrugged her shoulders. "Maybe you're perfect for each other. You can rub armors together. Because it's all you both got. More armor than fucking prince Gallahad. Oh, Tully," said Shakie, dispirited. "He will break your fucking heart."

"I'm ready," replied Tully.

Tully came back home from Shakie's around nine on Saturday night, and Robin wasn't home yet. Tully bathed Boomerang, read him three books, put him to bed, sat in the rocking chair in his bedroom, and then came downstairs. It was ten-thirty. She checked on her mother. Aside from saying that she thought Tully was staying at Shakie's overnight, Hedda did not want to talk to Tully, who then went to sit in her California room, but she was too restless to sit there long. She wanted Robin to come home. At eleven in the evening, she called Bruce and got Linda on the phone. After chatting for fifteen minutes, Linda finally said that the boys, as she called them, were out, and she didn't know when they were coming home. After another ten minutes, Linda said that Bruce was home and sound asleep. Tully asked Linda to have Robin call her when he got in. Midnight passed and one o'clock, and two o'clock, and three o'clock. Tully fell asleep downstairs on the couch and awakened to Boomerang's calling her from upstairs, asking her to come to bed so that he could lie down next to her. Tully went upstairs but then couldn't sleep and just lay there listening to Boomerang's even breathing.

Robin came home at around ten in the morning on Sunday.

"How come you didn't call me?" Tully wanted to know. "I asked you to call me."

"I know," he said, getting himself a glass of orange juice. "But we got in real late, and I thought you'd be sleeping."

"You're full of—" Tully looked over at Boomerang having cereal. "You're full of it. You know I don't go to sleep till, like, three. Are you telling me you got in after that?"

"I really don't remember, Tully," he said. "It was late, we all had a bit to drink, and I didn't want to wake you. Okay?"

"Where do you go in Manhattan until all hours in the morning?" she demanded. "I mean," she said, trying to make her voice sound milder, "what kind of fun stuff do you guys get up to?"

Robin eyed her coolly and went to sit by his son. "This and that. Not much of anything. Play pool. Go to the movies. Sit and talk."

"So just you and Stevie went out, huh?"

"Yeah," Robin said. "Just me and him."

"Where did you go?"

"Nowhere special," Robin said vaguely, feeding Boomerang oatmeal. "So Boomer, what do you want to do today? It's a great day. What do you want to do?"

"Go to the lake," said Boomerang, and Tully's face fell. Fortunately, Robin didn't look up.

"Listen, son," Robin said. "Daddy is playing in a rugby sevens game today. Why don't you and your mom come and watch?"

"Yeah!" exclaimed Boomerang

"Robin," said Tully carefully, "I was going to go to church and then do a little shopping. I spent all day with Shakie yesterday and didn't get anything done."

"Of course you didn't," said Robin, standing up. "It's okay. I'll take Boomer. Maybe you can buy me a T-shirt or something."

Guilt stabbed at Tully. Boomerang seemed so happy when he thought his mother might come. But the summer was almost over. There would be plenty of time to go with Robin and Boomerang to Manhattan once the summer was over.

One Saturday in the beginning of September, Tully and Jack went to Kansas City for the night. After a sweet dinner at their old French place, they went dancing. At the end of the night, somewhere around two A.M., they entered a dancing contest, "for old times' sake" but *together*, and won! Incredibly! Won some tickets to a comedy show, a bottle of champagne, and a couple of T-shirts. "Sure beats those bad old days when you used to get a hundred bucks for winning a dancing contest," said Jack, opening the champagne in their hotel room. "What did you do with all that money, anyway? Spend it?"

"Some," she said, hanging on to him. "Most. I made a lot of money, Jack."

"I believe it," he said, grabbing her around the waist and dipping her over. "I fucking believe it."

In their Holiday Inn bed at three in the morning, having made love twice, Jack spoke into Tully's tangled hair. "It's September, Tully."

Tully stiffened and lay very still in his arms. "Yeah. So?" she said after a few minutes of trying to control her throat. "Topeka doesn't close in September, you know."

"Painting season is over," he said.

"So?"

"I have to work, Tully," said Jack. "Like you have to work, I have to work."

"So? You can find something to do in Topeka. You can paint inside, can't you?"

"Tully, Tully." Jack ran his fingers through her hair. "You have such beautiful hair. I'm not an inside man. I like the air."

"I see," she said, still stiff, still trying to catch her throat.

Jack kissed her. "I'll be back in December. For Christmas."

Tully didn't answer him, counting sheep one after another. One sheep, two sheep, three sheep, four sheep.

At last she said, "Is that what we're going to have?"

Jack was quiet. "As opposed to what?" he asked, moving slightly away from her.

As opposed to what. Good question. Good question. Tully didn't really have an answer to a good question like that. She wasn't thinking beyond this week, beyond seeing him this week. And next. And the next after another.

So she remained silent, five, ten, fifteen minutes, having no answer for him. Finally, Tully recounted to Jack the conversation she'd had with Shakie a few weeks earlier.

"Armor, huh?" mused Jack. "Armor."

"Is she right?" Tully asked him.

Jack ran his fingers from her shoulders to her hip. "About you? Absolutely."

She poked him. "About *you*."

He lay on his back staring at the ceiling. "How can you not have armor?" he said. "Where would we be without our armor?"

"Dead?" said Tully.

"Dead." Jack nodded sadly, kissing her shoulder. "Your Jen. She didn't have a lot of armor."

"You can say that two times," said Tully.

"Yeah," Jack continued. "She was completely open. She had no protection from the world."

Tully flinched a little, turning her head away from him, and said, "Wrong. No protection from you."

"Is it that simple?" said Jack. "Because then I could kill myself or have her father kill me or marry her sister to alleviate my guilt."

"You could," said Tully. "But you know, she didn't have a sister."

Jack smiled. "Yeah, but she had you."

"Yes, but dear Jack, you forget," said Tully, "I'm already married." They laughed a little.

"You don't know this," said Tully, "but I actually did save your life once."

"Of that I have no doubt," said Jack.

"No, seriously. Many years ago. Mr. Mandolini came to me to ask me who 'J.P.' was. And I was going to tell him, but he had a crazy look in his face. Have you ever seen *The Great Gatsby*?"

"I did better than that. I read *The Great Gatsby*."

"Well, remember George Wilson?"

"Of course."

"That's the look Mr. Mandolini had in his face. The George Wilson look."

"I see. So you feel you had actually been a help to me by not telling him who J.P. was?"

"Yes. Of course," said Tully, surprised. "Don't you?"

"I don't know," said Jack thoughtfully. He looked softly at her. "Sometimes yes. Sometimes no."

"When no?"

"When . . ." Jack said slowly, "when I'm trying *to beat back death.*"

"I didn't know," said Tully, holding on to him, "that you were . . . trying to do that."

"No." He smiled ruefully. "You thought you were the only one."

Tully studied him for a moment. Demons? Not Jack. Tully stroked his chest. *"No matter,"* she whispered, quoting Fitzgerald. *"Tomorrow we will run faster—"*

"—stretch our arms a little farther," continued Jack, tightening his arms around her. *"And one fine morning—"*

"—so we beat on," Tully finished, *"boats against the current, borne back ceaselessly into the past."*

"You can say that two times," said Jack.

Outside their Holiday Inn window, they heard the predawn birds start to chirp when Tully said, "Jack, wasn't it possible for you to . . . like her back?"

"Sure, it was possible," he said.

"Jack? Why wasn't it possible?"

He turned onto his stomach and put his face on the pillow. Not lifting up his head, he said, "Tully, I was a young kid, a young jock kid. A young jock kid with an attitude and a family who thought I was God. I wanted to play football, to drink beer, to have lots of friends, to go out with lots of girls. I was told I could have it all, and all is what I wanted. Who knows why else? Ultimately, maybe because I wasn't attracted to her. Maybe because I knew her too well and sensed her intensity. She frightened me. I didn't want trouble . . ."

Tully stopped him by leaning down and kissing his mouth. "Why wasn't it possible with Shakie?"

Jack sighed. "Shakie was possible. She was very attractive. But in the end, I didn't think she was strong enough to withstand me. I really had nothing to give her. In the end, she'd have been so disappointed."

Tully whispered, "You had yourself to give her."

Touching her, Jack said, "Yes, but it's not enough."

Tully was barely audible. "It's everything."

Jack turned over to hug her and said resolutely, "Believe me, it's nothing. *Nothing.*" He cleared his throat and reached for the glass of water he liked to keep near the bed at night. "My dad, my real dad, was a wonderful man by all accounts. My mother certainly thought so. He was good-looking, much better looking than me, much more intelligent, and a brilliant artist on top of it. Yeah, my dad was a painter. He gave himself over totally to my mother, but he was poor and was never very interested in making a penny. He wanted only to create!" Jack said "create" nearly scornfully. "Wanted to paint for himself and for my mom. My mom says he adored her. I know he painted Kansas like poetry. His sunset over the prairie still hangs in our living room. He put my mother under his spell and she married him, thinking he was for changing. She soon realized he was not for changing and that in fact he became more and more like himself as the years went on. Now, she might have loved him when he was courting her and painting her, but when they were married and had a child—me—my mom understood they were going to forever have the prairie but never a penny. Mind you, it took her eight years to understand that. When she did, though, she promptly left him and married a man who could support her and me and her future children well." Jack let go of Tully, turning away on his side.

"Don't get me wrong, Tully. I don't blame her. But my dad, I think he blamed her. He had thought that what my mother loved most about him was his genius, his drifter's soul, his aesthetic values, his Christ-like principles of never having a shirt on your back." Again, Jack sounded scornful, and Tully couldn't quite figure out toward whom, his father or his mother.

"Ahhhh," she said gently. "So your mom remarried."

Jack nodded. "Remarried, and got cancer. God saw to it that she didn't have any more children."

"Just like he saw to Mr. and Mrs. Mandolini," said Tully.

"Yes. My mom never stopped torturing herself, either. For getting sick. She felt it was God's punishment and never stopped torturing herself. Or me. Or my stepfather. Never left Topeka, either."

"Never left Topeka?"

"No," said Jack. "The first time I myself saw the outside of this state was after my high school graduation."

"You've certainly made up for it now."

Jack was mute, staring into the wall.

"Do you know what happened to your dad, Jack?"

His back was still to her. "My dad, well, he left, you know. He left the state."

Tully clenched her fingers together, squeezing the bit between her teeth. Now, that's a palpable story, she thought, feeling the metallic taste in her mouth.

Jack continued. "I was eight. Didn't see him then for nine or so years. But then we heard he was back in town and not in such good shape, drinking hard, you know. My mother tried to find him, but he kept avoiding her, the local bars couldn't place him. He kept changing hotels on her. He must have tormented her this way for six months or so," he said, trailing off.

"Go on . . ." she prodded.

Jack spoke tonelessly without turning to her. "And then we found him one winter morning dead in our backyard."

"Oh, God," said Tully.

"Mmmm. Yeah. Just dead, you know? Lying there, in his ripped coat and bad shoes, frozen solid. John Pendel, Sr., forty-one years old. Came to my mother's house to die. To my mother's *white rosebushes*."

Tully closed her eyes. *Rosebushes*. "Is that where you got the white roses from? Your mother's garden?"

"Yes," replied Jack. "She has a greenhouse in the backyard. She grows the roses there all year round."

"Oh, God. Well, couldn't he have gone inside?"

"My mother, always cautious about her prize rosebushes, keeps the greenhouse locked at night."

Tully sat up, shaking her head. "That's terrible. I'm so sorry." And then she thought of something. "Did Jen know all this? Did you tell her about your dad?"

"I told her," he said. "She knew."

Tully muttered, "Fucking unbelievable." And all she could think of was, *He comes to St. Mark's to give her white roses because they mean so much to her but she liked them only because they mean so much to him*. Well, isn't that right out of fucking O'Henry. Tully stared at the wall, but before the wall was his bare back, and eventually she stared at him.

"Were you the one who found him?" Tully asked quietly.

"No, I didn't find him," said Jack. "We had a cocker spaniel. Barky. She found him."

The light outside changed from blue to gray before they spoke again.

"But Tully," Jack said at last, "you know so much about me, Tully, tell me, why don't I know anything about you?"

"Jack Pendel." Tully managed a smile. "You know everything about me. Too much. You are the man who knew too much. Even when I didn't know you breathed. You know I danced in clubs, you know about my mother, and you know about Jennifer. There's nothing else to know about me." She didn't look at him when she said that, and he turned around to face her, catching her in his arms, throwing her back on the bed, and kissing her eyes. "Tully, you are such a liar; even to me, you just can't stop. Please, let it down, let down your armor, let it down and tell me about *your* father. Tell me about him."

"Oh," she said. "Oh. And if I tell you, Jack Pendel, will you feel I've let down my armor?"

He looked at her very seriously. "No. Never. A little, yes, but all the way off? Why, Tully, you've never told me about these scars on your wrists, these scars that don't seem to go away. Now, I know something must have happened to you, something for you to pull away from Jennifer, to get these scars, to learn how to dance, and how to lie. Something. I have a feeling the secret of all that will die with you, Tully. But you know what? I don't care. I don't want to know. It would be enough for me if you slept at night, if you went to St. Mark's less, if you were with me more. If you were vulnerable to me a little."

Tully touched his hair and his face, overflowing inside. "Vulnerable? Jack Pendel, I love you."

He stared at her blankly. "*Love* me?"

"I love you," she repeated, and the words did not get stuck in her throat.

Jack grinned like a Cheshire cat, getting up and jumping up and down on the bed crying, "She loves me! She loves me! SHE! LOVES! ME!"

Tully pulled the hairs on his leg. "Get down, you fool. Somebody is going to call the police."

Jack jumped down on top of her and pinned her arms near her head. "She loves me," he whispered into her face. "She loves me."

Tully and Jack made love again, breathless love, and after they were done, Tully straddled him, her chest against his chest, and, stroking his arms, kissed his face. She kissed his hard forehead and his blond hair, his temples and his eyebrows. She kissed his nose and the sides of his nose and rubbed her face against his rough cheeks. She kissed his lips, she kissed his eyes and his lips, and breathed and breathed onto him . . .

"I love you, Jack, I love you, Jack Pendel, do you know what that means? I love you, why, it means everything, and how much I love you, if you only knew. I love everything that is you. Why, I would tell you my best friend's secrets, much less my own, I love you, I would tell you everything, everything, I would give you everything."

Jack Pendel, eyes closed and wet, whispered back, *"And I love you, my Tully. I love you. Do you know how much I love you? Do you know how long I've loved you? How long ago I lowered my defenses against you? How many years I came back and went to that stupid church for you and brought fresh flowers for you, how many years I looked for you and asked Shakie after you, and drove by Kansas Avenue looking for you, and went to White Lakes, and ate at Casa, because I wanted by chance to meet you, to see you, to see your lovely face, to see you walk, talk, bend down to kiss your boy. When I saw you at Jennifer's party, I was drunk, and more than a year had passed since I had seen you dance last, but when I saw you, I knew it was you and I remember thinking, I've met her finally, I've looked for her in school not knowing her name, but there she was and she was Tully. Jen's Tully. I didn't know your name,"* Jack sang, *"but I loved you just the same, even then, I loved you a little. Just a little, impersonally, the way we kind of like something that's far away, something outside our normal life. But all these years after she died, I wanted you to know I was not a nothing, I tried to be your friend, and then yes, miraculously, we were friends, and by that time I was lost in you, all I wanted was you, you were all I wanted. You had been so angry, so silent, so impenetrable, how I wanted you to let me in a little. I went away, came back, went away, came back, stayed longer, went away, and when I was away I looked forward to Christmas or to the summer when I could come back and see you, come back and take you to Lake Vaquero. I remember dancing with you at Shakie's wedding, and Robin coming over to rescue you from my grasping fingers. I've spent all this time trying to have you love me, I thought, she will change her heart, she will let me paint her house, finally, when she wants to be near me, and then I saw the time was near when I would paint your house, and all I thought was that I could indeed tell heaven from hell. . . ."*

"Well, Jack," Tully whispered back, "why did you wait so long to come near me in the end?"

"Because I wanted to be sure of you. I wanted you to be sure of you. What took you so long?"

"I love you, Jack Pendel. I didn't want in my short short life to be beaten with chains of pain."

But Jack had already fallen asleep underneath her, underneath her thighs, underneath her lips.

Sometime later Tully came to, still on top of him. Feeling her stir, Jack woke up. They made love again, had a quick shower, muttered at each other, and then got back into bed, bleary-eyed and exhausted.

"I gotta get home," said Tully. "I ought to at least make a pretense at some propriety."

"Who cares?" said Jack rudely. "He's never home, anyway."

That's true, thought Tully. But he is working, or playing rugby. It's not quite the same. "Still, though," she said vaguely.

"Still, though, nothing," said Jack. "You can't go. You said you would tell me everything."

Tully elbowed him in the ribs. "Did not. I said, what do you want to know?"

"I don't know," said Jack, smiling. "What is there?"

"This is not a restaurant," Tully declared. "Ask now, or I'm asleep in two seconds."

"Tell me about your father," he said quickly.

"Daddy, yes, uh-huh. Yes, he was with us awhile. You know, they were both uneducated and poor—"

"Kind of like me?" Jack interjected.

She smiled. "Nothing like you. Both worked in factories all day and we never had anything. But that was okay, you know, because, well, he was a real nice man. He always kissed me good night. I just think he never knew what to do with me. He didn't read very well, so he couldn't teach me to read. He was an only child, I think, and didn't know how to play with me. I think me going to school must have been the best thing that could have happened to them both. Suddenly, after five years, they breathed a sigh of relief that I was no longer just running around a fenced yard by myself all day while they weren't there. Anyway, it was when I started school that Hank was born. They didn't tell me I was going to have a brother, they just brought him home, like a done deal, and said, here, here's your little brother. There was none of that 'Come feel your brother or sister kick your mommy's tummy' nonsense beforehand.

"They named him Hank after my dad, Henry. He was kind of cute. He managed to outlive his infancy and was growing up into a little person. After school, Jen, Julie, and I used to come to the Grove and play with him.

"My dad, as you can imagine, flipped out over Hank. He still didn't know what to do with him, like feed him or bathe him or play with him, but he just had that look on his face of a smitten man—a man in love.

"Dad and Hank used to have this routine where every Saturday and Sunday morning after breakfast they would toddle to the candy store down the block and buy the newspaper and some candy. I used to have this routine where every Saturday and Sunday morning I would ask Dad to take me, too, and he would say, 'Natalie, we'll be right back. I'll bring you something, Natalie.'

"One Saturday morning, Dad had breakfast with us, washed his cereal bowl, put shoes on Hank and on himself, and said, like he always said, 'Hank and I are going for a little walk. We'll be right back.' I said, 'Take me with you.' He said, 'Natalie, Tully, we'll be right back. We'll bring you something, Tully. Right, Hank?' And Hank, who must have been around two, said, 'Yup, Tuwy wants candy.'

"Dad put on his hat and Hank's little cap. It was July—very hot and dry. 'I'll be right back, Hedda,' Dad said, as he said every Saturday. My mother nodded, didn't even turn from the sink.

"Leave your GI Joe's," Dad said to Hank. "We'll be right back."

"Every Saturday for about a year they had gone without me, but this particular Saturday, Dad came over to where I was sitting, bent down, and kissed me very hard on the top of my head, and kept his lips there for a moment. I saw his face in one of the glass cabinets. His eyes were shut tight. Then he scooped up Hank, and in his beige shorts, a white Topeka T-shirt, and old sneakers, walked out the kitchen door, down the steps, onto the driveway, and down the road to the corner."

Tully paused for breath while Jack stroked her leg with his fingers.

She continued. "Fifteen minutes went by. Mother and I cleaned the table. Half an hour went by, we washed the dishes. An hour went by, we started vacuuming. Two and a half hours later—at noon—my mother said, 'I'll be right back.' I said, 'I'll come with you.'

" 'I'll be right back, I said!' she told me, and left.

"I sat in the kitchen for a while, walked into the yard, walked outside to see if they were coming back. I rewashed the dishes and cleaned the windows. I changed my clothes. I packed my bag. I was seven. I just had no idea what was to happen next. I kind of walked around and imagined they all had left me— Henry, Hedda, and Hank, split and not looked back.

"I still remember I had this airless gut feeling for hours, this whooshing hole. I usually had it when I was by myself in the yard and no one was with me and the sun was going down. I never liked that much as a kid. I finally realized, though, that the whooshing noise wasn't actually inside me, it was just the din of the Kansas Turnpike. When I was little I used to actually like that turnpike. I used to look at it from the upstairs window and imagine all the places where it could possibly take me. There were so many places.

"But this time I wasn't thinking of the turnpike. I was inside the house and still heard the whooshing. So I sat there imagining monsters. I thought that if I had to be alone in that house when it got dark, I'd lose my mind. All I thought of was running into the street screaming, and being hit by the first passing car, the first passing car with *lights*.

"Hours went by, and then I kind of cheered up. I cheered up because I thought, Well, where would I go? And immediately thought, Jennifer."

"Why Jennifer and not Julie?" Jack asked her.

"Oh, there was never any question," said Tully. "Jennifer and I were just too much alike. When I was with Jen, I was home. I was never alone. Even at seven. For years we played together and we hardly ever talked. One might think we didn't know each other, but we knew nothing but each other. And I envied her her parents. Envied her their devotion.

"Anyway," Tully went on. "I almost started looking forward to my own parents not coming back. I started, in a kid kind of way, making up a life without them, without that yard, without those chickens and the chickenshit. I imagined another life and it didn't seem so bad, you know. I thought of all the sympathy, all the comforting, of all the people saying behind my back, 'There she goes, there's that girl whose parents ran away.' It started to seem funny to me. 'There is that girl, what do you think she could have done that they ran away from her?'

"So I sat on the couch, thinking all those things, and it began to get very dark and I got scared again. I didn't know what to do. I put my knees up to my chin and rocked myself back and forth on the couch and cried. God forbid I should have turned on any of the lights, right?"

"Did you believe in God then?" asked Jack.

"Hell, yeah," replied Tully.

"Was that what kept you from going nuts?" he wanted to know, kissing her shoulder.

"In the dark? No God could help me. No, not at all," Tully answered, kissing him back. "It was her coming back that did it. It must have been nine in the evening. I had been alone for nine hours.

"I kept saying, okay, I'll count to sixty and then I'll call Jen. Okay, I'll count to sixty again, slower, and then I'll call Jen. Okay, I'll count first to another sixty and then I'll definitely call Jen. I must have done that a hundred times.

"And then she came. She turned on the light in the living room and said, 'Natalie, take your feet off the couch.' And then she went to bed."

Jack stared at her.

Tully nodded. "Yes. Went to bed.

"I must have sat there and counted a thousand sheep before sleep slapped me. I woke up on the couch the next morning and then I went to bed."

Jack and Tully were silent.

After a while, he said, "Did she ever say anything to you about it?"

"Yeah," said Tully. "That Sunday. I asked her. I said, 'Ma, where are Daddy and Hank?' She said. 'I don't know.'

"I asked if they were coming back. 'I don't know,' my mother said to me. 'Would you?'"

"And that's it?" asked Jack.

"That's it," said Tully. "Needless to say, they never came back. Dad must have been planning it for some time because he disappeared off the face of the earth. The police looked for them for months. Dad must have known that unless he was meticulous, she'd hunt him down."

"Did anyone inquire at the candy store?"

"Of course," said Tully. "Apparently they came in as usual, bought the usual, and left. My dad tipped his hat, the saleslady said, and he never did that before."

"And that's it? No one saw them?"

"That's right."

"You've never heard from him at all?" asked Jack.

"That's right," replied Tully, her voice catching.

"Oh, hey, Tull, don't, babe, don't do it, please, hey, now, come on." He patted her back. She waved him off, fumbling on the floor for her bag and then feverishly rummaging through it.

"Tully, what are you looking for?"

"A cigarette," she said, and threw the bag on the floor.

"A cigarette? You don't smoke anymore."

"Yeah, right," she said. "I want to, though. I can't seem to get the cigarette out of my mouth."

He stroked her leg. "Take it easy, Tully," he said. "It's all right. It's the past. Forget it."

"Jack, you don't understand. You know what the worst part is?" She put her hand to her throat.

"The worst part is not him leaving us, leaving me, taking himself and my little brother who called me Tuwy away forever. The worst part is not even his running away and not leaving a note: 'Sorry, gal, couldn't close my eyes and imagine the futureless future with your mother.' No. The worst part is that he left without *me*! He left me with her. With HER! He didn't just run by himself, he took Hank, he took him because he loved him and didn't want him growing up with that monster, but he didn't take me! He didn't think enough about me, that I wanted to run away, too, and never come back! No, no, he abandoned me with her, and I could throw up my hands for a thousand years, but it won't change the fact that for five thousand days I did nothing but pay for his leaving. Won't change the fact that he did not think enough of me to take me with him . . ."

Tully lowered her head, furiously biting her lip, while all Jack could do was stroke her hair and whisper, "Tully, Tully, it will be all right, babe, it will be all right, I promise, it will all be all right."

She wiped her bleeding mouth with trembling hands. "Don't you see, Jack?" she said, shaking her head. "*Ceaselessly* into the past. It'll never be all right. It'll never be right. Never in my life, never between us, never. It will just come to pass, but my life will never leave the Grove."

"But that's not true, dear Tully," said Jack, wiping the blood off her mouth. "It will. One way or another, it will. Beat on."

IV

Natalie
Anne
Makker

But in Hope I breathe
Of course I don't believe
You're dead
And gone
All Dead
And gone

Brian May

All things betray thee who betrayest me

Francis Thompson

Breathe, breathe in the air
Don't be afraid to care
Leave, but don't leave me*

Roger Waters

*"BREATHE"
Words by Roger Waters; Music by Roger Waters, David Gilmour, and
Rick Wright
TRO—© 1973 Hampshire House Publishing Corp. New York, New York.
Used by Permission.

16

JENNY

October 1986

A month after Jack left, Tully spoke for the third year in a row in front of the Appropriations Committee, hauling every broken family she could think of into her entreaty for an eight-week training course for foster families. Tully pulled out every metaphor she had ever thought of, every analogy. She even, in a moment of great energy, lifted up her arms with wrists outward to show . . . she didn't know what. She was sure that gesture was lost on the eighteen committee members who sat at their long rectangular tables with their long poker faces. Though she certainly had their attention for the third year in a row.

But Tully must have worn them down. In November, the committee passed her amendment to the budget, 10–8, and gave Tully what she wanted. The training session for new foster families in the state of Kansas rose from six hours to eight weeks in 1987. This was a major step in the Foster Home Recruitment Agency and a major success for Tully, but all Tully could think of when she was being congratulated by Mr. Hillier was, We're treating the symptoms, we're treating the symptoms, we are treating the symptoms. That, and also that December was around the corner.

Tully thought of quitting after she got her training period, but stayed on as associate director of Special Projects. She actually got to hire two new people for herself, whom she trained for about fifteen weeks before she sent them out to train foster families for eight. Tully believed in her training program.

Statistics eventually bore her out and showed that truancy and delinquency for kids in new foster homes decreased by twenty percent from the year before. Tully was then given an even bigger staff budget, and she made Alan her assistant director. Sara and Joyce applied for the position, too, but Tully, while holding no grudges, never forgot their resistance to her efforts. The women remained, despite their doctoral training, at Lillian's capricious beck and call. Though Tully technically continued to report to Lillian, their paths rarely crossed and Lillian usually left Tully alone.

The week before Thanksgiving, 1986, Tully and Robin celebrated their fifth wedding anniversary. They had the party catered at the house on Texas Street and invited thirty people, all of them, with the exception of Shakie and Frank, Robin's friends from the soccer and rugby clubs. The festivities went on until three in the morning, and Robin had quite a bit to drink. After everyone had gone or crashed out and fallen asleep in the living room, Robin cornered Tully in the hall and then dragged her by the hand into the California room.

"Tell me, Tully, tell me," he said, leaning on her. "Has it been a good five years?"

Tully'd had considerably less to drink than he had. She gently pushed him away from her. "Go to bed. I would not call you sober as a judge."

"Answer me. Has it been a good five years?"

"Yes," she said. "It's been a good five years. Now go to bed."

Instead of going, he came up close and put his hands under her skirt. "Are you happy here with me, in your house on Texas Street?"

Tully was pinned against a wall and had nowhere to go. She didn't particularly want to go. "Well, this is the house of my childhood dreams," she said, holding on to his shoulders. Robin's hands were insistently rubbing her thighs. "Robin," Tully said quietly, "don't start anything you can't finish."

"Can't finish? Can't finish?" he said, pulling at her panties. "Just watch me."

They had sex on the floor of the California room, between the palm tree and the wicker loveseat, and afterwards Robin stared at the ceiling and said, "Do you want to get a divorce?"

Tully laughed. "Robin, what's wrong with you? We just made love, what are you saying?"

"I don't know what I'm saying," he said. "Would you tell me if you wanted to leave me?"

"I might let you know, yes," Tully said lightly. He was drunk and she was not taking him seriously.

"Do you think I work too much?" he asked her. "Bruce says I'm away too much. He says I have this young beautiful wife, and I'm away from her all the time. He says I'll be sorry when you take up with the gardener because you're alone all the time."

Tully lay on his chest. "We don't have a gardener," she said. "Except Millie. And trust me, I will not take up with Millie."

"Are you lonely, Tully?" Robin asked her.

She fell as quiet as the house.

"Sometimes," she answered. "But not because of you. If anything, you and Boomerang keep me from being alone."

Robin rubbed her hair, already falling into a drunken confusion. "Then why—are you—lonely, Tully?"

She didn't answer him, but it didn't matter. He had fallen asleep. She lay on him for a while, and then moved to get up. His hand came up and pushed her back down onto his chest. "Don't leave me, Tully," he mumbled. "Please . . . don't leave me."

Tully put her head back down on his chest and stayed there awake till morning.

Jack continued to return for Christmas and the summers. Tully held her breath and lived in between, cooking for her family and teaching Boomerang how to read. She even went dancing with Robin once or twice during the Cooking Season—the empty period between Jack's coming and going.

In the summers, Tully didn't cook. That was okay, because in the summers, Robin wasn't home much.

It was hard for Tully to let Jack go in 1986, but it was even harder in 1987 and 1988 after two more, intensely Jack-filled, summers. When Christmas, 1988, came around and Jack came around, too, Tully walked around with clenched fists for the month he was in Topeka, not wanting to explode, not wanting to make a scene. I'm not going to do it, she kept repeating to herself. I'm not going to do it.

"Jack," Tully said one Saturday night at their Meadow Acres Motel room on Topeka Boulevard. "I was thinking of going to Washington, D.C., this April."

"What for?"

"The Department of Health is having its annual foster care management seminar weekend. I thought I might go this year."

"That sounds great," Jack said, changing the TV channel.

Tully cleared her throat. "Is Washington nice in the spring?"

Jack looked away from the TV. "It's terrific. You'll like it."

"So . . . you've already been there, then?"

"Yeah, I've been there once or twice. Not warm enough for me."

He's being pretty obtuse, thought Tully. Well, I'm not going to ask him. Absolutely not.

"Jack, do you want to come to Washington for the weekend with me?"

He turned the TV off.

"You're giving me a weekend in Washington in the spring! That's nice, Tully."

She couldn't understand his tone. "Is that a yes or a no?"

"These seminars, they take all day?"

"No, no," Tully said quickly. "Well, Thursday and Friday they take all day, but at nights I'm free, and the whole weekend, except for a Saturday brunch."

"Ahhh," said Jack. "So I'll have my Sunday with you. That's nice."

She still couldn't read his tone. "Is that a yes or a no?"

"Sure," he said, lying back on the bed. "It'll be nice to see you in the middle of the year."

She moved next to him and stroked his face. "Not just see me, Jacko. But see me in Washington. And not just see me in Washington, but see me in Washington in the spring."

"Yes, I'm sure that will be delightful," said Jack tonelessly. "There is nothing quite like Washington in the spring. But it's not your *hometown*. Are you sure you'll be okay leaving Topeka?"

Topeka? What is he talking about? thought Tully. "Of course I'll be all right," she said, wanting to ask him what was the matter, but there were so many things inside that were the matter with her, she didn't want to give herself an opportunity to vent. So she kept her mouth shut.

April came, and Robin took Tully to Billard Airport. "We'll miss you," he said to her, and Tully smiled and hugged him, mouthing a reply. Something like, I'll miss you, too. But she was thinking only of the next four days. Jack had called her at work a few weeks ago, asking her if they were still on for D.C. Sure, she had replied, thinking, My God, I've been sustained by nothing else but this weekend for the last two months. What's going on with him?

The flight was three hours long with lunch and a movie. Tully lunched and slept, missing most of the film. She saw the ending: Meryl Streep was acquitted of killing her child.

Their room, registered in her name, was on the fourteenth floor of the Holiday Inn across the Potomac in Arlington. Tully dropped her bags near the door and called Robin before Jack arrived. While on the phone, Tully noticed the balcony. After hanging up, she went outside.

She had never been up so high in her life. Look at that. The city was sprawled out before her with the river at her feet. Not bad, she thought. Nice, even. But there were so many tall buildings, everywhere. Washington seemed really built up to Tully, compared with Topeka, where from the West Ridge Mall she could see horses grazing on the nearby hills.

Looking all the way down, Tully spotted what looked like a fountain glistening in the light. Coming close to the railing, Tully saw the highway several hundred feet below. The railing only came up to her waist. She leaned over it a little, thinking, What a long way down.

She heard Jack's voice. "Tully, what are you doing?"

She turned around and smiled. He dropped his bags on the floor and came up through the glass balcony doors. "Tull, why are you grinning like the Cheshire cat?"

Hugging her, he looked over the railing. "You're not thinking of making yourself into strawberry jam all over that highway, are you?"

"Jack!"

"That's what I thought. Okay, from now on, no unsupervised visits to the balcony." Jack bent his head down to hers, and when Tully felt his lips she closed her eyes and thought, I don't need this fucking city.

"Let's go eat," said Jack. But Tully, feeling faint at smelling him, had other ideas.

"Tully, man, what's gotten into you?"

"You," she mouthed to him, fumbling at his pants. YOU.

Afterwards, they had dinner in the hotel restaurant on the twenty-seventh floor. It was only five o'clock, and the place was empty. They sat at the best table, with a view that got to

Tully. She hardly touched her food. "I can't believe I ordered filet mignon, me, coming from cow country," she said. "Jack, let's go. Let's go, so I can smell what I see." She pointed with her hand to Washington.

They were sitting next to each other. Jack leaned over to Tully, putting his face into her neck. "I smell what I see," he whispered.

Tully was pleased with the way she looked. Her hair was halfway down her back, her gray eyes had on nothing but black mascara, and her lips red gloss. Tully was wearing a cream jersey tank top and a pink cotton skirt. She was flushed and excited, her neck was pale, and her hands, well, one almost didn't notice those scars, with her nails long and polished. She'd stopped biting them some years ago. Tully was pleased with the way she looked for him.

"Jack," she whispered back. "I look nothing like I did when you first saw me, do I?"

"Not much," he admitted, putting down his knife and fork. "You look better than ever."

She peered at him. "Do I look nearly thirty?"

"Tully, you just turned twenty-eight, for God's sake."

She pointed to her eyes. "See the wrinkles?"

"They're not wrinkles, they're laugh lines."

"That's funny," said Tully. "Because I never laugh."

He touched her lips. "You laugh sometimes. You laugh on Sundays."

She had to admit she sometimes did.

"How was your flight here?"

"Good, fine. I slept all the way."

"I guess you're an old pro at flying, huh?" And then, seeing her quizzical look, he said, "You have flown before, haven't you?"

"Never," said Tully.

The piano man played Beethoven's "Für Elise" to Jack and Tully, and then the *Moonlight Sonata* to Jack and Tully. Then the place started to get filled up with people and Jack and Tully left, without coffee or dessert.

It was seventy degrees out—a perfect April evening. They walked over to the Rosslyn train station of the newly opened Metro and, without knowing where to get off, alighted at L'Enfant Plaza.

"Where the hell are we?" said Tully, looking around. Every direction spanned block-long, six-story-high gray government buildings.

"I don't know," said Jack, looking at the map. "I guess we're right here."

"Guess so," said Tully.

The streets were deserted. "Just like Topeka," she commented. "What is it about capital cities?"

Tully and Jack strolled one block this way and one block that, until Tully pointed to a green patch a few blocks away.

"So this is the Mall, huh?" said Tully, coming out to the mile of grassy common surrounded by oak, running from the Washington Monument to the Capitol. The sun was behind the Monument, and the Capitol was bathed in golden light.

Jack and Tully slowly walked to the Capitol, then turned around and walked back to the Monument. He had his arm around her, and they both had little to say. Tully mentioned that in Topeka, she worked near the building fashioned after the nation's capitol, replete with a dome and everything, but she'd never seen the sun hit the Topeka City Hall in quite the same way.

"Could it be," inquired Jack, "that it's because at five o'clock you're always rushing away from the Capitol?"

Could be, Tully said.

They waited in line for forty-five minutes to get into the Monument. Open until midnight, it was the only option, besides dining, available to tourists in the late evening.

Tully liked it up there, but she couldn't see very much in the dark. In the gift shop, Jack bought her a picture of Washington with the full moon behind the Capitol, and then they took a taxi back to their hotel room.

"Look, we didn't even unpack earlier," said Tully, bending down to her suitcase.

"Who wants to unpack?" said Jack, coming up behind her.

"Not me," replied Tully.

After they had made love and were lying there on the verge of sleep, Jack said, "Is it safe?"

"Now you ask?" said Tully.

"Well, it only now occurred to me that you didn't take your little pill, like you usually do at night."

"Because this is my off week. I'm going to get my period any minute. I should've gotten it yesterday."

" Ah," Jack said. "Is it . . . safe, during your period?"

"Yes, Szell," replied Tully. "It's safe. What are you so worried about, Jack?" The question came out a bit shrill.

"I'm not worried much about anything," Jack assured her, but his tone was impersonal. Tully almost wished he would take her up on the challenge.

In the middle of the night, Tully woke up, feeling herself bleeding. Jack woke up, too, and came into the shower with her. They were sleepy but needy. He pulled her down into the bath and got on top of her. The water was beating down on his back and into her face, but she closed her eyes and held on to him as best she could.

"That was pretty neat," he said when they were all dry and in bed.

"Yeah," she agreed, but said no more, and then, later, when she had nearly drifted off, Tully asked, "Jack, do you like sleeping with me?"

"Sleeping with you or making love to you?" He didn't sound sleepy at all.

"Sleeping with me."

Lifting up his head to look at her, he said, "Yes, Tully, I like sleeping with you very much. I don't get to sleep with you very often, though, do I?"

"Not very often," she agreed, thinking, Well, maybe if you didn't insist on traveling eight months of the year . . .

"Tully, do you like sleeping with me?"

"Very much," she replied. "When I sleep with you, I don't wake up."

Jack put his hand on her belly. "That's because you're usually too exhausted."

"Maybe," said Tully, thinking, That's not it.

"What are you doing after this weekend?" she asked, and instantly regretted it, because he answered, "Flying back to California." And Tully didn't want to hear that. She didn't want to hear that at all. She lay and lay there; when she looked at the clock, it said four A.M.

"Jack," she said softly, looking up from the crook of his arm. "Are you asleep?"

His eyes were wide open, and he was staring at the ceiling.
"No," he said.

Boy, was Tully tired on Thursday. After barely sleeping, eight whole hours of the new social policy that affected local-level welfare work. Much of the seminar had little to do with her. If it did, she was too tired to notice. Thursday night, there was a reception Tully had to go to, so she didn't see Jack until eleven in the evening when she came back to the room exhausted and a little drunk.

"Did you dance?" he asked her as they got undressed.

"Of course I didn't dance. Who'd take me seriously if I danced?"

"Oh, you think they took you seriously wearing that?"

She looked at her dress. It was just a normal short black dress. "What's wrong with it?"

"Nothing," he said, turning on the TV.

Tully wanted to come over and slap down that fucking TV knob. What's wrong with it? she wanted to scream, but instead she clenched her fists and stormed into the bathroom.

Jack fell asleep, but she couldn't sleep very well. She went out on the balcony and breathed in the air. She liked the way Washington smelled. When Tully looked up at the sky, though, she was surprised by how dull it looked, how washed out, and the stars, why, she could hardly see them at all, they were just little sparks far away. The sky was not lit up. And there were noises. Car noises, people noises, city noises. There was not that great absorbent silence of the prairie at night.

Tully didn't stay on the balcony too long. She did not want to be not touching Jack. She didn't want to be so far away that she couldn't smell him. So she came back to bed and remained wakeful till dawn.

Friday was much the same, except Friday night, Jack and Tully ate at the upstairs restaurant again and listened to the piano. Danced once. Went to movies. Saw *Rain Man*, which had just won Best Picture of 1988 at the Oscars. After the film their conversation was limited to whether Dustin Hoffman gave a better performance in that than in *Kramer vs. Kramer,* and whether Tom Cruise held his own. Jack mentioned that Raymond seemed in worse shape than Jennifer had been. Tully wanted to point out, one, that Raymond was still alive, and two, that Raymond was fictional, but she let it pass.

Back in their room, Jack said, "Listen, why don't you not go to that silly brunch tomorrow?"

She shook her head. "I gotta go."

"No, you don't. Haven't you had enough of foster care for one week? You have to leave on Sunday. Come on. Let's have a full day, for fucking once."

He said it amiably enough, but Tully stared at him, perplexed. What *was* that in his voice? Jack smiled thinly.

Tully sighed. "Look, I'll see. Okay? Now, listen. I hope you don't mind, but I have to call Robin."

He said he did mind, actually.

"Jack, please. I have to talk to Boomerang. It's not a big deal. I haven't called home since Wednesday."

"I didn't know you called home on Wednesday."

"I called before you came," she admitted. "Called to say I arrived safely."

"I see," he said. "Well, would you like me to leave the room?"

What an odd question. "No," Tully replied slowly. "I'll only be a minute." Again the question came up in her throat. What the hell is wrong with you? she felt like shouting. Gritting her teeth, Tully sat by the bed and dialed Texas Street. Jack walked out onto the balcony.

"Robin! Hi. How's everything?"

"Hi, Tully. Boomerang! Mommy's on the phone!"

She talked to her son for about ten minutes. He couldn't get enough of her. In the background, she heard Robin muttering for Boomer to get off the phone.

"Hi again," he said when he finally got the receiver back. "Are you having a good time?"

"Yeah, it's okay," turning her back to the balcony. "I'll be home on Sunday."

"I'll pick you up," Robin said. "We miss you."

What could she say to that? And she couldn't lower her voice, either. "Well, I miss you, too, my guys," she said clearly. "I'll see you Sunday."

When Jack came back inside, his face was all distorted. My God, Tully thought. What's happening?

On Saturday, they got up at seven, and in the morning Jack seemed happier. Tully cheered up herself; she didn't go to brunch.

They made love—with the curtains open!—had room service in bed, showered together, made love again right there in the bath, and were miraculously out by nine-thirty.

They took in the White House, Lafayette Square, and Pennsylvania Avenue. Lunch was tuna sandwiches in the secluded courtyard of the National Portrait Gallery, and afterwards they walked across the Mall trying to find Archie Bunker's chair, but had failed to find it by five in the afternoon when all the museums closed.

"Let's walk to the Lincoln Memorial," said Jack.

Tully scrunched up her face and whined. "My feet are killing me."

"Why are you wearing high-heeled sandals?" he demanded.

"I want to look nice for you," she said.

"I like you barefoot. Like you are at Vaquero. The less you have on, the better."

They slowly trod to the Reflecting Pool. The winding line for the Washington Monument was three times as long as Wednesday night's. "I bet they're going to see more than we saw," said Tully.

"Yes, but they'll have to wait three hours to see it," said Jack.

At the Reflecting Pool, Tully and Jack ran into a black girl of about four, trying to get the little baby ducks to swim over to her. Tully crouched down to the girl and Jack took some pictures.

"Where is your mommy?" Tully asked "Over there," said the girl, Samantha, and over there was a football field away, where on a bench, hidden behind the oak trees and bushes, sat a black woman paying a lot of attention to a black man.

"Samantha," said Tully, peering into the girl's face. "Maybe you should go back to your mommy and daddy."

"That's not my daddy," said Samantha. "My daddy is in the West Indies. That's Peter."

"So why don't you go back to them, honey?" said Tully.

"No. He might be mad I ran so far," said Samantha.

Jack pulled on Tully and she reluctantly resumed walking toward the Lincoln Memorial. The girl followed, talking to them about the ducks and the cherry trees and the water, which, apparently, did not look very clean to Samantha. Jack took more pictures. Samantha asked if she could borrow Tully's

newly bought funky yellow baseball cap that said I LOVE
WASHINGTON, which Tully wore backwards. Tully immediately took the hat off, and Samantha put it on backwards,
too. Tully anxiously looked back to the bench. Out of sight.
The mother couldn't even see Samantha now, couldn't see her
talking to strangers. Jack and Tully continued to walk as slowly
as they could, and the girl followed; then—finally—there was
a distant "SAMAAAANTHA!"

In a while, a robust, smiling young woman caught up with
them and said, "Samantha, how come you go so far?"

"I'm sorry, Mama," said Samantha. "Will Peter be mad?"

"No, babe, he'll not be mad," said Mama, glancing at Jack
and Tully. "Now, let's go back. Give the nice lady back
her hat."

Samantha looked at Tully and reluctantly started to take off
the cap. Tully shot Jack a quick look. He had bought her the
cap in the morning, while they were having hot dogs near the
White House. Jack rolled his eyes and nodded. Tully leaned
down and said, "Keep the hat, Samantha. It's yours."

Satisfied, Samantha plopped it back on her head. "Thank
you," she grumbled, then turned around and ran back. "I hope
she's been no trouble," said Samantha's mother.

"No, no trouble," said Tully, and Jack put his arm around
her.

Tully stared in wonder at the plaque above Abe Lincoln's
head that read *"In the hearts of the people for whom he
saved the Union, the memory of Abraham Lincoln is enshrined
forever."*

"Boomerang loves Lincoln," she said to Jack. "He'd love
to see this."

"Yeah," said Jack. "Maybe you can bring Robin, too."

God!

But Tully knew, if she opened her mouth, if she reacted,
there'd be no going back. They'd have to stand and fight right
under the memory to Abraham Lincoln.

It was six o'clock and nearly sunset when they walked to
the back of the Lincoln Memorial, sat on the grass, and looked
onto the Potomac and Memorial Bridge that led to Arlington
Cemetery.

"Is that Robert E. Lee's house up there?" asked Tully.

Jack nodded.

"In the dark, I wonder if you can see the light on Kennedy's grave," Tully mused.

"I don't think so. It's only a little flicker."

"Hey, an eternal little flicker, okay?"

"Okay," said Jack, pulling her down on the grass. "Let's go and see those cherry blossoms at the Tidal Basin. Let's go before it gets dark."

"I want to go up there," said Tully, pointing to Arlington.

"Of course you do. How silly of me to think you'd rather see cherry blossoms than a grave," Jack said, getting up and extending his hand to her. "Tully, you don't want to go up there when it's getting dark. We'll go tomorrow."

Tully did not move. Okay. This was as good a place as any.

"What's the matter with you, Jack?"

He continued to loom over her, blocking her view of Arlington Bridge and of the cemetery.

"Nothing is the matter with me," he said coolly. "What's the matter with you? Why do you keep clenching your fists and gritting your teeth all the time?"

"Because I have no idea what the hell is going on."

"Nothing's going on," Jack said, sitting back down on the grass. Ah, now, that's better, she thought. The sun to the right of her felt warm on her face. "Nothing at all, right, Tully?"

"What's going on between us, Jack? What's happening?"

"Nothing is going on between us. Nothing is happening to us. Right, Tully?"

Right? Right what? "What do you mean by that?" she demanded.

Jack was quiet. "Tully, let's go and see the cherry blossoms. Please. We're leaving tomorrow and we won't get a chance to see them again. Let's go. We'll have plenty of time to talk about all this."

"When? You're constantly away! No, I want to talk about this now. Fuck the cherry blossoms. What do you mean, nothing is happening between us?"

"I mean," Jack said pointedly, "that nothing's happened between us in two and a half years."

"Yeah, well, maybe if you were actually in Topeka and didn't keep running away every couple of months, something would happen!" she exclaimed.

"Well, maybe if you weren't married"—he raised his voice—
"I wouldn't keep running away and something *would* happen,
hey, Tully?"

Tully opened her mouth to shout back but suddenly had
nothing to say.

"Okay," she said, getting up. "Let's go and see the cherry
blossoms."

Utterly silent, they walked along the Potomac.

Tully's feet were sore. She took her white sandals off and
walked barefoot for a while, but the pebbles and the rough
pavement hurt the soles of her feet, and when she walked on
the grass, the blades cut them, forcing her to put her shoes
back on.

Finally Jack carried her, and Tully rubbed her cheek against
his.

"I'll just call you my porcupine face," she whispered.

"Careful," said Jack. "Porcupines leave hair in their victims."

Tully rubbed her face harder against his. "So leave some in
me, Jacko," she said.

When Tully and Jack crossed the road to the Tidal Basin
at dusk, they started to notice an odd assortment of people
lining the sidewalk with their friends and their cigarettes and
the roads with their beer cans and their loud, nearly alive
cars. Tully wanted to go to the bathroom but immediately
reconsidered, seeing the clientele and the smelling the odor,
both emanating from said bathroom.

"Jack," said Tully, taking his arm. "Maybe we could get up
extra early tomorrow and come see the cherry blossoms?"

"Sure," Jack said, and hailed a taxi.

"So Tully," he asked when they were safely inside the cab,
"tell me, why did you take me to Crack Row?" Pointing to the
road they had just walked.

"I wasn't the one who carried you, Jacko," said Tully, and
felt better.

They had dinner at a French restaurant in Georgetown.

"Want to resume our talk?" asked Jack. "What are we going
to do about us?"

Tully sighed. Oddly, she didn't want to resume their talk.
She wasn't prepared for Jack's gripe. She had thought she was
the only one entitled to be indignant.

Jack repeated his question. "What are we going to do about us?"

"I don't know, Jack," she said, irritated. "I didn't think you wanted to do anything in particular about us."

"Right. And you certainly don't want to do anything in particular about us. Wait," he added. "That's not entirely true. You'd like me to hang around Topeka for you to see on Sundays. But remember, Tully, it's cold in Kansas in the wintertime. Besides Lake Vaquero, we have nowhere else to go."

"We can go someplace else," she said feebly.

"Like where? Burger King? Or a motel that rents by the hour?"

Tully sat there stunned. "Wow," she said at last. "I didn't know you could be this nasty."

He sneered. "You have no idea what you want, do you?"

"I know precisely what I want," she retorted uncertainly. She pointed to him across the table. "Do you know what you want?"

"You. That's it. Nothing else. Why do we have this problem?"

Because! she wanted to shout. You keep going away and breaking my heart to pieces, making me not want to live, making me want to roam the earth until I find you or die, making me as blue as the fields at dawn. That's why.

"Because you keep going away," she said in a small voice.

"I'm in Topeka for the whole summer."

"You keep going away," she continued, "and I miss you. I never know if you're coming back."

"I call you nearly every week!"

"You keep going away," she said doggedly.

They had long ago stopped eating their food, that now lay cold before them.

"Yeah? And what would you have me do, Tully Makker? What, precisely? Would you have me live with my mother and see you on Sundays at church? For lunch on the weekdays? On Saturdays when you can get away from Shakie? Once a year we'd come here for two days? Exactly what would you have me do?"

Tully was mute, staring at her food. "You don't like Topeka," she said at last. "You don't want to settle there."

"Settle to what?" he said sharply. "Oh, and you do?"

Tully didn't look at him. "You never asked me to come away with you," she said.

"Well, you never asked me to stay in Topeka," he countered.

She folded and refolded her napkin. "Would you if I asked you?"

"Would you come away with me if I asked you?"

Tully's hands began to shake.

Jack leaned over the table, grabbing her fingers. "Tully, what about Robin?"

Tully started picking at her old food so that she'd have something to do with her hands. "What about him?" she said.

"We don't talk about him."

"What's to talk about?"

He held the fingers on her left hand, touching the diamond ring and the wedding band. "You never take the rings off," he said quietly.

Tully smiled apologetically. "I know. My fingers got fat. The rings are permanently meshed into my skin." And tried to take her hand away.

Jack let go. "Why do you stay married?" he asked.

"Stay married?" The question made no sense to Tully. "As opposed to what?"

"As opposed to leaving him," Jack replied.

"Leaving him?" Tully was incredulous. "Whatever for?"

"Whatever for?" Jack snapped up his fork. "Whatever fucking for?"

Tully reached out, but he pulled roughly away.

"Jack," she said quietly. "Okay, okay, I understand you have to go away from Topeka once in a while. I just miss you, that's all."

"Is that all? I thought you wanted to go away from Topeka, too, Tully."

Tully really wanted to stop talking about this now. They had laid so many plans when they were together, but they were all dreams. Dreams of peace and freedom and swimming every day and teaching their kids to swim, and living in a white house. Dreams. The kind that everybody made after breathless sex.

What about Robin, indeed? Tully could kick herself for bringing up her stupid complaints at the Lincoln Memorial.

Why did she have to open her big fat mouth? Everything was so much easier when they weren't discussing what was wrong. God, nothing was so wrong that this conversation couldn't make wronger. Why did she open her mouth?

"How long am I supposed to keep coming back in the summers for you, Tully?"

I don't know, she wanted to say. Forever?

Summers, how she looked forward to the summers! Last summer must have been the happiest summer of her life, the very happiest. Last summer and the one before that and the one before that one . . .

Every grain of sand that got between her toes at Lake Vaquero, every duck they fed and each time they rowed the boat reminded her then and there that she was in love for the first time in her life. She had never been happier than when she was with him. As Tully tearfully made love to him and fed him and watched him paint, she was fully aware that her house of little illusion had the illusion of happiness that was as real as the pebbles between her toes.

How long am I supposed to keep coming back for you, Tully? The implied threat in his question made her sick with fear. Fear that her life before him would return. All those days in the yard, all those nights at Tortilla Jack's, all those locker rooms, all those boys, all those years she went doggedly about her day, looking only to get through one and not think about what was ahead. She had had little hope, she had had little future, a girl from the Grove, from the beaten houses, from a life she deserted when Henry Makker deserted her, when Jennifer Mandolini deserted her. How could she go back to having nothing again?

For the last thirty months Jack Pendel had been the sound of California and the sound of Jen. The only thing that was missing was the surf. Ah, but the sound of him.

Deciduous Tully. Her leaves fell and died when he would leave her, but yet, the gloom of sitting on the bathroom floor with the rugs all moved out, pressing towels to her wrists, well, that hadn't happened in a long time.

Also, she slept better.

In the winters, Tully cooked for Robin, who came home early to sit at their table together and eat the food she cooked for him. Then, on the floor, they would sit and play Candy

Land with Boomerang and help him do his homework.

Robin would bathe him and then Tully would read to him as Robin sat rocking behind her in the wooden chair. Then they would talk, in the bathroom or in the kitchen or in bed. They talked about his business and her work, they talked about their son, and about her mother. Hedda was feeling much better. She was walking again and talking, too, unfortunately.

In the winters Robin and Tully watched a movie, ate a late snack, and then went to bed and made love. Tully found that when Jack was away, she wanted to make love to Robin more than ever.

Summers were a different story . . . Tully hardly saw Robin in the summers. He worked late, played a lot of sports, took Boomerang with him on the weekends, and often stayed with Bruce or Steve until late on Sunday. Tully did not cook much, and they did not make love much, or talk. In the summers, Robin left her alone and that was enough for Tully. But when Jack wasn't there, Robin was there all the time, and that was enough for Tully, too.

"How long do you want to keep coming back in the summers, Jacko?" she finally asked.

He grabbed her hands from across the table. "Tully!" he whispered intensely. "California, Tully! California! Us, together, all the time, and sunshine all the time, too, and the sea, you've never seen such a sea until you've seen the Pacific. We'll get a house, I'll paint, you'll work, or whatever, we'll have some babies, and they'll grow up on the beach, and we will, too, in heat and on the beach. That's what I want, Tully, that's what I want with you."

Her heart was beating so fast. She tried to pull her hands away, but he was holding on to them tight.

"Are you asking me to come away with you, Jack?"

"Yes, Tully, yes."

She again tried to pull her hands away. This time he let her.

"I'm sorry, Jacko," she said. "I'm just a little surprised, that's all. This is a little all of a sudden, isn't it?"

"Sudden?" Jack glared her incredulously and then laughed. "You are really something else! Something else, Tully Makker. We've talked about it for three years, we talk about it every summer. What the hell are you talking about, sudden?"

For some reason, Tully wanted to correct him this time. *DeMarco*. How ridiculous. I haven't wanted to correct him in years.

"Why don't we talk about it later?" she said. "Let me sleep on it awhile."

"Okay, Tully," he said gravely. "But we're going to talk about it before the weekend is over."

"What do you mean?" she said. "The weekend is over tomorrow." And seeing his raised eyebrows, Tully sighed. "Let me ask you. If I hadn't brought up what was wrong, were you ever going to talk to me about all this?"

"God, Tully! Yes, I would have talked to you about this. How long do you think two people can go on like this? I think three years is just about my limit. I would've had to talk to you about it sooner rather than later."

"And say what?" Tully wanted to know. "And do what?"

"No ultimatums. Tully. No nothing," said Jack, waving the waiter down for the check. "No. If you felt like you wanted to stay with your husband, then I would bow out of the picture. If you wanted me, then we'd go to California. But Tully," Jack said, "I cannot go on this way much longer. I need to wake up with you more than twelve times a year. I need . . ." he trailed off.

"You all have so much need," Tully said quietly.

He paid the check.

"Yes, and you? You need two men."

"Do you?" she asked, smiling uncomfortably. "I mean, do you need two women to satisfy you?"

"No, Tully," Jack replied.

"So what do you do for the eight months of the year when you don't see me?"

"Well, tell me, what does your husband do for the four months of the year you're checked out of the marriage?"

She was thrown back by that question. I'm not checked out of the marriage, she wanted to say, but, fearing he was right, she said nothing.

They walked back down Connecticut Avenue looking for a way to get to Francis Scott Key Bridge. The night was warm, but there were few people on the street. After they got to Dupont Circle, Jack and Tully turned down New Hampshire and then again at M Street, and finally, there it was—the

Potomac, with the city reflected in its waters, and all the streetlights dancing on its shiny surface. They stopped on the bridge and looked to the left at the Kennedy Center for Performing Arts and, farther on down, the Lincoln Memorial, always lit, always drowning in light, and across the river, on the south bank, Arlington Cemetery, and as hard as Tully looked she could not see the light at Kennedy's grave. Jack must be right. It must only be a little light.

"We're two miles away from it, Tully," said Jack, as if reading her mind. "On the other side of the river. We can barely see our hotel, which is a twenty-seven-story building."

As they neared their hotel, Jack said to her, "We missed the parade. There was a parade today, cherry blossom parade, where were we?"

"Together," said Tully.

Then she kissed his upper arm, adding, "We also missed the cherry trees."

"Well, if you hadn't insisted on showing me Crack Row . . ."

Upstairs in their room, he said, "Cherry blossoms tomorrow morning?"

"Arlington tomorrow morning."

"Ah, I forgot," said Jack. "Arlington, of course."

"I'll show you, Arlington," she said, grabbing on to him, and they could hardly wait to get their clothes off. They made love between the bathroom and the closet, right on the carpet near the door.

After making their way to the bed a little while later, they lay quietly, and as the silent television flickered cold blue light on them, Tully circled Jack's lips with her fingers, murmuring, while he lay on his back and stared at the ceiling.

"Jack," she whispered, "we're together. Isn't that everything?"

"So everything," he said, "that I'd like to have it every day."

"But Jack, you're a loner. You're twenty-nine years old and been on your own since you were nineteen. You told Shakie you couldn't take care of anybody. She believed you. And I kinda do, too."

"I didn't want to be taking care of Shakie," said Jack.

"So what's changed?"

"I didn't love Shakie."

Tully moved away from him on the bed. He lifted himself up and got on top of her. "What, Jacko, what?" she whispered.

"Tully, do you love me?"

"Jack, I love you."

"How much?"

"Like I love myself," she answered.

"Is that a lot?"

"Jack," said Tully, "the kinship I feel with you is closer than any bond I've ever felt with anyone."

"Except for her."

"Because of her," said Tully.

"Except the bond you must feel to Boomerang."

All of a sudden, Tully had trouble breathing. She tried to get out from underneath him. Tried to move her head from side to side so she wouldn't be so close to him.

She caught her breath and said quietly, "Jack? Have you ever wanted a baby of your own?"

"What, so that he or she could live in a tent with me? Run around in my Mustang with me? Drink tequila with me?"

"Never even a little?"

"I guess a little. I don't think much about it. I guess I don't want to die and have nothing left of me. But I belong nowhere and to no one, how could I even think about babies?"

"Yes, but the baby would belong to you. And you would belong to it."

"Does Boomerang belong to you?"

To me, and to Robin. Tully had to, *had to* get out from under him. She felt herself suffocating. "Get off me, please," she whispered. "Get off me."

Jack rolled off her. "Did you want a baby before you had one?" he asked.

"Not much," she said, breathing hard.

Jack turned to her. "You're my baby," he whispered. "*Be-bop-a-loola . . .*"

She turned her back to him, and he sidled up close, rubbing against her, kissing her, playing with her hair.

"Come away with me, Tully," he whispered into her back. "Please come away with me."

Tully closed her eyes. If she could've, she would've shut her ears, too.

"Why, Jack?"

"Because I love you, Tully, and I don't want to be alone anymore."

After lying in bed for a while with the TV on mute, Jack said, "Do you ever think about her?"

She clutched at the blanket. "Not when I'm with you. Don't need to."

"We don't talk much about her anymore."

"'What's there to talk about?" Tully said.

"Are you still angry at her?"

Tully shook her head slowly. "No." And moved closer to him on the bed, putting her head on his chest. She listened to his heart beat, and thought, I'm not so lonely anymore, either.

"Tell me a story about her, Tully. Something new."

Tully had stories to tell him, all right, but she wasn't going to tell him those stories. She thought of an easier story. All of a sudden, remembering and then talking about Jennifer was easier than talking about themselves.

When we were nine or ten or so, we were lying in her backyard, we were supposed to be in the tent, sleeping, but you know slumber parties in the summer. We were lying on the grass, and she said to me, "Imagine if the sky was the ocean, and all the water would just fall on us right now."

And I said, "There's no ocean in America."

She said, "That's where you're wrong, Tully Makker. There's the Atlantic on one side, and the Pacific on the other. The Pacific is bigger. It's also closer, I think."

"There is no ocean in Kansas," I said.

"No," she said, "but do you know why it's called the Pacific?"

"Because it's so calm all the time?" I said. I didn't want to talk about the silly ocean anymore.

"No," she said. "Because it's so stormy all the time. Because the worst storms, the worst tidal waves, the worst sea disasters happen on the Pacific."

"Whoopee," I said.

"I want to see it," she said. "I want to go to the ocean and see the very worst disaster ever. Like a big tidal wave swallow up California whole. And I'd be standing there watching it."

"I didn't know California was so small."

"It isn't. It's huge. Don't you know anything? But the Pacific is even bigger than California. It could swallow it up."

"Well, California's not bigger than Kansas," I said. I was feeling pretty grumpy.

"Sure it is," she said.

"No it isn't! Kansas is the biggest state. It's huge. I know it is. There is no place bigger than Kansas! Not even your stupid California."

She shrugged. "Have it your way, Tully Makker. But I still want to stand on the edge of the world and see the Pacific ocean."

A few weeks after that, she got her parents to subscribe me to National Geographic.

I didn't read them for the first year, I was still so upset for my poor Kansas. Then I read them. The subscription continued until I was eighteen. I subscribed myself after I got married, but it just wasn't the same. I hardly ever had time to read them after I got married.

"Thank you, Tully," said Jack. "That was a good story. About you."

"It was about her, too," she said defensively.

"About you, Tully. Everything you've ever told me about her has been about you. Also," he added, "that wasn't the story you wanted to tell me. You had another story, but picked this one. Why?"

"There is no other story," Tully said quickly.

"Yeah, and there are no scars on your wrists, either."

Jack got on top of her again, and Tully was running her nails on his back. She closed her eyes and imagined she was Jennifer. Imagined she was Jennifer on New Year's Eve, touching her first guy, and not just her first any guy. Touching *him.*

"Jacko," Tully whispered. "I love you. How incredible that life and death should both be wrapped up in you." She rubbed his chest with her hands. "How was it for you to make love to her?"

"Good, I think. I was quite drunk. It seemed pretty good. Did she say anything about it?"

"Not much," said Tully. "I meant, how was it to touch her?"

"I don't know," Jack said. "Nice. She was a big girl. I remember that pretty well. She had terrific breasts."

Tully rolled out from under him, rolled on her back, and shut her eyes. "She did, didn't she?" said Tully.

Jack nudged her, and when she didn't move, he nudged her again, turned her on her stomach, and lay on top of her back, whispering into her neck.

"You're better now, Tully," he said. "Those years you lived on Kansas Avenue, you seemed devoid of feeling."

"Yeah," said Tully, once again having the tingling sensation in her fingertips. Numb. "You know, back then I couldn't even pronounce her name out loud."

"What do you mean, then? You still can't. Not without flinching. Like every time you say her name you get a toothache."

"Yeah, well . . ." she trailed off. "Did you know that last week was ten years? Ten years since that Monday."

"Ten years, it's a long time, Tully," Jack said softly, rubbing against her. "Tull, back then did you think it all was going to end *that* badly?"

"I don't know, Jack," she said. "I don't know anymore. In those days, I came home every day and every day I couldn't sleep, and every day I wanted to know where was my way, and what was there for me. I kept my head close to the ground, who was I to know anything? What could I see, with my own soul half in the grave, half in the past?

"She always talked about the future, incessantly. She had all these hopes, all these plans, she never stopped: working, studying, planning, never . . . until . . . and when she did, I think now that nothing could have brought her back. I couldn't help her, and that's my shame."

Jack didn't say anything, and Tully turned her head to look at him. His hands were over his eyes, and all of a sudden a surf, a tidal wave of pity knocked her over, washed over her, and when Tully surfaced again there he was, Jack Pendel, with his hands over his eyes. Tully wiped her face and whispered, *"Oh, Jack, oh, Jack, Jack, no."* She got on top of him, removed his hands, and then kissed his face. *"No, Jack, no. I love you, I love you,"* she whispered adoringly, rubbing his face with her face. *"I love you."*

And when they made love again, it was all she could do to hang on to the headboard with both her hands, hang on, rough and tight and hard. Hang on so she wouldn't slip away from him. Her eyes closed, she moaned and smelled him as he moaned into her mouth and she held on held on tight hard held on—

There was a crashing noise.

What the hell happened? Oh, my God, the headboard broke!

Just broke. It was down on the floor between the wall and the bed not doing anybody any good, and Jack and Tully laughed. Tully said, "I have nothing to hold on to now," and Jack replied, "Hold on to me," offering her his arms as he leaned over her, and she thought, Yes, yes, oh, yes.

"Have you seen this bed, Tully?" Jack said the next morning, smiling at her. Tully chuckled. Besides the broken headboard, the sheets were a mess.

"Jack," she said, touching the sheets, "we better check out in a hurry, or the police—and all the maids—will be after you."

It was seven in the morning. They must have slept for only two or so hours, but there was so much to do still and this was their last day.

Jack and Tully had some hash browns, eggs, and oatmeal in the breakfast café downstairs, then checked out, leaving their bags at the reception desk. The Iwo Jima statue was their first stop, but the taxi driver was new and couldn't find the right road. They drove past the Pentagon instead. Tully shook her head, glaring at the driver and at the map.

Finally, Iwo Jima. So proud, the monument to the men who fought in all the wars since World War I. Huge, too. "It dwarfs even you, Jack," Tully said, taking photos.

"Dwarfs, huh?" he said. "I'll show you, dwarfs."

At nine in the morning, Arlington opened. Tully and Jack walked over from Iwo Jima. That wasn't too bad, but then the hike up was long.

"I see you're still wearing your extra comfortable shoes," said Jack, looking at Tully's white sandals.

"Have to look good for you, even in a cemetery," she replied, limping up the hill.

He grabbed her around the waist. "You always looked good for me in a cemetery, Tully."

"Don't be such a romantic," she said.

There weren't too many people this time on a Sunday, only a few stray couples and a family heading up.

Kennedy's grave was so plain. JOHN FITZGERALD KENNEDY, the plaque said. 1917–1963. A single artificial rose, no other flowers, lay there. A few feet above, the eternal flame burned and flickered in the early morning breeze.

They stood there for a while, and Tully, in a gesture more convulsive than conscious, crossed herself, and then, with embarrassment, looked around. Another woman saw her, smiled, and crossed herself, too. Tully stood closer to Jack, who put his arm around her.

Tully gazed at the city that lay in the valley beyond Kennedy's grave. "What a sight to see this at your feet, every day and every night for eternity."

Jack gently prodded Tully to walk on. "Yes, did you know that when Kennedy saw the view from Robert E. Lee's house for the first time, he said that when he died, that's where he would like to be buried, on top of Washington, D.C.?"

"I didn't know that," said Tully. "Let's go up to Robert E. Lee's house."

They walked to the left, past Robert Kennedy's grave and up to Robert E. Lee's house. And then they sat on the grass and looked down over the city.

"Don't you think it's amazing how long people can grieve?" said Tully.

"Astounding," he agreed. "What do you mean?"

"Did you know that Ted Kennedy comes every November twenty-second to kneel at his brother's grave?"

"He loved his brother," said Jack.

"Of course," Tully said. "But that was twenty-six years ago. You'd think he'd be over it."

Jack glanced at her. "You'd think that, wouldn't you?" he said. "But you'd be wrong."

Tully was quiet and then turned to face him. "Jack," she said, "I don't want to lose you. I don't want to ever lose you."

He took her hand. "You won't lose me, Tully. You won't ever lose me."

"I want to be with you more than anything, but I need to tie up my life. You understand?"

Squeezing her hand, he said, "I understand. If I know you'll come with me, I'll wait."

"Jack, listen to me. What about Boomerang?" When Tully spoke her son's name aloud, she felt herself suffocating.

"What about him? He comes with us, of course. I love Boomer. He comes, too. He'll love the beach. We'll get him a dog. Boys love to run with their dogs on the beach."

Her throat constricted, Tully said, "Yeah, good. That sounds nice."

They spent a long time at Arlington. After meandering through the graves, going up, up, up, through the trees and a bridge, walking around a medium-sized white amphitheater, they came to the changing of the guard at the Tomb of the Unknown Soldier. Tully was so impressed with the ceremony that she wanted to stay another half hour for the next guard change. Jack sighed but obliged her.

They never managed to get to the Tidal Basin. They didn't have enough time, for Tully's plane was leaving at one. A taxi took them to the airport.

Jack held her bags while she pressed her face against his chest. "I had a great time," she said into his shirt. Jack cupped her head with his free hand and said, "We came here to have a great time. And we talked, at last."

"Yes," she said. "At last."

"Did you like Washington?" he asked her.

"It was great," Tully replied gaily, but she was thinking about being able to see the cottonwoods from West Ridge Mall.

Jack watched Tully disappear through the departure gate, and then took a taxi to the Lincoln Memorial. He trod their yesterday's path along the Potomac, toward the Tidal Basin. He sat on the white marble steps of the Jefferson Memorial, and looked at the basin, the little paddleboats, the Washington Monument, the White House, and the cherry blossoms.

A few months later, in June, Tully and Robin were having pizza. He had gotten home around six and there was nothing to eat. It was summer. Millie had already left for the day so they ordered half sausage, half plain, with some garlic rolls,

Tully was quiet. Preoccupied. She hardly listened even to Boomerang.

"How's work?" Robin asked her.

"Great," she said. "Worse than usual."

"What's up?"

What's up. Tully quickly glanced at Robin. What did he ask me again? Oh, God, yes. Work.

"The Slatterys got their kids back," she said.

"Oh, no. Tully, that's awful. I'm sorry. How?"

"Lillian, you know. And Dr. Connelly, too. They both felt that after three years, Mr. and Mrs. Slattery had been punished long enough and deserved another chance. So Jason, Kim, and Robbie went back two weeks ago."

"What did you do?"

"There was nothing I *could* do. Strangely, they didn't ask me to sit in on any counseling sessions this time around."

"Tully, you should have pressed charges."

"There are a lot of things I should've done," she snapped. Robin fell quiet. Boomerang excused himself and left the table.

Tully changed her tone. "I got my second written warning from the department the other day," she said brightly.

"One more and you're out? What for this time?"

"I sat in on parent-child evaluation. I hate those interviews, but I must attend them. I'm the one assigning foster families to these kids."

"You didn't think the parents should have their kid?"

"Of course I didn't. When do I ever?"

"Sometimes kids *should* go back to their parents," said Robin.

"Sometimes," allowed Tully. "Do you know how many permanent parent-child relocations there have been in the eight years I've been with the agency? Six. That's not even one a year. Not good odds, would you say? Anyway, this Miss Connor wanted her little girl back. She said she was a changed woman, a woman who saw the error of her ways, and was now going to take good care of Karen Connor."

"Error of her ways?"

"Yeah, you know, small things, like freebasing in her relatives' homes with her daughter watching. Miss Connor had never held down a job for longer than a couple of weeks and has been a patron of Social Services for most of her life. She probably spends most of that money getting higher than a Learjet. When the relatives found out about Miss Connor's creative pharmacology, they reported her to Social Services, who took her benefits away. So she left her four-year-old Karen with a distant great-aunt and went to Wichita, where she bartered for drugs. Finally, she got pregnant, came back to Topeka, and that's when I met her, trying to claim young Karen as her own to, I presume, get more aid for parents with dependent children."

"Sounds stable to me," said Robin.

"Solid as a rock," agreed Tully. "She was now claiming that she was off drugs, was going to get a regular job in no time, and wanted her daughter reunited with her soon-to-be-born sibling. But the distant great-aunt a couple of months ago applied to adopt the child and didn't want to let Karen go."

"So you—"

"I patiently outlined Miss Connor's mothering career to Miss Connor, making no conclusions but mentioning young Karen's best interests. She said, 'Oh, really? If you feel that way about me taking care of Karen, what do you recommend then that I do with my unborn child?' So I said, 'Have you considered abortion?' "

"Oh, Tully!"

"Well, needless to say, Miss Connor stormed out in tears, complained to Lillian, who complained to Mr. Hillier, who regretted having to inform me that the next time this sort of thing occurred I would be respectfully let go."

"You should be careful, Tull. You know Lillian is looking for any excuse to get rid of you. You don't want to lose your job, do you?" asked Robin.

Tully shrugged. Once she didn't. Now she had other things to think about.

"So what happened to Karen?"

Tully picked up her Coke glass in a mock toast. "Cheers," she said. "The girl was given back to the mother."

Robin shook his head. "Midwest," he said.

"Children," corrected Tully. "Young Karen *wanted* to go with her mother."

"How could that be?" Robin exclaimed.

"Because," Tully said glumly, "children always want to go to their parents. Their capacity for hope is astounding."

"Greater than yours," said Robin.

"Much," agreed Tully. "Neither the kids nor the State of Kansas can believe that mothers and fathers might not love their kids, or might love them and hate them at the same time, might love them and beat them, love them and abandon them, love them but hate themselves more or love themselves more or love drink more or the farm more. The State is as bright-eyed and idealistic as the babies. They all think moms and dads will come around in the end."

Robin drank and ate and was quiet. At last he said, "Adoption is hard."

She glanced at him again, then reached out and patted his hand. "You were so loved, Robin. So loved. God, what is so hard about that?"

Robin and Tully put Boomerang to bed and then came back downstairs. She slumped down to the floor in the kitchen, back against the wall.

Robin said, "Tully, what are you doing? What's the matter? Those kids will be all right. They'll recover."

Tully shook her head. "Forget it," she said. kneading her hands. "Robin, I have to tell you something."

She saw him pale and then crouch down on the floor beside her. "Good news?"

Tully looked at him hard and said in a drained voice, "Robin, I'm pregnant."

He sat for a while and stared at her, then nodded, got up, and went to get a cigarette, fumbling with the light. Robin smoked half of it before he stubbed it out and said, "Is it mine?"

Tully didn't look up. "Robin," she said, "what kind of a question is that?"

He lit another cigarette, barely smoked it before he stubbed it out and lit another. "You're right. What kind of question is that? Okay, I'm very happy to hear that. Are you?"

Tully was sitting vanquished on the floor.

Robin lit another Marlboro. "No, how silly of me. How silly. A baby. Why, it's the last thing you want. Nothing's changed."

He poured himself a Chivas. "Well, Tully, don't just sit there. What do you want to do?"

Tully didn't answer him. She was thinking of how close her life had been to . . . something.

"Let's see," he said caustically. "What did you recommend for Miss Connor? Should I recommend it for you? You gave me Boomerang. He is enough for me."

"Stop it!" she screamed. "Stop it! Don't say this to me, you bastard. Don't say this to me." She covered her face. Her mind was a blank. She was barely functioning. Two weeks ago she was functioning, before the little piece of paper unmistakably changed color. Before Tully bought three more tests of different brands and they all changed every color of the rainbow—none stayed white. She stopped functioning then. Stopped thinking. Now only images flickered through her head. Images of sand—endless sand and endless beach. Endless smell of salt water washing the air all the way to the desert. That was the way! . . . Jack, blond like the beach, like the sun, gray-eyed like the Pacific, tall and lean like the most beautiful palm tree. His breath when he kissed her.

. . . There was a shadow behind her in darkness. A shadow with panting breath.

In the middle of June, Jack came back home, and Tully and he went to Lake Vaquero.

"Look! Shit, look at that!" exclaimed Jack. "Look what's happened to our lake!"

There were five finished houses on the banks of Lake Vaquero. With a couple more under construction. Since the building of West Ridge Mall, the western side of Topeka had built up at the expense of the east side of Topeka, which Tully thought was *this* close to having tumbleweeds roll lazily through it.

Tully and Jack scrambled down to the embankment.

"Lake Sherwood is nearly all covered with developments," Tully said.

"It always was," said Jack. "But this lake was deserted. It was empty. Indian Hills Road was barely paved. Look at this now," he said sadly.

He waded into the lake, still in his high tops. "Tully, look, someone took our boat."

Tully sat down on the sand. "It was an old boat, anyway," she said.

Jack kicked the water and came out. "It was our boat," he repeated ardently. Sitting down next to her, he said, "What was that poem we had made up?"

"We made up three poems." Tully smiled.

"That last one."

"*Jack Pendel and Tully Makker/ Jumped together in the lake* . . . that one?"

"Yes!" he said, kissing her cheek. "That one. *Jack Pendel and Tully Makker/ Caught Boomer, too, and his small rake . . .*"

Tully continued. "*They said/ Watch this,/ They said/ Jump high—*"

"And then what?"

"Remember?" she said. "We couldn't think of an ending. I said, *'Please give me back my tie.'* "

"What did I say?"

"You said," answered Tully, "*It's time to say good-bye.*"

Shaking his head vigorously, Jack said, "I've got a better ending now. *They said/ Watch this,/ They said/ Jump high/ They said I love you with their eyes.* How's that?"

She half smiled. "I've got a better one too. *They said/ Watch this,/ They said/ Jump high/ They said I love you till I die.*"

Jack knocked her over on the sand. "I like that," he whispered into her face. "When did you think of that?"

Tully let him kiss her. "Back then," she replied. "All the way back then."

July and part of August passed. Tully's stomach was looking and feeling more and more like a hard basketball. Jack, ever the gentleman, never mentioned it. He must think I'm just getting a little pudgy, Tully thought. But she wished he would ask her. She wanted to tell him.

When they were into their third August week, Tully realized that September was around the corner and became afraid that Jack would leave again.

One Sunday at their little enclave at Vaquero, Jack said, "Tully, you look particularly beautiful today."

She took that as an opening, lousy opening that it was.

"Could it be," she said, "because I'm six months pregnant?"

"Pregnant?" he mouthed. *"Pregnant?"*

Jack didn't speak after that, didn't look at her, just sat there in silence and threw rocks into the water. Then, after a while, he spoke again. "Is it mine?"

"I don't know, Jack," Tully replied. "I hope so."

He stared at her coldly. "You assure me that when I'm here you don't have sex with him."

Tully, taken aback, muttered, "Well, no, I don't have much sex with him."

"Tully! For God's sake! Much? Tully, a baby? When is it due?"

"The beginning of January."

She saw him counting on his fingers, and then his face softened. "It could be mine, I guess. Washington."

Yes. Washington. This summer they had not talked about what they talked about in Washington.

"I thought you said it was safe."

"I guess I was wrong. I'm not God." She gritted her teeth. This baby. Nobody at all in the whole wide world is happy about it. Nobody.

"What do you intend to do, Tully?"

"About what?" she mumbled.

"Let's take this one question at a time. What do you intend to do about this baby?"

"I don't know," she said coldly. "What would you say are my options?"

Jack didn't answer her. Maybe something in Tully's face scared him away, because he looked as though he were going to answer her.

"Okay, second question. What are you going to do with me?"

"I want to come with you."

"Come with me now."

"I can't now."

"Yes, you can. Pack up your bags, tell Robin you're leaving, take Boomerang, and let's go."

She shook her head. Or was her head shaking all by itself? "I can't now," she repeated. "You have nowhere for us to live, you said so yourself. Me, without work, and two kids. No insurance—what if something went wrong? I want to wait till the baby is born."

"No," Jack said. "I don't want you to. What could go wrong? What if when it's born you find out it's his?"

"What are you saying, Jack? Are you saying you won't take me with two children?"

"I'll take you with ten children," Jack said. "But will he let you go with two children?"

Tully squeezed her hands between her knees so that Jack wouldn't see how tense her fingers were. Arthritic tense. "I don't know," she said quietly. "Will he let me go with one?"

They sat there, silent and awkward. From the other side of the lake, they heard children's laughter.

"Jack, I can't up and take one or two or a dozen children from him without a divorce or at least a separation agreement."

"I understand," he replied. "Do you intend to come with me?"

"Of course. When the baby is born," she said with difficulty. "All I want to do is be with you. But I want to leave him properly."

"Is there a proper way to leave somebody?" asked Jack.

"I don't know," said Tully. "I'll find out, won't I?"

Then, a little later, she said, "Jack, are you going away again?"

"Tully, are you leaving Robin? Tomorrow? And moving in with me? If you are, then I'll stay in Topeka."

Placing her two palms on her belly, her kicking belly, Tully said no more about it. Jack softened. He touched Tully's pregnant stomach with his fingers. "A baby, Tully. How can it be?"

Jack stayed in Topeka a whole extra month. His mother died of the breast cancer she had been battling for years. Jack buried her in the middle of September, and stayed for another two weeks.

"Tully, I'll be back. I promise." They were at his house on Lakeside, and he was packing.

She was quiet. "You're not going to come back, are you?"

Jack looked into her face. "I promise. I promise. I promise. You're not going to leave Robin, are you?"

"I promise. I promise. I promise," said Tully. "Why do you have to go?"

Jack, bending down over his suitcase, looked up to see her towering over him. He reached over and kissed her belly, then straightened up and smiled. "Don't be upset, babe, don't be upset. I have to go because you won't leave your husband. But I'll be back, Tully. I'll be back for you. In December. You look great, by the way."

Tully said she didn't believe him.

"You really do, Tully," he said seriously. "You look wonderful. You glow."

Coming closer to him, she shoved him with her stomach. "I didn't mean that."

Taking Tully by the shoulders, Jack said, "I know. Tully Makker, I have nowhere in the world to go except back to you, and I want you to stay here so that I can come back to you. December. I promise. I'll be here for the birth of your baby."

"And your baby," she said.

"And mine, too," he said, pressing his hand to her belly.

"Can't you come back in November?" she said. "Can't you be here so I can watch you turn thirty?"

"The fewer people watch me turn thirty, the better," replied Jack.

He came back after Thanksgiving and Tully spent a crazy ninth month of her pregnancy making love to two men and dreaming crazy dreams.

One Saturday night late in December, when Robin was away in Manhattan, Jack and Tully stayed in his house on Lakeside Drive. They used to stay at the Meadow Acres Motel, but since Jack's mother died, they stayed at Jack's Lakeside house. Tully liked staying there. She liked the rosebushes outside and liked the nearness of St. Mark's. She liked the double bed where Jennifer lay down once. It used to be harder for Tully to stay overnight with Jack, but Robin was home less and less, if less were possible. Tully told her mother she was staying over Julie's—who was home for Christmas, again without Laura—and made sure to disconnect the downstairs phone before she left for the evening. Robin never once came home before Tully on Sundays.

On this Saturday night, Tully was lying naked on Jack's bed with her belly upturned and navel sticking out. Jack, also naked, was lying with his head on her belly, trying to hear. "I think it's going to be a girl, Tully, I think it is."

"I'd like for it to be a girl," she whispered. "I'd like for it to be yours. Things would be so simple then."

"Oh, Tully," Jack whispered sadly back. "Now, how could things ever be simple? You're married to someone else and have a son by him. He is never going to give Boomerang up. I wouldn't."

Paling, Tully turned slightly away. She felt the cold dark and heard the *heavy breathing of the shadow get closer*. Tully didn't speak and tried not to breathe. She just held her kicking child with one hand and Jack's head with the other. Her chest was tight. *"Be-bop-a-lula,"* she started to sing, drowning out all the other noises. *"She's my baby, be-bop-a-lula, and I don't mean maybe, be-bop-a-lula, she's my baby doll . . .* Jack, if you were trying to make me feel better, it didn't work," Tully said into the flickering lights of the TV.

They fell asleep. Jack was on top of her belly, and Tully had one hand on him. They slept this way until dawn, when Jack got up and looked outside. There was no sun yet, but there was lots of falling snow. It covered the steps and the cars. No roads were visible, no people, no traffic, no trees, only snow-covered silhouettes. Pulling back the curtain, Jack went back to lie down next to Tully. She was sleeping restlessly in the middle of the bed, so he tried to move her. When he did, he noticed that the sheet beneath her was soaked.

Scared, Jack touched underneath her; it was sopping wet warm, from the middle of her back to her thighs. Jack snapped on the table lamp. "Tully, Tully, wake up, wake up, look! What's this?"

She awoke with a start, looked into his panicked eyes, and touched herself underneath her back. "Oh, God," she said, and closed her eyes. "Oh, my God."

"What? What? For God's sake, what?"

"Jack, my water broke." And as if to confirm that, Jack watched Tully suffer a full-blown, shattering contraction that lasted what seemed like minutes, and as soon as she came off that one, he saw her body tense into a diving board for another.

"We're in trouble, Jacko," she groaned. But he already knew that. Tully had yet to see the snow.

He started to run around, looking for his clothes.

"Jack, call an ambulance!"

"Okay, Tully, okay. Anything you say."

"Jack!" she screamed. "Forget it! Call them, quickly, then forget them! Come here and help me . . . We have no time," she panted. "No time at all . . . I don't even have space—space between the— Aaahhh . . . Jack, get me up, sit me up, sit me up! Call an ambulance . . . sit me up, then call them."

His hands barely connecting with the buttons, Jack dialed 911 and gave them the address. "Tully," he said quickly, "they want to know how many minutes apart the contractions are."

Tully screamed. "Jaaaaack! No minutes, no minutes at all! Come here!" He hung up and slowly walked over to her. Through his haze, he saw her contorted face. "Jack, help me, help me."

"Oh, God, Tully," he breathed out, crouching between her legs on the bed. "Wait till the ambulance gets here!"

Her response was a piercing scream. Jack sat her up, propped her up with pillows, and she whispered, nearly delirious now, her body heaving violently. *"Go on, go on, take it from me take it, turn up the heat, turn it up, get some water to wash it with, get some water, some blanket to wrap it with, scissors, get, scissors no scissors, oh God take it from me, get a knife, wash your hands with scalding water, wash your hands and come near to me, come here and help me, Jack . . ."*

He did as he was told, and then sat on the corner of the bed, near her feet, and looked at her as she held on to the headboard, eyes closed and panting in pain.

"Jack, get on the bed, get on it, are you clean? Get on it and take it from me. It's here, God, it's here, here it is, one more push, give me your hand, give me your hand, no wait, I got to hold on to something, hold on to my legs, Jack, listen listen listen, put my legs in your hands, let me push against your hands . . . let me push against your hands . . ."

He took each of her feet into each of his hands and she bore into him with all her weight, screaming. Jack could tell she was near. Oh, God, she was so strong, but he held on to her feet while she held on to the headboard, and he didn't know how much time passed, five minutes, maybe seven, maybe longer as she pushed against his hands while he watched and breathed and breathed and breathed and then he said inaudibly, "God, Tully, I think it's coming out, I think that's the top of the head."

She let go of the headboard for a moment, and put her hand between her legs. *"Feel it,"* she whispered. He put his hand between her legs to feel a wet soft sticky top.

"It's here, it's here, next push the head will come out, Jack, you got to hold the head. You got to make sure it doesn't doesn't fall. Let go my feet, go and wash your hands and catch her head," she panted. *"Go! Now!"*

And he washed and then ran back to sit between her legs, his hands near the treacly crown. Next contraction, oh, here, pushing, no, it will never come out, not this time, here, in a moment, no, here it is, yes, pushing, pushing, Tully screaming, but he doesn't hear anything anymore, the noise is like deafness, sight is like blindness, he is deaf and mute to everything, but he sees in a push, a screeching push, a head pop out, just slide out, right out, facing downward, he cannot see its face, oh, how can it breathe? How can it, and why is it just waiting there, where is the rest of it? He reaches out with his fingers to touch the little head that fits into the palm of his hand and his hand is bloody and he hears Tully whisper—or scream?— *"The neck the neck, hold it by the back, and the neck,"* but there is no back and neck, there is only the head, a bloody head covered with beige film. *"Take it, take it from me, take it, take her, help me . . ."* and he reaches in and holds the head with his hands and he feels the body start to come out and here are the shoulders and he pulls, cradles the head, pulls some more, and then one push and it's out, out this bloody squirming cocoon, and he is still holding it, but it's all out, lying on its side in the dark of the room in the dark of the bed, still attached to Tully, still purple, lying on its side in his hands, and he says, "It's a girl," and begins to cry, and she, too, fills her lungs up with air and begins to cry, wahhh, waahhh, waaaaahhh, but he hardly hears because he is crying himself and he hears Tully who is saying *"Give her to me give her to me, put her on me,"* but he is afraid to pick her up having just delivered her, he is afraid to pick her up. He does, umbilical cord and all, and puts her on Tully's stomach and she touches the baby's head as the little girl writhes and moves, her little mouth covered with film, and he cleans it with his finger, clears it for her, and Tully wants to put her on her breast but can't—the umbilical cord isn't long enough and Jack gets his knife and lets Tully cut it because he could never, never. Jack cuts a piece of rope off the curtains and clamps the cord. *That* he can do. Then Tully ties what's left of the cord on the baby and puts the little one to her breast, and the baby opens her mouth. At first she can't find the nipple, but here it is and she pops it into her mouth and sucks, eyes open, and Tully's eyes are open and his, too, he is between her legs again, she is bleeding heavily. What's this? Is this the placenta? He looks at a chunk of flesh that slid out all by itself that looks like liver. I guess that must be it, but Tully is bleeding, so he gets a towel and puts it between her legs to stop the flow, and Tully, holding the baby with one hand, reaches out to him. *"Come here,"* she says, and he comes and Tully cradles his face to hers and he kisses her lips, still crying, he would die for her at this moment the way he is feeling now, and she murmurs something and he murmurs something back. "A girl," he says, "a girl." And for the first time he can hear her, loud. The sound comes back. The sound and the sight. It's lighter. The bed is covered with blood. And they are, all three of them, naked, and covered in blood. And Tully Makker says, "Not just a girl. *Jennifer.*"

17

CALIFORNIA

December 1989

The blue reel of the ambulance lights startled him. He jumped up off the bed and looked outside. Yes, here they were. How long had it taken them? Jack quickly put on a pair of jeans, running his hands over his blood-covered body, and threw a blanket on Tully and the baby before he let in the two paramedics.

"Well, well," said one of the men, taking the baby from Tully's arms. "You hardly need us."

"What do you mean?" said Jack. "I called forty-five minutes ago. We couldn't wait."

"Have you looked outside?" said the second paramedic testily. "Snow."

"Forty-five minutes," said Jack immutably.

The paramedic ignored him and bent over an unresponsive Tully. "Wake up," he said. "Wake up, ma'am." He lifted the blanket covering her.

"I think you were wrong, Joe," the paramedic said to his partner. "She does need us. Look how heavy she's bleeding." He wrapped the baby tightly. "Let's get the stretcher. Cover your wife a little better, won't you? Don't you feel the draft from downstairs?" he said on the way down. Jack grunted and covered Tully with more blankets. Putting clothes on her was out of the question. Her limbs were all flaccid.

The paramedics returned with the stretcher. They tied some towels around Tully's stomach and between her legs. After they lowered her on the stretcher and took her and the baby downstairs, Jack looked at the bed. There was a big dark glistening stain on the sheets. It probably soaked all the way through, Jack thought, and then, There sure is a lot of blood during birth.

Outside, some of Jack's neighbors came out in their bathrobes to see why the sharp blue and red lights blinked on New Year's Eve day at seven in the morning.

Jack's next-door neighbor, Mr. Edward, came over. He was Jack's mother's age. "Is everything all right?" he asked Jack.

Jack looked Mr. Edward over. *I couldn't get this man to open the door for me in the middle of the afternoon to lend me some Mazola, and now it's the break of dawn and he is out here so curious.*

"Why, yes. Fine. Thank you," said Jack.

"What's happened?" asked Mr. Edward.

What's happened? Jack thought. What's happened? What to tell this man, crabby and gray, in an old overcoat, standing there with furrowed brows? Jack said, "She just gave birth," pointing to a shape being pushed inside the ambulance.

"Hey, I didn't know you were married, Jack," said Mr. Edward.

Not answering, Jack stepped away—cautiously, lest Mr. Edward notice and follow him. Moving from foot to foot to keep warm, Jack tried to flake off the dried blood on his hands.

"She gave birth right in the house?" said Mr. Edward, walking over to Jack.

"Everything is fine," Jack said, keeping his voice calm.

Mr. Edward pointed to Jack's hands. "What about that?"

"Would you excuse me?" Jack said. "We're going to the hospital."

Mr. Edward's face grew increasingly cheerless. "Who is it?" he asked.

"Have a nice day," replied Jack, feeling exhausted.

But there was something else, too. A feeling rose out of the mess, out of the cauldron, out of the full lungs of other very identifiable feelings. A feeling that was not like the others he had felt this morning. This was more akin to the frustration he had felt as a kid running through a maze in the middle of the night in an amusement park in Kansas City. One dead end after another, one wrong way, then a long way but still the wrong way. He had thought it would be easy. He had thought there would be nothing to it, but here it was, night now, and he still had not found his way. Jack imagined the questions might be worse at the hospital.

In the ambulance, Jack held the baby in one hand and Tully's hand in the other. Tully was delirious: murmuring, mumbling, drifting off. He tried to listen to what she was saying, but it was all gibberish. After the first few minutes in Stormont-Vail, Jack wished for the warmth and quiet of the ambulance. The nurses and doctors were asking him all sorts of questions, from the routine to the routinely unanswerable. Her name. Her age. His name. Okay, those weren't so bad. Though he did, in his automaton way say her name was Tully *Makker*, and then forgot to change it. Was he her closest living relative? That was tougher. No, he said. She had a mother. Were they related? She and her mother? He hoped so, he said. No one smiled. Was she his wife? No, he said, and nothing more. Was the child his? Yes, he said, deciding to be bold. She was. What was the child's name? My God, what an endless barrage. Was there someone else they needed to contact in case of an emergency?

What emergency, said Jack, feeling as vague as Tully was after the birth. The nurses looked at him oddly. Heavy blood loss, they said. Abnormal. Somehow, that almost made Jack feel better. He didn't want to believe that a two-foot-diameter stain in the middle of his double bed was normal.

Jack said he'd be glad to help. They took him to an empty room and rolled up his sleeve to test his blood, for all sorts of things. It was nearly 1990, after all. Everything must have checked out okay, because after about fifteen minutes, they allowed him to roll up his sleeve again. When the nurse was done, she thanked him and took the blood sample away. Jack sat quietly for a few minutes and then wandered out of the room and walked down the hall to see where Tully was. Finally he had to walk back to the nurses' station and ask. After the initial questioning, no one talked to him willingly anymore. One of the nurses did suggest he go and wash himself off.

Jack went to the men's showers. Undressing, he stood naked in front of the mirror and touched the dried blood on his body. Yes, he guessed a shower was a good idea, but as he ran the cold water, he was already regretting having one. Regretting washing Tully and the baby off him.

While Jack was showering and watching the water run down the drain at his feet, a cold thought washed over him and made him shudder.

He had to call Robin.

He had to call Robin and tell the man who never did Jack any harm that Tully Makker—Tully DeMarco!—just had a baby in the dawn of morning at Jack Pendel's house and was now in Stormont-Vail, not doing very well. Could he, Robin, please come and claim her?

Jack dried himself off, put back on his old dirty jeans, his shirt, and sweater and went to look in on Tully before he called Robin. She looked like she was sleeping, despite the IV tube going into her nose. Sitting down on the bed, Jack caressed her hand. "Tully," he whispered. "Tully, wake up. Wake up, babe, I need your help, please wake up."

"Mr. Pendel," said a nurse who looked and acted disconcertingly like nurse Ratched out of *One Flew over the Cuckoo's Nest*, "You promised you would not try to wake her up. I really must hold you to that, or ask you to leave." Tully was in a room with seven other beds, though only four were occupied. Jack closed the dividing curtain tighter around the corners and sat back on the bed, whispering, "Tully, I'm begging you, please wake up. Tell me what you want me to do. I need you to tell me what you want me to do, so I can do the right thing. Please wake up and tell me what the right thing to do is, Tully."

He left eventually. Tully didn't look as if she would be waking up soon.

Jack went in to check on Jennifer in the infants' ward. She lay there on her side, bundled up tight in white hospital linens, asleep. Her little mouth was slightly open. Jack tilted his head to look at her. She had blond hair. He had an overwhelming urge to cradle her soft downy head in his hands. Instead he steeled his jaw and went to call Julie. He got her number from information. It was eight-thirty on Sunday morning.

"Julie, this is Jack. I'm sorry to bother you this early. Jack Pendel."

"I know who you are, Jack," said Julie sleepily. "How is Tully?"

He liked that. No nonsense.

"She is okay. She had the baby."

"Baby! Oh wonderful!" Julie livened up. "Wow! Boy or girl?"

"Girl. Eight pounds. Twenty inches."

"Way to go, Tully! What have they named her?"

Jack skipped a beat before he said, "Jennifer."

Now a beat from Julie. "Jennifer? Oh, my dear. Well, okay, cool. So how come *you're* calling me up? Where is Robin?"

Jack swallowed. "Well, this is the thing. Robin isn't here."

"Oh." Then, "Where is he?"

"I don't know. Manhattan, probably."

"Oh." Then, "How do you know she had the baby? She call you?"

"No," said Jack. "She didn't call me. I was with her."

"At her house?" Julie said incredulously.

"Nooo," answered Jack. "At my house."

"Oh." Then, "Oh, my."

Jack rolled his eyes. Maybe she wasn't as no-nonsense as he first thought.

"Julie, I need your help. Tully is out cold. She needed blood and stitches. Do you understand what I'm saying? She can't call him herself."

There was no response from Julie, and Jack could almost see her closing her eyes and shaking her head. "Oh, what've you done?" she said at last. "What has she done?"

Jack was silent.

"Why didn't you call Robin before you brought her to Stormont? So that at least he could be with her when the baby was born."

Jack almost hung up. It was that fucking maze. He had to find the way out. "Because," he said slowly, "he would have had to come to my house. The baby was born there."

"Oh." Then—*again!* "Oh, my."

"Julie!"

"Jack, Jack, calm down," said Julie. "I'll get dressed and be right over. I understand. But I can't call for you, Jack. You've got to call him and tell him yourself. Just tell him that Tully went into labor and gave birth. I mean, think about it. It'd be ridiculous coming from me."

"Julie, you could say she was with you."

"Jack, she didn't give birth at the hospital! There is nothing I could say to him. He's going to talk to the doctor, the nurses. Come clean. Just tell him his wife gave birth. Is she okay?"

"No," he said. "She's not well. She's hemorrhaging."

"Tell him that. I think she told me she lost a lot of blood with Boomerang, too. Robin will be concerned. It'll be okay."

"Thanks," Jack said. "I'll be seeing you."

"Hold on! Hold on. I'll be right over. But Jack, you gotta call him, you gotta call him and tell him. What else can you do? I'll lie for Tully till the earth gets cold, but you can't ask me to lie for you, Jack."

"Julie. I wasn't going to lie to him. I just wanted it to be easier for him. Coming from you."

Julie didn't say a word at first. "Look at it this way. If Tully hadn't been with you, she would have been alone in that house of hers, while Robin was God knows where despite his nine-month-pregnant wife, and then she would have had to deliver that baby all by herself, or worse, with the help of her mother! Think about that. It could've been worse. I'll be right over."

When Jack hung up, he thought, Tully has good friends. Then Jack began to wonder, as he searched his pockets for another quarter, if Robin, upon hearing from Jack, would agree with Julie that it could indeed have been worse. Jack doubted it, dialing Tully's number.

After eleven rings, a woman's out-of-breath voice answered. Jack guessed it was Tully's mother. "Is Robin there, please?"

"I don't think he's home yet," said Hedda, breathing heavily into the phone. "Who is this?"

"Do you know what time he usually comes home?"

"I don't know," said Hedda. "Who is this?"

"Thank you, I'll call back."

"Tully will be home soon," Hedda said.

Jack closed his eyes, thinking, I hope so. "Yes, thank you," he said. "Have a good day."

Robin's not home yet. Well, that was interesting. Where could a man be when his wife is due to give birth any minute? Jack felt marginally better about calling Robin back.

He got a cup of coffee from the vending machine and then sat for an hour staring into space. Before he called again, Jack went to check on Tully and on Jennifer. How is the baby going to eat, he wondered, if Tully is unconscious? And does this mean Tully will lose her milk? He went to one of the nurses with his questions. She was busy, but no, she told him, the milk doesn't even come in for three days. Longer, and yes, she might lose it then, but the baby would be fine on formula until Tully came around. Infants eat very little the first few days, anyway, the nurse said. They're usually sleeping off the mother's anesthetics.

What anesthetics? thought Jack. Can *I* have an anesthetic while I run through this fucking thing? he thought, trying to find the exit.

2.

Robin walked in the door, Boomerang in front of him. "Mom!" Boomerang shouted, running upstairs. "Mom!"

Robin walked through to the kitchen, where he found Hedda drinking a cup of coffee. "What's up?" said Robin, taking off his coat.

"Tully's not home yet," said Hedda.

Blackness covered Robin's eyes for a moment, but it was only for a moment, and he quickly recovered. "Okay," he said. "She's staying over at Julie's. She'll be home soon."

Robin was anxious. Now that she was so very pregnant, he made it a point of calling her several times a day to make sure she was all right. Oh, no. Yesterday, he didn't even call once.

"Julie's, huh?" said Hedda. "Well, around eight forty-five this morning, a man called asking for you. The phone downstairs was disconnected. I had to go all the way upstairs to pick it up."

"Oh, really?" said Robin nonchalantly, but inside, panic rose up inside him like vomit. "Did he say who he was?" he asked.

"No," replied Hedda. "He said he'll call back."

Robin reconnected the phone cord to the jack and then poured himself a cup of coffee. Boomerang walked into the kitchen. "Mommy isn't home," he said ruefully.

"Mmmm," said Robin, patting his son on the head. "She'll be home soon."

"Where is she?" asked Boomerang.

"She is with her friends, Boomer. She'll be home soon."

Just then the phone rang. Never did it sound so loud, never did it beckon so much not to be picked up, never did it scream so loud to be picked up, never did Robin jump up so fast to go and answer it, and yet when he got to it, he could not pick up the receiver. It rang, three, four, five, six, seven—

"Pick it up, Dad!"

"Hello?" said Robin into the phone in a small voice.

"Robin?" The voice on the other end was unfamiliar, but just as small. "It's Jack, Jack Pendel."

"I know who it is," said Robin. "What's happened?" As he asked this, Robin turned to the wall so that his son and his mother-in-law could not see his face.

"Tully is at Stormont. She had the baby. A girl."

"Why didn't she call me?" Robin asked quietly.

"She was busy having the baby, I guess. I'm sorry, man."

"Why are you calling me? Why isn't she calling me?"

"She's not well. You should come and see her."

Don't tell me what the fuck to do! Robin screamed inside. But outside, Boomerang was pulling on his arm. "Dad," he was whispering. "How is Mom? What's happened to Mommy?" Robin jerked his arm away from his son, looking at nothing but the wall.

"She's not too good," said Jack. "She keeps losing blood. The baby is fine, though."

At hearing those words, Robin pressed his forehead to the kitchen tiles, pulled back, and struck his head against them once, twice, once, twice, harder each time, wanting nothing else at that moment but to crack his skull open and end all of this so that his head would be the only thing broken, the only thing cracked open and unfixable. Unfixable. Un-fix-able. How easy it would be then for all of them and for him.

"I'll be right there," he finally said.

"I'm sorry, man," said Jack.

"Yeah," said Robin, and hung up. He stood there, head still against the wall, trying to collect himself before he opened his eyes and looked into his child's face. Okay, okay, do this, do this now, do this now for him, come on, for him, won't you smile for your boy?

"Boomerang," Robin said, kneeling down and taking his son by the shoulders. "Mommy is in the hospital. She just had a baby, and so she's not feeling very well and this upsets Daddy. I'm going to have to go and see her, okay, Boomer?"

"I'll come with you," Boomerang said.

"No!" Robin flashed a look at Hedda. "No, you stay here with Nanna, okay?"

"Why can't I come with you?" said Boomerang, with an I'm-about-to-cry expression.

"Son, Mommy is not well, she may be connected to a bunch of tubes, they may not even allow Mommy to have visitors. Let me go and see. We'll go and see her together later, I promise. Okay?"

Kissing Boomerang on the head, Robin was putting on his coat when Hedda asked, "Did she have a boy or a girl?"

"A girl," said Robin. "A baby sister," he said to Boomerang, managing a grimace.

Boomerang clapped his hands together. "That's fantastic, Dad. What are we going to call her?"

"Knowing your mother, Boomer? We'll probably call her Jennifer. Jenny. Wouldn't that be nice?" And got out of the house as fast as he could.

Robin was still way at the other end of the long maternity wing when he saw Jack's back and Julie, sitting in the far-off waiting room.

Jack was just about the last person Robin wanted to see, so he turned around and walked back to the nurses' station.

"I'm here to see my wife," he said. "Tully DeMarco. She just had a baby."

"Let's see. Danilo, Davidson, Debenez, Dister . . . no, no DeMarco."

Bastard, thought Robin. Goddamn it. "Try Makker, please."

"Makker, Makker, ah yes, here. Natalie Anne. Yes. She was brought in this morning."

"Thank you. What time?"

"About seven or so. We had trouble getting to her in the snow." She smiled kindly.

"Of course. Is she all right? Can I go and see her?"

"Of course. Room four-seventeen. Ninth on the left. Quietly, though. She hasn't come around yet."

Robin was about to walk away when he turned around and said, thinking, Sounds just like an afterthought, doesn't it? "And the baby? The girl?"

The nurse smiled again. "She is in the infants' ward. All the way down and make a right. You'll see the glass. Ask someone there, they'll take her out for you."

"And her name?" asked Robin, steeling himself not to clutch at the counter. "What have they named her?"

"Hmm, she is not listed here as a Makker . . ."

"Maybe DeMarco?"

The nurse kept looking. "No, no DeMarco. I'm sure the nurse there will clear up the confusion. Don't worry. So I guess your wife didn't take your name, huh? A liberated lady." And the nurse smiled for the third time.

Oh, she took my name, all right, thought Robin, starting to walk to room 417.

"Sir, wait a minute, wait!"

Robin reluctantly turned around. A doctor came up to him. "Hello," he said. "I heard you asking about Tully Makker. I'm Dr. Brunner. And you are . . . ?"

Robin didn't know what to say. "Robin DeMarco?" he said at last.

"Are you related to her?" Dr. Brunner squinted suspiciously at Robin.

What the fuck is going on here? "Well," he let out, "I don't know if I'm related to her. I'm her husband."

"Husband." Dr. Brunner raised his eyebrows. "I see. Your wife is losing quite a bit of blood."

"Yeah . . . last . . . time . . ." Robin said slowly, "she lost a lot of blood, too."

"Yes, I've seen her medical records. Her uterus seems to have a problem contracting. We've given her a second injection of oxytocin, so we'll see. Did you know your wife was anemic? Everything should be okay. But her heart rate is way up. We're probably going to have to move her to ICU if she doesn't improve soon. Just as a precaution," Dr. Brunner added. "She may develop an infection."

Robin didn't understand. "Wait, wait, infection? Why would she get an infection?"

The doctor looked at him calmly. "Mr. DeMarco. Childbearing is a little risky. Ms. Makker's—umm, Mrs. DeMarco's—water's broke some time before she gave birth, and she had the child in nonsterile conditions. Infections happen. Quite treatable, not to worry. The bleeding I'm more concerned about. We already gave her one transfusion—" here, the doctor stopped and looked at Robin peculiarly before continuing. "She should be fine."

"Wait, wait," said Robin sharply. "I don't get it. Why would a hospital have nonsterile conditions? You don't sterilize your equipment here?"

Dr. Brunner's peculiar look came back. It sat uncomfortably on his long thin face. The doctor touched Robin on the arm. "I'm sorry, Mr. DeMarco. Your wife didn't have the baby in the hospital. By the time the ambulance got to her, she had already had the child. A lot of snow. Have you been out there? There was nothing our men could do." He smiled awkwardly. "But she should be all right," he finished, and scurried away.

Robin turned to the nurse. He began to understand what Jack Pendel was doing in the hospital on Sunday morning.

After a minute or so, Robin let go of the counter and stumbled outside, where he sat on a hospital bench in the howling cold and let the Kansas wind and snow hit his face and throat and eyes.

What Robin felt now when his snow-blinded eyes had finally seen the lie that was his life blowing up into his face was not rage or anger, nor jealousy or disgust. What invaded and tore at his throat and chest was pain and regret.

Regret for all those nights he was away from Tully, who was herself away, regret for all those Saturdays spent playing ball while Tully was away herself, for those Sundays in front of the TV while Tully was in church praying, those long evenings away while the dinner she had cooked was waiting for him, those many nights he slept turned away from her while she tossed and turned, tossed and turned, while she sat by the window. Regret that he did not say the house does not need painting, IT DOES NOT NEED PAINTING! It had pleased Robin to come home in the twilight and see his whitewashed beautiful house, with its sprawling front porch and the flower beds and the new white picket fence, and bay windows, and Tully. When she was home, her face always smiled to greet him, her lips were always there to kiss him; she sat with him while he ate, and washed his dishes, and washed his son, and washed him sometimes, too, in the night.

Pain and regret that he went away from his Tully and let another man bring forth a baby from his wife, a girl from Tully, a *Jennifer* from Tully. It was nearly too fucking much.

After sixty or seventy minutes, when the snow had made him sufficiently numb, he walked back inside, rose up the stairs to the fourth floor, and again walked down that corridor, to room 417. She wasn't there; Robin checked all eight beds. Five of them empty.

Before he went to ask someone about her, Robin thought, Tully died. She just up and died on me, right now. She died because I wasn't there to take her to the hospital. In the time Robin was outside numbing himself to face her, she had died.

When Robin saw Dr. Brunner coming out of 420, he walked up to him and said, "Is she dead?"

Dr. Brunner tried to inch past him. "Of course she isn't. She's been moved to the ICU. Mr. DeMarco, please."

Robin stepped away and walked to the double doors that said INTENSIVE CARE UNIT, and then through another set of double doors, before he was blocked by a stiff-necked nurse with a severe face. Robin stared.

"Who are you?" she said gruffly.

"Tully Makker. I'm here to see Tully Makker," he replied, still staring.

"She's already got a visitor. You're going to have to wait. She is in an ICU, not a recovery ward. She is not really allowed any visitors in ICU. You will have to scrub."

But Robin walked back out through the double doors. He wanted to see Tully, but Tully *already had visitors*.

Outside, in the far waiting room, Robin saw Julie.

She turned around, quickly got up, and hugged him. Robin struggled against wanting to sit down. "Robin, you okay?" she said.

"Great," he replied. "How's Tully?"

"Not so good. Did you see? They just moved her to ICU."

"I saw," he said. "I thought she was dead."

Julie looked at him reproachfully. "Oh, Robin."

He sat down.

"Do you want to come and see the baby?"

He stood up. And dutifully followed her.

Julie led him along the long glass wall, against which fathers, mothers, brothers, and grandmothers stood gazing with reverence at cots and cots of sleeping, crying, writhing infants that all looked exactly the same.

Robin gritted his teeth. He would get through this, he would get through this, and then he would go home.

Julie pointed out a wrapped bundle to him.

"That's her," she said lovingly.

"Is that her?" said Robin. He couldn't see anything. Either she was too far away or his eyes were going. "She looks beautiful," he said anyway, not wanting to appear callous. "Doesn't she?"

"Incredibly beautiful," said Julie, and then squeezed Robin's arm. "It'll be okay, Robin," she said. "It will all work out. Tully needs you now. Everything will be okay."

"Of course it will," he said, then adding, "Could you tell him to leave, please, so I could see my wife before she dies? He's in the ICU with her now."

"She's not going to die, Robin!" Julie whispered. "And I can't get in to see her in the ICU. They're very strict there with visitors."

"So how did *he* get in to see her?"

Julie lowered her head. "He's registered as the father."

Robin stared at the wrapped bundle in the window. She was in the second row—too far away for him to read the tag line. "You're telling me she is Jennifer *Pendel*?" he said hollowly.

"I'm sorry, Robin."

Robin looked one way, then another. He tried to take a deep breath, but the gritted teeth wouldn't let any breath out. And then he smashed the glass with his fist. Smashed it again. The tempered glass didn't break, but the noise made everyone turn around, everyone, and they all stared blankly at him.

Julie grabbed him. "Robin! Please!"

He wrenched himself away from her. "Goddamn it!" he hissed. "God-fucking-damn it!"

"Robin, please!" Julie was still holding on to him. He wouldn't be able to get her away from him without pushing her to the floor. A nurse rushed over.

"Please!" she said loudly. "What's going on? Why are you disrupting hospital activity? I don't want to ask you to leave."

"I don't want to ask you to shut the fuck up," Robin said just as loudly.

"Robin! Please!" Julie looked beseechingly at the nurse. "He's upset, that's all. He's not feeling well, he's sick, I'm sorry," she explained hastily. Finally Julie pulled Robin back into the waiting room.

"Robin, have you lost your mind?"

"That's it. I'm going home, getting my gun, and then I'm going to come back and shoot them both."

"Stop it, stop it!" Julie exclaimed. "Calm down! Nothing is so bad that you can't make worse, Robin."

His eyes were glazed over.

"Robin! She is the mother of your child. She is the mother of your son. Please, for his sake, calm down! For God's sake! You won't be much good to him like this."

Robin roughly pushed himself away from her. Julie was still trying to hold on to him.

"I'm going home," he said.

"If she wakes up, she might ask for you."

"Oh, yeah, that's likely, I'm sure," he said.

Julie stared at him hard. "Robin. You're probably feeling worse than I can imagine. But you have a son who needs to see his mother and his little sister. Will you please get a grip on your senses?"

He started to walk away from her, and then turned around and said, "How long have you known about this? Tell me, how long have you been in on this little joke?"

Julie's face was contorted. "Please," she said quietly. "I am here two weeks out of the year. I've always liked you, Tully knows how I felt about you. But she is my friend. She is the only friend I have left in the world."

"Well, isn't that just cozy?" Robin said.

Julie grabbed his arm. "Robin, God! Why don't you save it for when she gets better? Listen to me, if you had ever wanted to say two words to me, I would've told you, she had not grieved when the rest of us grieved. If you had wanted to know what was up with her, I would have told you not to judge her too harshly. Because when the rest of us were doing our grieving, she was numb and had been numb for years. Cut her some slack. She is in the ICU now. There'll be plenty of time to scream and yell."

He pulled his arm away from her. "Goddamn you all," he said. "I'm leaving. Tell him I don't want to see him here when I come back."

"Tell him yourself," snapped Julie. "Who do you think I am?"

Robin left then, leaving his car in the parking lot, and walked home from the hospital. On the way to Texas Street through snow, he realized he was no longer feeling pain and regret.

"Goddamn it," he muttered, kicking the snow as he walked. "Goddamn it!"

The cold air revived some of his senses but didn't abate his rage. He nearly ran home. All I want to do is hurt her, hurt her until she cries, until she screams from all the pain.

When Robin was at 1501 Texas Street, he saw Tully's Camaro, white with snow, and it was then he knew what to do. Without stopping to think, he rushed over to the car and found his set of keys for it.

He had to get in and drive it somewhere, he couldn't let his son see him go *mad*.

That sounds so rational, doesn't it? he thought, starting up the car after several tries. I have to drive it someplace else because I don't want Boomerang to see me. That sounds so sane. Almost calm. So why don't I just turn off the car and go inside the house?

He put the Camaro into drive. The wheels spun briefly in place. He noticed the heat wasn't working properly. Without clearing the snow off the car, Robin drove it to the empty parking lot near Frito-Lay, where Tully and Robin used to go to have sex years ago. Getting out of the car, Robin thought of Tully. And screamed. It was Sunday, the lot was empty, and Robin screamed and screamed. He ran around the car, screaming things he forgot immediately, kicking the car and the snow.

Spent, nearly mute, but still enraged, still out of control, Robin opened the Camaro and looked in the backseat for the iron pipe he always told Tully to carry just in case. She never needed it. Now he did.

3.

"Let's go and see Mom, Dad," said Boomerang, getting off the couch when he saw his father walk in the front door.

Robin, still in his coat, walked over to Boomer and patted his head. "Let's wait a little while, okay? Mommy is not feeling well at all."

"How is she?" asked Hedda, slowly hobbling in from the kitchen.

"She's in ICU," said Robin, taking her by the arm into the kitchen. He lowered his voice so that Boomerang wouldn't hear him. "They can't stop the bleeding."

"Oh," said Hedda. "Are you hungry? You want a sandwich?"

Robin shook his head and went to have a shower. He took a long, hot shower and then went into the bedroom. The bed was made from Saturday morning.

Neither of us slept in this bed last night, he thought, the salt of guilt running into his throat.

Robin called the store to make sure everything was all right. He thought about calling Stevie and Bruce and telling them about Tully, but he couldn't. He thought of calling Shakie and telling her, but he couldn't do that, either. So he cleaned the bedroom and vacuumed it, though it took him a while to find where Millie kept the vacuum. Then he cleaned Boomerang's bedroom and went downstairs to do some laundry. After folding the cleaned clothes and putting them away, Robin looked at the bedroom clock.

It said three o'clock. There was still a whole Sunday left, and Robin couldn't face it.

"Son," he said, putting on his coat. "I'm going to go and see Mommy again, okay? Then I'll come back, and maybe at night, or tomorrow, we'll go together."

"But Dad, tonight is New Year's Eve," said Boomerang, his voice cracking. "I don't want Mom to be alone on New Year's Eve."

"Boomerang, she is asleep right now. She won't be able to talk to you anyway."

"That's okay," he said. "I just want to see her."

Robin sighed. "I left my car at Stormont-Vail, Boomer."

"We can take Mom's car."

"Umm . . . Mom's car is in the shop." It didn't feel good lying to a seven-year-old.

"No, it isn't! We brushed snow off it this morning."

"I had to take it in an hour ago."

"Okay," said Boomerang. "Let's walk."

"It's a long walk."

"I don't mind."

"It's freezing outside. Must be twenty below with the wind."

"I'll bundle up," Boomerang said, putting on his coat. "Do you think they'll let me hold the baby?"

Sighing, Robin tied a scarf around Boomer's neck. "I'm sure they will, son," he said. "I'm sure they'll let you do anything you want."

Boomerang smiled. "Mom taught me that. She said, be . . . reasonable . . . and keep on. Sooner or later, they'll give in or lose their temper. Either way you win."

"Mom taught you that, did she?" said Robin, smiling back, forgetting for a moment that Mom was Tully, and that he hated Tully. "I'll have to have a talk with Mom, won't I?"

It was a long walk all the way from Texas Street to Stormont-Vail. And the wind was strong. But Boomerang didn't complain once, walking bravely, holding his father's hand.

"When we see Mommy," Robin said, "she is probably going to be attached to a lot of tubes and things."

"It's called IV, right?"

Robin glanced at his son. "Right. Is that what they teach you in school?"

"No, Mom taught me that when Nanna was in the hospital. What's IV, Dad?"

"It means intravenous," Robin explained. "So don't be frightened."

"I'm not going to be frightened," said Boomerang.

But seeing Tully lie there, completely immobile, hardly breathing, connected to every machine it seemed the hospital was capable of hooking her up to, frightened Robin. He sank into a chair next to her bed. Boomerang took Tully's hand.

"It's warm, Dad," he said encouragingly. "She's gonna be okay."

Robin touched Tully's hand. The hand wasn't just warm. It was hot.

"It feels like Mommy has a fever," said Robin.

Boomerang pressed his face to his mother's. "Dear Mommy," he said. "I hope you can hear me. I will pray tonight that you won't have a fever tomorrow anymore."

The stiff-necked nurse walked in, saying in a very business-like manner, "You will have to go now. Only a few minutes at a time. And children really shouldn't be brought into the unit."

Robin got up. "Thank you for your help and cooperation," he said, taking Boomerang's hand.

"Dad, let's go and see the baby, okay?"

They went. The nurse remembered Robin's earlier burst of temper and wouldn't give out a Jennifer Pendel to a Robin DeMarco.

Robin felt himself losing control again. Thank you, God, he thought, taking large gasping breaths and looking intently at Boomerang, whose face was pressed to the glass. Thank you for Boomerang. Because of his being here, I can breathe.

Robin walked back to the waiting room with Boomerang. Julie was there now with a cup of coffee. Julie wasn't the only one in the waiting room.

"Jack!" said Boomerang loudly, rushing over to the man sitting next to Julie. "You here to see my mom?"

Jack nodded. Robin wanted to sit down. "They wouldn't let us see her," Robin said hoarsely. Julie rose, putting her hand on Boomerang's shoulder. "Boomer, what do you say we go and see your little sister?"

About to walk away, she turned to Robin, who stood there like a pillar, watching Jack. "Coming, Robin?" she said.

"Yeah, come on, Dad," said Boomerang.

"I'll be right there," Robin said tonelessly. "Go on, now."

And then they were alone, staring at each other in terrible silence. Robin continued to stand. Jack sat in the chair. Jack spoke first.

"I'm sorry, man. I'm really sorry," said Jack.

"Fuck you to hell and your sorry," snapped Robin. His eyes glazed over again with a haze he couldn't see straight through. He took a moment to collect his sight.

"Can't you just go the fuck away?" Robin said. "Why are you here?"

Jack stood up and put his hands in his pockets. "Somebody should be here," he said. "You're not here."

"Fuck you," said Robin vehemently. "If you'd get the hell out, I'd be here."

"Listen, I can find another waiting room. But when she comes around, I want to be here. And the baby . . ."

"The baby," said Robin. "The baby. I should shoot you right now, shoot you, goddamn it. How dare you, you bastard, how dare you put your name on that child? Who the fuck do you think you are? You're a nothing, you're just scum. How dare you put your name on that child?"

Jack stepped away a little from Robin, who could barely see him. Though Robin did see that Jack had taken his hands out of his pockets.

"I am not scum," Jack said. "I didn't know what to do."

"You bastard, do you understand, they won't let me go and see her because my name is not on her? Not on her and not on my wife?" And he felt something hot and wet in his eyes, and immediately clenched his fists, canting inside, *It's okay, it's okay, it's okay.*

"I didn't know what to do," repeated Jack. "Look, I'm sorry. I'll go right now and change it."

"You bastard," said Robin. "Why can't you just leave us alone? What do you want from us?"

"I'm sorry, Robin," Jack said. "You don't deserve this."

"Go the fuck to hell," said Robin, backing away. "I never want to see your face again."

Jack put his hands back in his pockets and continued to stand there. Robin couldn't read the expression on Jack's face because he couldn't see Jack's face well. Haze was covering his eyes.

When Robin walked over to the infants' ward, Julie and Boomerang were already inside, and Boomerang was holding the baby. Robin was allowed in, now that Julie was there to "monitor" him, and after he washed his hands, he was allowed to hold the baby, too.

"Dad, she is so cute," whispered Boomerang. "Isn't she?"

Jennifer was bundled and asleep and light. "Yeah, she is, Boomer," agreed Robin, thinking this child was like an alien from outer space, a UFO sighting at Stormont-Vail. Who is this baby?

"Look, Dad, she looks exactly like Mom! Look at that blond hair. I wonder what color eyes she has?"

The baby did have blond hair. "I'll bet she's got Mommy's eyes," said Robin. "Well, let's go, Boomerang. Let's go home."

And that night, when Robin was putting Boomerang to bed, the boy asked, "Dad, is Mom going to be okay?"

"Yes, of course she will."

"Is that why you're not very happy about the baby? Because you're worried about Mom?"

"Yes, Boomerang, that's it," said Robin. "And I am," he added with difficulty, "happy about the baby."

Afterwards Robin sat in the rocking chair in the nursery listening to his son toss and turn.

"Dad?" said Boomerang. Robin opened his eyes.

"Dad, I think it will be difficult for the baby to say 'Boomerang,' do you think? It's such a long name. Maybe you and Mom should start calling me Robin. That is my name, right?"

"It *is* your name, my dear one," said Robin, getting up and coming over to sit on the bed. "But we've called you Boomerang all your life. That's your name, too."

"I know, Dad," said Boomerang firmly, turning away. "But Jennifer won't be able to say it."

New Year's Eve became New Year's Day, just another Monday. Monday morning, Monday afternoon, Monday evening. Tully's pulse was fast and weak, her blood pressure low. She was still not waking up, and she was still seeping blood. Tully needed another two transfusions on Monday. Robin volunteered on Monday evening. He didn't ask who gave Tully blood on Monday morning.

The name tag on the baby was changed. Jennifer *Pendel DeMarco* was the concession Jack Pendel made to Robin. I wonder what Tully will have to say about this? Robin thought. I hope she wakes up soon. I've got to go and register the baby's birth.

Shakie called Sunday evening. Pretty routine, but Boomerang—Robin, Jr.—told her over the phone Tully had the baby. His father wished he hadn't. Shakie effused for a few minutes on the phone, then got extremely concerned about

Tully's condition. So Robin lied. He told Shakie that Tully was not allowed any visitors in the ICU and that the baby was in quarantine to prevent infection and couldn't be seen, either.

"She'll never forgive me if I don't come and visit her or the baby," said Shakie.

"Don't worry, Shake. She's a very forgiving person."

Monday morning Robin went to the hospital and stayed through Monday evening. Hedda and Millie took care of Boomerang. Millie came by the hospital briefly to tell Robin she could stay overnight; he didn't have to worry. Thank God for Millie, Robin thought. And then Millie placed her hand on Robin's shirt and said meaningfully, "It'll be all right, Mr. DeMarco. Everything will work out. My prayers are with you."

Robin wasn't sure what she meant. Somehow, Robin doubted Millie was talking about Tully's getting better. She said her prayers were with Robin, not with Tully.

Robin sat in the waiting room, either by himself or with Julie, and took care of nothing. Occasionally he went downstairs to the cafeteria to take care of his thirst or to buy a Tylenol to take care of the throbbing ache above his left ear. Eating was out of the question. When Tully's blood pressure dropped further on Monday evening, going home was out of the question. Tully was given another dose of sulfa drugs, and when her hands stopped being hot, Robin wanted to know if that meant she was getting better. Seeing the look on Dr. Brunner's face, he knew she wasn't. He didn't want to leave the ICU but was told to. Apparently Tully had other visitors.

When Robin dozed off, he dozed off in the sitting position, head slumped to one side. The constant intercom announcements kept waking him up. He kept expecting to hear, *Mr. Robin DeMarco please report to the ICU on the fourth floor*.

There was a lot of time to think. Jack, thank God, had found himself another place to wait. Robin did most of his thinking in the waiting room. Some of it he did while holding baby Jennifer in the infants' ward.

"Your mom will be pretty proud of you, little one," Robin would whisper, touching the wisps of blond hair on the baby's head. "I think she wanted Boomer to look like her. But it's even better that *you* do. 'Cause you're a girl and everything."

And sometimes Robin thought, *Why would Jack put his name on this child?* Is he here, year in and year out? Does he never leave Topeka anymore? Robin counted back nine months. April. April is not a good painting month, you bastard. Why would you name the baby *Pendel*?

"I'm sorry, Mr. DeMarco. Your wife has taken a turn for the worse."

This was Tuesday morning, 8:30. Robin stared into Dr. Brunner's long face. Is mine just as long?

"I'll be glad to give more blood."

"Yes, thank you. That won't be necessary. We've nearly replaced her entire blood supply. We've done a CBC and it continues to show a presence of toxic bacteria in the blood-stream. Last night we gave her sulfa drugs and a fourth injection of oxytocin. But nothing is working as well as we'd hoped. She has gotten worse, I'm afraid. I'm sorry. She seemed so routine at first."

"How much worse?" Robin wanted to know.

"Much worse," replied Dr. Brunner.

"So give her some more antibiotic."

Dr. Brunner shook his head. "She's weakening fast, Mr. DeMarco. Her uterus has not contracted, her body is not responding to the antibiotics."

Robin stared away from the doctor's lowered head. "How weak?"

"Her blood pressure's dropped dramatically this morning. Seventy over forty-five. And her pulse rate, which for the last two days was a shallow one-fifty, has fallen . . ." The doctor looked away from Robin, and Robin stepped away from him, hoping the glaze over his eyes would help him not see a registered physician unable to look into his face.

"Fallen," Dr. Brunner continued, "to forty. I'm sorry."

"Forty, huh," repeated Robin dully. "What's normal?"

"Seventy-two to ninety-two is normal. During sleep, fifty-five to sixty-five is normal. Forty is not normal. I'm sorry."

Robin tried to collect his scattered thoughts.

"How not normal?"

Again the long face glanced away when its mouth moved. "Close to coma. I'm terribly sorry."

"God!" exclaimed Robin. "Why do you keep saying that? Don't say you're sorry. She's not dead yet. Help her, god-damn it."

"We're trying to, Mr. DeMarco. We're doing our best."

Dr. Brunner started to walk away. Robin followed him. "Wait," he said. "This is a difficult situation, I understand and appreciate your professionalism."

Dr. Brunner nodded.

"But," said Robin, "have you spoken to Mr. Pendel?"

"About what?" asked the doctor gently.

"About the birth, of course."

"Yes, we got all the information we needed from Mr. Pendel."

"Everything?"

"Yes."

"Infection, you said infection last Sunday. Did you ask him from what?"

"Mr. DeMarco, I wasn't sure. Infection was possible. Nonsterile conditions during childbirth are a breeding ground for bacteria. Mr. Pendel told us everything he knew. And Mrs. . . . Natalie seemed to be okay on Sunday other than the bleeding."

"Yes, yes, yes," said Robin, breathing hard. "But maybe there is something you overlooked."

"Mr. DeMarco, I know you're trying to help, but we've done nearly all we can."

Robin scrubbed and went to sit by Tully. It was 9:15.

He sat in his usual chair. Occasionally he got up to look at her up close, as he often did, but this morning some-thing gnawed at Robin, gnawed at him, just scratched him up inside, scratch, scratch, like fingers on glass. What the fuck is that?

He looked around, his heart sicker by each scratch, scratch. What, what? What is it? Taking off his gloves, he took Tully's hand. It was cool.

"Tully?" he whispered, leaning over her face. "Tully?" he said, louder, trying to wake her up, bringing his face to her face to try to feel her breath. "Tully?"

There was breath.

And that's when Robin knew what it was. Knew the SCRATCH SCRATCH.

It was the heart monitor. That fucking heart monitor, going . . . BLEEP . . . BLEEP . . . BLEEP . . . BLEEP . . . bleep . . .

Robin clawed at his chest to get at the scratching, clawed at his shirt, at the shirt buttons, at his bare chest, finally, scratch, scratch, stop it, stop it, STOP IT! He grabbed her, tubes and all, and started shaking her and screaming. A feeding tube fell out of Tully's nose. Her mouth opened in an O.

The nurse ran into the glass room. "What are you doing?" she panted, trying to pry his hands off her. "What are you doing to the patient? She's sick, what do you think you're doing?"

Robin let go, let Tully fall back on the bed. "She is not a patient," he said, breathing breathing breathing. "She is my wife."

Robin went out into the waiting room and sat next to Julie, who was haggard and unkempt, looking in many ways worse than Tully. At 9:35, Dr. Brunner came up to Robin.

"Mr. DeMarco. I'm sorry for the trouble in the ICU. I forgot to warn you about the heart monitor. A heart beating at forty beats per minute is a slow heart indeed. The monitor is sometimes distressing to listen to."

Robin's chest was still exposed. He fumbled with his shirt buttons. "It didn't sound . . . steady," he said haltingly.

Dr. Brunner cleared his throat, and then he pressed his palms together as if in prayer. "Mr. DeMarco, it's not very steady. Not at all. The pulse has dropped down to thirty-five." He bowed his head and his voice got quieter. "We have a priest in the chapel, if you—"

"Goddamn it!" Robin exploded. "Don't tell me to get a priest! Help her!"

Dr. Brunner said quietly, "We've done all we can. I'm very sorry. Maybe you have your own priest. . . ."

Robin stared blankly . . . *Our Father which art in heaven, hallowed be Thy name* . . .

"I can't leave her," he said.

"May God be with her and with you, Mr. DeMarco," said Dr. Brunner.

God, the scratching, the SCRATCHING.

"Yes," said Robin inaudibly. "But I can't leave her."

"Robin!"

He turned around. Julie was standing beside him. She wiped her face. "Father Majette, Robin," she said. "You can go and get Father Majette."

"Julie, you go and get Father Majette."

Julie sank to the floor. "I can't, Robin." She was weeping. "I can't."

"Go and get him if you want, Julie," Robin whispered, trying to keep everything out of his voice.

"I can't, Robin! I can't leave her, either! I wasn't there for our Jennifer . . . please! I can't not be there for Tully, too, I just can't!" she said, weeping. "She's my Tully, too, Robin," she whispered. "I knew her before any of you knew her. She is my Tully, too. . . ."

At 9:40 A.M., Robin went back to the glass room. He didn't walk in this time, just stood outside the glass and looked at Tully's face. It's all right, Tully, he thought. It's all right, my dear one, everything will be all right. God will bless you and keep you and keep me, too . . .

. . . *The Lord is my Shepherd, I shall not want . . . He maketh me to lie down in green pastures: He leadeth me beside the still waters . . .*

But the gnawing inside his chest did not abate, not even outside the glass. This glass may be tempered but it's not soundproof, and though haze is veiling my sight, I can still hear that detached distant sound of fingers on the board of the bleep of the heart monitor. I hear it as it gets farther and farther away and I feel lonely. Lonely lonely lonely. Robin blinked and quickly glanced to his right and then to his left.

And to his left he saw Jack.

It was the first time Robin had seen him since they spoke in the waiting room on Sunday.

Robin swallowed hard to get rid of that numbing snowball in his throat. "She's worse," he said to Jack.

"I know," Jack replied.

Robin glanced at him. Jack was unshaven, his eyes bloodshot and circled with black from lack of sleep. He looks like I feel, thought Robin. *The Lord is my Shepherd . . .*

"What's wrong with her?" Robin asked.

"Loss of blood," said Jack. "I don't know."

"She's got more blood in her than me and you put together. There has to be something else. She's got blood poisoning, and no one's sure where it's coming from."

Jack lifted a blue surgical mask over his face. Robin noticed Jack's hands were unsteady. It took him a while to get the mask just right. "I don't know, man. What can I say? Everything was clean, everything seemed to be okay."

"Have they—has anyone talked to you about it?"

"Yeah, on Sunday. Not since then."

Robin shook his head. "There is something they've overlooked. They, and you, too. There is something everyone's forgetting. There has to be. Her body is losing out because there's something you all overlooked."

Jack looked down at the floor. "I told them all I know."

Robin stepped closer to Jack. Robin was not looking away. "Well, think hard," he whispered. "Think of something!"

Jack twitched, moving toward the glass door that led to Tully. "I told them all I know. I don't know anything else. What do I know from babies?"

Only how to make them, you bastard, thought Robin, going after Jack into Tully's glass room.

"One at a time," said the nurse, looking at both of them with her eyebrows permanently raised. "I said one at a time."

Robin pushed her away. "Go and get Dr. Brunner, if you want. She can't hear us, anyway."

"You're disturbing her."

"Who?" snapped Jack. "Who are we disturbing, *nurse Ratched*?"

"My name," the nurse said icily, "is Jean Crane. R.N. You're disturbing my patient."

They both ignored her. Jack was already at Tully's bedside.

Nurse Jean Crane grabbed Robin by the arm. "Please go and wait and let him be done," she whispered angrily. "He's been standing outside the door waiting for you to be done when you're in here for hours at a time. Let him have a few peaceful moments with her, will you?"

Robin stared at the nurse and then looked back to see Jack. In the glass room, in the soundless sleepy ICU, next to Tully's bed, Robin saw Jack. And Jack was on his knees.

Robin turned around and went back into the waiting room.

* * *

At 9:47, Robin saw Jack rush out of the ICU, heading toward him.

"I know what it is! I bet I know what it is," Jack panted. "The umbilical cord—what's happened to the rest of that umbilical cord?"

"It came out, didn't it?" said Robin, standing up. "It's not attached to her anymore, so it must've come out, right?"

"Yes, but what is it attached to inside her?"

"Nothing! It's out."

"What *was* it attached to? The placenta, I think, right?"

Robin just nodded, barely keeping up.

"And the placenta is live tissue, right? Live tissue?"

"I guess," said Robin, confused. "Well, it came out, didn't it?"

"Yes, it did," said Jack, cracking his knuckles. "But we pulled on it a little. What I'm saying is . . . *what if part of it is still inside her?*"

And then they were both running full speed down the long corridor. Robin had forgotten the doctor's name. Jack didn't forget, though, ah, yes, of course. Dr. Brunner. With the long face. He was nowhere to be found, but the sight and sound of two grown desperate men spurred the nurses to find Dr. Brunner, and Jack, panting, forgetting his words, saying *imbecilical* instead of *umbilical,* finally got across what he wanted to say, while Dr. Brunner's face got longer. He ran back to the ICU, screaming to the nurses behind him, "Makker in ICU, O.R. One! O.R. One! Now! I need two to prep, hurry! Jean, we'll need blood"—pointing to Robin and Jack—"as soon as you can, please! Hurry!"

And then Robin and Jack stood by the double doors of the ICU, waiting for Tully to be wheeled out. There she was with all her tubes, with her eyes closed, and with that fucking heart monitor, still going bleep . . . bleep . . . SCRATCH . . . SCRATCH.

They gave blood again. Both of them, in the same little room with their sleeves rolled up. This was Robin's second Band-Aid. He noticed it was Jack's third.

And then they both got Julie. The three of them went down to the second floor and sat in the O.R. waiting room.

. . . Give us this day our daily bread, and forgive us our trespasses, as we forgive those who trespass—

"She'll be all right, won't she?" Robin said to no one in particular, not even looking up. Julie didn't answer, busy blowing her nose.

Jack looked up and replied, "Of course. She's strong like a bull."

Robin nodded. And just as stubborn. Stronger than me. All his sharp feelings with edges had given way to a general malaise of nonfeeling, of a slow anesthetic, *Novopain,* that dulled his senses. Robin heard himself asking, "The little girl, she must've come out quick?"

"Oh, yes," said Jack, looking at Robin steadily. "She did. Tully nearly missed the whole thing."

"Mmmmm," said Robin. "She nearly missed it with Boomerang, too." Lord knows I missed it. "Boomerang was fast. Very fast."

Jack smirked. "She said Boomerang took two days to come out and even then they had to induce labor."

Robin fleetingly smiled back. "Yeah, that's what she says to everyone." It pleased him somewhat to know that Tully did not divulge the truth to Jack. What a funny animal man is, thought Robin, trying always to find something, anything, any goddamn thing to rid himself of pain. But just as fast, the small satisfaction disappeared when Jack said, "Listen, man—"

Robin waved him off immediately, his eyes half closing. "No," he said, getting up, helping himself up. "This is about as much as I can stand. Thanks for remembering about the placenta, though."

He moved slowly to the window . . . *And lead us not into temptation but deliver us from evil . . . I will fear no evil: for Thou art with me; Thy rod and Thy staff comfort me . . . but Thy loving kindness and mercy shall follow me all the days of my life: and I will dwell . . . my God, my God, look upon me; why hast Thou forsaken me . . . ?* Robin wasn't sure if that was a psalm or an old Simon and Garfunkel tune called "Blessed." He sat back down in the corner of the waiting room near a window.

Blessed are the meek, for they shall inherit . . .
Blessed is the lamb whose blood flows . . .

Blessed are the sat upon, spat upon, ratted on . . .
Oh Lord, why have you forsaken me?

Robin wanted a smoke, but he didn't want to leave the room. But, oh, how he wanted a smoke. *"Kathy's Song,"* he thought. *"Tully's Song."* . . . *And so you see, I've come to doubt, all that I once held as true; I stand alone without beliefs, The only truth I know is you . . .*

Taking out his lighter, he flicked it on and off, on and off, on and off, thinking . . . *Have mercy upon us, miserable sinners* . . . Let's see . . . what else is there? Thank you, Mom, for dragging me to church when I was young, and for making me memorize these prayers I haven't needed in thirty years. . . . *From all evil and mischief; from sin, and from everlasting damnation, Good Lord, deliver us. From all blindness of heart; from pride, from envy, hatred, and malice; from fornication, and all other deadly sin, from all deceits of the world; from lighting and tempest; from battle and murder, and from sudden death . . . Good Lord, deliver us. I hope you don't die, Tully, and leave me lonely, like she left you, and left you lonely. . . .*

Over two hours passed. One hundred and thirty-nine minutes. Eight thousand three hundred and forty seconds . . . forty-one . . . forty-two . . . forty-three . . .

The doctor came out.

Robin and Jack both stood up. Julie remained sitting.

"All right. All right," said Dr. Brunner, taking off his surgeon's gloves. "Let's calm down, now. She's going to make it."

Robin sank back down into his chair. But Jack continued to stand. "It was the placenta, wasn't it?" he said.

"Yes, Mr. Pendel, you were right. Part of the placenta remained inside the uterus. Life-threatening. Endometritis. Hard to pick up on X rays, and as a dead and useless organ, it decays and festers very quickly, causing all sorts of problems, as you saw. Hemorrhaging, high fever, blood poisoning, not to mention a serious deterioration in the uterine wall. Ms. Makker's uterine lining had always been weak, damaged. She had problems before with the expulsion of the placenta. This time, with a home birth, it was much worse. But anyway, the worst's behind us.

Her pulse is up to fifty-three now and gaining. Her blood pressure is still low—but she should be okay. Oh, one more thing . . ." Dr. Brunner faced Robin. "We had to remove her uterus in order to save her. The surrounding tissues are fine, but the uterus, I'm afraid, is gone. I'm sorry," he added, turning away from Robin's stricken face. "Thank you again for the blood, gentlemen. And for your help, Mr. Pendel," said Dr. Brunner, extending his hand.

Jack shook it. Robin sank into the chair. It was 1:05 in the afternoon, the second day of 1990.

4.

Robin came home Tuesday night. Three women in his house were taking care of Boomerang: Millie, who arched her eyebrows and repeated about her prayers being with Robin; Hedda, who paddled into the kitchen and asked if Robin wanted something to eat; and Shakie, who was upstairs putting Boomer to bed.

"Thanks, Shake," said Robin gratefully.

Shakie patted him on the arm. "How's Tully?"

Shakie was the only one of the women who asked Robin about Tully. Maybe Shakie's prayers are actually with *Tully*.

"Great," said Robin. "You can come and see her and the baby soon."

"Is she still unconscious?"

"*Less* unconscious," said Robin, stretching his lips into a nominal smile.

"You didn't sound so hot when you called me this afternoon," commented Shakie. "Is she all right?"

"Fine. I was probably a little tired, that's all," said Robin, feigning a yawn. "Well, it's late."

And then afterwards, he sat by his son's side.

"How's Mom, Dad?" Boomerang asked.

"She's better, Boomer. Sorry. *Robin*. She'll be waking up soon."

"Boy, will she be surprised she had a baby girl, won't she, Dad?"

"Stunned," agreed Robin.

"The baby, she's kind of cute," said Boomerang. "When does she start to talk and do stuff?"

"In a little while," said Robin. "Maybe next week."

"Next week? Get out of here, Dad. I gotta ask Mom, you don't know anything about kids."

Robin smiled a little bit. It *will* seem like next week, he thought, before she, too, is saying, "Get out of here, Dad," and then he thought, Will she be saying it to *me*?

"Robin, Jr.," he whispered, "I'm lucky to have you, son."

"Dad," said Boomerang, patting his father on the back and turning away. "Stop kissing me. Good night."

5.

When Tully awoke, the first person she saw in front of her was Robin. She was groggy, feeling sleepy, but she opened her eyes and saw Robin sitting across from her. It was almost like the Robin she had been dreaming of when her eyes were closed, but she knew this one was real. He looks like hell, thought Tully as she focused. He looked gaunt and drawn. His lips were parched, and the dark circles under his eyes covered nearly half his face. His chocolate eyes went liquid when she moved her lips.

"Robin," she mouthed, "how is the baby?"

"She is fine," he said, trying to sound calm. "Doing better than you."

Tully saw the glass bottle of Lucosade connected to her arm. "God, look at me," she whispered. "I've turned into my mother."

Robin just sat there, his hands folded on his lap, so she said, "How is Boomer?"

"Great," said Robin. "He thinks his sister is pretty cute."

"I'm sure she's lovely. What day is this?"

"Wednesday."

"Wednesday . . ." she echoed dully, touching her breasts. An unbearable thought floated by. I must've lost my milk by now. My milk must all be gone.

"What have they been feeding her?" she asked, wanting to cry.

"She is doing fine, Tully," he repeated. "Better than you."

"How *am* I doing?"

"Better now."

"What was the matter? Last thing I remember was an ambulance . . ."

"Yeah. Apparently not all of your placenta came out. A part got stuck, and it kind of poisoned you. You're okay now," he said, looking away.

Tully tried to think of something comforting to say to him. He looked so forlorn. "Happy New Year's," she said. "She was born on New Year's Eve, you know."

"I know," he said.

Tully felt all constricted inside. "Robin," she said quietly, almost apologetically. "Where's Jack?"

A beat. Another beat. Only the sound of water running, and metal clanging somewhere. "Outside," said Robin. "Do you want me to get him?"

Tully didn't answer. Everything was so vague, so confused, sweaty, feverish, otherworldly. But Jack's was the face she last remembered seeing. It was a beloved face, and she wanted to see it again.

Tully glanced over at Robin. He looked utterly alone. She fought an impulse to ask him to come closer to her, to hold her. I guess there isn't that much milk left in me after all, she thought, saying aloud, "Please. Please. Just for a few minutes."

Robin got up and put his hand to his throat in a gesture Tully didn't understand and didn't want to. Unable to look at him anymore, Tully closed her eyes and whispered, "I'm sorry, Robin," but she didn't think he heard her, having already closed the glass door behind him.

A nurse came in and Tully asked her to bring in her little girl. And in a moment, she saw Jack through the glass walls, walking towards her and smiling. She felt happier. "Jacko," she murmured. He came over, sat on the bed, and leaned over her, his arms flanking her.

"Hey, babe. Time to wake up, sleepyhead. I think this is a record even for you."

Tully emitted a guttural sound that was more like a baboon than a human, but Jack seemed pleased by it because he smiled and put his face to hers. She lifted up her free hand and patted him gently on the head. "Jacko, how is she?"

"Tully, she is so beautiful."

He pulled up, and she saw his face up close. Black sleepless marks underneath those gray eyes, and blond stubble from well into last week. Even his mouth was pale. Jack looked as bad as Robin.

"Have both you guys been in here all this time?"

Jack nodded.

"Oh, God," said Tully, not letting go of Jack's head. "Poor Robin."

"Poor Robin," agreed Jack. "He's been okay. You were kind of tough on both of us."

"Was I okay?"

"Yeah, sure," Jack said, averting her gaze. "Did Robin tell you? A chunk of the placenta didn't want to leave that nice womb of yours."

"He told me some. Did they get it?"

"Yeah, they got it," Jack said, putting his head on her chest. "But they had to give you a hysterectomy, Tull. I'm sorry."

Tully felt her whole body tense up into a knot. She pushed him off her. Jack got up and went to sit on a chair.

When she could speak, she said, "Why did they have to go and do a thing like that? What about some antibiotics or something?"

Jack shook his head. "Nothing was helping, Tully. You weren't doing so good."

Tully studied Jack's face, remembered Robin's face, looked around the sterile glass unit, and said quietly, "Did they ask what religion I was?"

"No, I don't think so," replied Jack.

Tully waved him off. "Well, then I couldn't have been doing that badly, could I?" she said. "Too bad about my uterus, though." She rubbed her belly. It hurt. "It's gonna make it difficult to have more babies, huh?" she said.

Jack just stared at her sadly.

In a few minutes, Nurse Crane came in with Jennifer. She said nothing, but slowly unhooked Tully's arm from the drip and handed her the infant. Jennifer was asleep, but through Jack's and Tully's efforts, quickly woke up and began to wail. Jack propped Tully up. His big arms practically lifted her off the bed. And Tully pulled down her hospital gown and pushed Jennifer's face to her breast. "God, is there anything left?" she whispered.

Nurse Crane came back with a bottle of formula. "Forget about that," she said briskly. "You've got nothing in there. Here, she's been drinking this."

When she left, Tully said to Jack, "What the hell is wrong with her?"

"Don't pay attention to her. But they're all pretty rotten, though. They all have raised eyebrows. They wear them like fucking armament."

"Why?"

"Why? Tully, there's been two of us here. Constantly. I brought you in, and then Robin came in and said he was your husband."

"He is my husband."

"Yes, and that's why all of them wear those raised eyebrows along with their uniforms. Two of us at the ICU. Two of us at the infants' ward asking to hold the baby. Actually, the nurse in the infant ward was the only decent one, but I think it's because she was the only one who hadn't figured it out."

Tully looked down at the baby, sucking on a bottle. "I'm a failure," she said. "Such a shame I won't be able to breast-feed her," she said, hurting. "That's it now for me, isn't it? I'm never going to breast-feed again. Boomerang was my first and last." She tried to swallow the lump in her throat. "Had I known, I would have fed him twice as long. . . ."

"Oh, Tully," Jack said, caressing her blanket. "Didn't you nurse him till he was two?"

"Twenty months. But I didn't know it was to be my last twenty months, did I?"

"Cheer up, Tully," Jack said. "It could be worse."

"Not much," whispered Tully, trying not to cry.

They listened to Jennifer's feeding noises. "She is pretty lovely, isn't she?"

"Beautiful."

"Look at her blond hair."

"You mean, look at her bald head! Where's the hair? I don't see it."

"Here! And here! Look at her eyes."

"Yeah, where are her eyelashes?"

"Jack! You're incorrigible. Have you been looking in on her much?"

"All the time."

Tully stroked the baby tenderly. "Have you held her?"

"All the time," said Jack. A look passed between them, a look that transcended the ocean and the prairie.

They sat there quietly and after a while, Jack said, pushing farther away on the chair, "Tully, who's going to be taking you home?"

Tully shut her eyes to shut out his question and with it her whole life. But Jennifer kept sucking on the bottle too loudly. It wasn't possible to shut *her* out. Tully stretched her hand to Jack. "Jacko, I gotta go home. I gotta see my boy, I gotta get better. I don't feel too good, you know."

"I know," he said.

"As soon as I'm better, as soon as I have some strength in me, I'll talk to Robin. We'll figure out what's best. Okay?"

Jack shook his head. "I don't have much choice, do I?"

"Please, Jack," Tully whispered. "Be patient."

"Patient? I ought to be canonized," replied Jack.

The ceiling and the roof pressed down on Tully's insides when she saw the expression on his face—bitterness and love.

"I'm so sorry, Jacko," Tully whispered again. Ten minutes later, Jennifer was finally asleep.

Nurse Crane came in, took the baby, and said, "You must go, Mr. Pendel. Her husband," she said, with raised eyebrows. "Her husband wants to see her."

"Fuck you," Jack muttered under his breath, getting up to hug Tully, hard.

"Was that to me or her?" Tully smiled. He kissed her head.

"Jack? Did you call Robin to tell him I had the baby?"

Jack took a slight bow, his eyes the color of rained-on slate. "Who else? Who else did you leave that to, Tully Makker? You were so out, I couldn't even ask you how to do it best. So I did it the best I could."

"I'm sure you were splendid as always," she said, her voice cracking. "In all ways."

Jack pressed his fingers to his lips, blowing her a kiss, and was out. And Tully pressed her fingers to her eyes, as Jennifer once did, trying to keep at bay the sea of sadness. I am worn out, she thought. I am so worn out. I am so tired. Well, at least no more secrets. No more lies. No more non-phone calls. No more pretending, one way or the other. But she wasn't thinking clearly, so she drifted off, imagining she was still holding Jennifer in her arms.

6.

When Tully awoke, Robin was sitting in the chair again, dark and desperate. He looked so forsaken that Tully nearly cried aloud. She stretched out her free arm to him, and he got up and came over. Sitting on the bed, he hugged her with both arms, and she stroked the back of his head and his back, his trembling shoulders.

Tully was moved from the ICU to the post-op ward Thursday evening and spent a week there. During the week she had lots of visitors. Besides Robin, Jack, and Julie, Tully saw Julie's mother and father, Shakie and Frank, Bruce and Linda, Steve and Karen, and Tony Mandolini. Tully also saw her son every day after school.

Shakie and Frank came. When Shakie had a few moments alone with Tully, she said, "I saw Jack's car in the parking lot, Tully."

"Did you? Good," said Tully.

"Why is *he* here? Haven't you done enough to poor Robin?"

"Oh, Shakie! Cut the shit. Robin doesn't need your pity. I don't need your judgment. Everything is going to be just fine. Lest you forget, he came to see *you* when you had your babies."

"He did not come alone."

"He didn't come alone here, either. He came with Julie."

"Oh, Tully—"

"Oh, Tully, nothing! Save it, Shakie. Besides, you don't understand anything."

"Tully! That's what I had said to you."

"Great! You win! Now, do us both a favor and shut up. You're like a broken record."

"Tully, I told you once, and I'm going to tell you again. He'll break your heart."

"Oh, Shakie. So the fuck what? Who cares about my stupid heart?" *There is Robin's poor heart. And Boomerang's. And Jennifer's. And Jack Pendel's.* Who cares about my stupid heart anymore?

* * *

Hedda came. Robin drove her: she wanted to see her daughter. Tully pretended to be asleep.

"And I'll tell you honestly," Tully heard Hedda saying. "You are the biggest disappointment of my life. First place you hold. Your father is in second place. I took him when he was twenty-two years old, and he was somebody's before me—mommy's, daddy's, grandma's. But you began with me—and look what a misfortune. I don't even want to talk to you about this. To talk about this with you is disgusting to me, sad, and insulting. I don't know why you torture me like this. I feel sorry only for your poor Boomerang and the girl. I feel sorry for Robin. You've ruined everybody's life, everybody's, including your own, and you don't even care. You think things will ever be the same? You think they *could* ever be the same? You think if your father came back and I took him back, things would be the same then? So often I wished I raised a different daughter. Had a different daughter. We never connected, me and you. How I wish I had a daughter I connected to. Sometimes you don't seem like a daughter to me at all, you don't treat me well, you wish I was dead, I know you do. You don't want me in your house, I know. You pointed a gun at your mother. How could you do that? What kind of daughter does that to her mother? No, you are not a good daughter. You are not a good wife. That man loves you more than he loves the whole world and you don't care about him at all. Why Boomerang loves you so much, I'll never understand. And now this little girl. How will you be with her? My only satisfaction in my old age will come from her being as nasty a daughter to you like you were to me. Tully, I know you can hear me, you're clenching your fists, but you don't have to answer me. I'm used to having no answer from you. Everybody's used to having no answer from you."

7.

Tully came home.

The first thing Tully said when she got out of Robin's Beamer was, "Where's my car?"

Robin placed his hand on her back. "Come inside, Tully, it's cold out here."

"Where's my car?" she said, not moving.

"Come inside. The baby."

She came inside then. "Where's the car?"

"Dad says it's broke," put in Boomerang when Robin didn't answer.

Tully turned to Robin. "What do you mean *broke*, Dad?" she said.

"Take off your coat, Tully."

"Where's the car, Robin?"

"Boomerang, can you go upstairs, son? Mommy and Daddy need to talk."

"Talk about what?" said Tully, louder. "All I want to know is where's the car?"

"Dad says it's in the shop, Mom," said Boomerang. "It's no big deal."

"Is it in the shop, Robin?"

"Do you really want to know where it is, Tully?"

"Of course I do! Where is it?"

"Come with me, then," said Robin. "Don't take off your coat."

"I'll come, too," said Boomerang.

"*No!*" said Robin. "You stay here with Nanna. We'll be right back."

Tully had little Jennifer in her arms as they drove off.

"For the millionth time, where's the car, Robin?"

"Tully, I'm sorry."

She punched the dashboard. "What did you do with my car, you bastard? What did you do with Jennifer's car?"

"Tully, I'm sorry. I was unbelievably angry."

"Oh, Robin, don't give me that shit, what did you do with it?"

"I'll show you in a minute," he said, and sure enough, in a minute they drove into the Frito-Lay parking lot. It was early Sunday morning, and the parking lot was completely empty. No other cars. Not even the Camaro.

"What did you bring me here for?" asked Tully, wiping her face. "I don't want to have sex with you."

"I brought you here to show you your car," Robin said. "But someone must've taken it."

"You left it here?" Tully gasped. "You left it here to be *stolen*?"

"No, Tully, after I was done with it, no one would have wanted to steal it."

"So what did you do with it?" she said in a small voice.

"I'm sorry. I smashed it to bits. I'm glad you can't see it. I took the lead pipe you carry and broke all the windows, and—"

Tully waved at him to be quiet. For a while she couldn't speak. "How could you have done that to me?" she said at last.

"Tully! How could you have done *that* to me?"

"You bastard."

"Call me names if you want. At least I *am* sorry."

"You bastard. I'll never be sorry for anything I do to you now."

"Oh," said Robin bitterly. "You have something else planned?"

"Let's go," Tully said, turning as much as she could away from him. "I'm glad I can't see the car. You shouldn't have brought me. You should have just told me. In front of our son. Let's go."

Days passed. Days of sleep and feedings, and not being able to pee properly because of the stitches. Days of not getting dressed. Days of visitors. Julie came nearly every day before Laura arrived in Topeka and took her. Came every day, bawling, trying to talk Tully into something, or out of something, Tully wasn't sure. She was barely listening. Though apparently Julie was grateful to God that Tully lived. Like I had a choice, thought Tully.

Days upon days. One of the days, Tully turned twenty-nine and no one remembered, except for Jack, who called. A few days later everybody remembered, but too late. Millie cooked a birthday dinner and was asked to stay by Robin. Hedda, Robin, Tully, Millie, and Boomerang all sat at the table and ate the chicken cutlets that Millie had prepared, while Jennifer lay in a bassinet in the living room. "It almost makes me nostalgic," Tully said, "for those days when I went from seven to fifteen and never knew it. I thought I was eight years old and in high school." Everyone glanced at Hedda and then down into their food, except for Robin, who watched Tully with unwavering eyes.

"Do you have to?" he said to Tully later when they were alone. "Do you have to make everyone feel bad? Haven't you done enough?" Tully didn't respond but went out of the room to sit in the rocking chair in Jenny's nursery. She fell asleep there. It was three in the morning when she came back to bed, and Robin wasn't in the room. She went downstairs, but he wasn't there, either. She found him finally in Boomerang's bedroom. Waking him up, she whispered, picking up the ashtray on Boomer's nightstand, "Robin, how many times have I asked you? Don't smoke when you are here, or open the goddamned window, or something, it is so bad for him to breathe this shit."

"Yeah, yeah, yeah," he said. "You told me."

Days of having food brought up by the ever-loyal Millie, of having Jennifer brought in by the ever-loyal Millie, of having Jennifer changed and dressed by Millie. It was too bad Millie didn't dress adults. Tully could have gone downstairs then. Or outside. But she just lay there in her bed. The only TV in the house was downstairs and she did not want to go downstairs. Robin asked her if she wanted the TV upstairs, but she did not.

Occasionally Tully talked to Millie. Briefly. Mostly Tully lay in bed. Millie would come in and open the windows.

"What's the weather like, Mill?" Tully would say.

"Cold, Mrs. DeMarco," Millie would reply. "It's cold."

"You can say that two times," Tully would mumble.

Robin finally went back to work. There was nothing he could do for her anymore, she said. Go and make money. Tully slept a lot, tossed and turned a lot, stared out of the window that Jack had painted. Ran her fingers over the ragged vertical scar that reminded her every minute Boomerang and Jenny were to be her only children.

Now Tully couldn't bring herself to call Jack. She knew he was waiting for her call, but she just couldn't call him. She didn't know what to say to him. Didn't know what to say to Robin, either. Tully talked mostly to Millie and to Boomerang. She also babbled whatever vague endearments she could think of to little Jennifer. Tully didn't speak to Hedda at all, not even when her mother limped up to her bedroom and asked Tully if she needed anything. "Millie gets me everything I want," said Tully, her head turned away.

It was early February when Tully finally let Jack come over. She became afraid if she didn't, he might leave for California and leave her behind.

Tully didn't bother sending Millie away. What was the point, when Hedda lurked in the house? Tully even got out of bed and took a shower and got dressed for him, but she trod downstairs as slowly as someone who had just learned to walk.

Hedda and Millie were sitting in the kitchen and looked surprised to see her. "Mother, could you go to your room, please? Jack is going to be here any minute. Millie, take a break, why don't you? Go shopping, or whatever," Tully said weakly. It was hard to be out of bed. She held on to her stomach.

"Do you think that man should be coming to this house?" said Hedda, while Millie looked into her cup of tea.

"Mother, I want you to go to your room. I don't think it's a good idea that you should be living in this house, yet here you are."

"What are you doing, Tully?" Hedda said. "What are you doing?"

"Not explaining myself to you. Now, Mother, please, I don't feel well enough to argue. Please."

Hedda got up, but not before she said, "You are worse now than you have ever been."

"Yes, and out of your hands," said Tully.

When Hedda left, Tully looked at Millie, who was still staring into her tea, and said, "Go on, Millie. It will be all right. Don't judge me."

"No, Mrs. DeMarco. I'm not judging you," Millie said. "I want to help. But what's Mr. DeMarco going to say?"

"Hopefully as little as possible," said Tully. "Now help me by helping Shakie, Mill. Go to Dillard's. Offer Shakie some money. She'll give you some lipstick in return."

When the bell rang and Tully opened the door, her heart jumped a little, stopped, breathed a little, screamed when she laid her eyes on him. She nodded hello and let him in.

They went upstairs to see Jennifer. What used to be the exercise room was now converted into a nursery and Jennifer's bed was in the far corner.

Tully looked at the window and remembered standing on a ladder outside that window with a paintbrush in her hand one hot July.

Jack held Jennifer to him, rocked with her, put her on the changing table, and took off her playsuit and diaper, and when she was all naked he looked over her face and body: her nose and lips and eyes and forehead, her head and thin hair, her neck and shoulders, her arms and hands and fingers, her chest and stomach and ribs, her thighs and knees and calves and feet, her toes. Tully felt tired. And broken.

"Look," Jack said quietly to Tully. "Look," pointing to her toes, thick and wide. "Is there any doubt whose baby she is?"

Tully glanced away. "No," she said.

Jack changed Jennifer's diaper, dressed her, and they took her downstairs, where Tully warmed up a bottle and Jack fed her.

"How are things?" he asked her.

"Great!" She tried to sound cheerful. "How are things with you?"

"Okay. I'm not doing much, as you can imagine," he said.

"Wintertime is hard on you, isn't it?"

He stroked Jennifer's head.

"I can see you haven't talked to him yet."

"I haven't felt up to it."

"No, of course not. What would you like me to do in the meantime? I can't keep coming here, or he's liable to shoot me for trespassing."

"I'll talk to him as soon as I can. Please stay in Topeka."

"Oh, Tully," he said. "Enough already."

"Maybe you'll learn to like it again?" she said hopefully.

"Tully, stop," said Jack. "You know there is no life here for me. I don't want to stay here, and you don't, either. Look, we can go to California, we can go there and I will rent us a house in a great town, and I will work all year round there, and when you want to go back to work you will. Tully, it's the only thing we both want. What are we waiting for?"

"I'll talk to him," she said doggedly. "I haven't been feeling well."

"I know. Think of what the sunshine and warm weather will do for you."

She lowered her eyes and settled them on Jennifer. "It certainly does sound good," she whispered.

"So, what are you waiting for?"

She shook her head. "Jack, it just isn't as easy as all that."

"What else is there?"

She tried to think of what else there was. There was something. There was something that felt as big as Mount St. Helens to her. As big and wide as the dried-out Gobi. As parched. As insurmountable. "Robin will not let Boomerang go," she said grimly.

The only sound in the room was Jennifer's drinking. Tully thought she heard *the shadow with panting breath.*

At last, Jack said, "Tully? Will you?"

No response from Tully.

"I will not let Jennifer go," said Jack, hands shaking, touching the baby's head.

Still no response from Tully.

"Tully," Jack said softly, leaning over and looking into her face. "Will you let *me* go?"

No! cried Tully, but couldn't speak.

After putting Boomerang to bed that night, Robin came into the bedroom and sat on the window seat. He sat there, while she lay staring off into the wall.

"So Tully. Hedda tells me Jack was here."

Tully nodded, without looking at him.

Robin just sat there until her eyelids fluttered. "Okay, Tully," he said, coolly. "Let's do it. What do you want to happen?"

I want things to be the way they were, Tully instantly thought. I don't want anything to happen at all.

Robin continued. "Now, I know you, Tully. I know you wish things were as neat and stacked as before. I look the other way, you continue to do as you please. But here we are. If I had looked the other way in the past, if I did avert my gaze, it was because I was hoping you'd come to your senses. But here we are. You haven't come to your senses, and I can't look the other way anymore.

"I almost wish that I could continue to wade through our marriage with half-open eyes, not paying too much attention to your comings and goings, but you've made sure that I absolutely can't do that. He called the girl Jennifer *Pendel*. Why did he do that, Tully? Why would he fly in the face of decency like that? I counted back. Could she possibly be his child?"

Tully nodded. "She could possibly." She wasn't prepared to tell Robin the whole truth.

"How? Is he here all year round nowadays?"

"Washington," said Tully bleakly. "We went to Washington together."

Robin pressed his palms between his legs and then lit a cigarette.

"I see. Could she also be mine?"

"She could," said Tully, turning from the window. She couldn't tell him.

"Should we do a paternity test?"

"If you wish."

"What do you wish?"

For things to be the way they were, thought Tully, but said, "I don't want a paternity test."

"Why?"

Because I know, she wanted to say. "Because it's not important to me."

"Do you want the child to be registered as Jennifer Pendel?"

"No," Tully said. "We're married. Boomerang is her brother. Register her as Jennifer P. DeMarco."

Tully wasn't looking at him when she heard him say, "What are you doing to me, Tully?"

"I'm sorry, Robin," said Tully, still not turning to him. "Please forgive me."

"I will forgive you, Tully. I have no choice. But we have to decide about us. We can certainly not talk and not eat and not drink and not look at each other and not touch each other for a couple of days, weeks, maybe months. But I think it'll get to be a drag year after year. Besides, we can't ignore Jennifer *Pendel* DeMarco."

"So register her as just Jennifer DeMarco."

"Like what's that going to change?"

Nothing, I guess, thought Tully, asking, "Robin, if you suspected, why didn't you say anything?"

"What for? And say what?"

"Say it was important to you that it not happen."

"Tully, what was important to me was that it be important enough to you that it never happen. I wanted you to want to stay with me because you wanted to. Besides, I really had no idea. For all I knew, all you could have been doing is burying and reburying Jennifer."

Tully did not say anything. There was nothing to say.

"But now it's kind of late for pretend, though I see by your blank stare that you still entertain some idiotic hope, like I had entertained, that some*how,* some *way* this will just all correct itself and I will once again close my eyes. But I tell you, Tully, that's impossible. I'm not dead yet. You have not killed me yet."

"Robin, you know," said Tully, "I haven't questioned you, either, all those nights you came home late and stayed in Manhattan Saturday nights, I almost never called Bruce, never wanted to know. I just assumed that if you wanted to change your life, you would let me know."

Robin smiled thinly. "Well, Tully, I'm here asking you the same question. . . . If you wanted to change your life, would you let me know?"

She was silent and still.

"You know what I think?" He smirked joylessly. "I think *you* wouldn't. I think you're too scared. You were always too scared."

"You're right," she said faintly. "But this is all too much for me to take right now."

"Tully, okay. But he cannot come to this house in the meantime. That cannot happen again."

She nodded. "Or what?"

"Or I will have to throw you out."

"Just me?" she said. "Or my children, too?"

"Just you, Tully."

She was silent. "He won't come here again," she said.

Robin stubbed out his cigarette and immediately lit another. "For once, just once in your fucking life! can't you be honest with me? Be honest with me, Tully, tell me what you really want."

And Tully had to turn away from him before she said, barely audible even to herself, "I want to change my life."

She heard him jump off the window seat and come around the bed. He sat down on the corner. "Did I hear you right?"

She nodded.

"You're being honest. Can I stand some more? I don't know if I can. But tell me honestly, Tully. Look at me. Do you love him?"

She nodded, unable to look into his face. Broken by him, broken by Robin DeMarco's decade-long inability to ask her if she loved *him*!

"Tully!" He leaned closer to her, turning her on her back. "Tully, I need you to look at me. That's better. Tell me again. Do you love him?"

"Yes," she whispered, "I love him."

He sat back. "I see. I thought you were friends because of Jennifer. I thought you might've been burying Jennifer."

"I was," said Tully.

"I see. But that was then. Do you want to go with him?"

"Yes," she said. "I want to go with him."

He sat farther back and finally stood up.

"So what are you waiting for, Tully? Permission?"

"I wanted to talk to you. Wanted to figure out—"

"Figure out what? Who gets the TV? Take everything, Tully, I'll buy myself three more."

"Not the TV, Robin," Tully whispered. "Boomerang."

Robin just stared at Tully. "What about Boomerang?"

"Will you let me . . . take Boomerang?"

Robin cursed and rushed up to her, leaning over her face and wrenching her arm. "Fuck you, Tully, fuck you!" he spat out. "Why don't you just get out the Colt you have up in the attic and blow my fucking brains out, and make it easy on yourself! After a couple of years in the slammer you can be reunited with your kids and with him. Or better yet, let me break your nose and your arm first and then kill me in self-defense! That way at least I will get some satisfaction from you." He let go of her, and grabbed the pillow and quilt off the bed. "Tully, leave if you want," he said, going out of the room. "But you are never—never!—getting my son."

8.

Tully saw Jack a week later. They did not meet at the house. Tully took a bundled-up Jennifer and met Jack at Washburn University, where they went to the student union and walked around with Jennifer strapped to Tully's chest.

"Jack, what do we do? Robin will not let me take Boomer."

"Of course not," Jack said. "It's what we expected. You'll have to fight for custody."

Tully shook her head. "No court is going to award custody to me, when I'm taking a child from his home and dragging him fifteen hundred miles to the great unknown. If they'd give me custody at all, they'd stipulate I have to live in Topeka. Look, I've been to enough family court. I know. The court weighs only the best interest of the child."

"The best interest of the child is to be with his mother," declared Jack.

"I agree," said Tully. "But Robin is going to think otherwise. He's going to pull out all the stops. He doesn't want to lose his boy. He'll tell them about my wrists, and I'll never get custody. Besides," Tully added, "I'm not even sure Boomerang would rather go with me than stay with his dad. No, the custody thing is a silly point. I can't go to court to fight for my boy. Solomon might as well take a knife and cut him in two. No, I need to figure out a way to talk Robin into letting me have Boomer, or—" she broke off.

"Or what?" Jack said.

"Or talk myself into leaving without him," Tully finished with effort.

"Are you going to come with me either way?"

"Yes," said Tully into the wind. "I will come with you either way."

Later she said, almost as an afterthought, "There is also the issue of my mother. Somebody's got to take care of her. I'm certainly not taking her to California with me, but I can't expect Robin to take care of her, either."

"Why not?" Jack said. "It can be part of your divorce settlement."

Divorce. My God. "It all needs to be worked out, I guess. I don't really want to hurt anybody." *Don't want to hurt Robin.*

"Robin's already been butchered, Tully," Jack said. "What else can you do to him?"

"Jack, I wish you wouldn't say that," Tully said.

They walked around a little while longer. "Tully, I know a place where you'd like to live. Carmel-by-the-Sea. It's a white-roofed little town, right on the ocean. Could you tell that from the name? I want to go and find us a place to live there, a nice place close to the water, if I can. So that we'll all have a place to stay when we go to California."

"Go? By yourself? What do you mean, go?"

"Tully, you need this time to settle your affairs peacefully. We can't see each other, there's no pretending now, no running around, and that's good in a way, but bad in another way. Besides, I really do need to find us a home. We can't be living in a van, you know."

"I know," she said tearfully. "But what if I get divorced and you don't come back?"

"Tully, I swear to you I will come back. I'll call you every week to tell you I'm coming back."

"Jack, I don't want you to go," Tully said, fighting back tears.

Jack stopped walking in front of Tully and held them both to his chest. "I'm no good to you here. I sit around all day and watch TV or read the paper or walk the malls. I can't stand winter. I wait for you to call, wait for you to say you'll see me. I'm miserable and you are miserable. I can't do it, sitting around here, waiting for you to decide my life. I'm not Jeremy, Tully. I am going to go and find us a home in Carmel. You'll like Carmel. So will the kids."

"I'm sure they will," mumbled Tully against his chest. "When you come back, Jenny will be six months old!"

"Tully, Jenny will be six months old whether I go away or not. I don't get to see her anyway. It's not like I have any rights or anything. No, God forbid. I get no time with you at all, or with her, and I'm tired of having snatches of time. I've had nothing but snatches of your time for the last three years," he said. "I'm tired of it. I want you all to myself."

They walked in circles around the campus. It was cold, but Tully wanted to sit down for a minute. Sit down next to him.

"Let's go and sit down over there, Jack," Tully said, pointing to the football stadium—the Home Bowl.

They sat high up in the bleachers. Tully blew on Jennifer's forehead and pulled her little hat down.

"Remember being on that field, Jacko?"

"Sure," he replied. "Nothing quite like it. The crowd, the noise, the ball. Football's a great game." He fell quiet. "I remember high school."

"Yeah, who doesn't," Tully said tonelessly.

"No, I mean," he said, "I remember it *well*. Even the winter. It wasn't so bad back then somehow."

"No, of course not," Tully said. "You were the stud of the school. The captain of the football team." A boundless, ageless, timeless captain of the football team, and every time you look at that field you're still there, and every time I look at you my throat aches. Jack Pendel, I don't want you to go.

"Jack, if you stay," Tully said uncertainly, "I'll move in with you."

"You what?"

"I'll move into your mother's house with you. I'll stay with you if you stay with me, and I'll get divorced and we'll go away when it's all done."

"You'll leave Texas Street?"

She thought of Boomerang's nursery. Of Jenny's nursery. "I'll leave Texas Street," she said, even more uncertainly.

"You'll leave Robin?"

Tully's throat ached more than ever. "I'll leave Robin."

Jack put his arm around her. "We won't have much money."

"Don't need much," she answered.

"All the money I have will have to go on getting a place in Carmel."

"That's good."

"I will still have to go and get us a home, Tully. I'd say come with me, come with me right now, but you've got to end your life here. You can't be running out on a whole life, now can you?" He smiled lightly. "You need to detach yourself from Robin, and from your house, and from your mother, and from your job, too. You said so yourself."

"No problem," Tully said.

Jack shook his head. "Go easy on yourself, Tully," he said. "You're coming with me. That's the important thing. I'll be back in a few months. With a home for us. And in California we'll have plenty of money because I can work all the time."

"You just don't want to stay here for a minute longer than you have to, do you?" said Tully. "Not even to be with me, not for a minute."

Jack sighed. "Tully, I'm going to go and find us a house. And I need to work. I can't make money here right now. I need to make some."

"I don't care about money, Jack," said Tully. "I just want things to work out for the best."

Jack drew her closer to him. "Tully, if you won't be able to take Boomerang with you, will you think things have worked out for the best?"

"No," she replied. "But I don't want to think about that just yet." *I don't want to think about that just* ever.

18

MOTHER

February 1990

Tully walked in the house and headed for the kitchen. "Oh, Millie, Millie," she said, handing the housekeeper the baby and taking off her coat. "It's so cold."

"I can turn the heat up, Tully," said Millie.

Tully shook her head. "What good will that do?" She sat down at the table and stared into the yard. She always liked the way the yard looked from the kitchen, through those criss-crossed Georgian windows. Through those *painted* windows.

"Millie. He's going back to California," she said dully.

Millie sat down at the table and said, "The baby is crying. She needs to be fed." Tully got up and warmed up a bottle. Upstairs, Tully changed Jenny, and then came back to the kitchen table, where Millie was still sitting, with a cup of tea.

"Mrs. DeMarco, let me know if it's none of my business, but will you be leaving us soon?"

"Millie, what kind of a question is that?"

"It's on our minds, Mrs. DeMarco," said Millie. "I'm sure Mr. DeMarco wants to know."

"I'm sure he does," said Tully. "Mr. DeMarco is not making it very easy for me, though, is he?"

"Once he realizes you want to go, I'm sure he'll give you a divorce."

"Oh, yes," said Tully. "I'm sure he'll give me a divorce."

"You know," said Millie carefully, "I think it's good *he's* gone away for a little while. Him being here drives Mr. DeMarco to distraction."

"Yeah, yeah," said Tully. "Who doesn't it drive to distraction? Mr. DeMarco. Me. Shakie. My mother, who would just love to call me slut again, except she is afraid of becoming a homeless statistic."

Cautiously, Millie offered that Hedda didn't much care what happened to her life.

"You can say that again," said Tully. "No, actually, I disagree. She's still ticking away, isn't she?"

"You're not saying you want your mother to stop living, are you, Tully?"

"No, no," Tully said hurriedly. "I suppose not." Sipping her tea, Tully looked out of the window. She saw in the yard the evenings that ran on and on when she and Robin sat outside and ate hamburgers and watched Boomerang jump about. She saw many winter Sundays when they built snowmen and snowladies and snowbabies, threw snow in each other's faces and played mad ball. She closed her eyes and said, "Millie, how am I going to make this all go away?"

"Go away, Tully?"

"Things got so screwed up," Tully said, and didn't say any more. What if Jack doesn't come back? What if he just decides not to? she thought, watching her little girl suckle and splutter. He'll come back, she thought. He'll come back for Jennifer.

"I pray you do the right thing, Mrs. DeMarco."

"Oh, and what do you think that might be?"

Millie was thoughtful. "Learning from our past might be a right thing to do."

Tully got the sneaking suspicion that Millie had talked to Hedda at some length.

"You've got to stop talking to my mother, Millie. It'll do you no good."

"Believe it or not, your mother loves you."

"Millie, do you think this is helping? I'll tell you right now it's not. Besides, what's to love? I've become so unlikable. How has Robin stood me for this long? What did it cost him?"

"A great deal, Mrs. DeMarco, I'm sure."

Tully glanced over at Millie. What does she mean by that? Is she agreeing? Have I become *that* unlikable? But the questions faded away quickly. Tully was thinking about Boomerang.

Holding baby Jennifer close to her chest, Tully whispered, "Millie, I don't think he'll let me take Boomerang."

Millie stroked the polished wooden table and without looking at Tully said, "Mrs. DeMarco. Tully. His life's already gonna be so broken. Why do you want to kill him, too?"

"Well, you think it wouldn't kill me to go away without Boomer?" Tully said loudly. "You think it's possible for me to go away without my boy? What kind of a life could I have with anyone, anywhere—after having sacrificed my son!" Tully wrung her hands over Jennifer, while Millie stood up, picking up the teacups and putting them in the sink.

"Mrs. DeMarco, I know it's hard for you. A mother shouldn't have to part with her child. But then you should stay here. Stay for Boomerang's sake."

"Millie, I can't stay," Tully said, startled. "I'd be giving up Jack."

Millie sighed. "Mrs. DeMarco. Abraham was ready to sacrifice his only begotten son to prove his love for the Lord—"

Tully bolted up out of her chair.

"See, I don't want to fucking sacrifice anybody. That's the whole point. Nobody."

"Good luck," Millie muttered under her breath. Tully heard but chose to ignore it. Actually, didn't choose so much. She just couldn't talk anymore.

She took Jennifer upstairs and lay down with her.

My sacrificial lamb, thought Tully. My little lamb. "Okay, my darling, okay, my little one. Okay," she whispered, holding her daughter to her. "Maybe we won't have to sacrifice *you*."

And then Tully lay on the bed until Robin, Jr., came home at three o'clock. Tully fed Boomer and helped him with his homework. At four o'clock, they all got bundled up, Tully, Jenny, and Boomerang, and went outside. Boomerang played in his jungle house, and then kicked a soccer ball to Tully as Jennifer slept in her carriage.

"Mom, Dad said when I am eight he is going to teach me to play rugby."

"He said that, did he?" said Tully. "Over my dead body."

"Mom! He told me you were going to say that. Mom, it's a man's game."

"Yes," said Tully. "A dead man's game."

"Mom! Dad says you just don't understand."

"I understand plenty. Have you ever seen your father after he comes home from a rugby match? Does he look pretty to you?"

"No, but he looks like a man, Mom. Besides, he plays scrum-half. You always get beat up in that position. I want to be a fullback," said Boomerang. "The star!"

"Go on and play ball, Boomerang. I'll talk to your father when he gets home."

"Robin, Mom. I want to be called Robin."

"Robin, son. Robin."

Boomerang continued to kick the ball around by himself

while Tully sat, rocked Jenny's stroller, and watched him. And as she watched her seven-year-old boy, her heart got smaller and smaller while the lump around it got bigger and bigger.

They were still outside when Robin came home around six. He walked through the kitchen into the yard. Tully turned around when she heard the screen door slam. Boomerang ran to him and said, "Dad, you were right, you were so right! Mom doesn't want you to teach me how to play rugby!"

"Of course she doesn't, Boomer," said Robin, ruffling Boomerang's hair but looking at Tully. "She's your mother. She doesn't want you to get hurt."

Tully looked away into the darkness.

After a few minutes they all went inside. Tully sat at the table and watched Robin at the refrigerator. Tully liked to look at Robin when he came home from work. He was always so impeccably dressed. And today, in his two-color double-breasted dark blue Pierre Cardin suit, he looked especially good.

"Like my suit, Tully?" Robin asked, noticing her gaze.

"Very much," she said.

"Want me to get one for him?" he asked. "I'll give him a good price."

Tully stood up and went into the living room without saying another word.

At night after they put Boomerang to bed, Tully wanted to watch TV. Actually she wanted to talk to Robin, but he said, "I'm tired. I'm going to bed."

"But it's only nine o'clock!" exclaimed Tully.

Robin looked at her steadily. "I'm tired."

She put her head back down on the sofa pillow and turned to the TV. "Okay," she said. "Don't smoke in bed."

Tully came up a few hours later and woke Robin up. "Robin," she said, kneading the quilt between her fingers, sitting on his side of the bed. He looked so sleepy, so out of it.

"He's left, Robin, he's gone back to California."

"Good," Robin said. "Wonderful. Would you like me to clap?"

"Have you been thinking any more about what we'd talked about?"

"I don't know. What did we talk about? We talked about so many things."

This was difficult for Tully. She was not accustomed to begging.

"What, Tully?"

"Robin . . . have you . . ." she broke off.

"Have I what?"

"Thought anymore about Boomerang?"

He looked at her coldly, pushing her away from him. "I think about Boomerang every day."

"What about the other thing?"

"Tully, I already gave you my answer. I haven't changed my mind. It's impossible."

She backed away from him and scrunched down on the floor. "Robin. Please," she whispered. "You know I can't leave without him."

"I didn't realize you were so close to going."

"I'm not," she said quickly. "But I can't leave without him."

"So don't leave," said Robin.

"Robin. Listen, you've got so much money. You can come and visit him every weekend if you want to—"

"Tully!" he screamed, shooting out of bed. Tully scrambled out of his way. He came up to her, into her face again. "Tully, I don't think you understand me. This conversation is over. Boomerang is the only thing I have. I will never, I repeat, since you've obviously ignored me the first time, *never* give him up."

"He's the only thing I've got, too, Robin," Tully said into her hands.

"Why, that's not true, Tully! You've got so many other things. You've got Jack. You've got Jennifer. You're going to have California. You, Jack, and Jennifer are all going to go to live in California. See how many things you have?"

"I have nothing without Boomerang," said Tully.

"Okay. So let Jack have California. And you stay here with Boomerang, Jenny, and me."

"Robin, stop," she begged.

"Oh, I see, then he won't have anything. Poor Jack."

No, thought Tully, sitting brokenly on the floor. Then *I* won't have Jack.

Robin sat down on the edge of the bed. "Think about what you're saying to me. You want to leave me with nothing. What have I done to you, Tully, in my life that you need to be so deliberately malicious to me?"

"I'm sorry, Robin," Tully said in a dead voice.

"You've made up your mind, then? You're leaving. How soon?" he asked flatly.

"I haven't made up my mind at all," she said. That was a lie. But what could she do? She couldn't see reason. "There are many things we still have to work out."

"Yes, like your mother."

"Like my mother," she agreed. And then, "Robin," she began again, "we could go to court and fight for his custody."

"We could, yes. Is that something you want to do?"

"No," she answered.

"That's right," he said. "No. You know why? Because you haven't fought for a single blessed thing in your life, Tully. Not a single thing. And you're not going to fight for this one, either. You're just going to hope it falls into place somehow, you'll never lift a finger to do anything about it. And when he comes in the summer, you will leave, and you will leave it all behind, and feel as sorry for that as you have for your whole sorry life, but no, you won't fight."

Tully glanced around to find a close corner she could crawl to, to feel sheet rock instead of open space. But she just sat there, immobile. "Robin," she said, looking at the carpet so he wouldn't see her tears. "You don't seem to understand. I can't leave him. I know you say leave him, I know you say I'll have all the things I want, I know you say that my dreams will come true, but it's all meaningless if I leave him behind. Can you understand that?"

"No," he said, getting off the bed and taking his pillow and quilt with him. "Go ahead. Take me to court. I will fight you for him, Tully, and you know and I know that I will win. So go right ahead and do it," he said, slamming the bedroom door behind him.

A few hours later, when Tully ventured into the hall, she found Robin asleep in the rocking chair in Boomerang's room.

"Come to bed, Robin," she said tiredly. "Come to bed."

2.

Slow, exhausting weeks passed. Miserable weeks during which Tully and Robin hardly spoke. Tully hung on to every word Boomerang said and followed him around the house trying to find stuff for them to do. She lost weight and sat in the California room after lunch with Jenny, holding her up to the trees. Tully loved her California room. To make the palm trees grow, the south-facing, sunlit room had to be always hot and humid. Tully sat in the room in the middle of winter barely dressed and imagined what it would be like to be barely dressed in Carmel-by-the-beautiful-Sea.

Tully sat outside in the yard, too. She wrote to Julie once, in New Orleans, but had nothing to say, so she sent her some pictures of Jennifer being held by Boomerang. "It reminds me of the photo of me holding little Hank," Tully wrote on the card.

Boomerang saw the postcard on the kitchen table, and later that night, in bed, when Tully was sitting on his bed and Robin was rocking in the chair behind her, Boomerang asked, "Mom, who is little Hank?"

"Did you read the card?" she asked. "Hank was my little brother."

"Oh. Where is he now?"

"Somewhere nice, I hope. He's with his daddy."

"Oh. Where's your daddy?"

Tully looked back at Robin. "With Hank, I hope."

"Oh," said Boomerang for the third time, turning his back to his mother and father. "You must miss them, Mom."

On Valentine's Day, Robin came home with two dozen long-stemmed red roses, only to find Tully sitting in the kitchen holding on to two dozen long-stemmed white roses. Robin stood there and watched her for a few moments, roses in his hand, then turned around, went into the garage, and threw his red roses in the trash. He went for dinner by himself at Casa Del Sol, where he was lucky to get a table after a twenty-minute wait, and then sat there and ate his fajitas amid a sea of smiling faces. He nursed two or three margaritas until Casa closed and it was time to go home. He did not want to go home, but he had nowhere else to go. Coming back to a dark house, he saw that the white roses were not in the kitchen anymore. His were. Tully had dug them up, straightened them all out, and put them in a vase in the middle of the table. The white roses he found in the hot and humid California room. Tully was upstairs in

Jennifer's nursery. "Come to bed, Tully," he said. She shook her head.

"As you wish," he coldly said, about to leave.

"Robin," she said quietly. "Why do you never look in on her? Why do you so rarely pick her up? Why don't you look at her? She is a little baby, how can you be angry with her?"

He lowered his head, his hand still on the doorknob. "Tully, I'm not angry with her. I just don't want to get too attached to her, that's all."

When Tully came to bed a little while later, she asked Robin, "Is that why you don't touch me anymore when we sleep? You don't want to get too attached to me, either?"

"It's too late with you," he replied. "I'm trying to get *un*attached to you."

Shakie came over with her kids once or twice. There was nothing to discuss with Shakie. Shakie was reserved, and all they talked about were their kids. That's all they could talk about now, though once, before December, they could also talk about their husbands. And once they could talk about everything but Jack.

Hedda sometimes came out of her room and sat in the kitchen with Tully, or watched a little TV with her. She asked Tully to read to her once, but Tully shook her head and said, "No, Mom, I am just too tired."

Tully called the office nearly every day at first, then every other day, then on Mondays and Thursdays, and then on Fridays only, and she had to force herself to do even that. They were difficult phone calls. Alan, who had taken over Tully's responsibilities and cases, asked once during each phone call when Tully would be returning to work, but Tully had no answer. When, indeed? She missed her job. Not her job so much, but the kids. Alan said the kids asked for her nearly every week. Tully believed that. She hadn't forgotten them. But when indeed would she be returning? She was going to Carmel-by-the-Sea.

In early March, Hedda Makker had another stroke, bad enough to impair her walking and again necessitate hiring a full-time nurse. The odor of Hedda came back, but Tully hardly noticed, so busy she was counting the days, running to the phone, and checking her mail.

Jack wrote to Tully often. Small things on postcards. Sometimes letters, but short ones. "Dear Tully, I'm working and missing you. What are you doing? I miss you both. Don't sit around the house and drive yourself nuts. How's Boomerang? I'm waiting to hear on a fantastic house! Keep our fingers crossed. How's that divorce going? How I wish you were here. Jack." Tully kept all his letters in the California room, under one of the palm trees. There were many cards under there, collected over three years. The tree was no longer standing straight on the floor.

The divorce was going nowhere. She hadn't even approached Robin with it. She never even mentioned it. Thinking about talking to Robin about a divorce filled Tully with dread.

Tully's only consistent thought, the sole feeling that had any lasting identifiable meaning to her, was Boomerang. Boomerang was her paperweight, as heavy as a block of cement, sitting inside her, rendering her immobile.

Tully would go from Jenny's bedroom to Boomerang's and lie down with him. She would brush his hair away from his sleeping face and kiss him, kiss his feet and his hands, kiss him until he woke up and mumbled, "Mom, please. I'm trying to sleep."

Tully would get up with him and dress him for school, iron his clothes herself, make him breakfast herself despite Millie's anxious restlessness. Tully would meet him at the bus and walk home with him, until he finally told her that he was the only second grader whose mom still picked him up from the bus. So Tully stopped, but when he came home, Tully would sit in the garden and watch him.

And when she watched him, she thought, This is what my life has become. Winter. I'm alone. My husband can't look at me, my lover has left me and I don't know when or if he is coming back. My daughter is upstairs. Did I mention it's winter? Only my boy and I are outside. I look old and tired and heavy. I've been scarred for life. She looked at her wrists. By someone else. She thought of Jennifer. I'll never have another child as long as I live. I have to have hormone treatments for the rest of my life. I'm sitting in the cold every afternoon, freezing my butt off, looking at an eight-year-old who mostly ignores me. I'm sitting here looking at him and I'm trying to figure out if my little boy would be okay if I just upped and left him, or would he miss his mother?

3.

In mid-March, Boomerang asked his mother to come watch him play soccer in Manhattan as part of his birthday present. Tully agreed. Boomerang was so excited, for days he could talk about little else and made his father come home from work early for a few days so they could practice. "I want to impress Mom," Boomer said. "Otherwise she might not come again."

Tully was glad to be going with them, and even Robin seemed livelier than usual.

"I hope Jenny won't be too cold out there," said Boomerang on the way to Manhattan. "It's windy."

"I'm sure she'll be fine, Boomer," said Robin. "She'll be tied to Mommy. And Mommy is a furnace."

"Yeah, Mom, you are," said Boomerang. "I remember in the hospital. How hot you were. You were really burning up."

Tully glanced at Robin. "I'm not that hot anymore, Boomerang," she said. "I'm better now."

"Robin, Mom. *Robin*," corrected Boomerang.

It was a good day at first. But it was blustery and the young boys couldn't control the ball too well. It kept being blown away. Tully cheered her son's team anyway, jumping up and down with Jenny tied to her chest. Boomerang had one assist and his team won the game 1–0.

After their sons were finished, the dads couldn't resist playing a short game themselves. Tully and Boomerang sat in the front row of the bleachers and watched Robin run around in his shorts. Tully watched him and thought, Don't his legs look nice, all muscular and dark. She imagined that's what Boomerang's legs were going to look like when he grew up because Boomer looked a lot like his father.

At halftime, Robin ran over to them, and Tully said, "You look very sexy in your shorts."

"Do I indeed?" Robin said. "Well, thank you." Tully wanted him to lean over and kiss her, but he didn't.

Tully's sister-in-law Karen came over and sat next to Tully, and said after making some small talk, "You guys look so normal together, so happy. How are you doing?"

"Like always," said Tully.

"Robin's been saying there's been some trouble. Is everything okay?"

"Everything is fine," said Tully. Except I can never have more children and the thought of leaving my son is hauling me down to the bottom of the Marianas Trench.

"You're not thinking of splitting up or anything, are you?"

"No, of course not," Tully said absentmindedly, but she was no longer paying attention to Karen. Instead she was trying to focus on a young woman talking to Robin. Wasn't it a little cold for a woman to be out in shorts? It's not as if she was playing soccer. Tully strained to see Robin better. He stood a polite distance away, but the woman came up close and kind of looked up at him, kind of smiled, kind of . . .

Something squeezed Tully as she watched them and she lowered her eyes but just for a moment. She wanted to see.

"Umm, Karen," said Tully, trying to sound as casual as possible. "Who's that talking to Robin?"

Karen stared across the field. "I don't know. Don't know her name. She is here all the time, though. I think she is going out with—" Karen pointed to some guy in the field, "him, I think."

But Tully was no longer listening.

She couldn't even sit still anymore. She jumped up off the bench and started pacing quickly from one end of the bleachers to another.

"Mom! Come back and sit down with us!" Boomerang shouted. Tully didn't.

I have no right, no right, no right, no right, Tully was drumming to herself, trying not to look at Robin anymore. No right. But what's going on? she thought, feeling herself lose control inside. What's going on? Who is she? Is it possible? Could Robin have been having an affair in Manhattan all these years?

The thought staggered Tully. She tottered unsteadily on her feet and then strained to see her or him or both. Robin was on the field, and she was on the sideline, laughing.

Here, in Manhattan? Right here, minutes away from our home, what, what am I thinking, what am I doing? Tully said to herself, trying to steady her legs. Stop it.

Time passed on the field and in front of the bleachers. Time passed everywhere around Tully, but she just kept pacing back and forth, trying to get hold of her senses.

She vaguely recalled Jack. I have no rights, she droned to herself. Forfeited all those *rights*. Never confronted Robin, never asked him, never called, never wanted to know. I get all I deserve.

Inside, something stabbed and stabbed her.

Tully had no idea how she got through dinner at Steve and Karen's. All evening she clamped that metal bit between her teeth, and she did not eat well.

They drove back home late, around eleven. Boomerang was still awake, chatting about the day's events. Tully wished he would go to sleep so that she could talk to Robin, but it was probably for the best that Boomer was awake. What was inside Tully didn't feel very *conversational*.

What could she bring up anyway? How dare you? That seemed so feeble. Who is she? that's all I want to know. Who the fuck is she?

She was thinking in her dark silence, What kind of a marriage do we have, anyway? He with someone in Manhattan, me with someone in Topeka.

At home, Boomerang said, hugging his mother good night while Robin rocked behind her in the chair, "Mom, did you have fun?"

"Yes, I did, Boomer," Tully said with some difficulty. "I'm . . . so glad I came. Happy birthday, little one."

"Mom, it's Robin. And I'm not your little one anymore. Jenny is your little one."

"Boomerang, till the day you die, you'll be our little one."

"Like you're Nanna's little one."

"Yes," said Tully. "Just like that."

The rocking chair behind her creaked and creaked.

"Mom," said Boomerang, "will you come again next week?"

"I'd like to, Boomer, but it's up to your daddy."

"Dad, can Mom come next Saturday?"

Creak, creak. "Of course. She's always been welcome."

Yeah, like shit, I was welcome, thought Tully as she stormed out of the room and downstairs.

In a while, Robin came down after her. "Are you okay?" he asked.

"Oh, sure," she said through her teeth. "I'm just great."

He stood by the wall. She was ten feet away from him. "Tell

me, goddamn it," Tully said, still trying to sound calm. "Who the fuck was she?"

Robin didn't move a muscle. "What are you talking about?"

"This is what I'm talking about!" Tully shouted, and swiped three tall glasses off the oak table. They fell on the tile floor and broke. "Who the fuck is she, Robin?"

His face got harder. "I have no idea what you're talking about," he said.

"Oh, I'm sure you don't," yelled Tully. "I'm sure as shit you don't have any idea!" She quickly walked over to the counter and picked up the dish drainer. Dropping the whole thing with plates and glasses at his feet, she said, "Let's try again. Who the fuck is she?"

Hedda was calling, panicked, from her room, but neither Robin nor Tully paid her any attention.

"How could you?" she screamed. "How could you have? Taken me with you, with our son, with our little girl, how could you have stood beside me? Like we were some kind of family or something!" Tully said with scorn. "How could you have done that? Goddamn you, how could you have taken me with you?"

"Tully, what the fuck are you talking about?" he said.

"Robin! Have you been fucking some slut all these years, have you been fucking her all this time? These eleven years, is that what you've been doing?" Tully screamed.

Robin, standing at the kitchen entrance, raised his hands in supplication, entreaty, anger, what? She didn't know. She hurled a plate at his feet.

"Tully, calm down, you're hysterical."

"I am not hysterical!" she shrieked, and briefly thought, I don't recognize myself. Who am I?

But Tully's eyes and heart were full of *red mist*, and she ran screaming to him, trying to claw at him. Robin grabbed her arms and pushed her away, but she was livid and he wasn't. Her madness made her stronger, and she nearly knocked him down with the force of her hands.

"Tully, you're crazy," Robin panted, pressed against the wall, keeping her off him. "You've gone mad! What's wrong with you?"

"You bastard, you bastard," she kept repeating. "How could you? How could you! For eleven years!"

He squeezed her hands tightly. "What is it that bothers you, Tully?" he said with venom. "That I could, or the eleven years?"

Tully fought then to get away from him, tried to kick him, even, tried to do the unthinkable—kick him in the groin. "You bastard," she hissed. "Let go of me, you bastard. Let go of me!"

"Oh, I'll let go of you, all right," he said, pushing her off him and away. She staggered back, looked around, and grabbed a piece of broken glass off the floor.

"Don't even think about it, Tully," Robin said. "Calm down, goddamn it! Calm down, and maybe then we can talk."

"There's nothing to talk about, you fuck," she panted, lunging for him, but Robin was quicker, grabbing her wrists and squeezing them so hard that she involuntarily let the glass drop.

"Think about what you're doing," he breathed. "How's this all going to look to a judge in a custody hearing?"

"Get your fucking hands off me!" she screamed, and Robin pushed her away again. Harder.

"Custody hearing!" Tully shouted. "What are you talking about, custody hearing? What's the point of a hearing when you won't let me have my children? Won't let me keep my children?"

"You can have Jennifer," said Robin in a hoarse voice.

"But Boomerang?" Tully cried. "He is my children, too! He is my children, too!"

And then they just stood there, he with his arms crossed on his chest, looking at the floor, not looking at her standing there helpless and panting. They stood there like that amid all the broken glass, he against the wall, she in the middle of the kitchen, until she wiped her mouth, came up to him, hit him hard across the face, and then ran upstairs.

Robin stayed downstairs and cleaned up. In fifteen minutes he was up at the bathroom door. "Come out," he said.

"Get lost," she said.

Their bathroom door did not have a lock, ever since that episode before Boomerang's birth, and so Robin opened the door and walked in. Tully was sitting on the toilet.

"Get out," she said.

"Have you calmed down?" He closed the door behind him.

"Will you please leave?"

He sat down at the edge of the tub.

Her eyes were swollen, her lips were swollen from all the salt on them. All of a sudden, Tully got up, opened the cabinet, got out a pair of scissors, and started to chop off her long hair.

"Tully, stop," said Robin, not getting up. "What are you doing?"

"Leave me alone," she said roughly, unevenly lopping off chunks of hair. "You destroyed my car. I can do anything I want."

Ten minutes it took Tully to cut off eight years' worth of hair. Just over a minute per year. And now the hair was jagged all around her scalp. "There," she said. "I hate that hair." Then she sat back down on the toilet seat, and they sat there mutely, staring at the hair on the floor until Jenny started to cry.

Tully went to get her while Robin went downstairs to warm up her bottle.

In their bedroom, he started to say something, but Tully cut him off. "Robin, please. I am feeding the baby. Just leave me alone."

He undressed, got onto the bed, and waited for Jenny to finish.

"How could you humiliate me in that way, Robin?" Tully let out a dry sob. "How could you, in front of all your brothers and their wives? They all know, don't they? How could you have taken me there, and not tell her not to come?"

"I did not humiliate you," Robin said carefully. "*I* was not the one who humiliated *you*, Tully. You don't know what humiliation is. Let me tell you, I couldn't get Boomerang to see his sister because she was named Jennifer Pendel."

"So it's true, then," Tully said lifelessly, holding on to Jenny. "You've been with her for eleven years."

"No, Tully," replied Robin. "I've been with *you* for eleven years."

"What is she, then? A feel-good thing once in a while?"

"Well," said Robin. "Don't you think somebody has to be? Somebody has to be *my* feel-good thing."

Tully didn't say anything. She put Jenny in between them and turned her back to both of them, rolling up into a ball.

"Do you love her, Robin?" she said after a while.

He was silent for a good five minutes before he answered her. "Tully," he said. "You've lost your mind. How could you even ask me that?"

"Then what the hell did you need to call that slut up for? So that she can laugh at me? Is that why you brought me? So that she can giggle and think that here I am sitting in my perfect world, thinking it's perfect, while she is fucking my husband!" She covered her face and began to drone.

"You're a fine one to talk," Robin said gently.

"Fine, then let's not talk about it," she said.

"Tully, in these last three years, I hardly saw you. I don't know where you were for three years."

"What are you talking about? We spent all winter together, we spent all fall and spring together."

"Well, then if we were together all the time, as you say," he said sarcastically, "then what are you so worried about?"

"I'm not fucking worried," she snapped. "I just want to know who she is."

Robin didn't answer her. "What did you expect me to do, Tully? Sit and wait for you to come home?"

"I don't know what I expected you to do," she said dejectedly. "Stand up for yourself. Say something. Why didn't you ever say something?"

"Say something? Like what?"

"I don't know. Why didn't you try, 'stop'?"

"Why?" Robin threw up his hands and got up to walk out, but Tully saw rage on his face. "Why?" He quickly walked back to the bed and grabbed her by the shoulders and shook her so hard, so hard, she thought he would hit her, hit her head on the headboard, on the wall, and his own, too, he shook her with all his anger and clenched teeth and tight fingers.

"Why?" he shouted. "Oh, you selfish, selfish woman! You selfish, heartless woman! Because I love you, goddamn your tortured soul to hell! Because I love you more than anything because I want you for my own more than anything because I never wanted to lose you! I became blind so that you would find your own way. I wanted you to stop feeling that you had made a terrible mistake marrying me! It has not been a terrible mistake, Tully, despite all your fucking self-pity and your wallowing. It's been our life, and it's the only life I ever wanted!"

Robin stopped shaking her. "In eleven years, I've never asked you if you love me, I was happy enough to be with you, and despite your best efforts, we built something. Maybe it doesn't seem much to you, but you and our son and this house was my life. I paid dearly just to keep my sanity around you. I paid with my pride and with my hopes for the future. You think I want someone else? I only want *you* to be glad to see me! I never wanted you to leave me, and never wanted to threaten you with leaving. I wanted you to choose me on your own," he finished, out of breath. Minutes passed. "And I still do," he said. "I still do, goddamn you. Still love you, God help me. Still want us to work out somehow. But you made sure you fucked things up real good, haven't you? You made sure to get us into as big a hole as you possibly could."

"I got us into a hole?" Tully shouted. "I? Listen, you asshole, maybe if you weren't out every goddamned Saturday night fucking some slut, you might have been home! And then I would have been home! And then maybe you wouldn't have let another man deliver our baby!"

Robin screamed and pushed Tully off the bed with his left arm. Pushed her to the floor, and when she was still on the floor, he bent over her and hit her across the face with his right hand.

"How dare you!" he screamed. "How dare you say that to me! You bitch! How could you say that to me!" He stood over her, naked, panting panting panting. "You'll drive anybody to anything, won't you?" he said. "Anything!" And stepping over her, he opened the bedroom door and slammed it behind him.

Tully got up. She picked up Jenny, who slept through everything, and put her into her crib.

Then Tully went to find him. He was downstairs, sitting on the couch covered by a blanket.

"Robin," she whispered, coming close to him. "I'm sorry."

"I'm sorry I hit you," he said, his voice trembling. "You'll drive anybody to anything, won't you? Anything."

She sat down on the couch next to him. "Robin," Tully repeated. "I'm sorry."

"We're raw," he said. "It's all right. We're not used to this."

She kneeled down on the carpet in front of him and moved his legs apart. "Not used to what, Robin?"

"To talking. Tully, what are you doing?"

She pulled on the blanket, to remove it from his body. Robin tried to move away. "What the hell is wrong with you?" he said. "I don't want to touch you, Tully."

"I don't blame you," she whispered. "But I want to touch *you*." She pulled the blanket away until she saw him completely naked, and then she moved closer to him, still on her knees. "I'm sorry, Robin," she whispered, burying her face in him.

Robin pulled her up to the couch and then got on top of her, thrusting against her, his hand on her head, holding her in one place, thrusting hard against her, while Tully just moaned and whispered, *"Robin, Robin, Robin."*

"Is this what you want?" he whispered back. "Is this it, is this what you want? An angry fuck? Or is this a pity fuck?"

And Tully held on to his neck with both hands and continued to whisper his name. "Neither, *Robin*," moaned Tully.

Afterwards, spent, they fell asleep on the couch. Robin was on top of Tully, she with her legs around his legs, her arms on his back. Tully woke up because she felt someone looking at her; woke up, and saw Boomerang standing next to the couch staring at them. "Mom," he said. "Didn't you hear? The baby is crying."

Robin woke up, too, hearing his son's voice, pushed off Tully, and stood up. He looked for the blanket to cover her, but it was somewhere on the floor and in the dark and he couldn't find it. Boomerang just stood and stared at his naked mother. "Boomer, go upstairs, son," said Robin. "Go on. We'll be right up." Helping Tully up, Robin said, "Go on upstairs. The baby's crying."

Upstairs, Robin lay down in bed next to Tully and Jennifer, stroking the baby's head, and then lifting his fingers and stroking Tully's cheek. "Had I known," he whispered, "that *such* treatment from me would precipitate *such* treatment from you, I would have treated you this way long ago."

"Har-de-har-har," said Tully.

But she wasn't laughing afterwards. When Jenny fell asleep, Tully carried her into the nursery and remained there with her. She lay down on the carpet near the crib and closed her eyes.

After about half an hour, she heard Robin open the door. His footsteps on the carpet stopped near her face on the floor.

"Why didn't you ever confront me?" Tully spoke into the beige pile, spoke not expecting an answer. "Why didn't you ever talk to me? We talk so much, we sit and do nothing but talk, why didn't you ever talk to me about this?"

"Oh, Tully," said Robin, crouching. "You had set these rules. I didn't set them, but I kept to them because you made it clear it was either keep the peace or lose you." He paused. "And we never talked. Oh, we talked about books and movies and Boomerang. We talked about your job and my job and what to have for dinner. But we never talked about you and me, we never talked about you or what you needed or what was wrong. We never talked about anything that mattered."

Tully turned back to him. "I didn't think there was anything to talk about."

"No, you never do, do you?" said Robin. "We never talked about Jeremy, we never talked about Jennifer, we never talked about anything. You closed your eyes, because you did not want to be bothered with me. I closed my eyes, because I did not want to lose you. So what are you asking me these things for? What's the point?"

"You're right. There is no point," she said, thinking, I just want to feel better, that's all I want, just something to feel a little better. But the layers are piled up so high, I don't even know what hurts. God! It was so much better, so much better, the absence of feeling, better even to battle the pain of the past than to have to feel this about *now*—

But how in the world can I feel better when Jack is not here, when I am tearing my son away from me, when my Robin has been sleeping with that slut for a decade—

She yelped, like a puppy dog who's had her paws broken and crushed, yelped miserably. He put his hand on her back, but she pushed him away and he fell over, while she crawled away to another part of the room, continuing to make a heartbroken noise. "No point," she sobbed. "No point at all. But I counted on you. I thought you were faithful to me. It's the one thing I counted on. Your faithfulness was a rock in my life."

He crawled to her in Jennifer's nursery. "It still is, Tully, it still is," he whispered. "I'm still here. I don't want you to go."

When she didn't answer, Robin continued. "Tully, I'm sor-

ry. Do you want to kick me? Because I deserve kicking. But
Tully, maybe three years is too long to avoid this kind of thing.
Maybe ten years is too long to avoid it."

"No, Robin," Tully said heavily. "We could've avoided it
forever."

He tried to touch her. "But at what cost?"

Finally he got up off the floor. "Coming to bed?" he asked.

"No, Robin," replied Tully, looking into the carpet. "I can't
bear to be in the same bed with you. Can't bear to have you
near me."

"I'm sorry, Tully," he said again, but colder now. "Would
you like me to pack my things and go?"

"What's the point?" she said quickly. "We've been pretending this long for Boomerang, we can pretend a little longer."

"Yes, why not?" said Robin.

4.

After that night, Tully stopped sleeping in their bed. Without
a pillow or a blanket or a mattress, she continued to wander
between Boomerang's and Jennifer's bedrooms, falling asleep
on the carpet near Jenny's crib.

March became April, but Tully did not want to come to
the games again, despite Boomerang's pleas. Finally Robin
pleaded for his boy.

After days and days of Robin the father's and Robin the
son's entreaties, Tully came with them.

The girl was there. Tully watched her from across the field.
The girl did not approach Robin in any way, but when his
team scored, she jumped up and cheered and laughed, and
Tully was sure she was looking straight at Robin DeMarco.
Tully couldn't stand it anymore. She walked around the large
football field, being careful not to step in the mud, dug out by
soccer spikes, and headed toward the girl.

It was good that Tully was carrying Jenny in the sling: she
looked so *motherly*.

Tully stopped near the girl, who tensed immediately. "Listen," Tully said. "Let me tell you something. If you want
him, you're going to have to take his two kids, too, do you
hear me?"

The girl flinched and remained silent.

"I don't know who the fuck you are," said Tully, "but he is still my husband."

The girl spoke. "Well, maybe if you took better care of him—" she began.

"Him and his two kids," Tully interrupted. "You're going to have to take the whole fucking package. Do you understand? Just stay the fuck away from him. He is still my husband."

"Not for long, Tully Makker," said the girl.

That was sharp. Tully winced and whirled around. "It's Tully *DeMarco*, you ignorant slut."

"Girls, girls!" Robin ran over, shooting the girl a quick, uncomfortable glance and then leading Tully away with his arm around her.

"Tully, I'm surprised at you," Robin said. "Making such a loud spectacle of yourself. It's not like you."

"Stay away from her, Robin," Tully warned. "You are still my husband."

Robin's chocolate eyes got deeper. "Not for long, Tully *DeMarco*," said Robin.

And a week later, continuing their old conversation as if nothing had been said between the sentences, Tully asked, "So what does she do, your girl?"

Robin sighed. "She is not my girl, Tully. Stop it. She is just someone who talks to me on Saturdays. Really. Sometimes she goes to the pool hole Stevie and I hang out in, but that's it."

Tully rolled her eyes. "Yeah, right. What does she do?"

"She works in a haircutting salon."

Tully laughed meanly. "She's a hairdresser, Robin? Are you fucking a hairdresser?"

"Are you fucking a house painter, Tully?" Robin said quietly.

Deep down, Tully felt awful hearing him say that, and she knew that afterwards his would be the only words she would remember out of the whole useless fight, but that was deep down. On the surface, Tully was furious.

"Robin! Are you telling me she cuts your hair? Does she? Is that what she does?"

"Sometimes," he replied.

Tully cursed and yanked hard at Robin's hair. He knocked her hand away roughly. "Don't fucking touch me, Tully," he said, getting out of bed. "Don't provoke me."

"Your hair," Tully said, feeling the fight ooze out of her. "I love your hair. I touch it when we make love. How could you let her cut your hair!"

Robin leaned over her. Tully thought he was going to hug her or kiss her or something, but he just said, "Make love? You mean fuck, Tully. You mean we fuck."

She pushed him away from her weakly. "Get away from me. I don't know what you're still doing here. Why aren't you with her? Huh? Why don't you go to her now and let that slut suck your cock?"

"Oh, Tully, just stop it," Robin said, taking his pillow and the quilt. "You're so boring."

Turning to the window, she said, "I know they all know. Bruce and Stevie and all of them. Because Karen or Linda had to be taking care of Boomerang while you went with *her*. How could you have done it? How could you have? I can't look at you anymore without shouting this question at you. How could you have done it?"

Robin grimaced. "Tully, I didn't think you cared about anything I did. I didn't think you gave a good goddamn."

"You are not answering my question," said Tully. "I want to know. How could you have done it?"

"How could *you*?" he said.

"I never said I loved you!" she cried. "I never held my feelings over your head, like you did over mine, as if to say, 'Here they are, and now I am going to beat you with them'! I didn't sleep with anyone in the time we were married—"

Robin raised his eyebrows.

"Not until," Tully continued, "Jack."

"And this is supposed to make me feel better?" said Robin darkly.

"I fell in love!" cried Tully. "That's my excuse! What's yours?"

"I am not making any excuses. I don't have to. You did not love me," Robin said.

"God!" she whispered fiercely. "Are you really that faithless? Is that really what you're all about, does your faithlessness have no bounds? No, don't answer that. I've had enough."

*   *   *

Tully and Robin's relationship ground down. Tully regressed deeper into her well. She did not eat dinner with Robin anymore, or watch TV with him, or go to bed with him. When they talked, the conversation usually erupted into bile, yellow and free-flowing. Tully continued not to sleep well and wandered out of Jenny's nursery periodically to come and lie down with her son. Robin and Tully had not made love since the night he hit her. They did not talk anymore about anything, but they bickered about everything. One night, when Robin made his automatic stop in the nursery to ask her to join him, she stopped him before he went out the door. "Robin, we never used to fight like this, we sure do fight a lot," she said, full of dry misery.

"There's a lot to fight about," said Robin.

"We got along so well for more than a decade," she said softly.

"We did not talk for a decade," he replied.

"We don't get along so well anymore."

"There's a lot not to get along about."

She rubbed her cheek on the cream carpet. "You don't love me as well as you used to," she whispered.

"There is a lot not to love you for, Tully," Robin said bitterly.

Despite it all, every night, Robin came in and mechanically asked her if she was coming to bed, and every night Tully said no. In the mornings when she woke up, she occasionally found herself covered with a blanket.

Late one evening, Tully suggested seeing a lawyer. Jack had called her earlier in the day, and Tully had lied and told him she and Robin were in the process of getting officially separated. So she brought it up to Robin, as casually as she could.

"Lawyer?" asked Robin, as if hearing the word for the first time. "Lawyer," he repeated, and then fell quiet.

Tully wasn't looking at him, trying to concentrate on "Lonesome Dove."

"Sure," he said in the end. "Let's go and see one. I had been wondering what was taking you so long," he added.

She felt so badly, she nearly told him to forget it. She wanted to go over to his chair and touch him. But the thought of Jack sprung up, in California, in Carmel, near the sea, and Tully steeled herself, willed herself to be still, leveling her gaze on the TV with eyes that refused to focus. He won't let me go without my boy, she thought. He can't.

At the lawyer's they sat quietly and answered some questions about the length of their marriage and the number of their children and the quantity of their property. Robin said they had been married eight years, had two children, and property was not an issue. Tully could have anything she wanted. No, he said, they did not want separate lawyers, they had nothing to divide but the kids. No, said Tully, they did not really want a separation agreement first, they wanted to go ahead and get it over and done with.

No, said Tully, there need not be a special visitation agreement during the divorce proceedings because Robin would continue to live in the house.

"Are you planning to sell the house?"

Robin and Tully stared at each other. "We haven't thought about it," he said. "Eventually."

"Boomerang really likes that house," said Tully faintly. "Maybe you could stay in the house."

Robin didn't answer.

"You said you have two children. Are you agreeing on joint custody?"

Robin nodded.

"Who are the children going to live with?"

"The girl with her mother," Robin said. "The boy with me."

The lawyer, a nice man by the name of Andrew Hofmann, glanced quickly at Tully. She wasn't sure what kind of a face she must have worn, but she could tell by Mr. Hofmann's expression it was not a totally impassive one. Tully felt salt on her lips. She lifted her trembling hand to touch them. Tears? No. Blood.

"I see," he finally said. "Splitting up the children is very hard on them sometimes. How old are they?"

Tully couldn't speak.

"The boy is eight," said Robin. "The girl is a couple of months."

"I see," said Mr. Hofmann, his kind blue eyes shifting uncomfortably around the room, as if he were trying to avoid looking at the defendant and plaintiff.

"The grounds for the divorce?" he asked.

Abandonment? Abuse? Adultery? What was next in alphabetical order? California?

"No fault," said Robin.

Mr. Hofmann shook his head. "Can't do it. Not when there are kids involved."

"Abandonment, then."

"Okay," said Mr. Hofmann, getting a box of tissues from the drawer and handing it to Tully. "Let me see what I can come up with. No division of property, you said?"

"None," said Robin. Tully just wiped her mouth.

5.

Jenny got big. She was lifting her head up and looking around. Tully's one specific regret that she could actually put a word to was the inability to breast-feed her little girl. Jack's little girl. Jennifer, Jack's little girl.

Missing Jack was one more feeling that implanted itself into the general fabric of Tully's king-size quilt of pain; her mosaic, her handmade patchwork. Her stained-glass soul hurt in every one of its intricate pieces, and she couldn't give adequate vent to any of its particulars. Missing Jack felt pretty much like the feeling of Robin's betrayal, and everything else felt like Boomerang.

Tully missed the end of March.

She totally forgot the Monday in March that marked eleven years since the day Tully had grown old.

When Tully went to St. Mark's in April with two bouquets of flowers, she tried to find the patch of grief on her quilt that once was as big as her entire being, tried to find the crushing quilt of raw grief that once covered her completely.

Tully found it, all right, but it was only a patch now and it was next to some other barely identifiable things that were all just so much bigger than eleven-year-old grief. Things that were *unbearable*. That were *impossible* to think about.

That desert, Jen, thought Tully. *Is it a peaceful place?*

That night, Tully climbed into the attic, turned on the light, and painstakingly went through all of Jennifer's milk crates, through all the stuff Tully had not touched in a decade. Eight crates of stuff. Books. Records. I need to throw away the records, she thought. No one listens to records anymore; Jen missed the CD revolution.

. . . Cheerleader uniforms. Yearbooks from elementary and middle schools. Drawings. Photo albums. Journals. Looking through the photo albums, Tully found a picture of herself when she was little. "Tully, 1962," it said on the back. She also found a picture of Jack, at roughly the same age. She didn't know it was Jack, but on the back, in Jennifer's early teenage handwriting, it said, "Jack, July, 1963." He was four in the photo, platinum blond, standing shirtless, in a pair of red swimming trunks, holding a football. He was thin and smiling. Tully took that picture with her. Little Jennifer looked like her dad.

There was other stuff in the crates. Letters, postcards, presents, little knickknacks from the shelves of the Sunset Court room.

It wasn't the looking through the crates and it wasn't the memory of Jennifer, living and breathing through every knickknack, that made Tully dizzy with grief, it was the memory of the minutes and the hours that Tully had spent in Jen's bedroom putting it all into milk crates, the memory of stripping the Sunset Court room of Jennifer, the memory of putting Jennifer into these eight red milk crates. When Tully was able to get her hand away from her lips, she put everything back in the crates, everything, even the dusty old records, taking only the pictures of herself and Jack. Tully had come up to get the picture of Jennifer smiling and blond and chubby, a happy thirteen-year-old, flanked by Tully and Julie. She left that, too, up in the attic.

6.

At the end of April, Mr. Hillier called Tully, asking her to come and see him. Tully's old work clothes were too small for her, so she had to go out and buy herself a size-eleven suit. Eleven! She was such a five in high school. After Boomerang, she filled out to a nine, but then lost weight back down to a seven. But an *eleven*! Twelve in ladies' suits.

And according to the scale, I've lost twenty pounds since Jenny was born. My God, what a porker I must have been in January.

Tully thought Mr. Hillier seemed nervous. Folding her hands on her lap, Tully sat as calm as a willow on a windless day at Lake Vaquero.

"How have things been for you, Tully?" he said. "Good, I hope?"

"Great," replied Tully.

"How is your little girl?"

"Still little. Only three and a half months old."

"Yes, of course." He coughed. "Umm, Tully, there is something I wanted to talk to you about. Were you considering returning to work for us?"

. . . by the sea, by the beautiful sea . . .

"Sure," said Tully. "Would be a shame to waste a masters, wouldn't it?"

"Oh, absolutely," he said, blowing his nose. "Especially for you. You've come such a long way."

Tully looked at him. He was nearly all gray now, and heavier. He didn't look like Mr. Cunningham anymore.

"Tully," Mr. Hillier began again. "I have a proposition for you. I hope you will think about it."

"Sure," she said. "What's up?"

"Lillian's no longer with the FHRA," he blurted out.

Tully was surprised. "Really?" she exclaimed, and then tried to subdue her voice. "Gee, that's very strange. I didn't think she'd ever leave that place."

"Well, she didn't quite," said Mr. Hillier, "leave. She was let go."

"Really?" Tully was now even more surprised. "What's happened?"

He coughed again and could not meet her eye.

"I, as the president of Social and Rehabilitation Services of the State of Kansas, want to ask you on behalf of myself and the department to accept the position of director of the Foster Home Recruitment Agency." He cleared his throat.

Tully stared blankly at him and then looked around the office. "Are you serious?"

"Couldn't be more serious. I know how you've felt about things in the past. But they're different now. Lillian's gone. You've a chance to make a real difference. I think it's a good opportunity."

"Mr. Hillier," said Tully, buying time to collect her thoughts.

"Why me? I am so young. I'm sure you have more qualified people than me."

"More qualified than Lillian, certainly." Mr. Hillier smiled. "But more qualified than you? No one. And you know it. I knew you'd be hedging. You hedge on everything. Will you think about it?"

"Sure," Tully said, buying more time. "I'll think about it. But you know, this is all very sudden." Tully shook her head, trying to ward off her all those *patches of pain* from rising to her throat. "I have a lot of things to think about right now."

"It's not the money, Tully, is it?" asked Mr. Hillier.

Tully waved him off. "No, Mr. Hillier. It's never been the money. I have more money than I know what to do with."

"Well, what is it, then?"

"I don't know," Tully replied evasively. What to say? "Sometimes," she said slowly, "I feel as if I'm running around in circles from nine to five." *Running in circles around the clock,* she thought. "Like we muddle in the affairs of these kids, taking them away from their parents, thinking we're helping them, and in the meantime, all these kids want is their moms and dads to love them. Can we help them with that? Not really. I used to think," she continued, "that maybe if I cared enough I could, but I've begun to realize I cannot address their problems in any meaningful way. In *any* way. I used to think that if I cared enough, if I got them the best foster family, the best counselor, the best home, that somehow I'd cure some of them—"

"And you have," said Mr. Hillier. "Your kids ask for you. Your foster families ask for you."

Tully shook her head. "We now have the most efficient and positive program in Kansas for giving these kids a good foster home and counseling their parents. And yet, the children aren't any happier."

"Some of them are, Tully. It's true, many of them are just spinning their wheels. Many of them are truant, some are on drugs, some are JDs. But some of them are glad to be in a loving foster home. *Some* of them are doing better. Thanks to you, that's possible. Thanks to the better foster families, better recruitment. Better training. This year, the training period goes up to ten weeks. That's incredible, Tully, incredible! And some of those children will thank you when they grow up."

Who? she wanted to know, drifting down into her empty

well. Who will? Will my son thank me?

"Their faces are just as long," Tully said. "Their eyes just as lifeless. The only time I see animation in their faces is when their mommies and daddies come to take them home."

"Not all of them, Tully. Take heart."

She couldn't do that. Whose?

"I was thinking of going to work for the Gentle Shepherd adoption people," she said.

"You've been thinking about that for years. But why? Why would you want to do a thing like that?"

"Because," Tully said slowly, "I'm unhappy."

"When was this job ever about happiness?" said Mr. Hillier. "You do good work. You have a good heart. We'll give you all the resources you need. We'll work more closely with Gentle Shepherd, I know you've been fighting for that."

"Mr. Hillier, you know what's wrong with foster care? It's like Anbesol. Temporary care equals temporary relief. Adoption seems more hearty. Permanent care equals permanent relief."

Mr. Hillier shook his head. "People like you should not be in adoption. Happy people should be in adoption. Unhappy people should be doing unhappy jobs."

"Oh, great," said Tully, smiling wanly. "Mr. Hillier, you were going to fire me a year ago because you thought I was too rough on some poor mother. Now you want me to be the director of the whole agency? You think I'll be any gentler as the director?"

"You have a good heart," Mr. Hillier repeated. "You know your job. You're important to me."

"You were going to fire me," said Tully.

"No, Tully," said Mr. Hillier. "That was your twentieth second warning. I would've been giving you second warnings forever. You were always too important to me. I'd be proud to have you succeed this way," he said. "I recommended you."

"Well, thank you, Mr. Hillier," Tully said softly. "Thank you. I promise you I'll think about it, okay?"

He nodded. "Okay, Tully. I guess that's as much as I can expect from a hedger."

She shook Mr. Hillier's hand.

"Who, if not you?" Mr. Hillier said, holding her hand in his for a moment. "Tell me that."

His hand was warm, and Tully felt better for having touched it and for having come.

"So tell me what happened. What ghastly thing could Lillian have done to have you fire her?"

Mr. Hillier coughed into his hand. "Kim and Jason Slattery have died," he said.

Tully sat down like she was cut down. Something inside her broke suddenly, spilling cold pain all over. "Oh," she whispered. "Now I understand."

"That old Slattery shot them both during an argument with his wife."

"Is she still alive?" Tully asked.

"Oh, yes," said Mr. Hillier. "They've both been arrested. She as accessory to manslaughter. Why didn't he just shoot the wife? That's what I wonder."

"Manslaughter," Tully whispered. "Manslaughter. That man has been trying to kill those kids for years, and his wife was letting him for years, and that's all they call it? Manslaughter?"

"Slattery says he was mad. Didn't mean to shoot them kids. That's exactly what he said. 'Didn't mean to shoot them kids.' "

"What's happened to the youngest boy? Robbie?"

"Oh, he was sleeping somewhere. That's what saved him. The other two tried to intervene between mom and dad."

"How terrible," said Tully.

"You understand why Lillian could not remain director any longer? There is a criminal investigation under way, and the court requisitioned all our records on the Slatterys. You're in there, and what he did to you. The district attorney wanted to know how the kids ever ended up back with those people. We just barely avoided Lillian's being charged with being accessory to manslaughter herself," said Mr. Hillier.

"Yes," Tully said sadly. "She should have been arrested. That man was homicidal all his life. The kids had no place with them." She crossed herself. "They're in peace now," she whispered. "It's okay. They're at peace."

"Will you take the job, Tully?" said Mr. Hillier.

"Ironic, isn't it?" said Tully. "Because of their tragedy, my life could be a success."

"If you were director, it never would have happened. Think about that."

*   *   *

Tully went for a drive. A purposeful drive. Her ears were ringing, and she kept hearing Jack's voice.

Tully drove to Manhattan. And in Manhattan, she went to DeMarco & Sons and went out to lunch with Robin and Steve, who was now fully employed in the family business. Tully watched the two brothers and thought that Robin must have liked that—Stevie's coming around after all this time. Caring for the store that made them all rich.

Tully wanted to tell Robin about her talk with Mr. Hillier, but the lunch was so relaxed, so pleasant, Tully didn't want to spoil it. After she got back into her car to go home, she realized all she had really wanted to do was to sit with Robin.

Once the news got around that Tully was offered this position, everybody put in their unanimous two cents. A great opportunity. A fool not to take it. Everybody, that is, except Robin. Robin and Tully had just signed off on the court papers that Mr. Hofmann with his ever-kind blue eyes was going to send off to the district court.

"I think I'm going to take it," Tully said to Robin one April evening. The windows were open. It was getting warm. Spring was here.

"I'm not surprised in the least," he said. "You always loved that crazy job. But tell me something. What's the point of taking it now?"

Tully rubbed her hands together. "I don't know," she said.

"Of course," said Robin, opening up the paper and turning his back to her. "It'll all seem so normal to you. It'll be just like a regular life. What a fucking sham."

"They've offered me a lot of money," Tully said, as if that explained anything.

"What do you need money for, Tully?" he said. "Don't worry," he added sarcastically. "I won't let you and Jack starve out on the beach. Besides, money never meant anything to you, anyway. Otherwise you would've cared for me a long time ago." He faced her then, dark and quiet. He stood up before her, arms folded, and asked, "Tully, has our life really been so bad?"

"No," said Tully, thinking, blinking, numbing. "It hasn't been so bad."

At the end of April, Tully doubled Millie's salary, left Jenny with her so Millie could bring the baby to Docking at lunchtime, and returned to work as the director of the Foster Home Recruitment Agency.

7.

It had been four long months since anyone had touched Tully, and Tully missed being touched. One night in May, when her heart was particularly hurting, she came to Robin. Tully came into their bed and spooned him and smelled his hair. He didn't turn to her that night, but the following night he did.

Afterwards, when she was lying in his arms, Robin asked her, "When is he coming?"

"I don't know," she said.

"Are you hoping he'll come soon?"

"I don't know," replied Tully. "I guess so."

"You guess so," Robin mimicked her, disentangling himself. "And how soon do you think you'll be going?"

"I don't know," said Tully. "Are you going to let me have my son?"

"For Christ's sake, Tully! It is not about your son!"

"Yes, it is," she said weakly. "I can't leave without him."

"Oh, I see," Robin said. "You can't go until you have him. I don't get it. You're ready to dispense with your entire life— your great new job, your house, your friends, your mother. Me. Why not him, too?"

"He's my son!" she cried.

"Shhhh!" he hissed.

"He is my son! He is not a dog! I cannot just dispense with him! He is not a lamb I can just burn and sacrifice!"

"I see," said Robin. "But we are all dogs, the rest of us."

"I'm still here, aren't I?" she said, lying on her side, away from him.

"Ah, yes, but not by choice. Well, I hope he comes for you soon, Tully. Tell me, do you think he has been faithful to you?"

"If *you* haven't been," Tully said brokenly, "no one in the world could be."

A few weeks later, Tully was sleeping on the floor of the nursery again. It must have been early morning, three or four.

When she woke up she was covered by a blanket.

Tully couldn't understand at first what woke her. She had not had a bad dream and Jenny was quiet. So she closed her eyes and tried to drift off, but drifting off scared her. Being half asleep, however, she couldn't figure out what it *was* that scared her. There were no images running around in her head, but there *was* something else, something unidentifiable. What *was* that?

Tully thought she was dreaming at first, but the panic feeling was so real, the fear so fresh that she opened her eyes and sat up. Tully sat up and inhaled and smelled smoke.

Throwing the blanket off her, she scrambled on all fours to the door, reached for the handle, pulled herself up, and swung the door open. The hallway smelled like smoke.

And then Tully yelled. She screamed, and afterwards couldn't remember *what* she had screamed, but Boomerang remembered because he told her later that what woke him up was his mother's voice screaming his father's name.

"ROBIN! ROOOOOBIIIN! ROOOBIIIN!" Tully ran past the bathroom, past Boomerang's bedroom, straight into their bedroom. The room was filled with smoke, and it appeared to Tully that the bed was on fire.

She fell to her knees, took one deep breath, held it, and crawled to the bed, around the bed. He slept on the side farthest from the door and closest to the window, where she used to sleep. Tully's eyes were burning, and she couldn't see him very well, but the curtains were blowing open, blowing the smoke around the room, blowing spring-air to the flames on the bed. She grabbed Robin's arm, but he was not moving. Afraid to shout his name, afraid to breathe, Tully yanked him by his arm from the bed, and Robin kind of slouched forward, his head falling off the edge. Tully yanked him again, pulling, pulling, until he fell off the bed in a heap but did not awaken. It's okay, it's okay, it's okay, Tully's mind was spinning. It's okay, he's only unconscious. She dimly heard Boomerang's whimper next door. Dragging Robin by his arms, she managed to pull him to the window, and then, with an effort that made her grunt fiercely, she pulled half of Robin up on the window seat. Flinging the window open all the way, she shoved his head into the fresh night air and gasped for breath herself. Tully did not wait to see if he would come around. Those seconds were ticking by while the room was getting more and more filled with smoke. The bed was nearly all ablaze now, the blankets, the pillows. I've got to get him out of this room, she thought. If I leave, he'll never get out of here. Tully started to shake him and blow air in his mouth, shake, blow, shake, blow, shake, blow. "Come on, Robin, come on, COME ON!" she screamed.

The lights in the house across the street went on. A neighbor leaned out of her window. "Fire!" she shouted. "Oh, my Lord, fire!"

"Call someone, please!" Tully shouted back. Blow, shake, blow, shake, blow, shake, goddamn it! Finally, Robin stirred, and as soon as he stirred, Tully shook him with renewed might, shouting at him, "Robin, wake up! Please! Help me, please, wake up, Robin!" He coughed and threw up all over the windowsill, shaking violently all by himself. "Help me, Robin, help me, come on!" cried Tully.

"Okay, okay," he whispered. "The babies?"

"Let's go! Please," panted Tully, helping him stand up.

They crawled out of the room though Robin kept falling down. Behind him, Tully pushed him forward. Boomerang was not in his bedroom, and Tully, desperately scared, ran to the window. Robin ran to Jenny's room and found Boomerang under the crib, holding his little sister. He took Jenny, helped his son out, screamed for Tully, and they all ran downstairs, Robin still in his underwear, wet and smelling of vomit, Tully in an old blue sweat suit, the kids hardly dressed. But it was May and warm. Downstairs, opening the front door and ready to get outside, Tully remembered Hedda. "My mother," she said to Robin, who turned back to go and get her. Tully stopped him, hearing the fire engines.

The firemen rescued Hedda Makker, paralyzed, heavy, unable to help herself. The men laid her down on the grass to wait for the ambulance. "What's happened?" Hedda asked, looking up from the grass.

"Robin smoked in bed," replied Tully.

The paramedics took the family to the hospital, while the firemen put out the fire in fifteen minutes. The fire, although confined to the bedroom, destroyed nearly everything there, burning the wooden bed to a crisp, scorching the carpet and the curtains and leaving black soot all over the ivory-painted walls.

*   *   *

"A fire!" Shakie exclaimed. The DeMarcos, except for Hedda, who was taken to Topeka State, were staying with the Bowmans for a few days. "A fire, for God's sake! What kind of people are you? Why does nothing ever happen to anyone in Topeka, except you guys?"

Not true, thought Tully, still shaken up and not wanting to be alone. Just a few months ago, two young children lost their lives for no good reason at all. All we had was a burning bed.

Robin said, "Tully, if you don't mind, I'll just call you Farrah."

Tully rolled her eyes. "Yeah?" she said. "If I'm Farrah, you know what that makes you? A loud, boorish, abusive drunk."

"Not to mention divorced," said Shakie. "They were divorced when Farrah scorched him."

"Not an altogether bad idea," said Tully. "I'll bet you he wasn't snoring away while Farrah was trying to pull his dead weight to the window to save his ass." But Tully couldn't quite look at Robin when she said that. She could barely look at Shakie.

"I still can't figure out," said Shakie to Tully, "why Robin lost consciousness but not you."

Tully and Robin exchanged looks.

"She was feeding Jenny in the nursery and fell asleep," explained Robin.

"What the hell were you doing smoking in bed, man?" said Frank.

"Yeah, and what the hell were you doing letting him?" said Shakie to Tully.

"Letting him!" exclaimed Tully. "I've been yelling at him for years."

"Yeah, ever since you stopped smoking you've been getting on my tail," said Robin.

Tully ignored his remark and turned to Shakie. "Do you know," she said, "he even smokes in Boomer's room, right next to his own son's bed!"

"Robin!" said Shakie. "Tsk, tsk. I'll just have to call Social Services, won't I? Oh, wait. Tully *is* Social Services. Well, she'll just have to take your son away from you, won't she, and give him to a nonsmoking family."

Again, Robin and Tully looked at each other, and Tully

lowered her eyes, for what there was between them at that moment was impossible to put on somebody else's kitchen table and chew over like scrambled eggs. Unspoken. It was just like the old days.

The DeMarcos stayed with Shakie and Frank for several weeks, well into June.

Tully and Robin kept going back to their house and, with Millie's help, slowly cleaning out all the debris, throwing away the burned furniture, pulling up the carpet, washing and scrubbing the floor and the walls. There was some water damage to the floorboards and to the ceiling downstairs in the living room. The flooring upstairs was pulled out and new floorboards were put in. Tully liked the way the bedroom looked with a brand-new parquet floor. The ceiling downstairs was also replastered and repainted.

"It's too bad," said Robin, "that your friend Jack isn't here. He could paint the bedroom for us."

"Robin, please," said Tully. "Yeah, too bad your hair doesn't need cutting."

Robin and Tully went shopping together and bought a whole new bedroom set, a beautiful whitewashed maple. New lamps, shelves, radios, chairs. A Persian area rug. New cushions for the window seat, new curtains for the three windows. Tully looked at the calendar. June 10. Thirty thousand dollars to fix the floor and redecorate one room. For how long? For how many days? Thirty thousand dollars divided by how many days?

8.

On Friday, June 15, Tully ran into the bathroom before she left work for the weekend. She smiled at herself in the mirror. Power dressing. Powerful yet accessible, that's the image she tried to project. She had to admit, she liked being boss. Mrs. DeMarco, they all called her. And on her door was written NATALIE ANNE DEMARCO.

Her dark blue suit and white blouse with a lace collar looked quite sophisticated, she had to admit. Maybe Robin can start a women's line, she thought, quickly stopping herself. What am I thinking? She ran her fingers through what was left of her hair. Tully rubbed her mouth to remove any residue of lipstick: she didn't want to be kissing her Jenny with lipstick on. Rushing to the elevator, she said good-bye to the few people still left in the office, and down on the first floor she waved 'bye to the building clerks.

On the way to her car, she thought of vague things: dinner, the weekend, maybe if the weather was nice they could all go to Lake Shawnee, and further on to the summer, hazy nonverbalized thoughts, and then she heard his voice.

"Tully? Tully Makker? Is that you?"

Tully knew that voice. She squinted and opened her eyes and squinted again, but it was not a mirage. There he was, leaning against his car in the warm June evening.

"Jack," she whispered.

He opened his arms.

"Oh, Tully, man," he said. "What have you done to your beautiful hair?"

"I cut it," she said. "Do you like it?"

"I don't know," he said. "I need to get used to it. You looked like this at your graduation."

"So I look young? That's good."

"As I remember, the whole graduation thing wasn't such a great time for you," Jack said.

"I'm grown up now," she said. "I am nearly thirty."

"I am thirty," he said. "But I'm not grown up at all."

He hugged her hard and tight, and Tully forgot everything. It was as if Bruce Springsteen had come and took off that quilt he kept covering her with . . . *Cover me, cover me . . . I'm looking for someone who will come on in, and cover me* . . . But she didn't want to be covered. The stupid quilt was heavy.

Jack hugged her and lifted her up, spinning her around. "Tully, Tully, Tully."

"Oh, Jack, oh, Jack," Tully kept saying, her fingers in his hair, on his face, around his neck, around his shoulders. "Aren't you a sight for sore eyes."

"Me? Wait till you see what I got us!" He smiled. "I got us a house in Carmel that's so cute."

She pulled away from him a little. "It's nice, is it?"

"It's wonderful. And right down the street is the ocean. You can see it from the second-floor windows."

"Wow," she said, trying to muster up some enthusiasm. "A whole ocean from the second-floor windows. All I can see from my window now is Mrs. Palmer's house."

"Which needs painting, by the way," said Jack. "Where do you want to go?"

"Go? I gotta go home, Jack. The kids are waiting."

He pulled away from her. "Is Robin waiting?"

"Well," she said vaguely, "he's with the kids, I suppose."

Tully didn't like him pulling away from her. Rubbing herself against him, kissing his bare chest right above the last button on his white shirt, she said, "Tomorrow is Saturday, right? We'll meet tomorrow. Early."

He sighed. "Need a ride home?"

"No, uh-uh. I drive now. How did you know I was here, by the way?"

"Called the house," Jack said curtly. "Millie told me. What are you doing working, by the way?"

"Killing time, mostly," she said. "Waiting for you. Making some money."

"All the money you're making I'm sure is going right back into your clothes," Jack said, tugging at her skirt. "How's Jennifer?"

"Great," Tully said, and meant it. She took out a couple of photos from her purse. "Look."

"Look how chubby she is," Jack said. "Where did that come from?"

"I don't know. She never stops eating."

"I was never that chubby," Jack said. "Though I have to say, I was a pretty cute little kid."

"'Cause look at you now." Tully smiled, rummaging through her purse and pulling out an old frayed photograph.

"What's this?" Jack asked. "My God, didn't my mother feed me? Where did you find this?"

"Jennifer's milk crates."

He glanced at her. "You went up in the attic? What else happened while I was gone?"

Nothing, she wanted to say. Absolutely nothing. My bedroom burned down. I was made director of FHRA. Robin's been betraying me for years. My mother is still alive. My son . . .

"Who's this?" asked Jack, taking another photo out of Tully's hands, of a toddler, about a year old, round as a beach ball, blond and red-lipped, sitting on the grass, beaming. "Is this Jennifer?"

"No," she replied. "That's me."

"You!" Jack exclaimed. "You're so chubby."

"Why, thank you."

"What's this picture doing with Jen's stuff?"

"I don't know," she answered. "I must have given it to her when we were young. I certainly don't remember giving it to her. And my mother has no other photographs like it."

"I like it," said Jack.

"This is what your daughter looks like," said Tully. "She looks like me."

"What color eyes does she have?" he asked.

"Oh, puppy eyes. Slate gray."

"I hope they stay that way."

Wordlessly, Tully nodded her agreement.

"Nice car," Jack said, pointing to Tully's black Corvette.

"It's not mine, it's Robin's old car. 1985 or something."

"1985?" said Jack. "Oh, well, then it can't be nice, right?"

"Right." She smiled thinly.

Driving home, Tully thought of all the furniture she and Robin had bought for their new bedroom. They'd had it for five days. Five days into thirty thousand dollars.

Nonetheless, she felt better for having seen Jack again. She was full of high spirits until she walked into the kitchen and saw Boomerang playing baseball with Robin in the backyard.

"Hi!" they both yelled.

"Dad doesn't want to eat at home!" Boomerang shouted.

"Doesn't he?" said Tully, propping herself up by the kitchen door. "That's good. Because there's nothing to eat. Where's Jenny?"

Robin and Boomerang pointed to the baby swings they had set up for the baby. "We're hungry as hell," said Robin. "Where've you been?"

"I'm sorry," she said. "I went to White Lakes. I needed another suit."

"Another one? But you have about two dozen!"

"I lost weight. I don't have enough in size eight," said Tully, going to Jennifer. Robin came up to her, in shorts, bare-chested. "Where's the shopping bag?" he asked.

"Couldn't find anything I liked," Tully replied, picking up Jennifer. "Come, let's go eat."

The guys went to get pizza. The four of them ate—though Jenny mostly slept—outside on the patio and then Robin, Boomerang, and even Tully played soccer until the sun went down.

When they were getting undressed, Robin looked at Tully and said, "Well, that's something. That's an expression I haven't seen in your eyes before."

"What expression is that?" said Tully, glancing away.

"Guilt," said Robin.

They got into bed and lay there for a few minutes, not touching, not breathing.

"He came back, didn't he?"

Tully nodded in the dark. She heard Robin swallow. She almost wanted to cover her ears.

At last Robin spoke. "We have to go to court in July."

"August," she said.

"Will you stay here until then?"

"Of course," said Tully, clutching the sheet. Bruce Springsteen was back, covering her with the quilt of pain. Well, being uncovered didn't last long.

"I *mean*," said Robin slowly, "will you stay in this house?"

"As opposed to what?"

"As opposed to moving in with him."

Tully was far away. She was thinking about the ocean. She was hearing the water slap against her feet. She was tasting salt. Of the ocean, she hoped, but she wiped her mouth anyway. She knew it wasn't the ocean.

"Robin," Tully said, not turning to him. "I beg you. Please. Please. I can't leave—" her voice broke.

"So don't go," he said quietly.

"I can't leave without him," she whispered. She had no voice. "I can't go without my boy."

"So don't go," he repeated.

"Robin, I can't stay . . ."

"For the wrong reasons?" he finished for her. "So stay for the right reasons. Stay for Boomerang."

"Robin, I beg you," she whispered. "Every weekend. Come every weekend. I'll join you guys in a soccer league there, in a softball league. Anything you want. Just . . . please."

"Stop it," he said coldly, turning his back to her. "Stop begging. It doesn't become you. You can come here every weekend. I'll pay for you to come here every weekend."

"Robin!" Tully wiped her face, her mouth on the pillow. Clutching the pillow, closing her eyes, trying to ward off . . . the ocean. "Please. Please let me have my boy."

"Stop being a selfish pig for once in your life, Tully," Robin said.

Tully was thinking about the girl on the soccer field. "Robin, that girl, if you wanted to, I don't know if you do, but if you did, you could marry her. You could have kids with her. You could have kids with whoever you want. As many kids as you want. But me . . . Boomerang and Jenny are all I'll ever have. Ever. Please let me have him."

Robin shot out of bed. "God, will you just shut up already! What are you even talking about! More kids. Don't you understand? He is *all* I have. At least you have Jenny. I have only one child, one son, you and your Jack *Pendel* have made sure of that. So stop talking to me about this, I'm sick and tired of hearing you."

After he left, Tully lay in bed and the whole night wished for the oblivion she had been in when her pulse rate was thirty-five and her life was bleeding out of her.

Saturday was a magnificent day. Boomerang asked her to come with them to Manhattan, but Tully declined.

After Robin and Boomerang left, Tully got herself and Jenny ready and drove to the Washburn parking lot, where Jack was already waiting for them. His face lit up when he saw Jennifer. He picked her up and held her above his head, peering at her, cooing at her, kissing her face. Jennifer laughed uncontrollably when Jack stuck his nose into her neck, tickling her, while Tully wanted to weep uncontrollably.

The three of them went to Lake Vaquero. Tully watched Jack's face when they came upon the lake, with house after house built upon its shallow shores. The sand they once sat on was gone. It had become somebody's pier. The tree trunk they had once sat on was gone, too, and a shed had been built in its place. They saw this all from the road from the car. Finally they parked on Indian Hills Road and walked all the way around El Cerrito Drive and then Lagito Drive before they found a patch of woods that looked like it belonged to no one. There was no access to the water, just trees on the embankment and then a sharp four-foot drop. Jack took off his clothes and immediately jumped into the water. "Okay," he shouted to her. "It's safe!"

"What do you want me to do?" Tully asked, unstrapping Jenny from the baby sling. "Jump into the lake with an infant? Or wait till she falls in by herself?"

"She's not even six months yet, she can't possibly be mobile!" Jack shouted, making circles with his hands in the water.

"Speak for yourself," Tully said. "This kid is like Boomerang—she can't sit still."

"It's not that they can't be still," Jack said, climbing up the embankment and grabbing a towel. "It's that they can't be still when you're not with them. You're forgetting why you called Boomerang Boomerang. He followed you around like a puppy."

"And now I follow him around like a puppy," Tully said sadly.

Tully and Jack made love, and afterwards, a buck-naked Tully jumped in the lake and Jack jumped after her. Jenny was asleep—her car seat served wonderfully as a bed and as a feeding chair.

Then they ate lunch and lay on the blanket. Jenny slept through their lovemaking and most of the lunch, too.

Jack pressed his face into Tully's naked breasts. "I'm hungry," he said softly. "Feed me."

She pushed him away. "Get out of here, you big child," she said. But he persisted. His strong arms didn't let her go, and she didn't want him to, anyway. She wanted nothing more in the world at that moment than for Jack to be able to taste her milk. It had been six long months since he had touched her, and she had missed him to pain.

"What would it taste like, Tully?" he crooned. "The milk? What's it like?"

"Sweet," she said, trying to push him away from her. "Sweet and warm. Nothing like regular milk."

"Better, I expect," he muttered, still buried in her breasts.

"Much better," Tully muttered back, and stopped protesting.

Hours went by, numbingly fast hours, rapturous and blissful, hot and slow, abandoned and deserted hours, hours in which they played with Jennifer and splashed water on each other.

Hours in which they ate and fed one another. Hours in which Jenny slept again while they made love. Once, twice, three, four, five times, she lost count of the hours, lost count of the minutes, of the sun above their heads, and the trees covering them from the rest of the world. When Tully sat on top of his stomach and stroked his chest, when she swung her breasts into his face and kissed his wet blond hair, when she kissed his eyes and his chest under which his heart beat, when she felt the heart beat up and down fast fast fast under her lips, it seemed to Tully that she had lost her sense of everything else in the universe except the sense of him, and of her, and of their baby, peacefully asleep. She forgot her job and her mother and her life, and her husband, and Boomerang, too. She forgot them all as she cried into his face.

"Tully, why are you crying?" Jack asked her.

"Because I'm so happy," Tully told him.

"What's wrong, Tully?" he whispered. "Tell me, what's wrong?"

"Everything is a-okay, Jacko," Tully whispered back.

He pushed her face slightly away from his shoulder to take a look at her.

"Then why don't I believe you?" he said.

9.

Kansas was hot, rainless, burned to the ground. Another Fourth of July came and went. Jack was finishing up the sale of his mother's house. Tully was still working and still seeing Jack at lunches and on the weekends, and sometimes weeknights, too. Robin and Boomerang and Tully were still playing soccer in the backyard and making barbecues. Tully and Robin were still pretending to their son that they had a normal life. And there were times—when Tully's mangled lips would fight not to betray what was behind them—when it truly *appeared* as if they had.

Finally, on Tuesday, July 17, Tully dragged herself to see her mother, who had remained at Topeka State since the fire in June.

"I need to talk to you, Mother," Tully said.

"I'm not well, Tully," Hedda replied. "Maybe some other

time. When are you taking me home?"

"Well, that's kind of what I gotta talk to you about, Mom," said Tully.

"Let me guess," said Hedda. "You're not taking me home?"

"Ma," said Tully, sitting down in the chair next to Hedda's bed. She hoped no one could hear them.

"I want to go away, Ma," Tully said. "You see, I want to go to California, and I don't know what to do with you."

"You're going with Robin?"

"No," said Tully. "Robin is staying here."

"You're going with that other man?"

"He is not that *other* man."

"What about your children?"

"Yes, leave it to you to question me about my children!" Tully laughed and fell quiet. "So what am I going to do with you?"

"I don't know, Tully," Hedda said wearily. "Why do you have to do anything?"

"I am going away. Do you understand? I'm going away, and I'm not taking you with me."

"Are you taking your children with you?"

"Ma! I don't want to talk about my children with you, okay?"

"You're leaving him behind, aren't you? You are leaving Boomerang behind."

Tully clenched her fists as her heart had clenched. "Mother," she said through gritted teeth, "you are the last person on earth I want to talk about this to. Now be quiet!" She took a deep breath. Released her fists, though her heart stayed put and tight. "What am I going to do with you?"

"Is Robin staying on Texas Street?"

"I don't think so," answered Tully. "Maybe. In any case, you are not his responsibility."

"No, I'm not," said Hedda. "I'm yours."

"Yes, Mother, yes," said Tully tiredly. "So what do I do with you? Aunt Lena doesn't want you. She is not too well herself. Menninger, Mom?"

Hedda turned her face away. She lay there very still, and then said, "Whatever you wanna do, Tully. Whatever you want."

"What about a private place? Somewhere really snazzy?"

"Snazzy?" Hedda repeated dully, like she didn't know what the word meant. "Who will pay for snazzy?"

"Don't worry about that. *You*, Robin and I will settle somehow," replied Tully.

"When do you plan on going?"

"Soon," said Tully. "Soon." What an awful word, Tully thought. What an awful word, holding with it so much time, and so little, so many questions, so many answers. Soon. Robin and she hadn't been to court yet. Hadn't disposed of each other yet.

"You're such a disappointment to me, Tully," said Hedda.

Tully laughed. "I'm a disappointment? Yes, go on. You've already told me this, Mother, remember? But thank you for bringing it up again." Tully paused before she said, "I never blamed you for anything."

"Like hell, you didn't," said Hedda. "Since you were just a little kid you blamed me. You and your unblinking gray eyes. Following me everywhere, accusing me, judging me, blaming me. You never said anything, no. You didn't have to. Besides, you weren't honest that way, you still aren't. But you did blame me!"

"There was a lot to blame you for," said Tully softly.

"I was your mother!" Hedda yelled, her hands twitching. "Your mother! How can you blame me for anything? I did the best I could, the very best, I couldn't do any better—"

"Though I'm sure you've tried," interrupted Tully.

"You don't know what I've lived through, you don't know what I've been through, what kind of life I had—"

"Oh, yes, I do," Tully interrupted again. "I'm not stupid, and Aunt Lena was kind enough to explain you away to me. I feel for you, Mom. But you, on the other hand, don't know what *I've* been through. You don't know what kind of life *I've* had."

"Who cares about you?" said Hedda. "It's not all about you. Besides, I know what kind of life you had. Milk and honey every day since you married Robin."

"Indeed, Mother, indeed."

"I've led a tortured life," said Hedda, her eyes shut, her face turned away from Tully, her hands at her sides. "A tortured life. A meaningless life. Nothing good has come of my life, and look at me now. Nothing ever will. I just want to stop living now. I'm done with it."

"Oh, don't I know how that goes," said Tully with fierce sympathy and fierce self-pity. "Don't I know what that's like."

"You have no idea," said Hedda, turning her head away.

"No, you have no idea!" exclaimed Tully. *I* will never stop being tortured by my past, she thought. Never. No talking, no crying, no carrying on will make me better. No psychiatrists, no help. No time. No palm trees. Nothing will bring me peace except death.

"My entire life, the only life I've known," said Tully, "has been one big fat rope on which I've hanged. I've put my lowered head into the noose and looked on as it tightened around my neck. That was the bottom, that was the end." Tully took a deep breath, and so did Hedda.

"I've been where you are every day of my life, Mom. I couldn't imagine how I could live another day. But yet, just when my vision was blurring and my breath was leaving, just when my heart was missing its beats and my body grew whiter, just then, something—not much, but something—would pull on me, work on me. Just then I would remember Jennifer's or Julie's funny faces, or Jeremy's care, or Boomerang's kisses, or Robin's, or Jack's. I would remember Jack's eyes and smile, and it would lift my heart. Just then. And I would slowly free my head out of the loop. I'd take a deep breath. The air would smell so clean, so cool—air after rain. And I would lick my wounds, grateful to myself that I found a way to go on another day. I never wanted to die, you see. I just wanted to live a little better."

"You've been lucky," Hedda said. "You've had something to pull you back."

"I haven't been lucky!" Tully said, nearly weeping. "I haven't been lucky!" she repeated. "Just stronger, Mother, that's all." She showed Hedda the scars on her wrists. "These? I taste my own blood and imagine what it's like not to see, not to smell, not to hear the wheat fields of Kansas rustling with the wind, not to see the prairie or the prairie sky, not to hear my son's voice, or my daughter's cry, or Robin's laugh, or Jack's . . . and so I live, resigned that there are some things I will never get over.

"How could I ever get over my dad leaving and not taking me? I can't. If he'd stayed, it'd be a different story. If he took me along with Hank? Then, too. But to have left me? To have sacrificed me? Well, here I am. Sacrificed. I try to dwell on everything as little as possible, but at night there is no life, there is nothing to do but dwell, and I can't help myself. I wish there was only day, so that I could do, do, do, and never have to lie there, terribly awake. I wish I could do, do, do, and be tired for anything else but sleep. But frankly even sleep brings little relief, with my visions of suffocation and hanging. Suffocation. Where do you think that might've come from, Ma?"

Hedda looked on at Tully with cold eyes and shook her head.

"Mmmm. Yes, I may have been a bad daughter to you when I was a teenager, and certainly am a bad daughter and a huge disappointment to you now, but tell me, Mother, was I a bad daughter to you when I was *two*?"

Hedda opened her eyes and stared at Tully blankly.

"What? Was I not blond enough, not happy enough, not chubby enough? What was it?"

"What the hell are you talking about?"

"Well, tell me," said Tully. "Did you feel that I was complicating your life just a little too much? Did you feel I was taking too much out of you? Was it like a post facto abortion? Did you think that with me out of the way, Dad would pay more attention to you? Johnny was already gone, did you think it was one down, one to go?"

When Hedda did not reply, Tully said loudly, clearly, "Mother, don't tell me you are going to say I imagined that pillow on my face and the smell of your hands. Please don't tell me I imagined it!"

"Tully, I'm not going to tell you anything. You've always had bad dreams, always," said Hedda. "Your father frequently ran into your bedroom to calm you down."

"I'm sure my father did," said Tully. "So it was a dream, Mother? Did my bad dreams start perhaps after I was two?"

"Tully, what the hell are you talking about?"

"Oh, yes, pretend. Well, what else can you do, really? I'm marginally lucky to have been left alive. Johnny certainly didn't make it, though Hank fared a little bit better than all of us."

"Johnny died from crib death, and your father took Hank with him. Your father split you kids up. Don't blame me."

"Well, gee, I wonder why, Momma. I wonder just why Daddy felt he had to go and take Hank, too."

"I don't think your father was ever prepared for a family," said Hedda, who had closed her eyes again.

"Hmm, well, certainly one of you was not prepared for a family. But Dad took Hank with him, after all."

"It got to be too much for him."

"Yes, it must have," said Tully. "Hearing me night in and night out describe my dreams to him must have gotten too much for him, my dreams which were always the same, I mean, I never dreamt that *he* was the one suffocating me."

Hedda was silent.

"I know he told you about them, Mother. I heard him once, telling you how he could not understand why a six-year-old child would be dreaming such horrible things, night after night, year after year, and you said I was pretending, just crying out for attention. You told him to ignore me, just ignore me, or I'd sit all over you both, and he listened to you and didn't come to my bed anymore then. Didn't come to me anymore."

"Your father and I had to go to work. We could not be woken up by you every goddamn night."

"Of course. Maybe you could have avoided that little problem by being more successful. After all, Johnny never had to wake you up."

"Yes," said Hedda flatly. "And then I wouldn't have had to hear this shit. How could you say such a terrible thing to your mother?"

Tully was unmoved. "Mother!" she whispered cruelly. "I know you killed Johnny. You tried to kill me and, if Dad didn't come in, you would've succeeded. Maybe you tried with Hank, too, I don't know, though I certainly kept watch. Luckily that was easy for me, for you've ensured that I can never go to sleep, not even nearly three decades later, so maybe Hank's life was saved, just like my own was saved. And you say I am a bad daughter to you? Mother, I am nobody's daughter. You're my mother in name only, and I am your daughter in name only. I have a father in name only. In reality, I am an orphan, and I wear the makeup of an orphan, and I pity myself just like an orphan. What can I do about that? Nothing. So I come home and play with my son and give him a bath and give my daughter a bath and read to my children and sit on the floor with them and kiss them, and hope I will do a little better by them."

"I doubt you will, Tully," said Hedda. "You have the wandering spirit, just like your father did."

Tully stopped. Leaning forward in her chair toward her mother, Tully said, "Ma? Do you think Dad and Hank are dead?"

"I try not to think about your father, Tully," replied Hedda, her face turned away toward the curtain.

"Well, think about him now."

"I think they're out there somewhere," said Hedda. "I didn't know you still thought about them, Tully."

"I don't much," said Tully.

"I didn't think so. You hardly seemed to notice they left. Much like your friend Jennifer."

Tully was aghast. "You're wrong, Mother," she said, shaking her head. "So wrong. How in the world can you say that?"

Hedda shrugged in bed. "You never even told me. And you went on in the same sulky silent way. Nothing changed. It was like you didn't notice. You never seemed to notice very much. Except yourself."

Tully leaned back. "I was, I admit, self-absorbed, inadequate. I despise the four walls that contain me. But, Mom, Jennifer? I noticed she was gone, Ma," Tully said with feeling. "How did I go on? I couldn't have, if not for the four walls that contained me."

"You have a good life now," said Hedda.

"Can I help that I want a different one?" said Tully. "A different life, a different past, a different future. Can I help wishing that Lynn Mandolini was my mother? Pretty futile of me, isn't it? I never wanted to take care of you, that's true. I never wanted you in my house, and when Robin brought you there, wishing he, too, had a different past, I hated him and hated you. I fed you and didn't want to. I brought you tea, and didn't want to. I looked at you and didn't want to. And you know what? I still don't want to. Eight years have passed. And I just don't want to, Mother. So what do I do with you?"

Hedda turned to look at Tully. Tully was rocking back and forth in the chair.

"Whatever you like," said Hedda, closing her eyes and pulling the blankets to her chin. "Whatever's best for you. I'm tired now. Let me sleep."

"Ma," said Tully beseechingly. "You had another stroke,

you can't walk again, with each stroke you get further and further back from being able to function normally. Eight years is a long time. What do you want me to do?"

"Nothing, Tully," said Hedda. "Let me sleep."

Tully got up to go and then came over and sat on the edge of Hedda's bed.

"They've made me head of the Foster Agency," she said quietly. "Not even thirty, and I am head of the whole agency! One hundred people. Who would have thought?"

"That's great, Tully," said Hedda, without opening her eyes.

"I can do better now for those kids—"

"Well, that's really good, Tully," replied Hedda. "But you're leaving. And I'm really tired."

Tully leaned closer to Hedda and said, "Ma? you know all that other stuff, all this stuff we just talked about? All that stuff is bullshit. Meaningless. I mean, okay, it might have brought me here, it might all have brought me to this point in time and abandoned me here. Just left me here as if to say, this is your life. And you're going to have to decide for yourself what you want your future to be. 'Cause you're going to have to spend a long time in it."

Getting no response from Hedda, Tully continued. "I can't even use Jennifer, or my dad, or you, or Uncle Charlie as my excuse. I've got no excuses now because I've got to take my head out of the fucking sand that's been my entire life and . . . just deal! I've got all this mess weighing on me like a fucking stone: this mother mess, this house mess, this Robin mess, Boomerang mess, and Jenny mess, and Jack mess, and I'm having trouble dealing. So that's why I'm here. I'm trying to deal with you. I'm sorry we talked about that other stuff at all. It's over. It's been dealt with, not well, maybe. It's been endured. I've gritted my teeth and went on, but now I've come to this, and I don't want the rest of my life to become another unhealed wound like everything else around me. I don't want this to become another thing I can't talk about! I want, need, to be able to talk about my life! I want to be able to look people in the face and not turn away from them, not flinch from them. I don't want *this*, cannot have *this* become another open sore! An open sore . . . like you, Mommy," Tully added in a whisper.

"Like me," Hedda echoed.

"Like you," said Tully, wringing her hands. "You know, I've nearly gotten over your hands around my throat thing. It stopped meaning anything to me long ago. It just gives me bad dreams. And I got over my dad, and my brothers, too. Believe it or not, I even got over Uncle Charlie. I'm not sure if you even remember Uncle Charlie, Mother. Jennifer's mom remembers. After all, what happened helped me decide to have Boomerang, and that can't be a bad thing."

A short, hard silence. "Even Jennifer. Don't get me wrong, I don't make the climb to the attic too often. On the other hand, you, Mommy, you are like a canker sore to me, you're like a scab that I pick at every day, you are like my mother. And how could that be, when I'm sure I never had one? How could you be my mother and never have loved me? As long as I live, I won't understand, but as long as you live, I will see you, talk to you, read to you, turn off your lights when you are asleep and think, This here is my mother, but she does not love me. I have a mother who did not love me. How can that be true? How is that possible? And yet, every day, I see you, and every day I am exposed to this sore. Thank God for my job for making me feel less sorry for myself. Still, though, it does not change the fact that you did not love me when I was little and do not love me still, and you know what? I just do not want to be reminded of that any longer. I don't hate you, Mother, I just don't want to hang my head every day I see you. Can you understand that?"

"All too well, Tully," replied Hedda.

Tully got up again to go.

"Mom, tell me something, won't you?" Tully said, almost as an afterthought. "Tell me. Aunt Lena says all those years you kept me, you didn't even want me with you, you thought of giving me into foster care yourself. Tell me, why? Why didn't you do it? Why didn't you give me to a family that might have taken care of me? Lynn Mandolini told me she asked you if I could come and live with them and you refused. Why, Mom? Why did you refuse?"

Hedda did not open her eyes, did not stir. "Because," she said faintly, "you were my daughter, Tully. You were my daughter. How could I give up my child? Yes, I wasn't fit much for motherhood, I wasn't fit much for anything, I did the best I could, and I just didn't have the energy for you, or the heart, but how could I, how could I give up my child? My mother gave me up. How could I give you up? You were my daughter, after all. . . ."

Hedda lay there with her eyes closed, while Tully watched her with her eyes open, standing over her, and then she bent down over Hedda's face and kissed her mother's forehead. "Okay, Mom," she whispered. "Okay."

10.

After Tully left, Hedda lay there and did not stir for hours and hours. Her eyes were open, then closed, open then closed. She did not eat her dinner, she did not drink her tea. She did not turn on the TV, nor did she ask to go to the bathroom. She just lay there and stared at a space on the wall, closing her eyes once in a while, opening them again, closing them.

At ten o'clock at night, she buzzed the nurse and asked if she could have a bath. The nurse refused, saying it was much too late. But Hedda insisted. She said she had not had a bath in a long time and felt dirty. After hearing Hedda out, the nurse called the doctor, who was much too busy to be bothered with trivialities, and then she called Tully, who said, of course, give my mother a bath if she wants a bath.

The nurse ran a lukewarm bath for Hedda, wheeled her into the bathroom, and undressed her. Hedda's legs did not move, and she weighed 190 pounds. The nurse was unable to get Hedda into the bath and was nearly going to forget the whole thing until Hedda, in a superhuman effort, lifted herself by her arms off the wheelchair and fell into the bathtub, drenching the nurse with the bathwater.

"I'm all right," said Hedda, straightening herself out in the bath and pulling up to a sitting position. "I'm all right. Please give me a little privacy."

Leaving, the nurse said she would check back with Hedda in twenty minutes.

After she left, Hedda sat for a few moments with her eyes closed and then sank down until the water covered her. She held on to the stainless steel side grips and lowered her head under the water. She tried to stay under for as long as she could, but it wasn't that long. Even Hedda, who had lost all sense of self-preservation, was instinctively propelled upwards.

The force of wanting to die was not equal and opposite to the force of wanting to live.

It was not enough. Hedda's head popped up like a float. She took a deep breath and sat there for a while, thinking, breathing, thinking.

When the nurse came back in twenty minutes, Hedda was running the water.

"What are you doing?" asked the nurse.

"The water is nearly cold. I need some hot water, I'm freezing here."

"Well, be sure to turn the faucet off when you're done," the nurse said, and left.

Upon checking on Hedda thirty minutes later, the nurse observed that Hedda was sitting silently in the bath, water up to her chin, her face flushed pink and hot. The nurse beckoned Hedda to get out, but Hedda didn't budge. "I haven't had a bath in seven years," Hedda said. The nurse decided there was no harm in letting an infirm woman enjoy the water for a few minutes longer. It was nighttime and quiet. She walked back to her station, got herself a cup of coffee, read *People* magazine for a little while, and went to check on a few of her other patients. About forty-five minutes later, she went back to the bathroom to get Hedda out of the bath.

Hedda sank deeper into the hot water. She knew it was very hot because the steam was rising and fogging up all the mirrors. It was oppressively hot. Hedda could hardly breathe. Still not hot enough, Hedda thought. I gotta get some of this bathwater out. She turned on the taps and ran the scalding hot water again. It took a long time to close her fingers around the taps, to apply enough strength to turn them, just enough and no more because Hedda had no more, and she feared she might even not have enough. But after a supreme effort and a couple of grunts, the hot water flowed, and Hedda sat back and closed her eyes. Still, she could not relax. The water needed to be turned off soon. It could seep out, flood out, flood the bathroom, and the sound of running water would be enough to alert even the night nurses, who usually couldn't be alerted with a fire. They would come in droves, empty the bath, put Hedda back in her bed, and then where would she be? Back in her bed. Back in her bed, on her back, lying there in her bed, watching TV, eating, sleeping, more TV. Hedda forced herself to open her eyes. In the bathroom fog, she could hardly see the water running, and she could hardly hear it—it reminded her of hearing the Kansas River for the twenty-one years she lived at Grove Street. I think it's hot enough, she thought, turning off the taps, and slinking back. She lowered her body fully under the water. How nice, and she thought she heard the sound of the ocean, but she had never heard the ocean, it just sounded like a whoosh whoosh in her head, distant, distant, and she opened her eyes slowly and tried to lift her hand to wipe her sweating forehead, but her hand would not lift, she looked at it, underneath the blue water, and sluggishly thought that she had forgotten the command for the hand, and couldn't even wipe her own brow. *Hand hand hand.* Or the nurse will come in and wipe me. That lifted her hand up. Hedda didn't want to be disturbed, she was feeling so dozy now, so relaxed, so easy. What did it matter if she was sweating? She was feeling so serene. She felt something liquid and peaceful running all inside her. She laid her head against the bath tiles, and tried to sink lower, but she was too big; her feet were firmly up against the other side of the tub. So her head remained just where it was, tilted to one side against the white porcelain. Hedda felt such tiredness, such sleepiness; she smiled weakly, so happy to be drifting off, and then a slow thought swam up to her: wonder if this is how my Tully felt when she let blood, wonder if this is what she was looking for. It's so nice, this.

The following morning, Tully handed Robin a cup of coffee before he left for work.

"Tully, why aren't you dressed?" Robin said. "It's eight o'clock."

"I'm not going in today," she replied.

"Did you quit?"

"No, I did not quit. My mother died."

Silence. "Oh," he said. "My God, I'm sorry." Then, "When were you going to tell me?"

"Now. I am telling you now."

"When did you find out?"

"Last night. The hospital called at three in the morning."

"Where were you at three in the morning?"

"Downstairs," Tully said.

"Why didn't you wake me and tell me?"

She shrugged. "What for?"

Robin backed away from her and put the cup of coffee down, untouched. "Of course. You needed time to think, didn't you?"

"No," she said. "You needed time to sleep."

He went on as if he hadn't heard her. "How nice for you," he said coldly. "How convenient. How did she die?"

"Had a massive brain hemorrhage while sitting in a tub of scalding hot water."

"I'm sorry. Let me guess," said Robin, watching Tully's face. "You were really upset in the night, but didn't want me to see it, and now you've calmed down."

She returned his cold stare. "What the fuck is wrong with you this morning?" she said.

"This morning?" he said, leaving the kitchen. "*This* morning?"

Died, Hedda Makker, of Texas Street, 47, of brain hemorrhage, at Topeka State Hospital, Wednesday, July 18, 1990, at 2:30 A.M. Mrs. Makker was an esteemed worker for the City of Topeka from 1959 until 1981. Memorial services and cremation will be held at Penwell-Gabel Funeral Home on SW 10th, Saturday, July 21, at 10 A.M. Mrs. Makker is survived by her loving daughter Natalie Anne DeMarco, her loving son-in-law Robin DeMarco, and her loving grandchildren: Robin DeMarco Jr. and Jennifer P. DeMarco.

This appeared in Thursday's edition of the *Topeka Capital-Journal*.

Tully came to the funeral home Thursday morning promptly at nine, as if she were going to work. She let Jack take care of Jenny during the day. He came by Thursday afternoon, Jennifer in tow, to pay his respects. Tully was glad he didn't stay long. She didn't want Jennifer to be looking at dead people.

Tully stayed in the medium-sized, oak-paneled, subdued parlor room for eight hours, on a comfortable chair in the very back, and listened to a young boy of about nineteen, new apprentice at Penwell-Gabel, recite the New Testament in a low drone. At five o'clock Tully left to pick up Jenny and go home. She had dinner with her family, did homework with Boomerang, bathed Jenny, and was back at the parlor by seven, until ten at night. After ten, she went over to Jack's for a few hours.

Tully herself went up to the coffin only once. On Thursday morning, with some fresh flowers, to start Hedda off. Hedda looked very well. Penwell-Gabel did a good job making her up. Hedda certainly didn't look any worse than she looked in real life. Yes, they were good, Mr. Penwell and Mr. Gabel. Tully was glad to give them her business, again.

She was frankly surprised by the turnout Hedda received at Penwell-Gabel Thursday and Friday. People from the old sewage plant came, neighbors from the Grove, and from Texas Street. All the nurses and physical therapists who treated her. Even the nurse who had found Hedda came, crying and apologizing.

Millie and all of Robin's family came, replete with the kids. Shakie came, put flowers down, and then went over to Tully and whispered, "What does the P. stand for?"

"The P?" said Tully.

"The P. As in Jennifer *P*. DeMarco."

Tully looked up at Shakie steadily. "Penelope," she replied.

"Oh, really?" Shakie said. "Jennifer Penelope DeMarco?"

"Exactly right," said Tully.

Aunt Lena came. Threw some flowers down near the coffin and then walked over to Tully and said, "She is also survived by her sister, by me, Lena Kramer."

"You're not her sister," said Tully.

"I am her sister," said Lena, blustery.

"You're not her sister," repeated Tully calmly. "You're the daughter of the woman the man who is not her father lived with. A pretty tenuous connection, wouldn't you agree?"

Tony Mandolini came; sagged, bald, old, but holding his head up high, he put his flowers down, and went to kiss Tully. "Dear Tully, you'll be all right," he said.

"Of course I will," she said, smiling lightly.

"I think Lynn might come to the cremation," Tony whispered into Tully's ear. "It's not a done deal yet. But I think so."

"I hope so," said Tully earnestly. "I really hope so."

Angela Martinez came, with Julie. Angela cried loudly, wiping her eyes with a handkerchief. "Poor Tully," she sobbed, pressing her face against Tully's face, making it all wet. "You truly are an orphan now."

"I'm nearly thirty with a husband and two children," said Tully, squeezing Angela's hand. "Besides, I've had *you* for most of my life."

"You're a good daughter, Tully, doing this for your mother, despite your differences. Look at all the flowers Hedda's got."

Tully patted Angela's hand, mute for a moment. "I hope she's in peace now," Tully said.

Julie hugged Tully. "Dear Tully," she said. "Look on the bright side. I'm here to stay for the rest of the summer. I'll tell you all about it later, okay?"

Look on the dark side, thought Tully. I'm not.

Late afternoon on Friday, Tully was sitting there, looking at her watch. Nearly five o'clock. Time to go home and eat, thought Tully. Just one more evening, and it's over.

The room was empty. Except for young Jeff in the corner near the coffin reading from St. Matthew. More people would come later, though you'd think they had better things to do Friday night.

Tully impassively watched a tall man walk into the room, glance at her briefly, and proceed up the isle to the coffin. She would have paid him no attention at all, except the man had glanced at Tully one heavy moment too long. He put his flowers down gently. They were yellow carnations, Tully noticed, for lack of anything else to notice. The man tilted his head, peered at Hedda's face, and crossed himself. Backing away slightly, he slumped into a chair.

Tully looked at her watch again. Four fifty-five. Almost.

She looked at the man again. From the back he was gray and wearing a suit. Tully was ready to get up.

All of a sudden, the man turned around and from across the room, from the front to the back, stared at Tully.

Tully's blood stopped coursing through her veins. All activity stopped inside her and drained out of her, and the only thing Tully heard in her now hollow gut was the echo of her heart. Then the blood rushed to her face and hands. The hands began to shake. Tully pressed them in between the folds of her long black skirt.

The man stood up and began to walk toward her. In the moments before she stood up herself, Tully noticed he had a serious pale face and a receding hairline. His suit was dark gray. His tie was black-and-white striped. He had a green Adidas sports bag with him.

"Hello, Tully," the man said, and Tully's legs started shaking so badly at the sound of his voice that she had to quickly sit down. Her heart echoed. No other activity had resumed itself in Tully's body.

"They still call you Tully? Or do you prefer Natalie nowadays?" He smiled.

"They call me Tully," she said.

"You look well," he said. "I'm sorry for your mother."

Tully cleared her throat. No sound came out. She tried to stand up again. Couldn't. She felt ridiculous sitting down while he was standing.

"What—what—" she stammered, "are you doing here?"

"I came to pay my respects to your mother."

"How—how—" she couldn't get the rest of the sentence out.

"How did I know she had died?" the tall gray man said. "Because I have the *Topeka Capital-Journal* delivered to me every day. It doesn't get to me till a day late, which is why I'm here a day late."

She didn't say anything.

"I read recently in the appointments section that you were made director of Foster Care for the State of Kansas."

Tully vacantly nodded. "But wait," she said, confused. "How did you know? It said Natalie Anne DeMarco."

"It said, 'Natalie Anne "Tully" DeMarco.' I knew you by your name."

"Ahh," she mouthed.

"That's a good position. Congratulations."

She nodded again. "Are you staying?"

He shook his head. "I'm flying back tonight."

"Flying to where?"

He looked down at her oddly. "New Mexico. Santa Fe."

"Is that where you've been?" Tully muttered.

"Yes. Some of the time. I've moved around a lot. Settled down finally in Santa Fe about ten years ago. I see you've gotten married. Had kids. Your husband a good man?"

"He's great," said Tully. "The kids are great, too."

"Of course they are."

There was an awkward silence. Then Tully said, "Do you want to come to the house?"

The tall gray man shook his head. "It wouldn't be a good idea. I got to fly back tonight." Then, "Do they look like you?"

"Robin, Jr., looks exactly like his father. The girl looks like me."

"Jennifer," the man said. "I read in the obits your friend Jennifer Mandolini died. When was that?"

"1979," Tully said.

"I'm sorry for that. She was a cute kid."

Tully wished she were deaf. "How's . . . Hank?"

"Hank is fine." He smiled. "He likes to be called Henry now. He's doing well. He's a projects contractor for commercial real estate."

"What does that mean?"

"He looks at blueprints and hires a crew that builds office buildings around Santa Fe."

"Oh, good," said Tully. She didn't know what else to say. She couldn't swallow.

"Why didn't he come with you?"

"I didn't think it would be a good idea."

"Why did you come, then?"

"Tully, Hank thinks his mother died a long time ago. That's why we left Topeka, I told him. Because I didn't want to live amid the bad memories, I said. What's he now going to think of me if I tell him I took a two-year-old away from his mother and his sister? You think he'll understand? Or do you think he'll never speak to me again?"

"I don't know," said Tully tonelessly. "Why don't you just tell him and see?"

"I might one day. Really. But I got myself a young family now. Got myself married again, after bumming around for twelve years. Got four kids now. The youngest girl was just born in January. Like you. The oldest is ten. What's my family going to think of me?"

"I don't know," repeated Tully. "Tell them and see."

He didn't answer.

"What'd you wait for her to die for? I turned eighteen over ten years ago. You could've seen me when I became an adult. Why didn't you just come?"

"Tully, you've been an adult since the day you were born," the man said. "And I didn't want to see your mother again, except in death. I would've looked in the *Capital-Journal* every day for the rest of my life, trying to catch her obituary. So I could come and see you."

"You could've come before."

"I didn't know anything about you. For all I knew, you were still living with her. Hating my guts. Your mother, she still was refiling missing reports with the state police departments in all fifty states as late as 1981. She even contacted the FBI. Didn't know that, did you? I didn't want her somehow to slap me with kidnapping a minor. And she would've if she could've."

"Yes," said Tully, nodding her head. "She would've. Did you have to change your name?"

"Believe it or not, no. Only in Topeka was I the only one. Everywhere else there are dozens of me. I'm one of four in Santa Fe."

Tully bit down on her lip. "I thought you'd forgotten me."

"How could I? I have all your baby pictures, Tully. I took them all."

"Ah," she said. "So you took them. The *pictures* you took. Well, you could've left some for me."

He shifted on his feet. Still holding the green bag. "You've grown up so nice, Tully. You're a fine young woman. You look just like your brother." His voice broke.

Tears spilled down Tully's cheeks. She stood up and didn't bother to wipe them. "Come and see my kids," she said.

"No, Tully," he said, catching himself quickly. "I can't. You've done all right for yourself. You'll do all right for yourself again. I'll keep in touch with you from time to time, now that your mother's dead, God have mercy on her soul. I won't lose touch. And someday I'll talk to Hank." His eyes glistened. "I think he'd be pleased to meet you."

Tully ran her lips around her mouth to taste the salt. "I'm sure he would." How sore and broken her mouth was from the clamping down it received at Tully's teeth.

The man looked around. "Look at all you've done for your mother. I can't believe she got so many flowers. Many people turn up?"

"More than I thought knew her."

"Had she changed much . . . your mother? In the last few years?"

"Not much," said Tully. "Please don't go," she said.

The tall gray man reached over and rubbed Tully's cheek. With the hand that wasn't holding the green bag. She did not flinch. "I *have* to go, Tully. I have a family now. I've got a wife and four kids besides Hank. Henry," he corrected himself, and smiled. "My wife will think I have a lady on the side if I don't come home on Friday night. I told her I was going for a game of pool after work. If my family finds out, they'll hate me. They'll think I'm a monster for what I've done."

"You are a monster," said Tully. "Johnny's dead."

The tall gray man took his hand away. "But you and Hank are alive and well. I'm not a monster, Tully," he said quietly. "You should know that better than anyone."

"I know no such thing," she said loudly. The apprentice stopped reading his Scriptures, looked up briefly, and then resumed reading. "You left me behind. You're a monster."

"Tully, I'm not. I *had* to leave you behind. I had to leave her something, someone. I couldn't just take your mother's entire life from her and leave her absolutely nothing, could I? I knew she wouldn't harm you. Not when you were the only thing she had left. And I was right. You grew up fine, despite her best efforts, I'm sure. And Tully, *you* knew your mother. My son is never going to know his. Think about that. *Never*."

"Please don't go," Tully said again tremulously. "I want to see my brother."

The man dug into his jacket pocket. "Here," he said, handing Tully a photograph. "I took it just this morning. For you." Tully glanced at it. It was a Polaroid shot of a smiling clean-shaven face of a light-haired, light-eyed young man. A young man who looked like Tully.

Henry cupped Tully's hand. "Don't shake. All I wanted was to show you I haven't forgotten you. You were always strong as an ox, Tully. Strong, even as a kid. You were the only one who could survive her. I wanted you to know I didn't leave you behind. I left you *for* your mother."

The following morning, the coffin was finally and blissfully closed, and Hedda was cremated. Tully brought Jennifer to Jack's, and then walked to Penwell-Gabel. Robin and Boomerang met her there. Boomerang insisted on going to the funeral of his Nanna.

Tully barely listened to the sermon, thinking only of the tall man's face from yesterday.

Gazing around the parlor with restless, wandering eyes, Tully caught a sideview glimpse of Lynn Mandolini.

Tully could not very well forget *that* face, which stared at her for a moment and then stared away. Lynn's once raven-black hair was gray now, and her face, once so thin and delicate, was an overblown mask of caloric and alcoholic excess.

Tully, startled by Lynn's appearance, hung on a little to Boomer, who pushed her away and moved to the other side of the bench, as if to show her that an eight-year-old boy *could* not, *would* not be pawed by his mother in public. Not even in front of God. Not even at his Nanna's funeral.

The sermon, Tully decided, did not comfort her. Despite the promise of burning embers, there was something cold and Dachau-like about burning her mother in a stove. It was what Hedda wanted, and Tully gave her mother what she wanted, but sitting there, watching Hedda's coffin being carried away by a mechanical belt, much like the ones at Dillons Supermarket, Tully shuddered at the *dis*comfort she felt with the service. She longed for the smell of incense, longed to stand outside and see earth beneath her feet, not parquet, longed to see her mother returned to the earth whence she came. What a fucking mistake, she thought. Thank God, Jennifer Mandolini, we didn't give you what you had wanted.

After the coffin was slid away, Tully got up and turned around. She saw Lynn Mandolini get down on her knees, and Tony put his steady hand on her back.

Tully waited for her. Boomerang was getting impatient. Robin stood silently next to Tully. She touched his black suit lightly to show him Lynn and he nodded. "I'll go and get the urn, okay?" he whispered to her.

"Good idea," she said. She certainly didn't want to be doing it. Tully wanted Jack to be here.

Finally, the crowd cleared out. It was an unbelievably hot, arid Kansas day, but Tully reckoned it was better outside than it would've been inside St. Mark's, with all those tightly shut stained-glass windows.

Tully came up to Lynn. "Come here, Tully," said Lynn,

stretching her arms out. Tully held her. How different Lynn felt. How heavy.

"Would you like to come back to my house?" asked Tully, disengaging herself.

Lynn shook her head. "I don't think it's a good idea. I think I will go and say hello to Angela. She's been good to me over the years."

"And me," said Tully, tilting her head and peering into Lynn's face.

Mrs. Mandolini held her head high and squared her shoulders. "I'm very well, Tully," she said, without being asked. "I went back to work six months ago. In Lawrence. For First National. Tony says he hasn't seen you in a while."

"Once in five years," said Tully. "I haven't seen you in seven."

She shrugged. "What's to see? Nothing to see, Tully."

Lynn looked down at Boomerang. "Well, well, Boomerang. Aren't you grown up? Last time I saw you, you were a baby in your mother's arms."

Tully felt her face muscles tighten at the mention of Boomerang.

"Robin, Jr.," said Boomerang, holding on to his mother's hand.

Lynn stared at Tully inquisitively. "I thought you called him Boomerang."

"His proper name is Robin, Jr.," Tully explained.

"I'm eight now," said Boomerang. "Boomerang is a child's name."

Tully smiled sadly, patting her son on the shoulder.

"How've you been, Tully? Are you working?" asked Lynn. Tully told her.

"Wow," said Lynn, without any enthusiasm. "Director of the Foster Home Recruitment Agency. Well, I'm pleased you made something of yourself, Tully." She paused, and Tully wondered what Lynn must have been thinking. "How is Robin?" Lynn asked.

Tully's heart compressed, as if it were possible to compress an already clenched fist. "Good," she replied. "Fine." She looked around the front yard. Robin was standing talking to Tony Mandolini with an urn in his hand.

"I have a sister now. Jenny," Boomerang blurted out suddenly.

Lynn gazed at Tully, and the twitch in her left eye became more prominent. "Ah, yes. I . . . Tony told me. Jennifer P. DeMarco. What's the P. for?"

"Pendel," Tully told her. Why not? Lynn would not remember.

But Lynn's left eye twitched and stared into something vague and dim in its valiant effort to search the brain for a memory the synapses to which died long ago.

"Well, isn't that good," said Lynn, her eye twitching uncontrollably. "Good to see you, Tully," she said, moving away. "Keep in touch."

What could Tully do? What could Lynn do? Eleven years. Eleven years, after which Lynn's eyes still groped for some light, her skin for some air, her heart for some life, at the mention of her dead daughter's name. And it's not like Tully didn't understand. But what could she do? You'd think people could rebuild their lives, Tully thought. You'd think they could. Eleven years. Another few months, and Tully will have lived without Jennifer as long as she had lived with her.

Lynn stopped suddenly, turned around, and beckoned Tully to come near.

"Tully," she said. "I'm so selfish. Thinking only of myself, as usual. I'm sorry about your mother. I came here to tell you how sorry I am."

Tully waved her off. "Mrs. Mandolini. You know how I felt about my mother." In many ways, thought Tully with a heavy heart, it's such a relief she is gone.

"Yes. It's a shame, Tully. I kind of hoped that maybe you and Hedda, you know, as you got older, maybe you had remembered she was your mother, recalled she was your mother, recalled your daughter's love for her."

"Mmmm," said Tully, holding her black hat in one hand and Boomerang's hand in the other. "Did you hope she recalled her mother's love for me?"

Lynn wiped her forehead and upper lip. The sun was beating down, and she seemed to be having difficulty standing up. She was a little out of breath. All that smoking, thought Tully. All that drinking. And when she looked into Lynn's eyes again, the expression seemed familiar to Tully, the expression of that dogged exhaustion with life, of knowing that there would be no improvement, no light, just days and days of waiting for life to be done with her. My mother carried that expression until the day she died.

"Tully," said Lynn. "*Did* you recall your love for her?"

Tully scrunched up her face, and Lynn laughed lightly. "You're so funny, Tully. You always used to make that face. That face of distaste, like after the first and only time you tried escargot. And then Jennifer started to make that face. Why did you just make that face, Tully?"

"She made that face better than I did," Tully said. "She perfected that face."

"She did, didn't she?" said Lynn. "She had those chubby cheeks that were just made for that look."

They fell quiet. Then Lynn took Tully's hand. "Tully," said Lynn in a soft voice. "Do you remember when I took you to Wichita in 1973? Do you remember?"

Tully looked at her son, who had let go of her hand and was playing with the earth and the rocks in the flower bed. She could not look back at Lynn Mandolini for some time, finally nodding into the ground.

Tully remembered.

"Tully, I took you there, and I stood by you, I stood by you the whole time you were there, I never left your side, and all I kept thinking was, Poor girl, poor baby, I'm going to adopt her. I was going to ask the city to make you a ward of the court and then I was going to fight tooth and nail to adopt you, because I loved you, because I could not stand to feel sorry for you, because you deserved to be loved by someone, by us, to be taken care of by us. That's how I felt, Tully, that's how I still feel when I remember you as a twelve-year-old child. Even now, I remember how much I felt for you at that moment, when I stood by you in your hospital bed."

As Lynn was talking, Tully had fumbled in her bag for some sunglasses and put them on. Now Tully's eyes were shielded by the sunglasses, black and wide, but behind them, Tully was still unable to look at Mrs. Mandolini.

"Do you remember what you did when you came out of the anesthetic?" Lynn continued, quieter now. "You came out of it so violently, nearly falling off the bed, and you screamed and screamed and screamed. Do you remember?"

Ever so slightly, Tully nodded.

"Do you remember what you were screaming, Tully?" Lynn asked, barely audible.

Tully shook her head a little and cleared her throat. "I thought it was just general, generic, all-purpose screaming," she said.

Now Lynn Mandolini shook her head. "No, Tully. You were screaming something very particular. Do you remember?"

MOMMY! MOMMY! MAMA! MAMA! MAMA! MAMA! MAAAAAMMMMMA! MOMMMMMMEEEEEE! She writhed and scratched, she flailed and tried to get away, she looked at every face around her with streaming, desperate eyes, but all that was coming out of her mouth was an obscenely guttural sound, a two-syllable word, screamed over and over. MOMMY! MAMA! MAMMMMMAAAAAA!

O, wretched memories.

"You're wearing sunglasses, Tully, but I can see that you remember," said Lynn, squeezing Tully's hand tightly. "I'll tell you, I was shocked. I couldn't believe that you were crying for her, for that animal, who was never there, never there for you, never took care of you, never offered you anything, and you! You were always so blasé, so unemotional, so kept! You kept inside yourself all the time I knew you. I guess you reminded me of my Jennifer in this way, so contained, the two of you. You were like a tomb, into which no one ventured, no one, not even you yourselves. And this at twelve! I thought, It's a miracle you found each other, and Julie, too, who was so sweet and light, a hundred and eighty degrees from the both of you. But then, I heard you scream in Wichita, scream for her! And I got so scared. I knew then you'd never want to come and live with me, never want another mommy. You just wanted your own, despite it all, you just wanted your own, and all I could do was offer you my house."

Tully was silent.

"But you know how that scared me? Do you have any idea? I mean, there you were, a twelve-year-old impenetrable wall, and you're still like that, I see, but in a child, it's so strange. At least Jennifer had an excuse, but you! And yet, the most frightening feeling came over me when I heard you in that unguarded moment: the fear that inside your tomb, inside yourself, you screamed like this all day long, all night long! Every minute of every day!"

Lynn started to cry. "It's okay, it's okay," she said to Tully, who offered Lynn a tissue and an arm.

It took Lynn a couple of seconds to speak again. "But even more than you, I thought of my Jennifer, and thought, Well, what's inside her? What's inside my own baby if this is what's inside Tully? As you know, Jennifer didn't speak a word when she was two, or three." Lynn shuddered and then said, "Now I know what was inside."

"Jennifer had your love," Tully said.

"And a lot of good it did her," said Lynn spiritlessly.

Tully bowed her head. "It's better to have it," she said. "Given a choice."

"She would've been thirty years old this September," said Lynn. "Thirty."

Tully listened to Boomerang chatting to himself as he dug up the flowers. "May she rest in peace," Tully said.

Tully and Lynn had a small silence, and then Lynn said, "Again, I'm sorry about your mother, Tully."

Tully just nodded. Me, too, she thought.

She drove with Boomerang to pick up Jenny, stayed with Jack at his house for a few minutes, and then went back to Texas Street.

During the reception, right in between the little shrimp croquettes that Millie made and the glass of rosé that Millie poured, intense loneliness sat down on Tully's chest.

She went to look for her son. "Boomer, what do you say we get out of here for a few minutes?" she whispered.

Boomerang immediately assumed a conspiratorial tone. "And go where?"

"Lake Vaquero."

He looked pensive. "Mom," he continued to whisper. "It's not a bad idea, but I'm wearing my best suit. And you've got on your best dress."

"It's not my best dress, Boomerang," she said. "It's my saddest dress. And we'll take our clothes off and go swimming in our underwear. What do you say?"

"I say," said Boomer, "why don't we just go to Burger King and call it a day?"

But he went with his mother.

She parked at Lagito Drive and found that little space Jack

and she had managed to find and keep for themselves in recent weeks. The small clearing was covered by trees, with a sandless embankment and a drop from which she and Jack had bounded gleefully into the water, scaring all the ducks nearby. Now Tully took off her clothes, leaving only her bra and panties, and Boomerang undressed to his underwear. She heard him muttering under his breath, but then they jumped into the water, and it felt so good, against their heat and sweat that Boomerang appeared to forget about his irritation and continued to jump and swim long after Tully had gotten out.

Sitting on the grassy mound, Tully watched Boomerang and thought, *I can't leave him. I can't leave him. I can't leave him.*

She hit herself in the chest. Hard. But the loneliness would not get off.

I can't leave him. I can't leave him. I can't leave him.

She sat there and chanted this catatonic mantra to herself, rocking back and forth, precluding all rational thought *I can't leave him. I can't leave him. I can't leave him.*

It was as if saying it over and over and over would render the words meaningless when Tully finally had to sacrifice her boy.

"This was a great idea, Mom!" Boomerang shouted from the water.

I can't leave him I can't leave him I can't leave him I can't leave him.

Wasn't it, though? she tried to shout back, except her voice didn't obey her.

19

HUSBAND AND WIFE

July 1990

Robin was sitting downstairs in the dark when Tully came down.

"Come to bed, Robin," said Tully. "Why are you sitting here in the dark?"

She heard him take a deep breath. "So, Tully. What are your plans?"

"Plans?" she repeated. "My plans are to go to bed. I'm tired."

"What are your plans for tomorrow?" Robin persisted wearily. "And for Monday? And for Monday the following year?"

"Robin, I've just buried my mother! Can you give me a little break, please? I don't know what my plans are. Work hard at my job, be a good person, respect old people. Now come on," she said. "I'm tired."

"Tully, I need to know what's going on," he said. "I need to know when you're planning on going."

When you give me my boy! she wanted to cry. When you give me him, I'll go.

"Planning?" she said feebly. "I was planning to go to bed."

"You refuse to be honest about this, don't you, Tully? What's holding you back?"

Yes. Yes, I do. I do refuse to be honest, she thought. What's holding me back? What's holding me back is the child that's lying in this house sleeping.

"Your mother was a big roadblock for you, wasn't she?"

Not that big, thought Tully. Compared to all my other roadblocks, she was a can of Coke on the open road. Maybe a six-pack.

Robin sat turned away from her in the armchair, smoking and stroking his chest. Tully saw his contours in the night light, blue and black, naked chest, shorts, the profile of his face, turned away from her. She bent her head and went upstairs. What Tully needed to do she could not do: she could not approach him again about taking Boomerang.

Having approached him countless times since February, Tully could not subject herself to his answer again, and she could not subject him to her question, either.

I tiptoe into his room. I tiptoe in, and I shut the door behind me, it creaks, but better that than the noise from TV downstairs, or Jenny's crying. I walk up, and as usual, he's uncovered, he gets so hot when he sleeps. It *is* the Kansas summer, and it's a hot one this year, but the air-conditioning is on, and he gets cold. So I cover him up, automatically. I check him, yes, he's sweating, but I can't help covering him. It's like breastfeeding. Instinctive. I have to cover him up. Just a sheet. But before I do, I pull back the cover all the way and I look at him while he sleeps. He's all stretched out, legs apart, he's on his back. His day was long today. He buried his grandmother and went swimming. He's a brave boy, he didn't cry once. I touch his legs, they're smooth and soft. He's getting hair on them already. He's only eight. I feel his feet. They're warm. His hair is matted and wet, and his mouth is slightly open. I bend my face to his mouth, and I . . . smell his breath. His sleeping boy breath. His breath that's as familiar to me as sunset. I've been breathing in his breath since he was an infant. Now I ask him in the mornings, "Breathe on me, Boomerang," and he says, "Oh, Mom," but he does. Still. Sometimes, when he thinks I'm mad at him, he comes over and says, "Mom, do you want to smell my breath?" as if, if I say no, I'm really mad at him. As if I ever say no. Come here, I say. Come here and breathe on me. And tonight I'm leaning over him, smelling him breathe, and I realize my tears are dripping on his face. I wipe them off him, gently, and then I nudge him to move over, and I lie down next to him. I lie down next to him and I press my face against his wet hair. It smells like Finesse. It is obvious— Boomerang has to stay with Robin. Dear Boomerang. What are you going to do without your mommy? You'll just play rugby all day and eat popcorn and hamburgers. You'll like that, won't you? Dad, you'll say, I don't want to have a bath tonight. Okay, your father will say. Dad, you'll say, I don't want to go to bed yet. Okay, your father will say. Dad, can I have some more chocolate, a cigarette, a condom? Okay, your father will say. Son, what am I going to do without you? The thought of leaving you is making me paralytic, I feel like your Nanna must have felt. Each day, of the last two hundred days, is one unending, slow-mo dream sequence, where I move but can't remember moving, speak but can't remember speaking, cry but can't remember crying. Going without you is unthinkable. But what's your daddy going to do without you? Who is he going to torture in the middle of our living room? Who is he going to get dirty with in the middle of a disgusting muddy field? Who is he going to eat popcorn with? Taking you from your father is equally unthinkable. However ... given the choice ... I would not leave you *for* your father, Boomerang. That's what he said to me, you know. I left you *for* your mother. Like I was an old book. He looked inside and saw her name in there and thought, Oh, all right, I guess I'll leave this one, after all. What did he see when he looked into Hank's book? Did he see his own name in there? Well, son, my name is in you. Mine *and* your father's. So I remain from waking up to restless sleep, from morning showers to your nighttime bath, in a perpetual state of suspended motion, while inside me the only coherent thought is, *I cannot leave you! I cannot leave you! I cannot leave you!*

Tully heard the door creak open and Robin come in and sit down in the rocking chair.

"Come to bed, Tully," he whispered.

"I am ... in bed ... Robin," she replied spasmodically.

Tully felt Robin watching her. "Come, Tully."

In a few minutes, Tully did get up. She closed Boomer's door gently behind her, but couldn't stand still. She walked into Jenny's room, adjusted her blankets, turned the air conditioner down, then walked downstairs, into the living room, into the kitchen, into the California room, across the house into her mother's old rooms—they still smelled like her—back into the living room, into the kitchen, back into the unbearably humid California room, she paced and paced, with her arms wrapped around herself, she paced and rocked as she paced, paced and rocked. I may be catatonic, she thought, but I'm not *numb*.

"Tully, what are you doing?" Robin asked her, catching her on one of her passes into the living room.

"Nothing," she answered. "Go to bed."

"What, Tully? What's the matter? What's wrong?"

"I miss my mother," she said instantly, looking away from his expression.

"You do?" he said.

"No," she said. "I meant I wish she were here. No, I didn't mean that, I meant, it's hard not to have one. No, I didn't mean that, either."

"You don't know what you meant," Robin said gently.

Oh, I know exactly what I meant, Tully cried inside. I know.

"I know what you meant," Robin said.

"No, you don't! You don't have a clue."

"I know," he said, sighing. "I know." Then, "You saw your father."

She walked up to him, startled. Her arms were still wrapped tight around her. "How did you know that?"

Robin pulled out a postcard. "I got this in the mail on Friday. It was in an envelope addressed to me. No stamp. He must have driven over and put it inside the mailbox."

It was a picture of a long-grass prairie. Flint Hills in sunrise. On the back it said, "Robin, Get in touch if you ever need anything. Tully's gonna need family around her now. Henry Makker, Santa Fe."

"Why didn't you tell me you saw him?"

"What's to tell? He came, gave my mother some flowers, and left."

"You didn't speak?"

"Oh, we spoke," she said disconsolately. "We spoke, *then* he left."

"You saw your father and you didn't tell me? God, Tully, what the hell is wrong with you?"

"What's to tell, Robin?" Tully said.

Robin took a deep breath. "Listen, Tully—"

She interrupted him. "No, you listen, Robin. There are more important things for us to talk about than my silly father. That's all past. That's talk for peaceful times."

"What else is there for us to talk about?"

Tully walked off into the kitchen. Robin followed her. "Listen to me," he said, grabbing her arm. "I can't do this anymore."

"Do what?"

"Pretend. Lie. Fake it. Can't do it."

"Pretend what?"

"Play this marriage charade for Boomerang. Yes, Mommy and Daddy are going to play like hell is normal and everything's okay, and when Mommy is packing to go, we'll say she's going on a trip and will be back soon, and when Mommy takes Jenny, we'll say Jenny was sick and needed her mommy and when Mommy doesn't come back to live, we'll say Mommy has to work and will see you soon. I don't want to play anymore."

"So don't," she snapped.

"Soon, Mommy and Daddy won't be married anymore. Were you ever planning to tell him that?"

"He's eight years old, for God's sake! He doesn't need to be privy to every ugliness we go through. Why don't you tell him about your bit on the side!"

"Why don't you tell him about Jack?"

"He knows! Jack is his friend. Jack is not a stranger. He's not some hairdresser stranger slut!"

"Tully, look," said Robin. "When are you going? I can't stay here with you anymore."

Why not? she wanted to ask him. But what she said was, "How can I go when you won't give me my son?"

"How can you go and leave your son behind?"

"Am I going?" she shouted. "Am I leaving?"

"What the fuck are you waiting for? Pack up! Get the hell out of here. Go and stay with your Jack until the divorce is final. Go on!"

"How can I!" Tully cried. "How can I leave without my boy! I can't go, I just can't! And you know I can't, that's why you're tormenting me. He is my son." She covered her face with her hands. "Mothers don't leave their children. Mothers don't leave their little boys!"

At last she straightened up and said, "I can't leave him, Robin. And you know that. You held him over my head, knowing full well that I could not leave him—"

"Tully, that's not true, you never even wanted him! How could I know that?"

"You knew! Because you knew how much I loved him!" she yelled. "Well, I can't go. Can't! Is that what you want? You want me on these terms? You think *that* wouldn't be a sham, a farce, a charade, huh? You think if I stay with you because of him, you won?"

"It would be a hollow victory indeed," said Robin, shaking his head and retreating from her. "No, Tully. I don't want you to stay with me at all."

*   *   *

The following Saturday, Tully went with Jenny and Jack to Lake Vaquero for the afternoon. There was no one at home when she returned to Texas Street around five. Tully wandered around the house for a while, holding Jenny in her arms, going from room to room, sitting in all the chairs, touching all the tabletops and bookshelves and counters. She went into the California room, turned on the grow lights, and stared at the cacti for a while. But then she got too hot and left. It was quiet quiet in the Texas Street house. The only sounds were of dripping water, of Jenny's breathing, of Tully's breathing. And of loneliness, panting on Tully's chest.

Tully sat down in Robin's rocker-recliner and fell asleep. Jenny fell asleep, too, on her mother's stomach.

When Tully woke up, she was disoriented. She didn't know where she was. She recalled Jennifer's tent, and Julie's backyard, and a Christmas tree, and Washington, but she couldn't place herself for a few moments. It was quiet. Then she felt Jenny on top of her, soundly asleep, and felt the arms of the chair, and she was okay. Almost okay, but not quite. Something didn't feel right. Gently getting up out of the chair, she went upstairs to put Jenny in her crib and then called Robin from the kitchen phone.

"Robin, what's up?" Tully said.

"Not much," he replied, but she thought he sounded awkward.

"What's the matter? Are you guys going to be home soon?"

She heard Robin sigh into the phone. "Tully, I'm going to be staying here for a while," he said.

Tully's heart fell to the floor. She bent down and picked it up. It was only Boomerang's ball lying on the kitchen floor, but Tully thought she was picking up her heart.

"What do you mean?" she said, beginning to shake. "Where is Boomerang?"

"He is here with me," said Robin.

Tully screamed then. Shrieked. Screamed and screamed into the phone and into the kitchen, dropped the phone, ran wildly into the living room, upstairs, downstairs, screaming and screaming.

Her teeth were chattering when she picked up the phone again.

"R-r-r-r-o-bin, you c-c-c-a-nt t-t-t-t-a-ke him, R-r-o-bin. You jus-s-s-t c-c-a-nt!"

"Tully," he said. "Please stop being hysterical."

"R-r-obin, p-p-lease, p-p-lease bring him home," said Tully.

"Tully, I wasn't taking him away. I just wanted to spend the weekend with him. He has school on Monday. I was going to bring him to school on Monday."

Tully was still trembling. "Come back tonight," she said.

"No, Tully," said Robin. "I'm going to be staying at Bruce's awhile."

"What about B-b-b-boomerang?" she asked.

"Boomerang will be going to school on Monday."

"Robin, what's going on? When are *you* going to be home? Monday?"

He sighed into the phone again. "Tully, you just don't get it, do you? I've had enough. I am not coming back."

She hung up the phone and ran to get Jenny; she then stuffed her into the backseat of the Beamer and sped to Bruce's near Manhattan. Tully had Springsteen on full volume, so that she did not have to think about anything, and for the most part, she succeeded.

At Bruce's farm, Boomerang ran out to meet her. Tully's heart fell again, but she didn't have any time to pick up Boomer's toys this time because he was on her, and she was clutching him around the neck. "Hey, Mom," he said. "What are you doing here? We went shopping. We bought me a new mitt, and a new ball, and new sneakers. We bought me a lotta stuff."

"Of that I have no doubt," said Tully, and felt a stab of guilt for using Jack's patented phrase. She held him tight against her, until he patted her on the back. "All right, Mom, all right."

"What are you doing here?" said Robin, walking down the steps of the farmhouse into the front yard.

"I came to see you guys," she said. "What are you doing here?"

"I told you," Robin replied coldly. "I'm spending some time with my son. I was going to take him to school on Monday."

Tully was a little calmer now, less full of pain, and a little angry. "What's going on? You leave, don't tell me where you're going or when you'll be coming back—"

"Yeah?" Robin said. "What else is new?"

"What are you doing, Robin?" she asked. "I don't understand. What are you up to?"

"I'm tired of you," he replied. "I'm worn out and tired," he went on, unaffected by her expression. "You've beaten me down, and I've had enough. I've left."

Tully looked around to see if Boomerang was within earshot. He wasn't. He was getting Jenny out of the backseat.

"Why?" she said.

"Oh, goddamn it, Tully," Robin exclaimed. "Why are you being so dense? I've left so that you can go."

She bowed her head. "Robin, what are you talking about? I already told you. I can't go. How can I go?"

"How can you go? Easy. You pack your bags, quit your job, and off you go. Wednesday we go to court. Thursday you go."

"Robin," she said quietly, looking not at him but at the hem of her gray cotton skirt, at her black sandals, at the burned grass beneath her feet, "what are you saying? There is no point to Wednesday, to court, to divorce, to anything. I can't go without my boy."

Boomerang, having taken Jenny out of the car, came by and stood with both his parents.

"Can't go where, Mom?"

"Go and play in the back, Boomer," said Robin. "Mom and Dad will be done in just a minute."

"Come out back with me, guys," Boomerang said. "Mom, Uncle Bruce got this great new horse!"

"Go and play, Boomerang, we'll be done in just one moment," said Robin a little louder.

"Go on, son," said Tully. "We'll be there soon."

Mumbling that his name was not Boomerang but Robin, Boomerang slowly went to the backyard, while Tully and Robin stood in the front yard of the farm, and all around them were wheat fields and the prairie.

"Come back home, Robin."

Robin contemplated her coldly. "Well, it looks like you only have two choices, Tully," said Robin. "Go with Jack and leave Boomerang, or let Jack go and stay with Boomerang."

"Yes," she whispered. "It looks like I only have one choice. I can't go without my boy."

Robin was impenetrable, standing there in front of her with his black eyes, with black rings around them. Then, affecting a light tone, he said, not looking at her anymore, "Tell you what, then, Tully. I'll make it real easy for you. You can take him. You can take him with you. Do you hear me? I will let you take him with you."

Moments passed in a soundless vacuum. She looked up at him then, looked into his face, stamped with exhaustion, clad in suffering, into his eyes, black with pain. Robin couldn't say his son's name as he was giving him away.

"Robin—" she began.

"TULLY!" Robin screamed. Tully put her hands to her ears. "Tully! What are you doing? You're not going to try to talk me out of it, are you? I mean, that wouldn't be very hard, and it would be really stupid of you. I said you can take him, and you can. Take him, goddamn it, take him."

"Robin, you can't part with him," said Tully, squeezing her hands together in desperation.

"Tully, I just did," he said. "You know, somehow, you want this all to turn out so nicely! In such a way that there aren't any losers. Tully, I gotta tell you, grow up. This is how it is. Jack won't stay in Topeka, you don't want to stay in Topeka, you want Jack but you don't want to leave Boomerang. Deal with it. There are real losers here. Something for something. You don't want to sacrifice Jack, you don't want to sacrifice Boomer, you don't want to sacrifice Jenny, you don't want to sacrifice you. The only one left is me. But better you sacrifice me, better I be the big fucking loser than Boomerang. Boomerang should know his mother," Robin said through gritted teeth. "Boomer should not be without his mother."

"Robin!" she cried. "What are you saying? You can't part with him, you love him just as much as I do!"

"No, Tully," replied Robin. "I love him more."

Tully saw Robin's face. "Oh, Robin," she whispered, coming close to him. "Oh, God, Robin . . ."

He backed away fast, putting up his hands against her. "Don't touch me, man," he said. "Don't touch me, Tully. I'm through with you touching me. I don't want you to touch me again."

"Robin," Tully said pleadingly, holding her hands as if in a prayer. "Please come back with us, please come home with us."

He laughed then. A loud, unnatural, forced laugh. "Home?" he said. "Oh, yes, I bet. Home." He was silent for a couple of seconds and then said, "Tully, you just don't get it, do you? We don't have a fucking home. We haven't had a fucking home since you let your lover paint our house. We have nothing except a lot of furniture. I am *never* coming home."

"Robin, please," Tully said. "You shouldn't be without us."

"I better start getting used to it, hadn't I?" he said. "Look, back in January, you nearly died. You were *this* close. And I made my peace with it. I thought you would die, and I wasn't surprised when you were dying, and the only thing that surprised me was that you didn't die. I had been expecting you to die since the first time I saw your wrists at The Village Inn. I knew I couldn't save you from yourself."

"I haven't touched my wrists since before Boomerang was born," she said quietly.

"Yes, but that has had nothing to do with me. I'm not saying Boomerang can't save you, because he did. And I'm not saying that Jack can't save you, because he did, too. That's why I can't hate him. Because he saved you."

"You gave me the only life I have," Tully whispered.

"A fat lot of good that did me. Nothing I ever did for you was equal to what Boomerang did for you and what Jack did for you. So go, Tully. This is the only way."

"Robin, *you* gave me Boomerang," said Tully. "Come with us. Spend these few days with us."

Now it was Robin's turn to put his hands over his ears. And Tully backed away, wanting only to throw her arms around him.

Robin put Boomer's stuff in the trunk and promised he would come and see him on Wednesday.

"Aren't you coming with us, Dad?" Boomerang asked.

"No, son," Robin answered, glancing at Tully. "I have to go to work really early tomorrow. I'm going to stay with Uncle Bruce for a few days."

Robin stared through the passenger window at Tully as if to say, I guess I'm not through pretending yet, and then he kissed Jenny on the head and stepped away from the car.

"Honk, Mom," said Boomerang. "Honk for Dad."

On the way back home, Tully tried to hear the screaming in her head, to discern the usual, customary noises, the peripatetic chant that had replaced sane thought for the last half year. But tonight, instead of hearing the endless *I cannot leave him!* Tully heard the endless *I am never coming home.*

The hours stretched out for Tully like the Kansas fields: burned and all around her. She came home with her children and put them to bed and wandered around the house, looking in all the closets in all the rooms, sitting at the kitchen table staring into a cup of tea, sitting on the couch looking into the TV. Then night, long night, and she finally had to go upstairs, had to feed Jenny, and then had to go to bed, her bed, their bed, the bed in which there was no Robin. How did she do it, how did she lift herself off the couch? How slowly she took every one of the fourteen steps upstairs, one after the other. How unpolished the wood looked to her, how worn the carpet.

Tully lay down on the floor next to Jenny's crib for a while, but couldn't sleep there, couldn't, imagining that at any time Robin would walk in and ask her in his weary, familiar voice to come to bed. She lay there on the floor and looked outside onto the trees and the half moon, tried to feel some nightly breeze on her skin, but there was no breeze, just heat and night. Finally she got up and went to lie with Boomerang, but she couldn't manage to fall asleep with him, either. She sat in the rocking chair and looked at her sleeping boy, and though she tried to think about California and the sea and the salty air, all she could think about was that Robin would no longer be creaking in this chair watching her read to Boomer. She came to sit by the bed, adjusting Boomerang's covers. He is hot, she thought. And soon he will be nine years old. Ohmigod, was it just his father's birthday? Her mind reeled frantically through the days. July 26, what were they doing? Oh, my God, she missed his birthday. Robin turned thirty-seven years old and no one noticed. Her shoulders sagged, and she left the room, closing the door softly behind her.

In their bedroom, she stopped at the door. What is wrong with me? she thought tiredly, painfully. Is it because I've hurt him? Am I just crushed because I've hurt him? Man, he'll be so young and so single, and so free. He'll be so many things, and he won't be with me and he won't worry about me, about whether I'm happy, whether I'm sleeping, whether I'm liking my work. He will just not have to worry anymore at all about us, and he will be so alone. She pressed her head against the door.

Tully thought about the girl on the soccer field. He could take up with her. Is that why he left? Did she promise him something I didn't give him? Is he going to be with her now, when I leave him alone in Kansas, without his family? Tully walked into the bedroom.

She opened his closet. It was empty. His jackets, his shirts, his trousers were all gone. He took all his suits. His chest of drawers was also empty, of all his jeans and T-shirts and Polo shirts, all the cotton shorts, all the underwear and white tee-shirts that she smelled when she saw them folded on top of the washing machine downstairs. Nothing of him even to smell, she thought desperately. Nothing of him even to smell.

Sunday morning, Tully stumbled around the house with two kids and no Millie and no Robin. She went to St. Mark's, she went to the Lakeside Drive house to get Jack, and they all went to Lake Shawnee. It was impossible to go to Lake Vaquero now with two adults and two kids. There wasn't enough clear space for all of them. So they rented a paddleboat and paddled out into the middle of Lake Shawnee. Tully paddled, with Jenny strapped to her chest. Jack paddled. And Boomerang paddled, too.

"It's just not the same as Lake Vaquero, is it, Tull?" asked Jack.

"No, it isn't," Tully agreed sadly. Jack studied her face briefly and then turned away to run his hands in the warm water.

In the evening, she went over to Julie's for dinner. Boomerang didn't eat much, and neither did Vinnie: all they wanted to do was play Nintendo. Tully didn't eat much, either: all she wanted to do was crawl away to someplace other than Kansas.

"Thanks for coming over, Tull," said Julie. "I haven't seen too much of you this summer."

No kidding, thought Tully. "Well, I haven't seen too much of you these past ten summers," she said.

"Guess not," said Julie. "I didn't think you really cared," with mock jealousy. "Shakie did very well to replace me."

"Nobody replaced you, Jule," said Tully. "Nobody can replace your childhood friends. The feelings you have for them . . . they're like family."

"Not so much me, though, Tull, huh?" said Julie. "I was always like a poor second."

Tully pinched her. "Stop it."

"Admit it, Tully," said Julie. "You never felt anything for me like you did for her."

"I admit," said Tully, pinching Julie harder. "But Martinez, don't give me this martyr shit. You never felt for me like you did for her, either."

"But that's not true, Tully," said Julie. "I've always loved you best."

Tully carefully studied Julie's face. "Well, I'll be damned," she said softly. "You're not joking."

"Of course I'm not."

Tully coughed. "When you say *loved* . . ."

Julie pinched Tully's arm hard. "You are my oldest friend. You are the sister I never had, Tully Makker. I'm glad I'm back home."

Later, Julie added, "I think I might stay here for good. I don't know if I can stand living in my mother's house." She smiled. "But I was thinking of getting a real job or something. I think if I get into one more combine, I'll just puke."

"Hey," said Tully. "Don't be too hasty. How long have you had now to 'think' about things since you've left Northwestern? A decade? Maybe it's not enough time. You might miss those Iowa cornfields."

"Cornfields, shmornfields, nothing," said Julie. "I miss you."

"Well, here I am," said Tully. "I haven't gone anywhere."

Julie ruffled Tully's cropped hair. "Yet, Tull," she said sadly. "Yet."

Sunday night, Tully tried to sleep but couldn't. The bedroom, empty of Robin, was making her sick with misery.

Midnight passed, and two in the morning also passed. Eventually three o'clock passed, and then Tully heard the first birds. It wasn't like she was alone. There was the water dripping somewhere, and there was Boomerang's breathing. Thank God he was back in the house with her. There was Jenny's breathing, and her own. And plus, there was the *panting of the shadow,* the panting of loneliness, that was so close to her, that sat so firmly on her chest, that it almost felt as if there were someone else in the house besides her and her two children.

Tully sat downstairs on the edge of the sofa, hands between her knees, and stared at Robin's chair. At five in the morning, Jenny woke up and Tully stumbled upstairs to feed her. She then had a very long shower and spent extra time ironing her clothes for the week. Boomerang woke up at seven-thirty and Tully made him breakfast. At eight, Millie came and Tully walked Boomerang to his bus stop at the corner of Texas and Maine.

"You look like hell, Tully," said Millie when Tully returned.

"Mmmm," said Tully, bleary-eyed.

"You said you weren't going to work today."

"No. You know, they gave me a couple of weeks off for bereavement."

"Then why are you dressed for work?"

"Oh. You know. I thought I'd go in, anyway. It's probably good to keep moving, right? Less time to sit around and think. You'll be okay with Jenny?"

"I'll be fine, Mrs. DeMarco. Where is Mr. DeMarco this morning?"

"He's left, Millie."

"Left for work?"

"No," said Tully, through a burning throat. "Just left."

At Docking, Tully chaired the Monday morning staff meeting, or the "pep" meeting, as she called it. She interviewed a prospective foster family and sat in on a counseling session with the mother of a five-year-old boy. The mother had been having revolving father figures and even quicker revolving bottles of Jack Daniel's in the past, many times just leaving the boy alone in the house when she went revolving for the weekend. During the weekdays she was a good mother and held down a full-time job at Waldenbooks. Finally, after the fifth time she brought her son to Stormont for dehydration, the SRS was notified and the child was taken away. That was about three months ago.

She was now sitting pleading to Dr. Connelly that she had not touched liquor since they took her little Tommy and that she would never never never ever never ever ever but never leave him alone again. Dr. Connelly looked skeptically at Tully. She was in a trance.

"Tully?" the doctor said quizzically.

She stared blankly at the mother and then at Dr. Connelly.

"Yes," she said. "Yes, of course. Six months probation. You understand we will have to send someone over to your house every weekend to make sure the boy is not alone?"

"Yes, of course, anything. I understand."

"And you will have to go for counseling on a weekly basis. We can arrange something for you if you can't make the payments."

Dr. Connelly opened his mouth but was too dumbfounded to speak.

Tommy's mother started to cry. "You mean—I can have my boy?"

"Yes," said Tully. "You can have your boy."

Monday, Tully met Jack for lunch. She didn't feel like going to lunch with him, but went anyway. When she saw him, her heart felt a little lighter; she forgot for one hour what was eating her—just looking into his happy face seemed plenty. That face and the ocean, she thought. That face and the ocean. She felt salt on her mouth, but it was only the tortilla chips. Tully wanted to tell him as soon as she saw him about being allowed to take Boomerang, but she couldn't tell him about that without also telling him that Robin had left, and Tully was just unable to speak Robin's name aloud, for fear she might break down or otherwise reveal what was inside her. She remained quiet about it until the check came.

"Oh, so good news," she said as evenly as she could. "Robin is letting me take Boomer."

Jack pounded his fist on the table. "Well done!" he exclaimed, reaching over and touching her. She leaned into his hand. "Tully, that's *great* news, not just good news. I didn't think you'd leave without Boomerang."

"I don't think I would've," she admitted glumly. The umbilical bond has turned out to be made of tougher stuff than me.

"So why so sad? A few days, you go to court, get your custody, and we can be off."

"Great," said Tully, without any enthusiasm.

Jack stopped smiling. "So what are you so sad for?"

"I don't know . . ." she drew out, "poor Robin."

Jack contemplated her for a moment. "He'll be fine. He was an ox when you were on your deathbed."

"That's because he's been at my deathbed for eleven years. He was used to it."

"He'll be okay, Tully," said Jack. "Really. He'll be out there every weekend visiting Boomer. Maybe he'll even move there."

"He'll never move there," said Tully. "His life is here. He grew up in Kansas, his parents are buried in the Kansas soil, his family is here. He loves it here."

"So what are you saying, Tully?" Jack wanted to know. "How sorry do you feel for him, huh?"

"Pretty sorry," said Tully, barely getting the words out. "He doesn't want to lose his boy."

Jack slapped his money on the table. "No, who would?" he said. "It's hard to let go of your children."

Tully tried to smile. He patted her shoulder quickly. "So maybe he'll move, Tull."

She shook her head. "His parents are buried here."

Jack said, trying to smile himself, "So now do you see the advantage of cremation? With cremation you can always take your family with you."

Tully laughed a little. "Yes, Hedda's always wanted to travel."

And then she kissed his lips and went to finish her workday, and went home afterwards to her children. Without asking any questions, Millie offered to stay, but Tully declined. It wasn't Millie she needed.

Another evening.

Tully and the kids watched a Mickey Mouse marathon on the Disney channel from six to eight. She bathed Jenny, and then she bathed Boomerang. She still loved to bathe him, and he still loved to be bathed by her. Tully was having an okay time until she remembered that Robin used to help bathe Boomer and sometimes even got in the tub with him while Tully bathed them both.

"Where's Dad, Mom?"

"At Uncle Bruce's, honey. You talked to him earlier. You know where he is."

"Mom, why isn't Daddy here? Are you guys fighting?"

OhGod, ohGod, ohGod, ohGod. "We're not fighting, honey," she said, touching Boomerang's soapy forehead. He moved away. "We're not fighting. But I tell you, though, I think your dad and me aren't going to be staying together so much anymore."

Boomerang stopped filling his boats up with water. "Why?"

"Well, we're just not getting along so good."

"Mom! Just days ago you were chasing each other over my ball in the backyard."

"Yeah, I know, honey, but it's really hard to understand. Listen, here's how it goes. You, Mommy, and Jenny will be moving. How do you feel about California?"

"California!" Boomerang exclaimed. "Great! When do we go?"

"Soon," said Tully, closing her eyes. "Soon."

"Is Dad gonna come with us?" asked Boomerang.

"No, honey," said Tully. "Daddy will be staying here. His store is here and Uncle Bruce and Uncle Stevie. He's going to be coming to see you every weekend, though. And you can visit him anytime you want."

"Anytime?" said Boomer. "Even during school days?"

"Sure," said Tully. "Why not?"

"Are we gonna go by ourselves?"

"No, Boomer, you know Jack? Uncle Oz? He'll be coming with us. You like him, don't you?"

"Yeah, he's cool," said Boomerang, looking around the bathroom. "Can you hand me my towel, Mom? I want to get out now."

The fucking thing sitting on her chest felt as heavy as she imagined massive cardiac arrest would feel.

Another night. She wandered around the house, sat on the couch, watched Johnny. Robin Williams was on, talking about his new baby girl. And David Letterman. She couldn't remember who was on Letterman.

A cup of coffee at three in the morning, and then she looked through some old photos. Not so old—she found them in a desk downstairs. For really old ones, she'd have to go up to the attic, and she didn't want to do that.

Photos of her and Robin when they first moved to this house. Tully pregnant, not smiling, standing in front of the weeds. Robin holding up three-month-old Boomerang, who looked very unhappy to be up so high. Year-old Boomerang asleep in his stroller, head hanging down, mouth open. Hedda. Sitting outside under the shadow of the trees in the garden, not smiling, but letting her picture be taken. What a funny picture, thought Tully. How typically like my mother. Tully touched Hedda's face. Shakie's wedding. Shakie and Frank, both beaming at Tully's Instamatic. Tully and Robin at Shakie's wedding, his arm around her, smiling formally into the camera. Tully remembered that picture being taken. She remembered standing next to him and wanting only to dance, for the first time in a year.

Where is my yearbook? Tully thought. When was the last time I looked in that? Tully realized that she had never actually looked at it, never looked at it at all. Never even had it signed by anyone. Senior year. Who needed it?

Where is it, though? And at four in the morning, Tully, obsessed, climbed up to the attic and searched through her own old milk crates, through high school papers and *National Geographic*s and *People* magazines, and found it—big, black, dusty. Topeka High School, 1979.

The inscription on the inside cover read: "It was the best of times, it was the worst of times, it was a year of so many things, but we must move on."

She brought it downstairs with her, sat in Robin's chair, and looked through it. The cheerleaders were on the flap, raising their pom-poms. There was Shakie, long-limbed and beautiful. There was Jennifer. Tully's heart squeezed in pain at Jennifer, in a short white skirt and white blouse, permed blond hair all over the place, smiling. She looked shy but not out of place.

Then came the Mostest and the Bestest pictures. Oh, look! Tully couldn't help taking her breath in, there he was. The Best Looking guy in the school, standing in his football uniform, holding his helmet under his arm, all white teeth and blond hair and lips. She had kissed those lips, had touched that face. Reaching out with her fingers, she touched his face, his hair, and then bent down and pressed her lips to his. God, I love you, Jack Pendel, she thought tearfully, numbly. God, I love you. I've never considered myself lucky, but I'm lucky to have known you.

And then the Best Looking girl—Shakie's face was plastered all over the white glossy page. A face so young, so fresh, a face happy always, happy to be happy, a face which never entertained anything but happiness.

The Smartest girl was Suzanne something. Suzanne Frankel. Who is she? I've never even heard of her, thought Tully. And where is Jennifer? Why isn't she the smartest girl? Then Tully realized why not.

Most Athletic guy, Jack again; Best Smile; Best Teacher; Class Clown; and then, to her surprise, her own body! under Best Dancer. Best Dancer, it said. Natalie Anne Makker. And there was a full shot of her, in a leotard, skinny as a rail and just about as attractive, standing with her hands gracefully above her head, making a pirouette.

Tully laughed. I should have looked in this silly book long ago and laughed, she thought. I could have used the laugh.

And then individual photos. "Martha Louise 'Shakie' Lamber," it said. "Cheerleader, Junior Prom Queen, Junior Homecoming Queen." Dream: "To be happy," wrote Shakie.

Natalie Anne Makker, Jennifer Lynn Mandolini, and Julie Maria Martinez all came on the same page. Tully was first. She looked at herself, a seventeen-year-old kid, looking seriously into the camera, trying to look grown up. Her hair was short and bleached, she was wearing tons of mascara and black eyeliner, tons of rouge, tons of lipstick. Tully squinted. Was that me? Boy, did I look like a railroad girl. She remembered having that picture taken. All the soon-to-be-seniors showed up loud and obnoxious in the school auditorium, cracking gum and bad jokes. "Natalie Anne Makker," the inscription read, "dancer."

And her dream? "To be dream-free," wrote seventeen-year-old Tully.

Twenty-nine-year-old Tully pressed the open book to her chest.

Jennifer's photo was framed in black. "Jennifer Lynn Mandolini," it read. "1962–1979. Middle School Valedictorian, Cheerleader." Dream: "California."

Having read that, Tully put the yearbook down on her lap and listened to her house and looked all around her, at the curtains and the bookshelves, at the stereo and the TV, shaking her head ever so slightly, unblinking eyes filled with tears.

Mandolini, Tully thought, *I miss you. I will miss you every day until the day I die and if we don't run into each other in the great beyond, I shall miss you every day of my eternity. For the rest of my life, no matter how much I may gain or what loves shall come my way, because of you, I will never be whole. I will never have everything. That's the canyon your death exploded inside me. And it's not the missing you, it's not the anger, it's not the grief that will ultimately live forever inside me. It is the canyon that your death made in me, and the canyon is loss. Eternal, irreplaceable, unhealable loss. A canyon no earth can cover. No time. No white roses. When I lost you, Mandolini, I lost everything, and I have stood in front of the canyon day after day, staring in.*

Since then, I've realized there are forty-nine other states that I can go to and feel all right. Because of Jack. Because of Jenny. Because of my son and my husband. But in that fiftieth state, the canyon lies, vast and unchanged.

You pig, Mandolini. What a wasted life, yours. Your young life, cut short by idiocy, by stupidity. All your hopes severed at the root, and mine, and your poor mother's. I regret not knowing you anymore, my Jennifer. You would have been worth knowing.

"Julie Maria Martinez," Tully at last resumed. "Debate Club, Politics Club, Chess Club." Dream: "To have as good a family as my mom and dad did." Tully shook her head. Dreams.

She leafed through some pages. The rest of the Ms, the Ns, the Os, and then Ps. Finally she found him. "John Pendel, Jr. Football Captain." Dream: "California," wrote John Pendel, football captain, in 1978.

She threw her head back and closed her eyes. She tried to imagine her life, her new upcoming life, in Carmel-by-the-Sea, by the sea by the beautiful sea. She tried to imagine her children running on the beach after Jack running with a kite and a golden retriever named Rover, Jack's tanned legs kicking up the white sand. She tried to imagine how the air would smell, how the salt water would taste in her mouth, how the white roof of their house would look in the Pacific sunset. How it would feel sitting under a palm tree, legs up, eyes closed, face up to the sun. She tried to imagine all these things, but the only noise in her head that came through like a scratched 45 was *I can't leave him! I can't leave him! I can't leave him!* And the only image burned into her mind's eye was Robin's face.

Oppressive heat, no sleep. No AC downstairs. Tully didn't want to go upstairs. She lay face down on the stairs, and then called Jack.

"Tully, are you crazy? What time is it?" said Jack's sleepy voice.

"Jack, I wanted to ask you something. Do you ever look through your high school yearbook?"

"Not often," he said. "What for? Do you?"

"Tonight. For the first time ever," she replied. "I liked your dream."

"Dream? What was my dream?" he said.

"Funny, it was just the same as Jennifer's dream. One word."

"Ah, I remember now," said Jack sleepily. "California."

"Right."

"Jennifer's?" he asked. "You mean yours."

"Haven't you ever looked at it?" she said impatiently. "No, that's the whole point. Not mine. Jennifer's."

"Well, you never looked at it, either," Jack defended himself. "What was yours?"

"To be dream-free," said Tully.

"Well, I guess you haven't gotten your dream," said Jack.

No, Tully thought, hanging up. I can't sleep anymore, even to dream. Dreaming would be a relief compared to this.

She dialed again.

"Bruce, I'm sorry to call you at this late hour. Nothing is wrong."

"Tully, this is not a late hour," said Bruce. "This is a farm. We're just getting up. Though Robin might think it is a late hour."

"Could I talk to him, please?" asked Tully.

A few minutes passed.

"Are you crazy?" Robin said when he picked up the phone.

"Who can sleep in this heat?" said Tully petulantly, waiting to hear his voice again.

"I don't know, I was managing quite nicely until five minutes ago. What's wrong?"

"I can't sleep," said Tully.

"Yeah, and? If you called people every time you couldn't sleep at five in the morning, you wouldn't have any friends left."

"How you doing, Robin?" she asked.

"I was doing a little better five minutes ago. Take one of Hedda's sleeping pills."

"Robin," Tully said, "you never let me take a sleeping pill before."

"That was before. Now I'm dog tired. How are the kids?"

"Fine. Boomerang misses you."

"Yes. Well."

"Robin, want to come tomorrow for dinner?"

"No, thanks, Tully."

"Please. I'll even cook."

"Not a good idea," said Robin. "What time is our court date on Wednesday?"

"One o'clock. Come tomorrow. I'll make your favorite. Pot roast. We can talk then."

"What, at the dinner table? In front of Boomerang? I don't think so. Listen, Tully—"

But she had hung up already, moving to lie at the foot of the stairs, where she finally fell asleep after an unbearable hour.

Tuesday was the same. Except instead of going out with Jack for lunch, Tully went over to Lakeside Drive and made love to him.

The Lakeside house was nearly empty now, except for the mattress upstairs and a card table downstairs.

"You must be sad about selling this house," said Tully, lying on top of him.

"It's time. I'm a little sad about the roses. But I've already planted some at the Carmel house. They should bloom in about five years."

"Is that how long it takes?" She laughed.

"Under the best of circumstances."

Then later, Jack said, "I was thinking of getting a puppy for Boomerang. You think he'd like that?"

"He'll love it," said Tully. "A golden retriever named Rover."

"I don't know," said Jack. "Golden retrievers named Rover may be hard to find."

She ran her fingers down his chest.

"Tully, have you given your notice at work?"

"No, you know, I was thinking of just not showing up on Monday."

"Have you packed?"

"No, not yet. I was thinking of just packing Monday. Or buying all new stuff."

"New clothes?"

"New everything," Tully said. Otherwise how could I get any peace, looking at the things I had on Texas Street with Robin's money? She kissed his ribs and got up.

Jack moved away from her a little. "Tully, what's going on?"

"Nothing."

"No, nothing. Exactly," said Jack. "I feel like you're having second thoughts."

"No second thoughts," she said. "I'm just a little down. Things will be fine," she said hurriedly. "I gotta go."

He pulled her back down on the mattress, kissing her. Tully closed her eyes. "Have I told you," she said tenderly, "that I love your lips?"

"Only every day," Jack said. "But tell me again."

"I love your lips."

"What else?"

Tully held him with both her hands. "I love," she said, "every fucking *inch* of you."

"Show me how much," he whispered huskily.

Tully showed him.

Afterwards, she got up off the mattress. "I really gotta get going."

"Spend the rest of the afternoon," offered Jack. "What are they gonna do? Fire you?"

Tully put on her underwear. "No, they'll call my mother," she said. "And she'll call me a slut."

"May she rest in peace."

"Amen," said Tully.

Tuesday night, Tully took the kids and went to visit Shakie.

"Tully, you look like hell," Shakie told her.

"Well, I thank you," Tully replied.

"What's wrong with you?"

"Haven't been getting much sleep," offered Tully.

The women talked mostly about the children and school and Tully's work. Yes, she was pleased with it, Tully told Shakie. Yes, it was working out very well. Yes, everyone was treating her great. Hard work, not often rewarding, but she supposed the only work she was ever born and raised to do. *Meant* to do.

"You look like the Grim Reaper, Tully," said Shakie. "The only thing you look *meant* to do is wear a black cloak, carry a staff, and knock on people's doors at night. What's wrong?"

Tully was quiet for a moment. "Robin left," she said.

"Ahhh." Shakie drew out her breath. "Why did he do a thing like that?"

"Because I'm going to California," said Tully.

The women were silent. "Ahhh," said Shakie. "Have you come to say good-bye?"

Tully nodded.

"Are you taking both kids?"

Tully nodded.

"He let you take Boomerang? This is just unbelievable!" Shakie exclaimed. "You're a witch, Tully. What kind of a spell did you cast on that man?"

"I couldn't leave without Boomerang," Tully said.

"When are you going?"

"Soon," said Tully. How I hate that word, she thought. "Soon."

"Well, good, I guess. So why the hell do you look like hell? Why don't you look glorious?"

I can't leave him! I can't leave him! I can't leave him! cried Tully inside.

"Just getting my bearings," Tully breathed out, with none of her bearings around her at all. "Need to give notice at work. Need to pack. Tie a few loose ends. I think God's given me a conscience late in life."

"What conscience, Tully?" said Shakie, patting Tully's hand. "I'm sorry. I'm sorry you're going. I'll miss you. So he's decided to take you with him. That's pretty amazing."

"I've decided to come. That's even more amazing," said Tully uncertainly.

"I guess," said Shakie. "You got a place to stay?"

"Sure. He rented us a house in Carmel. Carmel sounds nice, don't you think?"

"It sounds wonderful," Shakie said, but her eyes didn't glimmer.

Tully nodded weakly and then asked, "Shake, do you ever look through your yearbook?"

"All the time," replied Shakie. "It's a lot of fun to see what we all looked like back then. You look much different now, Tull. Much better."

"Much fatter, you mean," said Tully.

"No, better," said Shakie. "And though you wouldn't know it, I have gray in my hair."

Tully looked over her friend. "I wouldn't know it."

Shakie watched her. "Are you dream-free, Tully?"

Tully answered a question with a question. "Are you happy, Shakie?"

"Sure, I'm happy. It doesn't feel quite like it did in high school, but why not? Sure, I'm happy. Are you dream-free?"

"Yes," lied Tully.

"Well, that's a shame," said Shakie. "Because if you weren't, so many of your dreams would've come true."

Tully shifted uncomfortably in the chair.

"How does he look nowadays?" asked Shakie quietly. "I haven't seen him in four years. Does he still look the same?"

Tully nodded. "I think he still wears the same red football jersey he wore back then. But he's got weather lines all over his face. These craggy lines he never had before. Around the eyes and the mouth and the forehead. Also less hair."

Shakie smiled. "Well, there is a God, after all. Jack Pendel. Bald."

Tully stood up. Shakie stood up, too, and hugged her. "Good luck to you, Tully. Good luck to you both. Julie and I will miss you."

"Yeah, can you believe it? Just as I am about to go, she is back in Topeka to stay."

"What's happened to Laura?" Shakie asked. "I thought they were so tight."

"Laura apparently found herself another pasture to graze in. A male pasture. Getting married in August, I think."

"Poor Jule," said Shakie. "How's she taking it?"

"Like anybody would," said Tully. "Awfully."

"Well, that's really something," said Shakie. "I never liked that Laura person anyway. I hope Jule stays. I like her."

"Yeah, I like her, too," Tully said, smiling.

After Tully came home, she put the kids to bed and stayed up through a Jack Nicholson marathon on Channel 8. *Five Easy Pieces, Carnal Knowledge,* and *One Flew Over the Cuckoo's Nest.* Nurse Ratched reminded Tully of someone, that austere face and severe hair. Something jogged and got lost in her memory.

Tully fell asleep uncovered on the couch during the bus scene in *Cuckoo's Nest.*

During the night, Jenny sprang a fever. Tully sat with her downstairs. The little girl would doze off only in her mother's arms, and Tully, putting Jenny in the sling and cradling her to her chest, thought, Why can't someone put me to their chest so that I can doze off, too? I really need to be put to someone's chest so I can doze off.

She kissed the top of her daughter's head, felt the soft spot, kissed Jenny's fine blond hair, inhaled her baby smell. He won't know her! she thought. He won't know her at all, he won't have the pleasure of her, won't touch her, won't put her to bed, or bathe her, or watch her walk. He won't hear her say Daddy to him, he won't see her dressed up or dressed down. He won't see her naked in the bathtub, all flushed and wet. He will not know her, nor ever know how she turned out. Will never have a clue to all the wonders held in two little pudgy arms and pudgy legs and a head. God, how I wanted him to know her, how he deserved to know her! And she him! Tully pressed her fists tight to her eyes and shook her head endlessly from side to side. Her pain was intolerable. I will never see her riding high on his shoulders, drooling into his hair, I will never watch his face as she comes up to him in her Prom dress and says, "Dad, how do I look?"

I wanted to win so much! So much! I wanted us all to win. I never thought that all of us somehow would not be able to win, I never thought one of us would have to lose so much, why, everything he's ever had. And then have to get up and walk again, walk without me, and without his little, sweet girl, without her, without us. What an unlucky life. She stroked Jennifer's head, her back, her tiny little feet that fit twice into the palm of her hand. My little one, my little one, will you forgive me, will you forgive me? How could you ever forgive me for sacrificing your daddy? How could I ever forgive me?

Tully sat there, in Robin's chair, and rocked until Wednesday morning, her lips pressed into her daughter's feverish head.

On Wednesday morning before Robin came over, Tully left Jenny with Millie for a half hour and drove over to St. Mark's to put white roses on Jennifer's grave. Has my mother ever gotten roses on her urn standing on my mantelpiece like a decoration? No. I should bury my mother's ashes here, Tully thought emptily. My mother would like to get some flowers.

You'd be sad, Jen, if I weren't coming here anymore. You'd be sad if I weren't looking at the earth in which you're buried. Weren't smelling the earth that holds you.

Jennifer, Tully thought, Robin and I are supposed to be getting divorced today. Good idea, huh? We're going to court and the judge is going to ask us some questions and then he'll sign our divorce papers and Robin and I will no longer be married. Imagine that! No longer married to Robin. You know, all along I've said that I have nothing. I've walked— usually with eyes shut tight—from one illusion to another, but Robin is the realest thing I've ever had. Realer than you. I mean, here I am, talking to a grave, for God's sake. Robin is the Kansas earth beneath my feet. How can I give up the earth for the shiftless sea? I beat against him but he's stood strong, eroded with time with pain with wind but stood, and here he still is, how can I say I have nothing? I don't have nothing. I have someone to beat against. Every night.

While somewhere under Tully's thoughts but above Jennifer's tombstone was Jack Pendel's face.

Jenny was very feverish, and Tully spent the rest of the morning carrying her around in the sling, her hot head and heavy breathing drowning some of the merciless din inside her mother's chest. Tully gave Millie the rest of the day off. She wanted to talk to Robin and wanted to make dinner for tonight. She peeled the potatoes at the sink, with Jenny sleeping a disturbed hot sleep in the sling, tied to her mother.

Tully peeled the potatoes and cried.

Cried and wiped her wet face with her wet hands. The cold water ran as Tully peeled the potatoes and the only sounds in the whole house were the running cold water and Tully's crying.

At noon Robin came.

"No, I haven't quit. Jenny's sick," Tully said.

Robin walked over and touched the little girl's feverish head. Tully looked over at him. He was wearing a shirt and a tie. She smelled Paco Rabanne. She wanted him to touch her.

"You look like shit," Robin said, glancing at Tully. "We have to leave in fifteen minutes. Don't you have to get ready?"

"Robin," Tully said, ripping off a paper towel and wiping her hands and then her face. "I don't want to go."

"What are you talking about?"

Tully walked up to him, Jenny still strapped to her chest, and took his hand. "Robin," she said evenly, though quietly. "I don't want to go."

He stood there looking at her for a while. Then he tried to free his hand. She wouldn't let him.

"What do you want with me?" he said. "You're done with me. What are you doing?"

"Oh, no, I am not done with you, Robin DeMarco," said Tully. "I'm not done with you at all." She pulled him to her, but he resisted. She pulled him harder, he resisted still. They both looked into the backyard and then at each other.

"Robin," Tully said slowly, "I want you to come back."

"But Tully," he replied, freeing his hand from hers. "I don't want to come back. I'm happy where I am."

She shook her head. "Robin, I don't believe you. Come back."

"Tully," he said calmly. "Believe me. I'm all right."

"Robin! Come back to us!" she exclaimed. "We are your whole life! Why are you pretending that we don't matter?"

"No," he said. "I'm only pretending that *you* don't matter."

"But why would you do that?" she asked. "When you used to love me so much?"

Robin backed away from her, emitting a small, choked sound that sounded at first like a laugh. She came after him, Jenny strapped to her chest, but then stopped near the big oak kitchen table with the big oak kitchen chairs. "Robin, don't back away from me. Please, come back. Come back." Tully looked down at Jennifer's head, words and all her feelings stuck there, stuck at her throat, at her chest, at Jenny's head. "Come back, Robin. I will not leave you."

"What are you talking about, Tully? I've already begun to get over you," he said.

"What are *you* talking about?" she cried. "How can you get over me? Are you with your career hairdresser now? Is that how you're getting over me? Are you with her?"

Robin rolled his eyes. "Stop it, Tully," he said quietly. "She loves me."

"*I* love you!" Tully cried. "*I* LOVE YOU!"

Robin DeMarco stood there, straight against the kitchen wall, face to her, eyes on her, and then he said, "*You* love me?"

Unable to hold his disbelieving gaze, Tully looked away. "Yes," she whispered. "I love you."

Robin said unsteadily, "I don't believe you, Tully Makker. Since when?"

"Tully *DeMarco*," she corrected him. "Robin, I've always loved you," said Tully, stroking Jenny. "Except that there were all these things, clouding me a little bit. When have I ever been able to leave you?"

"Well, you never had so many things to leave me for before," he said.

"I still dragged and dragged my feet. And when I thought I couldn't leave here, Robin, I thought it was because I didn't know what to do with my mother. And when she died, I thought I couldn't leave because of my house, and my work, and my friends. And I thought all the while I couldn't leave my Boomerang, couldn't leave without him. But Robin," Tully continued, "when you left me alone, all those other things fell away from me, and it hit me that it wasn't my mother I couldn't leave, or my house, or my work, or even my son! It was you, it was you," she whispered. "I was free. I had nothing to leave but you, and I could not, cannot leave you."

He watched her carefully, still far away from her, backed up to the kitchen wall, while she stood near the table. He stared at her for the longest time and then said slowly, shaking his head, "I can't, Tully."

She nodded, worn out but resolute. "You can. Everything will be all right."

He shook his head. "You don't understand. I can't. I've got nothing left."

She waved at him. "There's nothing I want. Except you."

He remained as far away from her as was possible without being out of the kitchen. "Don't you see? I broke my plow on you, Tully."

She tried to sound cheerful. "I'll get you another one."

Robin shook his head again. "We're only given one plow. I'm convinced of that. You only have one, but yours," and the words did not come easily to him, "yours is made of something tougher than iron. But me, I'm not strong anymore, Tully. I cannot take care of you anymore. Not like I used to. Not like you need me to."

Tully tried to come closer to him, around the kitchen table. He lifted his hands and she stopped. "You won't have to be strong anymore, Robin," she whispered. "You won't need your plow."

"With you?" He emitted a silent laugh. "You've got to be joking."

"Robin, please," said Tully. "Don't make me beg you. You told me it doesn't become me. Please. Stay with us on any terms you like. Just stay."

Robin stood there shaking his head, and then Tully saw his legs start to tremble. He moved to the table, sat down across from her, and looked into his hands.

"Look what you've done to me," he whispered. "You've broken me."

"Please forgive me," Tully said faintly, holding on to her sleeping Jenny. "I know you still love me, please forgive me somehow."

Robin sat mutely at the table, looking doggedly into his hands, while Tully stood across from him, holding to the chair with one hand and Jennifer with the other.

"Tully, I don't know what you have in mind," he said at long last. "But I can't come with you."

Tully tried to smile but failed. "I don't want you to come anywhere but home," she said. "I will not go to California."

"All of a sudden you've decided this?" he said. "In three days?"

"In these three days I was without you and imagined a life without you, I felt the way I felt when Jennifer died and I looked ahead to a life without her. I felt indescribably lonely. I don't want to hurt for you, too, Robin. I don't want to grieve anymore for anybody."

"Except her."

"Robin, listen to me," said Tully. "I never had a life. Never even wanted a life. Never wanted anything. When you began to love me, I turned away from you. Not because I did not want *you*, but because there was *nothing* I wanted." Tully held Jenny closer to her. "I didn't care, I pulled away, because I had no life, and never saw a life for myself other than a railroad life, a life of wandering and longing, a life of bad dreams and gray skies. A rootless life. I wanted to go away from here to forget all the things that were keeping me awake at night, to forget so many things, you understand. That's all I have ever really wanted. Was to forget. To go away and forget. Forget my mother and my father, to forget Jennifer. Robin, all I wanted was to have a life Jennifer couldn't have. I wanted to live a life she would have liked to live. And when I got pregnant, it wasn't what I wanted. But Robin," she said, "please believe me when I tell you that I sort of grew to like my life." She smiled sadly. "I did grow to like it. I did not choose it. I did not choose this life. It was chosen for me—by who, I don't the hell know. By God or by the devil—by you, maybe? It was chosen for me, and I bucked it, but now I feel I want to have a little say myself. I choose you," Tully said, trying to shake off Jack in her eyes. "I choose you," she repeated, "because without you I have nothing. You gave me everything I ever needed, everything I ever wanted. You let me do everything I could do, and have everything I could have. You were proud of me the whole way. You stood by me when I was not much of anything and stood by me when I was not much of a wife. You gave me this boat and made yourself its anchor, and I am nothing without you, Robin," Tully said, looking at him, her eyes filling up with heartbroken relief.

"You are not nothing without me, Natalie Anne Makker," Robin whispered. "You are not nothing."

Tully held on to her daughter. "Forgive me, Robin," she said. "For everything."

"So what do you propose? To go back to the way it was?"

Tully tried to roll her eyes, but they hurt. "No. Now we're going to have to talk sometimes. Maybe go on vacation. Definitely go shopping."

Robin watched her. "Tully," he said. "What about Jack?"

"Please forgive me for Jack," Tully said, barely hearing herself.

"Don't tell me you only wanted him because he was what Jennifer wanted," said Robin. "Don't tell me you never loved him."

"I won't tell you any such thing," breathed Tully, now propping herself up by the oak table. "I did love him."

"And you still do," said Robin. "You still love him. Don't you?"

"I still do," said Tully brokenly. "I still love him. Please forgive me for him."

"So what are you going to do about him, Tully?" asked Robin quietly, and Tully, leaning against the solid oak table, whispered, holding on to the back of the oak chair with both hands so as not to fall, "I will get over him, Robin. I will get over him."

20

TULLY

Jack Pendel and Tully Makker said I love you till I die
Jack Pendel and Tully Makker loved so hard but said
good-bye
He went traveling; she unraveled
And then they had forever marveled
That they almost lived their lives
Without loving each other's eyes

N. A. DeMarco

August 1, 1990

Tully walked to Jack's house later that same afternoon. Robin stayed home and took care of Jenny.

Tully walked slowly. She dragged her feet up Macvicar, past Washburn, left on 17th Street. Tully almost made another left into Wayne to walk past Sunset Court, but didn't. Didn't have enough energy to walk past Sunset Court. She was going to go right to Lakeside but wanted again to go by Jennifer's, so she trudged up Oakley to Canterbury.

The St. Mark's gate creaked as always. Like Boomerang's bedroom door.

The bricked path was covered with hot summer dust. But it was as cool in the back underneath the oak trees as it had always been.

Tully saw Jack trimming the rosebush by the grave, and wished she had gone straight to his house. She would have had an extra couple of minutes.

He smiled. "Hi," he said. "What are you doing here? How was court?"

"It was fine," Tully lied, trying to get her bearings. But they creaked, too. Everything inside her seemed to creak. She slowly walked up to him. I want to sit down, but the seating's gone.

"Let's not stay long," Tully said. "I already came here this morning."

"So what are you doing here again? Are you looking for me?"

"Kind of," she evaded. "Guess so."

He caressed her cheek. "Come back to the house. I'll show you my maps," he said suggestively, kneeling down to pat the dirt down under the rosebush. "My maps of our trip. I figured we can take a couple of extra days and drive through the Grand Canyon."

"Drive through?" Tully said. "Isn't there a big crater in the middle?"

Tully looked at the white rosebush, breathed in the dry Grand Canyon air, imagined what Boomerang might have said at seeing the Grand Canyon.

She turned her gaze at Jack. Sunday after Sunday, summer after summer, winter after winter, he comes bearing flowers for Jennifer. Tully started to count sheep to try to compose herself in front of him because he was always composed in front of her and she wanted somehow to do right by him.

"Huge. But maybe there's a bridge," he said, getting up. He was no longer smiling. "What's wrong, Tully? You didn't go to court, did you?"

She stared intently at the rosebush. It was blooming beautifully. She shook her head. "Jack," she said, her voice faltering. "I can't go, Jack."

"What?" he said. "Look at me. What?"

Tully could not look at him. "I can't, Jack."

"He's changed his mind about Boomerang? Didn't he?" Jack said.

To stand up was as much as she could do. She was wearing his favorite dress. His favorite white sandals.

"Tully, will you please look at me?" Jack said seriously. "Thank you. Well?"

"I can't go, Jack Pendel," she said. He came close to her and caught her face between his two hands. Tully looked briefly into his face, then shut her eyes and said faintly, "I just can't." Jack held her face for a second more, then let go of her and moved back a little. He didn't say anything for a long time. Finally he said, "I knew it. I fucking knew it."

"Jacko, I'm really sorry."

"Tully, I got us a house," he said.

"I know," she said, looking around for something to hold on to.

"I've been coming back here for six years, and don't kid yourself, I've been coming here for six years only because of you."

"I know," she said sadly.

"Now that my mother died, I have no reason at all to be here. I don't want to be here anymore."

"I know," said Tully.

Jack took a deep breath. "What is it, Tully? It'll be all right. It's time."

When she didn't answer him and didn't look at him, he peered into her downcast face. "It's not Boomerang. There is something else," he said. "Isn't there?"

She searched the small graveyard, not just for something to hold on to but for something to fall into. Shifting on her feet, she searched for a sound to drown out the silence. She heard a distant police siren. Not good enough.

"Tully," he said, straightening up. "What? I'm not going to help you with this."

She looked away from him so he wouldn't see her face. Rather, Tully looked away from Jack so that she wouldn't see *his* face, his unchanged, unchanging, beautiful face, with those gray eyes as gray as her own. She wanted to touch his lips. You were right, Jack Pendel, captain of the High Trojans, our football captain, our football hero, give us a plan and lead us into battle. You were right. There is no good way to leave somebody. Have you loved me all this time in vain? Have you loved me, hoping your love would be enough for me, hoping I felt the same way about going away, and all this time it was in vain? And there *I* was asking *you* if you were going to break *my* heart.

"Oh, Tully," he said, stiffening.

She fought an impulse to weep. A short choking sound escaped anyway. She opened her mouth, but couldn't get the words out, and then, in a childish gesture, wiped her face with her forearm. Jack stopped demanding that she look at him.

"Tell me," he said hoarsely. "Tell me."

"Jack, Jacko," she whispered, her voice breaking. "I'm sorry."

"Just tell me, Tully," he said. "Why not?"

"Jack, I can't leave my life," she said intensely. "I can't do it, I just can't go chasing after some other life! How can I?"

"How can you, indeed?" he said. "When you have plenty of rainbows right here."

They were so quiet. "But Tully, what about California?" Jack said.

Tully shuddered. "I'll get over California, won't I?"

"Of course you will," he said. "You get over everything." And then, "What about me?"

Tully squeezed the palms of her hands together and put them to her lips.

"I can't leave *him*," she said.

"Robin?"

She nodded.

"Can't or don't want to?"

"Don't want to," she whispered.

He blew out a big painful breath. "What about me? Can you leave me?"

"Jack, I had a life with him, I had a child with him—"

"You had a child with me," he interrupted. "You had Jennifer with *me*," he added.

"I *can't* leave him," Tully repeated.

Minutes passed. "I'm not going to leave Jennifer," he said.

Tully pressed her palms tighter together. "Jack, please."

He stared at her. "Can I talk you out of it?" he asked.

"You can, yes," she said wearily. "But I don't want you to."

"Can I go to court and fight to have her?"

"You can, yes," Tully said. "If you want to put us all through the meat grinder. If you want to *hurt* me back."

"You don't think I'll win her, do you?" he said.

Tully shook her head. "I don't think you will. Besides . . . you know, and I know . . . Jennifer should be with her mommy."

"Of course she should," Jack said, and grabbed Tully by the shoulders. "Come with me!"

She tried to move away from his hands, but they held her in a steel grip. "I can't, Jack," Tully said. "I just can't."

Jack let go of her.

"I can't believe you're saying this. Can't leave him," Jack said dully. "You've wanted to for years."

Tully shook her head. "I've been dragging my feet for years."

"And his heart, and mine, right along with them," said Jack.

"And mine, too," said Tully.

"And *now* you've decided that you've wanted to stay with him all along."

"I'm sorry, Jack, I'm sorry. Please. I promise you, *he* promises you, you can come back and see Jenny anyt—"

"Okay, Tully, okay," Jack said. "Of course. I'll just show up for Sunday dinner in my best suit."

"I'm sorry. Please," she said. "You know how much I wanted to be free of . . . everything."

"Yes," said Jack. "I just didn't realize that *everything* meant me."

She sank down to her knees. He came up to her and knelt in front of her.

"What if I stay here?" Jack said desperately.

Tully, exhausted, shook her head.

"I'll stay here," he pressed. "We'll get a house, far away. You'll still work. He will still see his son. I'll stay, Tully."

Tully just numbly shook her head. "Jack, please . . ." she whispered.

"Are you saying you don't *want* me to stay here?"

She didn't answer.

He got up and looked down on her.

"Oh, Tully," said Jack. "I'm so stupid. I get it now. You are finished with me, aren't you? You have been finished with me for quite some time, haven't you? I just didn't know it, did I?"

Tully wiped her face.

Jack moved her hands away and lifted her chin. "Look at you. You're a mess." He wiped her cheeks with the palms of his hands. "It's okay, Tully," he said slowly. "I don't really want to stay here, you know that. Please," he said. "Please let me talk you out of staying."

"Please, Jacko," she said. "Please don't."

"Is this what you want? Is this it? You swear to yourself? You swear to me? Is this your peace?"

Tully barely nodded.

"I don't believe you, Tully Makker," he said. "Tully

DeMarco. Having been *there*, having known what you've never known, having heard what you've never heard—the sound of breaking waves that fill my head with noise and bring me peace. I don't believe you, but okay." He smiled sadly. "I thought you'd come with me, I really did. I had hoped we'd both get our dreams."

Tully looked up at him, her palms still pressed together. "Jacko, don't you realize? Out of all of us, you're the *only* one who had? Think about it. The only one who got his dream."

"Oh, yeah?" he said bitterly. "Then why do I feel like shit?"

Tully leaned over and pressed her lips to his leg. "It's gonna be all right, Jack Pendel. It's gonna be all right."

He stepped away from her. "For you, certainly. You're unbelievable. You live all your life so close to the edge that we're all afraid to blow on you, thinking at any moment you'll just blow the fuck over into the great abyss. And yet, I realize now, not only are you not blowing over, you're the only one who is still standing, like fucking flint, while the rest of us are bouncing off you like Ping-Pong balls."

"It's not true," she said. "I'm standing only because of you. You saved my life when Jenny was born."

Jack waved at her impatiently. "You're forgetting, dear Tully, that if you hadn't been with me, I wouldn't have had to save you at all."

"Jack, don't say that," Tully exclaimed. "That's not true. It's only because of you that I'm . . . here." Empty words.

"Yes, well, aren't you the lucky one?" said Jack bitingly. "Aren't *I* the lucky one? You know, I'm not naive. I knew that someone had to be sacrificed at the end of all this silly mess. But in all the years I lay on the beach at night and thought of you, of you being there with me and hearing the ocean, in all the years I've loved you and planned for you and returned for you, it didn't occur to me that I would be the one sacrificed."

"Me, either," said Tully.

"Ah, yet, here I am," said Jack. "Sacrificed." He tightened his mouth and set his jaw. She was still on her knees, looking up at him, burning his face in.

Jack gave her his hand and lifted her up. "Tully, don't you love me anymore?"

She reached up, touching his lips with her wet fingers. "Like I love myself." Tully looked into his beloved face. He was a grown man. He had seen enough pain, felt enough pain, *caused* enough pain to last two lifetimes. She hoped he was strong, hoped he would not break down in front of her, because she was so weak, so *worn* out. If he broke down, she would not let him go. *Could* not let him go.

"Do you love *him*?" Jack asked. "Wait," he said. "I don't want to know, I don't care, really. I know your answer already."

They were both mute. Tully tenderly touched his hair. "And I love my life, too, Jack. I never thought I'd say it, not about here, about Topeka, not about Kansas, but I do. I love it. I love Kansas. I love my Texas Street house, I love my work, I love my son . . . and . . ." she paused briefly, "my little girl."

"I hope so," said Jack fiercely. "I hope so."

In a while, Jack spoke again. "And I love you," he said.

"And I *you*," answered Tully, pressing her clenched fist to her heart. She pulled him to her and kissed his eyes, tasting salt. Tully took his face into her hands and kissed his lips, lips that had held her in thrall every hour of every day of the thousand days they had spent together. And then, closing her eyes, she rubbed her cheek against his stubbly cheek, to *feel* the roughness of his hair, to feel his cheek scrape hers. . . .When she had been next to him, she had been at peace. When she had slept next to him, she had slept dream-free.

Jack pulled away.

"Okay, Tully," he said. "It's gonna be all right. I'm gonna be all right. Go on, now. I'll stay here for a little while. Go on."

Tully wanted him to touch her but saw that something had surrendered inside him. Having done his level best, he could do no more. Jack folded his arms across his chest and turned his back to her.

"Thanks for wearing my favorite dress, Tully," he said. "And my favorite shoes. I remember when I carried you in those stupid shoes on the Potomac on the way *not* to see the cherry blossoms."

She made as if to come near him, but saw him, saw him turned away from her, and understood.

Saw his back—they were near the breaking point, Tully and Jack.

It was time to go. She stumbled toward the path, looking back at him. Jack stood there like a mountain of green trees and running rivers amid a desert. His blond head was up. Had it only taken fifteen minutes? Tully thought. In the blink of fifteen minutes, a whole imagined life gone. In the blink of fifteen minutes, the Pacific Ocean gone.

"We did it, Jacko," she said mournfully. "Me and you. We did it. We beat back death."

"We sure did, Tully," he replied, not turning around. "We beat back Jen."

She took a few steps away from the gate, toward him. She just couldn't stand to see him be unable to face her. "Jack, won't you please turn around?" she asked.

When he didn't answer her and didn't turn around, Tully hung on to the wall of St. Mark's. "Jack," said Tully, her voice barely audible. "Please come back sometime and see your little girl."

"Yeah, sure, Tully," said Jack.

Tully almost didn't leave then, almost had forgotten everything to run to him, to turn him around to her. She stepped toward him but tripped in her high-heeled white sandals, and grabbed on to the wall to stop herself from falling. Blinded.

"It's really too bad," said Jack. "I won't get to show you California, after all."

"Oh!" exclaimed Tully. "Don't be sad for that. I don't give a *damn* about California! You showed me Lake Vaquero, Jack Pendel. You showed me Lake Vaquero, and it was *everything*."

She saw him bow his head. "Yeah. Well," he said. "I'll see you, Tully."

"I'll see you, Jack," she thought she said.

The gate creaked once for open, once for close.

She walked haltingly down the stairs of the St. Mark's courtyard, nearly falling at the bottom step, her arms wrapped around herself, gripping her elbows.

There was no more sound. Except for the noise of a quiet Wednesday Topeka summer afternoon.

She wanted to turn around, to see if he was at the gate

watching her, but didn't. Couldn't. Tully wiped her f~
her bare arms and, crouching down, adjusted the str
her sandals. Straightening up, she tightened her arms
around herself, squared her shoulders as upright as she c
and went home.